Management:
Theory and Application

The Irwin Series in Management and
The Behavioral Sciences

L. L. Cummings and *E. Kirby Warren*   Consulting Editors

Management:
Theory and Application

Leslie W. Rue, Ph.D.
Professor of Management
College of Business Administration
Georgia State University

Lloyd L. Byars, Ph.D.
Professor and Chairman
Department of Management and Organizational Behavior
Graduate School of Business Administration
Atlanta University

1986   Fourth Edition

Homewood, Illinois   60430

Cover photo—© Robert Koropp 1983

ISBN 0-256-03364-1

Library of Congress Catalog Card No. 85–81466

Printed in the United States of America

1 2 3 4 5 6 7 8 9 0 K 3 2 1 0 9 8 7 6

To: Penny and Linda

Preface

The fourth edition of this book marks the ninth year since the first edition was published. Much has happened in the management field since that first edition. The proliferation of computers and the increased attention devoted to corporate culture are but two events that have significantly affected the management discipline.

After three previous editions and because of the changes that have taken place in the field, we decided that it was time to do major surgery on this book. Naturally, we tried to keep the strongest parts of the previous editions and to strengthen the weakest parts. In our efforts to accomplish this, we reorganized the entire text, eliminated some material, updated and revised some material, and added new material. The major changes are summarized in the following paragraphs.

This fourth edition is organized around the different types of skills necessary to be a successful manager. The book is still divided into six major sections; however, the content of these sections is significantly different from previous editions. Section 1, "The Management Process," still serves as an introduction to the management process. The major change in Section 1 is that the chapter on social responsibility and ethics has been moved to this section and the chapter on decision making has been shifted to Section 2. Section 2, "Decision-Making and Planning Skills," contains one chapter on decision making and three chapters related to the planning function. Section 3, "Administrative Skills," contains two chapters relating to the organizing function, one to the staffing function, and two to the controlling function. Section 4, "Human Relations Skills," contains chapters on motivation, leadership, work groups, and conflict and stress.

The first four sections deal with the knowledge and skills that we see as providing the basic foundation necessary to be a successful manager. Section 5, "Improving Organizational Performance," is concerned with those skills necessary to improve the performance of the organization as a whole. This section contains a chapter on communication, one on appraising and rewarding performance, and one on developing people in organizations. Section 6, "Contemporary Issues in Management," is the final section. It deals with the subjects of change and culture, management information systems, and international management.

Several other changes should be mentioned. We have reduced the chapters relating to operations management from three to two, placing one in Section 2 and one in Section 3. We have attempted to add realism to the book by adding numerous examples throughout. In addition to examples in the text itself, we have added an average of four major corporate or real-life examples, called "Management in Action," to each chapter. These examples are separated from, but relate directly to, the text material. We have also added an experiential exercise for each chapter that can be done in class. The section cases have been replaced by more comprehensive real-life cases.

Completely new chap ters have been added on the subjects of managing change and culture and on management information systems.

As in the previous editions we are indebted to our families, friends, colleagues, and students for the assistance we have received. Unfortunately, space limits us to mentioning only a few. Carmen Caruana, St. John's University; John Casey, Herkimer County Community College; Andrew Hoh, Creighton University; Timothy Matterly, Florida State University; and William Saalback, Washington and Jefferson College, all provided valuable reviews and guidance. Thanks are also extended to Noah Langdale, president; Bill Suttles, provost–executive vice president; Mike Mescon, dean, College of Business Administration; and Tom Clark, chairman, Department of Management, all of Georgia State University. Thanks are also due to Luther S. Williams, president, and to Johnnie L. Clark, dean, Graduate School of Business Administration, both of Atlanta University. Special thanks go to Caron St. John and Linda Byars for their invaluable assistance and major contributions to this project. Final thanks go to Sylvia Wyatt, Ardalia Green, and Carmen Whelchel for typing the manuscript.

We are excited about this edition and hope that it will excite you. We are interested in any feedback that you might be inclined to send.

Leslie W. Rue
Lloyd L. Byars

Contents

Reasons For Organizing. Division of Labor. Authority, Power, and Responsibility. Sources of Authority. Principles Based on Authority: *Delegation—The Parity Principle. Unity of Command. Scalar Principle. Span of Management. The Exception Principle.* Centralization Versus Decentralization.

Departmentation: *Functional. Product. Geographic. Customer. Other Types.* Line Structure. Line and Staff Structure: *Line and Staff Conflict.* Matrix Structure. Flat Versus Tall Structures. Committees: *Advantages. Disadvantages. Effectively using Committees. Boards of Directors.* What Determines the Best Structure? *Organization and Environment. Organization and Technology. Organization and National Culture.* Simple Form, Lean Staff. A Contingency Approach.

Human Resource Planning: *Job Analysis and Skills Inventory. Forecasting. Transition. Legal Considerations.* Integrating Organizational Objectives, Policies, and Human Resource Planning. Recruitment: *Promotion from Within. External Sources. Legal Influences.* Selection: *Who Makes the Decision? Legal Influences. Selection Procedure. Testing. Reference Checking. Employment Interview. Physical Examination. Personal Judgment.* Employee Development. Transfers, Promotions, and Separations. The Dynamics of Staffing.

11   Controlling: Comparing Results to Plan   294

Why Practice Management Control? Two Concerns of Control. The Management Control Process: *Three Requirements for Control. Control Tolerances. How Much Control? Behavioral Considerations. Where Should Control Reside.* Control Methods and Systems: *Budgets. Direct Observation. Written Reports. Audits. Break-Even Charts. Time-Related Charts and Techniques. Management by Objectives (MBO). Management Information Systems.*

12   Operations Control   318

Controlling Operating Costs. Inventory Control: *ABC Classification System. Reorder Point and Safety Stock. The Order Quantity.* Quality Control: *Quality Checkpoints. Types of Quality Control. Acceptance Sampling. Process Control Charts. Quality Circles.*

Section 3 Case   IBM   343

Section 4   Human Relations Skills   348

13   Motivating: Activating and Sustaining Human Behavior   352

The Meaning of Motivation. Traditional Theory. Need Hierarchy Theory: *Maslow's Need Hierarchy. The Need Hierarchy Theory: Other Considerations.* Achievement-Power-Affiliation Theory. Motivation-Maintenance Theory. Preference-Expectancy Theory. Reinforcement Theory. Integrating the Theories of Motivation. Job Satisfaction: *The Satisfaction-Performance Controversy.*

14   Leading: Influencing Human Behavior   378

Leadership: What Is It? Sources of Authority. Power, Authority, and Leadership. Leader Attitudes. General Approaches to Leadership: *Trait*

Communication Systems. Horizontal, or Lateral, Communication. Grape-vines.

18   Appraising and Rewarding Performance   490

Understanding Performance: *Determinants of Performance. Environmental Factors as Performance Obstacles.* Performance Appraisal: Definition and Uses. Performance Appraisal: Methods: *Essay Appraisal. Graphic Rating Scale. Behaviorally Anchored Rating Scale (BARS). Checklist. Forced-Choice Rating. Critical-Incident Appraisal. Work Standards. Ranking Methods. Management by Objectives.* Potential Errors in Performance Appraisals. Overcoming Errors in Performance Appraisals. Providing Feedback through the Appraisal Interview. Compensating Employees: *The Importance of Fair Pay. Pay Equity.* Job Evaluation. Wage Surveys. Pay Secrecy. Incentive Pay Plans.

19   Developing People within Organizations   518

Human Asset Accounting. Orientation: *Organizational Orientation. Departmental and Job Orientation. Orientation Kit.* Training Employees: *Determining Training Needs. Establishing Training Objectives.* Methods of Training: *On-the-Job Training and Job Rotation. Vestibule Training. Apprenticeship Training. Classroom Training. Programmed Instruction.* Making Training Meaningful. Management Development: *Needs Assessment. Establishing Management Development Objectives. Methods Used in Management Development.* Assessment Centers. Evaluating Employee Training and Management Development Activities.

Section 5 Case   The Coca-Cola Company   546

Section 6   Contemporary Issues in Management   552

20   Managing Change and Culture   556

Managing Change: *Employee Reactions to Change. Resistance to Change. Reducing Resistance to Change. Planned Change. Organizational Develop-*

Management:
Theory and Application

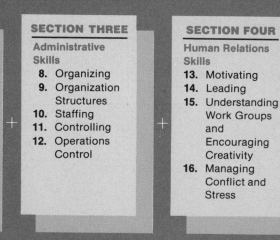

1

The Management Process

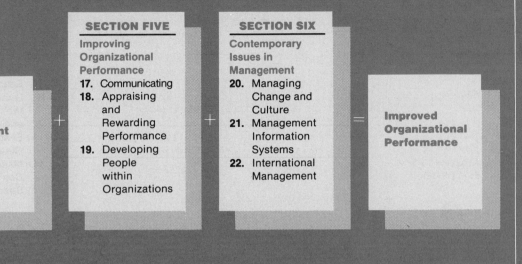

Management Foundation

+

+

=

Improved Organizational Performance

Section 1 serves as an orientation for this book. The purposes of Section 1 are to provide an understanding of the work that a manager does, to develop a historical perspective of how and why management evolved, and to develop an appreciation for the ethical and social responsibilities of a manger.

Chapter 1 discusses the concepts of management and manager. Management is discussed in terms of the basic functions that a manager performs—planning, controlling, organizing, staffing, and leading—the roles that a manager must assume, and the skills required of a manager. The increasing role of women and minorities in management is described. The characteristics of an entrepreneur are discussed, and the importance of entrepreneurship in larger organizations is stressed.

Chapter 2 presents a chronological development of the management discipline. The management pioneers are presented in perspective with the events of their day. Emphasis is placed not so much on what and when events happened as on why they happened.

Chapter 3 discusses the concept of social responsibility. Arguments for and against social responsibility are presented and analyzed. The concept of ethics as related to management is also discussed.

Help Yourself To A Book

Obtain the following information from
our MICROFICHE CATALOG:

Call No. _658 T_

Author _Townsend_

Title _Up the Organization_

Circle the initials listed beside the
call number, so you'll know which
branches own this book.

(G)	George Mason Regional NO	256-3800
(K)	Kings Park NO	978-5600
T)	Thomas Jefferson	573-1060
W	Woodrow Wilson	820-8774
Fx	Fairfax City Regional	691-2741
	Virginia Room	691-2123
P	Patrick Henry	938-0405
Ce)	Centreville NO Yes	830-2223
Ty	Tysons-Pimmit Regional No	790-8088
Rr)	Reston Regional No	689-2700
D)	Dolley Madison No	356-0770
Hw	Hunters Woods	860-2602
C)	Carter Glass NO	437-8484
He	Herndon	437-8855
S)	Sherwood Regional	765-3645
B)	Richard Byrd	451-8055
M)	Martha Washington	768-6700
J)	John Marshall	971-0010
	Lorton	339-7385

(over for directions)

1

Management and Entrepreneurship

Chapter Outline

SECTION ONE

The Management Process

The next day, Moses sat as usual to hear the people's complaints against each other, from morning to evening.

When Moses' father-in-law saw how much time this was taking, he said, "Why are you trying to do all this alone, with people standing here all day long to get your help?"

"Well, because the people come to me with their disputes, to ask for God's decisions," Moses told him. . . .

"It's not right!" his father-in-law exclaimed. "You're going to wear yourself out—and if you do, what will happen to the people? Moses, the job is too heavy a burden for you to try to handle all by yourself.

"Now listen, and let me give you a word of advice. . . .

"Find some capable, godly, honest men who hate bribes and appoint them as judges, 1 judge for each 1,000 people; he in turn will have 10 judges under him, each in charge of 100; and under each of them will be 2 judges, each responsible for the affairs of 50 people; and each of these will have 5 judges beneath him, each counseling 10 persons. Let these men be responsible to serve the people with justice at all times. Anything that is too important or complicated can be brought to you. But the smaller matters, they can take care of themselves. That way it will be easier for you because you will share the burden with them."

*The Living Bible**

What makes one organization more successful than others? For example, why has Delta Airlines consistently reported higher profits than other airlines? Numerous reasons can be given for any particular organization's success. Management in Action 1–1 outlines some of the reasons for the success of the Dallas Cowboys.

Unquestionably, an organization's management plays a critical role in its success or failure. The overriding purpose of this book is to identify, discuss, and show through examples the skills necessary to become a successful manager.

MANAGEMENT DEFINED

Management has been defined in many ways—and even today there is no universally accepted definition. One often used is "getting things done through others." Another popular definition holds that management is the

---

* *The Living Bible,* Exod. 18:13–22. Copyright 1971 by Tyndale House Publishers, Wheaton, Ill. Used by permission.

MANAGEMENT IN ACTION 1–1

"America's Team": The Dallas Cowboys

The Dallas Cowboys have had 17 straight winning seasons and have qualified for the play-offs in all but two of those years. What is the formula for this success story? Tex Schramm, the Cowboys' president–general manager, who has been with the team since its inception, explains as follows: "To start with, we don't always do everything right. We have had some mistakes along the way. But we believe you need three things—the organization, the players, and the coaches. If you lack any one of the three, you are not going to be successful. The elements have to come together. Players are essential. And coaches are more important, in my opinion, in football than any other sport. If you have a strong organization, you can go through years when you aren't so lucky or have problems with injuries or other factors. If you

have a strong base throughout the organization, you can withstand reversals."

Asked why the team has had so few changes in all phases, from coaching to the ticket department, Schramm answers, "I believe when problems arise it's wrong to start changing people. It's much easier and effective to alter the method."

In March 1984, the Dallas Cowboys were sold to an 11-member partnership headed by H. M. (Bum) Bright for a reported $80 million—the most ever paid for a sports franchise. The partnership reported that there would be no changes in the management of the club.

It will be interesting to see if this change in ownership will have an effect on the success of this organization.

Source: Adapted from John Steadman, *The Sporting News*, January 9, 1982. Used with permission of the Sporting News Publishing Company. Also, *Washington Post*, March 20, 1984, p. D1.

---

efficient utilization of resources. In this book, we will use the following definition of management:

Management is a process that involves guiding or directing a group of people toward organizational goals or objectives.[1]

> **Management**–process that involves guiding or directing a group of people toward organizational goals or objectives.

MANAGEMENT AND OBJECTIVES

A favorite story often told at management meetings is about three stone-cutters who were asked what they were doing. The first replied, "I am making a living." The second said: "I am doing the best job of stonecutting in the entire country." The third said: "I am building a cathedral."[2]

The third stonecutter has the potential to become a true manager, for he has a clear objective or reason for doing the work. The starting point of the management process is establishing objectives. Management must define the objectives of the organization, decide what must be done to achieve them, communicate them to the people who perform the work necessary to achieve them, and determine how progress toward reaching these objectives is to be measured. Evidence suggests that having specific objectives increases the performance not only of individuals within the organization but also of the organization as a whole.[3] It has also been found that individual employees who accept difficult objectives perform better than they do under less challenging objectives.[4]

Precisely what objectives should be set for a particular organization depends on the nature of the organization and its management philosophy. Obviously, the objectives of profit and nonprofit organizations will differ. Although they range widely among organizations, objectives normally fall into one of four general categories: (1) profits, (2) service to customers or clients, (3) employee needs and well-being, and (4) social responsibility. Chapters 5 and 6 discuss the objective-setting process in much more detail.

APPROACHES TO ANALYZING MANAGEMENT

Several approaches have been used to analyze the management process. Three common approaches examine management by categorizing the *functions* (work) performed by management, the *roles* that managers perform, and the *skills* required of managers in performing the job of management. Each of these categories is discussed below.

Management Functions

Management is a form of work. The *manager* is the person who performs this work; in doing it, the manager performs certain activities. These activities are often grouped into conceptual categories called the **functions of management.** These categories are:

1. **Planning**—deciding what objectives to pursue during a future time period and what to do in order to achieve those objectives.
2. **Controlling**—measuring performance against these objectives, determining causes of deviations, and taking corrective action where necessary.
3. **Organizing**—grouping activities, assigning activities, and providing the authority necessary to carry out the activities.
4. **Staffing**—determining human resource needs and recruiting, selecting, training, and developing human resources.
5. **Leading**—directing and channeling human behavior toward the accomplishment of objectives.

The functions of management are merely categories for classifying knowledge about management. Because management functions overlap, it is difficult to classify them purely as planning, controlling, organizing, staffing, or leading. In Figure 1–1, several managerial activities are classified under

Management functions–activities a manager performs in doing the work of management: planning, controlling, organizing, staffing, and leading.

Planning–management function that decides what objectives to pursue during a future time period and what to do to achieve those objectives.

Controlling–management function that measures performance against an organization's objectives, determines causes of deviations, and takes corrective action when necessary.

Organizing–management function that groups and assigns activities and provides the authority necessary to carry out the activities.

Staffing–management function that determines human resource needs and recruits, selects, trains, and develops human resources.

Leading–management function that directs and channels human behavior toward the accomplishment of objectives.

FIGURE 1–1
Functions of Management

Planning

1. Perform self-audit—determine the present status of the organization.
2. Survey the environment.
3. Set objectives.
4. Forecast future situation.
5. State actions and resource needs.
6. Evaluate proposed actions.
7. Revise and adjust the plan in light of control results and changing conditions.
8. Communicate throughout the planning process.

Controlling

1. Establish standards.
2. Monitor results and compare to standards.
3. Correct deviations.
4. Revise and adjust control methods in light of control results and changing conditions.
5. Communicate throughout the control process.

Organizing

1. Identify and define work to be performed.
2. Break work down into duties.
3. Group duties into positions.
4. Define position requirements.
5. Group positions into manageable and properly related units.
6. Assign work to be performed, accountability, and extent of authority.
7. Revise and adjust the organizational structure in light of control results and changing conditions.
8. Communicate throughout the organizing process.

Staffing

1. Determine human resource needs.
2. Recruit potential employees.
3. Select from the recruits.
4. Train and develop the human resources.
5. Revise and adjust the quantity and quality of the human resources in light of control results and changing conditions.
6. Communicate throughout the staffing process.

Leading

1. Communicate and explain objectives to subordinates.
2. Assign performance standards.
3. Coach and guide subordinates to meet performance standards.
4. Reward subordinates, based on performance.
5. Praise and censure fairly.
6. Provide a motivating environment by communicating the changing situation and its requirements.
7. Revise and adjust the methods of leadership in light of control results and changing conditions.
8. Communicate throughout the leadership process.

the different functions of management. However, this does not imply that managers perform each of these activities sequentially for each function. Figure 1–2 indicates the relative amount of emphasis placed on each function by different levels of management.

Management Roles

Henry Mintzberg has proposed another method of examining what managers do by introducing the concept of managerial roles.[5] A **role** is defined as an organized set of behaviors belonging to an identifiable job.[6] But remem-

Role—organized set of behaviors belonging to an identifiable job.

FIGURE 1–2
Relative Amount of Emphasis Placed on Each Function of Management

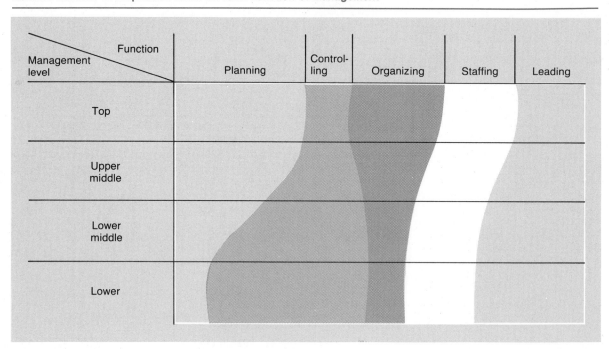

ber that the delineation of managerial working roles is essentially a categorizing process—just as it was with the managerial functions.

Mintzberg identifies 10 managerial roles, which he divides into three major groups: <u>interpersonal roles, informational roles, and decisional roles.</u> Figure 1–3 illustrates Mintzberg's approach to categorizing the roles of a manager. <u>The manager's position is the starting point for defining a manager's roles.</u> Formal authority gives the position status. <u>Authority and status together generate certain interpersonal roles for a manager.</u> The interpersonal roles in turn determine the informational roles of the manager. Finally, access to information, authority, and status place the manager at a central point in the organizational decision-making process. Figure 1–4 defines each of Mintzberg's 10 managerial roles.

Mintzberg further suggests that <u>the management level and the types of work that the manager directs significantly influence the variety of roles that the manager must assume.</u>[7] For example, managers at lower levels of the organization spend more time in the disturbance handler and negotiator roles and less time in the figurehead role. On the other hand, the chief executive of an organization concentrates more on the roles of figurehead, liaison, spokesperson, and negotiator.[8]

FIGURE 1–3
Roles of a Manager

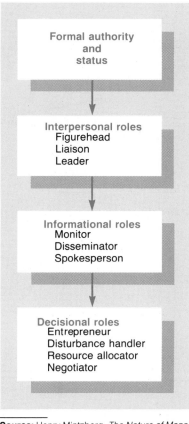

Formal authority
and
status

Interpersonal roles
Figurehead
Liaison
Leader

Informational roles
Monitor
Disseminator
Spokesperson

Decisional roles
Entrepreneur
Disturbance handler
Resource allocator
Negotiator

Source: Henry Mintzberg, *The Nature of Managerial Work* (New York: Harper & Row, 1973), p. 59.

Management Skills

Another approach to examining the management process is in terms of the types of skills required to perform the work. Five basic skills have been identified:

1. Decison-making skills—involve searching the environment for conditions requiring a decision, analyzing possible courses of action, and choosing a course of action.
2. Planning skills—involve deciding what objectives to pursue during a future time period and how to achieve those objectives.

FIGURE 1–4
Definitions of Managerial Roles

Interpersonal

1. Figurehead: Manager represents the organizational unit in all matters of formality.
2. Liaison: Manager interacts with peers and other people outside the organizational unit to gain information and favors.
3. Leader: Manager provides guidance and motivation to the work group and also defines the atmosphere in which the work group will work.

Informational

1. Monitor: Manager serves as a receiver and collector of information.
2. Disseminator: Manager transmits special information within the organization.
3. Spokesperson: Manager disseminates the organization's information into its environment.

Decisional

1. Entrepreneur: Manager's role is to initiate change.
2. Disturbance handler: Role the manager must assume when the organization is threatened, such as conflicts between subordinates, the sudden departure of a subordinate, or the loss of an important customer.
3. Resource allocator: Manager decides where the organization will expend its resources.
4. Negotiator: Role the manager assumes when the organization finds itself in major, nonroutine negotiations with other organizations or individuals.

Source: Adapted from Henry Mintzberg, *The Nature of Managerial Work* (New York: Harper & Row, 1972), pp. 54–99.

3. Administrative skills—involve understanding and performing the organizing, staffing, and controlling functions of management.
4. Human relations skills—involve understanding human behavior and being able to work well with people.
5. Technical skills—involve specialized knowledge, analytical ability within that specialty, and the ability to use tools and techniques of that specific discipline.

In practice, management skills are so closely interrelated that it is difficult to determine where one begins and another ends. However, it is generally agreed that lower-level managers need more technical skills than managers at higher levels. Human relations skills are essential to effective management at all levels. Finally, decision-making, planning, and administrative skills become increasingly important as a person moves up the managerial ladder.

Each approach to examining the management process looks at the process from a different perspective. Each has its merits. But in the final analysis, a successful manager must (1) understand the work that is to be performed (the management functions); (2) understand the organized set of behaviors to be performed (the managerial roles); and (3) master the skills involved in performing the job (the managerial skills). Thus, these approaches to analyzing management are not mutually exclusive—they are necessary and complementary approaches.

PRINCIPLES OF MANAGEMENT

Henri Fayol, a Frenchman, was one of the first writers to introduce the idea of principles of management. His contributions are discussed more fully in Chapter 2. Since Fayol's time, many concepts have been set forth as principles of management. A **principle** is an accepted rule of action.[9]

Principle–accepted rule of action.

Principles of management have been developed largely through observation and deduction. For example, Fayol drew upon more than 40 years of practical business experience in the development of his principles. However, a word of caution is appropriate. Management principles are much more subject to change and interpretation than are those in the physical sciences. For instance, the management principle of "unity of command" states that an employee should have one—and only one—manager. But some organizational structures violate this principle and still seem to work effectively. Thus, management principles must be viewed as *guides to action* and not laws that must be followed without exception. In summary, management principles should be followed—except where a deviation can be justified on the basis of sound logic.

MISCONCEPTIONS ARE COMMON

The practice of management is concerned with human behavior—and everyone seems to have their own ideas about management, especially its problems. Usually these ideas are based on personal experience and are defended with vigor.

To illustrate how each of us develops our own ideas about management and human behavior, a true-false test of human behavior is given in Figure 1–5. The answers to the questions have been empirically verified. However, the natural tendency is to believe our intuition even at the expense of refuting scientific investigation. The same is true in management. Many ideas and fads appear which are nothing more than seat-of-the-pants propositions. These do have some value, for they lead to hypotheses that can be researched. But the student and practitioner of management must learn to separate management fact from fiction.

INCREASING ROLE OF WOMEN AND MINORITIES IN MANAGEMENT

During the 1970s and 80s, increasing emphasis has been placed on the role of women and minorities in management. Government legislation has

FIGURE 1–5
True-False Test of Human Behavior

1. People probably never learn anything while they are deeply asleep.
2. Genius and insanity have little or no relationship to each other.
3. Better college students make less money after graduation than average students.
4. A person who learns rapidly remembers longer than a person who learns slowly.
5. All people in America are born equal in capacity for achievement.
6. Teaching a child to roller-skate very early in life gives the child a permanent advantage in this skill.
7. People are definitely either introverted or extroverted.
8. After you learn something, you forget more of it in the next few hours than in the next several days.
9. Famous people tend to be born of poor but hardworking parents.
10. Lessons learned just before going to sleep are remembered better than those learned early in the morning.
11. On the average, people of 45 are more intelligent than those of 20.
12. The tendency to imitate is probably learned.
13. There is a law of compensation in nature; for example, blind people are born with a highly developed sense of touch.
14. An especially favorable environment can probably raise a person's IQ a few points.
15. People born blind and having their sight restored as adults perceive the world almost immediately as we see it.

Answers: (1)T; (2)T; (3)F; (4)T; (5)F; (6)F; (7)F; (8)T; (9)F; (10)T; (11)F; (12)T; (13)F; (14)T; (15)F.

Source: Adapted from Gregory A. Kimble and Norman Garmezy, *Principles of General Psychology* (New York: Ronald Press, 1963), p. 4. Copyright © 1963 by the Ronald Press Company.

most certainly been one of the strongest factors in this emphasis. Table 1–1 shows the growth of the civilian labor force between 1973 and 1983. As you can see, the percentage of women and minorities in the civilian labor force has grown faster than the rate of growth of the total number of people employed. During the 1982–95 period, the number of women and minorities in the labor force is projected to continue to grow faster than the overall labor force. And women, both black and white, will account for about two thirds of the labor force *growth* during the 1980s and 90s.[10]

TABLE 1–1
Employed Civilian Labor Force

	1973*	1982*	Percentage Increase
Total employed	85,064	99,526	17.00%
Men (black and white)	52,349	56,271	7.49
Women (black and white)	32,715	43,256	31.34
Minorities (male and female)	8,128	9,189	13.05

* All numbers are in thousands.

Source: Adapted from *Handbook of Labor Statistics,* U.S. Department of Labor, Bureau of Labor Statistics, December 1983, pp. 44–48.

TABLE 1–2
Growth in Professional Technical, Managerial, and Administrative Employment

	1973*		1982*		Percent Increase	
	Professional and Technical	Managers and Administrators	Professional and Technical	Managers and Administrators	Professional and Technical	Managers and Administrators
Total employed	11,891	8,715	16,951	11,493	42.55%	31.87%
Men (black and white)	7,134	7,103	9,302	8,273	30.38	16.47
Women (black and white)	4,757	1,612	7,650	3,219	60.81	99.68
Minorities (male and female)	692	282	1,088	445	57.22	57.80

* All numbers are in thousands.
Source: Adapted from *Handbook of Labor Statistics*, U.S. Department of Labor, Bureau of Labor Statistics, December 1983, pp. 44–48.

Table 1–2 shows the growth in professional, technical, managerial, and administrative employment between 1973 and 1982. The percentage growth of women and minorities in these four job categories has been greater than the percentage growth in the total number of people employed in these areas. Top-level management jobs in most large organizations are still occupied mostly by white males. However, this will not likely be the case if the trends indicated in Tables 1–1 and 1–2 continue. And the trends *are* likely to continue.

ENTREPRENEURSHIP AND MANAGEMENT

A basic distinction is often made between a manager and an entrepreneur. The **entrepreneur** conceives the idea of what product or service to produce, starts the organization, and builds it to the point where additional people are needed. At this point, the entrepreneur can either make the transformation to a professional manager or can hire one. A *professional manager* performs the basic management functions for the ongoing organization. Entrepreneurs, then, are usually associated with relatively small organizations; professional managers are generally associated with medium- to large-sized firms. Note, however, that an entrepreneur must perform many—if not all—of the basic management functions in starting and building an organization.

The ability of managers and the style they use in performing their individual jobs are important for organizational success. The ability with which an entrepreneur performs the basic management functions also often has a strong impact on the entrepreneur's success. Time and time again, organizations have failed once they grew too large for the entrepreneur to manage alone effectively. This is not to imply that an entrepreneur cannot mature with the organization and remain in a top management position. But it is true that some entrepreneurs fail to recognize their management shortcom-

Entrepreneur–person who conceives the product or service idea, starts the organization, and builds it to the point where additional people are needed.

FIGURE 1-6
Characteristics of a Successful Entrepreneur

- Was the firstborn child in the family.
- Is married, with a supportive spouse.
- Began first company at the age of 30 or so (although years ago this happened as late as age 42).
- Tendencies to take risks and innovate showed up by the teenage years.
- Education varies. The technical entrepreneur often has a master's degree, while the garden variety of entrepreneur probably has at least a high school and probably a college degree.
- Primary motivation for becoming an entrepreneur is a psychological inability to work for anyone else.

- Personality developed mainly in interaction with the father's personality.
- Is often lucky.
- Is often in conflict with financial investors.
- Seeks advice, if it is needed, from other entrepreneurs, consultants, and college professors.
- Is essentially a doer, not a planner.
- Assumes moderate risks, not large or small ones.
- Has a never-ending sense of urgency to get things done.

Source: J. R. Mancuso, "What It Takes to Be an Entrepreneur," *Journal of Small Business Management,* October 1974, pp. 16–22; John A. Welsh and Jeffrey F. White, "Recognizing and Dealing with the Entrepreneur," *S.A.M. Advanced Management Journal,* Summer 1978, pp. 22–24.

ings. Figure 1–6 describes some general characteristics of successful entrepreneurs, as developed from data on 300 entrepreneurs. Management in Action 1–2 describes one of America's most successful entrepreneurs.

Entrepreneurship in Large and Medium-Sized Organizations

An increasing emphasis is being placed on developing the entrepreneurial traits of innovation and a willingness to take risks, among managers and employees in large and medium-sized organizations. The need for innovation and risk taking in larger organizations was illustrated in a National Science Foundation study. It found that small organizations produced about 4 times as many innovations per R&D dollar as medium-sized organizations and about 24 times as many as large organizations.[11]

Yet, many large organizations like IBM, 3M, GE, and Bristol-Myers have enviable records of innovation. They have done this by encouraging an entrepreneurial spirit among their people. In a study of America's "excellent companies," Thomas Peters and Robert Waterman, Jr. identified several characteristics essential for the development of an entrepreneurial spirit within larger organizations.[12] First, organizations must develop a system that supports and encourages people to champion their new ideas or products. Three types of champions have been identified. A *product champion* is a fanatic who believes in the specific product or idea that he or she has in mind. The *executive champion* shields the new product or idea from the organization's natural tendency to reject new products or ideas. The *godfather* is

MANAGEMENT IN ACTION 1–2

Mary Kay Ash
Founder & Chairman of the Board
Mary Kay Cosmetics, Inc.

In August 1963, Mary Kay Ash retired after a 25-year, direct-sales career. She was tired and disillusioned after years of hard work that had led only to the degree of success allowed women in the 1960s. "I thought that by starting a little business, I could give women an opportunity I had been denied." Her product was a homemade cosmetic that Mary Kay had been using since 1953. "I knew nothing about administration," Mary Kay admits. "Still don't. Luckily my husband did, and he agreed to take care of the business end of the company. I was free to handle everything else."

One month before the company was to open for business, while having breakfast and going over financial figures for the new venture, Mary Kay's husband and business partner suffered a fatal heart attack. Mary Kay was grief-stricken, confused, and scared.

However, with the help of her sons Richard and Ben, Mary Kay proceeded with her plans to open the company. It opened its doors on Friday the 13th in 500 square feet of rented space. "I never intended for the company to be more than a local business that gave women a fair chance to be successful," she says of the company that has spread to every state and several foreign countries, including Canada and Australia. In 1983, Mary Kay Cosmetics controlled about 3 percent of total cosmetics sales and 10 percent of total skin care sales nationwide. Mary Kay Cosmetics is also included in the recently published book *The 100 Best Companies to Work for in America*.

How did Mary Kay do all of this? She has four guidelines: (1) good use of time (when the company was young, she started the "five o'clock club," saying it was possible to gain ten hours each week by getting up two hours earlier than normal on five mornings); (2) organization (she makes a "must do" list every evening for the following day); (3) priorities ("When God is first, family is second, and job is third, everything goes right."); and (4) self-confidence ("You can do it!" is her motto.).

Source: Lynne Morgan Sullivan, "Mary Kay Ash," *Sky Magazine,* 1984, pp. 47–51.

typically an aging leader in the organization who provides the role model for championing.

Next, organizations that encourage entrepreneurship tolerate failures. These organizations seem to understand that some failures are to be expected when innovation is encouraged. Persistence in the face of failure and encouragement by management after a failure are key elements in developing entrepreneurship.

Finally, effective systems of communication encourage entrepreneurship. The absence of barriers to communication is essential.

MANAGEMENT AND PRODUCTIVITY

<u>**Productivity**</u> is normally defined as output per person hour of input. The Bureau of Labor Statistics (BLS) of the U.S. Department of Labor defines

Productivity—output per person hour of input.

productivity as the ratio between the production of a given commodity measured by volume and one or more of the corresponding input factors, also measured by volume.

Productivity has a profound impact on the economy. It affects our standard of living, rate of inflation, employment, and international competitive standing. Numerous factors influence the level of productivity. Figure 1–7 depicts some of the the more important factors. None of these factors is totally apart from the others. For example, the changing resource base has certainly affected the thrust of R&D efforts toward improving the fuel efficiency of automobiles. The efficiency of management and work force are, of course, interrelated. Government regulations affect all the variables.

The one factor with the potential for the greatest impact on productivity is the efficiency of management. For example, a former Motorola plant in Franklin Park, Illinois, illustrates what the U.S. worker can do under effective management. Under Motorola, the plant was having 140 defects for every 100 TV sets that passed down the assembly line. In 1974, Matsushita Electric Industrial Company bought the plant. The Japanese kept the same labor force; they even hired Motorola's vice president of engineering as president of the new subsidiary. In 1980, the reject rate was down to four to six per 100 TV sets. The number of warranty claims had been reduced eightfold. What happened? A new management made drastic changes. Automation was increased; workers were asked to think about what they were doing and how it could be done better.[13] Management in Action 1–3 illustrates how IBM improved productivity in its Office Products Division.

This book provides a logical framework for studying the job of management—with the ultimate goal of applying this knowledge to improve organizational performance.

FIGURE 1–7
Factors Influencing Productivity

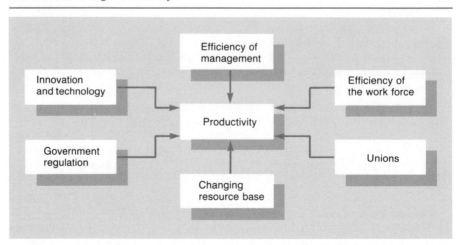

MANAGEMENT IN ACTION 1-3

Productivity at IBM's Office Products Division

IBM's productivity improvement program provides a system by which employees are paid for productivity improvements. The company's promotion policy is also based on productivity and performance. The company does not lay off people in slow economic times or when productivity improvements make their jobs unnecessary. The company also provides training and development for employees which emphasizes productivity. The results of IBM's efforts are summarized as follows:

If we were putting out today's production at our old productivity rate of 1955, our present plant would require an additional 1 million square feet of floor space, plus the expensive machinery to fill it—just for typewriters. Even more significantly, the improved productivity has financially permitted us to build a first-rate staff of development engineers, leading to the design and introduction of the Selectric, the copier, and other new office products and the building of new plants in Austin, Texas, and in countries overseas.

Source: Adapted from Clair F. Vough and Bernard Asbell, *Productivity: A Practical Program for Improving Efficiency* (New York: AMACOM, 1979), pp. 5–6.

ORGANIZATION OF BOOK

This book is divided into six basic sections:

Section 1: The Management Process.

Section 2: Decision-Making and Planning Skills.

Section 3: Administrative Skills.

Section 4: Human Relations Skills.

Section 5: Improving Organizational Performance.

Section 6: Contemporary Issues in Management.

Section 1 is an overview of the management process. In Chapter 1, management is defined; the functions, roles, and skills of management are described. The importance of entrepreneurship in organizations is also discussed. Chapter 2 presents a historical view of the management process. Chapter 3 discusses the important concepts of the social responsibility of organizations and of ethics in management.

Section 2 analyzes the decision-making and planning skills of management. Chapter 4 focuses on the manager as a decision maker. Planning skills are described in three chapters. Chapter 5 discusses the importance of objectives to developing effective planning skills. Chapter 6 describes the planning process in detail. Then, Chapter 7 discusses applying planning skills to the production and operations processes that produce an organization's goods or services.

Section 3 analyzes the administrative skills of management. Organizing and the development of organizational structures are described in Chapters

8 and 9. Chapter 10 is concerned with staffing. Chapter 11 describes the controlling function of management. The application of control in the production and operations process is described in Chapter 12.

Section 4 analyzes the human relations skills that are essential for managers. Chapter 13 develops an understanding of motivation. Chapter 14 describes the importance of leadership in achieving improved organizational performance. Chapter 15 develops an understanding of work groups and creativity in organizations. Finally, Chapter 16 describes approaches to managing conflict and stress.

Section 5 is designed around the philosophy that the successful manager not only must have knowledge of the decision-making, planning, administrative, and human relations skills but also must apply this knowledge to improve organizational performance. Chapter 17 describes the importance of communication to organizational performance. Appraising and rewarding performance is discussed in Chapter 18. The importance of developing people is described in Chapter 19.

Section 6 looks at the management process from a contemporary viewpoint. The topics of managing change and culture are examined in Chapter 20. The role and importance of management information systems are described in Chapter 21. Finally, the increasing internationalization of business is described in Chapter 22.

A sequential integration of the different sections of this book is summarized in Figure 1–8. This figure shows that the ultimate goal of understanding and applying the skills of management is to improve an organization's performance.

SUMMARY

Management is a process that involves guiding or directing a group of people toward organizational goals or objectives. Management must decide what the objectives of the organization are, determine what must be done to achieve them, communicate these objectives to the people whose performance is required to achieve them, and then determine how progress on the accomplishment of these objectives is to be measured.

Several approaches have been used to analyze the management process. To examine management, three common approaches categorize (1) the work that is performed (management functions), (2) the roles that managers perform, or (3) the skills required of managers in performing the job of management.

A principle is an accepted rule of action. Principles of management have largely been developed through observation and deduction.

During the 1970s and 80s, increasing emphasis has been placed on the

FIGURE 1–8

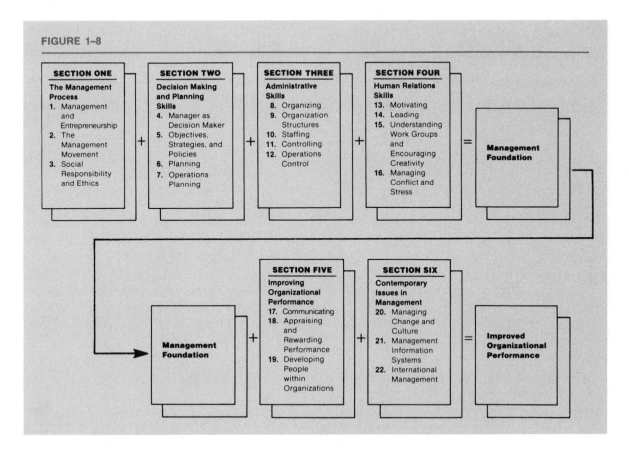

role of women and minorities in management. The numbers of women and minorities in management have been increasing and are likely to continue to increase.

The entrepreneur is the person who conceives the idea of what product or service the organization is going to produce, starts the organization, and builds it to the point where additional people are needed. Although entrepreneurship is mainly associated with small organizations, an increasing emphasis is being placed on developing the entrepreneurial characteristics of innovation and willingness to take risks, among managers and employees in large and medium-sized organizations.

Productivity is defined as output per person hour of input. Some of the more important factors influencing productivity are efficiency of management and of the work force, unions, changing resource base, government regulation, innovation, and technology. The one factor that has the potential to have the most significant impact on productivity is the efficiency of management.

References and Additional Readings

[1] Throughout this book, the terms *goals* an *objectives* will be used interchangeably.

[2] This entire story is adapted from Peter Drucker, *The Best of Peter Drucker on Management* (New York: Harper & Row, 1977), p. 61.

[3] Gary P. Latham and Gary A. Yukl, "A Review of Research on the Application of Goal Setting in Organizations," *Academy of Management Journal,* December 1975, p. 840.

[4] Ibid.

[5] Henry Mintzberg, "The Manager's Job: Folklore and Fact," *Harvard Business Review,* July–August 1975, pp. 49–61.

[6] T. R. Sarlin and V. L. Allen, "Role Theory" in *The Handbook of Social Psychology,* 2d ed., vol. 1, ed. G. Lindzey and E. Aronson (Reading, Mass.: Addison-Wesley Publishing, 1968), pp. 488–567.

[7] Henry Mintzberg, *The Nature of Managerial Work* (New York: Harper & Row, 1972), pp. 54–99.

[8] For more information on the roles of managers see John P. Kotter, *The General Managers* (New York: Free Press, 1982).

[9] *The Random House Dictionary of the English Language* (New York: Random House, 1966), under the word *principle*.

[10] *Employment Projections for 1995,* U.S. Department of Labor, Bureau of Labor Statistics, March 1984, p. 4.

[11] Lucien Rhodes and Cathryn Jakobson, "Small Companies: America's Hope for the 1980s," *Inc.,* April 1981, p. 44.

[12] Much of the following material is drawn from Thomas J. Peters and Robert H. Waterman, Jr., *In Search of Excellence* (New York: Harper & Row, 1982), pp. 202–9.

[13] Jeremy Main, "The Battle for Quality Begins," *Fortune,* December 29, 1980, p. 32.

Selected Management and Related Periodicals

Selected periodicals from this list are referenced throughout the text. This list is given so the reader will have a listing of the more commonly referenced management and related periodicals.

Academy of Management Journal

Academy of Management Review

Administrative Management

Administrative Science Quarterly

Business Horizons

California Management Review

Canadian Business Review

Columbia Journal of World Business

Decision Sciences

Forbes

Fortune

Journal of Small Business Management

Harvard Business Review

Human Resource Management

Industrial and Labor Relations Review

Journal of Applied Behavioral Science

Journal of Applied Psychology

Journal of Business

Journal of Human Resources

Journal of Management Studies

Journal of Systems Management

Management Accounting

Management of Personnel Quarterly

Management International Review

Management Review

Management Science

Managerial Planning

Michigan Business Review

Monthly Labor Review

Organizational Behavior and Human Performance

Long Range Planning

Organizational Dynamics

Personnel

Personnel Administrator

Personnel Management

Personnel Psychology

Public Administration Review

S.A.M. Advanced Management Journal

Sloan Management Review

Strategic Management Journal

Supervisory Management

Training and Development Journal

The Wall Street Journal (newspaper)

Review Questions

1. What is management? *guiding group toward org. goals/objectives*
2. What are the four general categories of organizational objectives? *profits, service, employee needs, social resp.*
3. Name and describe the basic management functions. *P C O S I*
4. Outline the roles of a manager. *Interpersonal, Informational, Decisional*
5. Define the three basic skills required in management.
6. Explain how the composition of the managerial work force is changing in terms of sex and race.
7. How are principles of management developed? *observation & deduction*
8. Distinguish between a professional manager and an entrepreneur.
9. What are three essential characteristics necessary for developing an entrepreneurial spirit in larger organizations? *communication, tolerance—innovation, exec. champ, godfather*
10. Define productivity. *output/hr of input*
11. What factors influence the level of productivity? *environment, efficiency of management, unions, technology, govt. regs*

Discussion Questions

1. Management has often been described as a universal process, meaning that the basics of management are transferable and applicable in almost any environment. Comment on this statement.
2. How does one decide who is and who is not a manager in a given organization? For example, is the operator of a one-person business, such as a corner grocery store, a manager?
3. Do you think that management can be learned through books and study or only through experience?
4. Discuss the following statement: "All entrepreneurs are managers, but not all managers are entrepreneurs."

Incident 1–1
Wadsworth Company

Last year, Donna Carroll was appointed supervisor of the small parts subassembly department of the Wadsworth Company. The department employed 28 people. Donna had wanted the promotion. She felt that her 15 years of experience in various jobs at the company qualified her for the job.

Donna decided to have two group leaders report to her. She appointed Evelyn Castalos and Bill Degger to these new positions. She made it clear, however, that they retained their present operative jobs and were expected to contribute to the direct productive efforts. Evelyn is ambitious and a highly productive employee. Bill is a steady, reliable employee.

Work assignment decisions were to be made by Evelyn. She took on this responsibility with great enthusiasm and drew up work-scheduling plans covering a period of one month. She believed productivity could be increased by 8 percent due primarily to work assignment improvements. She went regularly from workplace to workplace, checking the finished volume of work at each station. Bill assumed, at the suggestion and support of Donna, the work of training new employees or retraining present employees on new work coming into the department.

Donna spent most of her time preparing and reading reports. She made certain to be friendly with most of the other supervisors. She talked with them frequently and gave them assistance in filling out forms and reports required by their jobs. She also frequently circulated among the employees of her department, exchanging friendly remarks. However, when an employee asked a question concerning work, Donna referred the person to either Evelyn or Bill.

Some of the employees complained among themselves that the work assignments were most unfair. They contended that favorites of Evelyn got all the easy jobs and, although the present volume of work had increased, no extra help was being hired. Several times, the employees talked with Donna about this, but Donna referred them to Evelyn, each time. Likewise, many of the employees complained about Bill's performance. They based their opinions on the apparent lack of knowledge and skill the new employees have after receiving training from Bill.

Questions

1. Do you feel that the duties being handled by Evelyn and Bill should have been delegated by Donna?
2. What difficulties do you see for Evelyn and Bill in being both group leaders and operative employees:
3. Do you consider Evelyn and Bill to be managers? Why or why not?

Incident 1–2
The Expansion of Blue Streak

Arthur Benton started the Blue Streak Delivery Company five years ago. Blue Streak initially provided commercial delivery services for all packages within the city of Unionville (population 1 million).

Art started with himself, one clerk, and one driver. Within three years, Blue Streak had grown to the point of requiring 4 clerks and 16 drivers. It was then that Art decided to expand and provide statewide service. He figured that this would initially require the addition of two new offices, one located at Logantown (population 500,000) in the southern part of the state and one at Thomas City (population 250,000) in the northern part of the state. Each office was staffed with a manager, two clerks, and four drivers. Because both Logantown and Thomas City were within 150 miles of Unionville, Art was able to visit each office at least once a week and personally coordinate the operations in addition to providing general management assistance. The statewide delivery system met with immediate success and reported a healthy profit for the first year.

The next year, Art decided to expand and include two neighboring states. Art set up two offices in each of the two neighboring states. However, operations never seemed to go smoothly in the neighboring states. Schedules were constantly being fouled up, deliveries were lost, and customer complaints multiplied. After nine months, Art changed office managers in all four out-of-state offices. Things still did not improve. Convinced that he was the only one capable of straightening out the out-of-state offices. Art began visiting them once every two weeks. This schedule required Art to spend at least half of his time on the road traveling between offices. After four months of this activity, the entire Blue Streak operation appeared disorganized and profit had declined dramatically.

Questions

1. What is wrong with Blue Streak?
2. Do you think Art is a good entrepreneur? A good manager?
3. What would you suggest that Art do at this point?

Exercise

Required Attributes of a Manager

The following ads were taken from the Want Ads section of a newspaper. All company names and locations have been disguised.

A. Choose the job that is most attractive to you.

B. Your instructor will form you into groups with other students that selected the same job as you. Your group should then develop a list of required and desirable skills for the job.

C. Each group should be prepared to present and defend their list before the class.

Objectives

1. To explore the reasons why management did not emerge as a recognized discipline until the 20th century.
2. To develop an understanding of the events and persons that led to the development of modern management.
3. To provide a historical foundation for later chapters in the text.

2

The Management Movement

Chapter Outline

History is useful to us not because it provides us with final answers about the fate of man, but because it offers us an inexhaustible storehouse of lifestyles, civilizational modes, and ways of acting that we can draw on as we face the future. History gives us balance, patience, and a deeper understanding of what it means to live and die. History cannot save us in any ultimate sense, but it can deepen our understanding of humanity's potentialities and limitations.

Arthur N. Gilbert*

An understanding of the history of any discipline is necessary to understand where the discipline currently is and where it is going. Management is no exception. Many of today's managerial problems began in the early management movement. Understanding their historical evolution helps the modern manager to cope with them. It also helps today's managers develop a feel for why the managerial approaches that worked in earlier times do not necessarily work today. The challenge to present and future managers is not to memorize historical names and dates; it is to develop a feel for why and how things happened—and to apply this knowledge to the practice of management.

Although some management was needed centuries ago, very little sophisticated management was needed prior to the 19th century. Traffic lights were not needed—and therefore not invented—before automobile travel reached a certain level of sophistication. And management, as it now exists, was not needed or even known before the maturing of the corporate form of organization. The development of management thought and concepts is an example too of people responding to the needs of their environment. The environment that led up to and surrounded the emergence of management thought is the subject of this chapter.

U.S. INDUSTRIAL REVOLUTION

Daniel Wren has described the Industrial Revolution in America as having three facets: power, transportation, and communication.[1] The steam engine, developed and perfected by James Watt in England in the late 18th century, came to America shortly thereafter. The steam engine provided more efficient and cheaper power; it allowed factories to produce more goods at cheaper prices; it increased the market for goods. And the steam engine allowed factories to be located away from water power. This alone had a profound

---

* Arthur N. Gilbert, *In Search of a Meaningful Past* (Boston: Houghton Mifflin, 1972), p. 2.

effect on the development of this country. Now factories could be located near their suppliers, customers, and the most desirable labor markets instead of only near rivers.

Transportation growth began with the development of canals around 1755. America's first railroad charter was obtained by John Stevens in 1815. But he lacked financial support and did not build the first railroad until 1830.[2] A railroad boom then followed in the late 1840s. The track mileage increased from just under 6,000 miles in 1848 to over 30,000 miles by 1860.[3] As the railroad network grew, so did the size of individual rail companies. By 1855, at least 13 rail companies operated and maintained more than 200 miles of track. By the mid-1850s, the railroad industry had clearly established itself as America's first big business. It was the first industry whose scope of operations extended beyond the local area.[4] Although textiles were America's first entry into the industrial age, they were basically a local business with much smaller financial needs than rail companies.[5] Unlike local industries, railroad networks often spanned hundreds of miles, creating control and communication problems. Facilities could not be inspected in a matter of hours; decisions had to be made within a rapidly changing framework; scheduling became complicated. Beyond the day-to-day operating decisions, other management decisions became more complex. Long-range decisions had to be made about the expansion of facilities, new equipment purchases, and how to finance these operations.

Unlike the textile industry, which was transplanted from Europe, there were few precedents to guide the managers of the railroad companies.[6] Thus, rail company managers were the first in this country to need a sophisticated approach to management.

The railroads also made another significant contribution to the development of management: they created national and increasingly urban markets. Urban and industrial centers sprang up all along their miles of tracks. Thus, by providing rapid movement of raw materials and finished goods, railroads made a truly national market possible.

The third facet of the American Industrial Revolution—communication—was primed in 1844 by Samuel F. B. Morse's invention of the telegraph. Using the telegraph, managers could coordinate and communicate with speed and efficiency.

By 1860, the year generally thought of as the start of the Industrial Revolution in this country, power, transportation, and communication had advanced to the point that they served as an inducement to the entrepreneur.

CAPTAINS OF INDUSTRY

During the last 25 years of the 19th century, an important change took place in American industry. The economy shifted from mainly agrarian to one more involved with manufactured goods and industrial markets.[7] This

Captains of industry–
dominated and built
corporate giants during the
last 25 years of the 19th
century; included John D.
Rockefeller, James B.
Duke, Andrew Carnegie,
Cornelius Vanderbilt, and
others.

was a direct result of the urbanization brought about by a nationwide railroad system.

American business during this period was dominated and shaped by **captains of industry.** These captains of industry included men like John D. Rockefeller (oil—see Management in Action 2–1), James B. Duke (tobacco), Andrew Carnegie (steel) and Cornelius Vanderbilt (steamships and railroads). Unlike the laissez-faire attitudes of previous generations, these men often pursued profit and self-interest above all else. While their methods have been questioned, they did obtain results. Under these men giant companies were formed through mergers in both the consumer and producer goods industries. They created new forms of organizations and introduced new methods of marketing. For the first time, nationwide distributing and marketing organizations were formed. The birth of the corporate giant also altered the business decision-making environment.

For the empire building and methods of the captains of industry, previous management methods no longer applied. Government began to regulate business. In 1890, the Sherman Antitrust Act, which sought to check corporate practices "in restraint of trade," was passed.

By 1890, previous management methods were no longer applicable to U.S. industry. No longer could managers make on-the-spot decisions and maintain records in their heads. Corporations had become large-scale, with national markets. Communication and transportation had expanded and greatly helped industrial growth. Technological innovations contributed to industrial growth: The invention of the internal combustion engine and the use of electricity as a power source greatly speeded industrial development at the close of the 19th centruy.

However, despite what seemed an ideal climate for prosperity and productivity, wages were low.[8] Production methods were crude; worker training was almost nonexistent. There were no methods or standards for measuring work. Work had not been studied to determine the most desirable way to complete a task. The psychological and physical aspects of a job—like boredom, monotony, and fatigue—were not studied or even considered in the design of most jobs.

At this point in the development of management, the engineering profession made significant contributions. Engineers designed, built, installed, and made operative the production systems. It was only natural, then, for them to study the methods used in operating these systems.

SCIENTIFIC MANAGEMENT AND F. W. TAYLOR

The development of specialized tasks and of departments within organizations had come with the rapid industrial growth and the creation of big business. One person no longer performed every task but rather specialized in performing only a few tasks. This created a need to coordinate, integrate,

MANAGEMENT IN ACTION 2–1

John D. Rockefeller—Businessman and Philanthropist

John D. Rockefeller was born on July 8, 1839, in Richford, New York. He was the son of an itinerant, untrained (although fairly well off) doctor. Rockefeller took his first job as an assistant bookkeeper at age of 16 for a salary of $300 a year. Three and a half years later, a friend suggested that they form a partnership in a wholesale commission business in grain, meats, and produce. His partner Maurice Clark later described Rockefeller as "methodical to an extreme, careful as to details, and exacting to a fraction. If there was a cent due us, he wanted it. If there was a cent due a customer, he wanted him to have it."

Spurred by the needs of the army during the Civil War, the wholesale commission business grew tremendously. After looking around for a place to invest the profits, Clark and Rockefeller put $4,000 in a speculative, get-rich-quick oil refining business. On January 10, 1870, after many fast-growing, profitable years, the Rockefeller firm was reorganized as a corporation and named the Standard Oil Company of Ohio.

In 1916, the *New York Times* reported that Rockefeller's oil holdings were worth $500 million, with his total worth exceeding a billion dollars. One-day changes in the price of oil could cause his wealth to fluctuate by millions.

Source: Jules Abels, *The Rockefeller Million* (London: Frederick Muller, 1967).

and systematize the work flow. The time spent on each item could be significant if a company was producing several thousand items. Increased production plus the new need for integrating and systematizing the work flow caused engineers to begin to study work flows and job content.

The spark generally credited with igniting the interest of engineers to general business problems was a paper presented in 1886 by Henry Towne, president of the Yale and Towne Manufacturing Company, to the American Society of Mechanical Engineers. Towne stressed that engineers should be concerned with the financial and profit orientation of the business as well as their traditional technical responsibilities.[9] A young mechanical engineer named Frederick Winslow Taylor was seated in the audience. As you will see, Taylor later had a profound impact on the development of management.

Taylor's first job was as an apprentice with the Enterprise Hydraulic Works of Philadelphia.[10] Here Taylor learned pattern making and machining. Upon finishing his apprenticeship in 1878, Taylor joined Midvale Steel Company as a common laborer. In six short years, he rose through eight positions to chief engineer. During his earlier years at Midvale, Taylor worked with and observed production workers at all levels. It did not take him long to figure out that many workers put forth less than 100 percent effort. Taylor referred to this behavior of restricting output as **soldiering.** Because soldiering was in conflict with Taylor's Quaker-Puritan background, it was hard for him to understand and accept. He decided to find out why workers soldiered.

Taylor quickly saw that workers had little or no reason to produce more—

Soldiering—describes the actions of employees who intentionally restrict output.

most wage systems of that time were based on attendance and position. Piece-rate systems had been tried before but generally failed because of poor use and weak standards. Taylor believed a piece-rate system would work—if the workers believed that the standard had been fairly set and that management would stick to that standard. Taylor wanted to use scientific and empirical methods rather than tradition and custom for setting work standards. Taylor's efforts became the true beginning of scientific management.

Taylor first formally presented his views to the Society of Mechanical Engineers in 1895.[11] His views were expanded in book form in 1903 and in 1911.[12] **Scientific management,** as developed by Taylor, was based upon four main principles:

1. The development of a scientific method of designing jobs to replace the old rule-of-thumb methods. This involved gathering, classifying, and tabulating data to arrive at the "one best way" to perform a task or a series of tasks.

2. The scientific selection and progressive teaching and development of employees. Taylor saw the value of matching the job to the worker. He also emphasized the need to study worker strengths and weaknesses and to provide training to improve employee performance.

3. The bringing together of scientifically selected employees and scientifically developed methods for designing jobs. Taylor believed that new and scientific methods of job design should not merely be put before an employee; they also should be fully explained by management. He believed that employees would show little resistance to changes in methods if they understood the reasons for the change—and they saw a chance for greater earnings for themselves.

4. A division of work resulting in an interdependence between management and the workers. Taylor felt that if they were truly dependent on one another, then cooperation would naturally follow.[13]

Scientific management was a complete mental revolution for both management and employees toward their respective duties and toward each other.[14] It was a new philosophy and attitude toward the use of human effort. It emphasized maximum output with minimum effort through the elimination of waste and inefficiency at the operative level.[15] A methodological approach was used to study job tasks. This approach included research and experimentation methods (scientific methods). Standards were set in the areas of personnel, working conditions, equipment, output, and procedures. The managers planned the work; the workers performed it. The result was closer cooperation between managers and workers.

The scientific study of work also emphasized specialization and division of labor. Thus, the need for an organizational framework became more and more apparent. The concepts of line and staff were developed. In an effort

MANAGEMENT IN ACTION 2–2

A Steelworker Made Management History

In 1899, a man named Henry Noll loaded 48 tons of pig iron in one day as part of a scientific management experiment conducted by Frederick W. Taylor for Bethlehem Steel. From that experiment, Taylor developed a high-incentive work program with a set sequence of work and rest motions. The program—described in Taylor's *Principles of Scientific Management*—was designed to more than triple the amount a worker could load in a day. The Taylor method was adopted by companies all over the country.

When the results of the experiment were published, Henry Noll—under the pseudonym "Schmidt"—was described only as an ambitious and healthy 27-year-old man. In a social commentary published 12 years later, Upton Sinclair described Taylor's method as inhumane and accused him of unfairly inducing "Schmidt" to perform 362 percent more work for 61 percent more pay.

In response to the criticism, Taylor and others made several unsuccessful attempts to find Henry Noll, and rumors began to surface that he had died of overexertion. In 1914, he was finally found and pronounced healthy by a physician. Henry Noll—"Schmidt"—died a natural death in 1925.

Source: Ann Kovalenko, *The Sunday Call–Chronicle*, Allentown, Pa., December 6, 1964.

to motivate workers, wage incentives were developed in most scientific management programs. Once standards were set, managers began to monitor actual performance and compare it with the standards. Thus began the managerial function of control.

Scientific management is actually a philosophy about the relationship between people and work—it is not a technique or an efficiency device. Taylor's ideas and scientific management were based on a concern not only for the proper design of the job but also for the worker. This has often not been understood. Taylor and scientific management were (and still are) attacked as being inhumane and interested only in increased output. The key to Taylor's thinking was that he saw scientific management as benefiting both management and the worker equally: Management could achieve more work in a given amount of time; the worker could produce more—and hence he could earn more—with little or no additional effort. In summary, Taylor and other scientific management pioneers believed that employees could be motivated by economic rewards, provided that those rewards were related to individual performance. Management in Action 2–2 provides an interesting story related to Frederick Taylor.

OTHER SCIENTIFIC MANAGEMENT PIONEERS

Several disciples and colleagues of Taylor helped to promote scientific management. Carl Barth was often called the most orthodox of Taylor's followers. He worked with Taylor at Bethlehem Steel and followed him as a consultant when Taylor left Bethlehem. Barth did not alter or add to scientific management in any great manner. Rather, he worked to popularize Taylor's ideas.

Morris Cooke worked directly with Taylor on several occasions. Cooke's major contribution was to apply scientific management to educational and municipal organizations. Cooke worked hard to bring management and labor together through scientific management. His thesis was that labor was as responsible for production as management. Cooke believed that increased production would improve the position of both.[16] Thus, Cooke broadened the scope of scientific management and helped gain the support of organized labor.

Henry Lawrence Gantt worked with Taylor at Midvale Steel and at Bethlehem Steel. Gantt is best known for his work in production control; the "Gantt chart" is still in use today. Gantt was also one of the first management pioneers to state publicly the social responsibility of management and business. He believed that the community would attempt to take over business if the business system neglected its social responsibilities.[17]

Frank and Lillian Gilbreth were important to the early management movement as a husband-and-wife team and as individuals. Frank Gilbreth's major area of interest was the study of motions and work methods. Lillian Gilbreth's primary field was psychology. By combining motion study and psychology, the Gilbreths contributed greatly in the areas of fatigue, monotony, micromotion study, and morale.

Harrington Emerson, who coined the term *efficiency engineer*, was one of the first to recognize the importance of good organization. Emerson felt that waste and inefficiency were eroding the American industrial system. He believed that organization and scientific management could eliminate most waste and inefficiency. Emerson also developed organized management consulting at a time when consulting engineers were still mainly concerned with technical rather than managerial problems.

FAYOL'S THEORY OF MANAGEMENT

Henri Fayol, a Frenchman, was the first to issue a complete statement on a theory of general management. Born of relatively well-to-do parents, Fayol graduated as a mining engineer. He started in 1860 as a junior executive of a coal mining and iron foundry company. In 1888, the company was near bankruptcy. Fayol took over as managing director and rapidly turned the company into a financially sound organization. After retirement in 1918, Fayol lectured and popularized his theory of administration. He became especially interested in applying administrative theory to government. Fayol's major work *Administration Industrielle et Generale,* was published in 1916.[18] Unfortunately, this work was not translated into English until 1930 and then in only a very limited number of copies. The book was not readily available in English until 1949.

Possibly Fayol's greatest contribution was his discussion of management principles and elements. Fayol gave the following 14 "principles of management." (He stressed flexibility in the application of these principles and that allowances should be made for different and changing circumstances.)

1. Division of work—concept of specialization of work.
2. Authority—formal (positional) authority versus personal authority.
3. Discipline—based on obedience and respect.
4. Unity of command—each employee should receive orders from only one superior.
5. Unity of direction—one boss and one plan for a group of activities having the same objective.
6. Subordination of individual interests to the general interest—plea to abolish the tendency of placing individual interest ahead of the group interest.
7. Remuneration—mode of payment of wages was dependent on many factors.
8. Centralization—degree of centralization desired depended on the situation authority and the formal communication channels.
9. Scalar chain (line of authority)—shows the routing of the line of authority and formal communication channels.
10. Order—ensured a place for everything.
11. Equity—resulted from kindness and justice.
12. Stability of tenured personnel—called for orderly personnel planning.
13. Initiative—called for individual zeal and energy in all efforts.
14. Esprit de corps—stressed the building of harmony and unity within the organization.

Fayol developed his list of principles from the practices he had used most often in his own work. He used them as broad and general guidelines for effective management. His real contribution was not the 14 principles themselves—many of these were the products of the early factory system—but rather his formal recognition and synthesis of these principles.

In presenting his "elements of management," Fayol was probably the first to outline what today are called the functions of management. Fayol listed planning, organizing, commanding, coordinating, and controlling as elements of management. He most emphasized planning and organizing because he viewed these elements as primary and essential to the other functions.

The works of Taylor and Fayol are essentially complementary. Both believed that proper management of personnel and other resources was the key to organizational success. Both used a scientific approach to management. Their major difference was in their orientation. Taylor stressed the management of operative work, while Fayol stressed the management of organization.

PERIOD OF SOLIDIFICATION

The 1920s and most of the 30s was a period of solidification and popularization of management as a discipline. The acceptance of management as a respectable discipline was gained through several avenues. Universities and colleges began to teach management; by 1925, most schools of engineering were offering classes in management.[19] Professional societies began to take an interest in management. Much of the management pioneers' work was presented through the American Society of Mechanical Engineers; after the turn of the century, many other professional societies began to promote management. In 1912, the Society to Promote the Science of Management was founded. The society was reorganized in 1916 as the Taylor Society. In 1936, it merged with the Society of Industrial Engineers to form the Society for the Advancement of Management, still a viable organization. The American Management Association was founded in 1923.

The first meeting of management teachers, sponsored by the Taylor Society, was held in New York in December 1924.[20] The participants agreed that the first course in management should be called Industrial Organization and Management—they could not agree on what should be required in a management curriculum. After this meeting, professors began writing textbooks in the field of management.

During the 1930s, management teachers and practitioners began to stress organization. *Onward Industry!* by J. D. Mooney and A. C. Reiley appeared in 1931 and generated interest in the historical development of organizations. Several other books in this era focused on the organizing function. By the mid-30s, management was truly a recognized discipline. The major events leading to this are summarized in Figure 2–1.

THE HUMAN RELATIONS THRUST

The Great Depression saw unemployment in excess of 25 percent. Afterwards, unions sought and gained major advantages for the working class. In this period, known as the Golden Age of Unionism, legislatures and courts actively supported organized labor and the worker. Figure 2–2 contains a summary of the major pro-union laws passed during the 1920s and 1930s.

Organized labor and workers were attracting more attention. Therefore, emphasis began to be placed on understanding workers and their needs—it was the birth of the human relations movement. The earlier lack of emphasis on human relations was made prominent by the now famous Hawthorne Studies.[21]

FIGURE 2-1
Significant Events Contributing to the Solidification of Management

- First conference on "Scientific Management," October 1911.
- First doctoral dissertation on subject of scientific management by H. R. Drury at Columbia University, 1915.
- Founding of professional management societies: Society to Promote the Science of Management, 1912; Society of Industrial Engineers, 1917; American Management Association, 1923; Society for Advancement of Management, 1936.
- First meeting of management teachers, December 1924.

The Hawthorne Studies began in 1924 when the National Research Council of the National Academy of Sciences began a project to define the relationship between physical working conditions and worker productivity. The Hawthorne Plant of Western Electric in Cicero, Illinois, was the study site. First, the researchers lowered the level of lighting, expecting productivity to decrease. To their astonishment, productivity increased. Next they altered such variables as wage payments, and rest periods, length of workday—and production still increased.

Baffled by the results, the researchers called in a team of psychologists from Harvard University, led by Elton Mayo. After much analysis, the psychologists concluded that other factors besides the physical environment affected worker productivity. They found that workers reacted to the psychological and social conditions at work—such as informal group pressures, individual recognition, and participation in decision making. For the first time, research evidence had shown the potential impact of the behavioral sciences on management.

While the methods used and the conclusions reached by the Hawthorne researchers have been questioned, they did generate great interest in the human problems in the work place.[22]

FIGURE 2-2
Significant Pro-Union Legislation during the 1920s and 1930s

Railway Labor Act of 1926	Gave railway workers the right to form unions and engage in collective bargaining; established a corresponding obligation for employers to recognize and collectively bargain with the union.
Norris–La Guardia Act of 1932	Severely restricted the use of injunctions to limit union activity.
National Labor Relations Act of 1935 (Wagner Act)	Resulted in full, enforceable rights of employees to join unions and to engage in collective bargaining with their employer, who was legally obligated to do so.
Fair Labor Standards Act of 1938	Established minimum wages and required that time-and-a-half wages be paid for hours worked over 40 in one week.

At the same time, Mary Parker Follett spurred the human relations movement. Mary Follett was not a businesswoman in the sense of managing her own business. But her writings and lectures did have great impact on many business and government leaders. While concerned with many aspects of the management process, her basic theory was that the fundamental problem of any organization was to build and maintain dynamic, yet harmonious, human relations within the organization.[23] In 1938, Chester Barnard (president of New Jersey Bell Telephone for many years) published a book which combined a thorough knowledge of organization theory and sociology.[24] Barnard viewed the organization as a social structure. He stressed the psychosocial aspects of organizations. Effectively integrating traditional management and the behavioral sciences, Barnard's work has had a great impact on both managers and teachers of management.

THE PROFESSIONAL MANAGER

The career manager, or professional manager, did not exist until the 1930s. Until this time, managers could be placed into one of three categories: owner-managers, captains of industry, or financial managers. The owner-managers dominated until after the Civil War. The captains of industry controlled organizations from the 1880s through the turn of the century. The financial managers operated much the same as the captains of industry, except they often did not own the enterprises they controlled and operated. The financial managers dominated from around 1905 until the early 1930s, when public confidence in business organizations was severely weakened by the Great Depression.

During this time of weakened public confidence, people began to enter managerial jobs to perform those functions rather than because they owned the business. Thus emerged the professional manager. The **professional manager** is a career person who does not necessarily have a controlling interest in the enterprise for which he or she works. Professional managers realize their responsibility to three groups: employees, stockholders, and the public. With expanded technology and more complex organizations, the professional manager became more and more prevalent.

Professional manager–career manager who does not necessarily have a controlling interest in the organization and who realizes a responsibility to employees, stockholders, and the public.

CHANGING STYLES OF MANAGEMENT

As organizations grew in size and complexity, managers began stressing the importance of workers and their needs. As managers studied the worker and developed theories about worker behavior, new styles and methods of managing emerged.

One innovative style of managing was that of James F. Lincoln. The serious illness of his brother forced Lincoln to assume the top management position of the Lincoln Electric Company in 1913.[25] He knew little about managing a business and had no top management experience. But Lincoln remembered his former football days and the cooperation needed on the gridiron. He sought the help of his employees in managing the company.

Lincoln realized that effective cooperation required rewards. Therefore he designed a plan which coupled an incentive system with a request for cooperation. Lincoln emphasized the basic need of all individuals to express themselves. Specifically, the plan contained the following components:

1. An advisory board of employees.
2. A piece-rate method of compensation wherever possible.
3. A suggestion system.
4. Employee ownership of stock.
5. Year-end bonuses.
6. Life insurance for all employees.
7. Two weeks of paid vacation.
8. An annuity pension plan.
9. Promotion policy.

The development of the Lincoln Electric Company can be attributed to its innovative management. It certainly has been successful. For several decades, Lincoln workers have consistently been among the highest paid in their industry in the world—they have averaged almost double the total pay of employees in competing companies. Lincoln's selling price has consistently been lower than any comparable product. And the company has consistently paid a dividend since 1918. Management in Action 2–3 provides some additional information about Lincoln Electric.

Another innovative manager, Henry Dennison (1877–1952), felt that the strengths of an organization came from its members and that the sources of power are the incentives, habits, and traditions that influence people in an organization.[26] Dennison believed that an organization has greatest strength if: all of its members are strongly motivated; their actions lose no effectiveness by frictions, conflicts, or unbalance; and their actions move in a single direction, reinforcing each other. He believed that management's primary purpose was to provide conditions under which employees work most readily and effectively. Instead of designing an organizational structure first, Dennison advocated finding "like-minded" people, grouping them, and then developing the total organizational structure. In summary, Dennison believed that management attention must focus on causes and effects in the field of human behavior. Dennison successfully practiced his management approach in the 1920s and 1930s at the Dennison Manufacturing Company, which was also one of the early companies to implement the Taylor system of scientific management.

Charles McCormick and William Given, Jr., were top managers who applied a human relations philosophy to their organizations. Both McCormick's

MANAGEMENT IN ACTION 2–3

Innovation Management Practices at Lincoln Electric

The Lincoln Electric Company began in 1895 as a manufacturer of electric motors. Today it is the world's largest manufacturer of welding machines and metal electrodes. In 1981, Lincoln Electric employed 2,624 workers at an average annual wage of $44,000—substantially higher than the average for most production workers. There has not been a layoff in over 30 years.

Lincoln Electric employs an "incentive management" system. Many of Lincoln's production workers are paid by piecework. Bonuses are given for reliability and suggestions and have averaged 100 percent of base pay in many years. The company also practices a policy of continuous employment—

a minimum of 30 hours of work per week for each employee.

Why haven't guaranteed work and high wages put Lincoln in a poor competitive position in their industry? The primary reason is high productivity. According to Lincoln, their output per employee has always been 100 percent to 150 percent above that of most other companies.

Lincoln's financial performance has reflected its success. Between 1974 and 1981, sales rose steadily from $233 million to $527 million. Earnings in the same period increased from $17.5 million to $40 million.

Sources: William Baldwin, "This is the Answer," *Forbes*, July 5, 1982, pp. 50–52; Maryann Mrowca, "Ohio Firm Relies on Incentive Pay System to Motivate Workers and Maintain Profits," *The Wall Street Journal*, August 12, 1983, p. 50; Robert Fager, "Managing Guaranteed Employment," *Harvard Business Review*, May–June 1978, pp. 103–15.

and Given's styles of management were based on worker involvement in the decision-making process.

McCormick, the manufacturer of spices and extracts, developed and made famous the **McCormick multiple-management plan.**[27] This plan used participation as a training and motivating tool by selecting 17 promising young people from various departments within the company to form a junior board of directors. The junior board met with the senior board once a month and submitted its suggestions. Beside the immediate benefits of providing suggestions, the junior board provided early identification of management talent, opened communication lines, and relieved senior board members of much of the detailed planning and research. The huge success of the junior board led to the creation of sales and factory boards that operated in much the same way.

Using the term **bottom-up management,** Given, president of American Brake Shoe and Foundry Company, encouraged widespread delegation of authority to gain the involvement of "all those down from the bottom up."[28] Given's approach promoted considerable managerial freedom in decision making, the free interchange of ideas, and the recognition that managerial growth involves some failure. Given believed that the judgment, initiative, and creativeness of all employees in an organization provide a better end result than the autocratic administration of any single individual.

In 1938, Joseph Scanlon developed a productivity plan that gave employ-

McCormick multiple-management plan—developed by Charles McCormick; uses participation as a training and motivational tool by selecting promising young employees from various company departments to form a junior board of directors.

Bottom-up management—philosophy popularized by William B. Given that encouraged widespread delegation of authority to solicit the participation of all employees from the bottom to the top.

ees a bonus for tangible savings in labor costs. The **Scanlon plan** was unique in at least three respects: (1) Joint management and union committees were formed to discuss and propose labor-saving techniques. (2) Group rewards—not individual rewards—were made for suggestions. (3) Employees shared in reduced costs rather than increased profits.[29] Scanlon believed that participation was desirable not just to create a feeling of belonging but also to show clearly the role of employees and unions in suggesting improvements.

Many of the emerging styles of management of the 1930s and 1940s had distinct differences. But most were based on the human relations thrust, especially on participation. The emergence of the professional manager and the rapidly rising standard of living led to a greater concern for the employee and hence to the development of participative forms of management. The professional manager realized that a greater concern for the worker would most likely result in greater productivity and therefore greater profits. The rising standard of living made workers more mobile, increased the employment options open to them, and made them less likely to settle for a strictly authoritarian environment.

Scanlon plan—Incentive plan developed in 1938 by Joseph Scanlon to give workers a bonus for tangible savings in labor costs.

MANAGEMENT PROCESS PERIOD

During the late 1940s, management thought began to move toward the idea of a **process approach to management**.[30] This was an attempt to identify and define a process for attaining desired objectives. The process approach led management to become primarily concerned with identifying and refining the functions or components of the management process. For this reason, the process approach is sometimes referred to as the "functional approach."

As we have said, Henri Fayol was the first management scholar to present explicitly a functional analysis of the management process. Fayol listed planning, organizing, commanding, coordination, and control as functions of management.

Oliver Sheldon, an Englishman, also gave an early breakdown of the management process.[31] In 1923, Sheldon saw management as the determination of business policy, the coordination of the execution of policy, the organization of the business, and the control of the executive.

Ralph C. Davis was the first American to publish a functional breakdown of the management process.[32] He subdivided it into three functions: planning, organizing, and controlling.

All of these management scholars made early reference to a functional approach to management. But the concept was not widely accepted until Constance Storrs' translation made Fayol's work readily available in 1949. Thus Fayol was truly responsible for fathering the process approach to management.

At the same time, process management was gaining acceptance as a teacha-

Process approach to management—focuses on the management functions of planning, controlling, organizing, staffing, and leading.

ble discipline. Before, while accepted as a discipline, it had been modeled after certain successful individuals. The functional approach offered a new, logical, concrete method of presenting management.

A second generation of management process thinkers evolved after the 1949 translation of Fayol's work. They taught management via the functional approach. Most management texts of the 1950s presented management as a series of functions and principles that could be learned and synthesized in a logical fashion.

The early to mid-1950s was an era of almost complete agreement about the composition and teachings of management. The management process, or functional, approach was the accepted method for the study of management.

THE MANAGEMENT THEORY JUNGLE

The late 1950s saw a new era in the study of management. Uneasy with the process approach to management, production management and industrial engineering scholars began testing mathematical and modeling approaches to quantify management. As a result, mathematical and decision theory schools of thought developed for the study of management. The decision theory school was based largely on economic theory and the theory of consumer choice. The mathematical school viewed management as a system of mathematical relationships. At the same time, behavioral scientists were studying management as small-group relations; they depended heavily on psychology and social psychology. Drawing on the work of Chester Barnard and sociological theory, another school saw management as a system of cultural interrelationships. An empirical school of thought was developed by those scholars using the case approach. Their basic premise was that effective management could be learned by studying the successes and failures of other managers.

Harold Koontz was the first management scholar to discuss clearly this fragmentation movement.[33] Koontz accurately referred to this division of thought as the **management theory jungle.** Many conferences and discussions followed Koontz's analysis in an attempt to untangle the theory jungle and to unite the various schools of thought. While some progress was made, a unified theory of management has not been realized.

Managment theory jungle—term developed by Harold Koontz; refers to the division of thought that resulted from the multiple approaches to studying the management process.

THE SYSTEMS APPROACH

The fragmentation period of the late 1950s and early 1960s was followed by an era of attempted integration. Many management theorists sought to use a "systems approach" in order to integrate the various management schools. The **systems approach to management** was viewed as "a way of thinking about the job of managing . . . [which] provides a framework for visualizing internal and external environmental factors as an integrated whole."[34] The manager was asked to view the human, physical, and informational facets of the manager's job as linked in an integrated whole.

One popular thrust was to use a systems approach to integrate the other schools of management into the traditional functional approach. The idea was to integrate the human relations and mathematical approaches into the appropriate functional areas. Thus while studying planning, a systems approach might include mathematical forecasting techniques.

Other systems approaches were much more grand and were based on general systems theory. These versions attempted to analyze management in terms of other disciplines and cultures. "Comparative management" evolved because of the multinational firms and the need for managing in diverse fields.[35]

The term *systems appraoch* has been overused by many. Yet, a holistic view of the management process has special merit for today's students and practitioners of management. They must learn to integrate the different management functions and topics. For example, successful managers must understand both the function of planning and how to relate planning to the other management functions.

Systems approach to management–views the human, physical, and informational facets of the manager's job as linking together to form an integrated whole.

THE CONTINGENCY APPROACH

The 1970s were characterized by the so-called contingency approach. In the **contingency approach to management,** different situations and conditions require different management approaches. Proponents believe that there is no one best way of managing; the best way depends on the specific circumstances. Recognizing the rarity of a manager who thinks that one way of managing works best in *all* situations, one might ask, "What is new about this approach?"

What is new is that contingency theorists have often gone much farther than simply saying "it all depends." Many contingency theories outline in detail the style or approach that works best under certain conditions and circumstances. Contingency theories—many are discussed in this book—have been developed in areas such as decision making, organizational design, leadership, planning, and group behavior.

Contingency approach to management–theorizes that different situations and conditions require different management approaches.

INTERNATIONAL MOVEMENT

National and worldwide resource shortages appeared in the 1970s. These shortages were accompanied by poor local economic conditions and by communication and transportation advances. Many U.S. companies turned to

MANAGEMENT IN ACTION 2–4

Exxon: An International Giant

Virtually every American has heard the name Exxon. The huge oil company is an international manufacturer and marketer of energy and industrial products. Exxon explores for and produces crude oil and natural gas, mines for coal and other minerals, and manufacturers petroleum-based chemical and other industrial products. Exxon is such a mammoth presence in the American economy that it is frequently viewed as an all-American institution.

To the surprise of many, Exxon is more "international" than "American." Exxon has operations in 80 countries other than the United States. In 1983, a full 70 percent of Exxon's $88 billion in sales and over half of all its profits were made outside the United States.

Source: "The 100 Largest U.S. Multinationals," *Forbes*, July 2, 1984, pp. 129–33.

the international arena for new markets and profits. For example, in 1983, the 100 largest U.S. multinationals had sales of $422 billion outside the United States. As U.S. companies were expanding internationally, more foreign companies were entering the U.S. market. Leading this group were the Japanese. Because of Japan's phenomenal economic success since World War II, managers worldwide began to study Japanese management. Management in Action 2–4 describes some of the international operations of Exxon.

Japanese Management

Japanese management style–information and initiative flow from the bottom up; top management facilitates decision making rather than issuing edicts; middle management shapes solutions to problems; consensus decision making; fosters personal well-being of employees.

At least five factors have been credited for the success of the **Japanese management style:**

1. Emphasizing the flow of information and initiative from the bottom up.
2. Making top management the facilitator of decision making rather than the issuer of edicts.
3. Using middle management as the impetus for, and shaper of, solutions to problems.
4. Stressing consensus as the way of making decisions.
5. Paying close attention to the personal well-being of employees.[36]

Many American, Canadian, and European companies have adopted principles of Japanese management. William Ouchi has named this style of management "Theory Z." Theory Z organizations generally use the following principles:

1. Lifetime employment: Employees are not laid off during recessions. Rather, paychecks are pared down for all employees, including management.

2. Evaluation and promotion: Promotions often only come every 10 years in Japanese companies. But no one seems to resent this, since everyone is treated the same way.

3. Nonspecialized careers: Japanese managers do not specialize, and they regularly move from one department to another.

FIGURE 2–3
Major Components and Related Events of the Management Movement

Management Movement Component	Relative Major Events
U.S. Industrial Revolution (prior to 1875)	Steam power (1790–1810). Railroad boom (1830–50). Telegraph (1844).
Captains of industry (1875–1900)	Formation of corporate giants: John D. Rockefeller (oil). James B. Duke (tobacco). Andrew Carnegie (steel). Cornelius Vanderbilt (shipping and railroads).
Scientific management era (1895–1920)	Henry Towne, "The Engineer as Economist," 1886. Frederick W. Taylor's work (1895–1915): Carl Barth. Morris Cooke. Henry Lawrence Gantt. Frank and Lillian Gilbreth. Harrington Emerson. Henri Fayol, *Administration Industrielle et Generale,* 1916.
Period of solidification (1920 to early 1930s)	Founding of professional management societies (1920s). Mooney and Reiley, *Onward Industry!* 1931.
Human relations movement (1931 to late 1940s)	Hawthorne Studies, led by Elton Mayo (1924–32). Mary Parker Follett (1920–33). Chester Barnard, *Functions of the Executive,* 1938.
Management process period (early 1950s to early 1960s)	Storrs' translation of Fayol's work (1949). Ralph Davis, *Top Management Planning,* 1951. George Terry, *Principles of Management,* 1953. Koontz and O'Donnell, *Principles of Management,* 1955.
Management theory jungle (early to late 1960s)	Process approach. Quantitative approaches. Behavioral approaches.
Systems approach (late 1960s to early 1970s)	Integrating the various approaches to the study of management.
Contingency approach (1970s)	Theorizes that different situations and conditions require different management approaches.
International movement (1970s–1980s)	Worldwide interest in Japanese management.

4. Collective decision making: Japanese managers make decisions through a tedious process of collective decision making.[37]

There are many cultural differences between Western countries and Japan. Whether all aspects of the Japanese management system can be applied in the United States is still open to question; it will require much more research.

This chapter has summarized the major events that impacted the management discipline from the 19th century to the present. But the discipline did not develop and mature at the same rate in all parts of the country. Similarly, it did not develop from a series of discrete happenings; rather it grew from a series of major and minor events. Figure 2–3 presents a chronological summation of the major and related events in the management movement.

SUMMARY

Management today grew out of the American Industrial Revolution. Not until industry reached a certain level of sophistication was management recognized as a distinct discipline.

The railroads were the first big U.S. industry in terms of sophistication and capital requirements. The railroads also spurred the development of other industries. They provided rapid movement of raw materials and finished goods; this gave companies great flexibility. Taking advantage of the situation, men like Rockefeller, Duke, and Carnegie developed giant corporations in other industries by the end of the 19th century. These new corporate giants, along with the railroads, required new methods of management. No longer could businesses be run out of the home or on an informal basis.

At this point, the engineering profession made major contributions to the development of management thought. Challenging previous management methods, Frederick Taylor devised and popularized scientific management. Often misunderstood, his scientific management philosophy concerned the relationship of people to work. The basis for this relationship was finding the one best way to a do a job and the proper person for each job.

By the 1930s, the field of management had gained general acceptance as a discipline that could be taught and learned. Professional societies and related organizations had been formed and were contributing to the development of the discipline.

Following this period of solidification during the 1920s and early 1930s, the human relations movement made a significant impact on the management discipline. The Hawthorne Studies focused attention on human relations and specifically the psychological and sociological aspects of work. Meanwhile, Mary Parker Follett added push to the human relations movement.

Although his work was not readily available in English until 1949, Henri Fayol was the first to present a functional approach to the study of management. Fayol was also one of the first to develop principles of management.

By the mid-1950s, there was general agreement that management should be taught with a functional approach similar to that of Fayol. However, this period of general agreement was short-lived; it was followed in the early 1960s by a fragmentation era. During this time, several schools of thought were pursued by management scholars.

To reunify management thought, a systems approach was developed. It attempted to tie the various schools of thought together within a "systems framework."

The contingency approach followed the systems approach. It theorizes that different situations and conditions require different management approaches. Recent resource shortages coupled with advances in communication and transportation and adverse economic conditions caused many companies to enter the international arena to increase their markets and profits. Because of their worldwide economic successes, Japanese management systems have been widely studied and copied in recent years.

References and Additional Readings

[1] Daniel Wren, *The Evolution of Management Thought,* 2d ed. (New York: Ronald Press, 1979), p. 90.

[2] Dorothy Gregg, "John Stevens: General Entrepreneur," in *Men in Business,* ed. William Miller (New York: Harper & Row, 1957), pp. 120–52.

[3] Alfred D. Chandler, Jr., "The Railroads: Pioneers in Modern Corporate Management," *Business History Review,* Spring 1965, p. 17.

[4] Wren, *Management Thought,* pp. 93–94.

[5] Chandler, "The Railroads," pp. 17–19.

[6] Ibid., p. 21.

[7] Alfred D. Chandler, Jr., "The Beginnings of 'Big Business' in American Industry," *Business History Review,* Spring 1959, p. 3.

[8] Harry Kelsey and David Wilderson, "The Evolution of Management Thought" (unpublished paper, Indiana University, Bloomington, 1974), p. 7.

[9] Henry R. Towne, "The Engineer as Economist," *Transactions,* ASME 7 (1886), pp. 428–32.

[10] Frank Barkley Copley, *Frederick W. Taylor: Father of Scientific Management,* vol. 1 (New York: Harper & Row, 1923), pp. 77–79.

[11] Frederick W. Taylor, "A Piece-Rate System," *Transactions,* ASME 16 (1895), pp. 856–83.

[12] Frederick W. Taylor, *Shop Management* (New York: Harper & Row, 1903); Frederick W. Taylor, *The Principles of Scientific Management* (New York: Harper & Row, 1911).

[13] *Scientific Management: Address and Discussions at the Conference on Scientific Management at the Amos Truck School of Administration and Finance* (Norwood, Mass.: Plimpton Press, 1912), pp. 32–35.

[14] John F. Mee, *Management Thought in a Dynamic Economy* (New York: New York University Press, 1963), p. 411.

[15] John F. Mee, "Seminar in Business Organization and Operation" (unpublished paper, Indiana University, Bloomington), p. 5.

[16] Wren, *Management Thought,* p. 188.

[17] Henry L. Gantt, *Organizing for Work* (New York: Harcourt Brace Jovanovich, 1919), p. 15.

[18] Henri Fayol, *Administration Industrielle et Generale* (Paris: The Societe de l'Industrie Minerale, 1916). First translated into English by J. A. Coubrough, *Industrial and General Administration* (Geneva: International Management Institute, 1930). Later translated by Con-

stance Storrs, *General and Industrial Management* (London: Sir Isaac Pitman and Sons, 1940).

[19] John F. Mee, "Management Teaching in Historical Perspective," *Southern Journal of Business,* May 1972, p. 21.

[20] Ibid., p. 22.

[21] For a detailed description of the Hawthorne Studies, see Fritz G. Roethlisberger and William J. Dickson, *Management and the Worker* (Cambridge, Mass.: Harvard University Press, 1939).

[22] For example, see Alex Carey, "The Hawthorne Studies: A Radical Criticism," *American Sociological Review,* June 1967, pp. 403–16.

[23] Henry C. Metcalf and L. Urwick, eds., *Dynamic Administration: The Collected Papers of Mary Parker Follett* (New York: Harper & Row, 1940), p. 21.

[24] Chester I. Barnard, *The Functions of the Executive* (Cambridge, Mass.: Harvard University Press, 1938).

[25] Charles W. Brennan, *Wage Administration,* rev. ed. (Homewood, Ill.: Richard D. Irwin, 1963), p. 289.

[26] Henry S. Dennison, *Organization Engineering* (New York: McGraw-Hill, 1931).

[27] Charles P. McCormick, *Multiple Management* (New York: Harper & Row, 1949).

[28] William B. Given, Jr., *Bottom Up Management* (New York: Harper & Row, 1949).

[29] Joseph Scanlon, "Enterprise for Everyone," *Fortune,* January 1950, pp. 41, 55–59; Wren, *Management Thought,* p. 330.

[30] Mee, *Management Thought,* p. 53.

[31] Oliver Sheldon, *The Philosophy of Management* (London: Sir Isaac Pitman & Sons, 1923).

[32] Ralph C. Davis, *The Principles of Business Organizations and Operations* (Columbus, Ohio: H. L. Hedrick, 1935), pp. 12–13.

[33] Harold Koontz, "The Management Theory Jungle," *Academy of Management Journal,* December 1961, pp. 174–88.

[34] Richard A. Johnson, Fremont E. Kast, and James E. Rosenzweig, *The Theory and Management of Systems* (New York: McGraw-Hill, 1963), p. 3.

[35] Wren, *Management Thought,* pp. 463–64.

[36] Richard Tanner Johnson and William Ouchi, "Made in America (under Japanese Management)," *Harvard Business Review,* September–October 1974, p. 62.

[37] See, for instance, William Ouchi, *Theory Z: How American Business Can Meet the Japanese Challenge* (Reading, Mass.: Addison-Wesley Publishing, 1981); also William Ouchi and Alfred Jaeger, "Type Z: Organization Stability in the Midst of Mobility," *Academy of Management Review,* April 1978, pp. 305–14.

Review Questions

power, transportation, communication

1. What were the three facets of the Industrial Revolution in America? Discuss the impact of each of these facets on the development of industry as it is today.
2. What effect did the captains of industry have on the relationships between government and industry? corporate giants
3. What is scientific management? Discuss the four main principles of scientific management. Relationship of people/work

   1) designing jobs
   2) selection, training
   3) bringing together selected employees/jobs
   4) interdependence of managers, workers

4. Discuss the major contribution to scientific management of Morris Cooke, Henry Lawrence Gantt, Frank and Lillian Gilbreth, and Harrington Emerson.
5. What was Henri Fayol's major contribution to the management movement? functional approach
6. Discuss the impact of the Hawthorne Studies on management thought. human relations
7. Describe in detail the following approaches to the management process:

Lincoln Electric Company, McCormick multiple-management plan, bottom-up management, and the Scanlon plan.

8. What is the process approach to management? Discuss some of the major contributors to this approach.

9. Discuss the factors which led to the management theory jungle.

10. What is the systems approach to the management process?

11. Describe the contingency approach to managing.

12. Name five characteristics of Japanese management.

Discussion Questions

1. Why did the professional manager not emerge until the 20th century?

2. How were Taylor and Fayol's approaches to the management process different, and how were they similar?

3. Why do you think Taylor and scientific management have been misunderstood by many people as being inhumane?

4. "Successful managers adapt their style to the situation." Discuss your views on this statement.

Incident 2–1
Granddad's Company

The J.R.V. Company, which manufactures industrial tools, was founded in 1905 by James R. Vail, Sr. Currently, James R. Vail, Jr., is the president of the company; his son Richard is executive vice president. James Jr. has run the company for the past 30 years in a fashion very similar to that of his father.

When the company was founded, James Sr. had been a big supporter of scientific management. He had organized the work very scientifically with the use of time and motion studies to determine the most efficient method of performing each job. As a result, most jobs at J.R.V. were highly specialized and utilized a high degree of division of labor. In addition, there was always a great emphasis on putting people in jobs that were best suited for them and then providing adequate training. Most employees are paid on a piece-rate incentive system, with the standards set by time and motion studies. James Jr. has largely continued to emphasize scientific management since he took over. All employees now receive two weeks paid vacation and company insurance. Also, J.R.V. employees are generally paid an average wage for their industry. The present J.R.V. building was constructed in 1920. But it has had several minor improvements, such as the addition of fluorescent lighting and an employees' lunchroom.

James Jr. is planning to retire in a few years. Recently, he and Richard, his planned successor, have disagreed over the management of the company. Richard's main argument is that times have changed and that time and motion studies, specialization, high division of labor, and other company practices are obsolete. On the other hand, James Jr. argues that J.R.V. has been successful under its present management philosophy for many years. Change would be "foolish."

Questions

1. Do you agree with Richard?
2. Are the principles of scientific management applicable in today's organizations?

Incident 2–2
Return to Scientific Management

Recently, a professor at State University lectured in a management development seminar on the topic of motivation. Participants candidly discussed problems that existed in their respective organizations. Problem areas included absenteeism, turnover, and poor workmanship. The participants managed a variety of workers such as automobile assembly workers, clerical workers, computer operators, sanitation workers, and even some middle-level managers.

During the discussion, one participant made the following statement: "What we need to stop all of these problems is a little scientific management."

Questions

1. What do you think the person means?
2. Do you agree? Discuss.
3. Take one of the jobs in the above case and show how you could apply scientific management.

Exercise
What Have We Learned?

The following are excerpts from a speech made by Frederick W. Taylor in 1911:*

> If any of you will get close to the average workman in this country—close enough to him so that he will talk to you as an intimate friend—he will tell you that in his particular trade if, we will say, each man were to turn out twice as much work as he is now doing, there could be but one result to follow: namely, that one half the men in his trade would be thrown out of work.

> This doctrine is preached by almost every labor leader in the country and is taught by every workman to his children as they are growing up; and I repeat, as I said in the beginning, that it is our fault more than theirs that this fallacy prevails.

> While the labor leaders and the workmen themselves in season and out of season are pointing out the necessity of restriction of output, not one step are we taking to counteract that fallacy; therefore, I say, the fault is ours and not theirs.

A. Do you think that Taylor's position is equally applicable today? Be prepared to justify your answer.

C. Jackson Grayson, chairman of the American Productivity Center in Houston, has recently warned that if management and labor cannot make their relationship less adversarial, "then we won't get the full, long-term kick in productivity that we desperately need."†

B. Looking at Taylor's and Grayson's remarks which were made approximately 63 years apart, one has to wonder what we have learned. Many other similar comparisons could be made. Why do you think that managers don't seem to learn as much as they could from the past?

---

* *Scientific Management: Address and Discussions* (Norwood, Mass., Plimpton Press, 1912), pp 23–24.

† "The Revival of Productivity," *Business Week,* February 13, 1984, p. 100.

3

Social Responsibility and Ethics

Chapter Outline

"Business ethics," the father explained to his son, *"is something you couldn't do without. Take today for instance. A man comes in and pays me a hundred-dollar bill to clear up his account. After he leaves, I find two bills stuck together. He has paid me two hundred dollars instead of one. Now, son, here comes the question of ethics. Should I tell my partner or shouldn't I?"*

*William R. Gerler**

Today, organizations are more concerned about social responsibility and about questions of ethics in management than they have ever been. This chapter presents an overview of corporate social responsibility and examines the role of ethics in management.

DEFINING SOCIAL RESPONSIBILITY

Social responsibility is concerned with how individuals and organizations deal with current social issues. The general public has a rather broad and all-inclusive definition of the social responsibility of business organizations. The public seems to feel that managers and business organizations should provide leadership in rebuilding cities, wiping out poverty, controlling crime, and cutting government red tape. In short, social responsibility has come to mean participation in a multitude of issues and problems. Presently, no universally accepted definition exists for the term. In this book, **social responsibility** is defined as "the moral and ethical content of managerial and corporate decisions over and above the pragmatic requirements imposed by legal principle and the market economy."[1]

Social responsibility – moral and ethical content of managerial and corporate decisions over and above the pragmatic requirements imposed by legal principle and the market economy.

SOCIAL RESPONSIBILITY—A HISTORICAL PERSPECTIVE

The idea that business has a responsibility other than producing goods and services is not new. In 1919, Henry L. Gantt stated his belief that the community would attempt to take over business if the business system neglected its social responsibilities.[2] Another early management writer who discussed social responsibility was Oliver Sheldon. Writing in 1923, Sheldon stressed that management has a social responsibility:

---

* William R. Gerler, *Executive's Treasury of Humor for Every Occasion* (West Nyack, N.Y.: Parker Publishing, 1965). Copyright © 1965 by Parker Publishing Company, Inc.

It is important, therefore, early in our consideration of management in industry, to insist that however scientific management may become, and however much the full development of its powers may depend upon the use of the scientific method; its primary responsibility is social and communal.[3]

FIGURE 3–1
Historical Phases of Attitudes toward Social Responsibility and Value Systems of Managers

Attitudes	Phase 1 Profit-Maximizing Management (1800 to 1920s)	Phase 2 Trusteeship Management (late 1920s to early 1960s)	Phase 3 Quality-of-Life Management (late 1960s to present)
Orientation:	1. Raw self-interest.	1. Self-interest. 2. Contributors' interest.	1. Enlightened self-interest. 2. Contributors' interests. 3. Society's interests.
Economic values:	What's good for me is good for my country. Profit maximizer. Money and wealth are most important. Let the buyer beware (caveat emptor). Labor is a commodity to be bought and sold. Accountability of management is to the owners.	What's good for organizations and management is good for our country. Profit satisficer. Money is important, but so are people. Let us not cheat the customer. Labor has certain rights which must be recognized. Accountability of management is to the owners, customers, employees, suppliers, and other contributors.	What is good for society is good for our company. Profit is necessary, but. . . . People are more important than money. Let the seller beware (caveat venditor). Employee dignity has to be satisfied. Accountability of management is to the owners, contributors, and society.
Technological values:	Technology is very important.	Technology is important, but so are people.	People are more important than technology.
Social values:	Employee personal problems must be left at home. I am a rugged individualist, and I will manage my business as I please. Minority groups are inferior to whites. They must be treated accordingly.	We recognize that employees have needs beyond their economic needs. I am an individualist, but I recognize the value of group participation. Minority groups have their place in society, and their place is inferior to mine.	We hire the whole person. Group participation is fundamental to our success. Minority group members are people, as you and I are.
Political values:	That government is best which governs least.	Government is a necessary evil.	Business and government must cooperate to solve society's problems.
Environmental values:	The natural environment controls the destiny of people.	People can control and manipulate the environment.	We must preserve the environment in order to lead a quality life.
Aesthetic values:	Aesthetic values? What are they?	Aesthetic values are OK, but not for us.	We must preserve our aesthetic values, and we will do our part.

Source: Adapted from Robert D. Hay, Edmund R. Gray, and James E. Gates, *Business and Society: Cases and Text* (Cincinnati: South-Western Publishing, 1976), pp. 10–11.

However, concern for social responsibility was rare during this early period.

Changes began to occur in the late 1930s and early 40s. Shorter workweeks and safer working conditions were some of the first. Many of these early social responsibility changes were precipitated by labor unions. In effect, labor unions pressured organizations to consider factors other than just profitability.

In 1948, the theme of the annual Harvard Business School Alumni Association meeting was "business responsibility." In 1958, the American Management Association surveyed 700 companies concerning their "managerial creed or statement of basic objectives."[4] Nearly every company expressed the belief that they had a responsibility to society. In the 1950s and 60s, more and more organizations and managers expressed concern about the social responsibilities of organizations. However, few socially responsible programs were actually implemented until the late 1960s.

Looking back, the attitudes toward social responsibility and value systems of managers seem to have gone through three historical phases. Phase 1, which dominated until the 1930s, emphasized the belief that a business manager had but one objective—to maximize profits. Phase 2, from the 1930s to the early 60s, stressed that managers were responsible not only for maximizing profits but also for maintaining an equitable balance among the competing claims of customers, employees, suppliers, creditors, and the community. Phase 3, still dominant today, contends that managers and organizations should involve themselves in the solutions of society's major problems. Figure 3–1 describes these three phases in more depth.

SOCIAL RESPONSIBILITY TODAY

Today's organizations and managers still question the exact nature of their social responsibility. Major arguments for and against the social responsibility of business organizations are presented in Figure 3–2. The following sections of this chapter discuss in detail some of the more important arguments.[5]

Arguments for Social Responsibility

1. It is in the best interest of the business. The future of business organizations depends on good relationships with the society in which they operate. If organizations fail to act in the area of social responsibility, then society will act against business organizations. Boycotting products and picketing the organization and its customers—even violence against the organization—are examples of actions that can be taken. By extension, if public

FIGURE 3–2
Arguments for and against Social Responsibility

Major Arguments for Social Responsibility

1. It is in the best interest of the business to promote and improve the communities where it does business.
2. Social actions can be profitable.
3. It is the ethical thing to do.
4. It improves the public image of the firm.
5. It increases the viability of the business system. Business exists because it gives society benefits. Society can amend or take away its charter. This is the "iron law of responsibility."
6. It is necessary, to avoid government regulation.
7. Sociocultural norms require it.
8. Laws cannot be passed for all circumstances. Thus, business must assume responsibility to maintain an orderly legal society.
9. It is in the stockholder's best interest. It will improve the price of stock in the long run, because the stock market will view the company as less risky and open to public attack and therefore award it a higher price–earnings ratio.
10. Society should give business a chance to solve social problems that government has failed to solve.
11. Business is considered, by some groups, to be the institution with the financial and human resources to solve social problems.
12. Prevention of problems is better than cures—so let business solve problems before they become too great.

Major Arguments against Social Responsibility

1. It might be illegal.
2. Business plus government equals monolith.
3. Social actions cannot be measured.
4. It violates profit maximization.
5. Cost of social responsibility is too great and would increase prices too much.
6. Business lacks social skills to solve societal problems.
7. It would dilute business's primary purposes.
8. It would weaken U.S. balance of payments, because price of goods will have to go up to pay for social programs.
9. Business already has too much power. Such involvement would make business too powerful.
10. Business lacks accountability to the public. Thus, the public would have no control over its social involvement.
11. Such business involvement lacks broad public support.

Source: R. Joseph Monsen, Jr., "The Social Attitudes of Management," in *Contemporary Management: Issues and Viewpoints*, ed. Joseph W. McGuire (Englewood Cliffs, N.J.: Prentice-Hall, 1974 © 1974), p. 616. Adapted by permission of Prentice-Hall, Inc.

pressure becomes too strong, then government will force the organization to take responsibility.

2. Social actions can be profitable. No clear evidence now seems to support a cause-and-effect relationship between social responsibility and profits. Indirectly, though, it seems logical that donations to higher education, hiring disadvantaged persons, taking part in urban renewal projects, and aiding conservation programs should help the long-term profitability of all organizations.

3. Being socially responsible is the ethical thing to do.   Business is an integral part of society; so, many people argue that being socially responsible is a moral obligation of organizations. Proponents feel organizations are morally responsible to provide safe products, clean up streams, and conserve natural resources. Thus, if the public-at-large feels that being socially responsible is the ethical thing to do, it can be expected that managers and organizations will feel the same way.

Arguments against Social Responsibility

1. It might be illegal.   Milton Friedman has argued that the only responsibility of business is to maximize profits for shareholders.[6] This assumes that managers are agents of the stockholders and that the diversion of funds to activities that do not contribute to profits may be illegal. This viewpoint was held by most managers and was supported by the courts for a long time. For instance, in 1919, a Michigan court declared that business was to be operated primarily for the profit of stockholders. The court forced the company to declare a dividend, which it had not done for many years.[7]

This argument has been considerably weakened over the years. A 1935 amendment to the Internal Revenue code allowed corporations to deduct up to 5 percent of net profits for social purposes. And in 1953, the New Jersey Supreme Court upheld the right of the A. P. Smith Company to give funds to Princeton University against the desires of some stockholders. The court stated, "It is not just a right but a duty of corporations to support higher education in the interest of the long-range well-being of their stockholders because the company could not hope to operate effectively in a society which is not functioning well."[8]

2. Business plus government equals monolith.   Proponents of this argument feel that business should make profits and government should spend tax money to attack social problems. They argue that socially motivated business activities sublimate and compromise the profit motive. Theodore Levitt feels that if business assumes more and more social responsibility, then there could ultimately be very little functional difference between business and government.[9] Without this functional difference, society would be dominated by one unopposed and unstoppable monolithy.

3. Social actions cannot be measured.   If managers do have a social responsibility other than to maximize profits for stockholders, how do they know what it is? "Can they decide how great a burden they are justified in placing on themselves or their stockholders to serve that social interest?"[10] Also, who should decide what is good for society? Proponents of this argument feel that management cannot accurately measure the benefits of social action; also, it is fruitless to continue spending money without measuring the return on the investment.

The financial audit has been used traditionally to measure the profit performance of organizations. The need for measuring an organization's social responsibility has led to the idea of a social audit. A **social audit** attempts to report, in financial terms, an organization's expenditures and investments for social purposes. This is done by categorizing the socially related expenses and investments in terms of income, expenses, assets, and liabilities. However, the problems of placing a dollar value on social investments are complex and subject to individual interpretation.[11] Some business organizations have used the following methods to show socially responsible activities:

Social audit–attempt to report in financial terms the expenditures and investments made by an organization for social purposes.

1. Narrative disclosure of social responsibility efforts in footnotes of financial statements.
2. Adding to traditional financial statements to include the costs of specific social responsibility efforts.
3. Special reports covering pollution, occupational health, equal employment, and other areas of activity.

ACTIONS NECESSARY TO IMPLEMENT SOCIAL RESPONSIBILITY

The biggest obstacle to organizations assuming more social responsibility is pressure by financial analyists and stockholders. They push for steady increases in earnings per share on a quarterly basis. Concern about immediate profits makes it difficult to invest in areas that cannot be accurately measured and still have returns which are long run in nature. Furthermore, pressure for short-term earnings impacts on corporate social behavior; most companies are geared to short-term profit goals. Budgets, objectives, and performance evaluations are often based on short-run considerations. Management may state a willingness to lose some short-term profit to achieve social objectives. However, managers who sacrifice profit in their own departments and seek to justify it on the basis of corporate social goals may find superiors unsympathetic.

Organizations should also carefully examine their cherished values— short-run profits and others—to ensure that these concepts are in tune with the values held by society. This should be a constant process, because the values held by society are ever changing.

Organizations should reevaluate their long-range planning and decision-making processes to ensure that they fully understand the potential social consequences. Plant location decisions are no longer merely economic matters. Environmental impact and job opportunities for the disadvantaged are examples of other factors that may be considered.

Organizations should seek to aid both governmental agencies and voluntary agencies in their social efforts. This should include technical and managerial help as well as monetary support. Technological knowledge, organizational skills, and managerial competence can all be applied to solving social problems.

MANAGEMENT IN ACTION 3–1

Xerox Corporation's Social Service Leave Program

In September 1971, Xerox announced that it would allow 20 employees to take sabbaticals of up to one year to pursue social projects in their communities— at full salary and with complete job security. To date, Xerox has had a total of 258 employees participate in the program and has spent $3.5 million in replacement salaries on the program.

Projects worked on by Xerox employees in the leave program include:

- An employee in Stamford, Connecticut whose parents had both died of cancer founded a hospice for patients and their families.

- An employee in New York City whose infant son had died set up a help center for parents who had to cope with the devastation of crib death.

What does Xerox get out of the program. A Xerox spokesperson replied: "Generally, a good feeling among our employees. Even those who don't apply like to know that it's there."

Source: Adapted from "Ten Years of Social Service at Xerox," *Management Review*, December 1981, pp. 39–40.

Organizations should look at ways to help solve social problems through their own business. Many social problems stem from the economic deprivation of a fairly large segment of our society. Attacking this could be the greatest social effort of organizations. Management in Action 3–1 outlines some of Xerox Corporation's efforts to attack social problems.

In order for business organizations to implement social responsibility programs successfully, society must also meet certain basic responsibilities. These are summarized in Figure 3–3.

HOW SOCIALLY RESPONSIBLE ARE TODAY'S ORGANIZATIONS?

Regardless of the arguments against social responsibility, organizations— either on their own or through pressures from the government or consumers—are becoming more aware of their social responsibilities. Figure 3–4 summarizes many issues now seen as legitimate social concerns of organizations. The commitments of organizations in three of these areas are discussed next.

Consumerism–social movement that seeks to redress the perceived imbalance in the marketplace between buyers and sellers.

Consumerism

Consumerism is a social movement that seeks to redress the perceived imbalance in the marketplace between the buyer and the seller. Initially, the

---

FIGURE 3–3
Responsibility of Society to Business in Implementing Social Responsibility Programs

---

1. *Set rules that are clear and consistent.* Society must define organizations' boundaries; minimum standards expected to be met or exceeded; and performance criteria. Society must be consistent in its expectations for corporate social responsibility through the various governmental regulations affecting this area.
2. *Keep the rules within the bounds of technical feasibility.* Business cannot do the impossible. However, many of today's regulations are unworkable in practice. Extreme environmental restrictions have, on occasion, set standards surpassing those of Mother Nature.
3. *Make sure rules are economically feasible; recognize that society itself must be prepared to pay the cost—not only of their implementation by business but also their administration by government.* Ultimately, it is the people who must pay, either through higher prices or taxes.
4. *Make rules prescriptive, not retroactive.* There is a present trend toward retroactivity in an attempt to force retribution for the past—to make today's rules apply to yesterday's ball game.
5. *Make rules goal seeking, not procedure prescribing.* Tell organizations to devise the best, most economical, and most efficient way to get there.

Source: Adapted from Jerry McAfee, "Responsibilities Shared by Corporations and Society," *Credit and Financial Management,* May 1978, p. 31.

---

consumer movement sought to correct this through legislation; it was very successful in getting laws passed relating to product safety and consumer information. The **Federal Fair Packaging and Labeling Act of 1966** regulates labeling procedures for businesses. The **Truth in Lending Act of 1967** regulates the extension of credit to individuals. The **Consumer Product Safety Act of 1972** protects consumers against unreasonable risks of injury associated with consumer products. In fact, more consumer legislation was enacted during the past 15 years than during the previous 189 years.[12]

Spurred by the consumer movement and legislation, more and more companies are taking action on consumer affairs. One action establishes consumer affairs departments to handle consumer complaints and concerns. Well over 600 corporations and trade associations have formed consumer affairs departments. Firms such as Whirlpool, General Motors, Ford, American Motors, Zenith, Eastman Kodak, J. C. Penney, Sears, General Foods, and Giant Foods are generally thought to be effectively responding to consumers.[13] Furthermore, the **Society of Consumer Affairs Professionals in Business (SOCAP)** has been organized to promote professionalism among consumer affairs managers.

Federal Fair Packaging and Labeling Act of 1967–regulates labeling procedures for businesses.

Truth in Lending Act of 1967–regulates the extension of credit to individuals.

Consumer Product Safety Act of 1972–protects consumers against unreasonable risks of injury associated with consumer products.

Society of Consumer Affairs Professionals in Business (SOCAP)–promotes professionalism among consumer affairs managers.

Environmentalism

During the 1970s, protection of the environment became an important political issue. It resulted not only in stricter application of earlier laws

FIGURE 3–4
Issues That Are Social Concerns of Organizations

External issues—may or may not have been directly caused by business:
1. Poverty.
2. Drug abuse.
3. Decay of cities.
4. Community relations.
5. Philanthropy.
External issues—caused by economic activity of business.
1. Environmental pollution.
2. Safety and quality of goods and services (consumerism movement).
3. Social impact of facilities closings.
4. Site locations of new facilities.
Internal issues—directly related to economic activity.
1. Equal employment opportunity.
2. Occupational safety and health.
3. Quality of work life.

National Environmental Policy Act of 1969–committed the federal government to preserving the country's ecology, established a White House Council on Environmental Quality and required filings of environmental impact statements.

Council on Environmental quality–assists and advises the president on environmental issues.

Environmental impact statements (EIS)–written report required of federal government agencies on proposed actions that affect the human environment.

Environmental Protection Agency (EPA)–interprets and administers the environmental protection policies of the federal government.

but also in several new laws designed to improve the environment. Figure 3–5 outlines several key laws that influence business activities in relation to the environment.

The key legislation in environmental protection was the **National Environmental Policy Act of 1969.** The law went into effect on January 1, 1970; it committed the government to preserving the country's ecology, established a White House **Council on Environmental Quality,** and required filings of environmental impact statements (EIS) for any major federal action that could greatly affect the quality of the human environment. This law requires the president to submit an annual report to Congress on environmental quality. The Council on Environmental Quality assists in the preparation of the environmental quality report and advises the president on environmental issues. **Environmental impact statements (EIS)** require agencies of the federal government to submit a written report of proposed actions that affect the human environment. They must give an environmental analysis of the proposal, outline alternative methods of meeting the agency's goals, describe the existing environment, and analyze the environmental impact anticipated from the alternative proposals.

As a result of this legislation, the **Environmental Protection Agency (EPA)** was created in July 1970 by the order of the president. The EPA combines the environmental protection functions of the federal government which had been scattered among the Interior, Agriculture and Health, Education and Welfare departments and the Atomic Energy Commission. Today, EPA interprets and adminsters the environmental protection policies of the federal government; it also has authority to approve or disapprove all environmental impact statements.

Changing interpretations of the law by the EPA and complaints that the laws are too strict and costly have made environmental protection controversial. For example, the Council on Environmental Quality estimates the cumulative costs of environmental protection legislation to be $735 billion

FIGURE 3–5
Laws Relating to Environmental Protection

Date	Name	Purpose
December 17, 1963	Clean Air Act	To improve, strengthen, and accelerate programs for the prevention and abatement of air pollution.
November 3, 1966	Clean Water Restoration Act of 1966	To provide technical and financial assistance in the development of waste treatment, water purification, and water quality control programs.
January 1, 1970	National Environmental Policy Act of 1969	To establish a national policy on the environment and to establish a Council on Environmental Quality.
October 27, 1972	Noise Control Act of 1972	To control the emission of noise harmful to the human environment.
December 16, 1974	Safe Drinking Water Act	To assure that the public is provided with safe drinking water.
October 11, 1976	Toxic Substances Control Act	To regulate business and protect human health and the environment by requiring testing and necessary use restrictions on certain chemical substances.
October 21, 1976	Resource Conservation and Recovery Act	To provide technical and financial assistance to develop management plans and facilities for the recovery of energy and other resources from discarded materials and to regulate the management of hazardous waste.

between 1979 and 1988.[14] As a result, a growing number of people feel the need for reform of regulatory rules and procedures.[15] However, reform will not mean that environmental concerns will disappear. Environmental protection will continue to be a major social concern of business organizations.

Philanthropy

Corporate philanthropy involves donations of money, property, or work by organizations to needy persons or to socially useful purposes. Companies

Corporate philanthropy– donations of money, property, or work by organizations to needy persons or to socially useful purposes.

MANAGEMENT IN ACTION 3–2

American Express Corporate Philanthropy and Marketing

In October 1983, American Express Company's Travel Related Services (TRS) launched a national program that merged the two usually separate areas of corporate philanthropy and marketing. The program was the Statute of Liberty restoration. Over a period of three months, American Express earmarked one penny of every credit card transaction and one dollar for each new card member for the restoration.

The plan yielded good results. Over $1.3 million was raised for the restoration. American Express also benefited because during that same three month period, sales and card membership applications rose sharply.

Source: Adapted from Nancy Josephson, "AmEx Raises Corporate Giving to Marketing Act," *Advertising Age*, January 23, 1984, p. M–10.

can use one or more of three methods to make their donations. First, contributions can be made directly by the company. Second, a company foundation can be created to handle the philanthropic program. Numerous organizations use this approach. For example, Apple Computer Company has the Apple Education Foundation; General Electric has the General Electric Foundation. A final method for making contributions is for a company to establish a Clifford trust. Under a **Clifford trust,** the company turns over some of its assets for a set period–usually it is a little more than 10 years–during which all of the income earned by the assets goes to charity. At the end of the set period, the assets revert back to the company.

Clifford Trust–company turns over some of its assets for a set time period during which all of the income earned on the assets goes to charity.

In the past, companies have directed their philanthrophic efforts toward education, the arts, and the United Way. However, in the 1980s, the federal government has repeatedly exhorted private enterprise organizations to play a greater role in the support of nonprofit organizations and altruistic causes. Management in Action 3–2 tells how American Express uniquely addressed the Statue of Liberty restoration project.

How has business responded? Some say organizations have made significant contributions. Others argue that they have not done enough. Exact figures on total corporate giving are hard to determine. However, it was estimated that corporate charitable giving was over $3 billion annually in the early 1980s.[16] It is expected that corporate philanthropic efforts will continue to increase throughout the 1980s and 90s.

BUSINESS ETHICS

Social responsibility deals with how individuals and organizations handle current social issues. Business ethics are concerned with the day-to-day behavior standards of individuals and organizations. **Ethics** are standards or principles of conduct used to govern the behavior of an individual or group of individuals. Ethics are generally concerned with questions of right and wrong or with moral duties. Ethical standards can be developed by an individual, a group of individuals, or society. Laws are ethics formalized by a society; they are usually concerned with principles of conduct. Organizational ethics, however, generally deal more with the behavior of individuals or groups of individuals not covered by the law.

Ethics–standards or principles of conduct to govern the behavior of an individual or a group of individuals.

Why Is a Code of Ethics Needed?

Due to the adverse publicity that many organizations have received, society is demanding a code of ethics for organizations. Many people believe that if organizations do not develop their own code, the issue will be forced by public opinion or even government regulation.[17] In fact, the **Foreign Corrupt Practices Act** was passed in 1977. This law makes it illegal to obtain or retain business through payments to influence foreign officials and governments improperly. It is not, however, limited to businesses operating abroad nor to illegal foreign payments. It has significant internal accounting control and recordkeeping requirements that apply to the domestic operations of businesses. The act requires that the company's books and records accurately and fairly reflect transactions in reasonable detail. The company's internal accounting controls must provide reasonable assurances that:

Foreign Corrupt Practices Act of 1977– prohibits American companies operating abroad from bribing foreign officials, political candidates, and party leaders; requires that a company's books and records accurately and fairly reflect transactions.

- Transactions are carried out in an authorized manner.
- Transactions have been reported and recorded to permit correct preparation of financial statements and to maintain accurate records of assets.
- Access to assets is in accordance with management's authorization.
- Inventories of assets occur periodically and appropriate action is taken to correct discrepancies.

A code of ethics also reduces the organizational pressures to compromise personal ethics for the sake of organizational goals. One study indicated that managers do feel pressured to compromise personal standards to achieve company goals.[18] In this study, Archie B. Carroll found that 50 percent of top-level managers, 65 percent of middle-level managers, and 84 percent of lower-level managers feel this pressure.

Lastly, a code of ethics in organizations appeals to the ethical needs of people within organizations. Research shows that people generally want and need to be ethical in their business lives as well as their private lives.[19] Furthermore, most want to be part of an organization whose purpose and activity are beneficial to society.[20]

MANAGEMENT IN ACTION 3–3

Corporate Codes of Ethics

Judeo-Christian ethic—generally considered to be the basis of Western ethical codes and has love—including love of God and neighbor—as its primary goal.

The **Judeo-Christian ethic** is generally considered to be the basis of Western ethical standards. Its primary goal is love—including love of God and neighbor. James F. Lincoln, founder of the highly successful Lincoln Electric Company, commented on the ethics of organizations: "Do unto others as you would have them do unto you. This is not just a Sunday school ideal, but a proper labor-management policy."[21] His statement is a logical starting point for developing a corporate code of ethics.

Codes of ethics should be formal, written, and communicated to all employees. The Cummins Engine Company, for example, has given considerable time, thought, money, and energy to develope its corporate ethical codes. Their formal, written set of policies is called *Cummins Practices.* [22] *Cummins Practices* deal with ethical standards, questionable payments, meals, gifts and discounts, financial representations, internal distributor accounts, customs declarations, supplies selection, and employee involvement in political campaigns and noncorporate political activities. Each section discusses a practice, details responsibility for the practice, and lists persons to consult for more information and advice. The *Cummins Practice on Ethical Standards* is summarized in Management in Action 3–3.

A wide range of issues can be covered under a code of ethics; but rules in themselves are not always enough to handle all problems. For example, in the Gospel of Mark, Chapter 2, verses 23–28, and Chapter 3, verses 1–6, Jesus faced conflicting obligations. On the one hand, there was the obligation to follow the rules of the Sabbath observance, which forbade a wide range of activities. On the other hand, there were disciples who were hungry and followers to be healed. Jesus did not deny the validity of the rules of

MANAGEMENT IN ACTION 3–4

Code of Ethics
South Central Bell and
Southern Bell*

South Central Bell and Southern Bell's code of ethics outlines specific actions required of employees in the areas of privacy of communications, fair competition, conflict of interest, internal company accounting procedures, proprietary information, company funds, political contributions, company property, company records, computer systems, espionage, sabotage, and drugs.

The document also states:

Each employee, alone, is responsible for his or her actions. For each, integrity is a personal liability. No one will be permitted to justify an illegal act by claiming it was ordered by someone in higher management. No one, regardless of level, is ever authorized to direct an employee to commit an illegal or unethical act.

---

* Southern Bell and South Central Bell were reorganized in 1984 and are now Bell South.
Source: Public company documents.

---

the Sabbath. He decided that, in that case, the needs of life took priority over worship obligations and rest requirements.[23]

Codes of conduct do not end value conflicts. Organizations still need to have a formal mechanism to assist managers in resolving value conflicts in light of the corporate code. For example, Cummins Engine has a Department of Corporate Responsibility to assist its managers. Managers may also need more education in business ethics. One way of institutionalizing a corporate code of ethics is through an ethics training program within the management development program.

Finally, the corporate code of ethics must be followed by all levels of management. Having a written code does more harm than good if management does not put into practice what is written. "Actions speak louder than words" is an old statement that is especially true in codes of conduct. Management in Action 3–4 summarizes the code of ethics of South Central Bell and Southern Bell. It also specifically states that each person is responsible for their own behavior.

SUMMARY

Today's organizations are more concerned than ever before about social responsibility and questions of ethics in management. Social responsibility relates to the moral and ethical content of managerial and corporate decisions over and above the pragmatics of legal principle and the market economy.

Many arguments exist both for and against social responsibility on the part of business organizations. Favorable arguments are that it is in the best interest of business; social actions can be profitable; and being socially responsible is the ethical thing to do. Major arguments against social responsibility are that it might be illegal; business and government might become indistinguishable; and social actions cannot be measured. Many organizations have, however, participated in programs attempting to solve social problems.

Ethics are standards or principles of conduct used to govern the behavior of an individual or a group of individuals. Ethics generally involve questions of right and wrong and moral duties.

A code of ethics is needed within organizations because society is demanding it. One legislative attempt to establish a code of ethics in certain business activities was the Foreign Corrupt Practices Act of 1977. A code of ethics also reduces the organizational pressures to compromise personal ethics for the sake of organizational goals. And finally, a code of ethics appeals to the ethical needs of people within organizations.

Codes of ethics should be formalized in writing and communicated to all employees. Organizations also need to have a formal mechanism to assist managers in resolving value conflicts in light of the corporate code. Finally, the corporate code must be followed by all levels of management.

References and Additional Readings

[1] Robert H. Bork, "Modern Values and Social Responsibility," *MSU Business Topics,* Spring 1980, p. 7.

[2] Henry L. Gantt, *Organization for Work* (New York: Harcourt Brace Jovanovich, 1919), p. 15.

[3] Sheldon Oliver, *The Philosophy of Management* (Marshfield, Mass.: Pitman Publishing, 1966), p. xv (originally published in London in 1923 by Sir Isaac Pitman and Sons).

[4] Stewart Thompson, *Management Creeds and Philosophy: Top Management Guides in Our Changing Economy,* Research Study No. 32 (New York: American Management Association, 1958).

[5] For more discussion on the arguments for and against social responsibility, see Clarence C. Walton, "Corporate Social Responsibilities: The Debate Revisited," *Journal of Economics and Business* 34 (1982), pp. 173–87.

[6] Milton Friedman, "Does Business Have a Social Responsibility?" *Magazine of Bank Administration,* April 1971, p. 14.

[7] George A. Steiner, *Business and Society* (New York: Random House, 1971), p. 154.

[8] Committee for Economic Development (CED), "Social Responsibilities of Business Corporations," a statement on national policy by the Research and Policy Committee (Washington, D.C.: U.S. Government Printing Office, June 1971), p. 27.

[9] Theodore Levitt, "The Dangers of Social Responsibility," *Harvard Business Review,* September–October 1958, pp. 41–50.

[10] "A Changing Balance of Power: New Partnership of Government and Business," *Business Week,* July 17, 1965, p. 90.

[11] Neil C. Churchill and Arthur B. Toan, Jr., "Reporting on Corporate Social Responsibility: A Progress Report," *Journal of Contemporary Business,* Winter 1978, pp. 5–17.

[12] Hiram C. Barksdale and William D. Perreault, Jr., "Can Consumers Be Satisfied?" *MSU Business Topics,* Spring 1980, p. 19.

[13] Richard T. Hise, Peter L. Gillet, and J. Pat-

rick Kelly, "The Corporate Consumer Affairs Effort," *MSU Business Topics,* Summer 1978. p. 17.

¹⁴ Tom Alexander, "A Simpler Path to a Cleaner Environment," *Fortune,* May 4, 1981, p. 239.

¹⁵ Gustave Speth and Nicholas C. Yost, "SMR Forum: Simplifying Compliance with the National Environmental Policy Act," *Sloan Management Review,* Summer 1980, pp. 71–75.

¹⁶ James A. Joseph, "Directing the Flow of Corporate Largesse," *Business and Society Review,* Summer 1982, p. 42.

¹⁷ George K. Saul, "Business Ethics: Where Are We Going?" *Academy of Management Review,* April 1981, p. 275.

¹⁸ Archie B. Carroll, "Managerial Ethics: A Post-Watergate View," *Business Horizons,* April 1975, p. 77.

¹⁹ James Weber, "Institutionalizing Ethics into the Corporation," *MSU Business Topics,* Spring 1981, p. 48.

²⁰ Theodore V. Purcell, "Institutionalizing Ethics on Corporate Boards," *Review of Social Economy,* April 1978, p. 43.

²¹ C. Roland Christensen, Norman A. Berg, and Malcolm S. Salter, *Policy Formulation and Administration,* 8th ed. (Homewood, Ill.: Richard D. Irwin, 1980), p. 591.

²² This material is drawn from Oliver F. Williams, "Business Ethics: A Trojan Horse?" *California Management Review,* Summer 1982, p. 19.

²³ Ibid., p. 16.

Review Questions

1. What is social responsibility?
2. Outline three major arguments for social responsibility.
3. Outline three major arguments against social responsibility.
4. What are some obstacles to organizations becoming more socially responsible?
5. Categorize the issues that are now considered to be legitimate social concerns of organizations.
6. What is consumerism?
7. What actions have organizations taken in environmental protection?
8. What methods can companies use to make charitable contributions?
9. What are ethics?
10. Give some reasons why a code of ethics is needed in organizations.

Discussion Questions

1. Do you feel that organizations and managers should be evaluated with regard to social responsibility?
2. "Profits, not social responsibility, must be the primary concern of managers." Discuss.
3. What are some ethical questions that you have faced in college? What basis did you use to resolve them?
4. Do you agree with the statement of James F. Lincoln; "Do unto others as you would have them do unto you. This is not just a Sunday School ideal, but a proper labor-management policy"? Why or why not?

Incident 3–1

Poletown, USA*

In 1981, General Motors decided to invest $500 million for a new facility to boost its production of Cadillacs and Fisher body frames. The plant was to take 500 acres of land located in an old and historic area called Poletown, as well as part of an adjacent area and a portion of the site now occupied by one of Chrysler's defunct Dodge plants.

Since 6,000 new jobs and the potential for better dividends and better products are attractive prospects, Detroit's leaders worked hard to move the project forward; Michigan desperately needed jobs and Detroit needed tax income in the face of an impoverished state budget. But the people of Poletown, mostly elderly, protested. They wanted to keep their houses and their old church.

Since the early days of its formation, the United Automobile Workers (UAW) has had a reputation as being a socially responsible union. From 1979 to 1981, union membership had dropped from 1.5 million to 1.25 million. Its income had fallen by nearly a million per month. It had just sacrificed over $1 million in negotiated wages and benefits in a last-ditch effort to save jobs at Chrysler. Should the union support General Motors by favoring construction of the new plant? Or should it back the citizens of Poletown? The union wrestled with these questions. M. L. Douglas, vice president of Local 22, finally responded. "We have feelings about uprooting a lot of older people, but with the way things are going now, we cannot afford to lose those jobs."

The church faced another problem. John Cardinal Dearden, leader of the archdiocese, was known for his liberal views. By virtue of his own personality and priestly commitment, it could be reasonably inferred that because of the perceived needs of the poor and elderly, the Cardinal's response would be in their favor. Through a church bulletin, the parishioners learned that an agreement had been signed on February 16, 1981, with the city of Detroit. The diocese would sell the two churches of Poletown. Reactions were initially stunned surprise—and then anger. One parishioner expressed the common revulsion when he said, "They have sold us out to the city and to General Motors for 30 pieces of silver."

Questions

1. Were General Motors, the city of Detroit, the UAW, and John Dearden acting socially responsible?
2. Should the good of the larger number be used as rationale for social responsibility?

---

* Source: Adapted from Clarence C. Walton, "Corporate Social Responsibility: The Debate Revisited," *Journal of Economics and Business* 34 (1982), pp. 184–85.

Incident 3–2

When Should a Manager Lie?*

He's the number three person at the nation's second-largest insurance firm—a company whose gross revenues topped $6.2 billion last year. And he has just been asked a zinger: "Do you lie?"

John K. O'Loughlin, senior executive vice president at Allstate Insurance Co., Northbrook, Ill., gives it a whirl. "I probably have distorted the facts from time to time in my career," he admits. "But that was only to protect the innocent." Telling the unvarnished truth can be the more ignoble deed, he explains, when an executive ego is at stake. "Sometimes, it's hard to say to a guy, 'No, you'll never be chairman.'"

Questions

1. Do you agree or disagree with John O'Loughlin's statement? Discuss.
2. Where do you draw the line between distorting the facts and lying?
3. Is "protecting the innocent" a legitimate reason for distorting the facts?
4. Is telling the unvarnished truth the proper approach in all situations?

---

* Source: Adapted from B. Horovitz, "When Should an Executive Lie?" *Industry Week,* November 16, 1981, p. 81.

Exercise
Where Do You Stand?

Read each of the following situations and decide how you would respond.*
Be prepared to justify your position in a class discussion.

Situation 1:   Family versus Ethics

Jim, a 56-year-old middle manager with children in college, discovers
that the owners of his company are cheating the government out of several
thousand dollars a year in taxes. Jim is the only employee in a position to
know this. Should Jim report the owners to the Internal Revenue Service
at the risk of endangering his own livelihood, or should he disregard the
discovery in order to protect his family's livelihood?

Situation 2:   The Roundabout Raise

When Joe asks for a raise, his boss praises his work but says the company's
rigid budget won't allow any further merit raises for the time being. Instead,
the boss suggests that the company "won't look too closely at your expense
accounts for a while." Should Joe take this as authorization to pad his expense
account because he is simply getting the money he deserves through a different route, or should he not take this roundabout "raise"?

Situation 3:   The Faked Degree

Bill has done a sound job for over a year; he got the job by claiming to
have a college degree. Bill's boss learns he actually never graduated. Should
his boss dismiss him for a false resume? Should he overlook the false claim,
since Bill is otherwise conscientious and honorable and dismissal might ruin
Bill's career?

Situation 4:   Sneaking Phone Calls

Helen discovers that a fellow employee makes about $100 a month worth
of personal long-distance telephone calls from an office telephone. Should
Helen report the employee or disregard the calls, since many people make
personal calls at the office?

Situation 5:   Cover-Up Temptation

Bill discovers that the chemical plant he manages is creating slightly more
water pollution in a nearby lake than is legally permitted. Revealing the
problem will bring negative publicity to the plant, hurt the lakeside town's
resort business, and scare the community. Solving the problem will cost
the company well over $100,000. It is unlikely that outsiders will discover
the problem. The violation poses no danger whatever to people; at most,
it will endanger a small number of fish. Should Bill reveal the problem

---

* These situations are taken from Roger Rickles, "Executives Apply Stiffer Standards than
Public to Ethical Dilemmas," *The Wall Street Journal,* November 3, 1983, p. 33.

despite the cost to his company, or should he consider the problem as a mere technicality and disregard it?

Situation 6:   Actual Salary

Dorothy finds out that the best qualified candidate for a job really earned only $18,000 a year in his last job—not the $28,000 he claimed. Should Dorothy hire the candidate anyway, or should she choose someone considerably less qualified?

Section 1 Case
M&M Products

More than $4 billion is spent on hair care products each year by Americans. Over $1.5 billion of this is spent by blacks, who constitute only 12 percent of the U.S. population. "Ethnic" products—hair straighteners and relaxers, curling kits, oil sheen sprays, and special shampoos and conditioners—are usually more expensive than regular hair care items and carry operating margins of 40 to 70 percent. Yet, many retailers with a small amount of black traffic are hesitant to provide valuable shelf space for items they figure will appeal to only one in eight customers.[1]

The ethnic hair care business includes some 90 different minority owned ethnic hair care companies; most are local operations. The four largest ones that distribute nationwide are M&M Products, Johnson Products, Soft Sheen, and Pro-Line. The 90 companies account for 30 percent of sales in the ethnic hair care industry.[2]

The two primary main-line competitors of the minority-owned companies are Alberto-Culver and Revlon, which have special divisions that manufacture and sell products geared toward the ethnic consumer. Revlon, for example, uses Jayne Kennedy as a spokesperson for its Sophisticated Look relaxer. Alberto-Culver's product line, called TCB, continues to be one of the product leaders in black hair care. Procter & Gamble's Head and Shoulders and some of Revlon's general product lines like Flex and the higher-priced Jhirmack also court the ethnic hair care market. Ethnic hair care products are add-on products and not major lines for Alberto-Culver and Revlon.

M&M's number one minority-owned competitor is Soft Sheen Products Company of Chicago. In 1984, Soft Sheen had sales of $55 million, topping M&M Products' sales of $47 million. Soft Sheen was founded in 1964, and by 1979 had about 100 employees and sales of $2 million. This increase in sales prompted a change in strategy by Soft Sheen Products. It embarked on an extensive marketing campaign to increase sales even more through aggressive advertising on black radio stations and in other media to attract the attention of potential black customers.

M&M Products and the other Soft Sheen competitors sell permanent-wave kits on a retail basis; Soft Sheen limits its sales of permanents to salons. However, Soft Sheen does offer companion maintenance products on a retail basis. In fact, the activators and moisturizers that complement the permanent-wave kit make up a larger percentage of their sales than do the kits sold to beauticians. The permanent-wave kit, called Care Free Curl, is Soft Sheen's only product line. M&M Products has three product lines with a total of 77 different products. However, Soft Sheen's one line outsells M&M's three.

Johnson Products Company is the second main minority-owned competitor of M&M Products. Oldest of all the minority-owned companies in the black hair care industry, Johnson Products was established in 1954. The company did not experience the rapid growth in sales in its early years that M&M Products and Soft Sheen achieved, but its growth was basically stable.

Johnson Products has always advertised aggressively, using magazines like *Jet* and *Ebony* and buying spots on black-oriented radio stations. Sales for Johnson Products topped off at $35.5 million in 1982. In 1984, they were ranked third behind soft Sheen and M&M Products in the black hair care industry, but began losing ground because of the aggressive marketing practices of their competitors.

The third competitor of M&M Products is Pro-Line, which ranks fourth among the minority owned companies in the ethnic hair care industry. Sales for Pro-Line amounted to less than $10 million in 1984, even with extensive radio and billboard advertising.

M&M Products Company History

One of the best things that ever happened to Cornell McBride and Thurmond McKenzie occurred in 1974, when—a year out of Atlanta's Mercer University School of Pharmacy—they were turned down for a $7,000 loan to expand their young business. "You're pharmacists, you're not businessmen," the banker said. "You need to go to business school." The two men agreed and duly enrolled in night school business seminars. As a result, when they applied for—and got—a loan from another bank in 1975, they had learned the survival skills essential for a small business in an industry dominated by big names. They named their company M&M Products Company, standing for McBride and McKenzie.[3]

McBride and McKenzie are longtime friends who have always been looking for ways to make money together. In pharmacy school, they developed a hair spray particularly suited to the Afro style. The partners claimed that other sprays on the market in the 1970s tended to leave the hair hard and dry. "Our formula," says McKenzie, "left the hair soft and actually made it resilient and stronger." After graduation from Mercer, they held pharmacists' jobs in Atlanta by day and worked nights and weekends in McBride's basement, mixing batches of formula in a 55-gallon drum and stirring them with a pool cue. They decanted the liquid into eight-ounce plastic spray bottles and packed them into cartons that they used again and again.[4]

The partners began selling the product, which they called Sta-Sof-Fro, to barber shops and mom-and-pop stores. In the beginning, they insisted on delivering every bottle themselves. This not only saved distribution costs but enabled them to obtain prominent shelf display space and to get their cartons back for reuse.

In the early days, Sta-Sof-Fro was almost always left in beauty salons and barber shops on consignment. That paid off, according to McKenzie, because professional endorsements were the single most important factor in gaining product penetration. Once consumers learned about Sta-Sof-Fro in salons, they began to look for it in retail outlets. That demand enabled M&M eventually to place Sta-Sof-Fro in Woolworth and K mart stores nationwide. The philosophy of the two founders was to concentrate on one product. They added other product lines only when Sta-Sof-Fro began to reach the saturation stage.

Boosted initially by a modest series of TV commercials—"From the people who know your hair and care"—and on the bottle label's assurance that the product was "developed by black pharmacists," M&M sales jumped from $11,000 in 1973 (the first year) to $47 million in 1984, making M&M the 11th-largest black-owned company in the United States. The two partners have carefully expanded their line to include almost all hair care products used by black men and women.

Today M&M, which has 327 employees and attractive headquarters in suburban Atlanta, is owned equally by its two founders, each of whom is worth about $5 million. The partners make all important decisions. Early on, says McBride, "we decided that if we were going to make it, we were going to make it together."[5]

Products

M&M's three main product lines are Sta-Sof-Fro, Sof N' Free, and Moxie. Sta-Sof-Fro is aimed mainly at males aged 18 to 35; Sof N' Free, a new product still in its early stages of distribution, is for females in the same age bracket. Moxie, a lower-priced line, is not aimed at a specific age group but at the lower income population and rural areas of the United States. Moxie products retail for approximately $1.50 to $2.50; the other lines range from about $2.50 to $12.

McBride says the best sellers in all three product lines are the products that help maintain curly hair styles. He says M&M has about 50 percent of both the spray market and the oil sheen market. M&M also has between 20 and 25 percent of the curl activator market.[6]

Marketing Strategies

M&M Products are sold to salons and retail outlets—mainly supermarkets, drugstores, and mass merchandisers—by a sales force of 100 headed by sales and marketing Vice President Kay Osborne. Osborne joined the company in 1980 as an international sales account manager and is credited with much of the company's success in expanding overseas. Osborne, whose background includes marketing degrees earned in her native Jamaica and in London, assumed her present position in August 1982.

Although the manufacturing end of the ethnic hair care business is exploding, Osborne says, distribution is not. Very few distributors handle the products, so "they have a monopoly on servicing the stores, and they can dictate their own terms." M&M's strategy, she says, is to ensure consumer demand through continued advertising, promotion, and sampling, especially with the trial sizes that have become so popular for toiletries in recent years.[7]

One of Osborne's priorities is to complete the national distribution campaign for Sof N' Free products. M&M is aiming for distribution in eight markets in which its other products have the competitive edge.

M&M realized early the importance of advertising. As McKenzie says, "Coca-Cola and Crest have stayed number one because they constantly advertise, so we have continually earmarked a percentage of our sales for advertising." Today about 12 percent of projected sales goes into advertising and sales promotion; about 65 percent of that budget is spent on commercials on radio stations with a black audience. Print ads appear in industry magazines and such consumer magazines as *GQ, Ebony, Essence,* and *Jet.*

After 10 years of phenomenal growth between 1973 and 1982, M&M shifted its marketing strategy away from brand advertising to promotions. Believing that it would be foolish to try to compete with the brand advertising budgets of such giants as Revlon (whose revenues exceeded $2 billion) and Alberto-Culver (with more than $232 million in revenues), M&M Products has moved heavily into promotions. The promotions helped solve a major problem: in-store awareness of ethnic products. Most of M&M's advertising budget, estimated at more than $5 million, is spent in support of the promotions. Advertising is weighted two-to-one toward local radio spots, with the remainder spent on print advertising.

One high-profile advertising and promotion campaign is the African Journey Contest. During January and February 1983, this contest was promoted by four-color spreads in six magazines. Point-of-purchase displays carried entry blanks for the contest. To enter, consumers purchased Sta-Sof-Fro products and sent in cash register receipts plus the UPC number for the products purchased. Each product was assigned a point value. Five families— four persons per family—with the most points won the grand prize, a one-week trip to the Ivory Coast in West Africa. This promotion has since become an annual contest.

Third World countries represent a special marketing challenge. The ethnic consumer in the Third World is being weaned off soap as a shampoo, and M&M Products views this as a major opportunity for marketing its products. Consequently, its marketing strategy includes educating those consumers about hair care and hairstyles.

M&M has selected top-name people to promote its hair care products. It named this promotional campaign "the look of a leader"; M&M Products company president Cornell McBride calls it "the Andy Young look." Atlanta's Mayor Andrew Young and Los Angeles Lakers basketball star Magic Johnson are among the celebrity endorsers of M&M products.

Overseas

In 1982, M&M signed a manufacturing agreement with a Jamaican firm to distribute M&M products throughout the Caribbean. M&M products are also sold in London, Paris, Frankfurt, Nigeria, and the Ivory Coast. London is currently the company's largest foreign market, but a company spokesperson predicts that Nigeria will eventually be the biggest.

While in Zimbabwe in 1984 on a trip with Mayor Young, McKenzie met two men interested in setting up a joint venture with an American cosmetics firm. The men, a lawyer and an advertising agent, were already familiar with M&M's products, and they talked enthusiastically with McKenzie about becoming partners. As a result, M&M is presently considering doing business in Zimbabwe.

The Future

"The future is very, very bright—very positive," said McBride in a 1984 interview. Plans include acquisition of existing companies or existing lines of products such as a major skin care line. "We are presently selling mostly hair care products, but we envision selling other kinds of personal care items. Even going a step further, we plan to sell products to the general market some day."[8]

Notes

[1] Howard Rudnitsky and Jay Grissen, "Hair Wars," *Forbes,* December 6, 1982, pp. 132, 136.

[2] Ibid.

[3] "Formula for a Fortune," *Money,* November 1981, p. 32.

[4] Ibid., p. 32.

[5] Ibid.

[6] "M&M Products," *Sales and Marketing Management,* April 1983, p. 41.

[7] Ibid.

[8] Joe Brown, "Beauty," *Atlanta Constitution,* April 13, 1980, p. C–9.

2

Decision-Making and Planning Skills

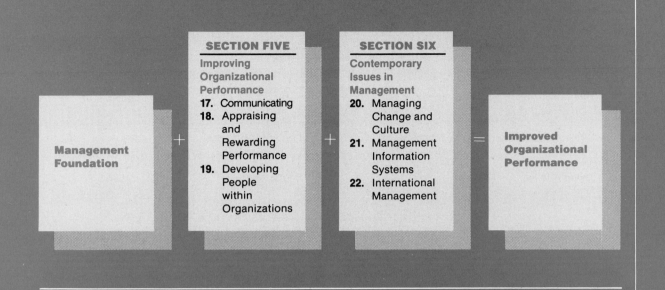

Management
Foundation

+

SECTION FIVE

Improving
Organizational
Performance
17. Communicating
18. Appraising
    and
    Rewarding
    Performance
19. Developing
    People
    within
    Organizations

+

SECTION SIX

Contemporary
Issues in
Management
20. Managing
    Change and
    Culture
21. Management
    Information
    Systems
22. International
    Management

=

Improved
Organizational
Performance

Section 1 introduced the skills required for successful management. Section 2 deals specifically with decision-making and planning skills.

Chapter 4 describes how all managers, regardless of their level in the organization, must make decisions. Both theoretical and practical approaches to decision making are explored. The role of values, as well as the manager's affinity for risk, is discussed. The chapter ends with a discussion of the special problems associated with making decisions in an organizational context.

Chapter 5 introduces and discusses the planning-related concepts of objectives, strategy, and policy. The primary intent is to define the concepts and clarify the relationships between each of these concepts as preparatory work before discussing the overall planning process in Chapter 6.

Chapter 6 discusses the various dimensions of the planning process as well as a step-by-step discussion of how to plan. Chapters 5 and 6 both emphasize that today's manager must be future oriented.

Chapter 7 applies planning concepts to the operations function. The operations function includes the design, operation, and control of facilities and resources directly involved in the production of the organization's goods or services. Chapter 7 concentrates on the planning of operating systems. Product/service design, process selection, site location, physical layout, and job design are all discussed, along with several methods and techniques for handling these tasks.

4

The Manager as Decision Maker

Chapter Outline

"Executive" derives from a Latin word meaning "to do," and the Oxford dictionary defines it in terms of "the action of carrying out or carrying into effect." Neither of these approaches would suggest that the main responsibility and function of the executive is to make decisions. Yet in modern business and industry, this is precisely what is expected. Executives are rewarded and evaluated in terms of their success in making decisions.

David W. Miller and Martin K. Starr*

Some authors use the term *decision maker* to mean manager. Although managers are decision makers, the converse is not necessarily true. Not all decision makers are managers. For example, a person sorting fruit or vegetables is required to make decisions, but not as a manager. However, all managers, regardless of their position in the organization, must make decisions in the pursuit of organizational goals. In fact, decision making pervades all of the basic management functions: planning, organizing, staffing, leading, and controlling. Although different types of decisions are required for these functions, they all require decisions. Thus, to be a good planner, organizer, staffer, leader, and controller, a manager must first be a good decision maker.

Herbert Simon, a Nobel prize winner, has described the manager's **decision process** in three stages: (1) intelligence, (2) design, and (3) choice.[1] The intelligence stage involves searching the environment for conditions requiring a decision. The design stage entails inventing, developing, and analyzing possible courses of action. Choice, the final stage, refers to the actual selection of a course of action.

Decision process—involves searching the environment for conditions requiring a decision, developing and analyzing possible alternatives, and selecting a particular alternative.

The decision process stages show the difference between management and nonmanagement decisions. Nonmanagement decisions are concentrated in the last (choice) stage. The fruit or vegetable sorter has only to make a choice as to the size or quality of the goods. Management decisions place greater emphasis on the intelligence and design stages. If the decision-making process is viewed as only the choice stage, then managers spend very little time making decisions. If, however, decision making is viewed as not only the actual choice but also the intelligence and design work needed to make the choice, then managers spend most of their time making decisions.

TYPES OF DECISIONS

Programmed versus Nonprogrammed Decisions

Decisions are often classified as programmed or nonprogrammed. Programmed decisions are reached by an established or systematic procedure.

* Adapted from David W. Miller and Martin K. Starr, *Executive Decisions and Operations Research* (New York: Harper & Row, 1960), p. 10.

Normally, the decision maker knows the situation in a programmable decision. Routine, repetitive decisions usually fall into this category. <u>Managerial decisions covered by organizational policies, procedures, and rules are programmed</u> in that established guidelines must be followed in arriving at the decision.

Nonprogrammed decisions have <u>little or no precedent</u>. They are relatively <u>unstructured</u> and generally require a more creative approach by the decision maker; the decision maker must develop the procedure to be used. Generally, nonprogrammed decisions are more difficult to make than are programmed ones. Deciding on a new product, a new piece of equipment, and next year's goals are all nonprogrammed decisions.

It should be realized that both decision types can have either major or minor consequences, depending on the nature of the decisions. For example, many personnel-related decisions are programmed. However, one involving disciplinary action could easily have major consequences. On the other hand, the nonprogrammed decision about how to arrange your office furniture would probably have minor consequences.

Organizational versus Personal Decisions

Organizational decisions are made by managers as a part of their organizational responsibilities. Such decisions ultimately relate to the organization's purposes and objectives. Personal decisions, on the other hand, relate to individual goals—a decision to leave one organization and join another would be a personal decision. Personal decisions may affect the organization and vice versa; however, the basis for the decision makes it either organizational or personal. Personal decisions are made from the standpoint of the individual; organizational decisions are made from the standpoint of the organization.

TIMING THE DECISION

To properly time a decision, the need for a decision must be recognized. That is not always easy. The manager may simply not be aware of what is going on, or the problem requiring a decision may be camouflaged. Once the need is realized, the decision must be properly timed. Some managers always seem to make decisions on the spot; others tend to take forever in deciding even a simple matter; another just seems to ignore the entire situation, acting as if it doesn't exist. The manager who makes quick decisions runs the risk of making bad decisions. Failure to gather and evaluate available data, to consider people's feelings, and to anticipate the impact of the decision can result in a very quick but poor decision. Just as risky is the other extreme: the manager who listens to problems, promises to act, but never does. Nearly as bad is the manager who responds only after an inordinate delay. Other

MANAGEMENT IN ACTION 4-1

There Is No Other Way

Back in 1978, Chairman Orin E. Atkins of Ashland Oil sold most of the company's crude oil–producing reserves and some chemical businesses for $1.2 billion. Immediately following the sale, crude oil prices continued to rise, and many people questioned whether Atkins made the right decision.

According to Atkins, he had to do it. Ashland did not have enough crude oil or cash to become a major force in the industry. In 1978, Ashland had to buy 94 percent of its oil on the open market, and its sales and assets were only a fraction of those of the industry leaders—Texaco and Exxon.

With the proceeds of the sale, Atkins paid off some debts and purchased a pollution control equipment business and an insurance business—all part of a plan to improve the company's financial condition and reduce the influence of the remaining petroleum business. Says Atkins, "There is no question that if we had held those assets, we could have got more for them. We simply had no choice."

Source: Maurice Barnfather, *Forbes,* March 30, 1981, p. 41.

---

familiar types are: the manager who never seems to have enough information for a decision; the manager who frets and worries over even the simplest decisions; and the manager who refers everything to superiors.

Knowing when to make a decision is complicated because different decisions have different time frames. For instance, a manager generally has more time to decide committee appointments than what to do when three employees call in sick. No magic formula exists to tell managers when a decision should be made or how long it should take. The important thing is to see the importance of properly timing decisions. Management in Action 4-1 and 4-2 show that managers sometimes must make decisions even when they know the timing is poor (4-1) and how the ability to make rapid decisions benefited Johnson & Johnson (4-2).

THE INTUITIVE APPROACH TO DECISION MAKING

Intuitive approach to decision making–approach to making decisions based on hunches and intuition.

When managers make decisions solely on hunches and intuition (the **intuitive approach**), they are practicing management as if it were wholly an art based primarily on feelings. Sadly, this happens in many situations. Managers sometimes become so emotionally attached to certain positions that almost nothing will change their minds. They develop the "don't bother me with the facts—my mind is made up" attitude. George Odiorne has isolated the following emotional attachments which can adversely affect decision makers:

1. They fasten on the big lie and stick with it.
2. They are attracted to scandalous issues and heighten their significance.

3. They press every fact into a moral pattern.
4. They overlook everything except the immediately useful.
5. They have an affinity for romantic stories and find such information more significant than any other kind, including hard evidence.[2]

Such emotional attachments can be very real and can lead to poor decisions. They most often affect managers or decision makers living in the past, who either will not or cannot modernize. An example is the manager who insists on making decisions just as the founder of the company did 50 years ago.

Odiorne offers two suggestions for managers and decision makers engulfed by emotional attachments.[3] First, become aware of biases and allow for them. Undiscovered biases do the most damage. Second, seek out independent opinions. It is always good to ask the opinion of some person who has no vested interest in the decision.

THE RATIONAL APPROACH TO DECISION MAKING

Fortunately, the physical sciences provide an alternative approach to decision making which is readily adaptable to management problems. The **rational approach** (sometimes called the scientific approach) to decision making includes the following steps:

> **Rational approach to decision making**—involves these steps: recognize the need for a decision; establish, rank, and weight criteria; collect data; identify alternatives; and make the final choice.

1. Recognize the need for a decision.
2. Establish, rank, and weight criteria.
3. Gather available information and data.
4. Identify possible alternatives.
5. Evaluate each alternative with respect to all criteria.
6. Select the best alternative.

Once the need for making the decision is known, criteria must be set for expected results of the decision. These criteria should then be ranked and weighted according to their relative importance.

Next, factual data relating to the decision should be collected. After that, all alternatives that meet the criteria are identified. Each is then evaluated with respect to all criteria. The final decision is based on the alternative which best meets the criteria. The following example illustrates the scientific approach to decision making.

Ms. Ryan, office manager for the TDY Company, is trying to reach a decision on a new supplier of office materials for her insurance business. The need for a new supplier has become evident over the last six months: the present supplier has been late on deliveries in seven out of the last nine orders. After consulting the office staff, Ms. Ryan chose the following criteria for the decision: dependability, price, delivery time, location of the

MANAGEMENT IN ACTION 4–2

Crisis Decision Making at Johnson & Johnson

In September 1982, a psychopathic killer laced 44 capsules of Extra-Strength Tylenol with fatal amounts of cyanide and randomly inserted the packages on store shelves in the Chicago area. Within a three-day period, seven people died.

Although the manufacturer Johnson & Johnson was completely blameless in the tragedy, corporate management was faced with a crisis of gigantic proportion. The Tylenol product had accounted for $450 million in sales the year before and contributed over 15 percent to company profits. How top management handled the crisis would impact the reputation of the company and, ultimately, the survival of the Tylenol brand.

Chairman Burke quickly formed a seven-member strategy team that met twice daily during the first six weeks of the crisis. A few of the many decisions the team made during the crisis were:

- To conduct an extensive product recall at a cost of $100 million.

- To stop all Tylenol advertising.
- To promote the trustworthiness of the organization through the use of the media. Burke appeared on the Phil Donahue Show, and "60 Minutes" filmed a strategy session.
- To modify product packaging to make it tamperproof.
- To begin the product comeback (several weeks later) with a 30-city video press conference via satellite.

In the weeks immediately following the tragedy, Tylenol's share of the over-the-counter analgesic market fell from 35 percent to 4.5 percent. By June 1983, Tylenol had recovered 27 percent of the market. As of January 1984, Tylenol had captured 32 percent of the market.

Sources: Mitchell Leon, "Tylenol Fights Back," *Public Relations Journal,* March 1983, pp. 10–14; "Speedy Recovery for Tylenol," *Marketing and Media Decisions,* June 1983, p. 36; Leonard Snyder, "An Anniversary Review and Critique: The Tylenol Crisis," *Public Relations Review,* Fall 1983, pp. 24–34; Johnson & Johnson, Annual Report, 1983.

suppliers, and variety of products offered. She then established the priorities, weights (relative importance of each item), and limits for the criteria, as shown in Table 4–1.

After looking through the city directory and talking with the managers of the local Office Suppliers Association, Ms. Ryan identified the possible

---

TABLE 4–1
Priorities, Weights, and Limits for Office Supplier Decision Criteria

Criteria	Priority	Weight (1–5)	Limit, If Any
Dependability.	1	5	—
Variety of products offered.	2	4	A full line of products.
Price.	3	4	Competitive.
Delivery time.	4	2	Less than four weeks.
Location of supplier.	5	1	Have at least one branch in the city.

candidates listed in Table 4–2. Using available data on these companies, Ms. Ryan evaluated each with respect to each criterion. Table 4–2 shows the results, using a scale of one (low) to nine (high). The totals for each line were found by multiplying each individual criterion evaluation by its respective weight and then summing all of these scores for the respective alternative. With each alternative evaluated, it is evident that Ms. Ryan should select Acme Supply Company since it received the highest point total.

Note that the first step of the scientific approach to decision making is analogous to Simon's intelligence stage; the next three steps of the scientific approach relate to Simon's design stage; and the final two steps compare with Simon's choice stage.

Limitations of the Rational Approach

The rational approach to decision making is certainly an improvement over the intuitive approach; but it is not without its problems and limitations. The rational approach is based on the concept of "economic man." This concept postulates that people behave rationally and that their behavior is based on the following four assumptions:

1. People have clearly defined criteria, and the relative weights which they assign to these criteria are stable.
2. People have knowledge of all relevant alternatives.
3. People have the ability to evaluate each alternative with respect to all the criteria and arrive at an overall rating for each alternative.
4. People have the self-discipline to choose the alternative which rates the highest (they will not manipulate the system).

TABLE 4–2
Evaluation of Alternative Suppliers

Weight	5	4	4	2	1	
Criteria / Alternative	Dependability	Variety of Products	Price	Time to Delivery	Location of Supplier	Total
Office Supply, Inc.	6	7	8	3	6	102
ABC Company	7	4	5	8	5	92
Acme Supply	9	3	9	8	5	114
University Supply	4	6	7	3	7	85
QTR Company	3	6	6	4	7	78

Often, these assumptions are not very realistic. First, problems arise in setting decision objectives because the decision maker may not always know the criteria to be used in evaluating the decision. Factors important to the person making the decision may not be important to superiors and subordinates. In selecting a new office supplier, it is entirely possible that Ms. Ryan and her staff might not agree on the proper criteria. Even if they did, they might disagree on the priorities, weights, or limits. Ms. Ryan's authority to overrule her subordinates doesn't simplify the situation they may very well try to undermine her decision at a later time.

Another problem is that most decisions are based on limited knowledge. In the example above, one or more alternatives could have been omitted due to a lack of knowledge—other suppliers who meet all the criteria may not even have been considered. Most decisions are based on less than perfect information; in many cases, a manager has very limited or no control over the information used to make the decision. Information over which the manager has no control might come from outside sources or even a competitor. With new products or innovative ideas, information may not exist. So the ability to evaluate each choice and to reach the best decision may suffer from a lack of information.

The most difficult step in the decision process may be the evaluation or the prediction of outcomes for the various alternatives. Even in the simple example above, it would be hard to evaluate accurately each criteria for each alternative. Since final selections are based on predicted outcomes, inaccurate predictions may lead to poor decisions.

A final problem is the temptation to manipulate the information and choose a favored—but not necessarily the best—alternative. This temptation may come from within the decision maker, or it may come from external forces. Ms. Ryan's staff might persuade her to select Office Supply, Inc. "just because they have the friendliest salesperson."

Due to the limitations of the rational approach, most decisions—even when the rational approach is followed—still involve some judgment. Thus, in making decisions, the manager generally uses a combination of science and art.

A SATISFICING APPROACH

Believing the "economic man" assumptions are generally unrealistic, Herbert Simon developed the *principle of bounded rationality,* which states: The capacity of the human mind for formulating and solving complex problems is very small compared with the size of the problems whose solution is required for objectively rational behavior—or even for a reasonable approximation to such objective rationality.[4]

Thus, the principle of bounded rationality states that there are definite limits to human rationality. Based on that, Simon has proposed a decision theory of the "administrative man," with the following assumptions:

1. A person's knowledge of alternatives and criteria are limited.

2. People act on the basis of a simplified, ill-structured, mental abstraction of the real world; this abstraction is influenced by personal perceptions, biases, and so forth.

3. People do not attempt to optimize but will take the first alternative which satisfies their current level of aspiration. This is called satisficing.

4. An individual's level of aspiration concerning a decision fluctuates upward and downward, depending on the values of the most recently found alternatives.

Satisficing—the practice of selecting the first alternative that meets the decision maker's minimum standard of satisfaction.

The first assumption is a synopsis of the principle of bounded rationality. The second assumption follows naturally from the first. If limits do exist to human rationality, then an individual must make decisions based on limited and incomplete knowledge. The third assumption also naturally follows from the first assumption. If the decision maker's knowledge of alternatives is incomplete, then the individual cannot optimize but only satisfice. **Optimizing** means selecting the best possible alternative; satisficing means selecting the first alternative that meets the decision maker's minimum standard of satisfaction. Assumption four is based on the belief that the criteria for a satisfactory alternative is determined by the current level of aspiration. **Level of aspiration** refers to the level of performance that a person expects to attain and it is determined by the person's prior successes and failures.

Optimizing—selecting the best possible alternative.

Level of aspiration—the level or performance that a person expects or hopes to attain.

Figure 4–1 represents the satisficing approach to decision making. If the decision maker is satisfied that an acceptable alternative has been found, it is selected. Otherwise, the decision maker searches for an additional alternative. In the office supplier example, the office manager would select the first satisfactory supplier rather than looking at all possibilities. If an additional alternative is required, it is evaluated. This evaluation is influenced by the value of the previous best alternative and by the current level of aspiration. In the office supplier example, the last supplier used and the last one considered for use would both influence the office manager's evaluation of a new supplier.

In Figure 4–1, the double arrows indicate a two-way relationship: The value of the new alternative is influenced by the value of the previous best alternative; the value of the best previous alternative is, in turn; influenced by the value of the new alternative. As indicated by the arrows, a similar two-way relationship exists between the value of the new alternative and the current level of aspiration. The net result of this evaluation determines whether or not the decision maker is satisfied with the alternative. Thus, the administrative man selects the first alternative that meets the minimum satisfaction criteria and makes no real attempt to optimize.

FIGURE 4–1
Model of the Satisficing Approach

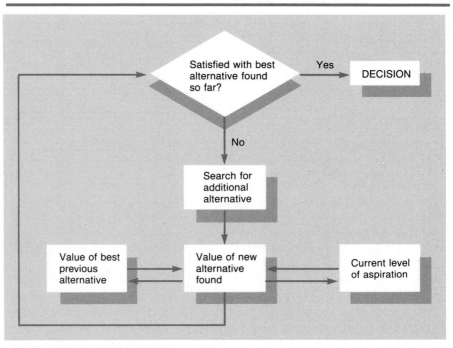

Source: Adapted from James G. March and Herbert A. Simon, *Organizations* (New York: John Wiley & Sons, 1958), p. 49.

CONDITIONS FOR MAKING DECISIONS

With any approach, decisions are not always made with the same amount of available information. The best decision often depends on what happens at a later point in time. Take the simple decision of whether or not to take an umbrella when going outside. The more desirable alternative is determined by whether or not it rains; but this is not under the control of the decision maker.

Table 4–3 gives combinations of alternatives and states of nature with their respective outcomes for the individual trying to decide whether or not to take an umbrella outside.

Certainty

Knowing exactly what will happen places the decision maker in a **situation of certainty.** In such a situation, the decision maker can often calculate the precise outcome for each alternative. If it is raining, the person knows

Certainty situation—
decision situation in which the decision maker knows the state of nature and can calculate exactly what will happen.

TABLE 4–3
Umbrella Decision: Alternatives and States of Nature

	State of Nature	
Alternative	**No Rain**	**Rain**
Take umbrella	Dry, but inconvenient	Dry
Do not take umbrella	Dry	Wet

the state of nature—and therefore knows the best alternative (take an umbrella).

Risk

Sadly, the state of nature is not always known in advance. The decision maker can often obtain—at some cost—information on the state of nature. The desirability of getting the information is figured by weighting the costs of obtaining the information against its value. A decision maker is in a **situation of risk** if the relative probabilities associated with each state of nature are known. If the weather forecaster has said there is a 40 percent chance of rain, the decision maker is operating in a situation of risk.

The precise probabilities of the various states of nature usually are not known. However, reasonably accurate ones based on historical data and past experiences can often be calculated. When no such data exists, it is difficult to estimate probabilities. In such cases, one approach is to survey individual opinions.

Under conditions of risk, expected value analysis can be used by the decision maker. With this technique the expected payoff of an act can be mathematically calculated. One shortcoming of expected value analysis is that it represents the average outcome if the event is repeated a large number of times. That is of little help if the act only takes place once. For example, airplane passengers are not interested in the average fatality rates. Rather they are interested in what happens on their particular flight.

Risk situation–decision situation in which the decision maker has some information and can calculate probabilistic estimates about the outcome of each alternative.

Uncertainty

With no knowledge of the relative probabilities of the respective states of nature, decision makers operate in a **situation of uncertainty.** For example, a person going to New York who had not heard a weather forecast for New York, would have no knowledge of the likelihood of rain and, hence, would not know whether or not to carry an umbrella.

If the decision maker has little or no knowledge about which state of nature will occur, one of three basic approaches may be taken. The first is

Uncertainty situation– decision situation in which the decision maker has no knowledge about the relative probabilities associated with the different possible outcomes.

to choose the alternative whose best possible outcome is the best of all possible outcomes for all alternatives. This is an optimistic, or gambling, approach—it is sometimes called the "maximax" approach. A decision maker using this approach would not take the umbrella, since the best possible outcome is no rain and no umbrella.

A second approach for dealing with uncertainty is to compare the worst possible outcomes for each of the alternatives and select the one which is least bad. This is a pessimistic approach—sometimes called the "maximin" approach. In the umbrella example, the decision maker would compare the worst possible outcome of taking an umbrella to that of not taking an umbrella. The decision maker would then decide to take an umbrella, since it is better to carry an unneeded umbrella than to get wet.

The final approach is to choose the alternative with the least variation among its possible outcomes. This is a risk-averting approach and makes for more effective planning. If the decision maker chooses not to take an umbrella, the outcomes can vary from staying dry to getting wet. By choosing to take an umbrella, the outcomes can vary from being dry but inconvenienced to being dry. Thus, the risk-averting decision maker would take an umbrella to be sure of staying dry. Figure 4–2 gives the different approaches to making a decision under conditions of uncertainty.

FIGURE 4–2
Possible Approaches to Making Decisions under Uncertainty

Approach	How It Works	Related to the Umbrella Example
Optimistic or gambling approach (maximax).	Choose the alternative whose best possible outcome is the best of all possible outcomes for all alternatives.	Do not take umbrella.
Pessimistic approach (maximin).	Compare the worst possible outcomes of each of the alternatives and select the alternative whose worst possible outcome is least bad.	Take umbrella.
Risk-averting approach.	Choose the alternative which has the least variation among its possible alternatives.	Take umbrella.

The specific approach used by the decision maker under conditions of uncertainty depends on the individual's aversion to risk and the consequences of a bad decision.

Management in Action 4–3 discusses several risky decisions that Peter Ueberroth (organizer of the 1984 Olympic Games and current commissioner of major league baseball) made regarding the 1984 Olympics.

MANAGEMENT IN ACTION 4-3

Decision Making under Risky Conditions

Peter Ueberroth, the organizer of the 1984 Olympic Games and Time Magazine's Man of the Year for 1984, is described by co-workers as a person not afraid to make a risky or unpopular decision. During the planning of the games, Ueberroth made several decisions that could have backfired. He dramatically reduced the number of TV sponsors to 10 percent of the 1980 level and raised the price to $4 million minimum per corporation. He implemented a one-shot bidding contest between the TV networks in what was described as a "white-knuckle showdown." When Eastman Kodak refused to pay the $4 million, Ueberroth switched to Fuji Photo without hesitation.

However, Ueberroth believed in delegating decision making when feasible. Ueberroth pushed decision making to the lowest possible level in the organization. If a subordinate pushed decisions upward, Ueberroth would push it back, claiming, "Authority is 20 percent given and 80 percent taken. Take it."

Source: Robert Ajemian, "Master of the Games," *Time*, January 7, 1985, pp. 32–39.

THE ROLE OF VALUES IN DECISION MAKING

A **value** is a conception, explicit or implicit, defining what an individual or group regards as desirable.[5] Values play an important role in the decision-making process. People are not born with values but rather they acquire and develop them early in life. Parents, teachers, relatives, and others influence an individual's values. As a result, every manager and employee brings a certain set of values to the workplace.

> Value—conception, explicit or implicit, defining what an individual or a group sees as desirable.

A person's values have an impact on the selection of performance measures, alternatives, and choice criteria in the decision process. Differences in values often account for the use of different performance measures. For example, a manager primarily concerned with economic values would probably measure performance differently from a manager primarily concerned with social values. The former might look only at profit, the latter might think only of customer complaints. Differences in values might also generate different alternatives. A viable alternative to one person might be unacceptable to another because of differences in values. Because the final choice criteria depend on the performance measures used, they are also affected by values. For example, consider the question of laying off excess employees. Managers with dominant economic values would likely lay them off much quicker than would managers with high social values.

George England—who has conducted very extensive research on the role of values in the decision-making process—has identified three major categories of values (see Figure 4–3).[6] He reported the following:

1. There are large individual differences in personal values within every group studied. In the different countries studied, some managers have a

FIGURE 4–3
England's Major Categories of Values

The pragmatic mode: Suggests that an individual has an evaluative framework that is primarily guided by success-failure considerations.

The ethical-moral mode: Implies an evaluative framework consisting of ethical considerations influencing behavior toward actions and decisions which are judged to be right, and away from those judged to be wrong.

The affect, or feeling, mode: Suggests an evaluative framework which is guided by hedonism. One behaves in ways that increase pleasure and decrease pain.

pragmatic orientation, some have an ethical-moral orientation, and some have an affect, or feeling, orientation. Some managers have a very small set of values; others have a large set and seem to be influenced by many strongly held values.

2. Personal value systems of managers are relatively stable and do not change rapidly. Edward Lusk and Bruce Oliver repeated one of Professor England's earlier studies and reported that values of managers had changed very little between 1966 and 1972.[7]

3. Personal value systems of managers are related to and/or influence the way managers make decisions. For example, those who have profit maximization as an important goal are less willing to spend money on cafeteria and rest room improvements than those who do not have profit maximization as an important value.

4. Personal value systems of managers are related to their career success as managers. Successful American managers favor pragmatic, dynamic, achievement-oriented values; less successful managers prefer more static and passive values.

5. There are differences in the personal values of managers working in different organizational contexts. For example, the personal values of U.S. managers were found to be different from those of labor leaders.

6. Overall, the value systems of managers in the different countries studied were similar; yet, there were some distinct differences. The data suggest that cultural and social factors—as opposed to level of technological and industrial development—are most important in explaining value differences and similarities.[8]

The work of England and others clearly establishes the importance that values play in the decision-making process of managers. His and other more recent studies show that values may differ from culture to culture and that these differences may have a profound effect upon resulting decisions.[9] To make sound decisions, today's managers must not only be aware of their own values; they also must know those of others inside and outside the organization.

PARTICIPATION IN DECISION MAKING

Most managers have opportunities to involve their subordinates and others in the decision-making process. One pertinent question is: "Do groups make better decisions than individuals?" Another is: "When should subordinates be involved in making managerial decisions?"

Group Decision Making

Everyone knows the old axiom that two heads are better than one. Empirical evidence generally supports this view—with a few minor qualifications. Group performance is frequently better than that of the average group member.[10] Similarly, groups can often be successfully used to develop innovative and creative solutions to problems. (Chapter 15 discusses several group-oriented approaches for improving creativity in organizations.) Groups also take longer to solve problems than does the average person.[11] Thus, group decisions are generally better when avoiding mistakes is more important than speed.

Group performance is generally superior to that of the average group member for two basic reasons. First, the sum total of the group's knowledge is greater; second, the group has a much wider range of alternatives in the decision process.

Group decision making also has other benefits. It facilitates and increases acceptance of the decision by group members—especially when a change is being implemented. A more complete understanding of both the decision and alternative solutions results from group decision making. This is especially helpful when those who must implement the decision participate in the process. Management in Action 4–4 presents an example of such a situation.

However, some potential drawbacks can greatly limit the effectiveness of group decision making. One person may dominate or control the group. This occurs frequently when the president or other higher-ups in the organization take part in the decision process. Because of their presence many other members become inhibited. The social pressures of conformity can also inhibit group members.

Competition can develop within the group to such an extent that winning an issue becomes more important than the issue itself. A final hazard results from the dynamics of group decision making. Groups tend to accept the first potentially positive solution and give little attention to others.

One other trait of group decision making compares the risk that people will take alone and in a group. Laboratory experiments have shown that unanimous group decisions are consistently more risky than the average of the individual decisions.[12] This is somewhat surprising since group pres-

Forming a New Company Takes Group Decisions

Biogen, a Swiss-based biotechnology firm, had an unusual beginning. In 1977, Raymond Schaefer, a venture capitalist, began to pull together a plan for starting a biotechnology company. He compiled a list of European and U.S. scientists that he wanted on his team and arranged for a preliminary negotiating meeting between the scientists and investors in March 1978. Shaefer and the other investors wanted to convince the scientists to join the venture.

The scientists were all experts in their fields but knew little or nothing about starting a company. However, the scientists, who were described as having "magnificently large" egos, pulled together and made several group decisions about what they wanted to accomplish and the value of their individual services to the potential new organization. They then proposed a corporate structure giving the scientific board the power to approve product development and set restrictions on the sale of stock so no one could sell out frivolously.

At the end of the negotiating meeting, the scientists asked the investors to leave the room. After a long, closed-door meeting, the scientists voted unanimously to participate in forming Biogen.

Source: Stephen S. Hall, "Biologist in the Boardroom," *Science 85,* February 1985, pp. 42–50.

sures often inhibit the members. Possibly people feel less responsible for the outcome of a group decision than when they act alone.

Figure 4–4 summarizes the positive and negative aspects of group decision making. Management in Action 4–5 illustrates the desire of employees to participate in the decision-making process.

A Model for Making Managerial Decisions

One key to effective managerial decisions is the ability of the manager to select the appropriate decision-making style for each decision faced. Re-

---

FIGURE 4–4
Positive and Negative Aspects of Group Decision Making

Positive Aspects
1. The sum total of the group's knowledge is greater.
2. The group possesses a much wider range of alternatives in the decision process.
3. Participation in the decision-making process increases the acceptance of the decision by group members.
4. Group members better understand the decision and the alternatives considered.

Negative Aspects
1. One invidivual may dominate and/or control the group.
2. Social pressures to conform can inhibit group members.
3. Competition can develop to such an extent that winning becomes more important than the issue itself.
4. Groups have a tendency to accept the first potentially positive solution, while giving little attention to other possible solutions.

MANAGEMENT IN ACTION 4–5

Workers Want to Participate in Decision Making

In 1983, Owen and Lee Associates Inc. conducted a survey of 350 laid-off workers in Pittsburgh. The consensus of the workers was that more worker input into decision making would have helped improve productivity in their former companies. Sixty-nine percent of the workers said their companies had sought their opinions "very little." Nine percent said they were not consulted at all. Seventy-five percent of the workers surveyed said they would take pay cuts in order to get their jobs back, but in exchange, they wanted some degree of ownership and involvement in decision making.

Source: "Unemployed Would Take Pay Cut for 'Ownership,'" *Industry Week*, May 16, 1983.

search and practice show that no single style of decision making works best in all situations. Successful managers learn to match the appropriate decision-making style with the situation.

Victor Vroom and Philip Yetton have addressed the problem with a very practical and useful model.[13] They developed the set of alternative decision styles shown in Figure 4–5. Each style has a code and is increasingly more participative: Style A–I has no subordinate participation, while Style G–II is almost totally participative.

Vroom and Yettan selected three variables bearing on the appropriateness of a given decision-making style: (1) the quality or rationality of the decision; (2) the acceptance or commitment by subordinates to execute the decision effectively; and (3) the amount of time required to make the decision.

FIGURE 4–5
Types of Management Decision Styles

A-I: You solve the problem or make the decision yourself, using information available to you at that time.

A-II: You obtain the necessary information from your subordinate(s), then decide on the solution to the problem yourself. You may or may not tell your subordinates what the problem is, while getting the information from them. The role played by your subordinates in making the decision is clearly one of providing the necessary information to you rather than generating or evaluating alternative solutions.

C-I: You share the problem with your subordinates as a group, collectively obtaining their ideas and suggestions. Then you make a decision that may or may not reflect your subordinates' influence.

G-II: You share a problem with your subordinates as a group. Together you generate and evaluate alternatives and attempt to reach agreement (consensus) on a solution. Your role is much like that of chairperson. You do not try to influence the group to adopt your solution, and you are willing to accept and implement any solution that has the support of the entire group.

Source: Victor H. Vroom, "A New Look at Managerial Decision Making," *Organizational Dynamics*, Spring 1973. © 1973 by AMACOM, a division of American Management Associations, New York, p. 67. Reprinted by permission of the publisher. All rights reserved.

FIGURE 4-6
Vroom and Yelton's Decision Model

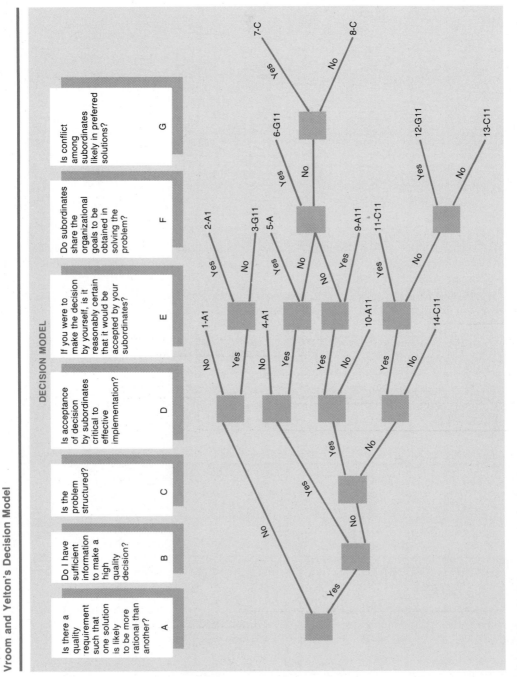

Source: Victor H. Vroom, "A New Look at Managerial Decision Making," *Organizational Dynamics*, Spring 1973. © 1973 by AMACOM, a division of American Management Associations, New York, p. 70. Reprinted by permission of the publisher. All rights reserved.

Figure 4–6 shows Vroom and Yetton's model as a decision tree. The problem attributes are shown across the top of the figure. For any decision situation, start at the left-hand side and work toward the right until a terminal node is reached. When more than one decision-making style is feasible, this model chooses the style requiring the least amount of time.

Vroom and Yetton found that most managers actually do use different decision-making styles in different situations. They also found that managers are much more likely to break decision rules about acceptance or commitment of the decision than those designed to protect the quality or rationality of the decision. One might then conclude that typical managers' decisions are more likely to suffer from a lack of acceptance by subordinates than from the quality of the decision. Similarly, managers who learn what decision styles work best in what situations are usually going to make better decisions than those who don't.

THE DECISION MAKER'S ENVIRONMENT

In addition to the situational factors of the Vroom and Yetton model, a decision maker's style is often affected by the environment. This includes the organization itself and groups and individuals within the organization.

A manager's freedom to make decisions depends largely on the manager's position within the organization and on its structure. In general, higher-level managers have more flexibility and discretion. The patterns of authority outlined by the formal organization structure also influence the flexibility of the decision maker.

Another important factor of decision-making style is the purpose and tradition of the organization. For example, a military organization requires a different style of decision making than does a volunteer organization.

The organization's formal and informal group structures affect decision-making styles. These groups may range from labor unions to advisory councils.

A final subset of the environment includes all the decision maker's superiors and subordinates. The personalities, backgrounds, and expectations of these people influence the decision maker.

Figure 4–7 shows the major environmental factors that affect the decision maker in an organization.

Successful managers must develop an appreciation for the different environmental forces that both influence them and are influenced by their decisions. They must develop a multilevel view (organization, group, and individual) of decision making. To always have a single-level view—whether it be the organization's, a group's, or the individual's—will not result in optimal decisions. Managers who view decisions only from the organizational perspective—who have no appreciation for the groups and individuals making up the organization—will eventually experience behavioral problems.

FIGURE 4–7
Environmental Factors Influencing Decision Making in an Organization

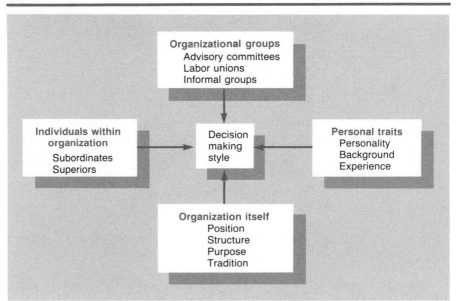

"Country club" managers, who are concerned only about their employees and neglect the organization's objectives in their decisions, will probably not keep their jobs. The same is true of managers who become overly concerned with organizational groups and neglect either the individual's or the organization's objectives. The key to good decision making is a balanced, multilevel perspective and the ability to match the decision situation with the appropriate decision-making style.

SUMMARY

Decision making pervades all management functions; therefore, all managers are decision makers. Decision making involves searching the environment for conditions requiring a decision, developing and analyzing possible alternatives, and then selecting the best alternative.

Programmed decisions are reached by following an established or systematic procedure. Nonprogrammed decisions are unique and have little or no precedent. Organizational decisions are those that managers make in carrying out their organizational responsibilities. Properly timing a decision is a major requirement for its success. Knowing when to make a decision is complicated by the fact that different decisions must be made within different time frames.

Making decisions strictly from intuition has many potential pitfalls. Decision makers can become so emotionally attached to a certain position that almost nothing will change their minds. The rational approach to decision making follows a structured method for making decisions: (1) recognize the need for a decision; (2) establish, rank, and weigh criteria; (3) gather available information and data; (4) identify possible alternatives; (5) evaluate each alternative with respect to all criteria; and (6) select the best alternative. However, the rational approach also has certain inherent weaknesses because of its reliance on the "economic man" concept.

The satisficing approach to decision making is based on Simon's principle of bounded rationality, which states that there are empirical limits to a person's rationality. Basically, a person does not attempt to optimize in the decision process but rather selects the first alternative that satisfies.

The state of nature coupled with the chosen alternative determine the outcome of a decision. Conditions of certainty exist when the state of nature is known. A situation of risk exists when the relative probabilities of the various states of nature are known. Conditions of uncertainty exist when nothing is known concerning the probabilities of the various states of nature. The personal value systems of managers also play an important role in the decision-making process.

Groups can be effective decision-making bodies—especially in situations where avoiding mistakes is more important than speed. Vroom and Yetton offer a very practical model for matching decision-making style to the decision situation. Their model is based on the fact that different decision-making styles work best in different decision situations.

A decision maker's style is often influenced by his or her environment. This includes the organization itself, groups within the organization, and individuals within the organization. Successful managers develop a multilevel perspective toward decision making. This multilevel perspective includes the ability to evaluate a decision from an organizational, group, and individual perspective.

References and Additional Readings

[1] Herbert A. Simon, *The New Science of Management Decision* (New York: Harper & Row, 1960), p. 2.

[2] George S. Odiorne, *Management and the Activity Trap* (New York: Harper & Row, 1974), pp. 128–29; George S. Odiorne, *The Change Resisters,* (Englewood Cliffs, N.J.: Prentice-Hall, 1981), pp. 15–25.

[3] Odiorne, *Management and the Activity Trap,* pp. 142–44.

[4] Herbert A. Simon, *Model of Man* (New York: John Wiley & Sons, 1957), p. 198.

[5] William D. Guth and Renato Tagiuri, "Personal Values and Corporate Strategy," *Harvard Business Review,* September–October 1965, pp. 124–25.

[6] George England, "Personal Value Systems of Managers and Administrators," *Academy of Management Proceedings,* August 1973, pp. 81–94.

[7] Edward J. Lusk and Bruce L. Oliver, "American Managers' Personal Value Systems Revisited," *Academy of Management Journal,* September 1974, pp. 549–54.

[8] England, "Personal Value Systems," pp. 82–87.

[9] For example, see H. S. Badr, E. R. Gray, and B. L. Kedia, "Personal Values and Managerial Decision Making: Evidence from Two Cultures," *Management International Review,* Fall 1982, pp. 65–73.

[10] Irving Lorge, David Fox, Joel Davitz, and Marlin Brenner, "A Survey of Studies Contrasting the Quality of Group Performance and Individual Performance, 1930–1957," *Psychological Bulletin,* November 1958, pp. 337–72; Frederick C. Miner, Jr., "Group versus Individual Decision Making: An Investigation of Performance Measures, Decision Strategies, and Process Losses/Gains," *Organizational Behavior and Human Performance* 33 (February 1984), pp. 112–24.

[11] M. E. Shaw, "A Comparison of Individuals and Small Groups in the National Solution of Complex Problems," *American Journal of Psychology,* July 1932, pp. 491–504; Lorge et al., "A Survey of Studies."

[12] M. Wallach, N. Kogan, and D. J. Bem, "Group Influence on Individual Risk Taking," *Journal of Abnormal and Social Psychology,* August 1962, pp. 75–86; N. Kogan and M. Wallach, "Risk Taking as a Function of the Situation, the Person, and the Group," in *New Directions of Psychology,* vol. 3, ed. G. Mardler (New York: Holt, Rinehart & Winston, 1967).

[13] Victor H. Vroom, "A New Look at Managerial Decision Making," *Organizational Dynamics,* Spring 1973, pp. 66–80; Victor H. Vroom and Philip W. Yetton, *Leadership and Decision Making* (Pittsburgh: University of Pittsburgh Press, 1973).

Review Questions

1. What are three stages in the decision-making process? *search, analyze, select*
2. What are the differences between programmed and nonprogrammed decisions? Between organizational and personal decisions?
3. Describe the intuitive approach to decision making. *emotional*
4. Describe the rational approach to decision making. *scientific*
5. What criticisms can be made concerning the rational approach to decision making? *Limitations: knowledge, criteria, manipulation, eval/prediction*
6. Describe the satisficing approach to decision making. *select 1st alternative which meets min. standard*
7. What is the difference between satisficing and optimizing? *select 1st min. sat. alt. / select BEST possible alt.*
8. What are values? Is there any relationship between values and managerial success?
9. Distinguish between the decision situations of certainty, risk, and uncertainty.
10. Describe some positive and negative aspects of group decision making.
11. According to Vroom and Yetton, what three variables have a significant bearing on the appropriateness of a given decision-making style? *1) quality/rationality of dec 2) acceptance by sub. to execute 3) amt. of time req. to make decision*

Discussion Questions

1. Do you subscribe to the belief that many managers only attempt to satisfice rather than optimize in making decisions? Support your answers with examples.

2. Specifically, how can managers' values affect their decisions?
3. What factors do you think affect the amount of risk that a manager is willing to take when making a decision?
4. Comment on the following statement: "Groups always make better decisions than individuals acting alone."
5. How does decision making within an organization differ from individual or personal decision making? Support your answer with examples.

Incident 4–1
Getting Out of the Army

Jay Abbott is confident that his future will be secure and financially rewarding should he decide to remain in the army. He entered more than 10 years ago as a commissioned officer after completing his college education on an ROTC scholarship. Jay, 31 years old, has progresssed to the rank of captain and is currently being considered for promotion to major. He has no reason to believe he will not be promoted. He has been successful in all of his appointments, is well liked by everyone—his peers, superiors, and subordinates—and has an unblemished record.

However, at the 10-year mark, Jay had second thoughts about staying in the army and has been thinking about leaving ever since. He has felt more and more resentful that the army has affected a large part of his personal life. Although he had always preferred to wear his hair shorter than that of most young men, he resented the fact that even if he wanted to let it grow out or have sideburns, he couldn't do it. It was the principle of the whole idea—the intrusion of the army into this personal life. The fact that this intrusion extended to the behavior of his wife and children bothered him even more.

Jay's wife Ellen was finishing her master's thesis. This took up a large portion of her free time; yet her lack of involvement in the officers' clubs was frowned upon. There was just no such thing as a private family life in his position. He didn't even have much time to spend with the family. His job required long hours of work, including weekend duty—which left little time for his wife and two daughters, aged seven and nine. Another problem was that Ellen, holding a degree in design engineering, was unable to pursue any kind of real career—something that was important to both of them.

These thoughts raced through Jay's mind over and over again as he tried to decide what would be best for him and his family. There were a lot of positive factors about the army, he kept reminding himself: he was already earning $27,000 a year; with his near-certain promotion, this would be raised to $31,000. Also he was being recommended for the Army's Command and General Staff College. There was little chance he would not be approved; completing the program would make his future even brighter. If he stayed, he'd be able to retire in just 10 more years (at age 41) with a permanent retirement income of half his final salary plus free medical and dental coverage. By then, he figured, he would probably be a lieutenant colonel with a base pay of around $41,000; at worst, he would retire a major. At 41, there would be plenty of time to devote to a second career should he so desire.

But, Jay could argue, regardless of how attractive the benefits seemed, salaries in the armed services had not kept pace with the rising rate of inflation: Congress had held the lid on raises at five percent. Furthermore, he did not look for any change in their posture in the next few years. In fact, Jay had read several newspaper articles indicating that Congress was considering reducing benefits for the armed services—the 20-year retirement specifically.

Jay had done some checking around. He learned that the training and experience received in the army was valuable to civilian employers. Commissioned in the signal corps, he had vast experience in the area of telecommunications. He had recently completed a tour as an instructor in a service school. He had also been in many positions of leadership during his term in the army. At 31, he probably had more firsthand managerial experience than most civilian managers. He knew that large organizations were currently hiring young ex-military officers at salaries of $5,000 higher than recent college graduates.

Questions

1. What should Jay do?
2. What factors should be considered in Jay's decision?
3. What role would values play in Jay's decision?

Incident 4–2
Going Abroad*

You supervise 12 engineers. Their formal training and work experience are very similar, so you can use them interchangeably on projects. Yesterday, your manager informed you that an overseas affiliate has requested four engineers to go abroad on extended loan for six to eight months. For a number of reasons, he argued and you agreed that this request should be met from your group.

All your engineers are capable of handling this assignment; from the standpoint of present and future projects, there is no special reason why any one engineer should be retained over any other. Somewhat complicating is the fact that the overseas assignment is in a generally undesirable location.

Questions

1. How would you select who should go abroad on extended loan?
2. Analyze this situation, using the Vroom and Yetton model.

---

* This case is adapted from Victor H. Vroom, "A New Look at Managerial Decision Making," *Organizational Dynamics,* Spring 1973. © 1973 by AMACOM, a division of American Management Associations, New York, p. 73. Reprinted by permission of the publisher. All rights reserved.

Exercise
Risk Aversion

This exercise illustrates how different decision makers react differently to similar risks. Draw the following set of axes on a piece of paper:

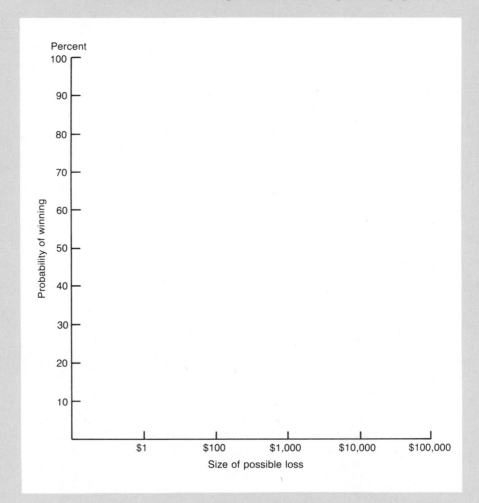

Assume you are faced with a decision on whether to play or not to play a game of chance. You will play the game once and only once. If you win, you will get $2. If you lose, you will have to pay $1. Would you be willing to play if the probability of winning the game is 80 percent? How about 50 percent? 40 percent? 30 percent? Find the lowest probability of winning for which you would be willing to play the game for one time only. Put a dot above the $1 on the graph at the probability that you select. Repeat the process for each of the following games:

Reward for Winning	Penalty for Losing
$ 20	$ 10
200	100
2,000	1,000
20,000	10,000
200,000	100,000

Note: Players cannot declare bankruptcy if they lose. They must give up one third of their earnings until the debt is fully paid.

A. Connect the dots on your graph and compare the curves drawn by various individuals in the class.
B. Do you consider yourself to be a risk taker or a risk averter?
C. How do you think that your affinity for risk might affect your ability to be a good manager?

Objectives, Strategies, and Policies

Chapter Outline

OBJECTIVES
    A Cascade Approach
    Organizational Purpose
    Long-Range and Short-Range
      Objectives
    Management by Objectives
      (MBO)
STRATEGY
    Types of Strategies
    Generic Corporate Strategies
    Generic Business Strategies

POLICIES
    Procedures and Rules
    Origin of Policies
    Formulating and Implementing
      Policy
INTEGRATING OBJECTIVES,
   STRATEGIES, AND POLICIES
SUMMARY

Of course, objectives are not a railroad timetable. They can be compared to the compass bearing by which a ship navigates. The compass bearing itself is firm, pointing in a straight line toward the desired port. But in actual navigation, the ship will veer off its course for many miles to avoid a storm. She will slow down to a walk in a fog and heave to altogether in a hurricane. She may even change destination in midocean and set a new compass bearing toward a new port—perhaps because war has broken out, perhaps only because her cargo has been sold in midpassage. Still, four fifths of all voyages end in the intended port at the originally scheduled time. And without a compass bearing, the ship would neither be able to find the port nor be able to estimate the time it will take to get there.

Peter F. Drucker*

Before studying the planning process in depth, it is necessary to clearly understand the terms *objective, strategy,* and *policy.* All are a part of, or relate directly to, the planning process.

Many differences exist about the meanings of these terms. Not only do the definitions and meanings of these terms vary widely but there is also much confusion over how the terms relate to each other. Hopefully, this chapter will help clear up some of this confusion.

OBJECTIVES

Objectives (goals)–
statements outlining what you are trying to achieve; they give an organization and its members direction.

If you don't know where you're going, how will you know when you get there? **Objectives** and **goals,** as stated in Chapter 1, are used interchangeably in this book. (Some authors describe objectives as being somewhat more specific and short range than are goals.) Objectives are statements outlining what you are trying to achieve; they give an organization and its members direction and purpose. Few managers question the importance of objectives, only what the objectives should be.

Management is a process or form of work that guides or directs a group of people toward organizational goals or objectives—the process centers around organizational objectives. Management cannot be properly practiced without pursuing specific objectives. Managers today and in the future must concentrate on where they and their organizations are headed.

---

* Peter F. Drucker, *The Practice of Management* (New York: Harper & Row, 1954), pp. 60–61.

A Cascade Approach

One desirable approach to setting objectives is to have the objectives "cascade" down through the organization.

1. The objective-setting process begins at the top with a clear, concise statement of the central purpose of the enterprise.
2. Long-range organizational goals are formulated from this statement.
3. The long-range goals lead to the establishment of more, short-range performance objectives for the organization. When tied to a specific time period, such as a year, these performance objectives become the basis for, and an integral part of, the objectives of the chief executive and the top management team.
4. Derivative objectives are then developed for each major division or department.
5. Objectives are then established for the various subunits in each major division or department.
6. The process continues on down through the organizational hierarchy.[1]

This cascade approach to goal setting, depicted in Figure 5–1, does not imply autocratic or "top down" management. It merely ensures that the objectives of individual units within the organization are in phase with the major objectives of the organization. It coordinates the entire objective-setting process.

Organizational Purpose

The **organization's purpose** outlines why the organization exists; it includes a description of its current and future business. Defining purpose, or mission, is crucial. It is also more difficult than one might imagine. Peter Drucker emphasizes that an organization's purpose should be examined and defined not only at its inception or during difficult times but also during successful periods.[2] If the railroad companies of the early 1900s or the wagon makers of the 1800s had made developing a firm position in the transportation business their organizational purpose rather than sticking strictly to the rail or wagon business, they might today hold the same economic positions that they enjoyed in earlier times.

✱ Drucker argues that an organization's purpose is not determined by the organization itself but by its customers.[3] Customer satisfaction with an organization's product or service defines the purpose more than does the organization name, statutes, or articles of incorporation. Drucker outlines three questions that need to be answered to define an organization's present business. First, management must identify the customers—where they are, how they buy, and how they can be reached. (Is the customer retail or wholesale?) Second, management must know what the customer buys: Does the Rolls-Royce owner buy transportation or prestige? Finally, what is the customer

Organizational purpose– outlines why the organization exists; it includes a description of its current and future business.

FIGURE 5–1
Cascade Approach to Objective Setting

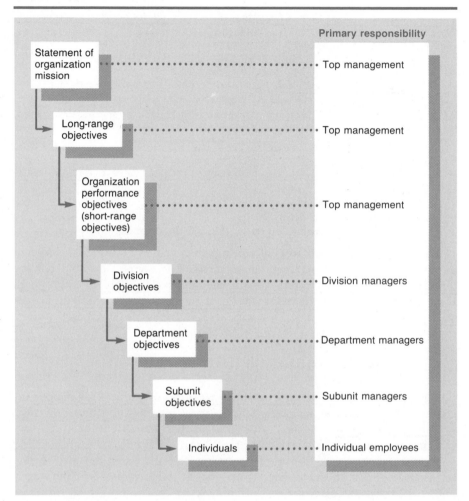

looking for in the product? For example, does the homeowner buy an appliance from Sears, Roebuck because of price, quality, or service?

Management must also identify what the future business will be and what it should be. Drucker presents four areas to investigate. The first is ① market potential: What does the long-term trend look like? Second, what ② changes in market structure might occur because of economic developments, changes in styles or fashions, or competition? For example, how have oil prices affected the automobile market structure? Third, what possible ③ changes will alter the customers' buying habits? What new ideas or products might create new customer demands or change old demands? Consider, for example, the impact of the minicalculator on the sale of slide rules and ④ hand-cranked adding machines. Finally, what customer needs are not being adequately served by available products and services? The success of the Xerox Corporation is a well-known example of identifying and filling a current customer need.

Long-Range and Short-Range Objectives

Long-range objectives generally go beyond the current fiscal year of the organization. Long-range objectives must support and not conflict with the organizational purpose. But they may be quite different from the organizational purpose and still support it. For instance, the organizational purpose of a fast-food restaurant might be to provide rapid hot-food service to a certain area of the city. One long-range objective might be to increase sales to a specific level within the next four years. Obviously, this objective is quite different from the organizational purpose; but it still supports the purpose.

Long-range objectives—objectives that extend beyond the current fiscal year of the organization.

Short-range objectives should be derived from an in-depth evaluation of long-range objectives. Such an evaluation should result in a listing of priorities of the long-range objectives. Then short-range objectives can be set to help achieve the long-range objectives.

Short-range objectives—objectives generally tied to a specific time period of a year or less and derived from an in-depth evaluation of long-range objectives.

All levels within the organization should set objectives based on the long-range and short-range objectives of the organization. Objectives at any level must be coordinated with, and subordinated to, the objectives of the next higher level. All objectives are then synchronized and not working against each other.

Objectives should be clear, concise, and quantified when possible. Affected personnel should clearly understand what is expected. Objectives should span all major areas of the organization, not just a single area. The problem with one overriding objective is that it is often achieved at the expense of other desirable objectives. While objectives in different areas may serve as checks on each other, they should be reasonably consistent with each other. Objectives should be dynamic; they should be reevaluated as the environment and opportunities change. As stated in Chapter 1, objectives for organizations normally fall into one of four general categories: (1) profit-oriented, (2) service to customers, (3) employee needs and well-being, and (4) social responsibility. Even nonprofit organizations must be concerned with profit in the sense that they generally must operate within a budget. The following areas represent potential areas for establishing objectives in most organizations:[4]

1. *Profitability* objectives can be stated in terms of profits, return on investment, earnings per share, or profit-to-sales ratios, among others. Objectives might be: "to increase return on investment to 15 percent after taxes within five years" or "to increase profits to $6 million next year."

2. *Market* objectives include share of the market, dollar or unit volume of sales, and niche in the industry. Marketing objectives might be "to increase share of market to 28 percent within three years," "to sell 200,000 units next year," or "to increase commercial sales to 85 percent and reduce military sales to 15 percent over the next two years."

3. _Productivity_ objectives may be expressed in terms of ratio of input to output; for example, "to increase the number of units to x amount per worker per eight-hour day." They may also be seen as cost per unit of production.

4. _Product_ objectives, in addition to sales and profitability by product or product line, include: "to introduce a product in the middle range of our product line within two years" or "to phase out certain products by the end of the next year."

5. _Financial resource_ objectives may be described in terms of capital structure, new issues of common stock, cash flow, working capital, dividend payments, collection period, etc. Examples include "to decrease the collection period to 26 days by the end of the year," "to increase working capital to $5 million within three years" and "to reduce long-term debt to $8 million within five years."

6. _Physical facilities_ may be described in terms of square feet, fixed costs, units of production, and many other terms. Objectives might be "to increase production capacity to 8 million units per month within two years" or "to increase storage capacity to 15 million barrels next year."

7. _Research and innovation_ objectives may be expressed in dollars as well as in other terms: "to develop an engine in the (specified) price range, with an emission rate of less than 10 percent, within two years at a cost not to exceed $150,000."

8. _Organization_ changes may be expressed in any number of ways, such as "to design and implement a matrix organizational structure within two years" or "to establish a regional office in the South by the end of next year."

9. _Human resource_ objectives include areas such as absenteeism, tardiness, number of grievances, and training. Examples are "to reduce absenteeism to less than 4 percent by the end of next year" or "to conduct a 20-hour, in-house management training program for 120 front-line supervisors by the end of 1978 at a cost not to exceed $200 per participant."

10. _Customer service_ objectives may be expressed as follows: "to reduce the number of customer complaints by 30 percent by the end of the year" or "to reduce delivery time from three to two weeks by the end of this quarter."

11. _Social responsibility_ objectives may be expressed in terms of types of activities, number of days of service, or financial contributions. An example might be "to increase contributions to charities by 50% within the next two years."

Management in Action 5–1 presents the objectives for Engraph, Inc.

Management by Objectives (MBO)

One approach to setting objectives that has enjoyed considerable popularity is the concept of **management by objectives.** MBO is a philosophy

Management by objectives (MBO)–the superior and subordinate jointly define the objectives and responsibilities of the subordinate's job; the superior uses them to evaluate the subordinate's performance; and the subordinate's rewards are directly related to performance.

MANAGEMENT IN ACTION 5–1

Objectives of Engraph, Inc.

Engraph, Inc. is a supplier of specialty packaging, labels, and covers to the consumer electronics, beverage, snack-food, textile, and personal care industries. Some of Engraph's 1984 objectives were:

1. Achieve a consistent 15 percent return on equity.
2. Increase sales 15 percent per year.
3. Perform in the upper quartile versus competitors in markets we select.

Source: Speech by Leo Benetar, chief executive officer, Engraph, Inc., Georgia State University, April 9, 1984.

based on converting organizational objectives into personal objectives. It assumes that establishing personal objectives elicits employee commitment, which leads to improved performance. The MBO process is summarized in Figure 5–2. MBO has also been called management by results, goals and control, work planning and review, and goals management. All these programs are similar and follow the same basic process.

The objective-setting process in MBO is best accomplished by using the cascade approach to objective setting that was outlined in Figure 5–1. Setting objectives from top to bottom creates an integrated hierarchy of objectives throughout the entire organization. It ensures that the various levels within the organization have a common direction.

In MBO, the objective-setting process requires great involvement and collaboration among the various levels of the organization. This results in several benefits. First, people at each level become more aware of overall objectives. The better they understand the overall objectives, the better they see their role in the total organization. Also in MBO, the objectives for an individual will be jointly set by the person and the superior; there are give-and-take negotiating sessions between them. Achieving self-formulated objectives can improve motivation and, thus, job performance.

Setting objectives in MBO is not always easy and problems occur frequently. Often the most difficult problem is deciding the specific areas in which to set objectives. The guidelines offered in Figure 5–3 should help in this process.

After the objectives have been jointly established, a plan of action for achieving them should be developed. This involves the following:

1. Determine the major activities necessary to accomplish the objective.
2. Establish subactivities necessary for accomplishing the major activities.
3. Assign primary responsibility for each activity and subactivity.

FIGURE 5–2
The MBO Process

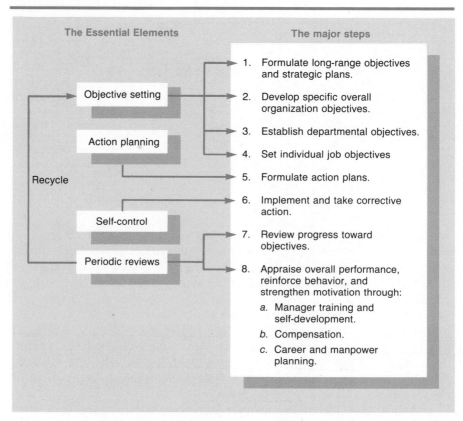

The Essential Elements

The major steps

Objective setting

Action planning

Recycle

Self-control

Periodic reviews

1. Formulate long-range objectives and strategic plans.
2. Develop specific overall organization objectives.
3. Establish departmental objectives.
4. Set individual job objectives
5. Formulate action plans.
6. Implement and take corrective action.
7. Review progress toward objectives.
8. Appraise overall performance, reinforce behavior, and strengthen motivation through:
   a. Manager training and self-development.
   b. Compensation.
   c. Career and manpower planning.

Source: Anthony P. Raia, *Managing by Objectives.* (Glenview, Ill.: Scott, Foresman). Copyright © 1974 by Scott, Foresman and Company. Reprinted by permission of the publisher.

4. Estimate time requirements necessary to complete each activity and subactivity.

5. Identify additional resources required for each activity and subactivity.

After establishing objectives and outlining the actions necessary to accomplish them, individuals are allowed to pursue their objectives essentially in their own manner. Therefore, MBO is largely a system of self-control. Of course, there are policy constraints on individuals; but basically, people achieve goals through their own abilities and effort.

Periodic progress reviews are an essential ingredient of MBO. This includes giving each employee feedback on actual performance as compared to planned performance (objectives). The importance of this personal feedback cannot be overestimated.

The manner in which the feedback is given is important. If it is hostile,

---

FIGURE 5–3
Guidelines for Establishing Individual Objectives

1. Adapt your objectives directly to organizational goals and strategic plans. Do not *assume* that they support higher-level management objectives.
2. Quantify and target the results whenever possible. Do not formulate objectives whose attainment cannot be measured or at least verified.
3. Test your objectives for challenge and achievability. Do not build in cushions to hedge against accountability for results.
4. Adjust the objectives to the availability of resources and the realities of organizational life. Do not keep your head either in the clouds or in the sand.
5. Establish performance reports and milestones that measure progress toward the objective. Do not rely on instinct or crude benchmarks to appraise performance.
6. Put your objectives in writing and express them in clear, concise, and unambiguous statements. Do not allow them to remain in loose or vague terms.
7. Limit the number of statements of objectives to the *most* relevant key result areas of your job. Do not obscure priorities by stating too many objectives.
8. Communicate your objectives to your subordinates so that they can formulate their own job objectives. Do not demand that they do your goal setting for you.
9. Review your statements with others to assure consistency and mutual support. Do not fall into the trap of setting your objectives in a vacuum.
10. Modify your statements to meet changing conditions and priorities.
11. Do not continue to pursue objectives which have become obsolete.

Source: Anthony P. Raia, *Managing by Objectives*. (Glenview, Ill.: Scott, Foresman). Copyright © 1974 by Scott, Foresman and Company. Reprinted by permission of the publisher.

---

then performance may be reduced. Reviews should not be used to degrade the individual. Performance appraisal under MBO is discussed further in Chapter 18, "Appraising and Rewarding Performance."

Many organizations proudly proclaim to have successfully implemented MBO when, in fact, they have met very few of the actual requirements. To summarize, an MBO system in its simplest form must meet the following three minimum requirements:

1. Individual objectives are jointly set by the subordinate and the superior.
2. Individuals are periodically evaluated and receive feedback concerning their performance.
3. Individuals are evaluated and rewarded on the basis of objective attainment.

Management in Action 5–2 describes how Alcan has implemented MBO.

STRATEGY

The word *strategy* originated with the Greeks around 400 B.C.; it pertained to the art and science of directing military forces.[5] A **strategy** outlines the basic steps that management plans to take in order to reach an objective

Strategy–outlines the fundamental steps that management plans to undertake in order to reach an objective or set of objectives.

MANAGEMENT IN ACTION 5-2

Management by Objectives at Alcan

Roy Gentles, president and chief executive officer of Alcan Aluminum Corproation, is proud of Alcan's MBO process. The steps they follow are:

1. Each divisional and functional head performs a needs analysis in his or her own area and generates a list of about 10 potential objectives.
2. The divisional and functional heads then whittle their lists down to the two or three objectives that are the most important to the total corporation and send that list to Gentles.

3. In a management meeting, Gentles and his staff reduce the list of 30–35 objectives down to the 8 or 10 most important corporate objectives.
4. The new corporate objectives then "cascade" back down through the organization. At this point, the divisional and functional areas are responsible for defining and coordinating any activities necessary to accomplish the objectives.

Source: Roy A. Gentles, "Alcan's Integration of Management Techniques Raises Their Effectiveness," *Management Review*, April 1984, pp. 31–33.

or set of objectives. In other words, strategy outlines how management plans to achieve its objectives.

Types of Strategies

Corporate strategies–address what businesses an organization will be in and how resources will be allocated among those businesses.

Business strategies–focus on how to compete in a given business.

Functional strategies–are concerned with the activities of the different functional areas of a business.

Grand strategy–overall strategy for the organization; describes the way the organization will pursue its objectives, given the threats and opportunities in the environment and its own resources and capabilities.

Strategies exist at different levels in an organization; they are classified according to the scope of what they are intended to accomplish. Strategies that address what businesses a multibusiness organization will be in and how resources will be allocated among those businesses are referred to as **corporate strategies.** They are established at the highest levels in the organization, and they involve a long-range time horizon. **Business strategies** focus on how to compete in a given business. Narrower in scope than a corporate strategy, business strategy generally applies to a single business unit. A third level of strategy is the *functional strategy.* Functional strategies are narrower in scope than business strategies. **Functional strategies** deal with the activities of the different functional areas of a business—production, finance, marketing, personnel, etc. Usually, functional strategies are for a relatively short period of time—often one year or less. They must support business-level strategies; but they are mainly concerned with "how to" issues. Management in Action 5–3 discusses some of the corporate, business, and functional strategies of Blue Bell, Inc.

Sometimes, the term *strategy* is used for the entire organization. Such overall strategy is also called its grand strategy. A **grand strategy** describes the way that the organization will pursue its objectives, given the threats and opportunities in the environment and the resources and capabilities

MANAGEMENT IN ACTION 5–3

Strategic Planning at Blue Bell

Blue Bell is the manufacturer of Wrangler jeans and Jantzen sportswear. During the heyday of the jeans craze in the 60s and 70s, Blue Bell was a strictly low-cost producer of jeans. During the last several years, as the sportswear business has become more market driven, Blue Bell has been forced to change their strategy.

According to the company's 1983 annual report, "the focus of the (corporate) strategy is that Blue Bell should concentrate on strengthening its position in its current core businesses." Blue Bell's business-level strategies are to "strive for a superior-quality product with a low *total* cost," "build a strong customer franchise with those in our targeted market segment," and "develop a mutually profitable partnership with retailers."

Some of the functional strategies for improving their marketing orientation include "research to determine consumer needs, product development to fulfill those needs, product testing, and quality control." The company also plans to broaden the role of the sales representative to include involvement in "everything from local advertising and promotion to actually stocking the shelves in retail outlets."

Sources: "Blue Bell's Mann with a Mission," *Sales and Marketing,* December 3, 1984, p. 28; and Blue Bell, 1983 Annual Report.

of the organization. A grand strategy outlines how the organization as a whole intends to compete. Three factors have a major impact on an organization's grand strategy: the external environment the internal situation, and the objectives being pursued. A grand strategy attempts to bring these elements together to provide direction for the organization in the face of changing conditions. Figure 5–4 summarizes the different types of strategies and illustrates the hierarchial relationships.

FIGURE 5–4
Pyramid of Strategies

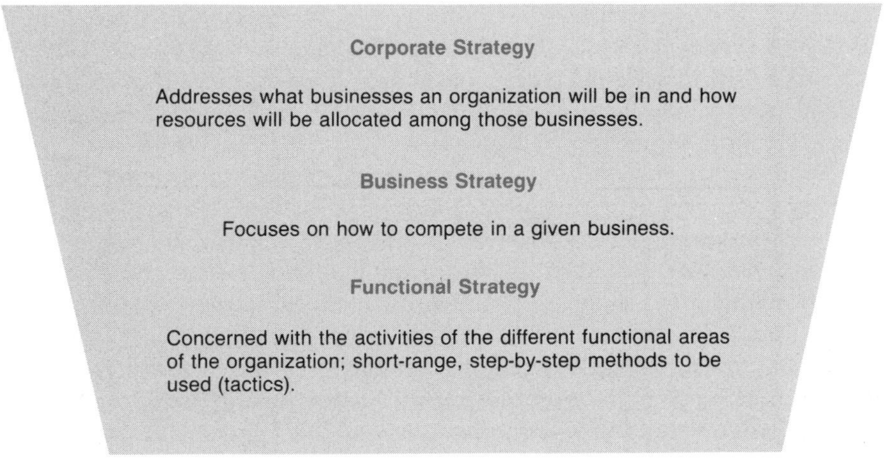

Corporate Strategy

Addresses what businesses an organization will be in and how resources will be allocated among those businesses.

Business Strategy

Focuses on how to compete in a given business.

Functional Strategy

Concerned with the activities of the different functional areas of the organization; short-range, step-by-step methods to be used (tactics).

Generic Corporate Strategies

Corporate strategy deals with what businesses an organization will be in and how its resources will be distributed among those businesses. Numerous corporate strategy alternatives exist; All can be placed into one of the following four basic categories:

1. Growth strategies. Growth strategies are used when the organization tries to grow or expand—as measured by sales, product line, number of employees, or similar measures. Growth strategies have dominated in many American organizations since World War II. Many who follow them are afraid not to grow. This usually occurs in rapidly changing environments where the product or service life cycle is relatively short. If the organization does not engage in a growth strategy, its product or service may become obsolete within a few years.

Another reason for pursuing growth strategies has to do with the personality and personal objectives of the chief executive. There is inherent pleasure in seeing an organization grow and become larger. The thought of providing new direction and growth to the organization is very satisfying to many executives.

An organization can grow in many ways. Most often encountered are concentration of current businesses, vertical integration, and diversification. Under a concentration strategy, an organization focuses on extending the sales of its current products or services. Kellogg and McDonald's are two companies that have been very successful with concentration strategies. Vertical integration occurs when the company moves into areas that serve either as suppliers to, or as customers for, its current products or services. For example, A. G. Bass—manufacturer of the famous Bass Weejuns and other sport shoes—has opened retail stores in several locations in the Northeast. Under a diversification strategy, an organization moves into areas that are clearly different from its current businesses. A significant example was U.S. Steel's purchase of Marathon Oil in 1982. Diversification can be a very profitable way to grow; yet more and more studies favor diversifying into areas having some relation to present businesses. For example, Thomas Peters and Robert Waterman, Jr., state in their best-selling book *In Search of Excellence*, "Our principal finding is clear and simple. Organizations that do branch out (whether by acquisition or internal diversification) but stick very close to their knitting outperform the others."[6]

2. Stability strategies. Stability strategies are followed when the organization is satisfied with its present course of action. Management may make efforts to eliminate minor weaknesses; but generally, its actions will maintain the status quo. When the organization is doing well, many managers are very reluctant to change anything. A stability strategy is not a "do nothing" approach; rather, it is a "do the same thing" approach. Growth is possible under a stability strategy. But, when it exists, it will be slow, methodical, and nonaggressive. Most organizations probably elect a stability strategy by default than by any conscious decision.

MANAGEMENT IN ACTION 5-4

Stability Strategy at E. L. McIlheney—Maker of Tobasco Sauce.

Tobasco Sauce, first produced commercially in 1868 by E. L. McIlheney & Company, has been manufactured and marketed in much the same way since its first factory opened in 1905. The overall strategy taken by the family firm has been one of stability. In fact, the second factory was not added until 1980. Between 1918 and 1928, McIlheney consolidated its position through various legal actions fighting use of the name Tobasco and label by rivals. By 1931, the name and label were patented and

remain uniquely their own. The sauce's ingredients and recipe, the way the sauce is manufactured (bottling, labeling, packaging, and materials handling), and distribution have remained stable. The company controls production of the basic ingredients and the formula so quality control is no problem. McIlheney has operated in international markets since its beginning. As a result of this stability strategy, Tobasco Sauce has a 95 percent share of the market. Only one price increase was made between 1928 and 1980!

Source: Phil Patton, "Tobasco Sauce: Hot Peppers and History in Every Bottle," *Companion*, July 1977, pp. 8–11; *Smithsonian*, May 1984, pp. 72–82.

Stability strategies are most likely to be sucessful in unchanging or very slowly changing environments. Organizations with a stability strategy usually have executives who feel comfortable with a slow-going, stable operation; they often have difficulty reacting to sudden or radical changes. Management in Action 5–4 describes how E. L. McIlheney—the makers of Tobasco Sauce—has been successful for many years, using a stability strategy.

3. **Defensive strategies.** Defensive, or retrenchment, strategies are used when a company wants or needs to reduce its operations. Most often, they are used to reverse a negative trend or to overcome a crisis or problem situation. Because of this, defensive strategies usually are chosen as a short-term solution or because no better solution exists.

Some of the most used defensive strategies include turnaround, divestiture, and liquidation. A *turnaround* strategy is designed to reverse a negative trend and to get the organization back on the track to profitability. Turnaround strategies usually try to reduce operating costs. Under *divestiture*, an organization sells or divests itself of a business or part of a business. Coca-Cola selling its Wine Spectrum to Seagrams in 1983 is one example. When an entire company is either sold or dissolved, *liquidation* occurs. It may come by choice or by force. By choice, it is usually because the owner or owners have an opportunity to sell the business at a substantial profit. For example, Charles Schwab sold his discount brokerage firm to Bank of America in 1983 for a personal profit of several million dollars.

4. **Combination strategies.** Most multibusiness companies use some type of combination strategy—especially those serving several different mar-

MANAGEMENT IN ACTION 5–5

A Combination Strategy at Holiday Inns

Holiday Inns, Inc. and its licensees constitute the largest hotel business in the world as measured by number of rooms. In the hotel business, Holiday Inns follows a concentration strategy. In addition to continuing support for the "Holiday Inn" hotels, it has recently developed the Holiday Inn Crown Plaza hotels for the luxury hotel market and Hampton Inns for the low-priced hotel market segment.

Holiday Inns also has a diversification strategy. As part of this strategy, Holiday Inns operates casinos in Las Vegas, Lake Tahoe, Reno, and Atlantic City.

Source: 1983 *Moody's Industrial Handbook.*

kets. Certain types of generic strategies combine well with other strategies. For example, divesting strategies are often combined with one or more strategies for other parts of the organization. Coca-Cola pursued a combination strategy in 1983 when it divested its Wine Spectrum while expanding Columbia Pictures and its soft-drink businesses. Management in Action 5–5 describes how Holiday Inns has used a combination strategy.

Generic Business Strategies

By nature, business strategies—which focus on how to compete within a given business—are less generic than corporate-level strategies. Almost all business-level strategies are tailored to some degree to the specific situation; but it is possible to categorize most business-level strategies as one of three major types: (1) overall cost leadership, (2) differentiation of the product or service, and (3) focus of the company.[7]

Overall cost leadership. The idea of an overall cost leadership strategy is to produce and deliver the product or service for less cost than the competition. Cost leadership usually comes through combined experience and efficiency. In the years before the digital watch, Timex prospered with an overall cost leadership strategy.

Differentiation of product or service. Differentiation strategy involves making the product or service unique in the industry. This may be attained through a quality image (Mercedes or Rolls-Royce), a brand image (Izod or Polo sportswear), or some other similarly perceived edge.

Focus of the company. This last type of business strategy focuses on a single market segment. The segment may be a special buyer group, a geographical market, or one part of the product line. With a focus strategy, the firm is able to serve a well-defined but narrow market better than competitors who serve a broader market. For example, Black & Decker has focused on the home market in the small-tool industry.

POLICIES

Policies are a broad, general guides to action which constrain or direct objective attainment. In this light, policies channel how management should order its affairs and its attitude toward major issues: they dictate the intent of those who guide the organization. In other words, policies define the universe from which future strategies and plans are derived. "It is the policy of the public relations department to answer in writing all written customer complaints" is an example of such a policy.

Policies are generally less action oriented than strategies and usually have a longer life. They do not indicate exactly how to attain objectives, rather, they outline the framework within which the objectives must be pursued.

Policy statements often contain the words *to ensure, to follow, to maintain, to promote, to be, to accept,* and similar verbs. For example, the ABC Company may have a policy "to accept all returns that are accompanied by a sales slip." Such a policy is a general guideline for pursuing company objectives related to profit and sales.

Policies exist at all levels of an organization. A typical organization has some policies that relate to everybody in the organization and some that relate only to certain parts of the organization. A policy such as "this company will always try to fill vacancies at all levels by promoting from within" would relate to everyone in the organization. On the other hand, the previously described policy requiring that all customer complaints be answered in writing relates only to departmental personnel.

Policies–broad, general guides to action which relate to objective attainment.

Procedures and Rules

Procedures and rules differ from policies only in degree. In fact, they may be thought of as low-level policies. A **procedure** is a series of related steps or tasks expressed in chronological order for a specific purpose. Procedures define in step-by-step fashion the methods by and through which policies are achieved. They outline precisely how a recurring activity must be accomplished. Procedures allow for little flexibility and deviation. A company's policy may be to accept all customer returns submitted within one month of purchase; company procedures would outline exactly how a return should be processed. Well-established, formal procedures are often known as standard operating procedures (SOPs).

Rules require specific and definite actions for a given situation. Rules leave little doubt about what is to be done. They permit *no* flexibility and deviation. Unlike procedures, rules do not have to specify sequence. For example, "No smoking in the conference room" is a rule.

Procedures and rules, then, are actually subsets of policies. All provide some kind of guidance. The differences lie in the ranges of applicability and the degree of flexibility. A no-smoking rule is much less flexible than

Procedures–series of related steps or tasks expressed in chronological order to achieve a specific purpose.

Rules–guidelines that require that specific and definite actions be taken or not taken in a given situation.

a procedure for handling customer complaints; the latter is likewise less flexible than a hiring policy.

Origin of Policies

Traditional policies–those that emerge from history, tradition, and earlier events. Some may be desirable; others may inhibit organizational performance.

Policies can also be classified into one of three categories, depending on how the policy evolved.[8] The first category includes policies formed by tradition. **Traditional policies** emerge from history, tradition, and earlier events. At worst, traditional policies may be very static and inflexible. In other cases, they may be very desirable. Such policies usually evolve for some logical reason. The reason for the policy often disappears, yet the policy remains in effect. In modern organizations, outdated, traditional policies may matter little and affect the organization only in minor ways. On the other hand, they can inhibit performance.

Policies by fiat–those that are arbitrarily announced by an individual or a group; they may lack precedence or clear-cut rationale.

The second category includes those policies that are arbitrarily announced by an individual or group of individuals. These are **policies by fiat.** They emerge from situations lacking precedence or clear-cut rationale. For instance, an individual may have to improvise policies to ensure order. In most instances, however, policy by fiat has unwanted effects. The potential problem is twofold: First, policy by fiat binds the subordinate to the policymaker. It is difficult for the subordinate not to be a "yes person" for the policymaker. Second, the policymaker can redefine and/or change the policy at any time; so the subordinate never knows what to expect. Policy by fiat can be very satisfying for the policymaker but very frustrating for those subject to the policy.

Rational policies–these include policies set by the board of directors or a policy committee and may be altered by conditions.

The final category, called **rational policies,** includes policies set by the board of directors or a policy committee. Unlike other policies, rational policies may be altered depending upon conditions and the situation. Rational policies are general guides to action and general guides for avoiding undesirable behavior. A rational policy may, through time and neglect, turn into a traditional policy. To guard against such deterioration, record the assumptions, conditions, and reasons for, the original policy and reevaluate it regularly.

Formulating and Implementing Policy

When setting policies, the policymaker must analyze several factors. First and foremost, the policymaker must understand the organization's purpose and objectives. To avoid conflict, the policymaker must consider both long-term and short-term objectives.

Because the organization must be concerned with its public image, formulators of policy must recognize the social and ethical responsibilities of the organization. Today's emphasis on social responsibility increases attention on the image of business organizations. Because organization policies directly reflect the ethical philosophy of the company, they often influence how employees, customers, competitors, the government, and others view the organization. For example, a company policy to actively support the United Way campaign might contribute positively to the public's view of the corporation.

The organization's culture can affect its policies, and vice versa. Culture, in the context of an organization, communicates how employees should behave; it establishes and conveys a value system through rites, rituals, myths, legends, and actions. The informal, free-flowing culture at Apple Computer—most employees and managers wear jeans to work—would not be conducive to a formal dress code.

The organization's structure also affects policy. A multilocation or multinational company may have different policies for each location because of environmental differences. The policies of a U.S. plant for working hours, employee selection, and so on, may not be appropriate for a Brazilian plant.

The policies of the competition may have a great impact. This is particularly true with personnel policies (such as employee benefits and reward structure), management development, and working conditions.

The final factor affecting policy formulation involves the general environment. This includes analysis and consideration of such factors as economic, social, and political trends, the competitive environment, and technological breakthroughs. Establishing policies without first considering such factors could be disastrous.

During policy formulation, affected personnel should be consulted; they should participate in making the policy. This does not imply that the affected people should have the right to dictate the policy. Rather, they have a right to be heard. Input by the affected employees greatly aids the implementation of a policy. If they feel that they at least have some input, they are much more likely to accept the policy.

INTEGRATING OBJECTIVES, STRATEGIES, AND POLICIES

Organizational objectives, strategies, and policies are not mutually exclusive parts of the management process. They are highly interdependent and inseparable. One cannot discuss attaining objectives without knowing the policy guidelines that must be followed.

A football game can be used as an analogy for showing the interdependencies of objectives, strategies, and policies. The purpose, or mission, is to win the game by scoring more points than the opponent. Everything that the team does is related to reaching its mission. Objectives derived from the mission might be to score 25 points and hold the opposition to no more than 10 points. Organizational performance objectives and other, sub-ordinate objectives might be compared to milestones to be reached during the game. Policies are analogous to the rules of the game. The rules do not dictate what play to call; they do set the boundaries within which the play must take place. Like the game's rules, policies remain in effect after the game is over. The team's game plan represents its grand strategy. The defensive formation or the offensive play used in a specific situation would be analogous to lower-level strategies.

SUMMARY

The management process centers around predetermined organizational objectives. The objective-setting process should begin at the top with a clear statement of the organization's purpose; it should then cascade down through the organizational hierarchy. For continuity short range objectives should be set only after an in-depth evaluation of the long-range objectives.

One approach to setting objectives is management by objectives (MBO). This philosophy of management is based on converting organizational objectives into personal objectives. The three minimum requirements of an MBO system are that (1) individual objectives are jointly set by the subordinate and superior; (2) individuals are periodically evaluated and receive feedback concerning their performance: and (3) individuals are evaluated and rewarded on the basis of objective attainment.

A strategy outlines the basic actions that management plans to take to reach one or more objectives. Corporate strategies address what businesses an organization will be in and how resources will be allocated among them. Business strategies focus on how to compete in a given business. Functional strategies deal with the activities of the different functional areas of a business; they usually cover a relatively short period of time. A grand strategy describes the way that the overall organization will pursue its objectives, given the threats and opportunities in the environment and the resources and capabilities of the organization.

Policies are broad, general guides to action which relate to objective attainment. Policies are not as action oriented as strategies and they generally have a longer life. Procedures and rules differ from policies only in degree. A procedure is a series of related steps or tasks stated in chronological order to achieve a specific purpose. Rules require specific and definite actions for a given situation.

When formulating policy, policymakers must analyze several factors: They must appraise the organizational objectives; they must be cognizant of the social and ethical responsibilities of the organization; they must know the general policies of the competition; and they must identify current economic trends in the environment.

References and Additional Readings

[1] Anthony Raia, *Managing by Objectives* (Glenview, Ill.: Scott, Foresman, 1974), p. 30.

[2] Drucker, *The Practice of Management* (New York: Harper & Row, 1954), p. 51.

[3] Ibid., pp. 50–57.

[4] Raia, *Managing by Objectives,* p. 38.

[5] George A. Steiner, *Top Management Planning* (New York: Macmillan, 1969), p. 237.

[6] Thomas Peters and Robert Waterman, Jr., *In Search of Excellence* (New York: Harper & Row, 1982), p. 293.

[7] Michael Porter, *Competitive Strategy: Techniques for Analyzing Industries and Competitors,* (New York: Free Press, 1980).

[8] Alan Filley, Robert House, and Steven Kerr, *Managerial Process and Organizational Behavior,* 2d ed. (Glenview, Ill.: Scott, Foresman, 1976), p. 310.

Review Questions

1. What is the purpose of organizational objectives?
2. Describe the cascade approach to setting objectives.
3. What questions must be answered in identifying an organization's present business? What area must be investigated in identifying an organization's future business?
4. List several areas in which objectives might be set by an organization.
5. What is management by objectives? What are the three minimum requirements of an MBO system?
6. What is a corporate strategy? A business strategy? A functional strategy?
7. What is the purpose of a grand strategy?
8. Describe four basic types of generic corporate strategies.
9. What are policies?
10. Define the following: traditional policies, policies by fiat, and rational policies.
11. What factors must be analyzed in formulating policies?

Discussion Questions

1. What percentage of managers do you think have a clear understanding of what they are supposed to do? How might this percentage be improved?
2. Is it possible to have policies that inhibit the attainment of organizational objectives? Explain and give an example.
3. "Policy should always be made at the top" is the belief of many managers. What do you think?
4. "How can we develop long-range objectives and strategies when we do not know where we are going tomorrow?" is a question often posed by managers. How would you answer this question?

Incident 5–1

Hudson Shoe Company

Mr. John Hudson, president of Hudson Shoe Company, and his wife spent the month of February on a long vacation in Santo Oro in Central America. After two weeks, Mr. Hudson became restless and started thinking about an idea he had considered for several years but had been too busy to pursue—entering the foreign market.

Mr. Hudson's company, located in a midwestern city, was started some 50 years ago by his father, now deceased. It has remained a family enterprise, with his brother David in charge of production, his brother Sam the comptroller, and his brother-in-law Bill Owens taking care of product development. Bill and David share responsibility for quality control; Bill often works with Sam on administrative matters and advertising campaigns. Many competent subordinates are also employed. The company has one of the finest reputations in the shoe industry. Their integrity of product and behavior is to be envied and is a source of great pride to the company.

During John's stay in Santo Oro, he decided to visit some importers of shoes. He spoke to several and was most impressed with Señor Lopez of Bueno Compania. After checking Señor Lopez's bank and personal references, his impression was confirmed. Señor Lopez said he would place a small initial order if the samples proved satisfactory. John immediately phoned his office and requested that they rush samples of their best numbers to Señor Lopez. These arrived a few days before John left for home. Shortly after arriving home, John was pleased to receive an order for 1,000 pairs of shoes from Señor Lopez.

John stayed in touch with Lopez by telephone; within two months after the initial order, Hudson Shoe received an order for 5,000 additional pairs of shoes per month. Business continued at this level for about two years until Señor Lopez visited the plant. He was impressed and increased his monthly order from 5,000 to 10,000 pairs of shoes.

This precipitated a crisis at Hudson Shoe Company, and the family held a meeting. They had to decide whether to increase their capacity with a sizable capital investment or drop some of their customers. They did not like the idea of eliminating loyal customers but did not want to make a major investment. David suggested that they run a second shift, which solved the problem nicely.

A year later, Lopez again visited and left orders for 15,000 pairs per month. He also informed them that more effort and expense was now required on his part for a wide distribution of the shoes. In addition to his regular 5 percent commission, he asked John for an additional commission of $1 per pair of shoes. When John hesitated, Lopez assured him that Hudson could raise their selling price by $1 and nothing would be lost. John felt uneasy but went along because the business was easy, steady, and most profitable. A few of Hudson's smaller customers had to be dropped.

By the end of the next year, Lopez was placing orders for 20,000 pairs per month. He asked that Hudson bid on supplying boots for the entire police force of the capital city of Santo Oro. Hudson received the contract and within a year, was supplying the army and navy of Santo Oro and three other Central American countries with their needs.

Again, several old Hudson customers could not get their orders filled. Other Hudson customers were starting to complain of late deliveries. Also, Hudson seemed to be less willing to accept returns at the end of the season or to offer markdown allowances or advertising money. None of this was necessary with their export business. However, Hudson Shoe did decide to cling to their largest domestic customer—the largest mail order chain in the United States.

In June of the following year, Lopez made a trip to Hudson Shoe. He informed John that in addition to his $1 per pair, it would be necessary to give the Minister of Revenue $1 per pair if he was to continue granting import licenses. Moreover, the defense ministers, who approved the army and navy orders in each country where they did business, also wanted $1 per pair. Again, selling prices could be increased accordingly. Lopez informed John that shoe manufacturers in the United States and two other countries were most anxious to have this business at any terms. John asked for 10 days to discuss this with his partners. Lopez agreed and returned home to await their decision. The morning of the meeting of the board of directors of the Hudson Shoe Company, a wire was received from the domestic chain stating that they would not be buying from Hudson next season. John Hudson called the meeting to order.

Questions

1. What were the objectives of Hudson Shoe?
2. What policies existed.
3. Do you agree with Hudson's strategy?
4. What would you do if you were John Hudson?

Incident 5–2
The Privileged Few

Jan Morgan was faced with a perplexing situation. Six months ago, Madison Business Machines had implemented a corporatewide no-smoking policy. There were, as anticipated, loud complaints voiced by the smokers at the Southeast Division headquarters, where Jan was director of employee relations. But gradually this vocal minority accepted the policy and even attended the "stop smoking" clinics made available to them by the company. For the first three months after the policy was announced, smoking was allowed in the general office area. After that, the employee lounge was partitioned off, creating a smoking area; smokers were permitted to smoke only on break. But this room was, as scheduled and announced earlier, done away with after the second three-month period following the announcement of the policy. This was just two weeks ago.

Jan was quite surprised with the growing acceptance of the policy. Some employees had competed with each other, seeing who could quit first. Others had even begun to form jogging groups that ran either before or after working hours.

All was fine until this morning. A sales managers' meeting had just been completed at the corporate offices in Chicago. Dan Wetcott, the Southeast Division sales manager, returned from the meeting in an uproar. It was evident that while Dan was in Chicago, he learned that the corporate officers were not complying with the new no-smoking policy. In fact, Dan claimed that smoking was permitted in the executive lounge and that "they didn't even try to conceal it"—not that concealing it would have made any difference to Dan. He had come storming into Jan's office early this morning, lit up a cigarette and stated that he was all for the new health kick, but "what's good for the rest of us is good for those turkeys up in Chicago—no matter who they are, right on up to the president!"

The news traveled fast. By early afternoon, ash trays appeared in their old places on desks and in the lounge areas. Even the nonsmokers appeared to be somewhat distraught with the apparent double standard that existed in the organization. Jan overhead one employee comment, "Why, that's enough to make me want to start smoking."

Questions

1. Should double standards exist in organizations, such as is depicted in this case?

2. What implications does the existence of double standards have for the behavior of the members of the organization?

3. What should be done in this case?

Exercise
Baker's Business

You are the manager of the Baker Company, a small national company engaged in the manufacture and distribution of household gadgets such as bottle openers, and ice crackers. The company is 60 years old and was founded by your spouse's grandfather. Baker became unionized six years ago and is still located in its original building (which has been slightly modernized and added on to). The company's income statement for last year and some additional information are given in Exhibits 1 and 2.

EXHIBIT 1

BAKER COMPANY
1985 Income Statement

	Units		Rate		
Total sales of 826,000 units at $5.60					$4,626,000
Cost of goods sold					
Raw materials					
Opening inventory	349,000	@	$2.308	$ 805,000	
Purchases	825,000	@	2.280	1,881,000	
Total available	1,174,000	@	2.288	2,686,000	
Less closing inventory	349,000	@	2.288	799,000	
Work in progress					
Material	825,000	@	2.288	1,888,000	
Labor (.382 hours per unit)	825,000	@	4.800	1,512,000	
Fixed costs	825,000	@	0.655	540,000	
Total	825,000	@	4.776	3,940,000	
Opening inventory	140,000	@	3.500	490,000	
Total in process	965,000				
Less closing inventory	132,000	@	3.500	462,000	
Finished goods					
Manufactured	833,000	@	4.764	3,968,000	
Opening inventory	441,000	@	4.768	2,103,000	
Total available	1,274,000	@	4.765	6,071,000	
Less closing inventory	448,000	@	4.765	2,135,000	
Cost of goods sold	826,000	@	4.765		3,936,000
Gross margin					690,000
Other expenditures					
Marketing				210,000	
Research and development				125,000	
Market research information				5,000	
Total other expenditures					340,000
Taxable income					350,000
Income taxes					182,000
Net profit after taxes					$ 168,000

EXHIBIT 2
Baker Company Statistics

Sales and net profits (for previous five years:

Year	Sales	Net Profit
1984	$4,649,000	$181,000
1983	4,760,000	188,000
1982	5,040,000	218,000
1981	4,561,000	119,000
1980	4,328,000	(48,000)

Miscellaneous data (1985):

Salaried workers	21
Wage-earning employees	180
Avoidable resignations	
Salaried	7
Wage earners	38
Worker-days lost	
Voluntary work stoppages	980
Accidents	12
Absences	620
Grievances filed*	19
New products introduced†	7
Increase in new customers	12%
Increase in customer complaints	19%
Market share	25%

* Eleven were settled at the local level. Of the eight grievances settled by arbitration, seven were in favor of the company.

† Average over the past five years has been four new products.

A. With regard to the Baker Company, rank the following general objectives in the relative order of importance that you think the company should follow (1 = Most important; 6 = Least important).

_____ 1. To continue to grow.
_____ 2. To provide for employee welfare (pay good wages, provide attractive fringe benefits, maintain present work forces, safety, etc.).
_____ 3. To increase profits by increasing sales and/or reducing costs.
_____ 4. To stay ahead of the competition.
_____ 5. To maintain satisfactory operations: smooth production, schedules, deliveries, etc.
_____ 6. To produce quality products and thus promote the reputation of the company.

B. Write a specific objective statement for each of the general areas listed in A. Make any assumptions necessary for realistic objectives.

Objectives

1. To emphasize the importance of planning in the management process.
2. To compare and contrast formal and informal planning as well as strategic and tactical planning.
3. To suggest a systematic approach to planning.

Planning: The Fundamental Function

Chapter Outline

Once upon a time there were two pigs (a third one had gone to market and disappeared) who were faced with the problem of protecting themselves from a wolf.

One pig was an old-timer in this wolf-fending business, and he saw the problem right away—just build a house strong enough to resist the huffing and puffing he had experienced before. So, the first pig built his wolf-resistant house right away out of genuine, reliable lath and plaster.

The second pig was green at this wolf business, but he was thoughtful. He decided he would analyze the wolf problem a bit. He sat down and drew up a matrix (which, of course, is pig latin for a blank sheet of paper) and listed the problem, analyzed the problem into components and possibilities of wolf strategy, listed the design objectives of his wolf-proof house, determined the functions that his fortress should perform, designed and built his house, and waited to see how well it worked.

All this time, the old-timer pig was laughing at the planner pig and vehemently declined to enter into this kind of folly. He had built wolf-proof houses before, and he had lived and prospered, hadn't he? He said to the planner pig, "If you know what you are doing, you don't have to go through all of that jazz." And with this, he went fishing or rooting or whatever it is that pigs do in their idle hours.

The second pig worked on his system anyway and designed for predicted contingencies.

One day the mean old wolf passed by the two houses (they both looked the same—after all, a house is just a house). He thought that a pig dinner was just what he wanted. He walked up to the first pig's house and uttered a warning to the old-timer, which was roundly rejected, as usual. With this, the wolf, instead of huffing and puffing, pulled out a sledge hammer, knocked the door down, and ate the old-timer for dinner.

Still not satisfied, the wolf walked to the planner pig's house and repeated his act. Suddenly, a trap door in front of the house opened, and the wolf dropped into a deep, dark pit, never to be heard from again.

Morals: 1.   *They are not making wolves like they used to.*
              2.   *It's hard to teach old pigs new tricks.*
              3.   *If you want to keep the wolf away from your door, you'd better plan ahead.*

Roger A. Kaufman*

Planning—process of deciding what objectives to pursue during a future time period and what to do to achieve those objectives.

Planning is the process of deciding what objectives to pursue during a future time period and what to do to achieve those objectives. Thus, the

* Roger A. Kaufman, "Why System Engineering? A Fable" (original source unknown).

process has two major segments: (1) setting objectives and (2) determining the course of action to be used in achieving those objectives. Planning is the management function that produces and intergrates objectives, strategies, and policies. Planning answers three basic questions:

1. Where are we now?
2. Where do we want to be?
3. How can we get there from here?

The first question calls for an assessment of the present situation. The second question involves determining the desired objectives. The final question requires an outline of actions and an analysis of the financial impact on those actions. It should be stressed that planning is concerned with *future implications of current decisions* and not with decisions to be made in the future.[1] The planner should examine how current decisions will limit the scope of future actions.

Many authors separate the objective-setting process from the planning process. In such cases, planning is viewed in the more narrow sense of determining a course of action toward some predetermined goal or objective. For example, it is not uncommon for top management to dictate the objectives for a division or department and then ask the respective manager to develop a plan for attaining the objectives. In this light, planning compares to the formulation of business and functional strategies as defined in the previous chapter. At the upper levels of management, the planning process usually does involve the setting of objectives. At the very top levels of management, planning compares to the formulation of a grand strategy. Whether or not the objective-setting process is viewed as an integral part of the planning process or as a precedent of it, objectives must be set before the planning process can be completed. It is not possible to outline a course of action for reaching some objective if one does not know what the objective is.

WHY PLAN?

The fable of the two pigs provided some insights into the reasons for planning. Planning is the primary management function; it is inherent in everything a manager does. It is futile for a manager to attempt to perform the other management functions without having a plan. Managers who attempt to organize without a plan will find themselves reorganizing on a regular basis. The manager who attempts to staff without a plan will be constantly hiring and firing employees. Motivation is almost impossible in an organization with continuous reorganization and high employee turnover.

Planning enables a manager or organization to affect rather than accept the future. By setting objectives and charting a course of action, the organization commits itself to "making it happen." This allows the organization to affect the future. Without a planned course of action, the organization is

MANAGEMENT IN ACTION 6–1

Planning Ahead at Merck

Merck Sharp & Dohme Company is a $3.2 billion drug company that achieved a leadership position in the pharmaceutical industry when it developed coritsone in the 1940s. Although the company has always been a leader in research, in recent years it has made an even stronger commitment to product development. In 1983, Merck spent 11 percent of sales on R&D, versus an industry average of 6.7 percent, and planned to spend $400 million on research in 1984.

The company's increasing commitment to R&D is not a response to poor financial performance but is part of an ongoing updating of their product line to position the company for future growth and stay ahead of the competition. Merck's newly revised research philosophy is to focus on basic research, using new biotechnology techniques.

Source: Christopher S. Ecklund and Judith H. Dobrzynski, "Merck: Pouring Money into Basic Research to Replace an Aging Product Line," *Business Week*, November 26, 1984, p. 114.

much more likely to sit back, let things happen, and then react to these happenings in a crisis mode. Management in Action 6–1 demonstrates how Merck Sharp & Dohme is trying to positively affect its future through planning.

Planning provides a means for actively involving personnel from all areas of the organization in the management of the organization. Involvement produces a multitude of benefits. First, input from throughout the organization improves the quality of the plans—good suggestions can come from any level in the organization. Involvement in the planning process also enhances the overall understanding of the organization's direction. Knowing the big picture can minimize friction between departments, sections, and individuals: Through planning, the sales department can understand and appreciate the objectives of the production department and their relationship to organizational objectives. Involvement in the planning process fosters a greater personal commitment to the plan; the plan becomes "our" plan rather than "their" plan. Positive attitudes created by involvement also improve overall organizational morale and loyalty.

Planning can also have positive effects on managerial performance. Studies have demonstrated that employees who stressed planning earn very high performance ratings from supervisors.[2] They have also shown that planning has a positive impact on the quality of work produced.[3] While some have proved inconclusive, several studies have reported a positive relationship between planning and certain measures of organizational success such as profits and goals.[4] One explanation that would fit all the findings to date is that *good* planning—as opposed to the mere presence or absence of a plan—is related to organizational success. The positive relationship between planning and performance appears to hold at all levels: the individual manager, decision-making groups, and the organization as a whole.[5]

A final reason for planning is the <u>mental exercise</u> required to develop a plan. Many people believe that the experience and knowledge gained throughout the development of a plan are more important than the plan itself. Preparing and developing a plan requires managers to think in a future- and contingency-oriented manner; this can result in great advantages over managers who are static in their thinking.

A DILEMMA

Planning is easiest where environmental change is least. <u>Planning is most useful where environmental change is greatest</u>. The environmental change since the Industrial Revolution has been unparalleled in human history. The increasing speed of change can well be appreciated if the entire span of human evolution is compressed into a 50-year time scale.

> It took man 49 years to get over being a nomad and settle down into established communities. It took a bit longer than that for us to get our first pair of pants. Only six months ago, we learned to read and write. Two weeks ago, the first printing press was built. And only in the last three or four days, we learned how to use electricity.
>
> Yesterday was a very busy day. We developed, radio, television, diesel power, rayon, nylon, motion pictures, and high octane gasoline. Since breakfast this morning, we have released atomic energy, built jet planes, and produced several dozen new antibiotics. We may now add that a few minutes ago we sent a man to the moon.[6]

There is no doubt that the rate of change of technology and the economy has been increasing at a staggering pace. This has made planning much more difficult but also much more necessary. John Argenti, a British planning consultant, sees it as creating a vicious cycle which results in an ever-longer planning horizon with increased risks:

> All types of planning, including strategic, have lately entered the vicious circle. Decisions are becoming more difficult; so it is necessary to spend longer on planning. If one spends longer on planning, one must plan further ahead. If one plans further ahead, it means making forecasts into the future. The further ahead one forecasts, the greater will be the level of uncertainty. The greater the uncertainty, the more difficult the decision—and so back to the start of the vicious circle of spending longer on the planning, planning still further ahead with still more errors in the forecast, and so on.[7]

This is exactly the trap that Thomas J. Peters and Robert H. Waterman, Jr., referred to in their best-selling book, *In Search of Excellence.*[8] They report that the so-called excellent companies avoid this trap by clearly favoring a <u>bias for action</u>. These companies are quick to try things out and careful not to be stymied by permanent committees, task forces that last for years, and long reports. In other words, plan—but don't plan forever.

Any good plan has built-in contingencies and alternatives. One real payoff in planning comes from the search for, and identification of, contingencies; planners consider events and evaluate their potential impact on the organization. If and when such events occur, the organization is in a much better position to take the proper actions. The pig fable clearly shows the need for contingency planning.

FORMAL PLANNING

Formal plan–a written, documented plan developed through an identifiable process.

All managers plan. The difference lies in the methods they employ and the extent to which they plan. Most planning is carried out on an informal or casual basis. This occurs when planners do not record their thoughts but rather carry them around in their heads. A **formal plan** is a written, documented plan developed through an identifiable process. Figure 6–1 compares formal to informal planning.

FIGURE 6–1
General Characteristics of Formal Planning versus Informal Planning

Formal Planning	Informal Planning
Rational.	Emotional.
Systematic.	Disorganized.
Regular intervals.	Sporadic episodes.
Future improvement.	Past evaluation.
Hard document.	Memory.

The absence of a formal planning system often results in continuous "fire-fighting" behavior by managers. Without a formal planning system with objectives and schedules, daily problems generally receive precedence over planning.

Formal planning also enhances the blending of managerial activity in organizations. A formal planning process forces collaboration between organizational subunits, such as the functional areas of marketing, production, finance, and accounting.

The need for formal planning is not limited to large organizations. Small ones can realize the same benefits. Of course, formal planning processes can vary greatly from large to small organizations and even among similar-sized organizations. One might have a two-page formal plan; another a 200-page document. The appropriate degree of sophistication depends on the needs of the individual managers and the organization itself. The environment, size, and type of business are factors which typically affect the planning needs of an organization.

Who Should Plan

Formal planning is not reserved strictly for top-level managers. Formal planning should be practiced by all levels of management—from first-line supervisors right up to the chairman of the board. Of course, the detail and type of plan varies greatly with the level and responsibility of the manager. For example, first-line supervisors normally prepare plans to aid in meeting the objectives of their departments. Such plans might include a day-by-day breakdown of what needs to be done. Middle-level managers also prepare plans to aid in the accomplishment of their objectives. Normally, the plans of middle management are for a longer duration and are more comprehensive than those of managers working beneath them. Top-level managers develop the plans that guide the entire organization.

Planning Horizon: Short-Range versus Long-Range

Short-range plans generally cover up to one year. **Long-range plans** start at the end of the current year and extend into the future. How long should a long-range plan be? The question cannot be answered specifically. The right time frame varies with the organization and the nature of the specific environment and activity. What may be long range when operating in a rapidly changing environment may be short range when operating in a relatively static environment. In practice, most long-range plans span at least three to five years, with some extending as far as 25 years into the future. While long-range planning is possible at any level in the organization, it is primarily carried out at the top levels of the organization.

Short-range plans— generally cover up to one year.

Long-range plans— generally start at the end of the current year and extend into the future.

Formal long-range planning did not become popular until after World War II. A 1939 survey by Stanford University found that about half of the 31 companies interviewed made plans in some detail up to a year in advance.[9] However, only 2 of the 31 firms made plans for as long as five years. A 1956 survey by the National Industrial Conference Board found that 142 out of 189 responding organizations used planning programs further than one year ahead.[10] A 1973 survey by one of the authors revealed that 328 out of 398 organizations (84 percent) did prepare some form of documented long-range plan covering at least three years.[11] Follow-up surveys conducted in 1979 and 1984 found 120 out of 142 organizations (84 percent) and 123 out of 139 (86 percent), respectively, with some kind of formal long-range plan.[12]

Several developments have contributed to this increased attention. First, the rate of technological change has increased continually since World War II. More recently, the development and availability of computers and sophisticated mathematical models have added to the potential and precision of long-range planning. Expenditures for research and development have increased dramatically. In many industries, this has resulted in the need for a longer planning horizon and huge investments in capital equipment. (The U.S. steel industry is an example of an entire industry that failed to plan far enough into the future.) Finally, the postwar economy has avoided the radical fluctuations experienced in the earlier decades of the 20th century. This has made longer-term planning more realistic. Figure 6–2 summarizes the differences between long- and short-range planning.

FIGURE 6–2
Short-Range versus Long-Range Planning

	Short-Range*	Long-Range†
Basic objectives, guidelines, and policies.	Profits and sales. Costs. Finance.	Growth. Reduction. Finance.
Capital expenditures.	Minor items, expendables, and short-life equipment.	Basic equipment, buildings, infrastructures, and land.
Sales.	By salesperson, products, customers and current markets, home sales and promotions.	By potential markets and industries. Exports.
Personnel.	Operating and clerical classes.	Supervisory, middle and top management.
R&D, design.	Fashion goods, short-life items, etc.	Basic research—especially associated with human, animal, and plant health—and items of high capital cost.

* Up to one year (qualified—included in quarterly budgets and action programs).
† More than one year (broadly quantified as long-range plans in corporate development).
Source: Adapted from Harry Jones, *Preparing Company Plans*, 2nd ed. (Aldershot, England: Gower Publishing, 1983), p. 42.

Functional Plans

Functional plans—originate from the functional areas of an organization, such as production, marketing, finance, and personnel.

In addition to being long-range or short-range, plans are often classified by function or use. The most frequently encountered types of **functional plans** are sales and marketing plans, production plans, financial plans, and personnel plans. Sales and marketing plans are for developing new products/services and selling both present and future products/services. Production plans deal with producing the desired products/services on a timely schedule. Production/operations planning is discussed in depth in Chapter 7. Financial plans primarily deal with meeting the financial commitments and capital expenditures of the organization. Personnel plans, discussed in Chapter 10, relate to the human resource needs of the organization. Many functional plans are interrelated and interdependent. For example, a financial plan would obviously be dependent on production, sales, and personnel plans.

Strategic versus Tactical Planning

Many writers and practitioners use the terms *strategic planning* and *tactical planning*. Strategic planning is synonymous with the formulation of a grand strategy (defined in Chapter 5) and is also the same as top-level long-range planning. The terms *strategic planning*, (top level) *long-range planning*, and *corporate planning* basically mean the same thing and are interchangeable.

Strategic planning covers a relatively long period of time and affects many parts of the organization. It includes the formulation of purposes and objectives, and the selection of the means by which the objectives are to be attained.

Tactical planning is short-range planning and concentrates on the formulation of functional strategies (defined in Chapter 5). Production schedules and day-to-day operational plans are tactical plans. However, the distinctions between strategic and tactical planning are relative, not absolute. Figure 6–3 gives terms that are often used to describe plans.

Strategic planning– covers a relatively long period of time; affects many parts of the organization; includes the formulation of objectives and the selection of the means by which the objectives are to be obtained.

Tactical planning– presupposes a set of objectives handed down by a higher level in the organization and determines ways to attain them.

FIGURE 6–3
Planning Terms and Their Respective Characteristics

Terminology Used	Characteristics
Grand strategy Long-range plan (top-level) Strategic plan Corporate plan	Covers a relatively long period of time; includes the formulation of objectives; affects many facets of the organization; general in nature.
Tactical plan Short-range plan Action plan Operational plan	Covers a relatively short period of time; primarily concerned with how to attain objectives (formulation of functional strategies); may affect a small part of the organization; specific in nature.

PLANNING IN PRACTICE

The practice of planning may vary from industry to industry, firm to firm, and even within different components of the same organization. But certain steps must be followed in developing and using all plans, regardless of the type of plan or the level of the organizational unit preparing it. The relative attention devoted to each step may vary—but not the value of their presence. The following steps for developing a plan should not be viewed as mutually exclusive events; they are overlapping and interacting components of the planning system.

Prepare Self-Audit

The first step in the planning process is a **self-audit** which is designed to answer part of the question "Where are we now?" A self-audit is actually

Self-audit–first step in the planning process; answers the question "Where are we now?" and is an evaluation of all relevant factors internal to the organization.

an evaluation of all relevant factors internal to the organization. To set realistic objectives, an organizational unit must know where it stands. In practice, a checklist of factors should be used in auditing the organization on a periodic basis. A typical checklist might include the following factors:

1. Financial position
2. Condition of facilities and equipment.
3. Quantity and quality of personnel.
4. Appropriateness of organizational structure.
5. Major policies and strategies in the past history of the organization.
6. Competitive position.
7. Profitability of various product lines.

Survey the Environment

The second step in the planning process is a **survey of the environment.** This step also answers the question "Where are we now?" Generally, this includes factors which influence the operation and success of the organizational unit but are not under its control. For top levels in the organization, the environmental factors include those factors external to, and not under the control of, the organization. For a department, the factors might include other departments within the organization as well as factors outside the organization. With an awareness of the external environment, the organization can better respond to change. Some general areas which might be surveyed are:

1. Population growth and movements.
2. Economic conditions and their effect on product or service demand.
3. Government regulation (taxes, wage and price controls, Occupational Safety and Health Administration [OSHA], pollution control, equal opportunity, etc.)
4. Labor supply.
5. Competitors.
6. Suppliers.
7. Financial community.
8. Social attitudes.

Management in Action 6–2 illustrates how a change in its environment has affected Avon.

Set Objectives

After the self-audit and environmental survey are complete, management can set objectives. The actual process of selecting objectives involves the

MANAGEMENT IN ACTION 6–2

Changing Environment for Avon

The typical Avon sales representative has always been a housewife who wants to earn pocket money on a flexible schedule. Her customers are other women in her community that, more often that not, are home during the day. The success of Avon's door-to-door sales business has been largely dependent on recruiting good sales representatives—and a lot of them.

In the 1970s, economic conditions dictated two paychecks for many families, and social changes brought about a greater variety of job opportunities for women. The result was record numbers of women entering the full-time job market. For Avon, the changes dealt a double blow—its customer base and potential sales force began to disappear. After suffering a sharp decline in sales and earnings, Avon is now beginning to rethink its sales approach.

Source: "For Avon, Everything Depends on Recruiting," *Financial World*, December 31, 1983, pp. 28–29.

---

application of the decion-making concepts of Chapter 4. Many different objectives are considered in the process of selecting the combination that best reflects the aims of the entire organization. Chapter 5 discussed in detail the objective-setting process.

Forecast the Future Situation

Almost all managers have some way of **forecasting** the future—especially as it relates to their jobs and areas of responsibility. For example, a top-level manager may want to forecast the future demand for a certain product. A first-line supervisor may need to forecast next week's production. Generally, a forecast tells a manager what to expect in view of the current and predicted situation.

Forecasting-fourth step in the planning process; involves making predictions about future demand.

Forecasting methods and levels of sophistication vary greatly. Many managers forecast the future based on experience and past events. Typically, a manager might examine what happened during the last few years and then project this into the future. This method has one obvious drawback: The past may not be representative of the future.

Another popular method of forecasting is to use a jury of opinion. Several managers get together and devise a forecast based on their pooled opinions. The advantage is simplicity; the disadvantage is that it is not necessarily based on facts.

Statistics and mathematical methods represent the most advanced and reliable approach to forecasting. The advent and recent adaptiveness of the electronic computer has made statistical and mathematical forecasting not only possible but accessible. (The use of computers in planning and forecasting is discussed later in this chapter.) A major drawback is the cost of gathering and analyzing data. Another drawback is that many such analyses require expertise in the field of mathematics, statistics, and the computer.

MANAGEMENT IN ACTION 6-3

Atari's Failure to Predict Market Downturn

Atari has the dubious distinction of being the video game industry's biggest loser. In 1982, the industrywide sales of video games were a strong 7 million units. At this time, Atari was the number one video game producer, owning approximately 43 percent of the market. In 1983, customer interest in video games waned considerably, and sales plummeted to 3 million units. Although industrywide losses from the decline in demand and price markdowns totaled $1.5 billion, Atari lost $539 million—roughly one third of the total industry loss. In order to survive, Atari was forced to cut back on virtually all long-term R&D projects and reduce personnel from 7,000 to 2,500 in less than one year.

Source: "A Game Plan for Survival at Atari," *Business Week*, April 9, 1984, p. 32; *The Wall Street Journal*, June 10, 1982, p. 33; *Advertising Age*, February 7, 1983, p. 3.

There are many specialized methods of forecasting, depending on the type of forecast desired. Sales forecasts, for instance, are often obtained through a sales force composite: combining the views of salesmen and sales managers as to expected sales. This method rests on the belief that those actually doing the selling should have the best knowledge of the market. Management in Action 6–3 tells how inaccurate forecasts led to major problems for Atari.

Setting objectives and preparing a forecast answer the second basic planning question "Where do we want to go?"

State Actions and Resources Required

With objectives and forecasts in place, the planner must decide what actions and resources are necessary in order to bring the forecast in line with the objectives. Suppose one objective is to increase sales by 15 percent; the forecast, based on the current sales force and advertising budget, predicts an 8 percent increase. The manager would then determine how many more salespeople would be needed and how much the advertising budget must be increased in order to bring the forecasted sales increase (8 percent) up to the objective (15 percent). This step of the planning process answers part of the basic question "How do we get there from where we are?" The planner should determine both *what* actions and resources are needed and *when* the actions and resources are needed. This allows the manager to better grasp the timing needed in carrying out a plan.

In this step and the next—evaluate proposed actions—different contingency approaches are considered. Several different mixes of resources may lead to the attainment of a given objective(s). The idea is to identify the most desirable mix of resources.

Evaluate Proposed Actions

Objectives have been set, forecasts made, and resource requirements determined. Now, the proposed actions should be evaluated for their feasibility and desirability. In most instances, this involves the preparation of a budget for the proposed actions and resource requirements. In addition to budgets, other pro forma statements—such as income statements, balance sheets, and cash flow statements—may be prepared as part of the evaluation step. Basically **pro forma statements** forecast the future financial impact of a particular course of action.

Pro forma statements—forecast the future financial impact of a particular course of action.

Control the Plan

All too often, a plan is developed and placed in a bottom file drawer, never to be looked at again. A plan should be periodically reviewed and compared with actual events to determine any major deviations between the plan and reality. Any that occur should be analyzed and proper adjustments made. Certain environmental factors beyond the control of the organization may have changed; thus, creating a need for updating. On the other hand, certain new problems within the organization may need to be corrected. How often a plan is formally reviewed varies with the application; a good rule of thumb is to review it at least quarterly.

Figure 6–4 outlines the sequence of events in the planning process.

PLANNING AND COMPUTERS

In the late 1970s, an IBM advertisement summarized the effect of computers on corporate planning. "Planning will never become an exact science. But it can now be less of a venture into the unknown. The future is a moving target. Computers can improve your aim."[13] Applications of computers in planning range from the simple storing of historical financial data to the elaborate simulation of total organizations.

In recent years, computers have dropped dramatically in price and become much less complicated to operate (user-friendly). As a result, they are used now in virtually every facet of the planning process in large companies. Even small companies can now afford to use a personal computer for storing performance data and developing financial plans.

One of the most common uses of computers is in market forecasting. Programs are readily available for performing time series, regression, and correlation analyses. One of the most sophisticated applications is the integrated corporate planning model. A corporate planning model expresses the financial, marketing, and production functions as one integrated system. In response to a series of "what if" questions, the computer will simulate

FIGURE 6–4
The Planning Process

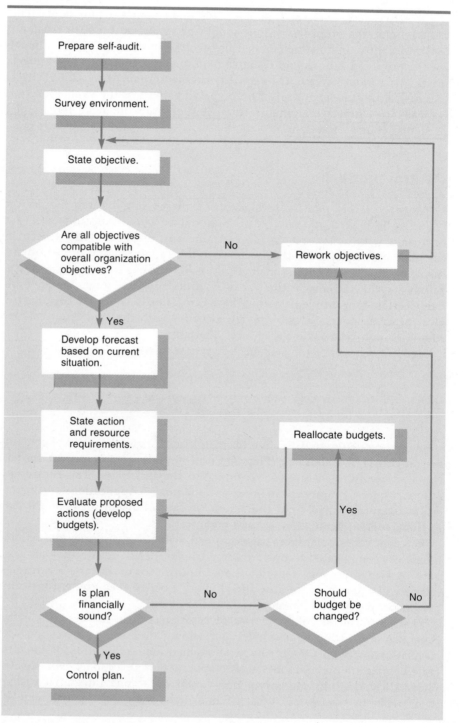

MANAGEMENT IN ACTION 6–4

Financial Modeling with a Microcomputer

Rocco Enterprises is an integrated poultry processor with five functionally independent divisions. The Feed Division purchases corn and soybean meal from outside vendors and sells finished feeds to the two 'growout' divisions (chicken and poultry). The growout divisions sell mature birds to the two processing divisions. Actual corporate sales are the processing divisions' sales to grocery stores.

Rocco has recently developed a profit-forecasting model, using Visicalc software and an Apple II computer to replace a manual forecasting procedure. The model has five separate operating units representing the five divisions. Inputs include assumptions about corn and soybean prices, production levels, and costs. Outputs include transfer prices between divisions and total corporate sales.

Source: James J. Darazski, "Financial Modeling for a Profit Forecast," *Managerial Planning*, January–February, 1985, p. 31.

the interactions between functions; this allows the user to model alternative future scenarios. Other applications of computers include financial portfolio planning and short- and long-range production planning. Management in Action 6–4 tells of one company's use of a microcomputer for planning.

STRATEGIC MANAGEMENT

The rate of change in the environment has increased in modern times. Therefore, it is more and more important for managers to keep their plans and strategies current. The process used to do this for the overall organization is referred to as *strategic management*. In essence, **strategic management** is the application of the basic planning process at the highest levels of the organization. Through the strategic management process, top management determines the long-run direction and performance of an organization by ensuring careful formulation, proper implementation, and continuous evaluation of plans and strategies.

It is entirely possible to prepare a formal plan with a well-defined strategy and not practice strategic management. With such a situation, the plan could become outmoded as changes occur in the environment. Avon (see Management in Action 6–2) is an example of how one company's plan became obsolete. Practicing strategic management does not ensure that an organization will meet all changes successfully—but it does increase the odds.

Although guided by top management, successful strategic management involves many different levels in the organization. For example, once top management has made top-level plans, different organizational units may

Strategic management—process through which top management determines the long-run direction and performance of an organization by ensuring careful formulation, proper implementation, and continuous evaluation of plans and strategies.

be asked to formulate plans for their respective areas. A proper strategic management process helps ensure that plans throughout the different levels in the organization are coordinated and mutually supportive.

SUMMARY

Planning is the process of deciding what objectives to pursue during a future time and what to do to achieve those objectives. Planning deals with the future implications of current decisions and how those decisions might limit future actions.

When properly practiced, planning has many positive effects on an organization. It allows management to affect rather than accept the future, provides a means of actively involving personnel from all areas of the organization, and can positively affect individual and organizational performance. Implementation of the planning process presents a serious dilemma for the planner. It is easiest where environmental change is least; yet it is most useful where environmental change is greatest.

Formal planning results in a written, documented plan and has several advantages over informal planning. Short-range plans generally cover up to one year; long-range plans start at the end of the current year and extend into the future.

Beside being either long range or short range, plans are often classified by function or use. Most frequent are sales and marketing plans, production plans, financial plans, and personnel plans.

Strategic planning covers a relatively long period of time, affects many parts of the organization, and includes the setting of objectives and the means for attaining the objectives. Tactical planning is concerned with a short timespan; it emphasizes the means and actions necessary to attain a given set of objectives.

The practice of planning may vary from organization to organization; yet certain steps must be followed in developing and implementing a plan. These steps consist of performing a self-audit; surveying the environment; setting objectives; forecasting the future situation; stating the actions and resource requirements; evaluating the proposed actions and resource usage; and controlling the plan.

In recent years, computers have dropped dramatically in price and have become very user-friendly. As a result, computers are used now in many facets of the planning process in both large and small organizations.

In essence, strategic management is the application of the basic planning process at the highest levels of the organization. Through that process, top management determines the long-run direction and performance of an organization by ensuring careful formulation, proper implementation, and continuous evaluation of plans and strategies.

References and Additional Readings

[1] David C. D. Rogers, *Corporate Strategy and Long-Range Planning* (Ann Arbor, Mich.: Landis Press, 1973), p. 12.

[2] J. J. Hemphill, "Personal Variables and Administrative Styles," *Behavioral Science and Educational Administration* (Chicago: National Society for the Study of Education, 1964), chap. 8.

[3] A. L. Comrey, W. High, and R. C. Wilson, "Factors Influencing Organization Effectiveness: A Survey of Aircraft Workers," *Personnel Psychology* 8 (1955), pp. 79–99.

[4] For a discussion of these studies, see Charles W. Hofer, "Research on Strategic Planning: A Survey of Past Studies and Suggestions for Future Effort," *Journal of Economics and Business,* Spring 1976, pp. 262–64; D. Robley Wood, Jr., and R. Lawrence LaForge, "The Impact of Comprehensive Planning on Financial Performance," *Academy of Management Journal,* September 1979, pp. 516–26.

[5] Alan C. Filley, R. J. House, and Steven Kerr, *Managerial Process and Organizational Behavior,* 2d ed. (Glenview, Ill.: Scott, Foresman, 1976), p. 457.

[6] "Future Shock Arrived Yesterday" (source unknown).

[7] John Argenti, *Systematic Corporate Planning* (New York: Halsted Press, 1974), p. 23.

[8] Thomas J. Peters and Robert H. Waterman, Jr., *In Search of Excellence* (New York: Harper & Row, 1982), pp. 119–55.

[9] Paul E. Holden, Lounsbury S. Fish, and Hubert I. Smith, *Top-Management Organization and Control* (New York: McGraw-Hill, 1941), p. 405.

[10] Arthur D. Baker, Jr., and G. Clark Thompson, "Long-Range Planning Pays Off," *Conference Board Business Record,* October 1956, pp. 435–43.

[11] Leslie W. Rue, "Tools and Techniques of Long-Range Planners," *Long-Range Planning,* October 1974, p. 1.

[12] William R. Boulton, Stephen G. Franklin, William A. Lindsay, and Leslie W. Rue, "How Are Companies Planning Now? A Survey," *Long-Range Planning,* February 1982, pp. 82–86; Leslie W. Rue, Lloyd L. Byars, William R. Boulton, and William M. Lindsay, "How Were Companies Planning in 1984" (unpublished paper, Georgia State University, 1985).

[13] Thomas H. Naylor, *Stimulation Models in Corporate Planning,* (New York: Praeger Publishers, 1979), p. 3.

Review Questions

1. What is planning? What questions does planning answer?
2. Discuss the relationship between objectives and planning. Give an example of this relationship.
3. Why is it necessary to plan?
4. Distinguish between formal and informal planning. How is most planning conducted?
5. Explain the difference between strategic and tactical planning.
6. Describe the most popular types of functional plans.
7. Discuss the steps in the planning process.
8. What is strategic management and how does it relate to the management function of planning?

Discussion Questions

1. Can you resolve the dilemma that planning is easiest where environmental change is least but more useful where environmental change is greatest? How?

2. If you were serving as a planning consultant, how might you answer the question: "How can I plan for next year when I don't even know what I'm going to do tomorrow?

3. With the rapid pace of change in today's world, why should management try to plan ahead?

4. What are some of the problems that a top-level manager might experience in attempting to coordinate the plans of various subunits?

5. Discuss the following statement: "Planning is something managers should do when they have nothing else to do."

Incident 6–1
First in the Market

Johnny Peron is a process engineer employed by Vantage Engineering, Inc., and assigned to the research laboratory in the Advanced Products Division (APD). Vantage is a well-established manufacturer of military hardware. The general purpose of APD is to conduct research for improving the military hardware products of Vantage. However, the laboratory director was recently given permission to develop spin-off products for possible sale on the open market.

Johnny spent his first year in APD assisting on various project assignments. Then he was put in charge of a special project to research a chemically processed wood for specialty applications. During the initial stages of the project, Johnny spent the majority of his time in the laboratory, becoming familiar with the basic aspects of the treatment process. However, he soon became tired of the long and tedious experimental work and became more and more anxious to move quickly into the promotion and marketing of the product. This desire was soon realized. An article in a national trade publication generated keen interest in a similar wood product; as a result, Vantage immediately allocated several thousand dollars to the development and marketing of the chemically processed wood. Simultaneously, a minor reorganization occurred, placing Johnny and his project under the direction of Greg Waites, a close friend of Johnny's. Thus came Johnny's opportunity to get out of the lab and become involved in the more desirable promotion and marketing aspects.

Johnny and Greg soon began traveling nationally, discussing the new product with potential customers. Traveling enabled Johnny to spend less and less time in the lab; as a result, many of the experiments required to determine the performance characteristics of the new product were left unfinished. As the number of companies grew that demonstrated an interest in purchasing small quantities for trial applications, Johnny suggested to Greg that a small pilot plant be constructed. In answering Greg's concerns regarding the performance characteristics of the wood, Johnny assured him that the preliminary tests indicated the wood could be successfully produced. Johnny contended that Vantage had to get a head start in the new market before everyone else got into the game; they should build the pilot plant immediately to fill the sudden influx of orders and then worry about completing the performance tests. Greg, seeing advantages associated with getting into the market first, finally agreed. Construction of the pilot plant began shortly thereafter.

During construction, Johnny and Greg continued traveling around promoting the wood. When the pilot plant was near completion, Johnny went to Vantage's personnel department and requested that three laborers be hired to operate the plant. Johnny personally intended to direct the technical operations and thus saw no need to establish elaborate job descriptions for the positions.

A week later, Johnny had his three employees. Due to a workload reduction in the Electronics Division of Vantage, the employees filling these positions had taken the laborer jobs in order to avoid being laid off. One had been a purchasing agent, and the others had been electronics technicians. At the beginning of the workday, Johnny would drop by the plant and give directions to the crew for the entire day before departing to make sales calls. No formal leader had been appointed, and the three laborers, knowing little about the chemical process involved, were instructed to "use common sense and ingenuity."

A month after the plant operations had gotten underway, a major producer of archery bows requested an order of 2,000 bow handles to be delivered in time to be sold for the upcoming hunting season. It was too good to be true. Johnny knew if they accepted the order, the first year of operations would be guaranteed to be in the black. Upon receiving the product specifications, Johnny persuaded Greg to sign the contract, arguing that they would be throwing all their hard work down the drain if they didn't. Subsequently, a crash program was established at the plant to get the order out on time.

One month after the final shipment of handles had been made, Johnny hired a junior engineer, Steve Adams, to conduct the performance experiments that had been disbanded while the plant had been getting the rush order out. Steve examined some of the experimental handles and discovered hairline cracks at various stress points that had not appeared during the initial examination. He immediately went to Johnny's office to inform him of the problem and found Johnny and Greg sitting there with a telegram from the archery company. It stated that several retailing merchants had returned bows with hairline cracks in the handles and that the archery company would seek a settlement for their entire investment in the handles.

Vantage paid the settlement and subsequently cancelled the wood project.

Questions

1. What caused the wood project to fail?
2. Would more effective decision making on the part of Johnny and Greg had aided in ensuring the success of the project?
3. At what stage of the planning process did the breakdown occur?
4. What general observations can be made so as to prevent such a situation occurring again?

Incident 6-2
Planning by a Student

Susan Good is a senior majoring in management at the local university. She has been an excellent student with a 3.4 out of a 4.0 grade point average. However, she really hasn't decided on what she wants to do. Her interviews for jobs through the university placement office have confused her even more. Each interviewer has asked her what she wanted to do, and she really had no adequate answer. Because of her dilemma, Susan went to see Professor Chapman, one of her management professors, and discussed the problem with him. His reply was, "Your problem is not all that unusual. Many students feel the same way. Why don't you use some of the planning concepts you have learned in management and develop a personal career plan?"

1. Can general planning concepts be used for personal career planning?
2. Develop a five-year career plan for your own career.

Exercise

Plan Development

Assume you have just purchased the Baker Company, discussed in Chapter 5's Exercise (pages 141–42).

A. Based on the information available in the exercise, current economic conditions, and your local environmental conditions, prepare a one-year plan for the Baker Company. Be sure to follow the planning format discussed in Chapter 6 and prepare a written analysis for each of the seven major steps in the planning process.

B. What additional information would you like if it were available?

C. What do you think are the weakest parts of your plan? How would you strengthen these parts?

D. Be prepared to present your plan to the class.

Operations Planning

Chapter Outline

THE IMPORTANCE OF
  OPERATIONS MANAGEMENT
OPERATING SYSTEMS AND
  ACTIVITIES
  Basic Types of Operating
    Systems
  Product/Service Design
PROCESS SELECTION
SITE SELECTION
PHYSICAL LAYOUT
  Basic Layout Classifications
  Computer-Assisted Physical
    Layout
JOB DESIGN
  Job Content

Job Methods
The Physical Work Environment
Sociotechnical Approach
DAY–TO–DAY OPERATIONS
  PLANNING
  Aggregate Production Planning
  Resource Allocation
  Activity Scheduling
  Material Requirements Planning
    (MRP)
SUMMARY
APPENDIX

An initial step in the planning process is to determine the character of the output of the enterprise. Once this decision is made, the way the output is created must be set. To complete the planning of the system, techniques for acquiring and using the necessary resources have to be chosen. The resources considered in making the planning decisions may be financial, may be physical (machinery or equipment), or may be human. The role of the human element is considered from a motivational standpoint and in regard to its importance in job design and job performance.

Arthur C. Laufer*

Operations management–application of the basic concepts and principles of management to those segments of the organization that produce the goods and/or services.

Operations planning–designing the systems of the organization that produce goods or services; planning the day-to-day operations within these systems.

Operations management, which evolved from the field of production or manufacturing management, deals with the application of the basic concepts and principles of management to those segments of the organization that produce the goods and/or services of the organization. Traditionally, the term *production* brings to mind such things as smoke stacks, machine shops, and the manufacture of real goods. Operations management is the management of the producing function in any organization—private or public, profit or nonprofit, manufacturing or service. **Operations planning** is concerned with designing the systems of the organization that produce the goods or services and with the planning of the day-to-day operations which take place within these systems. This chapter first discusses the basic design-related aspects of operations and then discusses the planning of the day-to-day operations.

THE IMPORTANCE OF OPERATIONS MANAGEMENT

The operations function is only one part of the total organization; however, it is a very important part. The production of goods and/or services often involves the largest part of an organization's financial assets, personnel, and expenses. The operations process also usually takes up an appreciable amount of time. Thus, because of the resources and time consumed by operations, the management of this function plays a critical role in achieving the organization's goals.

Effective operations managers directly influence worker output by (1) building group cohesiveness and individual commitment and (2) making sound technical and administrative decisions. Both have become more com-

* From Arthur C. Laufer, *Operations Management,* (Cincinatti: South-Western Publishing, 1975), p. 172.

MANAGEMENT IN ACTION 7–1

Poor Production Planning in the Computer Industry

The personal computer industry has an embarrassing record of missed shipments and delayed product introductions. Personal computer companies announce new products before they are half developed, in an effort to lure investors and encourage customers to put off buying a computer from another company. This optimistic technique called "preemptive marketing" has backfired on several occasions. Many companies, including IBM and Apple, have shipped products six months to a year after the original announced date of shipment. Those companies that do manage to ship on time frequently do so at the expense of product quality.

The industry is very unforgiving about product delays, regardless of whether the delay was caused by unforeseen technical problems or just poor planning. Some company losses have been catastrophic. Osborne Computers filed for protection from creditors under Chapter 11 of the Federal Bankruptcy Act after a premature product introduction hurt sales of existing products. After failing to ship its Adam computer in time for Christmas 1983 and problems with the early shipments in 1984, Coleco Industries is getting out of the computer business altogether. Microsoft had planned introduction of a new program for April 1984. After several delays caused by specification changes, the delivery date was changed to June 1985. Unfortunately for Microsoft, IBM and Digital Research then announced that they would have similar products available before March 1985.

Source: Dennis Kneale, "In Personal Computers, Delays in Production Take an Industry Toll," *The Wall Street Journal*, January 8, 1985, p. 1.

plex and important in recent years. Society wants not only improved productivity but also an enriched work environment. At the same time, social changes have increased the cultural gap between younger workers and established managers. The human problems confronting operations management have therefore become more important and more difficult.

Most operations managers no longer manage in a stable environment with standard products. Changing technology and a strong emphasis on low costs have altered the technical and administrative problems they confront. The modern operations manager must deal not only with low costs but also product diversity, high quality, short lead times, and a rapidly changing technology. As a result, their problems are now greater and require much more managerial talent than ever before. Management in Action 7–1 shows how poor operations planning has hurt the reputation of the personal computer industry. Management in Action 7–2 describes the role of operations planning in the success of McDonald's.

OPERATING SYSTEMS AND ACTIVITIES

Operating systems consist of the processes and activities necessary to turn inputs into goods and/or services. Operating systems exist in all organi-

Operating system—consists of the processes and activities necessary to transform various inputs into goods and/or services.

MANAGEMENT IN ACTION 7–2

Facilities Planning at McDonald's

The main function of each McDonald's hamburger outlet is the fast delivery of a consistently high quality product in a clean facility. One of the keys to McDonald's phenomenal success is the detailed facility layout and planned used of materials. Storage and preparation space are designed specifically for the existing mix of products, which discourages the owner from supplementing the menu. All products are prepacked and premeasured to ensure uniformity.

Food is cooked on equipment designed to make an optimum amount without waste. McDonald's even uses a special wide-mouthed scoop to fill a bag with exactly the right amount of french fries. The scoop prevents costly overfilling but creates an impression of abundance. The facilities are planned in such detail that employee discretion is virtually eliminated.

Source: Theodore Levitt, "Production-Line Approach to Service," *Harvard Business Review*, September–October 1972, p. 41.

zations; they are made up of people, materials, facilities, and information. The end result of an operating system is to add value by improving, enhancing, or rearranging the inputs. An automobile is a group of separate parts formed into a more valuable whole.

In some situations, the operating system breaks something down from a larger quantity to smaller quantities with more value. A metal shop cuts smaller parts from larger sheets of metal; a butcher produces steaks, hamburger, and other cuts from a side of beef. Both break down a larger quantity into smaller quantities with more value.

A third type of operating system produces services by turning inputs into more useful outputs. Here, emphasis is usually placed more on labor and less on materials. For example, a television repair shop uses some materials but the primary value results from the repairer's labor.

Figure 7–1 presents a simplified model of an operating system. The operating system is broader and more inclusive than just the conversion or transformation process. It includes not only the design and operation of the processs but also many of the activities needed to get the various inputs (such as product design and scheduling) into the transformation process. Many of the activities necessary to get the outputs out of the transformation process (such as inventory control and materials distribution) are also included.

Basic Types of Operating Systems

Two basic types of operating systems exist. One is based on continuous flows, the other on intermittent flows. Organizations with continuous flows generally have a standardized product or service. This product or service is often advertised and is immediately available to the customer. The post office, paper mills, petroleum refineries, assembly plants, and fast-food out-

FIGURE 7–1
Simplified Model of an Operating System

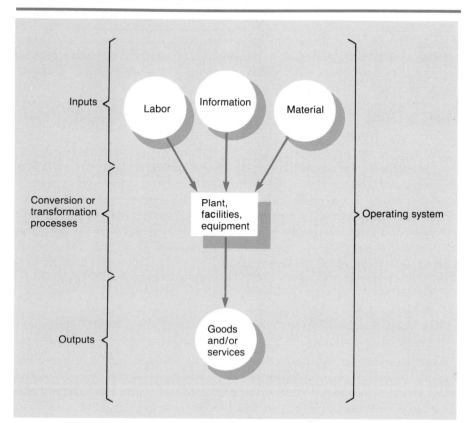

lets with standardized products (such as McDonald's) are examples. The
continuous type of operation has relatively large volumes of identical or
similar products/services flowing through similar stages of the operating
system.

The second type of operating system, the intermittent (or job shop) type,
produces customized products and services. Because of its customized nature,
organizations using an intermittent operating system usually do not have
inventories. Nor do they keep finished products or offer standardized services. Intermittent flow systems include special-order fabrication shops, hospitals, advertising agencies, and dental offices.

With economies of scale, specialized labor, and high equipment use, the
continuous flow system usually results in lower unit costs than the intermittent. However, continuous flow systems usually require special-purpose
equipment which is less flexible and usually more expensive than general-
purpose equipment. A continuous flow system therefore usually requires
a larger capital investment than does an intermittent flow system.

PRODUCT/SERVICE DESIGN

An organization's product or service determines the design of its operating systems. The design of a new product or service may cause extensive systems redesign, equipment change, new personnel, and so on. If so, it can greatly alter the attractiveness of the product or service. The design can be functionally sound, yet not economical to produce. Of course, specific functional design objectives must be achieved; however, several alternative designs are often available. When such choices exist, production costs should certainly be one criterion used in the decision.

Historically, design engineers have had conflict with operations managers. Design engineers are technically oriented and sometimes may lack concern for production methods and costs. On the other hand operations managers may care more about production costs and requirements than about the functional requirements of the product. Such conflict can be minimized through good communication which fosters an appreciation by both the engineer and the manager of the common objective of producing a functional product or service at the minimum cost.

PROCESS SELECTION

Process selection—specifies in detail the processes and sequences required to transform inputs into products or services.

Process selection includes a wide range of decisions about the specific process to be used, the basic sequences of the process, and the equipment to be used. As suggested earlier, the product/service design decisions and the process selection decisions should be closely coordinated.

The processes and equipment used can obviously play a large role in whether the product or service is competitive. The importance of the process selection decision has become magnified in some industries with the advent of robotics. This has clearly been shown in the steel and automotive industries: Japan's have much more modern production processes than their American counterparts. Management in Action 7–3 describes General Motors' most recent attempt to compete in the small-car segment of the auto industry.

Once the overall type of operations process is picked, specific decisions are needed regarding such factors as whether to use general or special-purpose equipment, to make or buy the components, and how much to automate. In equipment decisions, several factors beyond normal cost should be considered:

1. Availability of operators.
2. Training required for the operators.
3. Maintenance record and potential.
4. Availability of parts and services.
5. Supplier assistance in installation and debugging.

MANAGEMENT IN ACTION 7–3

Product and Process Planning at GM

In January 1985, General Motors announced plans to set up a new company, Saturn Corporation, to produce a full line of subcompact cars. The Saturn line will be GM's attempt to seriously compete with the Japanese in the small-car market. The plant will use the latest automation techniques, which should reduce costs and provide better quality—the two

areas where the Japanese currently have the advantage. According to GM's Chairman Roger Smith, the manufacturing process will be more important than any of Saturn's product innovations. "We hope this car will be less labor intensive, less material intensive, less everything intensive than anything we have done before."

Source: "Saturn Makes Its Debut at GM" *Time*, January 21, 1985, p. 50.

6. Compatibility with existing equipment.
7. Flexibility of equipment in handling product variation.
8. Safety of equipment.
9. Delivery date expected.
10. Warranty coverage.

In process selection, the overriding objective is to specify in detail the most economical processes and sequences required to transform the inputs into the desired product or service. Management in Action 7–4 tells how General Electric got unionized employees to agree to significant process changes.

SITE SELECTION

Management should carefully consider site location. It is easy to become overly engrossed in the operating details and techniques and ignore the importance of site location. Location is an ongoing question; it does not occur only when a facility is outgrown or obsolete. Location decisions relate to offices, warehouses, service centers, and branches, as well as the main facility. Each site selection decision involves the total production-distribution system of the organization. Therefore, not only the location of new facilities should be examined. The location of present facilities should also be regularly reviewed for the most effective production-distribution system.

Several options exist for expanding capacity when the present facility is overcrowded:

1. Subcontract work.
2. Add another shift.
3. Work overtime.
4. Move operation to a larger facility.

MANAGEMENT IN ACTION 7–4

Planning by Employees as Well as Managers

General Electric Co. is spending $52 million on an automated factory for aircraft engine parts. The factory will use robotic carts to move parts, and computer-controlled machining centers. For the plant to be profitable, it must operate 24 hours a day, seven days a week.

In order to persuade GE to build the plant in their area, unionized employees in Lynn, Massachusetts,

agreed to substantial concessions including consolidating the number of work classifications from 25 to 3 and allowing GE to set production goals. According to John W. Murphy, Jr., business agent for Local 201 of the International Union of Electronic Workers, "We could have stuck our heads in the sand and said, "We don't want to be a part of this, and wish (automation) would go away, or we could get in on the ground floor and help mold and shape it."

Source: "Swapping Work Rules for Jobs at GE's Factory of the Future," *Business Week,* September 10, 1984, p. 43.

5. Expand present facility.
6. Keep current facility and add another facility elsewhere.

A decision to move the entire operation to a larger facility or to add another facility elsewhere means management is faced with a location decision. Figure 7–2 lists several factors to consider when locating a new facility. The final site choice will have to be a compromise among these factors.

FIGURE 7–2
Factors to Be Considered in Site Location

1. Revenue.
    a. Location of customers and accessibility.
    b. Location of competitors.
2. Operating costs.
    a. Price of materials.
    b. Transportation costs: materials, products, people.
    c. Wage rates.
    d. Taxes: income, property, sales.
    e. Utility rates.
    f. Rental rates.
    g. Communication costs.
3. Investment.
    a. Cost of land.
    b. Cost of construction.
4. Other limiting factors.
    a. Availability of labor with appropriate skills.
    b. Availability of materials, utilities, supplies.
    c. Union activity.
    d. Community attitudes and culture.
    e. Political situation.
    f. Pollution restrictions.
    g. Climate.
    h. General living conditions.

PHYSICAL LAYOUT

Physical layout is essentially the process of planning the optimum physical arrangement of facilities, which includes personnel, operating equipment, storage space, office space, materials-handling equipment, and room for customer service and movement. Physical layout integrates all of the previous planning of the design process into one physical system. Physical layout decisions are needed for a number of different reasons:

1. Construction of a new or additional facility.
2. Obsolescence of current facilities.
3. Changes in demand.
4. Development of a new or redesigned product or process.
5. Personnel considerations: frequent accidents, poor working environment, or prohibitive supervisory costs.

Demand forecasts for the product or service must be considered in establishing the productive capacity of the organization. The costs of running short on space and equipment must be balanced with the costs of having idle space and equipment. A good approach is to match space needs with estimates of future demand but purchase equipment only as it is needed. This allows quick capacity expansion and avoids the costs of idle equipment.

Basic Layout Classifications

Most layouts are either process oriented or product oriented. Process layouts are generally used in intermittent flow operating systems. In a **process layout** equipment or services of a similar functional type are arranged or grouped together: All X-ray machines are grouped together; all reproduction equipment is grouped together; all drilling machines are grouped together; and so forth. Custom fabrication shops, hospitals, and restaurants are usually arranged in this fashion. With a process layout, a product/customer moves from area to area for the desired sequence of functional operations. When the product or service is not standardized or when the volume of similar products or customers in service at any one time is low, a process layout is preferred because of its flexibility.

Product layouts usually occur in continuous flow operating systems. In a **product layout** equipment or services are arranged according to the progressive steps by which the product is made or the customer is serviced. A product layout is generally used when a standardized product is made in large quantities. The assembly line is the ultimate product layout. Automobile assembly plants, cafeterias, and standardized testing centers are normally product layout oriented. In a product layout, all the equipment or services necessary to produce a product or completely serve a customer are located

Physical layout–process of planning the optimum physical arrangement of facilities, including personnel, operating equipment, storage space, office space, materials-handling equipment, and room for customer or product movement.

Process layout–equipment or services of a similar functional type are arranged or grouped together.

Product layout–equipment or services are arranged according to the progressive steps by which the product is made or the customer is served.

FIGURE 7–3
Advantages of Process and Product Layout

Advantages of process layout:
1. Lower investment in equipment and personnel because of less duplication (do not need the same machine or person doing the same thing in two different areas).
2. Adaptable to demand fluctuations.
3. Worker jobs are not as repetitive or routine.
4. Layout is conducive to incentive pay systems.
5. Allows for the production of a greater variety of products with a smaller capital base.
6. Failures of equipment or people do not hold up successive operations.

Advantages of product layout:
1. Relatively unskilled labor may be utilized.
2. Training costs are low.
3. Materials-handling costs are usually low.
4. Smaller quantities of work in process.
5. Operations control and scheduling are simplified.

in one area. Figure 7–3 lists the major advantages of both process and product layouts.

Computer-Assisted Physical Layout

Various computer programs have been developed to aid in designing physical layouts. Most computer approaches to a process-oriented layout stress the relative placement of like components subject to certain criteria; materials-handling cost is the most frequently used criterion. Computer programs for product-oriented layouts try to determine the optimum number of workstations to meet certain criteria. This approach is known as **line balancing**. Processing cost is normally the criterion used for line balancing.

Line balancing–process of determining the optimum number of workstations.

JOB DESIGN

Job design–designates the specific work activities of an individual or group of individuals.

Job design specifies the work activities of an individual or group of individuals. Job design answers the question of how the job is to be performed, who is to perform it, and where it is to be performed. As shown in Figure 7–4, the final job structure results from job design.

The job design process can generally be divided into three phases:

1. The specification of individual tasks.
2. The specification of the method of performing each task.
3. The combination of individual tasks into specific jobs to be assigned to individuals.[1]

FIGURE 7–4
Factors in Job Design

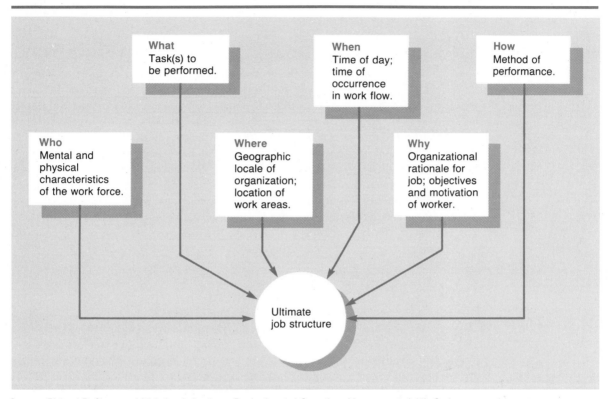

Source: Richard B. Chase and Nicholas J. Aquilano, *Production and Operations Management: A Life-Cycle Approach.* (Homewood, Ill.: Richard D. Irwin, Inc., 1981), p. 329.

Phases 1 and 3 determine the content of the job, while Phase 2 indicates how the job is to be performed.

Job Content

Job content is the sum of all the work tasks that the jobholder may be asked to perform. Starting with the scientific management movement, job content focused almost totally on the process by which the job was done. This usually meant minimizing short-run costs by minimizing the unit operation time. The obvious problem with this approach is that the job can become overly routine and repetitive, which leads to motivational problems in the form of boredom, absenteeism, turnover, and perhaps low performance. (These problems and some potential solutions are discussed in Chapter 14.) One fact greatly complicates the job design process: different people react

Job content–aggregate of all the work tasks the job holder may be asked to perform.

differently to similar jobs. In other words, what is boring and routine to one person is not necessarily boring and routine to another.

Job Methods

The next step is to determine the precise methods to be used to perform the job. The optimum **job method** is a function of the manner in which the human body is used, the arrangement of the workplace, and the design of the tools and equipment used.[2] The main purpose of job method design is to find the one best way to do a job. Normally, job methods are determined after the basic process and physical layout have been determined.

Motion study is used in designing jobs. It involves determining the necessary motions and movements for performing a job or task and then designing the most efficient method for putting these motions and movements together.

Job methods designers have traditionally concentrated on manual tasks. However, the basic concept of finding the one best way applies to all types of jobs.

Job method–manner in which the human body is used, the arrangement of the workplace, and the design of the tools and equipment used.

The Physical Work Environment

The physical work environment—temperature, humidity, ventilation, noise, light, color, etc.—can have an impact on employee performance and safety. Studies clearly show that adverse physical conditions do have a negative effect on performance; but the degree of influence varies from person to person.

The importance of safety in the design process was reinforced by the Occupational Safety and Health Act (OSHA) of 1970. Designed to reduce job injuries, the act gives very specific federal safety guidelines for almost all U.S. organizations.

In general, the work area should allow for normal lighting, temperature, ventilation, and humidity. Baffles, acoustical wall materials, and sound absorbers should be used to reduce unpleasant noises. Exposure to less than ideal conditions should be limited to short periods of time. This will minimize possible physical or psychological damage to the worker.[3]

Sociotechnical Approach

Sociotechnical approach–approach to job design that considers both the technical system and the accompanying social system.

The sociotechnical concept was first introduced in the 1950s by Eric Trist and his colleagues at the Tavistock Institute of Human Relations in London, England.[4] The **sociotechnical approach** rests on two premises:[5] (1) In any organization which requires people to perform certain tasks, there is a joint system operating—this joint system combines the social and technological systems and (2) The environment of every sociotechnical system is influenced by a culture, its values, and a set of generally accepted practices. The concept stresses that the technical system, the related social system, and the general environment should all be considered when designing jobs.

The sociotechnical approach is very situational; few jobs have identical technical requirements, social surroundings, and environments. This approach requires that the job designer carefully consider the role of the worker within the system, the task boundaries, and the autonomy of the work group. Using the sociotechnical approach, Louis Davis has developed the following guidelines for job design:

1. The need for the content of a job to be reasonably demanding for the worker in terms other than sheer endurance and yet provide some variety (not necessarily novelty).
2. The need for being able to learn on the job and to go on learning.
3. The need for some minimum area of decision making that the individual can call his own.
4. The need for some minimal degree of social support and recognition at the workplace.
5. The need to be able to relate what the individual does and what he produces to his social life.
6. The need to feel that the job leads to some sort of desirable future.[6]

DAY–TO–DAY OPERATIONS PLANNING

Designing an effective operating system does not ensure that it will operate efficiently. The day-to-day operations must also be planned and then carried out. This is called production planning. **Production planning** includes aggregate production planning, resource allocation, and scheduling. Its overriding purpose is to maintain a smooth, constant flow of work from start to finish—so that the product or service will be completed in the desired time at the lowest possible cost.

Production planning– concerned primarily with aggregate production planning, resoure allocation, and activity scheduling.

Aggregate Production Planning

Aggregate production planning deals with overall operations and with balancing the major parts of the operating system. Its primary purpose is to match the organization's resources with the demands for its goods or services. Specifically, the plan should find the production rates which satisfy demand requirements while minimizing the costs of work force and inventory fluctuations. Aggregate production plans generally look 6 to 18 months into the future.

The first step in developing an aggregate production plan is to obtain a demand forecast for the organization's goods or services. The second step

Aggregate production planning–concerned with overall operations and balancing major sections of the operating system; matches organization's resources with demands for its goods and services.

MANAGEMENT IN ACTION 7–5

Aggregate Production Planning With Computers at Honeywell

Honeywell's Small System and Peripherals Division manufactures circuit boards, subassemblies, cables and assembles terminals and minicomputers. In such a highly competitive market characterized by short product life cycles and complex manufacturing processes, planning is an essential but difficult task.

Honeywell has developed a comprehensive, computerized, medium- to long-range planning system to help estimate future manpower and equipment requirements. When market forecasts are entered as the independent variable, the system can be used to generate labor and equipment projections. The projected requirements are used to justify expenditures on new equipment and facilities and to plan manpower adjustments. The benefits of such a system are that manpower and equipment are added only when needed and that management has a realistic basis for making planning decisions.

Source: Kelvin Cross, "Manufacturing Planning with Computers at Honeywell, "*Long-Range Planning,* December 1984, pp. 66–75.

involves evaluating the impact of the demand forecasts on the organization's resources—plant capacity, work force, raw materials, and the like. The final step is to develop the best plan for using the organization's current and expected resources for meeting the forecasted demand. The aggregate production plan determines production rates, work force needs, and inventory levels for the entire operating system over a specified time period. Management in Action 7–5 describes how Honeywell has used computers in its aggregate planning process.

Resource Allocation

Resource allocation—efficient allocation of people, materials, and equipment in order to meet the demand requirements of the operating system.

Resource allocation is the efficient allocation of people, materials, and equipment in order to meet the demand requirements of the operating system. It is the natural outgrowth of the aggregate production plan. The materials needed must be determined and ordered; the work must be distributed to the different departments and workstations; personnel must be allocated; and time allotments must be set for each stage of the process.

Due to resource scarcities, resource allocation has become critical in recent times. Increased competition, both domestic and foreign, has also increased its importance. Proper resource allocation can mean great cost savings, which can give the needed competitive edge.

Numerous mathematical and computer-assisted tools and techniques can assist in resource allocation. Linear programming, critical path method (CPM), and program evaluation and review technique (PERT) are some of the most often used. (CPM and PERT are discussed in the Appendix to this chapter.)

Routing. Routing finds the best path and sequence of operations for attaining a desired level of output with a given mix of equipment and personnel. Routing looks for the best use of existing equipment and personnel through careful assignment of these resources. An organization may or may not have to analyze its routing system frequently; it depends on the variety of products or services being offered.

Flow charts and diagrams are used to aid in finding and ending inefficiencies in a process by analyzing the process in a step-by-step fashion. Most charting procedures divide the actions in a given process into five types; they are operations, transportations, inspections, delays, and storages. Figure 7–5 defines each of these types of actions. Two charts frequently used are assembly charts and flow process charts.

Assembly charts depict the sequence and manner in which the various parts of a product or service are assembled. A **flow process chart** outlines what happens to the product as it moves through the operating facility. Flow process charts can also map the flow of customers through a service facility. Figure 7–6 shows a flow process chart of the processing of a form for an insurance company.

Activity Scheduling

Activity scheduling develops the precise timetable to be followed in producing the product or service. It also includes dispatching work orders and expediting critical and late orders. Scheduling does not involve deciding how long a job will take (part of job design); rather it determines when the work is to be done. Scheduling is the link between system design and

Margin notes:

Routing–finds the best path and sequence of operations for attaining a desired level of output with a given mix of equipment and personnel.

Assembly chart–depicts the sequence and manner in which the various components of a product or service are assembled.

Flow process chart– outlines what happens to a product or service as it progresses through the facility.

Activity scheduling– develops the precise timetable to be followed in producing a product or service.

FIGURE 7–5
Flow-Charting Activities

Operation: Occurs when an object is intentionally changed in any of its physical or chemical characteristics, is assembled or disassembled from another object, or is arranged for another operation, transportation, inspection, or storage. An operation also occurs when information is given or received or when planning or calculating takes place.

Transportation: Occurs when an object is moved from one place to another, except when such movements are a part of the operation or are caused by the operator at the workstation during an operation or an inspection.

Inspection: Occurs when an object is examined for identification or is verified for quality or quantity in any of its characteristics.

Delay: Occurs to an object when conditions, except those which intentionally change the physical or chemical characteristics of the object, do not permit or require immediate performance of the next planned action.

Storage: Occurs when an object is kept and protected against unauthorized removal.

Source: William R. Mullee and David B. Porter, "Process-Chart Procedures," in *Industrial Engineering Handbook,* 2d ed., ed. H. B. Maynard (New York: McGraw-Hill, 1963), pp. 2–21.

FIGURE 7–6
Process Chart: Present Method for Completing Authorization-to-investigate Form

Operation	Complete authorization to	Sheet __1__ of __1__ Sheets	**Summary**	
Product	investigate form	Charted By Joe Millard	Operation	7
Depts.	Property Loss		Transport	4
Drawing No. N.A. Part No. N.A.		Date 9/14	Inspect	1
Quantity	One form in triplicate		Delay	1
		Approved By Jim Street	Store	—
			Vertical distance	—
Present ✓ Proposed		Date 9/15	Horizontal distance	180 ft.
			Time (hours)	16.000

No.	Dist. Moved (Feet)	Worker Time (Hours)	Symbols	Description
1		.200		Remove Claim Dept's. request from in-basket and identify client.
2	55	3.250		Walk to filing area, locate file, and return to desk. Locate pertinent information in client file.
3		.500		Type information on authorization to investigate form (form no. 3355).
4		4.750		Inspect form.
5		.500		Walk to section leader's desk.
6	35	.200		Wait for signature.
7		.500		Walk back to desk.
8	35	.200		Tear form apart into separate sheets.
9		.200		Prepare regional investigator's copy for mailing; place in mail basket on desk.
10		1.750		Prepare Claims Dept's. copy for routing; place in mail basket on desk.
11		1.500		Place one copy in client's file.
12		.200		Walk to filing area, refile, and return to desk.
13	55	2.250		
14				

Source: From *Production and Operations Management* by Norman Gaither. Copyright © 1980 by The Dryden Press. Reprinted by permission of CBS College Publishing.

operations planning and control. Once the initial schedule has been set, the system is ready for operation. Of course, scheduling is an ongoing activity in an operating system.

A scheduling system must be designed based on knowledge of the operating system for which it is being designed. Scheduling for intermittent systems is very complex because of the larger number of individual orders or customers which must flow through the system. Many types of scheduling tools—such as the Gantt chart, the critical path method and the program evaluation and review technique—have been developed to help overcome scheduling problems.

Scheduling for high-volume continuous flow systems is often a process of matching the available resources to the production needs as outlined by the aggregate plan. Computer simulation has been used to assist in the scheduling of continuous flow systems by estimating the impact of different scheduling decisions on the system.

Material Requirements Planning (MRP)

Material requirements planning (MRP) is a special type of scheduling system in which the needed amount of each component of a product is figured on the basis of the amount of the final product to be produced. When each component is needed depends on when the final assembly is needed and the lead time required to incorporate the component into the assembly.

The purpose of MRP is to get the right materials to the right places at the right time. It does little good to have some of the parts needed to produce a product if the organization does not have all of them. Because carrying parts that are not being used is costly, the idea behind MRP is to provide

---

FIGURE 7–7
Potential Advantages of Material Requirements Planning

1. It reduces the average amount of inventory for dependent-demand items (work-in-process inventory).
2. It improves work flow, resulting in reduced elapsed time between the start and finish of jobs.
3. It enables delivery promises to be more reliable.
4. It minimizes parts shortages.
5. It keeps priorities of work items up to date so that shopwork is more effective and appropriate.
6. It helps plan the timing of design changes and aids in their implementation.
7. It can simulate and evaluate changes in the master schedule.
8. It tells management ahead of time if desired delivery dates appear achievable.
9. It changes (expedites or deexpedites) due dates for orders.
10. It facilitates capacity requirements planning.

Source: James B. Dilworth, *Production and Operations Management*, 2d ed. (New York: Random House, Inc., 1983), p. 261.

either all or none of the necessary components. Some of the advantages of MRP are outlined in Figure 7–7.

Almost all MRP utilizes a computer. This is not because there are complex equations to solve. The computer has the ability to store and rapidly manipulate large amounts of data; as the number of items in the system begins to increase, it becomes necessary to utilize one. Of course, many versions of MRP programs are available.

SUMMARY

Operations management applies the basic concepts and principles of management to the operating systems of an organization. Large amounts of resources and time are used up by the operations function; so its management plays a critical role in achieving the organization's goals.

Operating systems consist of the processes and activities which turn various inputs into goods and/or services. Operating systems exist in all organizations; they are composed of people, material, facilities, and information. There are two basic types of operating systems: continuous flow and intermittent flow.

The product or service produced by an organization limits the design of its operating system. The operations manager and the design engineer must work closely to ensure an acceptable design—from both a functional and a production standpoint.

Process selection includes a wide range of decisions, including product design, the basic type and layout of the process system, and equipment selection. The main objective of process selection is to specify in detail the most economical processes and sequences required to transform the inputs into the desired product or service.

The location and layout of physical facilities are important decisions. The physical layout combines all of the planning of the design process into one physical system. Basically physical layouts are either process oriented or product oriented.

Job design sets the work activities of a worker or group of workers. It answers the questions of how the job is to be performed, who is to perform it, and where it is to be performed. Job content is determined by the individual tasks and by the manner in which these tasks are combined into a specific job. Job methods specify the precise methods for performing each task.

The more traditional approach to job design assumes that job content is fixed by the requirements of the process or by the organization structure. The sociotechnical approach considers both the task and social environment in designing jobs.

If an operating system is to be effective, its day-to-day operations must be properly planned. The purpose of production planning and control is to maintain a smooth, constant flow of work from start to finish, so that the product or service will be completed in the desired time at the lowest possible cost. Aggregate production planning, resource allocation, and activity scheduling are all part of production planning. Aggregate production planning is a process of determining work force requirements, production rates, and inventory levels over a specified time period for the whole operating system. Resource allocation refers to the efficient use of people, materials, and equipment in order to meet the demand requirements of the operating system. Activity scheduling develops the precise timetable for producing the product or service. Materials Requirement Planning (MRP) is a special type of scheduling system in which the needed amount of each component of a product is figured on the basis of the amount of the final product to be produced.

References and Additional Readings

[1] Louis E. Davis, "Job Design and Productivity: A New Approach," *Personnel,* March 1957, p. 420.

[2] Richard A. Johnson, William T. Newell, and Roger C. Vergin, *Production and Operations Management: A Systems Concept* (Boston: Houghton Mifflin, 1974), p. 204.

[3] Ibid., p. 206.

[4] Peter B. Vaill, "Industrial Engineering and Socio-Technical Systems," *Journal of Industrial Engineering,* September 1967, p. 535.

[5] Louis E. Davis and James C. Taylor, *Design of Jobs,* 2d ed. (Santa Monica, Calif.: Goodyear Publishing, 1979), pp. 98–99.

[6] Louis E. Davis, *Job Satisfaction—A Socio-Technical View,* Report 515–1–69 (Los Angeles: University of California, 1969), p. 14.

Review Questions

1. What is operations management?
2. Describe an operating system.
3. Describe the two basic types of operating systems.
4. What is the overriding objective of the process selection decision?
5. Discuss several factors that should be considered in site location.
6. What is a process-oriented layout? A product-oriented layout?
7. The job design process can generally be divided into what three phases?
8. What is the sociotechnical approach to job design? Give some guidelines for job design, using the sociotechnical approach.
9. What is production planning?
10. Define aggregate production planning.
11. What is the difference between resource allocation and activity scheduling?

Discussion Questions

1. Explain how you might take a production line approach (transferring the concepts and methodologies of operations management) to a service organization such as a fast-food restaurant.

2. Does process selection in service industries such as restaurants and hotels differ from process selection in manufacturing? If so, how?

3. Why should all of the phases involved in designing an operating system be integrated?

4. Discuss the following statement: "Most production planning is a waste of time because it all depends on demand forecasts, which are usually inaccurate."

Incident 7–1
The Lines at Sam's

Sam Baker owns and manages a cafeteria on Main Street in Dawsonville. He has been in business for almost two years. During his two years of operation, Sam has identified several problems that he has not been able to solve. One is the line that always seems to develop at the checkout register during the rush hour. Another problem is that customers are constantly complaining that the size of the helpings and the size of the pie slices vary tremendously from customer to customer. A third problem that has been disturbing Sam is the frequency with which the cafeteria runs out of "choice dishes." The final problem perplexing Sam is the fact that every Sunday at noon, when a large crowd arrives after church, Sam invariably runs short of seating space.

Sam has worked at other food establishments for the past 15 years; most of them have experienced similar problems. In fact, these and other related problems have come to be expected and are therefore accepted practice for the industry. After all, Sam's former boss used to say, "You can't please everybody all the time." Sam is wondering if he should take the industry's position and just accept these problems as an inherent part of the business.

Questions

1. Do you have any suggestions for Sam? If so, what are they?
2. Can you think of other service-oriented industries that seem to take the same view toward their problems as Sam's industry?

Incident 7–2
A New Building for Tot-Two

The Tot-Two Company manufactures clothes for children up to age five. Tot-Two has been growing rapidly for the past several years and is planning to build a new plant in a recently developed industrial park on the north side of town. Charles "Chubby" Shaver, the plant's operations manager, has been assigned the task of drawing up a new physical layout subject to the constraints that the new building cannot exceed 7,000 square feet including office space and that it must be a perfect rectangle in order to minimize the construction costs. Chubby developed the following list of departments with their respective approximate space requirements:

Shipping (400 square feet)—area for shipping all finished goods.

Receiving (400 square feet)—area for receiving all materials and supplies.

Materials supply room (200 square feet)—storage area for all incoming materials.

Spreading and cutting area (1,600 square feet)—area containing three 40-foot tables for spreading and then cutting the cloth. Many layers of cloth are spread on top of each other and cut at the same time with large portable cutters.

Pattern-making area (200 square feet)—area in which patterns are made.

Assembly area (1,200 square feet)—area for sewing together the various clothing parts.

Packing area (400 square feet)—area for packing the finished goods into boxes for shipping.

Finished goods storage (500 square feet)—area for storing finished goods prior to shipping.

Design area (200 square feet)—area occupied by designers.

Office space (800 square feet)—space for secretaries and company officers.

Wash facilities (300 square feet)—area containing men's and women's bathrooms.

Lunch/break area (400 square feet)—area with vending machines and lunch tables.

Chubby then drew up an initial layout as illustrated in Exhibit 1.

Questions

1. What are the strong points of Chubby's layout? What are the weak points?

2. Redesign the layout, based on your answers to Question 1.

EXHIBIT 1

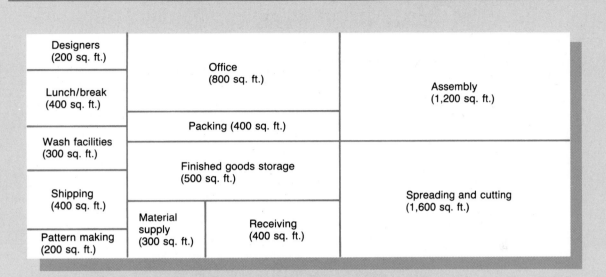

Exercise
Disseminating Confidential Information

Every month, you are responsible for collating and stapling 500 copies of a four-page document. The documents must then be placed in manila envelopes which are sealed and have the word *CONFIDENTIAL* written on each. The four pages are printed on one side only and are numbered sequentially.

A. Assume you have a manual stapler and a felt marker at your disposal. Draw a sketch of how you would arrange your workplace for doing this task and describe the procedure you would use.

B. Assume you have the authority (within reason) to make changes in the equipment, materials, and processes used, as long as the basic task of organizing the information and labeling it as confidential is accomplished. What suggestions would you make?

Chapter 7 Appendix
Gantt Charts

The **Gantt chart** is the oldest and simplest method of graphically showing both expected and completed production. Developed by Henry L. Gantt in the early 1900s, the main feature of the Gantt chart is that work planned and work accomplished are shown in their relation to each other and in relation to time. Figure 7A–1 presents a typical Gantt chart.

Gantt charts emphasize the element of time by readily pointing out any actual or potential slippages. One criticism of the Gantt chart is that it can require considerable time to incorporate scheduling changes such as rush orders. To accommodate such scheduling changes rapidly, mechanical boards using movable pegs or cards have been developed.

> **Gantt chart**–control device that graphically shows work planned and work accomplished in their relation to each other and to time.

Critical Path Method (CPM) and Program Evaluation and Review Technique (PERT)

The Gantt chart concept formed the foundation for network analysis.[1] The most popular network analysis approaches are the **critical path method (CPM)** and **program evaluation and review technique (PERT).** These two techniques were developed almost simultaneously in the late 1950s. CPM grew out of a joint study by DuPont and Remington Rand Univac to determine how to best reduce the time required to perform routine plant overhaul, maintenance, and construction work.[2] PERT was developed by the Navy in conjunction with representatives of Lockheed Aircraft Corporation and the consulting firm of Booz, Allen, and Hamilton to coordinate the development and production of the Polaris weapons system.

CPM and PERT are both techniques which result in a graphical network representation of a project. The graphical network is composed of activities and events. An activity is the work necessary to complete a particular event, and it usually consumes time. Events denote a point in time, and their occurrence signifies the completion of all activities leading into the event. All activities originate and terminate at events. Activities are normally represented by arrows in a network, while events are represented by a circle. The dashed arrows in a project network, called dummies, show dependencies

> **Critical path method (CPM)** planning and control technique that graphically depicts relationships between various activities of a project; used when time durations of project activities are accurately known and have little variance.

> **Program evaluation and review technique (PERT)**–planning and control technique that graphically depicts relationships between various activities of a project; used when durations of project activities are not accurately known.

---

[1] There is evidence that there were other forerunners to CPM and PERT. See Edward R. Marsh, "The Harmonogram of Karol Adamiecki," *Academy of Management Journal,* June 1975, pp. 358–64.

[2] Joseph J. Moder and Cecil R. Phillips, *Project Management with CPM and PERT* (New York: Van Nostrand Reinhold, 1970), p. 6.

FIGURE 7A–1
Gantt Chart with Heavy Lines Indicating Work Completed

Activity Description	Dec. 1972				Jan. 1973					Feb. 1973				Mar. 1973				Apr. 1973				May
	4	11	18	25	2	8	15	22	29	5	12	19	26	5	12	19	26	2	9	16	23	7 1
Process planning, routing, and scheduling																						
Materials procurement																						
Parts fabrication																						
Part No. 1																						
2																						
3																						
4																						
5																						
6																						
7																						
8																						
9																						
10																						
11																						
12																						
Subassemblies																						
A																						
B																						
C																						
D																						
E																						
Final assembly																						

Source: Adapted from Elwood S. Buffa, *Modern Production Management,* 4th ed. (New York, John Wiley & Sons, 1973), p. 576.

FIGURE 7A–2
Project Represented by Gantt Chart and a Project Network

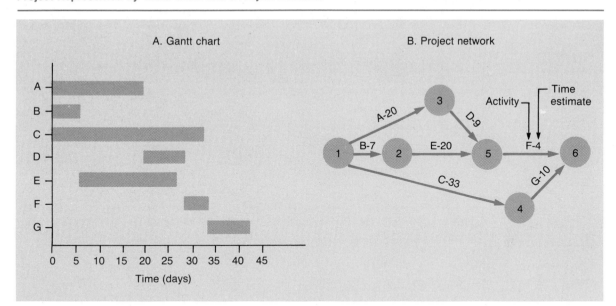

or precedence relationships. They simply denote that the starting of an activity or set of activities depends on the completion of another activity or set of activities.

Figure 7A–2 shows a simple project represented by both a Gantt chart and a project network. The project network has two distinct advantages over the Gantt chart: (1) The dependencies of the activities on each other are noted explicitly and (2) the activities are shown in greater detail.

The path through the network which has the longest duration (based on a summation of estimated individual activity times) is referred to as the critical path. If any activity on the critical path lengthens, then the entire project duration lengthens.

The major difference between CPM and PERT centers around the activity time estimates. CPM is used for projects whose activity durations are accurately known and whose variance in performance time is negligible. On the other hand, PERT is used when the activity durations are more uncertain and variable. CPM is based on a single estimate for an activity duration, where PERT is based on three time estimates for each activity: an optimistic (minimum) time, a most likely (modal) time, and a pessimistic (maximum) time.

Project network analysis can provide information beyond simple project planning and control. By knowing the critical activities, the project manager can best allocate limited resources and make more accurate time-cost trade-offs.

Section 2 Case
D'Lites of America*

During the next 24 hours, 6 out of 10 Americans will eat a fast-food meal. At stand-up counters and drive-through windows, orders for fast-food items will be placed, filled, paid for, and consumed by more than 35 million people. A few will taste, for the first time, fast food of a very different kind: Lite fast food, served by D'Lites of America.

D'Lites of America, a health-oriented fast-food chain, is one of the more recent entrants into the industry. The first D'Lites of America restaurant was opened in Atlanta on December 10, 1981. It immediately became a huge success.

Less than two years later, five D'Lites of America were in operation; more than 500 additional units were under development. By 1990, the company plans to have 1,000 D'Lites of America outlets, coast to coast.

Fast-Food Industry

From the small eateries and roadside stops of the past, the fast-food industry has become a giant with more than $38 billion in sales in 1983.

The reasons for the success of fast-food chains are clear. Consistency in the quality of food and service, convenient and well-maintained locations, and reasonable prices have combined to make fast food an integral part of the American lifestyle.

Restaurant chains have long been a part of the American scene—such companies as Nedicks, Chock Full O'Nuts, Stouffer, and Howard Johnson were some of the original entrants. McDonald's was the first to standardize physical layout, menu, price, and preparation on a national scale. Over 200 national fast-food franchises have developed since then. McDonald's, Burger King, and Wendy's currently hold their positions as the "Big 3."

With the exception of the drive-thru window by Wendy's in 1969, there have been few landmark innovations in the fast-food industry. The primary emphasis of the industry has been on marketing strategy.

Speculation on the future of the industry is interesting food for thought, as diversity in strategy is becoming apparent among the established chains. Confronted with conventional wisdom that the industry is maturing and that changing demographics (an aging baby-boom generation) are shifting demand away from traditional fast food, many chains are trying to develop "upscale" growth vehicles, usually full-service operations that offer liquor. Others are working to fine-tune their old concepts to suit the consumers of the 80s. Although "mature" is the adjective experts use to describe today's

---

* This case was prepared by Faramarz Parsa, Georgia State University.

fast-food marketplace, it appears that each company is pursuing a different strategy to capitalize on its target market segment. Continuing increases in advertising budgets and comparison advertising are telltale signs that the market is indeed in the mature stage of its life cycle.

The D'Lites Concept

The founder and chairman of D'Lites of America is Douglas Sheley. Sheley didn't mind admitting the obvious: "There's probably not room for another hamburger chain on America's fast-food–clogged boulevards." Yet, the obvious did not prevent Sheley from forming a new chain of fast food for health-concious customers who, he believed, have the same weakness for a good hamburger as everyone else.

The concept of D'Lites evolved out of Mr. Sheley's previous interests in health clubs and fast-food restaurants. In 1974, he sold three health clubs he owned in Michigan, Wisconsin, and Ohio. Later that year, he purchased a new franchise in Knoxville, Tennessee, from a small, growing chain of Columbus, Ohio–based restaurants named Wendy's. He built his Wendy's franchise to 18 locations by 1980—and in his spare time, he helped start another health club in Knoxville.

Nutrition-conscious customers kept asking Sheley when he was going to exchange his restaurants' highly processed white hamburger buns for more nutritious whole wheat buns and how many calories were in a Frostie. From those questions, a marketing idea was born.

The idea became Mr. Sheley's "Lite" concept: a new, different type of fast-food restaurant. Believing that fast foods were as much a part of American lifestyle as baseball and apple pie, he would continue to offer the traditional fast-food items—but they would have reduced salt, fats, cholesterol, and sugar carbohydrates. At the same time, he did not want a chain of "health food" restaurants. Middle America, he thought, was leery of such places. He calls his idea a "semihealth" concept. Combining Miller Beer's "Lite" and the first letter of his name (D) gave the new venture its name.

Beginning in 1978, when the concept of D'Lites of America was first formulated, until the first restaurant opened in Atlanta in 1981, the idea was nursed into being by clearly defining the business and formulating strategies for future growth.

Strategic Positioning

D'Lites mission, simply stated, is "to be a major contending force in the fast-food restaurant industry by offering light (low-calorie), nutritious food emphasizing quality, service, and cleanliness." This statement reflects Doug Sheley's personal objectives and his dominating influence over the organization. He views D'Lites as being in the restaurant industry while his major competitors are in the burger industry.

Extending from D'Lites' mission are its long-range objectives:

1. *Growth:* Establish 300 restaurants within 4 years and 1,000 within 10 years. A ratio of 20 percent company-owned and 80 percent franchised is a target for ownership. Quality will not be lowered to reach these goals if they prove not to be possible.

2. *Sales:* Each restaurant must realize $1 million or more in sales per year. Selection of properly evaluated sites will ensure this aim.

3. *Quality:* A high level of cleanliness, service, and consistency of product is expected. Quality will be evaluated by a field supervisor out of operations and then eventually through a field marketing manager.

D'Lites Operating Strategies

The main theme keying D'Lites' early success has been that "the idea sells itself." The recent rash of light food products and health consciousness allowed Doug Sheley to take the idea a step further. Fast food, which has become a mainstay of American life, is renowned for its poor nutrition. The newness and timing of D'Lites has allowed the company to adapt to the environment without having to shed a previous unhealthful image.

The following strategies are the result of D'Lites' objectives and mission:

Menu

The D'Lites menu denotes the main image of the firm's concept. The light, fast-food menu has several major criteria: (1) traditional taste cannot be compromised; (2) every item has to be competitively priced; (3) extending from this is customer choice or customizing of sandwiches and desserts; and (4) above all, the food items must be lower in calories and more nutritious.

Proving that D'Lites' food is lighter and healthier is the aim. For example, a typical fast-food order at a major chain could consist of a quarter-pound cheeseburger, french fries, and soft drink. These items total over 1,000 calories. A comparable D'Lites' meal of a cheesburger on a multigrain bun, baked potato, and sugar-free drink saves the consumer over 500 calories. The calories comparison of D'Lites to other standard fast foods shows D'Lites' to be 150 to 200 calories lower per item and about 400 to 500 calories lower per meal.

Coupled with lower calories is the criterion that traditional taste cannot be altered. The reason for this is to avoid the diet or health food image. Instead, the strategy is to promote D'Lites as having great tasting food that also has fewer calories. The good taste is maintained by leaner beef and ham, low-calorie frozen yogurt instead of ice cream, vegetable oil for frying, and lightly breaded chicken and fish. The food is still "fast food"—but unnecessary calories are removed.

The third criterion of menu diversity is related to the antihealth-food image. Keeping the basic fast-food staples—hamburgers, french fries, etc.—gives an option to even the nonconsumer of health food. The ability to be a fast-food restaurant to all customers is a driving theme. Family orientation is preserved by letting the diet-conscious eat with nondieting family members.

A reasonable price criterion is designed to keep D'Lites in the same price ranges as its competitors. An average meal at D'Lites does average slightly more than the industry average. A slightly higher cost, however, relates to the target market upper-end consumers with the ability to pay for extra quality and more healthful food.

D'Lites' menu strategy is not health food but less fattening and more nutritious versions of traditional fast-food items. The preparation to keep the calories lower has given D'Lites patent rights to several food-processing techniques.

Future Menu

Future expansion of D'Lites' menu will concentrate on introducing breakfast and dinner items. Presently, wine and beer are served in the restaurants to increase dinner traffic.

Traditionally, the fast-food industry has not penetrated into the dinner market, and McDonald's has a strong hold in breakfast fast food. To counter this situation, D'Lites plans to offer the following items at some point in the future:

- *Breakfast:* Multigrain biscuit, pita bread egg sandwich, fruit cup, light pancakes and syrup, lean sausage and ham, and fresh juices.
- *Dinner:* Chicken parmesan with low-fat cheese, hamburger Wellington, croissant stuffed with ground beef and mushroom sauce, baked chicken, and fish.

The purpose of this meal expansion is to reach the growing breakfast market and to attract new customers (not just health food eaters) who never eat at fast-food restaurants. Presently D'Lites dinner sales constitute 45 percent of total sales. This is significantly above the industry average.

Building Design

Corresponding to a nontraditional image for fast-food restaurants, the interior and exterior of all D'Lites restaurants are a contrast to the industry. This strategy again is based upon consumer research. The existing D'Lites restaurants are all free-standing and contain about 3,400 square feet and approximately 112 seats. The building itself is an unusual shape, emphasizing contoured corners and natural lighting from atrium glass windows. Natural blond wood construction and careful landscaping reinforces the theme of brightness.

Similarly, interior design includes wooden tables and padded chairs. Hanging baskets of plants give D'Lites a greenhouse affect. Completing the lightness theme is a highlighted salad bar surrounded by brass and etched glass. Sheley, drawing on his management experience at Wendy's, arranged the job station preparation and ordering areas in a similar fashion. Following typical industry practice, all D'Lites restaurants have a standard drive-thru service.

Research and Development

The overall strategy of R&D is to keep ahead of the competition's movement into the light food concept. Research and development for D'Lites has two main areas, food development and market research.

Food development. The first food product innovation was developed before the first D'Lites opened. D'Lites multigrain hamburger bun was the result of a $7,500 grant to the University of Tennessee and is a high-fiber, lower-calorie bun. The strategy of out-of-house product development continues today. Typically, a need for a new menu item is perceived, and suppliers are approached about producing a low-calorie, more nutritious version of a desired food. This allows the risk taking and expense to be shifted to the suppliers and soliciting innovators.

Many innovators offer their own variations directly to the company. One problem with this approach is that conflicts can arise in maintaining the secrecy of the product while allowing D'Lites to inspect it.

Market research. Market research is concerned with two main areas: test marketing of new food offerings and consumer research for particular markets. These areas are related to customer desires and affect one another. Test marketing of new products is extensive. The company-owned stores are used as test markets. Product results are monitored daily and tested for specific time periods.

Considerable expense is incurred in consumer research. The demographics of Atlanta provide a large test and target market of 25- to 45-year olds with annual salaries over $25,000. Future test markets for D'Lites will include Denver and possibly Cincinnati. Like Atlanta, these cities were chosen for demographics and customer type.

Advertising and Promotions

The key formulation is to communicate the correct image of the restaurant and sell people on the idea. Based upon Miller Lite's beer slogan, D'Lites' main slogan is "More of a good thing. And less." D'Lites' advertising strategy uses three main devices—public relations, radio, and print. The largest concentration of advertising effort is in public relations, because of the small advertising budget. The 1984 budget was estimated at around $600,000—well below industry levels.

The tactic of promoting D'Lites effectively through nonpaid media uses the unique story and concept of D'Lites. The measurable objective is to get an article about D'Lites in the news each week in various sources such as national and local television, newspapers, and magazines, stressing D'Lites' image to the fullest.

Print advertising is used irregularly and is not a mainstay of the overall strategy. Included in this area are limited billboarding, direct-mail coupons, and some print ads. At present, resources do not exist to exploit these sources heavily; neither is there a real desire by the company to use them.

Radio is a new media source for D'Lites. The jingles used on the radio communicate the quality of food and nutrition D'Lites' offers. One of the two company slogans—"Just What America Needs"—came from a radio campaign emphasizing lifestyle changes and the need for low-calorie, nutritious fast food.

Two other, less publicly noticeable ventures exist as a means of promotion: (1) the sponsorship of an Atlanta tennis and golf tournament and (2) point-of-sale tactics such as the calorie-counter menu next to cash registers and the stand-up cards on restaurant tables.

View of Competition

The restaurant business is highly competitive and is often affected by changes in taste and eating habits of the public, economic conditions, and traffic patterns.

D'Lites competes for restaurant locations, management personnel and other employees, franchises, and customers against a large number of national and regional restaurant chains. Many of the competitors operate with more-established products and greater financial resources. Nevertheless, management believes that D'Lites presently enjoys the competitive advantage of being the first to use the light-nutritious concept.

Going Public

In August 1984, D'Lites of America Inc. filed with the Securities and Exchange Commission an initial offering of 1.2 million common shares. This represented 26 percent of the company's stock, expected to be offered to the public at $6.50 to $8.50 a share. With the $8 million or so raised from the issue, D'Lites planned to go on an expansion spree.

D'Lites boosted its original offering of 1.5 million common shares at $9.50 each through underwriters led by William Blair and Co. They were also authorized to issue up to 1 million shares of preferred stock, $10 par value.

On March 8, 1985, the listed stock price of D'Lites of America traded in the over-the-counter market was 12¾.

What Lies Ahead?

With robust per-restaurant sales of $1.12 million just a little under McDonald's $1.17 million, D'Lites now is mainly concerned with managing its expansion and growth. "The company is walking a tightrope," asserts Michael Culp, an analyst with Prudential-Bache Securities, Inc. "They must expand quickly if they are to grab a share of the market, but they can't overdo it."

As of September 1984, D'Lites' return at its own restaurants, after general and administrative expenses, is less than 1 percent—not an unusual figure for a start-up operation, but way below the 10 percent for an established chain. To keep overhead down, Sheley wants at least 80 percent of D'Lites restaurants to be franchises, which requires little capital and produces margin-building development fees.

D'Lites' biggest test lies ahead, as it goes head-to-head with giant rivals and as new imitators pop up in this industry segment. Many big chains already offer salad bars and other items to health-conscious customers. Nevertheless, industry experts give D'Lites a solid chance at success—but only if it maintains quality and consistency.

3

Administrative Skills

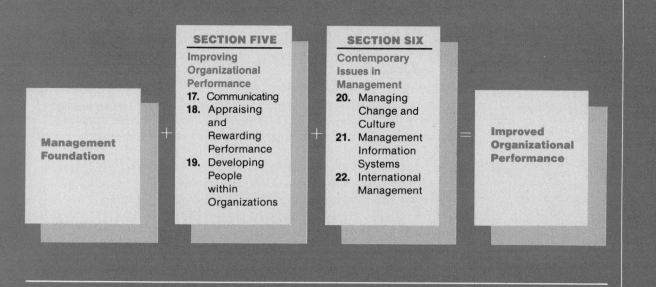

Management Foundation

$+$

SECTION FIVE

Improving Organizational Performance
17. Communicating
18. Appraising and Rewarding Performance
19. Developing People within Organizations

$+$

SECTION SIX

Contemporary Issues in Management
20. Managing Change and Culture
21. Management Information Systems
22. International Management

$=$

Improved Organizational Performance

Section 3 analyzes the administrative skills of management. Administrative skills are needed for the organizing, staffing, and controlling functions of management.

Chapter 8 is the first of two chapters related to the organizing function. It introduces that function through a discussion of division of labor. Authority is presented as the concept most central to the organizing function. The delegation process and its importance in the management process are discussed.

Chapter 9 builds on the basic concepts of Chapter 8 and presents several types of organization structures. This chapter also develops the idea that the most appropriate organizational structure depends on the organization's objectives, the particular technology employed, the rate of change in the environment, and other dynamic factors.

Chapter 10 deals with the staffing function of management. Human resource planning, recruitment, selection, and other personnel-related activities are discussed.

Chapter 11 is concerned with the controlling function. The reasons for management control are discussed along with the requirements of a control system. Several management control methods and techniques are explained and illustrated.

Chapter 12 deals with the controlling function as it applies to operations management. The point is stressed that an organization's operating system must be properly controlled. Operations control, inventory control, and quality control are all discussed.

Organizing: The Systematizing Function

Chapter Outline

REASONS FOR ORGANIZING
DIVISION OF LABOR
AUTHORITY, POWER, AND
  RESPONSIBILITY
SOURCES OF AUTHORITY
PRINCIPLES BASED ON
  AUTHORITY
   Delegation—the Parity Principle

Unity of Command
Scalar Principle
Span of Management
The Exception Principle
CENTRALIZATION VERSUS
  DECENTRALIZATION
SUMMARY

SECTION THREE

**Administrative
Skills**

 8. Organizing
 9. Organization
    Structures
10. Staffing
11. Controlling
12. Operations
    Control

If the employer fails to apportion the work among his assistants, it is likely that they will duplicate one another's work. If he neglects to distinguish between the kinds of work as promptly as the amount of endeavor permits, he will lose the advantages of specialization. If he delays too long in appointing supervisors, with the result that the task of oversight exceeds his capacity, the work will not be as well done as it might. Any of these errors reduces, if it does not prevent, the success of the enterprise. In each case, organization has been neglected; it has not performed its mission as a means to a more effective concerted endeavor.

*Alvin Brown **

Organization–group of people working together in some concerted or coordinated effort to attain objectives.

Organizing–the grouping of activities necessary to attain common objectives and the assignment of each grouping to a manager who has the authority necessary to supervise the people performing the activities.

Informal organization– aggregate of the personal contacts and interactions and the associated groupings of people working within the formal organization.

Most work today is accomplished by organizations. An **organization** is a group of people working together in some type of concerted or coordinated effort to attain objectives. As such, an organization provides a vehicle for accomplishing objectives that could not be achieved by individuals working separately. The process of **organizing** is the grouping of activities necessary to attain common objectives and the assignment of each grouping to a manager who has the authority necessary to supervise the people performing the activities.[1] Thus, organizing is basically a process of division of labor accompanied by appropriate delegation of authority. As illustrated in the above introductory quote, proper organizing results in the better use of resources.

The framework which defines the boundaries of the formal organization and within which the organization operates is the organization structure. A second and equally important element of an organization is the informal organization. The **informal organization** refers to the aggregate of the personal contacts and interactions and the associated groupings of people working within the formal organization.[2] The informal organization has a structure, but it is not formally and consciously designed.

REASONS FOR ORGANIZING

One of the primary reasons for organizing is to establish lines of authority. This creates order within the group. The absence of authority almost always leads to chaotic situations in which everyone is telling everyone else what to do.

Secondly, organizing improves the efficiency and quality of work through synergism. Synergism occurs when individual or separate units work together

* Alvin Brown, *Organization of Industry* (Englewood Cliffs, N.J.: Prentice-Hall, 1947), p. 15.

to produce a whole greater than the sum of the parts. Synergism results when three people working together produce more than four people working separately. Synergism can result from division of labor or from increased coordination, both of which are products of good organization.

A final reason for organizing is to improve communication. A good organization structure clearly defines channels of communication among the members of the organization. Such a system also ensures more efficient communications. The role of communication in the management process will be discussed in Chapter 17.

DIVISION OF LABOR

Organizing is basically a process of division of labor. The merits of dividing labor have been known for centuries. Taking the very simple task of manufacturing a pin, Adam Smith in 1776 demonstrated how much more efficiently the task could be performed through division of labor.[3]

Labor can be divided either vertically or horizontally. Vertical division of labor is based on the establishment of lines of authority and defines the levels that make up the vertical organizational structure. In addition to establishing authority, vertical division of labor facilitates the flow of communication within the organization.

Horizontal division of labor is based on specialization of work. The basic assumption underlying horizontal division of labor is that by making each worker's task specialized, more work can be produced with the same effort through increased efficiency and quality. Specifically, horizontal division of labor can result in the following advantages:

1. Fewer skills required per person.
2. Easier to supply the skills required for selection or training purposes.
3. Repetition or practice of the same job develops proficiency.
4. Efficient use of skills by primarily utilizing each worker's best skills.
5. The ability to have concurrent operations.
6. More conformity in the final product if each piece is always produced by the same person.

The major problem with horizontal division of labor is that it can result in job boredom and even degradation of the worker. An extreme example of horizontal division of labor is the automobile assembly line. It is not hard to imagine the behavioral problems associated with such an assembly line. When examining horizontal division of labor, it is necessary to identify two dimensions of the job: scope and depth.

Job scope refers to the number of different types of operations performed. In performing a job with narrow scope the worker would perform few operations and repeat the cycle frequently. The negative effects of jobs lacking

Job scope—number of different types of operations performed on the job.

in scope vary with the person performing the job but can result in more errors and lower quality.

Job depth refers to the freedom of employees to plan and organize their own work, to work at their own pace, and to move around and communicate as desired. A lack of job depth can result in job dissatisfaction and work avoidance which can in turn lead to absenteeism, tardiness, and even sabotage.

A job can be high in job scope and low in job depth or vice versa. For example, newspaper delivery involves the same few operations each time, but there is considerable freedom in organizing and pacing the work. Thus, the job is low in scope but high in depth. Of course, many jobs are low (or high) in both job scope and job depth.

Division of labor is not more efficient or even desirable in all situations. At least two basic requirements must exist for the successful use of division of labor. The first requirement is a relatively large volume of work. Enough volume must be produced to allow for specialization and also to keep each employee busy. A second basic requiremem is stability in the volume of work, employee attendance, quality of raw materials, product design, and production technology.

AUTHORITY, POWER, AND RESPONSIBILITY

Authority is the right to command and expend resources. Lines of authority serve to link the various organizational components together. Unclear delegation of authority is a major source of confusion and conflict within an organization.

Many people confuse power with authority. **Power is the ability to command or apply force and is not necessarily accompanied by authority**. Power is derived from the control of resources. A man with a pistol may have the power to shoot another, but he does not have the right to do so. Similarly, managers may have the power to make frivolous expenditures, but they do not have the right to do so. However, it is true that authority and power often accompany each other.

Responsibility is accountability for the attainment of objectives, the use of resources, and the adherence to organizational policy. Once responsibility is accepted, it becomes an obligation to perform assigned work. The term *responsibility* as used here should not be confused with the term *responsibilities* as in the context of defining job duties.

SOURCES OF AUTHORITY

Authority has traditionally been viewed as a function of position, flowing from top to bottom through the formal organization. According to this view, people hold authority because they occupy a certain position; once removed from the position, they lose their authority. Taking this theory one step further, one can say that the American people, through the Constitution and laws, represent the ultimate source of authority in this country. The Constitution and laws guarantee the right of free enterprise. The owners of a free enterprise organization have the right to elect a board of directors and top management. Top management selects middle-level managers. This process continues down to the lowest person in the organization. This traditional view of authority is also called the formal theory of authority.

A second theory of authority was first outlined in 1926 by Mary Parker Follett and popularized in 1938 by Chester Barnard.[4] Called the acceptance theory of authority, this theory maintains that a manager's source of authority lies with his or her subordinates, because they have the power to either accept or reject the manager's command. Presumably, if the subordinate does not accept the authority of the manager, it does not exist. Both Follett and Barnard viewed disobeying a communication from a manager as a denial of authority by the subordinate.

PRINCIPLES BASED ON AUTHORITY

Because authority is a key element in management and organizations, numerous related principles have been developed. Before proceeding, recall from Chapter 1 that management principles are suggested guides rather than ironclad laws.

Delegation—The Parity Principle

Can authority be delegated? Can responsibility be delegated? There is little debate concerning the delegation of authority—it can and should be delegated. For example, a manager might very well choose to delegate the authority to subordinates to make expenditures, without approval, up to a stipulated amount. However, considerable debate often arises with regard to the delegation of responsibility. A close analysis of this debate generally reveals that it is more the result of semantics than of a misunderstanding of the concepts involved. Those contending that responsibility cannot be delegated support their answer by stating that managers can never shed the responsibilities of their jobs by passing them on to subordinates. Those contending that responsibility can be delegated justify their position by pointing out that managers can certainly make subordinates responsible to them for certain actions.

Both parties are correct! Managers can delegate responsibilities to subordinates in the sense of making subordinates responsible to them. However, this delegation to subordinates does not make managers any less responsible to their superiors. Delegation of responsibility does not mean abdication of responsibility by the delegating manager. Responsibility is not like an object which can be passed from individual to individual. Suppose a loan manager for a bank decided to delegate to the loan officers the responsibility for ensuring that all loans are processed within a 10-day limit as stated by bank policy. Loan managers can certainly make loan officers accountable (responsible) to them in this matter. At the same time loan managers are no less accountable to their bosses.

Parity principle—states that authority and responsibility coincide.

The **parity principle** states that authority and responsibility must coincide. Management must delegate sufficient authority so subordinates can do their jobs. At the same time, subordinates can be expected to accept responsibility only for those areas within their authority.

Both authority and responsibility must be accepted by subordinates before the delegation process has been completed. Management sometimes expects employees to seek and assume responsibility that they have not been asked to assume and then to bid for the necessary authority. Such a system leads to guessing games which do nothing but create frustration and waste energy.

1   A manager's resistance to delegating authority is natural. There are several reasons why they are reluctant. Unfortunately, many managers subscribe to the old saying "If you want something done right, do it yourself!" Such an attitude reveals that the manager does not have a grasp of the management process and has done a poor job of selecting and developing subordinates. Managers who attempt to do everything themselves find that their time is continually consumed by rather unimportant tasks and that they do not have time to do important tasks. Newly appointed managers tend to adopt this attitude. They fear failure unless they do each task personally.

2   A second reason often given for not delegating is that it is easier for a manager to do a task than to teach a subordinate how to do it. This might be true the 1st time a particular task has to be done, but what about the 10th or 20th time? Delegating often does involve some initial investment of time; however, this investment is usually recouped quickly through subsequently saved time.

3   A third reason why managers are reluctant to delegate is the fear that a subordinate will look so good that he or she might replace the manager. To good managers, such fears are totally unfounded. A manager's performance is, for the most part, a reflection of the performance of subordinates. If a manager's subordinates look good, the manager looks good; if the subordinates look bad, the manager looks bad.

4   A fourth reason that causes managers to shy away from delegating is the human attraction for power. Most people like the feel of power which often accompanies authority. To many managers, there is a certain degree of satisfaction in having the power and authority to grant or not grant certain requests.

5   Yet another reason that managers are reluctant to delegate is that they often feel comfortable doing those things that should be delegated. This is especially a problem with people recently promoted into management. It is only natural that many new managers feel more comfortable doing the same tasks that they did before they became managers.

In spite of all the reasons for not delegating, there are some very strong reasons why a manager should delegate. Several phenomena occur when a manager successfully delegates. The manager's time is freed to pursue other tasks, and the subordinates gain feelings of belonging and being needed. These feelings often lead to a genuine commitment on the part of the subordinates. Another reason to delegate is that it is one of the best methods for developing subordinates and satisfying customers. Pushing authority down the organization also allows employees to deal more effectively with customers. For example, some department stores give their salespeople the authority to make exchanges and refunds right on the floor, while others force customers to go to the credit department. Most customers much prefer the first situation. The importance of satisfying the customer should not be minimized. Thomas Peters and Robert Waterman, in their study of America's excellent companies, identified "close to the customer" as one of the eight identifiable attributes of excellent companies.[5]

Unfortunately, the tendency of many delegating managers is to delegate only simple, unimportant tasks. The following quote from Robert Townsend illustrates this point:

> Many give lip service, but few delegate authority in important matters. And that means all they delegate is dog-work. A real leader does as much dog-work for his people as he can: He can do it, or see a way to do without it, 10 times as fast. And he delegates as many important matters as he can because that creates a climate in which people grow.[6]

Successful delegation involves delegating matters which stimulate the subordinates.

How to delegate. There are three major components of the delegation process: (1) the assignment of duties by managers to their immediate subordinates; (2) the granting of permission (authority) to make commitments, use resources, and take all actions which are necessary to perform the duties; and (3) the creation of an obligation (responsibility) on the part of each subordinate to the delegating manager to perform the duties satisfactorily.[7]

In order to best assign duties to subordinates, managers must be well acquainted with the skills of their immediate subordinates. The manager must also be able to determine the functions and duties that can be delegated and those that cannot.

The second and third components of the delegation process stress the parity principle. The still unanswered question is: "How much authority should be delegated? As mentioned previously, management must delegate sufficient authority to allow the subordinate to perform the job. Precisely what can and what cannot be delegated depends on the commitments of the manager and the number and quality of subordinates. A general rule of thumb is to delegate authority and responsibility to the lowest organization level that has the competence to accept them. Management in Action 8–1 describes how good delegation habits have contributed to the success of the chief executive officer of the McDonnell Douglas Corporation.

MANAGEMENT IN ACTION 8–1

Profile: Sanford N. McDonnell

McDonnell Douglas is the second largest defense contractor in the United States and the third largest commercial aircraft supplier in the world. Chief executive officer Sanford McDonnell is known for his keen perception and acute analytical ability as well as his easygoing, charming manner. "Sandy" McDonnell firmly believes the success of McDonnell Douglas is directly related to the delegation of decision making. He says, "I'm a team player. I like to think of myself not as someone sitting on top telling everybody what to do but someone who tries to put together the best combination of individuals to come up with the most synergistic team we can put together. A company this size cannot function with decisions being handed down from one office. I concentrate on bringing out the potential of our executives—to get them to work together toward the common goals of the corporation."

Source: Karol White, *Sky Magazine*, March 1982, p. 27.

Unity of Command

Unity-of-Command principle–states that an employee should have one and only one immediate manager.

The **principle of unity of command** states that an employee should have one and only one immediate manager. The difficulty of serving more than one superior has been recognized for thousands of years. Recall the Sermon on the Mount, when Jesus said, "No man can serve two masters."[8]

In its simplest form, this problem arises when two managers tell the same subordinate to do different jobs at the same time. The subordinate is thus placed in a no-win situation. Regardless of which manager the employee obeys, the other will be dissatisfied. The key to avoiding problems with unity of command is make sure that employees clearly understand the lines of authority that directly affect them. All too often, managers assume that employees understand the lines of authority when in fact they do not. For example, does the industrial relations manager in Plant A report directly to the general manager of Plant A or to the corporate vice president of industrial relations? In this type of situation, which is not unusual, the industrial relations manager in Plant A normally will report directly to the Plant A general manager and have a consultative type of relationship with the corporate vice president of industrial relations.

Scalar Principle

Scalar principle–states that authority in the organization flows, one link at a time, through the chain of managers ranging from the highest to lowest ranks; also called chain of command.

The **scalar principle** states that authority in the organization flows one link at a time, through the chain of managers ranging from the highest to lowest ranks. Commonly referred to as the chain of command, the scalar principle is based on the need for communication and the principle of unity of command.

The problem with circumventing the scalar process is that the link bypassed in the process may have very pertinent information. For example, suppose that Jerry goes directly above his immediate boss Ellen to Charlie for permission to take his lunch break 30 minutes earlier. Charlie, believing it to be reasonable, approves Jerry's request—only to later find out that the other two people in Jerry's department had also rescheduled their lunch breaks. Thus, the department would be totally vacant from 12:30 to 1 o'clock. Ellen, the bypassed manager, would have known about the other rescheduled lunch breaks.

A common misconception is that every action must painfully progress through every link in the chain, whether its course is upward or downward. This point was refuted many years ago by Lyndell Urwick, an internationally known management consultant:

> Provided there is proper confidence and loyalty between superiors and subordinates, and both parties take the trouble to keep the other informed in matters in which they should have a concern, the "scalar process" does not imply that there should be no shortcuts. It is concerned with authority, and provided the authority is recognized and no attempt is made to evade or to supercede it, there is ample room for avoiding in matters of action the childish practices of going upstairs one step at a time or running up one ladder and down another when there is nothing to prevent a direct approach on level ground.[9]

As Fayol stated, years before Urwick, "it is an error to depart needlessly from authority, but it is an even greater one to keep to it when detriment to the business ensues."[10] Both men are simply saying that in certain instances, one can and should shortcut the scalar chain if it is not done in a secretive or deceitful manner.

Span of Management

The **span of management** (also called the span of control) refers to the number of subordinates a manager can effectively manage. Although the British World War I general, Sir Ian Hamilton, is usually given credit for developing the concept of a limited span of control, there are numerous related examples throughout history (see Management in Action 8–2). Sir Ian argued that a narrow span of management (with no more than six subordinates reporting to a manager) would enable the manager to get the job accomplished in the course of a normal working day.[11]

In 1933, V. A. Graicunas published a classic paper which analyzed subordinate-superior relationships in terms of a mathematical formula.[12] This formula was based on the theory that the complexities of managing increase geometrically as the number of subordinates increases arithmetically. Graicunas's reasoning was that not only did the number of single relationships increase but so did the number of direct group relationships and cross relationships. Table 8–1 shows the total number of potential relationships envisioned by Graicunas. (Management in Action 8–3 provides some interesting personal information about Graicunas.)

Span of management – number of subordinates a manager can effectively manage; also called span of control.

MANAGEMENT IN ACTION 8-2

Historical Development of Span of Management

There is some evidence that the Egyptians practiced a form of "span of management." In the earliest Egyptian dynasties, a pharaoh's death meant that his workers and servants were killed and buried with him.

As the civilization evolved, that unusual custom was replaced with the idea of burying carvings that symbolized the servants. Interestingly, excavated carvings of servants have indicated that there was a ratio of about 10 servants to each supervisor.

Source: Daniel A. Wren, *The Evolution of Management Thought,* 2d ed. (New York: John Wiley & Sons, 1979.)

TABLE 8-1
Graicunas's Direct, Cross, and Group Relationships

Number of Subordinates	Number of Direct Single Relationships	Number of Cross Relationships	Number of Direct Relationships Between Groups	Number of Total Relationships
1	1	0	0	1
2	2	2	2	6
3	3	6	9	18
4	4	12	28	44
5	5	20	75	100
6	6	30	186	222
7	7	42	441	490
8	8	56	1016	1080

Based on personal experiences and the works of Sir Ian and Graicunas, Urwick first stated the concept of span of management as a management principle in 1938: "No superior can supervise directly the work of more than five, or at the most, six subordinates whose work interlocks."[13] As will be seen, Urwick's concept is not exactly applicable in all situations.

Since the publication of Graicunas's and Urwick's works, the upper limit of five or six subordinates has been continuously criticized as being too restrictive. Many practitioners and scholars contend that there are situations in which more than five or six subordinates can be effectively supervised. Their beliefs have been substantiated by considerable empirical evidence showing that the limit of five or six subordinates has been successfully exceeded in many situations.[14] Urwick has suggested that these exceptions can be explained by the fact that senior workers often function as unofficial managers or leaders.[15]

In view of recent evidence, the span-of-management concept has been revised to state that <u>the number of people who should report directly to any one person should be based upon the complexity, variety, and proximity</u>

MANAGEMENT IN ACTION 8-3

The Life of Vytautas Andrius Graicunas

Information about the life of Vytautas Graicunas, the developer of the span of control, is sketchy and often ambiguous. Although Graicunas is frequently described as a Lithuanian or French mathematician, he was actually born, raised, and educated in Chicago. After completing degrees in accounting and mechanical engineering, he helped start several factories in the United States and Europe. While attending a meeting of the International Committee for Scientific Management in Paris in 1929, Graicunas met Lyndall F. Urwick, and they collaborated on the classic essay about the span of control—"Relationship in Organization."

During the Second World War, Graicunas was a major in the U.S. Air Corps and advisor to the Lithuanian Air Force. Although little information is available about his activities between 1940 and 1947, it is suspected that he served with the U.S. Office of Strategic Services. While on a business trip to Moscow in 1947, Graicunas was arrested by the Soviet Secret Police. After iterrogation and torture, Graicunas went on a starvation strike and died.

Source: Arthur G. Bedeian, "Vytautas Andrius Graicunas—a Biographical Note," *Academy of Management Journal*, June 1974, p. 347.

---

of the jobs, the quality of the people filling the jobs, and the ability of the manager. Complexity basically refers to the job scope and job depth of the jobs being managed. Naturally, the more complex the jobs being managed, the lower the appropriate span of management. Variety relates to the number of different types of jobs being managed. For example, are all the subordinates doing the same or similar jobs, or are they doing very different jobs? The more variety that is present, the lower the appropriate span of management. The physical dispersion or the proximity of the jobs being managed also influences the span of management. If the subordinates are all working in rather close proximity, such as in one room, the span of management would be greater than if they are spread over the city or state. Quality of the people refers to the fact that some people need and require closer supervision than do others. The final contingent factor, the ability of the manager, refers to the skill of the manager in performing managerial duties.

Thus, in situations where workers are engaged in simple, repetitive operations in close proximity, the span of management could be very large. In situations involving highly diversified and technical work, the span of management might be as low as three or four.

While much thought is given to ensuring that a manager's span of management is not too great, the opposite situation is often overlooked. All too frequently in organizations, situations develop in which only one subordinate is reporting to a particular manager. While this situation might very well be justified under certain circumstances, it often results in an inefficient and "top-heavy" organization. The pros and cons of flat (wide span of management, few levels) organizations versus tall (narrow span of management,

FIGURE 8–1
Factors Affecting the Span of Management

Factor	Description	Relationship to Span of Control
Complexity	Job scope Job depth	Inverse*
Variety	Number of different types of jobs being managed	Inverse*
Proximity	Physical dispersion of jobs being managed	Direct†
Quality of subordinates	General quality of the subordinates being managed	Direct†
Quality of manager	Ability of perform managerial duties	Direct†

* As the factor of complexity (or variety) increases, the span of management decreases.
† As the factor of promixity (or quality) increases, the span of management increases.

many levels) organizations are discussed at length in the next chapter. Figure 8–1 summarizes the factors affecting the manager's span of management.

The Exception Principle

Exception principle– states that managers should concentrate on matters that deviate significantly from normal and let subordinates handle routine matters; also called management by exception.

The exception principle (also known as management by exception) is closely related to the parity principle. The **exception principle** states that managers should concentrate their efforts on matters which deviate significantly from normal and let subordinates handle routine matters. The idea here is that managers should concentrate on those matters that require their abilities and not become bogged down with duties that their subordinates should be doing. The exception principle can be hard to comply with when incompetent or insecure subordinates refer everything to their superiors because they are afraid to make a decision. On the other hand, the superior should refrain from making everyday decisions which have been delegated to a subordinate.

CENTRALIZATION VERSUS DECENTRALIZATION

There are limitations to the authority of any position. These limitations may be external, in the form of laws, politics, or social attitudes, or they may be internal, as delineated by the organization's objectives or by the job description. The tapered concept of authority states that the breadth and scope of authority become more limited as one descends the scalar chain (see Figure 8–2).

The top levels of management establish the shape of the funnels in Figures 8–2 and 8–3. The more authority that top management chooses to delegate, the less conical the funnel becomes. The less conical the funnel, the more decentralized is the organization. **Centralization** and **decentralization** refer to the degree of authority delegated by upper management. This is usually reflected by the numbers and kinds of decisions made by the lower levels of management. As they increase, the degree of decentralization also increases. Thus, an organization is never totally centralized or totally decentralized: it falls along a continuum ranging from highly centralized to highly decentralized. Looking at Figure 8–3, the organization represented by the diagram on the left is much more centralized than that represented by the right-hand diagram.

The answer to the question of how much an organization should decentralize depends on the specific situation and organization. Decentralization allows for more flexibility and quicker action. It also relieves executives from time-consuming detail work. It often results in higher morale by allowing lower levels of management to be actively involved in the decision-making process. The major disadvantage of decentralization is the potential loss of control. Duplication of effort can also accompany decentralization.

Because no magic formula exists for determining the appropriate degree

Centralization–little authority is delegated to lower levels of management.

Decentralization–a great deal of authority is delegated to lower levels of management.

FIGURE 8–2
Tapered Concept of Authority

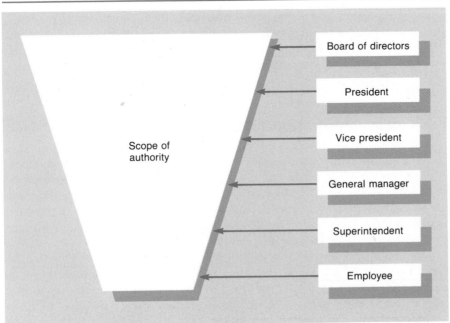

FIGURE 8–3
Centralized versus Decentralized Authority

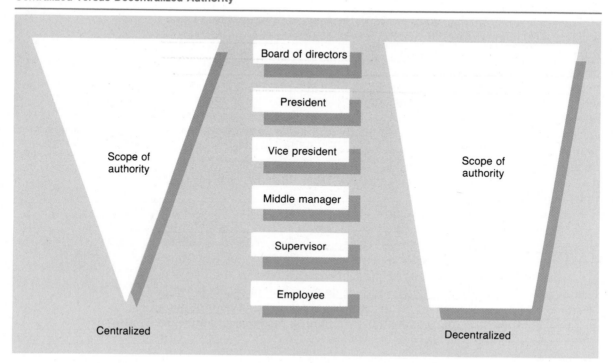

of decentralization, top management must periodically evaluate its particular situation in light of the advantages and disadvantages of greater decentralization. Management in Action 8–4 describes how Hewlett-Packard has recently moved toward more centralization.

SUMMARY

As a group of people working together in some type of concerted or coordinated effort to attain common objectives, an organization provides a vehicle for accomplishing objectives that could not be achieved by individuals working separately. Specific reasons for organizing include the need to establish lines of authority, improve efficiency and quality of work through synergism, and increase communication.

Horizontal and vertical division of labor are the means by which organization is accomplished. Job scope refers to the number of different types of operations performed. Job depth refers to the freedom of employees to plan and organize their own work, to work at their own pace, and to move around and communicate as desired.

MANAGEMENT IN ACTION 8-4

Centralization at Hewlett-Packard

In the 1970s, Hewlett-Packard was widely recognized as one of the technological leaders in the computer industry. During those years, HP was organized into autonomous divisions and placed a high value on individual innovation—a strategy that paid off. The company's many successful products during those years included the hand-held scientific calculator, the 3000 minicomputer and a nonimpact printer.

In the 1980s, HP began to experience difficulty introducing new products. New markets such as personal computers and office automation required that Hewlett-Packard's divisions work together in product development and marketing. Because of the independence of its divisions and its focus on the individual innovation, many of Hewlett-Packard's new product efforts were unsuccessful. In response to its changing business climate, HP is now moving away from a decentralized structure with an engineering focus to a centralized structure with a marketing focus.

Source: "Who's Excellent Now?" *Business Week*, November 5, 1984, pp. 76–88.

Authority is the right to command and expand resources. Power is the ability to command or apply force. Responsibility is accountability for the attainment of objectives, the use of resources, and the adherence to organizational policy.

Many management principles are based on the concept of authority. These principles include:

- The parity principle: Authority and responsibility must coincide.
- Unity of command: An employee should have one and only one immediate manager.
- The scalar principle: Authority in the organization flows, one link at a time, through the chain of managers ranging from highest to lowest ranks.
- Span of management: The number of people directly reporting to any one person should be based on the complexity, variety, and proximity of the jobs, the quality of the people filling the jobs, and the ability of the manager.
- The exception principle: Managers should concentrate on matters which deviate significantly from normal and let their subordinates attend to the routine matters.

While all managers should be familiar with the basic management and organization principles, they should be used as guides for action—not as laws.

Delegation is one key to successful management. Yet there are several reasons why managers are often reluctant to delegate. Fear of the subordinate failing, the "it's easier to do it myself" attitude, fear of the subordinate "looking too good," the human attraction for power, and feeling comfortable with doing things that should be delegated are some of the more frequently encountered reasons for failure to delegate.

Centralization and decentralization refer to the degree of authority delegated by upper management. This is usually reflected by the numbers and kinds of decisions made by the lower levels of management.

References and Additional Readings

[1] Harold Koontz and Cyril O'Donnell, *Management: A Systems and Contingency Analysis of Managerial Functions,* 6th ed. (New York: McGraw-Hill, 1976), p. 274.

[2] Chester L. Barnard, *Functions of the Executive* (Cambridge, Mass.: Harvard University Press, 1938), pp. 114–15.

[3] Adam Smith, *The Wealth of Nations* (New York: Modern Library, 1917) (originally published in 1776).

[4] Mary Parker Follett, *Freedom and Co-Ordination* (London: Management Publication Trust, 1949), pp. 1–15 (the lecture reproduced in *Freedom and Co-Ordination* was first delivered in 1926); Barnard, *Functions,* p. 163.

[5] Thomas J. Peters and Robert H. Waterman, Jr., *In Search of Excellence* (New York: Harper & Row, 1982), pp. 14, 156–99.

[6] Robert Townsend, *Further up the Organization* (New York: Alfred A. Knopf, 1984), p. 50.

[7] William H. Newman, *Administrative Action,* 2d ed. (Englewood Cliffs, N.J.: Prentice-Hall, 1963), pp. 185–86.

[8] The Holy Bible, Revised Standard Version, Matthew 6:24.

[9] L. F. Urwick, *The Elements of Administration* (New York: Harper & Row, 1943), p. 46.

[10] Henri Fayol, *General and Industrial Management* (London: Sir Isaac Pitman & Sons, 1949), p. 36 (first published in 1916).

[11] Sir Ian Hamilton, *The Soul and Body of an Army* (London: Edward Arnold, 1921), p. 229.

[12] V. A. Graicunas, "Relationship in Organization," *Bulletin of the International Management Institute* (Geneva: International Labour Office, 1933), reprinted in *Papers on the Science of Administration,* ed. L. Gulick and F. L. Urwick (New York: Institute of Public Administration, 1937), pp. 181–87.

[13] L. F. Urwick, "Scientific Principles and Organizations," *Institute of Management Series No. 19* (New York: American Management Association, 1938), p. 8.

[14] For a brief discussion of such situations, see Leslie W. Rue, "Supervisory Control in Modern Management," *Atlanta Economic Review,* January–February 1975, pp. 43–44.

[15] L. F. Urwick, "V. A. Graicunas and the Span of Control," *Academy of Management Journal,* June 1974, p. 352.

Review Questions

1. What is an organization? Define the management function of organizing. Define organizational structure. What is an informal organization?
2. Discuss the reasons for organizing.
3. What is the difference between horizontal and vertical divison of labor? What is the difference between job scope and job depth?
4. Define authority, power, and responsibility.
5. Discuss two approaches to viewing the sources of authority.
6. What is the parity principle?

*[handwritten: 1. assign duties
2. grant permission to make commitments
3. create respon. w/ empl.]*

7. Describe three components of the delegation process.

8. Why are many managers reluctant to delegate authority? *[handwritten: power, easier to do than teach, not comf. w/ subordinates, etc.]*

9. What is the unity-of-command principle? *[handwritten: 1 superv.]*

10. What is the scalar principle? *[handwritten: authority flows thru chain-of-command; high to low]*

11. What is the span of management? *[handwritten: ratio between superv: empl.]*

12. What is the exception principle? *[handwritten: mgrs. should not deal w/ routine]*

13. What is the difference between a highly centralized and a highly decentralized organization? *[handwritten: ∇ ⊔]*

Discussion Questions

1. Do you think that division of labor has been emphasized too much in today's highly mechanized and efficient society?

2. Comment on the following statement, which is attributed to Robert Heinlein:

   A human being should be able to change a diaper, plan an invasion, butcher a hog, conn a ship, design a building, write a sonnet, balance accounts, build a wall, set a bone, comfort the dying, take orders, give orders, cooperate, act alone, solve equations, analyze new problems, pitch manure, program a computer, cook a tasty meal, fight efficiently, die gallantly. Specialization is for insects.

3. The Que Company has 712 employees and annual sales of $11.2 million. The entire company is located in one office building on Main Street. Based on this information, what can you say about the degree of centralization of authority in this organization?

4. As a manager, do you think you would prefer a relatively large (more than seven) or small (seven or less) span of management? Why, and what are the implications of your choice?

Incident 8–1
Taking Over Dad's Business

Casey Ice Company had been in operation for over 50 years manufacturing ice for all purposes, ranging from crushed ice for sale in convenience stores to 300-pound block ice for industrial use. As with all seasonal industries, the company's daily operations were in a state of flux, with long hours of work required during the busy season. The company employed anywhere from 75 to 125 people ranging from unskilled labor to sales and supervisory personnel.

Mr. Albert had managed the plant for the past 30 years, ever since he had purchased it from an old friend. He performed all of the jobs in the plant, working right along with the workers and spending very little time in the office looking at "those figures and crazy ideas that have no business in an ice plant." Mr. Albert's philosophy was aptly described by his frequently made observation that "this is an old-fashioned business, and we're going to run it in an old-fashioned way." Mr. Albert's words were law. That he knew everything there was to know about making ice could not be disputed. He used his expertise and position to run all aspects of the operation, trusting few if any of the other employees. Recently he had fired Ben Porter on the spot for "laying out" on Labor Day. Ben tried to explain that he had worked 33 days straight with no time off and, further, that his supervisor had given him permission to take the day off. But his explanation was to no avail. Mr. Albert simply stated that no supervisor had the authority to give him the day off.

Two months ago, Mr. Albert suffered a heart attack and died while loading a truck with ice. His daughter, Christie, who had been living on the West Coast, had been considering going into business for herself for some time and was now considering the possibility of replacing her father. She hadn't been home much during the past few years, as she had been busy pursuing her own career in advertising. But she remembered how much the company had meant to her father and felt somewhat obligated to carry on and expand his organization.

In October, Christie arrived at the Casey Ice Company, walked in the door, and saw a sign posted on the wall directly in front of her: "We got one rule—do what you're told." It had been a long time since she'd walked through that door, but she knew she'd never seen the sign before. Tearing it down, she proceeded to walk through the plant talking to the employees and supervisors.

The situation was bordering on chaos; nobody seemed to be working. As the day progressed, she learned that nobody really knew what they were supposed to do. "Mr. Albert had always assigned the jobs first thing each morning" was the most common answer she received when asking what was going on. Absenteeism and tardiness were major problems; there were no policies, procedures, or rules for her to refer to. When she tried to get information from the supervisors, she learned that her father hadn't really used supervisors as subordinates who directed the work force.

Christie retreated to the office for the rest of the day to study the records regarding company operations. The investigation proved even more alarming than her conversation with the employees. Her father had kept all the books with the help of an old friend who was a CPA. It took some time to decipher the meaning behind the figures she found.

The annual turnover rate averaged about 75 percent over the past five years, which explained why the daily work log revealed that many employees spent a substantial part of their time training new employees. The financial statements revealed that the company had lost a considerable amount of money due to decreasing sales over the past two years. In fact, sales for last year were down $327,000 from the previous year. On the other hand, Christie knew that the Casey Ice Company was the only large ice company in the major metropolitan area (550,000 population). She later learned that many vendors, dissatisfied with late deliveries and even forgotten deliveries, discontinued buying ice from Casey and purchased ice machines. Further, one employee of Casey revealed to Christie that during the July 4 ice shortage last year, Casey Ice Company's prices rose 100 percent for a two-week period because Mr. Albert believed "if they want it bad enough, they'll pay for it." This, the employee suggested, resulted in even more vendors discontinuing use of the company's services.

The records also revealed a significant problem existed in the industrial market for ice. Casey Ice Company once served a large number of industrial users; in fact, over half of Casey's customers used to be industrial users. However, the number of industrial users had gradually dwindled over the years. Today, industrial ice services comprised a little under 12 percent of the total business.

Christie sat back in the leather chair, resting her feet on the desk. Her father had been so proud of Casey Ice Company. None of this made any sense—how could he have let things get into such a state? But more importantly, what could she do to get things moving again?

Questions

1. What can Christie do to straighten things out?
2. What principles of organization have been violated?

Incident 8–2
The Vacation Request

Tom Blair has a week's vacation coming and really wants to take it the third week in May, which is the height of the bass fishing season. The only problem is that two of the other five members of his department have already requested and received approval from their boss, Luther Jones, to take off that same week. Afraid that Luther would not approve his request, Tom decided to forward his request directly to Harry Jensen, who is Luther's boss and who is rather friendly to Tom (Tom has taken Harry fishing on several occasions). Not realizing that Luther has not seen the request, Harry approves it. Several weeks pass before Luther finds out, by accident, that Tom has been approved to go on vacation the third week of May.

The thing that really "bugs" Luther is that this is only one of many instances in which his subordinates have gone directly to Harry and gotten permission to do something. Just last week, in fact, he overhead a conversation in the washroom to the effect that "if you want anything approved, don't waste time with Luther, go directly to Harry."

Questions

1. What should Harry have done?
2. Who is at fault, Harry or Tom?
3. Suppose Luther confronts Harry with the problem and he simply brushes it off by saying that he is really only helping?

Exercise
Minor Errors

Recently you have noticed that one of the staff members on the same level as your boss has been giving you a hard time concerning reports that you submit to him. Having reviewed recent reports, you have discovered a few minor errors that you should have caught; but in your opinion, they are not significant enough to warrant the kind of criticism you've been receiving.

Your boss and this particular manager have a history of bad relations, which may be one reason for his attitude and actions.

As you think about how to best handle the situation, you consider these alternatives:

1. Talk to the manager in private and ask him why he is being so critical.
2. Do nothing. It is probably a temporary situation; to bring undue attention to it will only make matters worse.
3. Since your boss may get involved, discuss it with him and ask advice on what to do.
4. Simply work harder to upgrade the reports; make sure there will be nothing to criticze in the future.
5. Discuss it with your boss, but minimize or "play down" the situation by letting him know that you feel that constructive criticism of this type is usually healthy.

Other alternatives may be open to you, but assume that these are the only ones you have considered.

A. WITHOUT DISCUSSION with anyone, decide which of these approaches you would take now. Be prepared to defend your choice.
B. What principle of organization most closely relates to this situation?
C. To what extent do you think this is an organization problem as opposed to a personality problem?

Organization Structures

Chapter Outline

DEPARTMENTATION
  Functional
  Product
  Geographic
  Customer
  Other Types
LINE STRUCTURE
LINE AND STAFF STRUCTURE
  Line and Staff Conflict
MATRIX STRUCTURE
FLAT VERSUS TALL
  STRUCTURES
COMMITTEES

  Advantages
  Disadvantages
  Effectively Using Committees
  Boards of Directors
WHAT DETERMINES THE BEST
  STRUCTURE?
  Organization and Environment
  Organization and Technology
  Organization and National
    Culture
SIMPLE FORM, LEAN STAFF
A CONTINGENCY APPROACH
SUMMARY

One man draws out the wire, another straightens it, and a third cuts it, a fourth points it, a fifth grinds it at the top for receiving the head; to make the head requires two or three distinct operations; to put it on is a peculiar business, to whiten the pins is another; it is even a trade by itself to put them into the paper, and the important business of making a pin is, in this manner, divided into 18 distinct operations, which, in some manufactory, are all performed by distinct hands; though in others the same man will sometimes perform two or three of them. I have seen a small manufactory of this kind where 10 men only were employed and where some of them consequently performed two or three distinct operations. But though they were very poor and therefore but indifferently accommodated with the necessary machinery, they could, when they exerted themselves, make among them about 12 pounds of pins a day.

Adam Smith *

Chapter 8 discussed the basic organizational concepts of division of labor and the establishment of appropriate authority relationships. Authority relationships must be fused together in such a manner as to form an organizational structure which aids in the accomplishment of organizational objectives.

Many people believe that a good manager or a good employee should be able to perform well regardless of the organization structure and environment. The belief is that if managers or employees are good enough, then they can overcome any obstacles the organization structure might present. Others believe that given the right organization structure, anyone should be able to perform in an acceptable fashion. The truth lies somewhere in between. An appropriate **organization structure** certainly helps to achieve good performance.

Organization structure—framework that defines the boundaries of the formal organization and within which the organization operates.

DEPARTMENTATION

While thousands of different organization structures exist, almost all are built on the concept of departmentation. **Departmentation** involves grouping activities into related work units. The work units may be related on the basis of work functions, product, customer, geography, technique, or time.

Departmentation—grouping activities into related work units.

---

* Adam Smith, *An Inquiry into the Nature and Causes of the Wealth of Nations,* vol. 1 (London: A. Strahan and T. Cadell, 1776), pp. 7–8.

Functional

Functional departmentation occurs when organization units are defined by the nature of the work. Although different terms may be used, most organizations have three basic functions—production, sales, and finance. Production refers to the actual creation of something of value, either goods or services or both. The distribution of goods or services created is usually referred to as sales or marketing. Finally, any organization, manufacturing or service, must provide the financial structure necessary for carrying out its activities.

Each of these basic functions may be broken down as necessary. For instance, the production department may be split into maintenance, quality control, engineering, manufacturing, and so on. The marketing department may be grouped into advertising, sales, and market research. (Figure 9–1 charts a typical functional departmentation.)

The primary advantage of functional departmentation is that it allows for specialization within functions. It also provides for efficient use of equipment and resources. Functional departmentation, however, can be accompanied by some negative effects. Members of a functional group may develop

Functional departmentation—organizational units are defined by the nature of the work.

FIGURE 9–1
Functional Departmentation

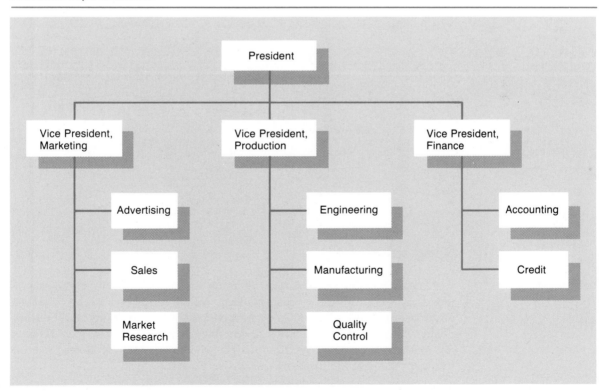

more loyalty to the functional group's goals than to the organization's goals. If the group's goals and the organization's goals are not mutually supportive, such activity can lead to problems. Conflict may also develop between different departments striving for different goals. This type of conflict is discussed in greater depth in Chapter 16.

Product

Product departmentation—all activities necessary to produce and market a product or service are under one manager.

Under **departmentation by product** or service, all the activities needed to produce and market a product or service are usually under a single manager. This system allows workers to identify with a particular product and thus develop esprit de corps. It also facilitates managing each product as a distinct profit center. Product departmentation provides opportunities for training for executive personnel by letting them experience a broad range of functional activities. Problems can arise if departments become overly competitive to the detriment of the overall organization. A second potential problem is that facilities and equipment may have to be duplicated. Product departmentation adapts best to large, multiproduct organizations. Figure 9–2 illustrates product departmentation at the Allied Corporation.

FIGURE 9–2
Product Departmentation

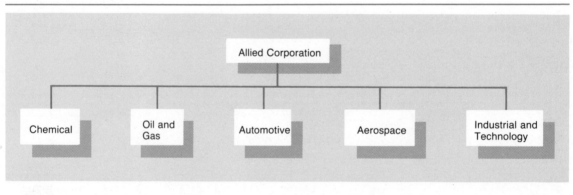

Geographic

Geographic departmentation—organizational units are defined by territories.

Geographic departmentation is most likely to occur in organizations which maintain physically dispersed and autonomous operations or offices. Departmentation by territories permits the use of local workers and/or salespeople. This can create customer goodwill and an awareness of local feelings and desires. It can also provide a high level of service. Of course, having too many geographic locations can be very costly.

Customer

Another type, **customer departmentation,** is based on division by customers served. A common example is an organization which has one department to handle retail customers and one to handle wholesale or industrial customers. (Figure 9–3 shows departmentation by customer for Johnson & Johnson.) This type of departmentation has the same advantages and disadvantages as product departmentation. For example, if the Professional Group and the Pharmaceutical Group in Figure 9–3 became too competitive with each other for corporate resources, the organization's overall performance could be damaged.

Customer departmentation–organizational units are based on division by customers served.

FIGURE 9–3
Customer Departmentation

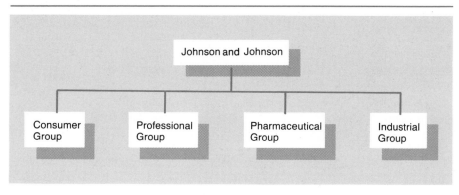

Other Types

Several other types of departmentation are possible. Departmentation by simple numbers is practiced when the most important ingredient to success is the number of workers. Organizing for a local United Way drive might be an example. Departmentation by process or equipment is another possibility. A final type of departmentation is by time or shift. Organizations that work around the clock may use this type of departmentation.

Departmentation is practiced not only for division of labor but also to improve control and communications. Typically, as an organization grows in size, it adds levels of departmentation. A small organization may have no departmentation at first. As it grows, it may departmentalize first by function, then by product, then by geography. As illustrated in Figure 9–4, many different department mixes are possible for a given organization. Which one is best depends on the specific situation. Management in Action 9–1 describes a recent reorganization at General Motors.

FIGURE 9–4
Possible Departmentation Mixes for a Sales Organization

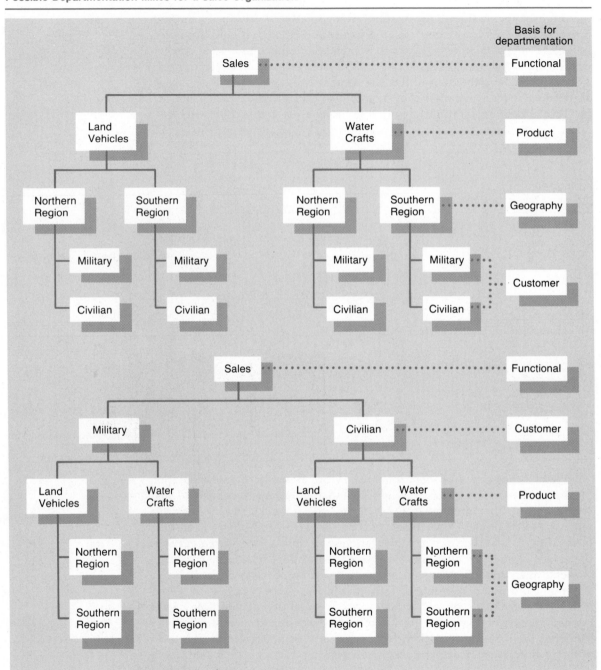

MANAGEMENT IN ACTION 9-1

GM's Reorganization

In January 1984, General Motors announced plans to reorganize operations. Over the next few years, the seven divisions of GM—Fisher Body, assembly, and the five car divisions—will be consolidated into two: a small-car division and a large-car division. According to GM chairman Roger Smith, the major reason for the reorganization is to enable GM to concentrate on the difference between small and large cars. Other benefits of the reorganization include reducing duplication of effort, improving communications, forcing decision making and responsibility to lower levels in the organization, and creating true profit centers.

Source: "GM Revamp Seeks to Solve Corporate Ills that Persist despite Rebound in Finances," *The Wall Street Journal,* January 12, 1984, p. 8.

LINE STRUCTURE

The most important aspect of the **line structure** is that the work of all organizational units is directly involved in producing and marketing the organization's goods or services. The simplest organization structure, it has vertical links between the different levels of the organization. All members of the organization receive instructions through the scalar chain. One advantage is a clear authority structure which promotes rapid decision making and prevents passing the buck or blaming someone else. A disadvantage is that it may force managers to perform too broad a range of duties. It may also cause the organization to become too dependent on one or two key persons who are capable of performing many duties. Because of its simplicity, line structure exists most frequently in small organizations. Figure 9–5 represents a simplified line structure.

Line structure–organization structure with direct vertical lines between the different levels of the organization.

FIGURE 9–5
A Simplified Line Structure

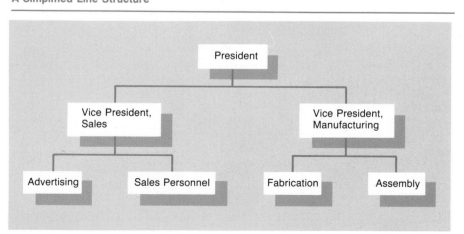

LINE AND STAFF STRUCTURE

Line and staff structure–organization structure that results when staff specialists are added to a line organization.

Staff functions–advisory and supportive in nature; designed to contribute to the efficiency and maintenance of the organization.

Line functions–functions and activities directly involved in producing and marketing the organization's goods or services.

The addition of staff specialists to a line-structured organization creates a **line and staff structure.** As a line organization grows in size, staff assistance often becomes necessary. **Staff functions** are advisory and supportive in nature; they contribute to the efficiency and maintenance of the organization. **Line functions** are directly involved in producing and marketing the organization's goods or services. They generally relate directly to the attainment of major organizational objectives, while staff functions contribute indirectly. Staff people are generally specialists in one field, and their authority is normally limited to that of making recommendations to line people. Typical staff functions include research and development, personnel management, employee training, and various "assistant to" positions. Figure 9–6 shows a simplified line and staff organization structure.

Line and Staff Conflict

The line and staff organization allows much more specialization and flexibility than the line organization; however it sometimes creates conflict. The potential problem of a line-staff conflict should not be taken lightly. A 1960s study by the American Management Association found that 41 out of 100 companies reported some form of line-staff conflict.[1] There is no reason to believe that this is any less of a problem today.

Some staff specialists resent the fact that they may be only advisors to line personnel and have no real authority over the line. At the same time, line managers, knowing that they have final responsibility for the product,

FIGURE 9–6
A Simplified Line and Staff Structure

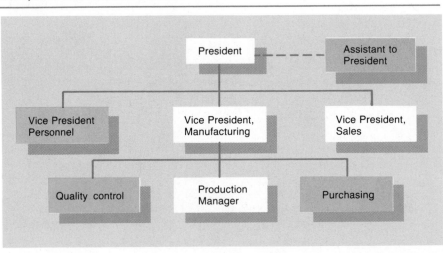

are often reluctant to listen to staff advice. Many staff specialists feel that they should not be in a position of having to sell their ideas to the line. They feel that the line managers should openly listen to their ideas. If the staff specialist is persistent, the line manager often resents even more the staff's "always trying to interfere and run my department." The staff specialist who does not persist often becomes discouraged because "no one ever listens."

Another factor in line and staff conflict is that line and staff personnel may be different in orientation and behavior. For example, line managers are often older, have worked their way up through the ranks, and do not have a college education.[2] Staff specialists usually are young and highly educated. Because they may lack line experience, they are often accused of not knowing anything about what the line does and therefore "living in ivory towers."

Reducing and ending line-staff conflict that is harming the organization depends on the building of mutual trust between line managers and staff. The first step in building this relationship is to develop a clear understanding of the lines of authority and the responsibilities of each group. If this is successful, each group should appreciate the fact that they can both maximize their performance only through cooperation.

In some organizations, staff specialists are encouraged to obtain some line experience by working on projects or committee assignments with line departments. With some experience in line management, staff specialists can better understand the problems facing the line managers that they work with and support. In other companies, corporate staff positions are occupied by line managers for a limited time period. For example, IBM fills most of its corporate staff positions with line managers who are rotated back to line jobs after a maximum of three years.[3]

MATRIX STRUCTURE

The matrix (also called project) form of organization has recently evolved; it is a way of forming project teams within the traditional line-staff organization. A project is "a combination of human and nonhuman resources pulled together in a temporary organization to achieve a specified purpose."[4] The marketing of a new product and the construction of a new building are examples of projects. Because projects have a temporary life, a method of managing and organizing them was sought so that the existing organization structure would not be totally disrupted and would maintain some efficiency.

Under the **matrix structure,** those working on a project are officially assigned to the project *and* to their original or base department. A manager is given the authority and responsibility for meeting the project objectives in terms of cost, quality, quantity, and time of completion. The project manager is then assigned the necessary personnel from the functional depart-

Matrix structure—hybrid organization structure in which individuals from different functional areas are assigned to work on a specific project or task.

ments of the parent organization. Thus, a horizontal-line organization develops for the project within the parent vertical-line structure. Under such a system, the functional personnel are assigned to and evaluated by the project manager while they work on the project. When the project or their work is done, the functional personnel return to their departments. Figure 9–7 shows a matrix structure.

FIGURE 9–7
Illustrative Matrix Structure

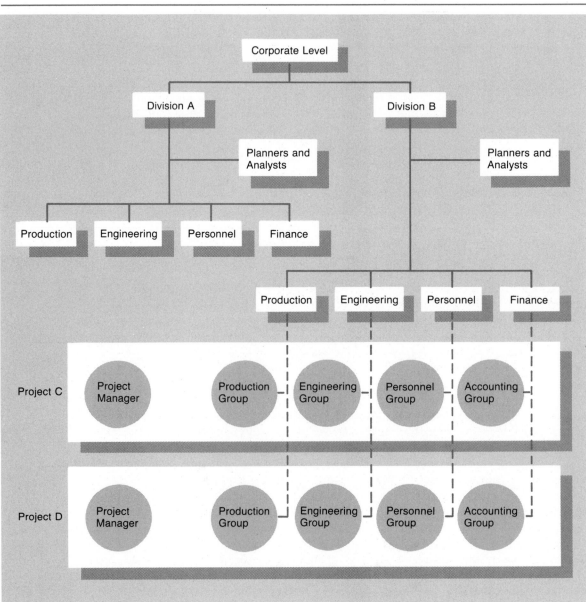

Source: David Cleland and William King, *Systems Analysis and Project Management*, 3d ed. (New York: McGraw-Hill, 1983), p. 279.

MANAGEMENT IN ACTION 9-2

Matrix Management at Dow Corning

Dow Corning has been practicing matrix management since 1972 and has found that bridging departmental barriers can frequently result in cost savings. For example, Dow Corning's Transportation and Physical Distribution Department reports to the vice president of material management and is responsible for goods following their scheduled release for shipment. Customer service reports to marketing and is responsible for overall service from order receipt until delivery. After the adaption of the matrix structure, customer service and traffic functions worked together as a project team to improve the coordination of services. Some results of the collaboration were a new generation of order-processing/shipping documents, modified terms of sale, and a new allocation of customer service representation—all of which combined to reduce order-filling times and costs.

Source: Jack W. Farrell, "Dow Corning Puts Matrix Management to Work," *Traffic Management,* October 1982, pp. 56–60.

A major advantage of matrix structure is that the mix of people and resources can readily be changed as project needs change. Other advantages include the emphasis placed on the project by use of a project team and the relative ease with which project members can move back into the functional organization once the project has ended.

One serious problem is that matrix structure can result in a violation of the principle of unity of command. A role conflict can develop if the authority of the project manager is not clearly delineated from that of the functional managers. In such a case, the people assigned to the project might receive conflicting assignments from their project manager and their functional managers. A second problem occurs when the personnel assigned to a project are still evaluated by their functional manager, who usually has little opportunity to observe their work on the project. Management in Action 9–2 describes how Dow Corning has successfully used a matrix structure in part of its organization.

FLAT VERSUS TALL STRUCTURES

Many studies have compared the desirability of flat structures versus tall structures. A **flat structure** has relatively few levels and relatively large spans of management at each level; a **tall structure** has many levels and relatively small spans of management (see Figure 9–8). A classic study in in this area was conducted by James Worthy.[5] Worthy studied the morale of over 100,000 employees at Sears, Roebuck & Co. during a 12-year period. His study noted that organizations with fewer levels and wider spans of management offer the potential for greater job satisfaction. A wide span of management also forces the manager to delegate authority and to develop more direct links of communication—another plus. Peters and Waterman emphasize that the number of middle-management levels is one of the big-

Flat structure– organization with few levels and relatively large spans of management at each level.

Tall structure– organization with many levels and relatively small spans of management.

FIGURE 9–8
Flat versus Tall Structures

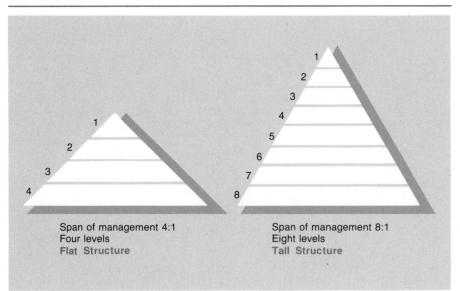

Span of management 4:1
Four levels
Flat Structure

Span of management 8:1
Eight levels
Tall Structure

gest contrasts between Japanese and American companies.[6] In general, the Japanese have far fewer middle managers and much flatter structures. For example, there are only 5 levels between the chairman and the first-line supervisor at Toyota; there are fifteen at Ford.

On the other hand, Carzo and Yanouzas found that groups operating in a tall structure had significantly better performance than those operating in a flat structure.[7] Other studies have also shown conflicting results. Therefore, one cannot conclude that all flat structures are better than all tall structures (or vice versa).[8] Recalling from Chapter 8 that the most appropriate span of management is dependent on several situational variables, this is exactly what one would expect to find. There are advantages and disadvantages associated with both flat and tall structures. Which is most appropriate depends on the specific situational variables. Management in Action 9–3 describes how Apple Computer has reduced the number of levels in its organization structure.

COMMITTEES

Committee—organization structure in which a group of people are formally appointed, organized, and superimposed on the line or line and staff structure to consider or decide certain matters.

A **committee** is a group of people formally appointed and organized to consider or decide certain matters. A form of matrix structure, they are superimposed on the existing line or line and staff structure. Committees can be permanent (standing) or temporary and are usually in charge of, or supplementary to, the line and staff functions.

A temporary, or ad hoc, committee is generally appointed to deal with

MANAGEMENT IN ACTION 9–3

Flat and Decentralized Apple Computer

Interestingly, Apple Computer took the opposite tack of Hewlett-Packard (see Management in Action 8–4). Before 1984, Apple was organized into five divisions with centralized manufacturing and marketing for all products. In 1984, Chief Executive Officer John Scully created two decentralized divisions organized around the company's two major products.

Another very important element of Apple's organization structure is the minimum number of management layers. Apple's sales per employee ratio is an amazing $300,000 per employee. A computer company of comparable size, Intel Corporation, has a sales-to-employee ratio of $100,000 per employee.

Source: "Apple's New Crusade," *Business Week*, November 26, 1984, pp. 146–56.

a specific problem or problems; it studies the problem, makes its recommendations, and then is dissolved. The permanent, or standing, committee usually acts more in a purely advisory capacity to certain organizational units or managers. When committees have the authority to order rather than just recommend, they are called plural executive committees. Plural executive committee privileges are usually reserved for very high-level committees such as the board of directors.

Advantages

Committees have many of the same advantages as matrix structures. Primary advantages are:

1. The formation of a committee places emphasis on the problem.
2. Expertise can be drawn from many areas of the organization; thus, better solutions often result.
3. Group decisions are often better than individual decisions.
4. Committee members are often motivated by being involved.
5. Better coordination and communication often result because all affected parties can be represented.
6. Consolidation of authority from several areas of the organization exists to make decisions.

Disadvantages

Everyone has heard the old sayings "A committee is a collection of the unfit appointed by the unwilling to do the unnecessary" and "A camel is a horse invented by a committee." Committees can have many positive features; they can also have many drawbacks if not properly managed. Some potential drawbacks are:

1. They can be excessively time consuming and costly.
2. They tend to compromise when aggreement is not easily reached. Such compromise decisions are often mediocre in quality.
3. They can result in divided responsibility with no one feeling personally responsible.
4. They can result in a tyranny of the minority. For example, one very strong-minded and vocal member can often control the entire committee.

Effectively using Committees

Managers can do many things to avoid the pitfalls and increase the efficiency of a committee. The first step is to define clearly its functions, scope, and authority. Obviously, the members must know the purpose of the committee to be effective. If it is a temporary committee, the members should be informed of its expected duration. This will help avoid prolonging the life of the committee unnecessarily.

In addition, careful thought should go into the selection of the committee members and chairperson. Size is always an important variable; generally, committees become more inefficient as they grow in size. A good rule of thumb is to use the smallest group necessary to get the job done. It is more important to select capable members than representative members. It is also important to pick members from the same approximate organizational level. Members from higher levels may inhibit the actions and participation of the other members. Figure 9–9 lists several methods for selecting commit-

FIGURE 9–9
Methods of Selecting Committees

Method	Advantages/Disadvantages
Appointment of chairperson and members.	Promotes sense of responsibility for all. May result in most capable members. Members may not work well together.
Appointment of chairperson who chooses members.	Will probably get along well. Lack of sense of responsibility by members. May not be most capable or representative.
Appointment of members who elect chairperson.	Lack of sense of responsibility by chairperson. May not choose best chairperson for the job. Election of chairperson may lead to split in the committee.
Volunteers.	Will get those who have greatest interest in the outcome (or those who are the least busy). Lack of responsibility. Potential is great for splits among members of the committee.

tee members and chairpeople and outlines good and bad points for each method.

Once a committee has been properly set up, there are other things a manager can do to ensure that it functions effectively. The manager should encourage participation from all members. All too often, one or two members do 90 percent of the work. Because much committee work involves meetings, emphasis should be placed by the chairperson on the conduct of all committee meetings. Each meeting should be carefully planned, with an agenda sent out in advance. This helps the members prepare for the meeting; they can also see that the meeting is not going to be a waste of time. It is equally important to stick to the agenda and not run the meeting past the allotted time. Once the meeting is in progress, careful minutes should cover the major points and recommendations. These minutes should be given to all committee members at a later date. The committee chairperson should design a reporting system to ensure that all follow-up actions are taken. Finally, the committee should periodically reevaluate the need for the committee.

Boards of Directors

A board of directors is, in reality, a type of committee that is responsible for reviewing the major policy and strategy decisions proposed by top management. Although most boards restrict their inputs to the policy and strategy level and do not participate in the day-to-day operation of the organization, their degree of involvement varies widely from board to board. Boards are used strictly as figureheads in some organizations, contributing little to the organization. However, because of the potential contribution that the board can make, its members should be carefully chosen. Directors do not necessarily need to own stock; they should be chosen primarily for what they can and will contribute to the organization. Usually boards of directors are paid a nominal fee for their services. Recent lawsuits against boards of directors concerning their liabilities regarding the day-to-day operation of the organization have increased the risks of serving on boards. (See Management in Action 9–4.) Thus, boards are becoming more active than they have been in the past. Moreover, some people now require liability insurance coverage before they will serve on a board of directors. Management in Action 9–5 shows that boards of directors do not always agree with top management.

WHAT DETERMINES THE BEST STRUCTURE?

Managers have often wondered just how their organization should be structured. Many factors have been studied to determine whether or not they influence the appropriateness of organization structure. The immediate environment in which the organization operates and the technology em-

MANAGEMENT IN ACTION 9–4

Stockholder Sues Board of Directors

A Martin Marietta Corp. shareholder sued the company's directors, charging they breached their fiduciary duties to the company and its stockholders in their fight against Bendix Corporation's tender offer. The shareholder charged the defensive tender offer by Marietta directors was made to perpetuate themselves in office—it denied holders the right to sell their stock at advantageous prices.

Source: "Marietta Holder Sues Board over Its Defense Against Bendix Offer," *The Wall Street Journal*, January 11, 1983, p. 12.

ployed by the organization are two variables that have been closely examined.

Organization and Environment

A landmark study relating structure to environment was conducted by Tom Burns and G. M. Stalker in the United Kingdom.[9] By examining some 20 industrial firms—both in a dynamic, changing industry and in a more stable, established industry—Burns and Stalker focused on how a firm's pattern of organization was related to certain qualities of the external environment. They identified two distinct organizational systems. "Mechanistic systems" have rigidly set functional duties, precise job descriptions, fixed authority, and responsibility and a well-developed organizational hierarchy through which information filters up and instructions flow down. "Organic systems" are characterized by less formal job descriptions, greater emphasis on adaptability, more participation, and less fixed authority. Burns and Stalker found that successful firms in stable and established industries tended to be mechanistic in structure. Successful firms in dynamic and changing industries tended to be organic in structure.

Paul Lawrence and Jay Lorsch conducted a later study of organizational structure and its environment.[10] Their study included 10 firms in three distinct industrial environments. Reaching conclusions similar to Burns and Stalker's, Lawrence and Lorsch found that in order to be successful, firms operating in a dynamic environment needed a relatively flexible structure; firms operating in a stable environment needed a more rigid structure; and firms operating in an intermediate environment needed a structure somewhere between the two extremes.[11]

Several other studies investigating the relationship between organization structure and environment have been conducted in the recent past.[12] In general, most have concluded that the best organization structure for a given situation depends somewhat on the conditions of the organization's environment.

MANAGEMENT IN ACTION 9–5

Board and CEOs Disagree on Merger Plans

In January 1985, Occidental Petroleum Corporation and Diamond Shamrock Corporation announced plans to merge. The merger was to involve a one-for-one stock exchange and the creation of a new holding company with Occidental's chairman Armand Hammer as the new chairman and chief executive officer. Diamond Shamrock's chairman and chief executive officer William Bricker and Armand Hammer had agreed to the merger and thought both boards would support it. However, when each board met to vote on the merger, there was very little support. Occidental's board reluctantly accepted the proposal over the adamant objections of two directors. Diamond Shamrock directors rejected the proposal unanimously. Within a few days of the initial announcement, all merger plans were cancelled.

Source: "Occidental, Diamond Shamrock Cancel Merger Plan Hours after Announcing It." *The Wall Street Journal*, January 8, 1985; "Diamond Shamrock Chief Says Concern Isn't for Sale but Notes Vulnerability," *The Wall Street Journal*, January 9, 1985.

Organization and Technology

Numerous studies have also explored potential relationships between technology and organizational structure. One of the most important was conducted by Joan Woodward in the late 1950s.[13] Her study analyzed 100 manufacturing firms in the southeast Essex area of England. She classified them along a scale of "technical complexity" with special emphasis on three modes of production: (1) unit or small-batch production (e.g., custom-made machines); (2) large-batch or mass production (e.g., an automotive assembly plant); and (3) continuous flow or process production (e.g., a chemical plant). The unit or small-batch production mode represents the lower end of the technical complexity scale, while the continuous flow mode represents the upper end.

After putting each firm into one of the above modes, Woodward investigated a number of organizational variables. Some of her findings are:

1. The number of levels in an organization increased as technical complexity increased.

2. The ratio of managers and supervisors to total personnel increased as technical complexity increased.

3. Using Burns and Stalker's definition of organic and mechanistic systems, organic management systems tended to predominate in firms at both ends of the scale of technical complexity, while mechanistic systems predominated in firms falling in the middle ranges.

4. No significant relationship existed between technical complexity and organizational size.

A similar study was done a few years later by Edward Harvey.[14] Rather than use Woodward's technical complexity scale, Harvey grouped firms along a continuum from technical diffuseness to technical specificity. Technically diffused firms have a wider range of products, produce products that vary from year to year, and produce more made-to-order products. Harvey's findings were similar to Woodward's: He found significant relationships between technology and several organizational characteristics.

The general conclusion reached in these studies was that a relationship was present between organizational technology and a number of aspects of organizational structure. Many additional studies have investigated the relationship between technology and structure.[15] Despite some conflicting results, most studies have found a relationship between technology and structure. And most researchers suggest that technology per se determines structure.

Organization and National Culture

As more and more organizations have become international, the importance of dealing with cultural differences has become evident. The study of organization structure as it relates to national culture is still in its infancy; but there is evidence that certain structures better fit a given national culture than others.[16] For example, studies have shown that the British have a high regard for the rights of the individual against collective power, whereas the West Germans subordinate the individual to the collective.[17] This difference is reflected in the fact that British organizations tend to be less centralized than do German organizations. Realizing that many cultural differences do exist between and among different countries, multinational companies should adapt their stuctures, where possible, to the local culture and values.

SIMPLE FORM, LEAN STAFF

As an organization grows and has success, it tends to evolve into a more and more complex structure. Just how this takes place varies; frequently, a major cause is an increase in staff positions, especially at high levels. Many managers seem to feel a need for more staff and a more complex structure as the organization grows. They seem inclined to equate staff size with success.

In their observations, Peters and Waterman found that many of the best-performing companies had managed to maintain a simple structure with a small staff (see Figure 9–10).[18] One reason for this is that a simple form with a lean staff better allows an organization to adjust to a fast-changing environment. A simple form with a lean staff is also conducive to innovation. A simple form and a lean staff are naturally intertwined, in that one breeds the other: A simple form requires fewer staff, and a lean staff results in a simple form.

FIGURE 9–10
Example of Companies with Lean Staffs

- Emerson Electric has 54,000 employees and fewer than 100 in its corporate headquarters.
- Dana employs 35,000 and reduced its corporate staff from about 500 in 1970 to around 100 in 1982.
- Schlumberger, the $6 billion diversified oil service company, has a corporate staff of 90.
- Intel, which enjoys $1 billion in sales has virtually no staff; temporary staff assignments are given to line officers.
- ROLM manages a $200 million business with about 15 people in the corporate headquarters.

Source: Thomas J. Peters and Robert H. Waterman, Jr., *In Search of Excellence* (New York: Harper & Row, 1982), pp. 311–12.

Peters and Waterman outline four characteristics or practices that enable organizations to maintain a simple form and a lean staff:[19]

1. Extraordinary devisional integrity. Each division has its own functional areas, including product development, finance, and personnel.

2. Continual formation of new divisions and rewards for this practice.

3. A set of guidelines which determine when a new product or product line will become an independent division.

4. Moving people and even products among divisions on a regular basis without causing disruption.

Peters and Waterman postulate that the successful organizations of the future will be variations of the simple, divisionalized line and staff structure and that they will have the above characteristics.

A CONTINGENCY APPROACH

Even if one accepts the merits of a simple form with a lean staff (as discussed in the last section), there is no one structure suitable for all situations. The most appropriate organization structure depends upon organizational objectives, the technology employed, the rate of change in the environment, the culture, and many other dynamic forces.

The knowledge that there is no one best way to organize—the design is conditional—has led to a **contingency (situational) approach** to organizing. In their study dealing with organization structure and environment, Lawrence and Lorsch concluded that different organizations in different environments require different kinds of organization structures at various stages in their growth.[20] Figure 9–11 depicts many of the variables that can have an impact on what is the most appropriate organization structure.

Contingency approach–states that the most appropriate organization structure depends on the technology used, the rate of change in the environment, and other dynamic forces.

FIGURE 9–11
Variables Affecting Appropriate Organization Structure

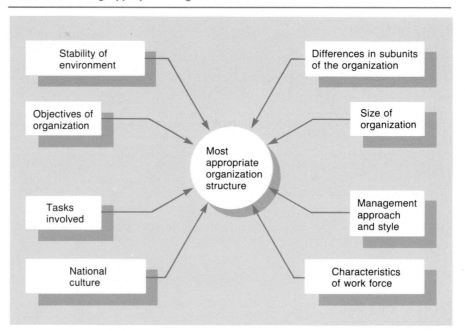

Once management adopts a contingency view, it will begin to thoroughly analyze the relevant variables and then choose the appropriate structure; it is essentially a matching process. Because each of the interacting forces is dynamic, top management should periodically analyze and appraise their structure in light of any relevant changes.

SUMMARY

The organization structure forms the framework within which the organization operates. An appropriate structure helps performance. While thousands of different organization structures exist, almost all are built on the concept of departmentation. This refers to the grouping of activities into related work units. The work units may be related on the basis of work function, product, customer, geography, or time.

The line structure is the simplest organization structure. It has direct vertical links between the different levels. The addition of staff specialists to a line structure creates a line and staff structure. Line functions are functions directly involved in the production and marketing of the organization's goods or services; staff functions are advisory and supportive in nature and are designed to contribute to the efficiency and maintenance of the line organization. A line and staff structure creates the potential for conflict. One of the major reasons for this is that staff specialists have no direct authority over the line personnel—they must persuade the line personnel to implement their ideas. Also, line and staff personnel often have different personal characteristics and backgrounds, and this can cause problems.

The matrix structure has recently evolved as a way of forming project teams within the traditional line-staff organization. Committees are a form of matrix structure in that they are superimposed on the existing line and staff structure. A committee is a group of people formally appointed and organized to consider or decide certain matters. Several advantages and disadvantages of committees were outlined. In addition, several steps were suggested for effective use of committees. A board of directors is, in reality, a type of committee; it is responsible for reviewing the major policy and strategy decisions proposed by top management.

Most studies conducted on the relationship between organization structure and environment have concluded that the best organization structure depends to some degree on the conditions of the organization's environment. Several studies have also found a relationship between technology and structure. Most researchers suggest that technology per se determines structure.

In their observations of excellent companies, Peters and Waterman identified simple form and lean staff as characteristics of successful companies. They also postulate that these same characteristics will be prevalent in the successful companies of the future.

In the contingency approach, the most appropriate organization structure depends not only on the organization's goals but also on the technology employed, the rate of change in the environment, the culture, and many other dynamic forces.

References and Additional Readings

[1] Ernest Dale, *Organization* (New York: American Management Association, 1962), p. 67.

[2] M. Dalton, "Conflict between Staff and Line Managerial Officers," *American Sociological Review,* June 1950, pp. 342–51; James A. Belasco and Joseph A. Alutto, "Line-Staff Conflicts: Some Empirical Insights," *Academy of Management Journal,* December 1969, p. 477.

[3] Thomas J. Peters and Robert W. Waterman, Jr., *In Search of Excellence* (New York: Harper & Row, 1982), p. 312.

[4] David Cleland and William King, *Systems Analysis and Project Management,* 3d ed. (New York: McGraw-Hill, 1983), p. 187.

[5] James Worthy, "Organization Structure and Employee Morale," *American Sociological Review* 15 (1956), pp. 169–79.

[6] Peters and Waterman, *In Search,* p. 313.

[7] Carzo Rocco, Jr., and John Yanouzas, "Effects of Flat and Tall Organization Structure," *Administrative Science Quarterly* 14 (1969), pp. 178–91.

[8] Dan R. Dalton, William D. Todor, Michael J. Spendolini, Gordon J. Fielding, and Lyman W. Porter, "Organization Structure and Performance: A Critical Review," *Academy of Management Review,* January 1980, pp. 49–54.

[9] Tom Burns and G. M. Stalker, *The Manage-

ment of Innovation (London: Tavistock Institute, 1962).

[10] Paul Lawrence and Jay Lorsch, "Differentiation and Integration in Complex Organizations," *Administrative Science Quarterly,* June 1967, pp. 1–47; Paul Lawrence and Jay Lorsch, *Organization and Environment* (Homewood, Ill.: Richard D. Irwin, 1969) (originally published in 1967 by Harvard University Graduate School of Business Administration, Division of Research).

[11] Ibid.

[12] For a review of these, see Mariann Jelinek, "Technology, Organizations, and Contingency," *Academy of Management Review,* January 1977, pp. 17–26; Peter H. Grinyer and Masoval Yasai-Ardekani, "Strategy, Structure, Size, and Bureaucracy," *Academy of Management Journal,* September 1981, pp. 471–86.

[13] Joan Woodward, *Industrial Organization: Theory and Practice* (London: Oxford University Press, 1965).

[14] Edward Harvey, "Technology and the Structure of Organizations," *American Sociological Review,* April 1968, pp. 247–59.

[15] For a summary, see David F. Gillespie and Dennis S. Mileti, "Technology and the Study of Organizations: An Overview and Appraisal," *Academy of Management Review,* January 1977, pp. 7–16; Louis Fry, "Technology-Structure Research: Three Critical Issues," *Academy of Management Journal,* September 1982, pp. 532–53.

[16] William I. Gorden, "Organizational Imperatives and Cultural Modifiers," *Business Horizons,* May–June 1984, pp. 76–83.

[17] John Child and Alfred Kiesar, "Organization and Managerial Roles in British and West German Companies: An Examination of the Cultural Free Thesis," in *Organizations Alike and Unlike,* eds. C. J. Lammers and D. L. Hickson (London: Routledge and Kegan Paul, 1979), pp. 25–271.

[18] Peters and Waterman, *In Search,* pp. 306–17.

[19] Ibid., p. 310.

[20] Lawrence and Lorsch, "Differentiation and Integration."

Review Questions

1. Describe:
   a. Functional departmentation.
   b. Product departmentation.
   c. Geographic departmentation.
   d. Customer departmentation.
2. What are line functions? What are staff functions?
3. Explain:
   a. Line structure.
   b. Line and staff structure.
   c. Matrix structure.
4. What factors contribute to the potential conflict between line and staff personnel in a line and staff organization? How can the potential for destructive conflict be reduced?
5. What are the advantages of a flat structure? What are the advantages of a tall structure?
6. What are the advantages associated with committees? What are the disadvantages? How can committees be made more effective?
7. Discuss the relationship between organization structure and environment.
8. Discuss the relationship between organization structure and the type of technology employed.
9. Describe four characteristics or practices than enable organizations to maintain a simple form and a lean staff.
10. What is the contingency approach to organizing?

Discussion Questions

1. How can you justify the use of a matrix structure, since it clearly violates the unity-of-command principle?

2. Do you think that the contingency approach to organizing is a useful concept that can be implemented, or is it really a cop-out?

3. Discuss this statement: "When the appropriate organization structure is determined, the firm no longer has to worry about structure."

4. How would you respond to the following statement: "There is no way to grow and keep the corporate staff small."

Incident 9-1
Who Dropped the Ball?

In October 1975, the Industrial Water Treatment Company (IWT) introduced KELATE, a new product that was 10 times more effective than other treatments in controlling scale buildup in boilers. The instantaneous demand for the new water treatment KELATE required that IWT double its number of service engineers within the following year.

The sudden expansion caused IWT to reorganize their operations. Previously, each district office had been headed by a district manager who was assisted by a chief engineer and two engineering supervisors. In 1976, this structure was changed. The district manager now had a chief engineer and a manager of operations. Four engineering supervisors (now designated as "group leaders") were established. They were to channel all work assignments through the manager of operations, while all engineering-related problems were to be handled by the chief engineer. Each group leader supervised 8 to 10 field service engineers (see Exhibit 1).

EXHIBIT 1
Partial Organizational Chart for IWT

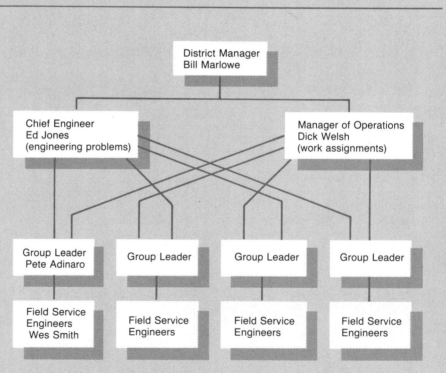

Bill Marlowe, district manager for the Southeast District, has just received a letter from an old and very large customer, Sel Tex, Inc. The letter revealed that when Sel Tex inspected one of their boilers last week, they found that the water treatment was not working properly. When they contacted IWT's service engineer for their area, Wes Smith, they were told "he was scheduled to be working in the Jacksonville area the rest of the week but would get someone else down there the next day." When no one showed up, Sel Tex was naturally upset—after all, they were only requesting the engineering service they had been promised.

Bill Marlowe, upset over the growing number of customer complaints that seemed to be crossing his desk in recent months, called Ed Jones, chief engineer; into his office and showed him the letter he had received from Sel Tex.

Ed: Why are you showing me this? This is a work assignment foul-up.

Bill: Do you know anything about this unsatisfactory condition?

Ed: Sure, Wes called me immediately after he found out. Their concentration of KELATE must have gone up, since they're getting corrosion and oxygen on their tubes. I told Peter Adinaro, Wes's group leader, about it, and I suggested he schedule someone to visit Sel Tex.

Bill: OK, Ed, thanks for your help. [*Bill then calls Peter Adinaro into his office.*]

Bill: Peter, two weeks ago Ed asked you to assign someone to visit Sel Tex because of a tube corrosion problem they are having. Do you remember?

Peter: Oh sure! As usual, Wes Smith called Ed instead of me. I left a message for Dick to assign someone there because my whole group was tied up and I couldn't spare anyone. I thought Dick would ask another group leader to assign someone to check it out.

Bill: Well, thanks for your help. Tell Dick to come on in here for a second.

Dick Welsh, manager of operations, came into Bill's office about 20 minutes later.

Bill: Dick, here's a letter from Sel Tex. Please read it and tell me what you know about the situation.

Dick: [*After reading the letter.*] Bill, I didn't know anything about this.

Bill: I checked with Pete, Wes's group leader, and he tells me he left a message for you to assign someone since his group was all tied up. Didn't you get the message?

Dick: Have you taken a look at my desk lately? I'm flooded with messages. Heck, I'm the greatest message handler of all times. If I could schedule my people without having all the engineering headaches unloaded on me, I wouldn't have all these messages. Sure, it's possible that he left a message but I haven't seen it. I will look for it though. Anyway, that letter sounds to me like they've got an engineering problem, and Ed should contact them to solve it.

Bill: I'll write Sel Tex myself and try to explain the situation to them. You and I will have to get together this afternoon and talk over some of these difficulties. See you later, Dick.

Questions

1. What are the problems that Bill Marlowe faces?
2. Are the problems related to the way IWT is organized or are they related to the employees?
3. How could these problems be resolved?

Incident 9–2
A New Organizational Structure

Yesterday, Tom Andrews was officially promoted to his new job as hospital administrator for Cobb General Hospital. Cobb General is a 600-bed hospital located in a suburban area of New Orleans. Tom is extremely excited about the promotion; at the same time, he has some serious doubts about it.

Tom has worked at Cobb General for three years as the associate administrator of the hospital. Although that was his official job title, he was really more of a "gofer" for the former administrator, Bill Collins. Because of his educational background (which includes a master of hospital administration degree) and his enthusiasm, Tom was offered the administrator's job last week after the hospital's board of directors had asked for Bill Collins' resignation.

Tom was now looking at the organization chart for the hospital, which had been pieced together over the years by Bill Collins (see Exhibit 1). In reality, each time a new unit had been added or a new function started, Bill merely had the person report directly to him. Tom is worried about his ability to handle all of the people that are currently reporting to him in his new position.

Questions

1. Do you agree with Tom's concern? Why?
2. How would you redraw the organizational chart?

EXHIBIT 1
Organizational Structure—Cobb General Hospital

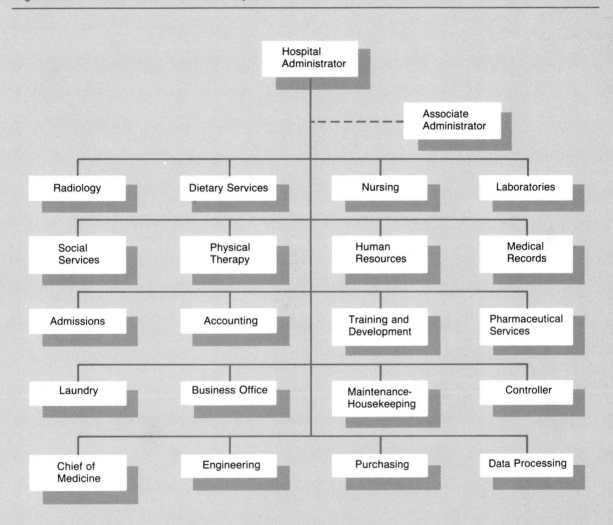

Exercise
Organize

Suppose you have just been hired as the vice president in charge of sales for COMBO Enterprise, Inc. COMBO manufactures, sells, and distributes both land and water vehicles. The land vehicles are bicycles powered by a two-horsepower, two-cycle engine. Basically, you have developed a method to adapt an off-the-shelf chain saw motor to a popular French-produced bicycle. The water vehicles use the same chain saw motor adapted to a standard canoe which is fitted with a special propeller and rudder.

The advantage over the available competition is that, due to the light weight of the motor being used, the bicycles and canoes can also be used manually with very little loss of efficiency as compared to nonmotorized bicycles and canoes. Your market surveys have shown that there is a large market for such a product.

COMBO serves both civilian and military markets for both the land and water vehicles.

Presently, COMBO has a plant in a medium-sized eastern city and one in a medium-sized western city. The eastern plant handles all business east of the Mississippi River, while the western plant handles business west of the Mississippi.

A. Design what you think would be the best way to organize the sales (marketing) division of the company.
B. Design an alternate structure for your division.
C. Why did you prefer one structure over the other?
D. Design a matrix structure (if you did not use one in A or B) for this situation. What would be the pros and cons of such a structure in this situation?

Staffing: Securing the Right People

Chapter Outline

"Whatever is in our future—people are the key to our success."

John P. Imlay, president
Management Science of America (MSA)*

Staffing–securing and developing human resources for the jobs created by the organizing function.

Staffing involves securing and developing human resources for the jobs which are created by the organizing function. The goal of staffing is to obtain the best available people for the organization and to develop the skills and abilities of those people. Obtaining the best available people generally involves forecasting human resource requirements and recruiting and selecting new employees. Developing the skills and abilities of an organization's employees involves employee development as well as the proper use of promotions, transfers, and separations. The staffing function is complicated by numerous government regulations. Furthermore, many of these regulations are subject to frequent change.

Unfortunately, many of the staffing activities have traditionally been conducted by human resource/personnel departments and have been considered relatively unimportant by line managers. However, securing and developing qualified personnel should be a major concern of all managers, as it involves the most valuable asset of an organization—human resources.

HUMAN RESOURCE PLANNING

Human resource (personnel) planning (HRP)–process of getting the right number of qualified people into the right job at the right time.

Human resource planning (HRP), also referred to as personnel planning, has been defined as the process of "getting the right number of qualified people into the right job at the right time."[1] Put another way, HRP is "the system of matching the supply of people—internally (existing employees) and externally (those to be hired or searched for)—with the openings the organization expects to have for a given time frame."[2]

HRP involves applying the basic planning process to the human resource needs of an organization. Once organizational plans are made and specific objectives set, the HRP process attempts to define the human resource needs to meet the organization's objectives.[3]

The first basic question addressed by the planning process—"Where are we now?"—is frequently answered in human resource planning by using job analyses and skills inventories.

---

* William P. Patterson, "Will the Lion Roar in 1984?" *Industry Week,* May 14, 1984, p. 62.

Job Analysis and Skills Inventory

Job analysis is the process of determining, through observation and study, the pertinent information relating to the nature of a specific job. The end products of a job analysis are a job description and a job specification. A **job description** is a written statement which identifies the tasks, duties, activities, and performance results required in a particular job. A **job specification** is a written statement which identifies the abilities, skills, traits, or attributes that are necessary for successful performance in a particular job. In general, it can be said that a job specification identifies the qualifications of an individual who could perform the job. Job analyses are frequently conducted by specialists from the human resource department. However, managers should have input into the final job descriptions for the jobs they are managing.

Through conducting job analyses, an organization defines its current human resource needs on the basis of current and/or newly created jobs. The purpose served by a **skills inventory** is to consolidate information about the organization's current human resources. The skills inventory contains basic information on all the employees of an organization, giving a comprehensive picture of the individual. Through analyzing the skills inventory, the organization can assess the current quantity and quality of its human resources.

Thomas Patten has outlined seven broad categories of information that may be included in a skills inventory:[4]

1. Personal data history: age, sex, marital status, etc.
2. Skills: education, job experience, training, etc.
3. Special qualifications: memberships in professional groups, special achievements, etc.
4. Salary and job history: present salary, past salary, dates of raises, various jobs held, etc.
5. Company data: benefit plan data, retirement information, seniority, etc.
6. Capacity of individual: scores on tests, health information, etc.
7. Special preferences of individual: location or job preferences, etc.

The popularity of computerized skills inventories has risen in recent years. Today, many large organizations such as IBM, RCA, and the U.S. Civil Service Commission have computerized skills inventory systems.[5] The primary advantage of a computerized skills inventory is that it offers a quick and accurate evaluation of the skills that are available within the organization. Combining the information provided by job analysis and the skills inventory enables the organization to evaluate the present status of its human resources.

Because the type of information required about management personnel sometimes differs from that required about nonmanagerial employees, some

Job analysis–process of determining, through observation and study, information relating to the nature of a specific job.

Job description–written statement that identifies the tasks, duties, activities, and performance results required in a particular job.

Job specification–written statement that identifies the abilities, skills, traits, or attributes necessary for a particular job

Skills inventory–contains basic information on all employees of an organization.

MANAGEMENT IN ACTION 10–1

Dun & Bradstreet's Computerized Management Inventory System (CMIS)

This system is intended to facilitate the transfer of managers among D & B's operating units. In using the system to select a particular person for a job, the user is asked a series of questions requiring only "yes/no" or "choose one" responses. Appropriate candidates for the job are identified by the computer, their names are produced, and long or short resumes are generated either on a screen or in hard copy.

Source: Adapted from Brian D. Dunn, "The Skills Inventory: A Second Generation," *Personnel*, September–October 1982, pp. 40–44.

organizations maintain a separate management inventory. In addition to biographical data, a management inventory often contains the following information: work experience, product knowledge, industrial experience, formal education, training courses, foreign language skills, relocation limitations, career interests, and performance appraisals. Management in Action 10–1 describes how Dun & Bradstreet uses a management inventory system.

In addition to appraising the current status of its human resources, anticipated changes in the current work force due to retirements, deaths, discharges, promotions, transfers, and resignations must be considered. Certain changes in personnel can be estimated accurately and easily, while other changes are not so easily forecast. Changes such as retirements can be forecast reasonably accurately from information in a skills inventory. Others, such as transfers and promotions, can be estimated by taking into account such factors as the ages of individuals in specific jobs and the requirements of the organization. Individuals with potential for promotion can and should be identified. Factors such as deaths, resignations, and discharges are much more difficult to predict. However, past experience and historical records can often provide helpful information in these areas. Planned training and development experiences should also be considered when evaluating anticipated changes.

Forecasting

Human resource forecasting–process that determines future human resource needs.

The second basic question addressed in the planning process is "Where does the organization want to go?" **Human resource forecasting** attempts to answer this question with regard to the organization's human resource needs. It is a process that attempts to determine the future human resource needs of the organization in light of the organization's objectives. Some of the many variables that are considered in forecasting human resource needs include sales projections, skills required in potential business ventures, composition of the present work force, technological changes, and general economic conditions. Due to the critical role human resources play in attaining organizational objectives, all levels of management should be involved in the forecasting process.

Human resource forecasting is presently conducted largely on the basis of intuition; the experience and judgment of the manager is used to determine future human resource needs. This assumes that all managers in the organization are aware of the future plans of the total organization. Unfortunately, this is not true in many cases. For instance, a decision to increase the number of sales representatives in an organization could very likely have human resource implications for all units of the organization. Ideally, an increase in the number of sales representatives would generate more sales, which would then require increased production and increased invoicing to customers. Then, the production and accounting departments would need to increase their human resources.

Various mathematical and statistical techniques are also used to project future personnel needs. A simple example of such a method is the use of sales forecasts to determine human resource needs.

Transition

The human resource forecast results in a statement of what the organization's human resource needs are in light of its plans and objectives. These human resource needs are referred to as aggregate human resource requirements. The skills inventory, management inventory, and job descriptions derived from job analyses define the current quantity and quality of the organization's human resources.

The final phase of human resource planning—the transition—is to determine how the organization can obtain the quantity and quality of human resources required to meet its objectives as reflected by the human resource forecast. The difference between the aggregate human resource requirements and the current level of human resources available to the organization is referred to as the net human resource requirements. The net human resource requirements may be either positive or negative.

The organization engages in several transitional activities in order to bring its current level of human resources in line with forecasted requirements. These activities include recruiting and selecting new employees, developing current and/or new employees, promoting or transferring employees, laying off employees, and discharging employees. Other factors that must be considered when determining how forecasted human resources will be attained include organizational policies on promotions, transfers, layoffs, and discharges. Generally, the coordination of these activities is delegated to a human resource or personnel department within the organization.

Legal Considerations

Government regulation now plays a vital role in human resource planning. Discriminatory personnel practices by many organizations led to this. Four significant government bills in this area are the Equal Pay Act of 1963; the Civil Rights Act of 1964; the Age Discrimination in Employment Act of 1968, as amended in 1978; and the Rehabilitation Act of 1973.

Equal Pay Act of 1963– effective in June 1964; prohibits wage discrimination on the basis of sex.

The **Equal Pay Act of 1963,** which became effective in June 1964, prohibits wage discrimination on the basis of sex. The law states: "No employer . . . shall . . . discriminate . . . between employees on the basis of sex by paying wages . . . at a rate less than the rate at which he pays wages to employees of the opposite sex . . . for equal work on jobs the performance of which requires equal skill, effort, and responsibility and which are performed under similar working conditions."[6]

Civil Rights Act of 1964– Title VII of this act was designed to eliminate employment discrimination based on race, color, religion, sex, or national origin in organizations that conduct interstate commerce.

Title VII of the Civil Rights Act of 1964 is designed to eliminate employment discrimination related to race, color, religion, sex, or national origin in organizations that conduct interstate commerce. The 1978 Civil Rights Act Amendment to Title VII prohibits discrimination in employment because of pregnancy, childbirth, or related medical conditions. The act as amended covers the following types of organizations:

1. All private employers of 15 or more people.
2. All educational institutions, public and private.
3. State and local governments.
4. Public and private employment agencies.
5. Labor unions with 15 or more members.
6. Joint labor-management committees for apprenticeship and training.

Equal employment opportunity–right of all people to work and advance on the basis of merit, ability, and potential.

The Civil Rights Act was passed by Congress to establish guidelines for ensuring equal employment opportunities for all people. **Equal employment opportunity** refers to the right of all people to work and to advance on the basis of merit, ability, and potential. One of the major focuses of equal employment opportunity efforts has been to identify and eliminate discriminatory employment practices. Such practices are any artificial, arbitrary, and unnecessary barriers to employment when the barriers operate to discriminate on the basis of sex, race, or other impermissible classification.

Two federal agencies—the Equal Employment Opportunity Commission (EEOC) and the Office of Federal Contract Compliance Programs (OFCCP)—have major responsibility for enforcing equal opportunity legislation. The EEOC was created by the Civil Rights Act. It investigates complaints of discrimination, develops guidelines to enforce the act, and takes legal action against organizations using discriminatory employment practices.

Actions required of organizations to remedy discrimination and effects of past discrimination are illustrated in the major agreement signed by AT&T

with EEOC and the Department of Labor after more than two years of litigation. This agreement's major provisions include:[7]

- Approximately $15 million in one-time payments to employees that suffered from discriminatory employment practices.

- An estimated $50 million in yearly payments from promotions and wage adjustments to female and minority employees.

- Specific hiring and promotion targets to increase utilization of women and minorities in every job classification.

- Goals for employing males in previously all-female jobs.

- Women and minorities in nonmanagement, noncraft jobs would be allowed to compete for craft jobs, based on their qualifications and company seniority.

- All female college graduates hired by the company since 1965 were to be assessed to determine their interest and potential for higher-level jobs, and a specific development program was to be implemented to prepare these women for promotions.

The OFCCP within the U.S. Department of Labor is responsible for ensuring equal employment opportunity among federal contractors and subcontractors, which includes most major businesses in the United States. A special clause in their contracts makes equal employment opportunity an integral part of their agreements. Women, minorities, members of religious and ethnic groups, handicapped persons, Vietnam veterans, and disabled veterans of all wars are protected by the equal opportunity requirements in federal government contracts.

The Age Discrimination in Employment Act went into effect on June 12, 1968. Initially, it was designed to protect individuals 40–65 years of age from discrimination in hiring, retention, compensation, and other conditions of employment. In 1978, the act was amended and coverage was extended to individuals up to age 70. Specifically, the act now forbids mandatory retirement at age 65 except in certain circumstances. The **Rehabilitation Act of 1973** prohibits discrimination in hiring of the handicapped by federal agencies and federal contractors.

Union contracts also influence human resource planning when they contain clauses regulating transfers, promotions, discharges, and so on.

Age Discrimination in Employment Act of 1968– amended in 1978; protects individuals from 40 to 70 years of age from discrimination in hiring, retention, compensation, and other conditions of employment.

Rehabilitation Act of 1973–prohibits discrimination in the hiring of the handicapped by federal agencies and federal contracters.

INTEGRATING ORGANIZATIONAL OBJECTIVES, POLICIES, AND HUMAN RESOURCE PLANNING

Figure 10–1 graphically illustrates the basic relationships among organizational objectives, policies, and human resource planning. As discussed in Chapter 5, organizational policies outline the ground rules and define the

FIGURE 10–1
Organizational Objectives, Policies, and Human Resource Planning

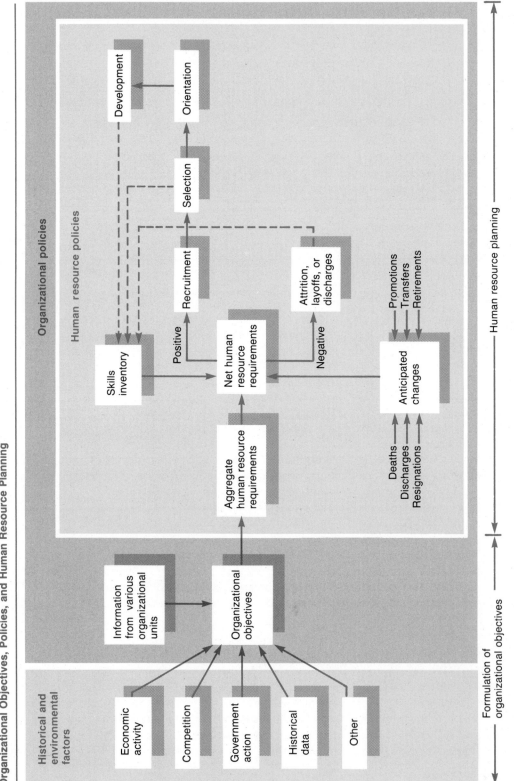

boundaries within which organizational objectives must be formulated and within which personnel planning must operate. Once the organizational objectives have been established, they are translated into a forecast of aggregate human resource requirements.

Net human resource requirements are determined by comparing the aggregate human resource forecasts to the present human resources in light of anticipated changes. If the net requirements are positive, the organization implements the processes of recruitment, selection, and training and development. If the requirements are negative, proper adjustments must be made through attrition, layoffs, or discharges. As these changes take place, they should be recorded in the skills inventory.

RECRUITMENT

Recruitment involves the activities of seeking and attracting a supply of people from which qualified candidates for job vacancies can be selected. The amout of recruitment that must be done by an organization is determined by the difference between the forecasted human resource needs and the talent available within the organization.

After the decision to recruit has been made, the sources of supply must be explored.

Recruitment–process of seeking and attracting a supply of people from which qualified candidates for job vacancies can be selected.

Promotion from Within

If an organization has been doing an effective job of selecting employees, one of the best sources of supply for job openings is its own employees. Promotion from within is a policy that many organizations follow. In fact, some of the best managed organizations, such as Delta Airlines and IBM, have a strict promotion-from-within policy.[8]

Promotion from within has several advantages. First, an organization should have a good idea about the strengths and weaknesses of its own employees. Employee morale and motivation are positively affected by internal promotions, assuming such promotions are perceived as being equitably related to performance. Finally, most organizations have a sizable investment in their employees; using the abilities of present employees to their fullest extent improves the organization's return on its investment.

Certain potential dangers must be acknowledged before adopting a policy of promotion from within. One danger has been popularized by Lawrence Peter: Managers tend to be promoted to their level of incompetence.[9] According to the **Peter Principle,** successful managers are continually promoted until they finally reach a level at which they are unable to perform. The Peter Principle can and does occur in organizations. However, knowing the present skills of employees (skills inventory) and knowing the skills required

Peter Principle–idea popularized by Lawrence Peter, that managers tend to be promoted to their level of incompetence.

by a new job (job analysis) minimizes the occurrence of the Peter Principle.

A second danger involves the inbreeding of ideas. When all vacancies are filled from within, caution must be taken to ensure that new ideas and innovations are not stifled by attitudes such as "we've never done it before" or "we did all right without it."

External Sources

Organizations have a wide range of external sources available for obtaining personnel. Probably the most widely used method for obtaining external personnel is the "Help Wanted" advertisement. Recruitment on college and university campuses is also used by many organizations. Other sources for obtaining personnel include employment agencies (public and private), management consulting firms, employee referrals, and labor unions.

Legal Influences

The previously discussed legislation has also had a profound impact on the recruitment activities of organizations. For example, reliance on "word of mouth" or "walk in" methods of recruitment has been ruled by the courts to be a discriminatory practice where females and minorities are not well represented at all levels within the organization.[10]

The EEOC has offered the following suggestions to help eliminate discrimination in recruitment practices:[11]

- Maintain a file of unhired female and minority applicants who are potential candidates for future openings. Contact these candidates first when an opening occurs.
- Utilize females and minorities in recruitment and the entire human resource process.
- Place classified ads under "Help Wanted" or "Help Wanted, Male-Female" listings. Be sure that the content of ads does not indicate any sex, race, or age preference or qualification for the job.
- Advertise in media directed toward women and minorities.
- All advertising should include the phrase "equal opportunity employer."

SELECTION

The purpose of selection is to choose from those that are available the individuals most likely to succeed on the job. The process is entirely dependent on proper human resource planning and recruitment. Only when an adequate pool of qualified candidates is available can the selection process function effectively. The ultimate objective of the selection process is to match the requirements of the job with the qualifications of the individual.

Who Makes the Decision?

The responsibility for hiring is assigned to different levels of management in different organizations. Often, the human resource/personnel department does the initial screening of recruits, but the final selection decision is left to the manager of the department with the job opening. Such a system relieves the manager of the time-consuming responsibility of screening out unqualified and uninterested applicants. Less frequently, the human resource/personnel department is responsible for both the initial screening and the final decision. Many organizations leave the final choice to the immediate manager, subject to the approval of higher levels of management. In small organizations, the owner or the top manager often makes the choice.

An alternate approach is to involve peers in the selection decision. Traditionally, peer involvement has been used primarily with professionals and those in upper levels of management, but it is becoming more popular at all levels of the organization. Under this approach, co-workers have an input into the final selection decision.

Peer and managerial involvement normally is desirable not only for identifying talent but also for facilitating the acceptance of the new employee by the work group. Experience has shown that co-workers may have negative reactions toward the new employee if the selection is made solely by the human resource department. On the other hand, supervisors and peer groups are often more committed to helping new workers succeed if they have some input into their selection.

Legal Influences

The selection process has been of primary interest to the government, as evidenced by the number of laws and regulations in effect that prohibit discrimination in the selection of employees. One action that is frequently required of organizations is the development of an affirmative action plan.

An **affirmative action plan** is a written document outlining specific goals and timetables for remedying past discriminatory actions. All federal contractors and subcontractors with contracts over $50,000 and 50 or more employees are required to develop and implement written affirmative action plans which are monitored by OFCCP. While Title VII and EEOC do not require any specific type of affirmative action plan, court rulings have often required affirmative action when discrimination has been found.

Affirmative action plan— written document outlining specific goals and timetables for remedying past discriminatory actions.

A number of basic steps are involved in the development of an effective affirmative action plan. Figure 10–2 presents the EEOC's suggestions for developing an affirmative action plan.

FIGURE 10–2
EEOC's Suggestions for Developing an Affirmative Action Plan

1. The chief executive officer of an organization should issue a written statement describing his or her personal commitment to the plan, legal obligations, and the importance of equal employment opportunity as an organizational goal.
2. A top official of the organization should be given the authority and responsibility for directing and implementing the program. In addition, all managers and supervisors within the organization should clearly understand their own responsibilities for carrying out equal employment opportunity.
3. The organization's policy and commitment to the policy should be publicized both internally and externally.
4. Present employment should be surveyed to identify areas of concentration and under-utilization and to determine the extent of underutilization.
5. Goals and timetables for achieving the goals should be developed to improve utilization of minorities, males, and females in each area where underutilization has been identified.
6. The entire employment system should be reviewed to identify and eliminate barriers to equal employment. Areas for review include: recruitment, selection, promotion systems, training programs, wage and salary structure, benefits and conditions of employment, layoffs, discharges, disciplinary action, and union contract provisions affecting these areas.
7. An internal audit and reporting system should be established to monitor and evaluate progress in all aspects of the program.
8. Company and community programs that are supportive of equal opportunity should be developed. Programs might include training of supervisors on their legal responsibilities and the organization's commitment to equal employment and job and career counseling programs.

Source: *Affirmative Action and Equal Employment,* vol. 1 (Washington, D.C.: U.S. Equal Employment Opportunity Commission, 1974), pp. 16–64.

Reverse discrimination– alleged preferential treatment for one group (minority or sex) over another rather than merely providing equal opportunity.

Organizations without affirmative action plans will find that it makes good business sense to identify and revise employment practices which have discriminatory effects, before the federal government requires such action. Increased legal action and the record of court-required affirmative action emphasize the advantage of writing and instituting an affirmative action plan.

However, the growing number of **reverse discrimination** suits (which results from alleged preferential treatment for one group over another for reasons other than equal opportunity) may have a significant impact on affirmative action programs. The first real test case in this area was the Bakke case of 1978.[12] Allen Bakke, a white male, brought suit against the medical school of the University of California at Davis. He charged that he was unconstitutionally discriminated against when he was denied admission to the medical school while some minority applicants with lower qualifications were accepted. The Supreme Court ruled in Bakke's favor but at the same time, upheld the constitutionality of affirmative action programs.

In another case in 1979, the Supreme Court heard a challenge—brought by a white worker, Brian F. Weber—to an affirmative action plan collectively bargained by a union and an employer.[13] This case questioned whether

MANAGEMENT IN ACTION 10–2

Memphis Fire Department and the Supreme Court

In 1974, the Memphis Fire Department was sued for alleged racial bias. The city settled the suit with a consent decree providing for interim hiring goals.

In 1977, Carl Stotts, a black fire captain, sued the department, charging that he and other blacks had been denied promotions because of their race. The suit was settled in 1980 by a consent decree in which the city pledged itself to a hiring goal of 50 percent blacks and promised to promote qualified blacks into 20 percent of the department's vacancies.

In 1981, the city proposed citywide layoffs of public employees. Stotts then asked the courts to ban layoffs or demotions of blacks as a result of the layoffs. Both the U.S. District Court and the Circuit Court of Appeals agreed to ban layoffs of blacks.

However, in June 1984, the Supreme Court ruled that the Memphis Fire Department could *not* insulate blacks from layoffs and demotions. The ruling indicated that employers may not be forced, when hard times hit, to scrap seniority plans that favor white men to protect "affirmative action" gains by minorities and women.

Title VII of the Civil Rights Act of 1964 as amended prohibited private employers from granting racial preference in employment practices. The Court, in a 5-to-2 opinion, held that it did not and that the voluntary quota was permissible. The Weber decision also hinted at the Court's criteria for a permissible affirmative action plan: (1) The plan must be designed to break down old patterns of segregation. (2) It must not involve the discharge of innocent third parties. (3) It must not have any bars to the advancement of white employees. (4) It must be a temporary measure to eliminate discrimination.

Some guidance on the issue of reverse discrimination has been given in both the Bakke and Weber cases. However, the issue is far from being settled, and more court cases are likely in the future. In fact, Management in Action 10–2 illustrates a court ruling that is likely to have a significant impact on affirmative action programs.

Selection Procedure

Figure 10–3 is a suggested procedure for selecting employees. The preliminary screening and preliminary interview eliminate candidates who are obviously not qualified for the job. In the preliminary screening of applications, personnel data sheets, school records, work records, and similar sources are reviewed to determine characteristics, abilities, and the past performance of the individual. The preliminary interview is then used to screen out unsuitable or uninterested applicants who passed the preliminary screening phase.

FIGURE 10–3
Steps in the Selection Process

Steps in Selection Process	Possible Criteria for Eliminating Potential Employee
Preliminary screening from application blank, résumé, employer records, etc.	Inadequate educational level or performance/experience record for the job and its requirements.
Preliminary interview	Obvious disinterest and unsuitability for job and its requirements.
Testing	Failure to meet minimum standards on job-related measures of intelligence, aptitude, personality, etc.
Reference checks	Unfavorable reports from references regarding past performance.
Employment interview	Inadequate demonstration of ability or other job-related characteristics.
Physical examination	Lack of physical fitness required for job.
Personal judgment	Intuition and judgment resulting in the selection of a new employee.

Testing

Test–sample of behavior used to draw inferences about the future behavior or performance of an individual.

One of the most controversial areas of staffing is employment testing. **Tests** provide a sample of behavior that is used to draw inferences about the future behavior or performance of an individual. Many tests are available to organizations for use in the selection process.[14] Tests used by organizations can be grouped into the following general categories: aptitude, psychomotor, job knowledge and proficiency, interests, psychological, and polygraphs.

Aptitude tests measure a person's capacity or potential ability to learn. Psychomotor tests are used to measure a person's strength, dexterity, and coordination. Job knowledge tests measure the job-related knowledge possessed by the applicant. Proficiency tests measure how well the applicant can do a sample of the work that is to be performed. Interest tests are designed to determine how a person's interests compare with the interests of successful people in a specific job. Psychological tests attempt to measure personality characteristics. Polygraph tests, popularly known as "lie detector tests," record physical changes in the body as the test subject answers a series of questions. By studying recorded physiological measurements, the polygraph examiner then makes a judgment as to whether the subject's response was truthful or deceptive.

Test validity–extent to which a test measures what it purports to measure (generally, how well it predicts future job success or performance).

Employment testing is legally subject to the requirements of validity and reliability. **Test validity** refers to the extent to which a test predicts a specific criterion. For organizations, the criterion usually used is performance on the job. Thus, test validity generally refers to the extent to which a test predicts future job success or performance. The selection of criteria to define

job success or performance is a most difficult problem, and its importance
cannot be overstated. Obviously, test validity cannot be measured unless
satisfactory criteria exist.

Test reliability refers to the consistency or reproducibility of the results
of a test. Three methods are commonly used to determine the reliability
of a test. The first method, called test-retest, involves testing a group of
people and then retesting them at a later date. The degree of similarity
between the sets of scores determines the reliability of the test. The second
method, called parallel forms, entails giving two separate but similar forms
of the test. The degree to which the sets of scores coincide determines the
reliability of the test. The third method, called split halves, divides the
test into two halves to determine if performance is similar on both halves.
Again, the degree of similarity determines the reliability. All of these methods
require statistical calculations for determining the degree of reliability of
the test.

*Test reliability–
consistency or
reproducibility of the results
of a test.*

In the past, organizations have frequently used tests without establishing
their validity or reliability. As a result of such practices, testing came under
a great deal of attack. The previously discussed Civil Rights Act of 1964
includes a section specifically related to the use of tests:

> nor shall it be an unlawful employment practice for an employer to give and
> to act upon the results of any professionally developed ability test provided
> that such a test, its administration, or action upon the results is not designed,
> intended, or used to discriminate because of race, color, religion, sex, or national
> origin.[15]

Two Supreme Court decisions have had a profound impact on the use
of testing by organizations. First, in the case of *Griggs* v. *Duke Power Company,* the Court ruled that any test which has an adverse impact on women
or minority group applicants must be validated as job related, regardless
of whether an employer intended to discriminate.[16] In *Albermarle Paper Company* v. *Moody,* the Supreme Court placed the burden on the employer to
show that its tests are in compliance with EEOC guidelines for testing.[17]

Finally, in 1978, the EEOC, the Civil Service Commission, the Department
of Justice, and the Department of Labor adopted a document titled "Uniform
Guidelines on Employee Selecton Procedures."[18] These guidelines established
the federal government's position concerning discrimination in employment
practices. The guidelines explain what private and public employers must
do to prove that their selection procedures, including testing, are nondiscrim-
inatory.[19]

Reference Checking

Reference checking can take place either before or after the diagnostic
interview. Many organizations realize the importance of reference checking
and provide space on the application form for listing references. Most prospective employers contact individuals from one or more of the three follow-

ing categories: personal, school, or past employment references. For the most part, contacting individuals who are personal references has limited value because generally no applicant is going to list someone who will not give a positive recommendation. Contacting individuals who have taught the applicant in a school, college, or university is also of limited value for similar reasons. Previous employers are clearly the most used source and are in a position to supply the most objective information.

Reference checking is most frequently conducted by telephone. However, many organizations will not answer questions about a previous employee unless the questions are put in writing. The amount and type of information that a previous employer is willing to divulge vary from organization to organization. The least that can be accomplished is to verify the previous employment. Other information that might be obtained includes reasons for leaving and whether or not the organization would be willing to rehire the person and why.

Government legislation has significantly influenced the process of reference checking. The Privacy Act of 1974 prevents government agencies from making their employment records available to other organizations without the consent of the individual involved. The Fair Credit and Reporting Act (FCRA) of 1971 requires private organizations to give job applicants access to information obtained from a reporting service. It is also mandatory that an applicant know that a check is being made. Because of these laws, most employment application forms now contain statements which must be signed by the applicant to authorize the employer to check references and conduct investigations.

Employment Interview

The employment interview is used by virtually all organizations as an important step in the selection process. Its purpose is to supplement information gained in other steps in the selection process to determine the suitability of an applicant for a specific opening in the organization. It is important to remember that all questions asked during an interview must be job related. Equal employment opportunity legislation has placed limitations on the types of questions that can be asked during an interview. The Appendix to this chapter outlines permissible questions and questions to be avoided in an interview with a job applicant.

Types of Interviews

Several different types of interviews are used by organizations. The structured interview is conducted using a predetermined outline. Through the use of this outline, the interviewer maintains control of the interview so that all pertinent information on the applicant is covered systematically. Advantages to the use of structured interviews are that it provides the same type of information on all interviewees and allows systematic coverage of all questions deemed necessary by the organization. Furthermore, research studies have recommended the use of a structured interview to increase reliability and accuracy.[20]

Unstructured interviews are conducted using no predetermined checklist of questions. Open-ended questions such as "Tell me about your previous job" are used. Interviews of this type pose numerous problems, such as a lack of systematic coverage of information, and are very susceptible to the personal biases of the interviewer. This type of interview, however, does provide a more relaxed atmosphere.

Three other types of interviewing techniques have been used to a limited extent by organizations. The stress interview is designed to place the interviewee under pressure. In the stress interview, the interviewer assumes a hostile and antagonistic attitude toward the interviewee. The purpose of this type of interview is to detect the highly emotional person. In board (or panel) interviews, two or more interviewers conduct a single interview with the applicant. Group interviews, in which several job applicants are questioned together in a group discussion, are also sometimes used. Board interviews and group interviews can involve either a structured or unstructured format.

Problems in Conducting Interviews

Although interviews have widespread use in selection procedures, a host of problems exist. The first and certainly one of the most significant problems is that interviews are subject to the same legal requirements of validity and reliability as other steps in the selection process.

Furthermore, research has indicated that the validity and reliability of most interviews is very questionable.[21] One of the primary reasons for this seems to be that it is easy for the interviewer to become either favorably or unfavorably impressed with the job applicant for the wrong reasons. Several common pitfalls may be encountered in interviewing a job applicant. Interviewers, like all people, have personal biases. These biases play a role in the interviewing process. For example, a qualified male applicant should not be rejected merely because the interviewer dislikes long hair on males.

Closely related is the problem of the **halo effect,** which occurs when the interviewer allows a single prominent characteristic to dominate judgment of all other traits. For instance, it is often easy to overlook other characteristics when a person has a pleasant personality. However, merely having a pleasant personality does not necessarily ensure that the person will be a good employee.

Overgeneralizing is another common problem. An interviewee may not behave exactly the same way on the job as during the interview. The interviewer must remember that the interviewee is under pressure during the interview and that some people just naturally become nervous during an interview.

Halo effect–occurs when interviewers allow a single prominent characteristic to dominate their judgment of all traits.

Conducting Effective Interviews

Problems associated with interviews can be partially overcome through careful planning. The following suggestions are offered to increase the effectiveness of the interviewing process.[22]

Careful attention must be given to the selection and training of interviewers. They should be outgoing and emotionally well-adjusted persons. Interviewing skills can be learned, and the persons responsible for conducting interviews should be thoroughly trained in these skills.

The plan for the interview should include an outline specifying the information to be obtained and the questions to be asked. The plan should also include room arrangements. Privacy and some degree of comfort are important. If a private room is not available, the interview should be conducted in a place where other applicants are not within hearing distance.

The interviewer should also attempt to put the applicant at ease. The interviewer should not argue with the applicant or put the applicant on the spot. A brief conversation about a general topic of interest or offering the applicant a cup of coffee can help ease the tension. The applicant should be encouraged to talk. However, the interviewer must maintain control and remember that the primary goal of the interview is to gain information that will aid in the selection decision.

The facts obtained in the interview should be recorded immediately. Generally, notes can and should be taken during the interview.

Finally, the effectiveness of the interviewing process should be evaluated. One way to evaluate effectiveness is to compare the performance ratings of individuals who are hired against assessments made during the interview. This cross-check can serve to evaluate the effectiveness of individual interviewers as well as the total interviewing program.

Physical Examination

Many organizations require a physical examination before an employee is hired. Its purpose is not only to determine whether the applicant is physically capable of performing the job but also to determine the applicant's eligibility for group life, health, and disability insurance. Because of the expense, physical examinations are normally given as one of the last steps in the selection process. Their expense has also caused many organizations to have applicants complete a health questionnaire when they fill out their application form. If no serious medical problems are indicated on the medical questionnaire, the applicant is not normally required to have a physical examination.

The Rehabilitation Act of 1973 has caused many employers to reexamine the physical requirements for many jobs. This act prohibits discrimination against handicapped persons; it requires government contractors to take affirmative action to employ qualified handicapped persons—persons who, with reasonable accommodations, can perform the essential functions of a job. This act does not prohibit employers from giving medical exams. However, it does encourage employers to make medical inquiries which are directly related to the applicant's ability to perform job-related functions and encourages employers to make reasonable accommodations in helping handicapped people to perform the job.

Personal Judgment

The final step in the selection process is the personal judgment required to select one individual for the job. (Of course, the assumption is that at this point there will be more than one individual qualified for the job.) A value judgment, using all of the data obtained in the previous steps of the selection process, must be made in selecting the best individual for the job. If previous steps have been performed correctly, the chances of success in this personal judgment are dramatically improved.

The individual making the personal judgment should also recognize that in some cases, none of the applicants are satisfactory. If this occurs, the job should be redesigned, more money should be offered to attract more qualified candidates, or other actions should be taken. Caution should be taken against accepting the best individual that has been seen, if the individual is not what is needed to do the job.

EMPLOYEE DEVELOPMENT

Employee development deals with the improvement and growth of the capabilities of individuals and groups within the organization. The goal of employee development is to facilitate the achievement of organizational goals. Included in this process are such activities as determining employee development needs, training and development programs, performance reviews, and employee counseling.

Employee development–improvement and growth of the capabilities of individuals and groups within the organization.

The importance of employee development cannot be overstated. It is frequently viewed by management as a nicety that is encouraged in good economic times but quickly reduced or eliminated in bad economic times. Such a shortsighted position often causes the organization to suffer in the long run.

Chapter 19, which focuses on developing people within organizations, discusses specific methods and techniques of employee and management development.

TRANSFERS, PROMOTIONS, AND SEPARATIONS

Transfer–moving an employee to another job at about the same level, with about the same pay, performance requirements, and status.

Recalling Figure 10–1, the final step in the human resource planning process involves transfers, promotions, and separations. **Transfers** involve moving an employee to another job at approximately the same level in the organization, with basically the same pay, performance requirements, and status. Planned transfers can serve as an excellent development technique. Transfers can also be helpful in balancing varying departmental workload requirements. The most common problem relating to transfers occurs when a "problem" employee is unloaded on an unsuspecting manager. Training, counseling, or corrective discipline of the employee may eliminate the need for such transfers. If the employee cannot be rehabilitated, discharge is usually preferable to transfer.

Promotion–moving an employee to a job with higher pay, status, and thus higher performance requirements.

A **promotion** moves an employee to a job involving higher pay, status, and thus higher performance requirements. The two basic criteria used by most organizations in promotions are merit and seniority. Union contracts often require that seniority be considered in promotions. Many organizations prefer to base promotions on merit as a way of rewarding and encouraging performance. Obviously, this assumes that the organization has a method for evaluating performance and determining merit. An organization must also consider the requirements of the job under consideration, not just the employee's performance in previous jobs. Success in one job does not automatically ensure success in another job. Both past performance and potential must be considered. This also lessens the probability of the occurrence of the Peter Principle.

Separation–voluntary or involuntary termination of an employee.

A **separation** involves either voluntary or involuntary termination of an employee. In voluntary terminations, many organizations attempt to determine why the employee is leaving, by using exit interviews. This type of interview provides insights into problem areas that need to be corrected in the organization. Involuntary separations should be made only as a last resort. When a company has hired an employee and invested resources in the employee, termination results in a low return on the organization's investment. Training and counseling often are tried before firing an individual. However, when rehabilitation fails, the best course of action is usually termination because of the negative impact a disgruntled or misfit employee can have on others in the organization.

THE DYNAMICS OF STAFFING

Because organizations are dynamic, the staffing process is subject to continual changes. The activities involved in the staffing function must continuously be reevaluated in light of changing conditions, both internal and external. Internal conditions include changing job requirements, changing technology, retirements, deaths, resignations, terminations, and promotions. External conditions include government regulations, general economic conditions, industry competition, and resource availability. These conditions and the changes they cause must be adequately considered so that the level of human resources can be maintained in order to achieve organizational objectives. The critical link between an organization's human resources and the achievement of organizational goals is reflected in the general consensus that even if the physical assets of an organization were suddenly destroyed, the human organization, if properly staffed, could rebuild and maintain an ongoing and viable organization.

This chapter has presented what could be considered an ideal staffing model. It should not be concluded, however, that most organizations follow this model: Many do not.

SUMMARY

Staffing involves securing and developing human resources to fill the jobs that have been created by the organizing function.

Human resource planning is the process of getting the right number of qualified people into the right jobs at the right time. The following activities and information are required in the human resource planning process: job analyses, skills inventories, human resource forecasts, recruitment, selection, employee development, promotions, transfers, and separations.

Job analysis is a process of determining, through observation and study, the nature of a specific job. The end products of a job analysis are a job description and a job specification. A job description is a written description of a job and its requirements. A job specification is a written statement of the necessary qualifications of the prospective job holder.

A skills inventory provides basic information on all the employees of an organization. Combining the skills inventory with the job analyses enables the organization to determine its present position with regard to its human resources. Human resource forecasting is an attempt to determine the future human resource needs of an organization. Recruitment involves the activities of seeking and attracting a supply of people from which qualified candidates for job vacancies can be selected.

The purpose of the selection process is to choose the individuals that are most likely to succeed from those that have been recruited. Steps involved in the selection process are preliminary screening and interviewing, testing, reference checks, employment interviews, physical examinations, and personal judgment. Several suggestions were made for improving the interviewing process.

Employee development is a process that is concerned with the improvement and growth of the capabilities of individuals and groups within the organization. The goal of employee development is to facilitate the achievement of organizational objectives.

Transfers, promotions, and separations are the final steps that influence the human resource planning process. Transferring an employee involves moving the employee to another job at approximately the same level in the organization, with basically the same pay, performance requirements, and status. A promotion involves moving an employee to a job involving higher pay, status, and performance requirements. A separation involves either voluntary or involuntary termination of an employee.

References and Additional Readings

[1] C. F. Russ, Jr., "Manpower Planning Systems: Part I," *Personnel Journal,* January 1982, p. 41.

[2] Ibid.

[3] For a description on how Robbins & Meyers, Inc. does human resource planning, see David R. Leigh, "Business Planning Is People Planning," *Personnel Journal,* May 1984, pp. 44–54.

[4] Thomas H. Patten, *Manpower Planning and the Development of Human Resources* (New York: John Wiley & Sons, 1971), p. 243.

[5] See also Brian D. Dunn, "The Skills Inventory: A Second Generation," *Personnel,* September–October 1982, pp. 40–44.

[6] "Equal Pay for Equal Work under the Fair Labor Standards Act," *Interpractices Bulletin* (Washington, D.C.: U.S. Department of Labor, 1967), Title 29, pt. 800.

[7] *Affirmative Action and Equal Employment,* vol. 1 (Washington, D.C.: U.S. Equal Employment Opportunity Commission, 1974), pp. 10–11.

[8] Herbert J. Sweeney and Kenneth S. Teel, "A New Look at Promotion from Within," *Personnel Journal,* August 1979, pp. 531–35.

[9] Lawrence J. Peter and R. Hall, *The Peter Principle* (New York: Bantam Books, 1969).

[10] *Parham* v. *Southwestern Bell Telephone Company,* 433 F. 2d 421 (8th Cir. 1970).

[11] *Affirmative Action and Equal Employment,* pp. 30–31.

[12] *University of California Regents* v. *Bakke,* 483 U.S. 265 (1978).

[13] *United Steelworkers* v. *Weber,* 99 S. Ct. 2721 (1979).

[14] For a detailed description of a large number of tests, see *Tests and Reviews* (Highland Park, N.J.: Gryphon Press, 1974).

[15] Title VII, Section 703(h), Civil Rights Acts of 1964.

[16] *Griggs* vs. *Duke Power Company,* U.S. Supreme Court (1971).

[17] Thaddeus Holt, "A View from Albermarle," *Personnel Psychology,* Spring 1977, p. 71. Also see "EEOC Guidelines on Employment Testing," *Federal Register,* August 1, 1970, p. 12333.

[18] "Uniform Guidelines on Employee Selection Procedures," *Federal Register,* August 25, 1978, pp. 38290–315.

[19] For a more in-depth discussion on the current state of testing, see Dale Yoder and Paul D. Staudohar, "Testing and EEO: Getting Down

to Cases," *Personnel Administrator,* February 1984, pp. 67–74.

[20] E. D. Pursell, M. A. Champion, and S. R. Gaylord, "Structured Interviewing: Avoiding Selection Problems," *Personnel Journal,* November 1980, p. 908.

[21] D. Yoder and H. G. Heneman, *ASPA Handbook of Personnel and Industrial Relations* (Washington, D.C.: Bureau of National Affairs, 1979), p. 4–125.

[22] Ibid., pp. 4–152 through 4–154.

Review Questions

1. How does staffing relate to the organizing function?
2. What is human resource planning?
3. What is a job analysis? A job description? A job specification? A skills inventory?
4. What is human resource forecasting?
5. Describe a model of the human resource planning process.
6. Describe the purpose of the following government legislation:
    a. Equal Pay Act of 1963.
    b. Civil Rights Act of 1964.
    c. Age Discrimination in Employment Act of 1968, as amended in 1978.
7. What is equal employment opportunity?
8. Define affirmative action plan.
9. What is recruitment? Describe some sources of recruitment.
10. What is selection? Describe the steps in the selection process.
11. What is test validity?
12. What is test reliability? What methods are commonly used to determine test reliability?
13. What is reference checking?
14. Describe two basic types of interviews.
15. Discuss some common pitfalls in interviewing.
16. What is employee development? Cite some of the activities involved in employee development.
17. What is a transfer? A promotion? A separation?

Discussion Questions

1. Discuss the following statement: "An individual who owns a business should be able to hire anyone and shouldn't have to worry about government interference."
2. Discuss your feelings on reverse discrimination.
3. Many managers believe that line managers should not have to worry about human resource needs and that this should be handled by the human resource department. What do you think?
4. One common method of handling problem employees is to transfer them to another department of the organization. Discuss your feelings on this practice.

Incident 10–1
To Promote or Not Promote?

Alice Franklin, president of Franklin Advertising Agency, was contemplating events that had transpired over the past several months. Her company had grown rapidly since she had started it on a shoestring just over 10 years ago. Today she has several large national accounts, with several more likely to close in the next six months. Her business has grown to over 100 employees with eight department heads reporting to her. The departments are the Creative Department, Media Department, Regional Buying Department, Yellow Pages Department, New Business Department, Account Services Department, Business Operations Department, and Marketing Department.

Alice had for a few months felt the need to create a position of executive vice president. She wanted this person to be responsible for the day-to-day operations of the company so that she could concentrate more on strategy formulation and long-range planning. The problem facing her was whether to promote someone from within the organization or go outside to find someone.

She had been thinking about offering the job to Tom Barnes, who had joined her agency about three months after she had started it. The first employee she had hired, he had joined Alice after dropping out of college. In college, he had been majoring in communications but left after two years to support his family. Tom was familiar with most facets of the business but had concentrated mostly in marketing and was presently heading up that department. He had been extremely loyal to Alice and had done a good job over the years. Alice knew that Tom would be really disappointed if she created the position of executive vice president and didn't offer it to him.

However, Alice had some real doubts about Tom's ability to handle the job. She had heard complaints from several of her people that Tom handled people as if they were machines. She was also concerned about his lack of formal education in business.

Questions

1. Should Alice promote Tom?
2. What are the potential consequences of promoting Tom? Of not promoting Tom?

Incident 10–2
The Employment Interview

Jerry Sullivan is the underwriting manager for a large insurance company located in the Southwest. Recently, one of his best employees had given him two weeks' notice of her intention to leave. She was expecting a baby within a very short time period, and she and her husband had decided that she was going to quit work and stay home with her new baby and her other two young children.

Today Jerry was scheduled to start interviewing applicants for this job. The first applicant was Barbara Riley. She arrived at the company's office promptly at 9 A.M., the time scheduled for her interview. Unfortunately, just before she arrived, Jerry received a phone call from his boss, who had just returned from a three weeks' vacation. He wanted Jerry to bring him up to date on what had been going on. The telephone conversation lasted 30 minutes. During this time, Barbara Riley was seated in the company's reception room.

At 9:30, Jerry went to the reception room and invited her into his office. The following conversation occurred:

> **Jerry:** Would you like a cup of coffee?
>
> **Barbara:** No, I've already had one.
>
> **Jerry:** You don't mind if I have a cup, do you?
>
> **Barbara:** No, go right ahead. [*Jerry pauses, and rings his secretary Dorothy Cannon.*]
>
> **Jerry:** Dorothy, would you fix me a cup of coffee?
>
> **Dorothy:** I'll bring it in shortly. You have a call on Line 1.
>
> **Jerry:** Who is it?
>
> **Dorothy:** It's Tom Powell, our IBM representative. He wants to talk to you about the delivery date on our new word processor.
>
> **Jerry:** I'd better talk to him. [*Turning to Barbara.*] I'd better take this call. I'll only be a minute. [*He picks up his phone.*] Well, Tom, when are we going to get our machines?

This phone conversation goes on for almost 10 minutes. After hanging up, Jerry turns again to Barbara to resume the interview.

> **Jerry:** I'm sorry, but I needed to know about those machines. We really do need them. We only have a short time, so why don't you just tell me about yourself.

At that point, Barbara tells Jerry about her education, which includes an undergraduate degree in psychology and an M.B.A. which she will be receiving shortly. She explains to Jerry that this will be her first full-time job. Just then the phone rings, and Jerry's secretary tells him that his next interviewee is waiting.

> **Jerry:** [*Turns to Barbara.*] Thank you for coming in. I'll be in touch with you as soon as I interview two more applicants for this job.

Questions

1. Outline the inadequacies of this interview.
2. What information did Jerry learn?
3. How do you think Barbara Riley feels?

Exercise

The T-Test

You will be given one minute to copy the letter T on a blank sheet of paper as many times as possible. The exercise is timed, and exactly one minute is permitted.

A frequency distribution will then be developed by your instructor (or the class) to show how well the class performed.

A. What is the shape of the distribution?
B. Why is the distribution shaped in this manner?
C. Why would some students have performed better and some worse?
D. How would you feel about using this test as a selection device? What problems can you see with using it?

Chapter 10 Appendix
Preemployment Inquiry Guide

This guide is *not* a complete definition of what can and cannot be asked of applicants. It is illustrative and attempts to answer the questions most frequently asked about equal opportunity law. It is hoped that in most cases the given rules, either directly or by analogy, will guide all personnel involved in the preemployment processes of recruiting, interviewing, and selection. This guide pertains only to inquiries, advertisements, etc., directed to all applicants prior to employment. Information required for records, such as race, sex, and number of dependents, may be requested after the applicant is on the payroll, provided such information is not used for any subsequent discrimination, as in upgrading or layoff.

These laws are not intended to prohibit employers from obtaining sufficient job-related information about applicants, as long as the questions do not elicit information which could be used for discriminatory purposes. Applicants should not be encouraged to volunteer potentially prejudicial information. The laws do not restrict the rights of employers to define qualifications necessary for satisfactory job performance, but require that the same standard of qualifications used for hiring be applied to all persons considered for employment.

It is recognized that the mere routine adherence to these laws will not accomplish the results intended by the courts and Congress. Employment discrimination can be eliminated only if the laws and regulations are followed in the spirit in which they were conceived.

Subject	Permissible Inquiries	Inquiries to Be Avoided
1. Name	"Have you worked for this company under a different name?" "Is any additional information relative to change of name, use of an assumed name or nickname necessary to enable a check on your work and educational record? If yes, explain."	Inquiries about name which would indicate applicant's lineage, ancestry, national origin, or descent. Inquiry into previous name of applicant where it has been changed by court order or otherwise. Inquiries about preferred courtesy title: Miss, Mrs., Ms.
2. Marital and family status	Whether applicant can meet specified work schedules or has activities, commitments, or responsibilities that may hinder the meeting of work attendance requirements. Inquiries as to a duration of stay on job or anticipated absences which are made to males and females alike.	Any inquiry indicating whether an applicant is married, single, divorced, engaged, etc. Number and age of children. Information on child-care arrangements. Any questions concerning pregnancy. Any such questions which directly or indirectly result in limitation of job opportunities.
3. Age	Requiring proof of age in the form of a work permit or a certificate of age— if a minor. Requiring proof of age by birth certificate after being hired. Inquiry as to whether or not the applicant meets the minimum age requirements as set by law, and requirement that upon hire, proof of	Requirement that applicant state age or date of birth. Requirement that applicant produce proof of age in the form of a birth certificate or baptismal record. The Age Discrimination in Employment Act of 1967 forbids discrimination against persons between the ages of 40 and 70.

APPENDIX *(continued)*

Subject	Permissible Inquiries	Inquiries to Be Avoided
	age must be submitted in the form of a birth certificate or other forms of proof of age. If age is a legal requirement, "If hired, can you furnish proof of age?," or statement that hire is subject to verification of age. Inquiry as to whether or not an applicant is younger than the employer's regular retirement age.	
4. Handicaps	For employers subject to the provisions of the Rehabilitation Act of 1973, applicants may be "invited" to indicate how and to what extent they are handicapped. The employer must indicate that: (1) compliance with the invitation is voluntary; (2) the information is being sought only to remedy discrimination or provide opportunities for the handicapped; (3) the information will be kept confidential; and (4) refusing to provide the information will not result in adverse treatment. All applicants can be asked if they are able to carry out all necessary job assignments and perform them in a safe manner.	An employer must be prepared to prove that any physical and mental requirements for a job are due to "business necessity" and the safe performance of the job. Except in cases where undue hardship can be proven, employers must make "reasonable accommodations" for the physical and mental limitations of an employee or applicant. "Reasonable accommodation" includes alteration of duties, alteration of work schedule, alteration of physical setting, and provision of aids. *The Rehabilitation Act of 1973 forbids employers from asking job applicants general questions about whether they are handicapped or asking them about the nature and severity of their handicaps.*
5. Sex	Inquiry or restriction of employment is permissible only where a *bona fide occupational qualification* exists. (This BFOQ exception is interpreted very narrowly by the courts and the EEOC.) The burden of proof rests on the employer to prove that the BFOQ does exist and that *all* members of the affected class are incapable of performing the job. Sex of applicant may be requested (preferably not on the employment application) for affirmative action purposes but may not be used as an employment criterion.	Sex of applicant. Any other inquiry which would indicate sex. Sex is *not* a BFOQ because a job involves physical labor (such as heavy lifting) beyond the capacity of *some* women nor can employment be restricted just because the job is traditionally labeled "men's work" or "women's work." Applicant's sex cannot be used as a factor for determining whether or not an applicant will be satisfied in a particular job. Questions about an applicant's height or weight, unless demonstrably necessary as requirements for the job.

APPENDIX *(continued)*

Subject	Permissible Inquiries	Inquiries to Be Avoided
6. Race or color	General distinguishing physical characteristics such as scars, etc., to be used for identification purposes. Race may be requested (preferably not on the employment application) for affirmative action purposes but may not be used as an employment criterion.	Applicant's race. Color of applicant's skin, eyes, hair, etc., or other questions directly or indirectly indicating race or color.
7. Address or duration of residence	Applicant's address. Inquiry into length of stay at current and previous addresses. "How long a resident of this state or city?"	Specific inquiry into foreign address which would indicate national origin. Names and relationship of persons with whom applicant resides. Whether applicant owns or rents home.
8. Birthplace	"Can you after employment submit a birth certificate or other proof of U.S. citizenship?"	Birthplace of applicant. Birthplace of applicant's parents, spouse, or other relatives. Requirement that applicant submit a birth certificate before employment. Any other inquiry into national origin.
9. Religion	An applicant may be advised concerning normal hours and days of work required by the job to avoid possible conflict with religious or other personal conviction. However, except in cases where undue hardship can be proven, employers and unions must make "reasonable accommodation" for religious practices of an employee or prospective employee. "Reasonable accommodation" may include voluntary substitutes, flexible scheduling, lateral transfer, change of job assignments, or the use of an alternative to payment of union dues.	Applicant's religious denomination or affiliation, church, parish, pastor, or religious holidays observed. Any inquiry to indicate or identify religious denomination or customs. Applicants may not be told that any particular religious groups are required to work on their religious holidays.
10. Military record	Type of education and experience in service as it relates to a particular job.	Type of discharge.
11. Photograph	May be required for identification after hiring.	Requirement that applicant affix a photograph to the application. Request that applicants, at their option, submit photograph. Requirement of photograph after interview but before hiring.

APPENDIX *(continued)*

Subject	Permissible Inquiries	Inquiries to Be Avoided
12. Citizenship	"Are you a citizen of the United States?" "Do you intend to remain permanently in the U.S.?" "If not a citizen, are you prevented from becoming lawfully employed because of visa or immigration status?" Statement that, if hired, applicant may be required to submit proof of citizenship.	"Of what country are you a citizen?" Whether applicant or parents or spouse are naturalized or native-born U.S. citizens. Date when applicant or parents or spouse acquired U.S. citizenship. Requirement that applicant produce naturalization papers. Whether applicant's parents or spouse are citizens of the U.S.
13. Ancestry or national origin	Languages applicant reads, speaks, or writes fluently. (If another language is necessary to perform a job.)	Inquiries into applicant's lineage, ancestry, national origin, descent, birthplace, or native language. National origin of applicant's parents or spouse.
14. Education	Applicant's academic, vocational, or professional education; school attended. Inquiry into language skills such as reading, speaking, and writing foreign lanugages.	Any inquiry asking specifically the nationality, racial, or religious affiliation of a school. Inquiry as to how foreign language ability was acquired.
15. Experience	Applicant's work experience, including names and addresses of previous employers, dates of employment, reasons for leaving, salary history. Other countries visited.	
16. Conviction arrest, and court record	Inquiry into actual *convictions* which relate reasonably to fitness to perform a particular job. (A conviction is a court ruling where the party is found guilty as charged. An arrest is merely the apprehending or detaining of the person to answer the alleged crime.)	Any inquiry relating to arrests. Any inquiry into or request for a person's arrest, court, or conviction record if not *substantially related* to functions and responsibilities of the particular job in question.
17. Relatives	Names of applicant's relatives already employed by this company. Names and address of parents or guardian (if applicant is a minor).	Name or address of any relative of adult applicant.
18. Notice in case of emergency	Name and address of persons to be notified in case of accident or emergency.	Name and address of *relatives* to be notified in case of accident or emergency.

APPENDIX *(concluded)*

Subject	Permissible Inquiries	Inquiries to Be Avoided
19. Organizations	Inquiry into any organizations which an applicant is a member of, providing the name or character of the organizations does not reveal the race, religion, color, or ancestry of the membership. "List all professional organizations to which you belong. What offices do you hold?"	"List all organizations, clubs, societies, and lodges to which you belong." The names of organizations to which the applicant belongs if such information would indicate through character or name the race, religion, color or ancestry of the membership.
20. References	"By whom were you referred for a position here?" Names of persons willing to provide professional and/or character references for applicant.	Requiring the submission of a religious reference. Requesting reference from applicant's pastor.
21. Credit rating	None.	Any questions concerning credit rating, charge accounts, etc. Ownership of car.
22. Miscellaneous	Notice to applicants that any misstatements or omissions of material facts in the application may be cause for dismissal.	Any inquiry should be avoided which, although not specifically listed among the above, is designed to elicit information concerning race, color, ancestry, age, sex, religion, handicap, or arrest and court record, unless based upon a bona fide occupational qualification.

Source: Clifford M. Koen, Jr., "The Pre-employment Inquiry Guide," *Personnel Journal,* Costa Mesa, Calif., October 1980, pp. 826–28. Copyright *Personnel Journal,* reprinted with permission. All rights reserved.

11

Controlling: Comparing Results to Plan

Chapter Outline

In many circumstances, the more managers attempt to obtain and exercise control over the behavior of others in the organization, the less control they have. Furthermore, often the less control they have, the more pressure they feel to exert greater control, which in turn often decreases the amount of control they have, etc., etc.

Gene Dalton and Paul Lawrence*

Control–process of ensuring that organizational activities are going according to plan; accomplished by comparing actual performance to predetermined standards or objectives, then taking action to correct for any deviations.

The basic premise of organizations is that all activities will function smoothly; however, the possibility of this being false gives rise to the need for control. Control simply means knowing what is actually happening in comparison to preset standards or objectives. The purpose of all management controls is to alert the manager to a problem or a potential problem before it becomes critical. **Control** is accomplished by comparing actual performance to predetermined standards or objectives and then taking action to correct any deviations from the standard. However, as the above quote implies, control is a sensitive and complex part of the management process.

Controlling is similar to planning. It addresses the basic questions: "Where are we now? Where do we want to be? How can we get there from here?" But controlling takes place after the planning is completed and the organizational activities have begun. Controlling is after the fact; planning is before the fact. This does not mean that control is practiced only after problems occur. It can be preventive. Control decisions can also affect future planning decisions.

WHY PRACTICE MANAGEMENT CONTROL?

As stated above, management controls alert the manager to potentially critical problems. At top management levels, a problem occurs when the organization's goals are not being met. At middle and lower levels, a problem occurs when the objectives for which the manager is responsible are not being met. These may be departmental objectives, production standards, or other performance indicators. All forms of management controls are designed to give the manager information regarding progress. The manager can use it:

1. To prevent crises. If a manager does not know what is going on, it is easy for small, readily solved problems to turn into crises.

---

* Gene Dalton and Paul Lawrence, *Motivation and Control in Organizations* (Homewood, Ill.: Richard D. Irwin, 1971), p. 5.

MANAGEMENT IN ACTION 11–1

Lack of Control at DeLorean Motor Company

According to an investigative report published in *International Management*, the collapse of DeLorean Motor Company was caused, in part, by a lack of basic management control. From the beginning, the market for the DeLorean sports car was substantially overestimated, and all financial matters were handled casually. The coordination of design and production engineering during the construction of the Belfast, Ireland, plant was extremely poor. Lines of responsibility were abused, delegation was mimimal, and secrecy was encouraged. Company management failed to control costs and to enforce quality standards. When it finally rolled off the line, the DeLorean sports car was more expensive and of much lower quality than John DeLorean had said it would be. Within 13 months of the plant start-up, the company was in receivership.

Source: George Bikerstaff, "The Trashing of the DeLorean," *International Management*, May 1983, pp. 23–30.

2. **To standardize outputs.** Products and services can be standardized in terms of quantity and quality through the use of good controls.

3. **To appraise employee performance.** Proper controls can provide the manager with objective information about employee performance.

4. **To update plans.** Remember (from Chapter 6) that the final step in the planning process was to control the plan. Controls allow the manager to compare what is happening with what was planned.

5. **To protect an organization's assets.** Controls can protect assets from inefficiency, waste, and pilferage.

Management in Action 11–1 describes how a lack of control greatly contributed to the demise of the DeLorean Motor Company.

TWO CONCERNS OF CONTROL

In controlling, the manager must balance two major concerns: stability and objective realization. To maintain stability, the manager must be sure that the organization is operating within its established boundaries of constraint. The boundaries of constraint are determined by policies, budgets, ethics, laws, and so on. The second concern, objective realization, requires constant monitoring to ensure that enough progress is being made toward the established objectives.

A manager may become overly worried about one concern at the expense of the other. Most common is a manager who becomes preoccupied with the stability of the operation and neglects the goal. Such behavior can lead to a lot of activity but very little output—a manager obsessed with the manner or style with which a job is done is an example. On the other hand, a manager may lose sight of stability and have glamorous but short-lived success. A manager who sets production records by stopping safety checks is an example of this behavior.

THE MANAGEMENT CONTROL PROCESS

Figure 11–1 is a simple model of the management control process. Outputs from the activity are monitored by some type of sensor and compared to preset standards (normally set during the planning process). The manager acts as the regulator; he takes corrective action when the outputs do not meet the standards. The manager's actions may be directed at the inputs to the activity or at the activity itself.

Such a system —where outputs from the system affect future inputs or future activities of the system—is called a feedback, or closed, system. In

FIGURE 11–1
The Control Process

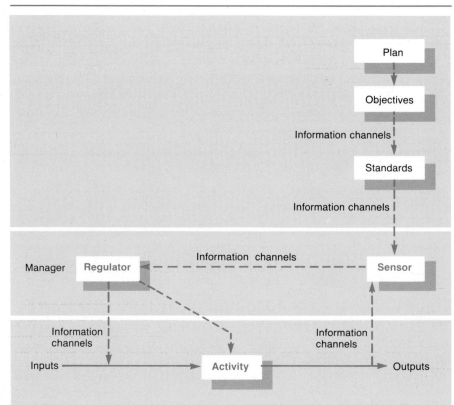

other words, a feedback system is influenced by its own past behaviors.[1] The heating system of a house is a common example of a mechanical feedback system. The thermostat sensor compares the temperature resulting from heat previously generated by the system to some predetermined standard (the desired temperature setting) and responds accordingly.

Feedback is a vital part of the control process. Although preventive, before-the-fact steps can often aid the control process, total control cannot be practiced without feedback. Managers may receive and act on facts about the inputs or the activity itself. But in the end, they must know what is happening in the organization; feedback gives them this information.

Three Requirements for Control

The process of control has three basic requirements: (1) establish standards; (2) monitor results and compare to standards; and (3) correct deviations. The first (setting standards) comes from the planning process, while the latter two (monitoring and correcting) are unique to the control process. All three are essential to having effective control.

Setting Standards

A **standard** is a value used as a point of reference for comparing other values. Standards, when used in management controls, come directly from objectives. As such, a standard outlines what is expected of the job and/or individual. In some instances, objectives may be used directly as standards. In other instances, performance indicators may be derived from the objectives. In either case, standards should be easy to measure and define. The more specific and measurable an objective is, the more likely that it can be directly used as a standard. Standards may deal with output per hour, quality level, inventory level, or other indicators of individual and/or organizational performance. The same guidelines presented in Chapter 5 for setting objectives should be followed for setting standards.

Standard—value used as a point of reference for comparing other values.

Monitoring Performance

Obviously, the entire control system is no better than the information on which it operates—and much of this information is gathered from the monitoring process. Monitoring is often considered to be synonymous with control. In fact, it is only part of the total control process. The main purpose of monitoring performance is to isolate problem areas. The nature and type of standard being used often dictates the type of checks to be made. Once actual performance has been checked and compared to standards, the proper corrective action can be taken.

The major problem in monitoring performance is deciding when, where, and how often to inspect or check. Checks must be made often enough to provide needed information. However, some managers become obsessed with the checking process. If overdone, monitoring can be expensive and it can result in adverse reactions from employees. Timing is equally important. The manager must recognize a problem in time to correct it. For example, inventory control must reorder stock before it has been depleted. Several techniques for monitoring performance are presented later in this chapter.

Correcting for Deviations

All too often, managers set standards and monitor results but do not follow up with actions. The first two steps are of little value if corrective action is not taken. It is entirely possible that the action that is needed may be to maintain the status quo. Action of this type would depend upon standards being met in a satisfactory manner. If standards are not being met, the manager must find the cause of the deviation and correct it. It is not enough simply to eliminate the problem itself or treat only the symptoms. This action compares to replacing a car battery when the real problem is a faulty generator. In a short time, the battery will go dead again. It is also possible that a careful analysis of the deviation will require a change in the standard. The standard may have been improperly set, or conditions may have changed so as to require a change. Figure 11–2 lists some potential causes of deviations between desired and actual performance. Management in Action 11–2 discusses how employees have been asked to make concessions in several industries as a corrective action to bring costs under control.

FIGURE 11–2
Potential Cause of Performance Deviations

- Faulty planning.
- Lack of communication within the organization.
- Need for training.
- Lack of motivation.
- Unforseen forces outside the organization, such as government regulation or competition.

Control Tolerances

Actual performance rarely conforms exactly to standards or plans. A certain amount of variation will normally occur. Therefore, the manager must set limits on the acceptable degree of deviation from standard. In other words, how much variation from standard is tolerable? The manner in which the manager sets control tolerances depends on the standard being used. If the activity being monitored lends itself to numerical measurement, statistical control techniques can be used. Often, the manager must make subjective judgments as to when the system or factor being monitored is out of

MANAGEMENT IN ACTION 11–2

Out-of-Control Costs Require Concessions from Employees

The airline, automobile, and steel industries are going through a painful process of adjustment to increased competition. Deregulation has opened the airline industry to new competition and price wars. The automobile and steel industries are facing fierce international competition. Unionized workers, accustomed to a protected environment of high wages and favorable working conditions, are now facing the

fact that high costs may force their companies out of business.

There have been several examples of "concessionary bargaining" in recent years. In December 1983, Eastern Air Lines pilots agreed to give up an average 18 percent of their pay for 25 percent of the company's stock. In 1982, the United Auto Workers granted GM and Ford $3 billion in contract concessions.

Sources: "In Detroit It's Jobs vs. Productivity," *Business Week*, July 30, 1984, p. 31; "Givebacks at Eastern and Greyhound" *Dun's Business Month*, January 1984, p. 241.

control. One element influencing how much deviation is acceptable is the risk of being out of control and not knowing it. In general, the lower the risk, the wider the tolerances. Figure 11–3 illustrates the idea of control tolerances. Note that tolerance levels may be formalized, or they may merely exist in the mind of the manager. The important point is that the manager

FIGURE 11–3
Control Tolerance Limits

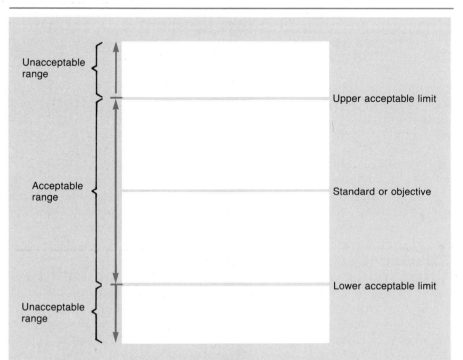

must develop some guidelines as to what deviation is acceptable (in control) and what is not acceptable (out of control).

How Much Control?

When deciding how much control should be exercised in an organization, two major factors must be appraised: (1) economic considerations and (2) behavioral considerations.

Economic Considerations

Installing and operating control systems cost money. A good-quality control system, for instance, requires additional labor, if nothing else. The equipment costs of sophisticated electronic and mechanical control systems can be very high. Ideally, control systems should be installed as long as they save more than they cost. Figure 11–4 shows the general relationship between control costs and the benefits gained. It makes several points:

- There is some optimum amount of control (Point A).
- There is some minimum amount of control necessary before the benefits of more control outweigh the costs (Point B).
- There is some maximum amount of control which, if exceeded, can be very costly (Point C).

The costs of implementing a control system can usually be estimated or calculated much more accurately than the benefits. For example, it is difficult to quantify and measure the true benefits of a quality control system. A good quality control system supposedly increases goodwill; but how does one measure this attribute? The decision is obviously much easier when the costs of not maintaining control are either very high or very low. Despite the measurement problems, management should regularly undertake such a study to ensure that gross misapplications do not occur.

Behavioral Considerations

Managers need to be aware of the possible impact of the control system upon employees. Most people do not like to work where they feel that their every move is being watched or questioned. Still, very few people like to work where there is no control: An absence of control creates an environment in which people do not know what is expected of them.

Many managers have a tendency to increase controls whenever things are not going according to plan. Figure 11–5 shows a simplified version of a model developed by Alvin Gouldner which explains this behavior.

Gouldner's model begins with top management's demand for control over operations. This is attempted through the use and enforcement of general

FIGURE 11–4
General Relationship between Control Cost and Benefits.

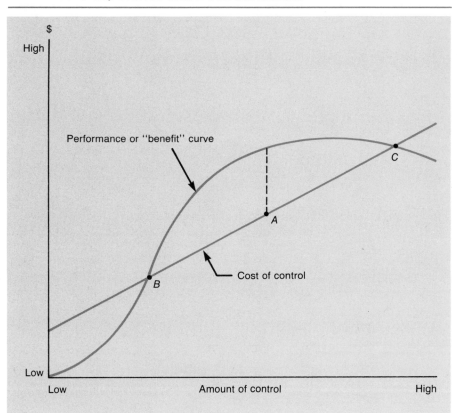

and impersonal rules about work procedures. These rigid rules are meant to be guides for the behavior of the organization members; they also have the unintended effect of showing minimum acceptable behavior. In organizations where there is little congruence between individual and organizational objectives or there is not a high acceptance of organizational objectives, the effect is a reduction of performance to the lowest acceptable level— people not highly committed to organizational objectives will perform at the lowest acceptable level. Managers view such behavior as the result of inadequate control; they therefore respond with closer supervision. This increases the visibility of power, which in turn raises the level of interpersonal tension in the organization. Raising the tension level brings even closer enforcement of the general and impersonal formal rules. Hence, the cycle repeats itself. The overall effect is increased control, increased interpersonal tension, and a lowering of performance.

One problem in deciding the right degree of control is that different people react differently to similar controls. Research has suggested that reac-

FIGURE 11–5
Simplified Gouldner Model of Organization Control

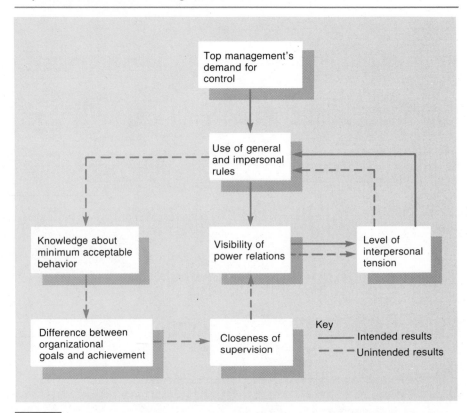

Source: James G. March and Herbert A. Simon, *Organizations* (New York: John Wiley & Sons, 1958), p. 45.

tions differ according to personality and prior experiences.[2] Problems can occur from unforeseen reactions to control because of both compliance and resistance.[3] Problems from compliance arise when people adhere to the pre-scribed behavior even when it is inappropriate. The salesperson who will not vary from prescribed procedures in order to satisfy a customer complaint is a common example of this. Problems resulting from resistance to controls arise when individulas attempt to preempt, work around, or sabotage the controls. Distorting a report or padding the budget is a form of control resistance.

Several things can be done to lessen negative reactions to controls. Most are based on good common sense. However, they require a real effort by the manager to carry out. The tendency is to take these suggestions for granted. They are:

1. Make sure the standards and associated controls are realistic. Stan-

MANAGEMENT IN ACTION 11-3

Trivial Pursuit Is a Major Problem for Its Manufacturer

When Parker Brothers and Milton Bradley decided not to market a new board game developed in Canada, Selchow and Righter—the 117-year-old supplier of Scrabble and Parcheesi—jumped at the chance. The new board game Trivial Pursuit became a phenomenal overnight success with retail sales of $750 million in 1984.

For Selchow and Righter, the success has been accompanied by certain problems. Since company management believes the demand for Trivial Pursuit will fall off eventually and they do not want to be faced with laying off people, they have added very few workers. The 300 employees are deluged with orders for Trivial Pursuit and frequently cannot meet those orders, much less support other promising new products. According to a buyer for a major catalog and retail chain, "It's pandemonium up there. There's no control. They struggle on a day-to-day basis to get their thing out."

Source: "Selchow and Righter: Playing Trivial Pursuit to the Limit," *Business Week*, November 20, 1984, pp. 118–26.

dards set too high or too low turn people off. Make the standards attainable but challenging.

2. Involve subordinates in the control-setting process. Many of the behavioral problems associated with controls result from a lack of understanding of the nature and purpose of the controls. It is natural for people to resist anything new, especially if they do not understand why it is being used. Solicit and listen to suggestions from workers.

3. Use controls only where needed. As suggested by the Gouldner model, there is a strong tendency to overcontrol, to be sure that all bases are covered. Periodically evaluate the need for different controls. A good rule of thumb is to evaluate every control at least annually. Things change, which makes certain controls obsolete. Remember, overcontrol can produce some very negative results. Management in Action 11–3 presents a situation in which a company's handling of a control problem was heavily influenced by employee considerations.

Where Should Control Reside?

For years, it was believed that control in organizations was a fixed commodity that should rest only in the hands of top management. This viewpoint naturally favored a highly centralized approach to decision making and controlling. However, as decentralized organizations have become more and more common, controls have been pushed further and further down the hierarchy. It is now recognized that where the controls reside is an important factor in how much control is desirable.

Evidence favors relatively tight controls as long as they are placed as far down in the organization as possible.[4] This approach has several advantages: it keeps higher-level managers from getting too involved in details; it shows why the control is necessary; and it elicits commitment from lower-level managers. When controls are spread through many levels of an organization, caution must be taken to ensure that there are no disagreements about how the controls are distributed.

CONTROL METHODS AND SYSTEMS

Behavior (personal) control–based on direct, personal surveillance.

Output (impersonal) control–based on the measurement of outputs.

Control methods can be either of two kinds: (1) behavior control or (2) output control. **Behavior (or personal) control** is based on direct, personal surveillance. The first-line supervisor who maintains a close personal watch over subordinates is using behavior control. **Output (or Impersonal) control** is based on the measurement of outputs. Tracking production records or sales figures is an example of output control.

Research has shown that these two categories of control are not substitutes for each other in the sense that a manager uses one or the other.[5] The evidence suggests that output control occurs in response to a manager's need to provide an accurate measure of performance. Behavior control is exerted when performance requirements are well known and personal surveillance is needed to promote efficiency and motivation. Thomas Peters and Robert Waterman strongly emphasize the need for managers at all levels to take a hands-on approach to managing.[6] By hands-on, they mean regularly mixing with subordinates and visiting them at their workplaces. Thus, organizations need to use a mix of output and behavior controls; each serves different organizational needs.

One of the most common mistakes made by managers is to assume that a new method or system of control will in itself solve problems. Methods and systems, by themselves, can not control anything! But together with good administration and intelligent interpretation, they provide control. The most appropriate control system is often worthless if not properly administered. Furthermore, an appropriate control system which is properly administered can only produce information which requires intelligent interpretation. Thus, the methods and systems discussed in this section should not be viewed as solutions to control problems; rather they are aids in the control process. Also note that many control tools (such as budgets) are developed as part of the planning process but used on a regular basis as part of the control process.

Before or after the fact?   In general, methods of exercising control can be described as either before the fact or after the fact. Before-the-fact methods attempt to prevent a problem from occurring. Requiring prior approval for purchases of all items over a certain dollar value is an example. After-the-fact methods of control are designed to detect an existing or potential problem before it gets out of hand. Written or periodic reports represent after-the-fact control methods. Most controls are based on after-the-fact methods.

Budgets

Budgets are probably the most widely used control devices. A **budget** is a statement of expected results or requirements expressed in financial or numerical terms. Budgets express plans, objectives, and programs of the organization in numerical terms. Preparation of the budget is primarily a planning function (see Chapter 6); however, its administration is a controlling function.

Budget—statement of expected results or requirements expressed in financial or numerical terms.

Many different types of budgets are in use (Figure 11–6 outlines some of the most common). Some may be expressed in terms other than dollars: Equipment budgets may be expressed in numbers of machines. Material budgets may be expressed in pounds, pieces, gallons, and so on. Budgets not expressed in dollars can usually be translated into dollars for inclusion in an overall budget.

While budgets are useful for planning and control, they are not without their dangers. Perhaps the greatest danger is inflexibility. This is a special threat to organizations operating in an industry with rapid change and high competition. Rigidity in the budget can also lead to ignoring organizational goals for budgetary goals. The financial manager who won't go $5 over budget in order to make $500 is a classic example. Budgets can hide inefficiencies. That a certain expenditure has been made in the past often becomes justification for continuing it when the situation has greatly changed. And managers may pad budgets because they will be cut by superiors. Since

FIGURE 11–6
Types and Purposes of Budgets

Type of Budget	Brief Description or Purpose
Revenue and expense budget	Provides details for revenue and expense plans.
Cash budget	Forecasts cash receipts and disbursements.
Capital expenditure budget	Outlines specific expenditures for plant, equipment, machinery, inventories, and other capital items.
Production, material, or time budget	Expresses physical requirements of production, or material, or the time requirements for the budget period.
Balance sheet budgets	Forecasts the status of assets, liabilities, and net worth at the end of the budget period.

Flexible (variable)
budget–allows certain
expenses to vary with the
level of sales or output.

the manager is never sure of how severe the cut will be, the result is often an inaccurate if not unrealistic budget.

Flexible budgets.   In order to overcome many of the shortcomings resulting from inflexibility, **flexible (variable) budgets** are designed to vary with the volume of sales or some other measure of output. Because of their nature, flexible budgets are generally limited to expense budgets. The basic idea is to allow material, labor, advertising, and other related expenses to vary with the volume of output. Because the actual level of sales or output is usually not known in advance, flexible budgets are more useful for evaluating what the expenses should have been under the circumstances; they have limited value as planning information for the overall budgeting program. Table 11–1 illustrates a simplified flexible budget.

TABLE 11–1
Simplified Flexible Budget

Sales (in units)	5,000	6,000	7,000	8,000	9,000
Product cost	$10,000	$12,000	$14,000	$16,000	$18,000
Advertising cost	5,000	5,000	6,000	6,000	7,000
Shipping costs	5,000	5,500	6,000	6,500	7,000
Sales commissions	2,500	3,000	3,500	4,000	4,500
Budgeted expenses	$22,500	$25,500	$29,500	$32,500	$36,500

Zero-base budgeting.   Zero-base budgeting is one approach to budgeting that has received attention over the last several years. It requires each manager to justify an entire budget request in detail, from scratch: The burden of proof is on each manager to justify why any money should be spent.[7] Under zero-base budgeting, each activity under a manager's discretion is identified, evaluated, and ranked by importance. Then, each year, every activity in the budget is on trial for its life and is matched against all the other claimants for an organization's resources.

Direct Observation

A store manager's daily tour of the facility; a company president's annual visit to all branches; a methods study by a staff industrial engineer: All are examples of control by direct observation. Although it is time consuming, personal observation is sometimes the only way to get an accurate picture of what is really happening. One hazard is that employees may misinterpret a superior's visit and consider such action meddling or eavesdropping. Also behaviors change when people are being watched or monitored. Another potential inaccuracy lies in the interpretation of the observation. The observer must be careful not to read into the picture events that did not actually occur. Visits and direct observation can have very positive effects when

Controlling through Active Involvement in Operations Details

Ray Kroc, the founder of McDonald's Corporation, was involved in every aspect of the operations of the McDonald's fast-food business. Known as a "detail person," Ray Kroc was personally involved in setting quality and housekeeping standards, suggesting menu changes, making purchasing decisions, and performing store inspections. When potential new store sites were identified, Kroc would drive around the area and visit the local shops to see how a McDonald's store would do there. In the early 60s, Kroc proposed that the company hold classes for new operators and managers to teach them "McDonald's method of providing services." According to Ray Kroc, "If I had a brick for every time I've repeated the phrase 'Q, S, C, and V' (quality, service, cleanliness, and value), I think I'd probably be able to bridge the Atlantic Ocean with them."

Source: Ray Kroc, "Grinding It Out: The Making of McDonald's," (Chicago: Regnery, 1977), p. 85.

viewed by the workers as a display of the superior's interest. Management in Action 11–4 describes how the founder of MacDonald's, Ray Kroc, used this method of control.

Written Reports

Written reports can be prepared on a periodic or "as necessary" basis. There are two basic types of written reports, analytical and informational. Analytical reports interpret the facts they present; informational reports only present the facts. Preparing a report is a four- or five-step process, depending on whether it is informational or analytical. The steps are: (1) planning the attack on the problem; (2) collecting the facts; (3) organizing the facts; (4) interpreting the facts (this step is omitted with informational reports); and (5) writing the report.[8] Most reports are prepared for the benefit of the reader, not the writer. The reader wants useful information not previously available.

The need for a report should be carefully evaluated. Periodic reports have a way of continuing long past their usefulness. Such unnecessary reports are a waste of organizational resources. Another tendency—even with necessary reports—is to include much useless information.

Audits

Audits can be conducted either by internal or external personnel. External audits are normally done by outside accountants and are limited to financial matters. Most are done to certify that the organization's accounting methods are fair, consistent, and conform to existing practices. Most outside audits

Audit–method of control normally involved with financial matters but can also include other areas of the organization.

do not delve into nonfinancial matters such as management practices. The internal audit similar to the external audit, is performed by the organization's own personnel.

When an audit looks at areas other than finances and accounting, it is known as a management audit. **Management audits** attempt to evaluate the overall management practices and policies of the organization. They can be conducted by outside consultants or inside staff; however, a management audit conducted by inside staff can easily result in a biased report.

Management audit–attempts to evaluate the overall management practices and policies of the organization

Break-Even Charts

Break-even chart–depicts graphically the relationship of volume of operations to profits.

Break-even charts depict graphically the relationship of volume of operations to profits. The break-even point (BEP) is the point at which sales revenues exactly equal expenses. Total sales below the BEP result in a loss; total sales above the BEP result in a profit.

Figure 11–7 shows a typical break-even chart. The horizontal axis represents output, the vertical axis represents expenses and revenues. It is not required, but most break-even charts assume that there are linear relationships and that all costs are either fixed or variable. Fixed costs are those that do not vary with output, at least in the short run. They include rent,

FIGURE 11–7
Break-Even Chart

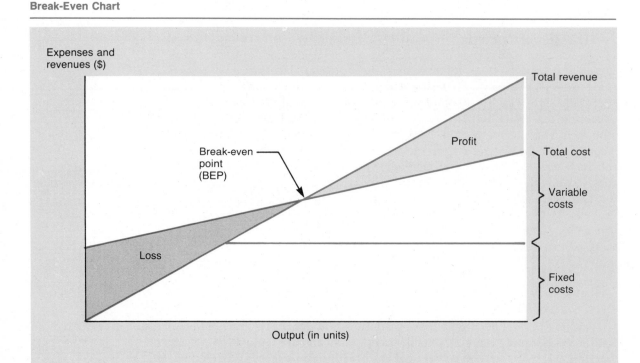

insurance, and administrative salaries. Variable costs are those that vary with output. Typical variable costs include direct labor and materials. The purpose of the chart is to show the break-even point and the effects of changes in output. A break-even chart is useful for showing whether revenue and/or costs are running as planned.

Time-Related Charts and Techniques

Gantt charts, the critical path method (CPM), and the program evaluation and control technique (PERT)—they were described in Chapter 7 and its Appendix—are tools used to plan and schedule. These same tools can also be used for controlling once the plans have been put into action. By tracking actual progress compared to planned progress, activities that fall behind schedule can quickly be spotted.

Management by Objectives (MBO)

Management by objectives (MBO) was discussed in Chapter 5 as an effective means for setting objectives. It also can be used for control purposes. As with many of the control techniques discussed in this chapter, the development of an MBO system is part of the planning function. However, once MBO is implemented, it is used for control purposes.

Management Information Systems

In recent years, the term *management information system* (MIS) has become popular. A MIS is a formal system for providing information to managers. While not essential, most management information systems include the use of a computer. The basic idea behind each MIS is to provide information in a systematic and integrated manner—rather than in a sporadic and piecemeal manner. A good MIS aids managerial control by giving managers better information on a timely basis. Chapter 21 is devoted entirely to MIS.

SUMMARY

The basic idea behind all management controls is to alert the manager to a problem or potential problem before it becomes critical. Management controls are used for several reasons: (1) to prevent crises, (2) to standardize outputs, (3) to appraise employee performance, (4) to update plans, and (5) to protect an organization's assets. The process of control has three basic requirements: (1) establish standards or objectives, (2) monitor results and compare to standards, and (3) correct for deviations. All three requirements are essential to maintaining effective control.

Because actual performance rarely conforms exactly to standards or plans, the manager must set limits as to which deviations from standards are acceptable and which are not. Such deviations are referred to as control tolerances.

Two major factors must be appraised when deciding the degree of control that should be exercised in an organization: (1) economic (cost) considerations and (2) behavioral considerations. Although the benefits from a particular system are often hard to calculate precisely, management should periodically attempt to measure the cost benefit of controls. Such an investigation ensures that gross misapplications do not occur. In order to lessen negative behavioral reactions to control, the manager should make sure that the purpose and nature of the controls are fully understood by all affected employees. Evidence favors relatively tight controls placed as far down in the organization as possible.

Control methods can be classified as one of two types: (1) behavioral or (2) output. Behavioral control is based on direct personal surveillance, while output control is based on the measurement of outputs.

Several control methods and systems were discussed. These included budgets, personal observation, written reports, audits, break-even charts, time-related charts, management by objectives, and management information systems.

References and Additional Readings

[1] Jay W. Forrester, *Principles of Systems,* 2d ed. (Cambridge, Mass: Wright-Allen Press, 1968), pp. 1–5.

[2] For a discussion of some relevant studies, see Arnold S. Tannenbaum, "Control in Organizations: Individual Adjustment in Organization Performance," *Administrative Science Quarterly,* September 1962, pp. 241–46; Klaus Bartolke, Walter Eschweiler, Dieter Flechsenberger, and Arnold J. Tannenbaum, "Worker Participation and the Distribution of Control as Perceived by Members of Ten German Companies," *Administrative Science Quarterly* 27 (1982), pp. 380–97.

[3] Dalton and Lawrence, *Motivation and Control,* p. 8.

[4] Timothy J. McMahon and G. W. Perritt, "Toward a Contingency Theory of Organizational Control," *Academy of Management Journal,* December 1973, pp. 624–35.

[5] William G. Ouchi and Mary Ann Maguire, "Organizational Control: Two Functions," *Administrative Science Quarterly,* December 1975, pp. 559–71; William G. Ouchi, "The Transmission of Control through Organizational Hierarchy," *Academy of Management Journal,* June 1978, pp. 174–76.

[6] Thomas J. Peters and Robert H. Waterman, Jr., *In Search of Excellence* (New York: Harper & Row, 1982) pp. 279–91.

[7] Stanton C. Lindquist and R. Bryant Mills, "Whatever Happened to Zero-Base Budgeting?" *Managerial Planning,* January–February 1981, pp. 31–35.

[8] C. W. Wilkinson, Peter B. Clarke, and Dorothy C. M. Wilkinson, *Communicating through Letters and Reports,* 7th ed. (Homewood, Ill.: Richard D. Irwin, 1980).

Review Questions

1. What is management control? What are the two major concerns in management control?
2. Describe a model of the management control process.
3. Outline the three basic requirements of control.
4. How much control should be exercised in an organization?
5. Describe two categories of control methods.

6. Describe the following control methods and systems:
   a. Budgets.
   b. Direct observation.
   c. Written reports.
   d. Audits.
   e. Break-even charts.
   f. Management by objectives.
   g. Management information systems.

Discussion Questions

1. What factors should you consider before installing tighter controls? How might you evaluate these factors?
2. If you were implementing a new control system designed to check more closely the expenses of your salespeople, what actions might you take in order to minimize negative reactions?

3. Why are many managers reluctant to take the actions necessary to correct for deviations?
4. How should you deal with managers who are so "married" to their departmental budget that they will not let you spend $1 in order to make $10?

Incident 11–1
"Bird-Dogging" the Employee

Ace Radio, Inc. is a small company located in Centerville. The owner Al Abrams, a highly experienced electronics man, founded the company in 1972.

Ace Radio's basic product is a walkie-talkie which is sold primarily to the U.S. military. The walkie-talkie units are relatively simple to produce; Ace merely purchases the parts—cables, wires, transistors, and so on—and assembles them with hand tools. Because of this fairly low level of complexity, Ace employs semskilled workers at low wages.

Although Ace has made a profit each year since production started in 1972, Abrams has become increasingly concerned. Over the past six years he has noticed a general decline in employee morale; at the same time, he has observed a decline in employee productivity and his company's profit margin.

Concerned, Abrams asked his supervisors to keep a closer watch on the hour-to-hour activities of the workers. In the first week, they discovered two workers in the restroom reading magazines. This "bird-dogging" technique (as it was called by management), or "slave driving" (as it was called by the workers), failed to increase production or productivity.

Abrams realized that the lack of performance on the part of some of the workers affected the production of everyone. This phenomenon was caused by the balanced assembly line under which the walkie-talkies were assembled. If an employee next to a normally productive employee did not work fast enough, walkie-talkies would back up on the line. Instead of a backup, however, what usually occurred was a readjustment of the assembly line to the production rate of the slower workers.

In addition, another situation developed which lowered productivity and increased unit costs. Ace was required by the government to meet monthly production and delivery schedules. If they failed, there was a very substantial financial penalty. In recent years the production and delivery schedule had become increasingly difficult to meet. As a matter of fact, for the last eight months, Abrams had scheduled overtime in order to meet the production and delivery schedule and thus avoid the financial penalty. This overtime not only increased unit production costs, but as a result of this consistent use of overtime, many employees began to realize that if they worked slower at the beginning of the month, they could receive more overtime at the end of the month.

This strategy to increase overtime wages was practiced even by senior employees. Abrams was very reluctant to fire anyone, especially senior employees. Even if he was inclined to do so, it was difficult to catch employees slowing down or to provide any reasonable evidence for such rash action.

Abrams was frustrated and perplexed.

Questions

1. Describe in detail the control dilemma that exists.
2. Are Abrams and the workers getting the same feedback?
3. What should Abrams do?

Incident 11–2
Mickey Mouse Controls

Bill: Hey, John, I could sure use some help. We regional supervisors are caught in the middle. What do you do about all this red tape we're having to put up with? The accounting department is all bothered about the way people are padding their expenses and about the cost of luncheons and long-distance calls. You know—their answer is nothing but more red tape.

John: Well, Bill, I don't know. I'm feeling the heat too. Upper management wants us to maintain our contacts with our brokers and try to get the money out in loans. So we push the district supervisors to see our best contacts or at least call them frequently. Yet lately, I've been having a heck of a time getting my men reimbursed for their expenses. Now the accounting department is kicking because we spend a few bucks taking someone to lunch or making a few long-distance calls.

Bill: I really don't know what to do, John. I'll admit that some of my people tend to charge the company for expenses that are for their personal entertainment. But how can I tell whether they're buttering up a broker or just living it up on the company? The accounting department must have some receipts and records to support expenses. Yet I think that getting a receipt from a parking lot attendant is carrying this control stuff too far. As a matter of fact, the other day, I caught a taxi at the airport and failed to get a receipt—I'll bet I have a hard time getting that money from the company even if I sign a notarized affidavit.

John: Well, the way I handle those things is to charge the company more for tips than I actually give—and you know they don't require receipts for tips. I just don't know how to decide whether those reimbursement receipts that I sign for my boys are legitimate. If I call a guy up and ask him about some items on a reimbursement request, he acts as though I'm charging him with grand larceny. So far, I've decided to sign whatever requests they turn in and leave the accounting department to scream if it wants to. The trouble is that I don't have any guidelines as to what is reasonable.

Bill: Yeah, but I don't want to ask questions about that because it would just result in more controls! It isn't up to me to be a policeman for the company. The accounting department sits back looking at all those figures—it should watch expenses. I ran into someone from the department the other day on what she called an internal audit trip, and she told me that they aren't in a position to say whether a $40 lunch at a restaurant is necessary to sell a loan. She said that the charge was made by one of my men and that I should check it out! Am I a regional production man or am I an accountant? I've got enough to do meeting my regional quota with my five district sales people. I can't go snooping around to find out whether they're taking advantage of the company. They may get the idea that I don't trust them, and I've always heard that good business depends on trust. Besides, our department makes the company more money than any other one! Why shouldn't we be allowed to spend a little of it?

John: Well, I say that the brass is getting hot about a relatively small problem. A little fudging on an expense account isn't going to break the company. I learned the other day that the accounting department doesn't require any receipts from the securities department people. They just give them a per diem for travel and let them spend it however they want to, just so long as they don't go over the allotted amount for the days that they're on trips.

Bill: Now that sounds like a good idea. Why can't we do that? It sure would make my life easier. I don't want to get a guilt complex about signing reimbursement requests that may look a little out of line. Why should I call a district man on the carpet for some small expense he swears really was the reason that he got the deal? Production is our job, so why can't the company leave us alone? They should let us decide what it takes to make a deal. If we don't produce the loans, we should catch flak about something that's important—not about these trifling details.

John: Bill, I've got to run now. But honestly, if I were you, I wouldn't worry about these Mickey Mouse controls. I'm just going to do my job and fill in the forms in order to stay out of trouble on the details. It's not worth getting upset about.

Questions

1. Has the company imposed overly restrictive controls?
2. Do you think the company has a good conception of control tolerances?
3. What should Bill do?

Exercise

Staying on Budget

As manager of the Ace Division of the Triple-A Company, you agreed to the following budget at the beginning of the current fiscal year: This budget was based on forecasted sales of 30,000 units during the year.

Fixed costs	$80,000
Subcontracting costs (variable, per unit)	$ 4
Other variable costs (per unit)	$ 2
Sales price	$10

You are six months into the fiscal year and have collected the following sales data:

Month	Actual Sales (units)
1	2,000
2	2,200
3	1,700
4	1,800
5	2,300
6	2,200

By shopping around, you have been able to hold your subcontracting costs to an average of $3.60 per unit. The fixed and other variable costs are conforming to budget.

A. What was the forecasted break-even point in sales for the Ace Division?
B. What is the revised break-even point?
C. What trends in the above information, if any, concern you?
D. Based on the preceding information, prepare a one-page report for your boss, summarizing the current status of the Ace Division.

Objectives

1. To emphasize the importance of properly controlling operating systems.
2. To apply the control concepts and principles presented in Chapter 11 to operating systems.
3. To introduce and discuss cost control, inventory control, and quality control.

Operations Control

Chapter Outline

CONTROLLING OPERATING
  COSTS
INVENTORY CONTROL
  ABC Classification System
  Reorder Point and Safety Stock
  The Order Quantity
  Material Requirements Planning
   (MRP)

QUALITY CONTROL
  Quality Checkpoints
  Types of Quality Control
  Acceptance Sampling
  Process Control Charts
  Quality Circles
SUMMARY

While the achievement of a steady state level of system performance implies that design and start-up problems have been solved, it does not mean that the pressure is off the production manager. Regardless of how careful the planning, few systems of any complexity can be expected to operate indefinitely without encountering some type of malfunction that must be corrected. This is true not only for the physical production process but for the production management system that monitors that process as well. Indeed, while machinery may produce scrap or break down, thus necessitating repairs, the operating and control system that governs the use of the machinery may provide faulty information and incorrect decisions, requiring that it, too, be overhauled.

Richard B. Chase and Nicholas J. Aquilano*

Product design, physical layout, and other design-related topics were discussed in Chapter 7. Unfortunately, designing an effective operating system does not in itself ensure that the system will operate efficiently. As indicated in the above quote, after the system has been designed and implemented, the day-to-day operations must be controlled. The system processes must be monitored; quality must be maintained; inventories must be managed; and all of this must be accomplished within cost constraints. In addition to ensuring that things do not get out of control, good operations control can be a substitute for resources. For example, good inventory control can reduce the investment cost in inventories. Similarly, good quality control can reduce scrap and wasted materials, thus reducing costs.

Effective operations control is attained by applying the basic control concepts discussed in Chapter 11 to the operations function of the organization. Operations controls generally relate to one of three areas: costs, inventories, or quality.

CONTROLLING OPERATING COSTS

Making sure that operating costs do not get out of hand is one of the primary jobs of the operations manager. The first requirement for controlling costs is to understand fully the organization's accounting and budgeting systems. The budgeting process was introduced in Chapters 6 and 11. Operations managers are primarily concerned with costs relating to labor, materials, and overhead. Figure 12–1 describes the major components of each of these costs. Variable overhead expenses are those that are assumed to change

---

* Richard B. Chase and Nicholas J. Aquilano, *Production and Operations Management: A Life-Cycle Approach,* rev. ed. (Homewood, Ill.: Richard D. Irwin, Inc., 1977), p. 579.

FIGURE 12–1
Budget Costs: The Basis for Cost Control

Type of Cost	Components
Direct labor	Wages and salaries of workers who are engaged in the direct generation of goods and services. This typically does not include wages and salaries of support personnel.
Materials	Cost of materials which become a tangible part of finished goods and services.
Production overhead—variable	Training new employees, safety training, supervision and clerical, overtime premium, shift premium, payroll taxes, vacation and holiday, retirement funds, group insurance, supplies, travel, repairs and maintenance.
Production overhead—fixed	Travel, research and development, fuel (coal, gas, or oil), electricity, water, repairs and maintenance, rent, depreciation, real estate taxes, insurance.

Source: Normal Gaither, *Production and Operations Management* (Hinsdale, Ill.: Dryden Press, 1980), p. 364.

with the level of production. Fixed overhead expenses are those that do not change appreciably with the level of production.

Normally, operations managers prepare monthly budgets for each of the major cost areas. Once these budgets have been approved by higher levels of management, they are put into effect. By carefully monitoring the ensuing labor, material, and overhead costs, the operations manager can compare actual costs to budgeted costs. The methods used for monitoring costs naturally vary, but they typically include many of those discussed in Chapter 11 (direct observation, written reports, break-even charts, etc.).

Usually, a cost control system only indicates when a particular cost is out of control; it does not address the question of *why* it is out of control. For example, suppose an operations manager determines from the monthly cost report that the labor costs on Product X are exceeding budget by 20 percent. The manager must then attempt to determine what is causing the cost overrun. The causes could be many: unmotivated employees, several new and untrained employees, low-quality raw materials, equipment breakdown, etc.

Determining the cause may require only a simple inspection of the facts, or it may require an in-depth analysis. Whatever the effort required, the operations manager must ultimately identify the source of the problem and then take the necessary corrective action. If the same cost problems continue

MANAGEMENT IN ACTION 12-1

Last Chance to Control Costs

Chapter 11 bankruptcy protection allows companies with severe financial problems the opportunity to get costs under control and try to make operations profitable rather than liquidate. Osborne Computer Corporation filed for Chapter 11 protection from creditors in 1983. Along with other changes, including a new strategy of finding market niches and

maintaining IBM compatibility, Osborne cut costs by reducing its staff from 1,000 in 1983 to 35. Osborne now has a positive cash flow and has to sell only 1,000 units a month to break even. According to President Ronald J. Brown, "In the old days, Osborne was selling 10,000 a month and still losing money."

Source: Deborah Wise, "Three Computer Makers and Chapter 11: Trying to Write a Happy Ending," *Business Week*, March 4, 1985, pp. 112–13.

to reoccur, chances are that the manager has not correctly identified the true cause of the problem or that the necessary corrective action has not been taken. Management in Action 12–1 describes how Osborne Computer used a form of bankruptcy to get their costs under control and avoid liquidation.

INVENTORY CONTROL

Inventory—quantity of raw materials, in-process goods, or finished goods on hand; serves as a buffer between different rates of flow associated with the operating system.

Inventories serve as a buffer between different rates of flow associated with the operating system. **Inventories** can generally be classified into one of three categories, depending on their respective location within the operating system: (1) raw material, (2) in-process, or (3) finished goods. Raw-material inventories serve as a buffer between purchasing and production. In-process inventories are used to buffer differences in the rates of flow through the various production processes. Finished-goods inventories act as a buffer between the final stage of production and shipping. Figure 12–2 illustrates these relationships.

Inventories add flexibility to the operating system and allow the organization to do the following:

1. Purchase, produce, and ship in economic lot sizes rather than in small jobs.
2. Produce on a smooth, continuous basis even though the demand for the finished product or raw material may fluctuate.
3. Prevent major problems when forecasts of demand are in error or when there are unforeseen slowdowns or stoppages in supply or production.

When making inventory decisions, management must answer three basic questions: (1) What items should be carried in inventory? (2) When should

FIGURE 12–2
Inventories as Buffers between Different Rates of Flow

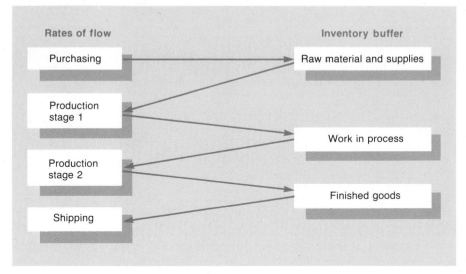

the items be ordered? (3) How many of the selected items should be ordered and carried?

If it were not so costly, every organization would attempt to maintain very large inventories in order to facilitate purchasing, production scheduling, and distribution. However, there are many costs associated with carrying inventory. Potential inventory costs include such factors as insurance, property taxes, storage costs, obsolescence costs, spoilage, and the opportunity cost of the money invested in the inventory. The relative importance of these costs depends on the specific inventory being held. For example, with women's fashions, the obsolescence costs are potentially very high. Similarly, the storage costs might be very high for dangerous chemicals. Thus, management must continually balance the costs of holding the inventory against the costs of running short of raw materials, in-process goods, or finished goods. Management in Action 12–2 describes how Toys 'Я' Us uses a computerized inventory control system to identify high- and low-demand items.

ABC Classification System

One of the simplest and most widely used systems for managing inventories is the ABC approach. The **ABC classification system** is a method of managing inventories based on their total value. In many organizations, a small number of products or materials, Group A, accounts for the greatest dollar value of the inventory. The next group of items, Group B, accounts for a moderate amount of the inventory value; and Group C accounts for

ABC classification system—method of managing inventories based on their total value.

MANAGEMENT IN ACTION 12–2

Computerized Inventory Control at Toys 'Я' Us

Toys 'Я' Us, the national discount toy retailer, operates over 180 stores in the United States, with over 18,000 items in each store. Every product in every store is tagged with an item number. When a customer makes a purchase, the item number is recorded on a computer as part of the checkout procedure. The store uses this detailed log of items sold when replacing stock. Corporate headquarters uses the computerized log to daily monitor sales by items as well as sales by store. Close attention to the buying patterns of customers allows Toys 'Я' Us to mark down slow-selling items, reorder high-demand items in larger quantities, and pick up on trends before the crucial Christmas buying season.

Sources: Subrata N. Chakravarty, "Toys 'Я' Fun," *Forbes*, March 28, 1983, p. 58.

---

a small amount of the inventory value. This concept is illustrated in Figure 12–3. The dollar value reflects both the cost of the item and its usage rate. For example, an item might be put into Group A through a combination of either low cost and high usage or high cost and low usage.

The purpose of grouping items in this way is to establish appropriate control over each item. Generally, the items in Group A are monitored very closely; the items in Group B are monitored with some care; and the items in Group C are only checked occasionally. Items in Group C are usually not subject to the detailed paperwork of items in Groups A and B. In an automobile service station, gasoline would be considered a Group A item and would be monitored daily. Tires, batteries, and transmission fluid would be Group B items and might be checked weekly or biweekly. Valve stems, windshield wiper blades, radiator caps, hoses, fan belts, oil and gas additives, car wax, and so forth would be Group C items and might be checked and ordered only every two or three months.[1]

One potential shortcoming of the ABC method is that although the items in Group C might have very little cost/usage value, they may be critical to the operation. It is possible, for instance for a very inexpensive bolt to be vital to the production of a costly piece of machinery. One way to handle items like this is to designate them as Group A or B items regardless of their cost/usage value. The major advantage of the ABC method is that it concentrates on controlling those items that are most important to the operation.

Reorder Point and Safety Stock

After the decision has been made concerning what items will be carried in inventory, a decision must be made concerning when to order each item. There are two basic methods for determining when to order: the fixed-

324

FIGURE 12–3
ABC Inventory Classification (inventory value for each group versus the group's portion of the total list)

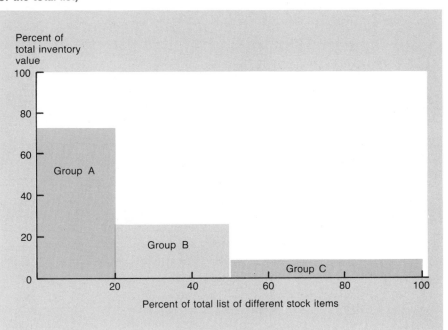

Source: Richard B. Chase and Nicholas J. Aquilano, *Production and Operations Management*, 4th ed. (Homewood, Ill.: Richard D. Irwin, Inc., 1985), p. 511.

order quantity method and the fixed-order period method. Under the fixed-order quantity method, illustrated in Figure 12–4, orders are placed whenever the inventory reaches a certain predetermined level, regardless of how long it takes to reach that level. In Figure 12–4, orders would be placed at times T_1, T_2, T_3, and T_4 under the fixed-order quantity method. Thus, the time between orders can vary depending on the demand. Fixed-order quantity systems usually assume continual monitoring of inventory levels. This is not an unrealistic assumption today, since many organizations have computerized their inventory records.

Under the fixed-order period illustrated in Figure 12–5, restocking orders are placed at predetermined, regular time intervals regardless of how much inventory is on hand. With this method, the amount ordered rather than the time between orders can vary, depending on the demand. The fixed-order period method requires that inventory be tallied only at the designated review periods. Both the fixed-order quantity method and the fixed-order period methods have certain advantages. The fixed-order period method is easier to administer because orders can be placed on a regular basis and inventory does not have to be continually counted. However, supplies in the fixed-order period method are more likely to run out if demand goes

FIGURE 12–4
Fixed-Order Quantity Method of Reordering

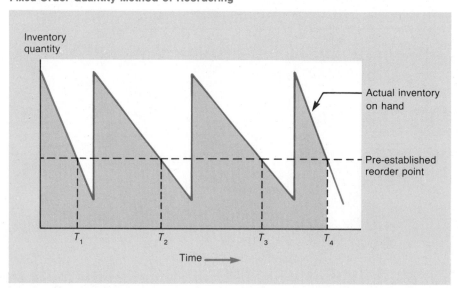

FIGURE 12–5
Fixed-Order Period Method of Reordering

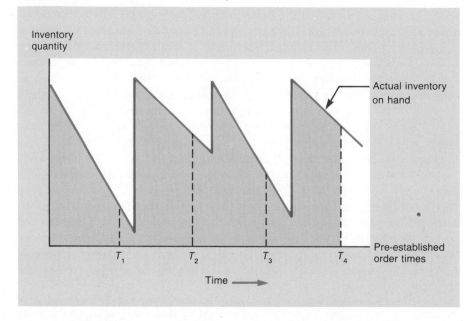

up unexpectedly. The fixed-order quantity method has the advantage of having all orders be of an equal and economical size. In general, the fixed-order period method lends itself to inventories where it is more desirable to physically count inventory on a regular periodic basis, such as in many small retail stores. The fixed-order quantity method lends itself to inventories that are easily computerized and can be continually monitored, such as with most wholesale suppliers.

Most organizations maintain **safety stocks** to accommodate unexpected changes in demand and supply and allow for delivery time. The optimum size of the safety stock is determined by the relative costs of a stock-out of the item versus the costs of carrying the additional inventory. The cost of a stock-out of the item is very often difficult to estimate. For example, the customer may go elsewhere rather than wait for the product. If the product is available at another branch location, the stock-out cost may be simply the cost of shipping the item from one location to another.

Safety stocks–inventory maintained to accommodate unexpected changes in demand and supply and to allow for delivery time.

The Order Quantity

Determining the amount to order is a decision that goes hand in hand with determining the reorder point. Most materials and finished products are consumed one by one or a few units at a time; however, because of the costs associated with ordering, shipping, and handling inventory, it is usually desirable to purchase materials and products in large lots or batches.

When determining the optimum number of units to order, the ordering costs must be balanced against the cost of carrying the inventory. Ordering costs include such things as the cost of preparing the order, shipping costs, and setup costs. Carrying costs include storage costs, insurance, taxes, obsolescence, and the opportunity costs of the money invested in the inventory. The smaller the number of units ordered, the lower the carrying costs (because the average inventory held is smaller) but the larger the ordering costs (because more orders must be placed). The optimum number of units to order, referred to as the **economic order quantity (EOQ),** is determined by the point where ordering costs equal carrying costs, or where total cost (ordering costs plus carrying costs) is at a minimum. Figure 12–6 graphically shows the inverse relationship between ordering costs and carrying costs. The total cost curve is found by vertically summing the ordering cost curve and the carrying cost curve. The lowest point on the total cost curve corresponds to the point where ordering costs equal carrying costs and determines the economic order quantity.

Economic order quantity (EOQ)–optimum number of units to order at one time.

The greatest weakness of the EOQ approach is the difficulty in accurately determining the actual carrying and ordering costs. However, research has shown that the total costs associated with order sizes that are reasonably close to the economic order quantity do not differ appreciably from the minimum total costs associated with the EOQ.[2] Thus, as long as the estimated carrying and ordering costs are "in the ball park," meaningful results can be obtained using this approach. Variations of this basic model have been

FIGURE 12–6
Inventory Costs versus Order Size

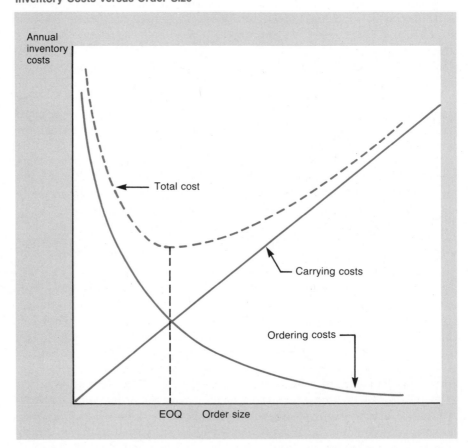

developed for taking into account such things as purchase quantity and other special discounts.

EOQ analysis is directly compatible with the fixed-order quantity method of reordering. Although the quantity ordered varies under the fixed-order period method, EOQ analysis can still be used to help set up the times between the designated order periods. The idea behind this approach is to calculate the average number of days required between orders so that the expected order size would approximate the EOQ. This method would work only in situations where the demand does not fluctuate appreciably.

QUALITY CONTROL

Quality is a relative term that means different things to different people. The consumer who demands quality may have a completely different concept than the operations manager who demands quality. The consumer is concerned with service, reliability, performance, appearance, and so forth. The operations manager's primary concern is that the product or service specifications be achieved, whatever they may be. For the operations manager, quality is determined in relation to the specifications or standards set in the design stages. Figure 12–7 lists some specific reasons for maintaining **quality control.**

When determining the most desirable level of quality, management must attempt to balance the marketability of higher levels of quality versus the cost of attaining this higher quality. Figure 12–8 graphically depicts the

Quality control–process of ensuring or maintaining a certain level of quality for materials, products, or services.

FIGURE 12–8
Quality versus Cost

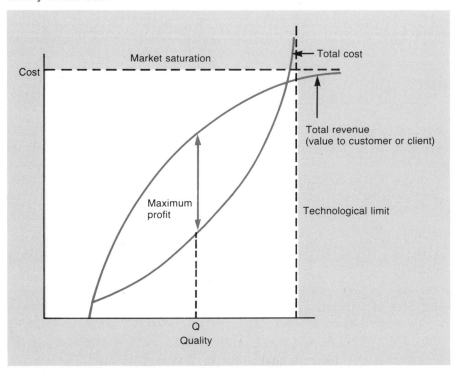

Quality Control in the Hotel Industry

In 1981, after 16 years as a five-star, five-diamond resort, the Boca Raton Hotel and Club lost one of the stars. In early 1982, management began development of a comprehensive quality assurance (QA) program. Management stated exactly what it wanted from a QA program—to reduce employee turnover, increase positive guest comments, improve labor productivity, and make quality the responsibility of every employee.

The quality assurance program involved forming QA committees, preparing detailed performance standards for every position at the resort, analyzing the types and costs of errors that occurred during operation, and recommending procedure changes in order to avoid errors.

The program was a success. Negative guest complaints dropped from 28 percent to 5 percent in the first three months after the program was implemented. Employee turnover dropped from 117 percent in 1981 to 50 percent in 1983. Total cost savings exceeded $1 million. In 1983, the Boca Raton Hotel and Club regained its fifth star.

Source: W. Gerald Glover, R. Scott Morrison, Jr., and Alfred C. Briggs, Jr., "Making Quality Count: Boca Raton's Approach to Quality Assurance," *Cornell Hotel and Restaurant Administration Quarterly*, May 1984, pp. 39–45.

general relationship between these factors. As shown in the graph, total revenue is a function of quality. Consumers may not be willing to pay for extremely high levels of quality. A cook may desire a mixer that has three to five variable speeds and is dependable for 5 to 10 years; however, the same cook is probably not willing to invest substantially more money to obtain a 20-speed, lifetime-guaranteed mixer. The shape of the total cost curve shows that the cost of quality generally is increasing at an increasing rate. Point Q where profit is at a maximum, is the most desirable level of quality.

While the costs represented in Figure 12–8 are very real costs, management's task of determining the most appropriate level of quality is often based on estimates. However, once a policy decision has set the desired level of quality, the operations manager is responsible to ensure that the stated level of quality is achieved. Management in Action 12–3 describes the results of a program to raise the level of quality at a major resort hotel.

Quality Checkpoints

If the desired level of quality is to be attained in the final product or service, checks or inspections may be required at several different points in the operating system. Figure 12–9 shows some of the more frequent inspection points in a manufacturing system. The first inspection point is when the raw materials are received. The quality of the raw materials must be compatible with the quality desired in the final product. The incoming materials should be checked for quality, quantity, and possible damage.

FIGURE 12–9
Potential Quality Control Checkpoints

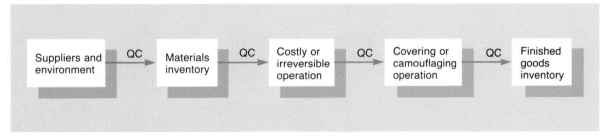

Depending on the operation to be performed, it may be desirable to inspect the materials again before they enter the operation. This is especially likely if the operation is costly or irreversible (such as with silverplating).

Other checks may take place prior to operations which cover or camouflage defects in the process. For example, painting may temporarily camouflage a flaw which resulted from an earlier operation.

A final inspection should take place before the product or service is distributed to the customer. This provides a check on the end product or service. It should be stressed that the optimum location and number of checkpoints depend on two separate costs: inspection cost and the cost of passing a defective. As the number of inspection locations increases, so do the inspection costs; however, the probability of passing on a defect decreases.

Types of Quality Control

Figure 12–9 suggests that variations in quality can occur in the inputs to the operating system, in the transformation operations, or in the final product or service. Quality control relating to the inputs or outputs of the system is referred to as *product quality control.* Product quality control is used when the quality is being evaluated with respect to a batch of products or services that already exists, such as incoming raw materials or finished goods. Product quality control lends itself to *acceptance sampling* procedures in which some portion of a batch of outgoing items (or incoming materials) is inspected in an attempt to ensure that the batch meets specifications with regard to the percentage of defective units which will be tolerated in the batch. Under acceptance sampling procedures, the decision to accept or reject an entire batch is based on a sample or group of samples.

Quality control relating to the control of a machine or an operation during the production process is called *process control.* Under process control, machines and/or processes are periodically checked to ensure that they are operating within certain preestablished tolerances. Adjustments are made as necessary to prevent the machines or processes from getting out of control and producing bad items. Process control is used to prevent the production of defectives, whereas product control is used to detect the presence of defectives.

Acceptance Sampling

Acceptance sampling—statistical method of predicting the quality of a batch or large group of products by inspecting a sample or group of samples.

Acceptance sampling is a method of predicting the quality of a batch or large group of products from an inspection of a sample or group of samples taken from the batch. Acceptance sampling is used for one of three basic reasons: (1) The possible losses or costs of passing defective items are not great, relative to the cost of inspection—it would not be wise to inspect every match produced by a match factory. (2) Inspection of some items requires destruction of the product being tested—as is the case when testing flash bulbs. (3) Sampling usually produces results more rapidly than does a census.

The procedure followed in acceptance sampling is to draw a random sample, of a given size, from the batch or lot being examined. The sample is then tested and analyzed. If more than a certain number (determined statistically) are found defective, the entire batch is rejected; it has an unacceptably large percentage of defective items. Because of the possibility of making an incorrect inference concerning the batch, acceptance sampling always involves risks. The risk that the producer is willing to take of rejecting a good batch is referred to as the producer's risk. The risk of accepting a bad batch is referred to as the consumer's risk. Obviously, one would desire to minimize both the producer's risk and the consumer's risk. However, the only method of simultaneously lowering both of these risks is to increase the sample size—which also increases the inspection costs. Therefore, the usual approach is to decide the maximum acceptable risk for both the producer and the consumer and to design the acceptance sampling plan around these risks.

Process Control Charts

Process control chart—time-based graphic display that shows whether a machine or process is producing items that meet preestablished specifications.

A **process control chart** is a time-based, graphic display which shows whether a machine or process is producing items that meet certain preestablished specifications. If the machine or process is producing items that do not meet specifications, then it is said to be out of control. Control charts do not attempt to show why a machine or process is out of control, only if it is out of control.

The most frequently used process control charts are called mean and range charts. Mean charts (also called $\overline{X}$-charts) monitor the mean or average value of some characteristic (dimension, weight, etc.) of the items produced by a machine or process. Range charts (also called R-charts) monitor the range of variability of some characteristic (dimension, weight, etc.) of the items produced by a machine or process.

The quality control inspector, using control charts, first calculates the desired level of the characteristic being measured. The next step is to calculate statistically the upper and lower control limits, which determine how much the characteristic can vary from the desired level before the machine or process is considered to be out of control. Once the control chart has been set up, the quality control inspector periodically takes a small sample from the machine or process outputs. Depending on the type of chart being used, the mean or range of the sample is plotted on the control chart. By plotting the results of each sample on the control chart, it is easy to identify quickly any abnormal trends in quality. A sample mean chart is shown in Figure 12–10.

A mean or range chart used by itself can easily lead to false conclusions. For example, the upper and lower control limits for a machined part might be 0.1000 millimeter and 0.0800 millimeter respectively. A sample of four parts of 0.1200, 0.1100, 0.0700, and 0.0600 would yield an acceptable mean of 0.0900; yet, every element of the sample is out of tolerance. For this reason, when monitoring variables, it is usually desirable to use mean and range charts simultaneously to ensure that a machine or process is under control.

FIGURE 12–10
Mean Chart

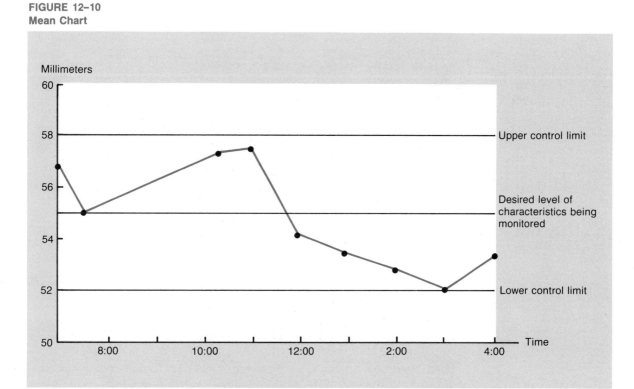

Quality Circle

Quality circle–members of a work unit who meet on a regular basis to discuss quality problems and generate ideas for improving quality.

The relatively new idea of quality circles was originated in Japan. A **quality circle** is composed of a group of employees (usually from 5 to 15 people) who are members of a single work unit, section, or department. The unit's supervisor or manager is usually included as a member of the quality circle. These employees have a common bond; they perform a similar service or function by turning out a product, part of a product, or a service. Membership in a quality circle is almost always voluntary. The basic purpose of a quality circle is to discuss quality problems and to generate ideas that might help improve quality.

A quality circle usually begins by exposing the members to specialized training relating to quality. Meetings of a quality circle are normally held once or twice per month and last for one to two hours. After the initial training, a quality circle begins by discussing specific quality problems which are brought up by either management representatives or by the circle members. Staff experts may be called upon by the circle as needed. Figure 12–11 outlines the major benefits of a quality control circle. As with other forms of participative management, the underlying objective of quality circles is to get employees actively involved. Management in Action 12–4 describes the positive impact that quality circles have had at the Milwaukee Road Company.

FIGURE 12–11
Potential Benefits of a Quality Control Circle

1. Problems—including some that have existed for years—do get solved.
2. Employees participate in changing things for the better.
3. Employees and managers broaden and develop as they receive special training and put it into practice.
4. Morale improves and is maintained as people become involved in helping to improve their work life and fulfill their potential.
5. The channel for upward and downward communication is strengthened.
6. Greater trust is built between levels in the organization and among units.
7. Managers are relieved of many worries and concerns without releasing control or having any of their authority diluted.
8. They are relatively inexpensive to start.
9. They can evolve into other forms of employee participation.

Sources: Adapted from Rich Tewell, "How to Keep Quality Circles in Motion," *Business*, January–March 1982, pp. 48–49; Edward E. Lawles III and Susan A. Mohrman, "Quality Circle after the Fad," *Harvard Business Review*, January–February 1985, pp. 65–71.

SUMMARY

If an operating system is to be effective, its day-to-day operations must be properly controlled. Effective operations control is attained by applying basic control concepts to the operations function of the organization. Operations controls can be classified in one of three general areas: costs, inventories, or quality.

The first requirement for controlling costs is to fully understand the organization's accounting and budgeting system. By carefully monitoring labor, material, and overhead costs, the operations manager can compare actual costs to budgeted costs. Normally, a cost control system only indicates when a particular cost is out of control; it does not address the question of why it is out of control.

Inventories can generally be classified as raw-materials inventories, in-process inventories, and finished-goods inventories. Raw-materials inventories serve as a buffer between purchasing and production. In-process inventories are used to buffer differences in the rates of flow through the various production processes. Finished-goods inventories act as a buffer between the final stage of production and shipping.

When making inventory decisions, management must answer three basic questions: (1) What items should be carried in inventory? (2) When should the items be ordered? (3) How many of the selected items should be ordered and carried?

The ABC classification system is a simple method for managing inventories in accordance with their value.

The fixed-order quantity and the fixed-order period are the two most common methods for determining the reorder point. The economic order quantity is one method for determining the optimum order size by finding the lot size that minimizes the total ordering and carrying costs of the inventory.

Quality is defined for the operations manager by the product or service specifications. When determining the most appropriate level of quality, management must balance the marketability of higher quality against the cost of attaining the higher quality. Generally, a minimum level of quality is necessary before the product or service can be sold. There is also usually a point of quality beyond which consumers are unwilling to pay.

Quality checks are appropriately performed at several points in the operating system. These points include: when the raw materials are received; before costly or irreversible operations are performed; before operations which may cover or camouflage defects; and after the product or service has been completed.

Quality control relating to existing products or services (including raw materials) is referred to as product quality control. Quality control relating to the control of a machine or an operation during the production process is called process control.

A quality circle is a group of employees that meets on a regular basis to discuss quality problems and to generate ideas for improving quality.

References and Additional Readings

[1] Chase and Aquilano, *Production and Operations Management,* 4th ed (Homewood, IL, Richard D. Irwin, Inc., 1985), pp. 511–12.

[2] John F. Magee, "Guides to Inventory Policy: I. Functions and Lot Size," *Harvard Business Review,* January–February 1956, pp. 49–60.

Review Questions

1. Name the three major categories of costs that operations managers are usually concerned about from a control standpoint. Give several examples of each category.
2. What is the difference between fixed and variable overhead expenses?
3. What are the purposes of inventories?
4. How does the ABC classification system work?
5. Describe two basic methods for determining reorder points.
6. What is the purpose of carrying safety stock?
7. What costs affect the economic order quantity?
8. Define quality.
9. List five possible reasons for quality control.
10. At what points in a manufacturing system might quality checks be appropriately performed?
11. What is a process control chart?
12. What is a quality circle?

Discussion Questions

1. Discuss the production control problems that can arise when demand is continually changing.
2. It has been said that good inventory management can make the difference between success and failure in certain industries.

Name several industries in which this statement is particularly applicable and discuss the reasons for your answer.

3. Since the cost of a stock-out of an inventory item is usually very difficult to estimate, how can the safety stock level be determined with any accuracy?

4. Since quality is a relative concept, how does a manager ever know if the quality level is optimum?

Incident 12–1
Production Problems

The Braddock Company of Sea Shore City fabricates stamped metal parts used in the production of wheelbarrows. Braddock fabricates two basic styles of wheelbarrow trays: one is for a deep, four-cubic-foot construction model and the other is for a shallow, two-cubic-foot homeowner's model. Braddock's process is simple: raw metal sheets are picked up from inventory (Braddock presently maintains about 7 days' worth of the large metal sheets for the construction model and about 10 days' worth of the smaller sheets for the homeowner model) and fed into a large machine which bends and shapes the metal into the desired tray. The trays are then inspected and packaged, 10 to a box, for shipping.

In the past few days, Braddock has been experiencing quality problems with both tray styles. Undesirable creases have been forming in the corners following the stamping operation. However, the problem with the construction model tray is more pronounced and appeared almost three full days before it did on the homeowner's model.

Several incidents have occurred at Braddock during the past week that Hal McCarthy, the operations manager, thinks may have a bearing on the problem. Shorty McCune, a machine operator and labor activist, was accused of drinking on the job and released a few days before the problem began. Since his release, Shorty has been seen in and around the plant talking to several other employees. About two weeks ago, Braddock also began receiving raw metal from a new supplier because of an attractive price break.

Presently the only inspection performed by the company is the postfabrication inspection.

Questions

1. What do you think is causing Braddock's problem?
2. Why is the problem more pronounced on the construction model than on the homeowner model?
3. How can Braddock eliminate its problem?

Incident 12–2
The Purchasing Department

The buyers for a large airline company were having a general discussion with the manager of purchasing in her office Friday afternoon. The inspection of received parts was a topic of considerable discussion. Apparently, several parts had recently been rejected six months or more after being received. Such a rejection delay was costing the company a considerable amount of money, since most of the items were beyond the standard 90-day warranty period. The current purchasing procedures state that the department using the parts is responsible for the inspection of all parts, including stock and nonstock items. The company employs an inspector who is supposedly responsible for inspecting all aircraft parts, in accordance with FAA regulations. However, the inspector has not been able to check those items purchased as nonaircraft parts, because he is constantly overloaded. Furthermore, many of the aircraft parts are not being properly inspected because of insufficient facilities and equipment.

One recent example of the type of problem being encountered was the acceptance of a batch of plastic forks that broke readily when in use. The vendor had shipped over a hundred cases of the forks of the wrong type. Unfortunately, all the purchase order specified was "forks." Another example was the acceptance of several cases of plastic cups with the wrong logo. The cups were subsequently put into use for in-flight service and had to be used, since no other cups were available. A final example was the discovery that several expensive radar tubes in stock were found to be defective and with expired warranty. These tubes had to be reordered at almost $900 per unit.

It was apparent that the inspection function was inadequate and unable to cope with the volume of material being received. Purchasing would have to establish some guidelines as to what material should or should not be inspected after being processed by the material checker. Some of the buyers felt that the material checker (who is not the inspector) should have more responsibility than simply checking quantity and comparing the packing sheet against purchase orders. Some believed that the checker could and should have caught the obvious errors in the logo on the plastic cups. Furthermore, if the inspector had sampled the forks, they would have been rejected immediately. As for the radar tubes, they should have been forwarded by the inspector to the avionics shop for bench check and then placed in stock. Some buyers felt that the inspector should be responsible for inspection of all materials received, regardless of its function or usage. It was pointed out, however, that several landing gears had been received from the overhaul/repair vendor and tagged by the inspector as being acceptable. These gears later turned out to be defective and unusable and had to be returned for repair. This generated considerable discussion concerning the inspector's qualifications, testing capacity, workload, and responsibility for determining if the unit should be shop checked.

Much of the remaining discussion centered around what purchasing should recommend for the inspection of material. One proposal was that everything received be funneled through the Inspection Department. Another proposal was that all material be run through inspection except as otherwise noted on the purchase order. Other questions were also raised. If purchasing required all material to be inspected, would this demand additional inspection personnel? Who would be responsible for inspection specifications? Furthermore, who should determine what items should be shop checked?

The meeting was finally adjourned until the following Friday.

Questions

1. What do you think of the current system of inspection?
2. Do you think the inspector is incompetent?
3. What would you suggest at the meeting next Friday?

Exercise
Out of Control?*

Situation 1

The manager of a fast-food hamburger chain must ensure that the hamburger that is advertised as a quarterpounder is actually 4 ounces, more or less. The company policy states that the quarterpounder must come within three 10ths of an ounce (.3 oz.) of being 4 ounces in order to be used. The chart below reflects the expected weight of the patty (4 oz.), the upper control limit (4.3 oz.) and the lower control limit (3.7 oz.). A sample of patties has been taken each day for the last eight days and the average weight recorded for each day is recorded on the chart below.

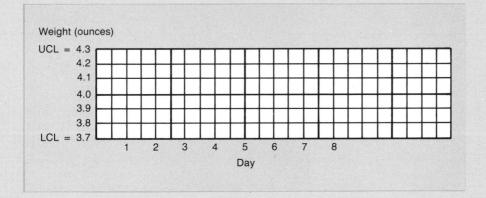

A.   Should the pattie preparation process be investigated?
B.   Why do you think so?

Situation 2

You are the owner of a car repair shop that specializes in tune-ups. On each work order, the mechanic records the time at which he began the tune-up and the time when finished. From these data, you can determine how long each mechanic spends on each job. You expect each job to take around 40 minutes; however, you know that if someone was in a great hurry, the job could be done in as few as 20 minutes. Also, you believe

* This exercise is adapted from Henri L. Tosi and Jerald W. Young, Management Experiences, and Demonstrations (Homewood, Ill.: Richard D. Irwin, Inc., 1982), pp. 45–47.

that under no circumstances should a tune-up take over one hour. A recently hired mechanic has recorded the times shown on the chart below for his last 11 tune-up jobs:

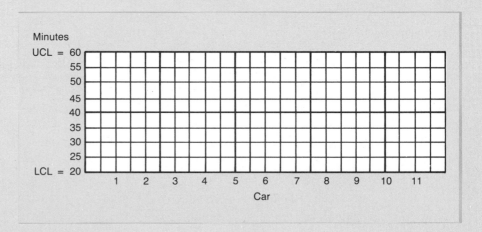

A. Should you have a talk with this person? Is there a problem?

B. Why do you think so?

Section 3 Case

IBM*

International Business Machines Corp. has stood as a symbol of the strengths and threats of big business for several decades, both in the United States and in the foreign markets in which it does 40 percent of its business. That image—and the reality behind the image—has proven to be a mixed blessing. On the one hand, IBM enjoys immense clout as the dominant force in the mainframe computer market and has long set the standards for customer service and support. In 1984, IBM ranked first for the second year in a row in *Fortune* magazine's survey of the most admired corporations. But IBM has been widely accused of abusing its power in order to obliterate its competitors and to force its technical standards on the market. Although the Justice Department dropped its antitrust suit in 1981, several firms have recently filed separate suits. IBM's new chief executive officer John F. Akers spends half of his time speaking and testifying in Washington and in capitals around the world in an attempt to soften IBM's image.

The Original Model of Success

Like many of those corporations that have enjoyed great success over the long run, IBM bears the imprint of the leadership of an individual with a distinctive vision. Thomas Watson, Sr., guided the destinies of IBM for three decades, passing control to his son Thomas Jr. in the mid-1950s. Among other things, the senior Watson established IBM's emphasis on marketing and customer service. Employees were well paid and superbly trained; but in return, they were expected to conform to a rigid code of corporate behavior and accept a high level of corporate paternalism. Watson also had a keen eye for new markets and opportunities, though Thomas Jr. deserves much of the credit for steering the firm toward computers.

Building on the firm foundations left by his father and profiting from the mistakes of several competitors who had a head start on IBM in the computer market, Thomas Watson, Jr., set the policies for IBM's computer operations. These policies, which remained essentially unchanged until the late 1970s, earned IBM about 60 percent of the worldwide market for large computer systems. That figure would probably be even higher if IBM had not felt constrained by antitrust considerations and had the company been willing to settle for lower net margins.

IBM developed and manufactured nearly all of its products in-house. Though strict controls over quality were maintained, IBM never led the industry in innovation. To the contrary, IBM had an interest in retarding

---

* This case was prepared by Benjamin Harrison, Georgia State University.

the development of both hardware and software. For many years, most large systems were leased. The leases provided a steady cash flow for the company and made computers available for many firms that would have been reluctant to make large capital investments. But to protect its own investments, IBM rarely cut prices of existing lines, even when it could have done so easily. For the same reason, new systems were expected to have a life cycle of four or five years, long enough to ensure a healthy return in the form of lease payments. IBM also developed its own software standards for operating systems and communications. Once a user installed IBM equipment, it was usually very difficult to install equipment that used different standards.

IBM's concentration on the large corporate customer who valued reliability and security above other considerations left several obvious opportunities open for other computer makers. One group of companies—the so-called "BUNCH" companies, consisting of Burroughs, Univac, National Cash Register, Control Data Corporation, and Honeywell—competed directly with IBM in terms of technical performance. IBM never entered the small but prestigious market for supercomputers. The rather long life cycle of IBM's systems gave other competitors time to develop and market "plug compatible" systems. By saving on research and development expenses, by providing lower levels of service, and sometimes by settling for lower margins, these systems could be sold for considerably less than the IBM systems on which they were modeled.

IBM was slow to appreciate the wide appeal of smaller systems, the minicomputers, which became technically feasible in the mid-1960s. Several very substantial companies have been built on minicomputers alone; other firms, well established in related industries, have become powers in the computer industry though their minicomputers.

Thinking Small at "Big Blue"

IBM's financial performance in the early 1970s remained well above industry averages. But signs of potential trouble were beginning to appear. The real growth rate, while enviable compared to that of nearly all firms of IBM's size in other industries, was slipping slowly and lagged well behind some of its much smaller competitors. The most obvious failure, as alluded to above, was IBM's late and not particularly successful entry into the minicomputer market. In fact, the mainframe or large-systems market which IBM dominated was the slowest growing major segment of the computer market.

By the late 1970s, IBM's stock was losing some of its luster. The underlying reason was a spreading impression that IBM had become too big to keep up with the computer marketplace. In a word, Big Blue seemed to be a "dinosaur," a victim of its own success. The unthinkable happened in 1979, profits actually fell for the first time since the depression. The conventional wisdom of the market, however, trailed management's foresight by several years. A significant shift in IBM's strategies was already under way. Despite the veritable industry of "IBM watching" that had developed, few analysts anticipated what was in store. IBM's penchant for understatement and secrecy is certainly one element of IBM's style that has not changed.

The individuals who deserve the greatest credit for shifting IBM's strategy are Frank Carey and John Opel. Carey was groomed for the presidency by Thomas Watson, Jr., and directed the firm through most of the 1970s. Opel, in turn, was Carey's protégé and served as CEO and president from 1980 to 1985. This deliberate process of succession continues with John Akers, whose appointment in 1985 was greeted favorably by the industry press and the stock market.

The new strategy implemented by Carey and Opel consists of several elements, whose relationships with each other became apparent only in the early 1980s. In terms of organizational structure, usually the most difficult aspect of any large firm's operations to change, the most striking feature of the revitalized IBM is the system of independent business units, or IBUs. IBUs have been used with considerable success by several large firms. But their appearance at IBM is especially remarkable because of IBM's traditions of tight controls and highly centralized corporate strategy.

Eleven IBUs were founded in 1980. Although the details of their organization vary somewhat from case to case and several have been substantially reorganized, they are broadly similar. They have what amount to independent boards, can set their own strategies for competing in particular markets, and are not always obliged to consult with corporate headquarters before making policy decisions.

It is apparent in retrospect that the rationale for the IBUs has been to achieve flexibility. In a technical industry like computers, flexibility has several dimensions. The first step is to develop new products quickly. That in turn requires that top management keep in close touch with the needs of customers and with the newest ideas coming out of the labs. It also means that managers must have the authority and the incentive to take risks on new, untested products. The element of risk taking within the context of a large corporation is sometimes called "intrapreneurship," in recognition of the special attributes of successful entrepreneurs. Finally, new products and new markets may make it desirable to implement new operating strategies for marketing and manufacturing.

Along with its IBUs, IBM has undertaken a wide variety of joint ventures and made several partial or complete acquisitions. The rationale again is to achieve flexibility. To advance quickly in the wider variety of markets in which IBM is competing, even a giant with IBM's resources cannot develop expertise as readily as it can acquire it through cooperation. The joint ventures and the new companies become something like IBUs themselves, or they can be integrated into ongoing operations. The most ambitious acquisition to date has been the purchase of Rolm, a maker of sophisticated communications switching gear, for $1.26 billion in 1984.

The Case of the Personal Computer

The IBUs at IBM reflect the firm's interest in the newest and most rapidly expanding markets, such as industrial robots, automatic teller machines, and microcomputers. By far the best known and the best documented of the IBUs has been the Entry Systems Division, which developed IBM's phenomenally successful microcomputer, the Personal Computer (or PC). Its story is worth relating in some detail because it illustrates so well the flexibility that an IBU can display.

The microcomputer emerged, to almost everyone's great surprise, as a significant segment of the computer market in 1978–79. The most conspicuous maker at that time was Apple Computer, which was launched by two young college dropouts working in a garage. Obviously, this was a special type of market. In 1980, IBM decided that the microcomputer market represented a challenge that should not be neglected as the minicomputer had been 15 years before.

The PC began as a small project in Boca Raton, Florida, where IBM already had a minicomputer manufacturing facility. Philip D. Estridge, a vice president, was put in charge of a team of 12 engineers and given a mandate to develop a microcomputer within a year. To save time and to avoid high start-up costs for what was essentially an experiment, the PC used mostly components purchased from outside suppliers. Another break with IBM tradition was that the PC was an "open" machine. That is, the PC was so designed that third parties could easily manufacture various accessories to be used with the new machine. The microprocessor was a relatively untried new model produced by Intel Corporation, in which IBM has since acquired a 25 percent interest. The software was equally open; in fact, IBM actively assisted software developers in writing applications programs. To sell the PC, IBM relied from the beginning on independent dealers, although its own sales force has recently picked up some of the large corporate accounts.

These decisions all proved to be very sound—so sound that the Entry Systems Division had grown to 10,000 employees and $5 billion in annual sales by 1984. In the process, the Entry Systems Division encountered some of the control and staffing problems that small companies experience with rapid growth. For several years, Estridge had almost a free hand and reported to corporate headquarters only every quarter; but in 1983, the division was integrated into one of the established operating groups. As frequently happens with engineers in the microcomputer industry, most of the original developers of the PC have left IBM to pursue more independent ventures.

More recently, IBM entered the volatile home computer market with its PC Jr. In the opinion of the microcomputer press and the marketplace, the PC Jr was at best a marginal product, with an inadequate keyboard and a relatively "closed" architecture that made it difficult to expand the capacities of the machine. Characteristically, IBM did not concede that a mistake had been committed. Within less than a year, however, IBM introduced a new version with an improved keyboard and greater expandability. The smoothness with which the new PC Jr. was introduced impressed the critics far more than anything about the computer itself. As a final example of flexibility, IBM announced in early 1985 that it was discontinuing production of the PC Jr. Apparently high sales could not be maintained without considerable discounts, which reduced margins below what IBM is accustomed to receiving.

The Challenge for the Future

In 1984, IBM had annual sales of $46 billion and 395,000 employees. Overall sales were growing at a rate of 15 percent a year; net margins averaged about 12 percent. The official corporate goal is to achieve sales of $100 billion by 1990. Soon after that, IBM may well be in a position to become the largest corporation in the world.

To fulfill such ambitious goals, IBM will have to continue to develop new products and undertake new ventures. IBM's traditional markets simply do not offer enough potential for the required growth. In technical terms, the greatest challenge will be to develop integrated systems for communications and the software to control them. In organizational terms, the challenge is no less daunting: Can Big Blue continue to innovate and adjust to new markets?

4

Human Relations Skills

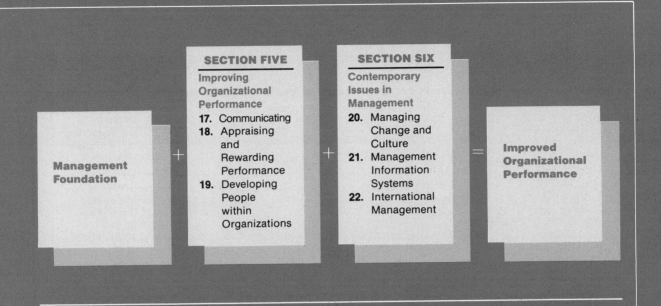

Management Foundation

+

SECTION FIVE

Improving Organizational Performance

17. Communicating
18. Appraising and Rewarding Performance
19. Developing People within Organizations

+

SECTION SIX

Contemporary Issues in Management

20. Managing Change and Culture
21. Management Information Systems
22. International Management

=

Improved Organizational Performance

All decision-making, planning, and administrative skills are implemented through people and depend on people for their success. Therefore, human relations skills are essential for building a sound management foundation.

It is difficult, if not impossible, to isolate completely human relations skills from other management skills. For example, appropriate managerial controls can only be determined in light of certain human relations considerations. Therefore, many human relations concepts are interspersed throughout all sections of the text. However, the purpose of this section is to discuss and emphasize the importance of human relations skills for effective management.

Chapter 13 discusses current concepts and approaches to motivating people. The relationship between motivation and satisfaction is also analyzed.

Chapter 14 focuses on the management skill of leading or influencing human behavior. Different styles of leadership are discussed and evaluated. Several contemporary leadership theories are also presented. A strong argument is made for a situational approach to leadership.

Chapter 15 discusses both formal and informal work groups. Informal work groups are shown to be assets of the organization if properly managed. The topics of conformity and creativity in organizations are also presented.

Chapter 16 focuses on conflict and stress in organizations. Conflict is presented as a normal and natural organizational activity which can produce positive results if properly managed. Stress is an inevitable occurrence in organizations. Suggestions are offered for managing stress.

Motivating: Activating and Sustaining Human Behavior

Chapter Outline

The early bird catches the worm. That fact
Has been into every young cranium packed
It's really absurd the talk that is heard
Of the wonderful thrift of that wonderful bird
And not the least mention is made of the worm
That equally early set out on a squirm
Except that within that most provident bird
The poor little fellow was thus early interred
Now it seems there's a word on both sides to be said
For had he but snugly remained in his bed
Or curled up for a nap
In mother earth's lap
The poor little chap
Would doubtless have lived to Methuselah's age
And another tale figured in history's page.

Moral: Maxims and rules
That are taught in the schools
Are excellent truly for governing fools
but you of your actions get up early of course
But if you're a worm don't be so absurd
As to get up at dawn to be caught by a bird. *

"Our employees are just not motivated." "Half the problems we have are due to a lack of personal motivation." "How do I motivate my employees?" Statements and questions such as these are often expressed by managers at all levels in organizations.

The problem of motivation is not a recent development. Research conducted by William James in the late 1800s indicated the importance of motivation.[1] James found that hourly employees could keep their jobs by using approximately 20 to 30 percent of their ability. He also found that highly motivated employees will work at approximately 80 to 90 percent of their ability. Figure 13–1 illustrates the potential influence of motivation on performance. Highly motivated employees can bring about substantial increases in performance and substantial decreases in problems such as absenteeism, turnover, tardiness, strikes, and grievances. Management in Action 13–1 describes Kentucky Fried Chicken's approach to motivating managers.

---

* The Early Bird" (source unknown).

MANAGEMENT IN ACTION 13-1

Motivating Managers at Kentucky Fried Chicken (KFC)

KFC has introduced a "Quality, Service, and Cleanliness" (QSC) program to assure clean facilities and a high caliber of service. The program consists of 103 quality control practices and a series of inspections to determine if KFC units are meeting company standards.

• A unit's composite QSC score directly affects the size of the unit manager's quarterly bonus. The bonus, which can be up to 40 percent of a manager's quarterly salary, is based on three criteria: cost of sales, labor costs, and sales increases over last year. However, no matter how well a manager performs in any of these categories, if the unit does not achieve a composite QSC score of at least 90, the bonus is lost. On the other hand, if a manager's unit scores better than 90, the bonus increases.

Source: Adapted from "Bonus Plan Motivates KFC Managers," *Restaurant Business*, January 20, 1984, p. 111.

THE MEANING OF MOTIVATION

The word *motivation* comes from the Latin word *movere,* which means to move. Numerous definitions are given for the term. Usually included are such words as *aim, desire, end, impulse, intention, objective,* and *purpose.* These definitions normally include three common characteristics of **motivation.** First, motivation is concerned with what activates human behavior. Second, motivation is concerned with what directs this behavior toward a

Motivation–causative sequence concerned with what activates human behavior, what directs this behavior, and how it is sustained.

FIGURE 13–1
Potential Influence of Motivation on Performance

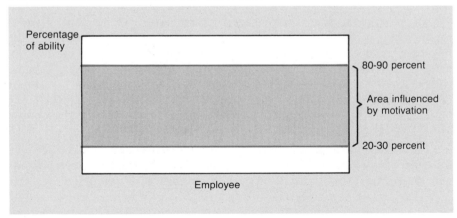

Source: Paul Hersey and Kenneth H. Blanchard, *Management of Organizational Behavior: Utilizing Human Resources,* 4th ed. (Englewood Cliffs, N.J.: Prentice-Hall, 1982), p. 4. Copyright © 1982 by Prentice-Hall, Inc. Adapted by permission.

particular goal. Third, motivation is concerned with how this behavior is sustained.[2]

Motivation can be analyzed using the following causative sequence:

Needs → Drives or motives → Achievement of goals

In motivation, needs produce motives which lead to the accomplishment of goals. Needs are caused by deficiencies, which can be either physical or psychological. For instance, a physical need exists when an individual goes without sleep for 48 hours. A psychological need exists when an individual has no friends or companions. Individual needs will be explored in much greater depth later in this chapter.

A motive is a stimulus which leads to an action that satisfies the need. In other words, motives produce actions. Lack of sleep (the need) activates the physical changes of fatigue (the motive) which produces sleep (the action, or in this example, inaction).

Achievement of the goal satisfies the need and reduces the motive. When the goal is reached, balance is restored. However, other needs arise which are then satisfied by the same sequence of events. Understanding the motivation sequence in itself offers a manager little help in determining what motivates people. The theories of motivation described in this chapter help to provide a broader understanding of what motivates people. They include traditional theory, need hierarchy theory, achievement-power-affiliation theory, motivation-maintenance theory, preference-expectancy theory, and reinforcement theory.

TRADITIONAL THEORY

Traditional theory of motivation—based on the assumption that money is the primary motivator: if the reward is great enough, employees will produce more.

The **traditional theory of motivation** evolved from the work of Frederick W. Taylor and the scientific management movement which took place at the turn of this century. Taylor's ideas were based on his belief that existing reward systems were not designed to reward individuals for high production. He felt that when highly productive people discover that they are being compensated basically the same as less productive people, then the output of highly productive people will decrease. Taylor's solution was quite simple. He designed a system whereby an employee was compensated according to individual production.

One of Taylor's problems was determining a reasonable standard of performance. Taylor solved the problem by breaking jobs down into components and measuring the time necessary to accomplish each component. In this way, Taylor was able to establish standards of performance "scientifically."

Taylor's plan was unique in that he had one rate of pay for units produced up to the standard. Once the standard was reached, a significantly higher rate was paid, not only for the units above the standard but for all units produced during the day. Thus, under Taylor's system, employees could in many cases significantly increase their pay for production above the standard.

The traditional theory of motivation is based on the assumption that money is the primary motivator. Financial rewards are directly related to performance in the belief that if the reward is great enough, employees will produce more.

NEED HIERARCHY THEORY

The **need hierarchy theory** is based on the assumption that individuals are motivated to satisfy a number of needs and that money can directly or indirectly satisfy only some of these needs. The need hierarchy theory is based largely on the work of Abraham Maslow.[3]

Need hierarchy theory–based on the assumption that individuals are motivated to satisfy a number of needs and that money can satisfy only some of these needs.

Maslow's Need Hierarchy

Maslow felt that several different levels of needs exist within individuals and that these needs relate to each other in the form of a hierarchy. Maslow's **hierarchy of needs** consists of the five levels shown in Figure 13–2.

The physiological needs are basically the needs of the human body that must be satisfied in order to sustain life. These needs include food, sleep, water, exercise, clothing, shelter, and so forth.

Safety needs are concerned with protection against danger, threat, or deprivation. Since all employees have (to some degree) a dependent relationship with the organization, safety needs can be critically important. Favoritism, discrimination, and arbitrary administration of organizational policies are all actions which arouse uncertainty and therefore affect the safety needs.

The third level of needs is composed of the social needs. Generally categorized at this level are the needs for love, affection, belonging—all are concerned with establishing one's position relative to others. This need is satisfied by the development of meaningful personal relations and by acceptance into meaningful groups of individuals. Belonging to organizations and identifying with work groups are means of satisfying these needs in organizations.

The fourth level of needs is composed of the esteem needs. The esteem needs include both self-esteem and the esteem of others. These needs influence the development of various kinds of relationships based on adequacy, independence, and the giving and receiving of indications of self-esteem and acceptance. Management in Action 13–2 illustrates General Food's approach to motivating employees through recognition.

The highest-order need is concerned with the need for self-actualization or self-fulfillment—that is, the need of people to reach their full potential in applying their abilities and interests to functioning in their environment.

Hierarchy of needs–Maslow's five levels of individual needs: physiological, safety, social, esteem (or ego), and self-actualization.

FIGURE 13–2
Maslow's Need Hierarchy

- Self-actualization needs:
  1. Self-fulfillment of potential.
  2. Doing things for the challenge of accomplishment.
  3. Intellectual curiosity.
  4. Creativity and aesthetic appreciation.
  5. Acceptance of reality.
- Esteem (or ego) needs:
  1. Recognition and prestige.
  2. Confidence and leadership.
  3. Competence and success.
  4. Strength and intelligence.
- Social needs:
  1. Acceptance.
  2. Feeling of belonging.
  3. Membership in group.
  4. Love and affection.
  5. Group participation.
- Safety needs:
  1. Security and safety.
  2. Protection.
  3. Comfort and peace.
  4. No threats or danger.
  5. Orderly and neat surroundings.
  6. Assurance of long-term economic well-being.
- Physiological needs:
  1. Food and thirst.
  2. Sleep.
  3. Health.
  4. Body needs.
  5. Exercise and rest.

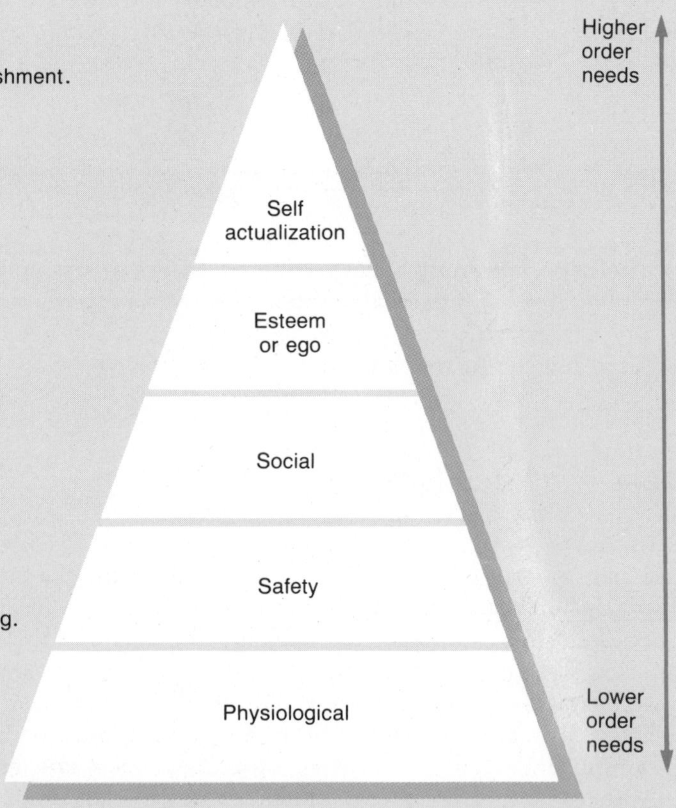

Higher order needs

Self actualization

Esteem or ego

Social

Safety

Physiological

Lower order needs

This need is concerned with the will to operate at the optimum and thus receive the rewards that are the result of that attainment. The rewards may not only be in terms of economic and social remuneration, but also in terms of psychological remuneration. The need for self-actualization or self-fulfillment is never completely satisfied; one can always reach one step higher.

The Need Hierarchy Theory: Other Considerations

The need hierarchy shown in Figure 13–2 adequately describes the general order or ranking of most people's needs. However, there are several other possibilities to be considered. First, although the needs of most people are arranged in the sequence shown in Figure 13–2, differences in the sequence

Pride Committee at General Foods

In response to employee suggestions for improving productivity and morale at its plant in Dover, Maryland, General Foods has established a Pride Committee. The committee—composed of management, union representatives, and hourly employees—awards the coveted Dover Pride Award each month. The award consists of a plaque and the choice between a day off with pay or dinner for the winner's family. Awards have been won by individuals single-handedly cutting inventory losses by 74 percent; reducing shipping costs through tighter scheduling; and achieving the lowest damage rate of any General Foods plant, for which an entire crew was cited.

Source: Adapted from "Management in Practice," *Management Review*, May 1984, p. 42.

can occur, depending on an individual's learning experience, culture, social upbringing, and numerous other aspects of personality. Second, the strength or potency of a person's needs may shift back and forth under different situations. For instance, during bad economic times, physiological and safety needs might tend to dominate an individual's behavior; in good economic times, higher-order needs might dominate an individual's behavior.

The unconscious character of the various needs should be recognized. In addition, there is a certain degree of cultural specificity of needs. In other words, the ways by which the various needs can be met tend to be controlled by cultural and societal factors. For example, the particular culture may dictate one's eating habits, social life, and numerous other facets of life.

Finally, different methods can be used by different individuals to satisfy a particular need. Two individuals may be deficient in relation to the same physiological need; however, the way in which each chooses to satisfy that need may vary considerably.

As far as motivation is concerned, the thrust of the need hierarchy theory is that a satisfied need is not a motivator. Consider the basic physiological need for oxygen. Only when an individual is deprived of oxygen can it have a motivating effect on that person's behavior.

Many of today's organizations are applying the logic of the need hierarchy. For instance, compensation systems are generally designed to satisfy the lower-order needs—physiological and safety. On the other hand, interesting work and opportunities for advancement are designed to appeal to higher-order needs. So the job of a manager is to determine the need level that an individual employee is attempting to attain and then provide the means by which the employee can satisfy that need. Obviously, determining the need level of a particular person can be a difficult process. All people do not operate at the same level on the need hierarchy. All people do not react similarly to the same situation.

It must be pointed out that little research has been conducted to test the validity of the need hierarchy theory. Its primary value is that it provides a structure for analyzing needs and, as will be seen later in this chapter, is used as a basis for other theories of motivation.

ACHIEVEMENT–POWER–AFFILIATION THEORY

Achievement-power-affiliation theory–holds that people have three needs: achievement, power, and affiliation; the level of intensity varies among individuals; and people are motivated in situations that allow them to satisfy their most intense need(s).

Closely related to the need hierarchy theory is the **achievement-power-affiliation theory,** primarily developed by David McClelland.[5] This theory holds that all people have three needs: (1) a need to achieve, (2) a need for power, and (3) a need for affiliation. The need for achievement is a desire to do something better or more efficiently than it has been done before—to achieve. The need for power is basically a concern for influencing people—to be strong and influential. The need for affiliation is a need to be liked—to establish or maintain friendly relations with others. McClelland maintains that most people have a degree of each of these needs but that the level of intensity varies. For example, an individual may be high in the need for achievement, moderate in the need for power, and low in the need for affiliation. This individual's motivation to work will vary greatly from that of another person who has a high need for power and low needs for achievement and affiliation. According to this theory, it is the responsibility of managers to recognize the dominating needs in both themselves and their employees and to integrate these differences effectively. An employee with a high need for affiliation would probably respond positively to demonstrations of warmth and support by the manager; an employee with a high need for achievement would likely respond positively to increased responsibility. Through self-analysis, managers can gain insight as to how they tend to respond to employees. They may then want to alter their response to employees to best fit the employees' needs. Table 13–1 shows the effect of the presence of certain characteristics within an organization on the need for achievement, the need for power, and the need for affiliation.

TABLE 13–1
Responses to Different Characteristics

Characteristic Present in Organization	Response		
	Need for Achievement	Need for Power	Need for Affiliation
Warmth	No effect	No effect	Aroused
Support	Aroused	No effect	Aroused
Conflict	Aroused	Aroused	Reduced
Reward	Aroused	No effect	Aroused
Responsibility	Aroused	Aroused	No effect

Source: Adapted from George Litwin and Robert Stringer, *Motivation and Organization Climate* (Cambridge, Mass.: Harvard Unviersity Press, 1968), chapter 8. Copyright © 1968 by the President and Fellows of Harvard College. All rights reserved.

MOTIVATION–MAINTENANCE THEORY

Frederick Herzberg, Bernard Mausner, and Barbara Snyderman developed a theory of work motivation which has had wide acceptance in management circles. The theory is referred to by several names: **motivation-maintenance theory,** dual-factor theory, or motivation-hygiene theory.

Initially, the development of the theory involved extensive interviews with approximately 200 engineers and accountants from 11 industries in the Pittsburgh area. The purpose of this work was summarized as follows:

> To industry, the payoff for a study of job attitudes would be increased productivity, decreased absenteeism, and smoother working relations. To the individual, an understanding of the forces that lead to improved morale would bring greater happiness and greater self-realization.[6]

In the interviews, researchers used what is called the critical incident method. This involved asking subjects to recall work situations in which they had experienced periods of high and low motivation. They were asked to recount specific details about the situation and the effect of the experience over time.

It was found through analysis of the interviewees' statements that different factors were associated with good and bad feelings. The findings fell into two major categories. Those factors that were most frequently mentioned in association with a favorably viewed incident concerned the work itself. These factors were achievement, recognition, responsibility, advancement, and the characteristics of the job. But when subjects felt negatively oriented toward a work incident, they were more likely to mention factors associated with the work environment. These included status; interpersonal relations with supervisors, peers, and subordinates; technical aspects of supervision; company policy and administration; job security; working conditions; salary; and aspects of their personal life that were affected by the work situation.

The latter set of factors was called "hygiene" or "maintenance" factors because the researchers felt that they are preventive in nature. In other words, they do not produce motivation but can prevent motivation from occurring. Thus, proper attention to hygiene factors is a necessary but not sufficient condition for motivation. The first set of factors were called "motivators." The researchers contended that these factors, when present in addition to the hygiene factors, provide true motivation.

In summary, the motivation-maintenance theory contends that motivation comes from the individual, not from the manager. At best, proper attention to the hygiene factors keeps an individual from being highly dissatisfied but does not make that individual motivated. Both hygiene and motivator factors must be present in order for true motivation to occur. Figure 13–3 lists some examples of hygiene and motivator factors.

Job enrichment programs have been developed in an attempt to solve motivational problems by using the motivation-maintenance theory. Unlike

Motivation-maintenance theory–states that all work-related factors can be grouped into one or two categories *maintenance factors,* which will not produce motivation but can prevent it; and *motivators,* which can encourage motivation.

FIGURE 13–3
Hygiene-Motivator Factors

Hygiene Factors (environmental)	Motivator Factors (job itself)
Policies and administration	Achievement
Supervision	Recognition
Working conditions	Challenging work
Interpersonal relations	Increased responsibility
Personal life	Advancement
Money, status, security	Personal growth

Job enlargement–involves making a job structurally larger by giving an employee more similar operations or tasks to perform.

Job rotation–practice of periodically rotating job assignments.

Job enrichment–upgrading a job with factors like more-meaningful work, recognition, responsibility, and opportunities for advancement.

job enlargement, which merely involves giving an employee more of a similar type of operation to perform, or **job rotation,** which is the practice of periodically rotating job assignments, **job enrichment** involves an upgrading of the job by adding motivator factors. Designing jobs that provide for meaningful work, achievement, recognition, responsibility, advancement, and growth is the key to job enrichment.

As can be seen from Figure 13–4, the motivation-maintenance theory is very closely related to the need hierarchy theory of motivation and so is subject to many of the same criticisms. Management in Action 13–3 (p. 364) illustrates how IBM uses motivational rewards in addition to the traditional hygiene type of rewards.

PREFERENCE–EXPECTANCY THEORY

Preference expectancy theory–holds that motivation is based on a combination of the individual's *expectancy* that increased effort will lead to increased performance which will lead to rewards, and the individual's *preference* for those rewards.

An additional theory of motivation was developed by Victor H. Vroom.[7] Called the **preference-expectancy (or expectancy) theory**, Vroom's theory is based on the belief that people act in such a manner as to increase pleasure and decrease displeasure. People are motivated to work if (1) they believe their efforts will be rewarded and (2) they value the rewards that are being offered. The first requirement—persons need to believe that their efforts will be rewarded—can be further broken down into two separate components: (1) the expectancy that increased effort will lead to increased performance and (2) the expectancy that increased performance will lead to increased rewards. These expectancies are developed largely from an individual's past experiences. For example, based on incidents that happened in the past, a person may feel that working harder does not produce any better results. On the other hand, even if employees believe that working harder does result in higher performance, they may not believe that higher performance is directly related to rewards.

The second part of the preference-expectancy theory is concerned with the value that the employee places on the rewards that are offered by the organization. Historically, organizations have assumed that whatever rewards

FIGURE 13–4
Comparison of the Need Hierarchy Theory with the Motivation-Maintenance Theory

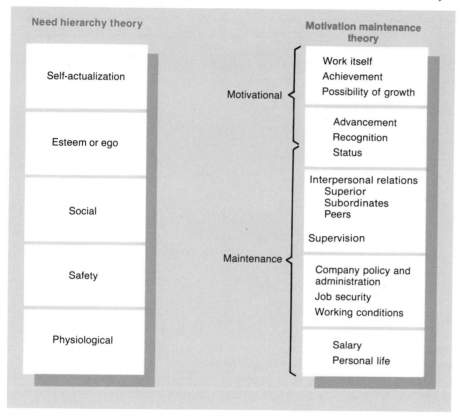

are provided will be valued by employees. Even if this were true, some rewards are certainly more valued than others. In fact, certain rewards, such as a promotion which involves a transfer to another city, may be viewed negatively.

Expectancy theorists believe that individual expectancies and preferences are formed either consciously or unconsciously but that they definitely exist in most people. The preference-expectancy theory is shown in model form in Figure 13–5.

The following example is intended to illustrate the preference-expectancy theory. Assume that John Stone is an insurance salesman for the ABC Life Insurance Company. John has learned over the years that he completes one sale for approximately every six calls he makes. John definitely perceives a direct relationship between his effort and performance. Since John is on a straight commission, he also perceives a direct relationship between performance and rewards. Thus, his expectation that increased effort will lead to increased rewards is relatively high. Further, suppose that John's income

MANAGEMENT IN ACTION 13–3

Motivating Salespeople at IBM

Salespeople get a quota of IBM products to be placed in their territory. Each year, the quota is raised or the territory cut or both. IBM takes back previously paid commissions if a customer decides to return rented equipment after a year.

Achievement of the quota is followed not only by monetary rewards but also by rewards such as having your name and quota on the bulletin board with a notation saying "100 percent." Letters of commendation are also issued in a steady flow for successful performance.

Source: Adapted from *The Wall Street Journal*, April 8, 1982, p. 1.

is currently in a high tax bracket such that he gets to keep, after taxes, only 50 percent of his commissions. This being the case, he may not look upon the additional money that he gets to keep (the reward) as being very attractive. The end result is that John's preference for the additional money may be relatively low. Even when this is multiplied by his relatively high expectation of receiving the additional money, his motivation to do additional work may be relatively low.

Each of the separate components of the preference-expectancy model can be affected by the organization's practices and management. The expectancy that increased effort will lead to increased performance can be positively influenced by providing proper selection, training, and clear direction to the work force. The expectancy that increased performance will lead to rewards is almost totally under the control of the organization. Does the organization really attempt to link rewards to performance? Or are rewards based on some other variable, such as seniority? The final component—the preference for the rewards being offered—is usually taken for granted by the organization. Organizations should solicit feedback from their employees concerning the types of rewards that are valued. Since an organization is going to spend a certain amount of money on rewards (salary, fringe benefits, and so on), it should ensure the maximum return from its investment.

FIGURE 13–5
Model of Preference-Expectancy Theory

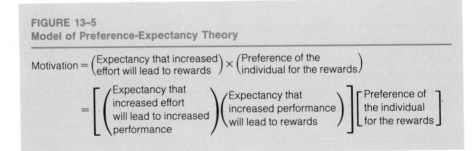

364

The development of the preference-expectancy theory is still in its infancy; many questions remain that must be answered. For example, critics attack the theory as being overly rational—i.e., humans often don't act rationally. Others say the theory ignores impulsive and expressive behavior. In spite of these criticisms, the preference-expectancy theory is currently one of the most subscribed-to theories of motivation.

REINFORCEMENT THEORY

The final theory of motivation to be explored is reinforcement theory, which is closely related to preference-expectancy theory.[8] The general idea behind **reinforcement theory** is that behavior which appears to lead to a positive consequence tends to be repeated, while behavior which appears to lead to a negative consequence tends to be repeated. A positive consequence is a reward.[9]

The current emphasis on the use of reinforcement theory in management practices is concerned with positive reinforcement. Examples include increased pay for increased performance and praise and recognition when an employee does a good job. Generally, several steps are to be followed in the use of positive reinforcement. These steps include:

1. Selecting reinforcers that are strong and durable enough to establish and strengthen the desired behavior.
2. Designing the work environment in such a way that the reinforcing events are contingent on the desired behavior.
3. Designing the work environment so that the employee has the opportunity to demonstrate the desired behavior.[10]

The key to successful positive reinforcement is that rewards must result from performance. In other words, the greater the level of performance by an employee, the greater should be the rewards. Several suggestions for the effective use of reinforcement have been proposed. These include the following:

1. All people should not be rewarded the same.
2. Failure to respond to an employee's behavior has reinforcing consequences.
3. A person must be told what can be done to be reinforced.
4. A person must be told what he or she is doing wrong.
5. Reprimands should not be issued in front of others.
6. The consequences of a person's behavior should be equal to the behavior.[11]

While positive reinforcement can be used by managers to elicit and strengthen desired behavior by employees, negative reinforcement is a

Reinforcement theory—motivation approach based on the idea that behavior which appears to lead to a positive consequence tends to be repeated, while behavior which appears to lead to a negative consequence tends not to be repeated.

MANAGEMENT IN ACTION 13-4

The "Golden Banana" Award

The Foxboro Company is a leading multinational manufacturer and distributor of instrumentation and control systems. In its early days, a technical advance was desperately needed for the survival of the company. Late one evening, a scientist rushed into the president's office with a working prototype. Dumbfounded at the elegance of the solution and bemused at how to reward it, the president bent forward in his chair, found something, leaned over the desk to the scientist, and said, "Here!" In his hand was a banana, the only reward he could immediately put his hands on. From that point on, the small "gold banana" pin has been the highest accolade for scientific achievement at Foxboro.

Source: Adapted from Thomas J. Peters and Robert H. Waterman, Jr., "How the Best-Run Companies Turn So-So Performers into Big Winners," *Management Review*, November–December 1982, p. 11.

method used to reduce the frequency of undesired behavior. Negative reinforcement is defined as either presenting a negative consequence or withdrawing a positive consequence, depending upon a response from the employee. Disciplinary systems within organizations are examples of negative reinforcers in that they are designed to reduce undesired behavior. Generally, it has been found that positive reinforcement is more effective than negative reinforcement in producing and maintaining a desired behavior.[12] Management in Action 13–4 gives an example of positive reinforcement.

INTEGRATING THE THEORIES OF MOTIVATION

All of the motivation theories previously presented contain the common thread that motivation is goal-directed behavior. Although the theories may appear to be quite different, most of them are not in conflict with one another. Rather, each looks at a different segment of the overall motivational process or at the same segment from a different perspective. Figure 13–6 presents a model which reflects the overall motivational process and indicates relationships among major motivational theories.

Vroom's preference-expectancy theory is shown at the heart of the model by the three factors that are shown to influence effort; note the arrows leading to the effort box. Maslow's need hierarchy theory and the achievement-power-affiliation theory are represented in the upper left-hand corner of the model by the variable labeled "Nature and strength of current needs." The nature and strength of current needs reflect the individual's needs, which in turn affect the value that the person places on the reward being offered. If the reward matches the individual's needs, that person will place more value on the reward than if it does not match the need level. The motivation-maintenance theory is represented by the variable "perceived nature and quantity of rewards," which is found in the upper right-hand corner of

FIGURE 13–6
The Overall Motivational Process

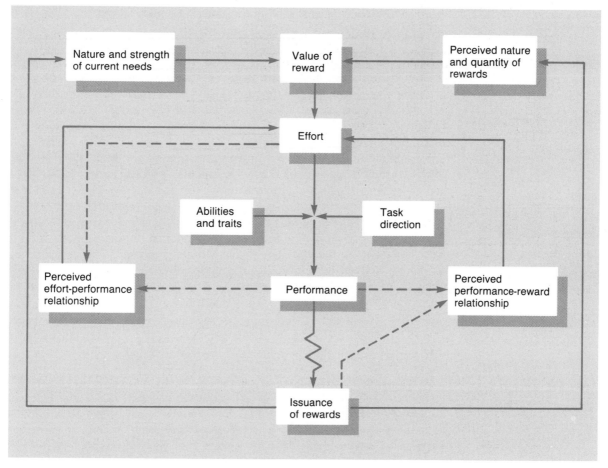

the model. Both of these variables reflect the need for rewards to consist of both hygiene and motivator factors. For example, if only hygiene factors are provided, then the perceived nature and quantity of the rewards would only be marginal, which in turn would result in a marginal or low value placed on the reward by the individual. Issuance of rewards based on performance reinforces the person's behavior. As suggested by Figure 13–6, no single motivation theory provides all the answers.

JOB SATISFACTION

Closely related to motivation is the concept of job satisfaction. In fact, managers often view motivated employees as being synonymous with satisfied employees. There are, however, important differences between motivated employees and satisfied employees.

Job satisfaction is an individual's general attitude about his or her job. The five major components of job satisfaction are (1) attitude toward work group, (2) general working conditions, (3) attitude toward company, (4) monetary benefits, and (5) attitude toward supervision. Other major components that should be added to these five are the individual's attitudes toward the work itself and toward life in general. The individual's health, age, level of aspiration, social status, and political and social activities can all contribute to job satisfaction. Therefore, job satisfaction is an attitude that results from other specific attitudes and factors.

Job satisfaction refers to the individual's mental set about the job. This mental set may be positive or negative, depending on the individual's mental set concerning the major components of job satisfaction. Job satisfaction is not synonymous with organizational morale. **Organizational morale** refers to an individual's feeling of being accepted by, and belonging to, a group of employees through common goals, confidence in the desirability of these goals, and progress toward these goals. Morale is related to group attitudes, while job satisfaction is more of an individual attitude. However, the two concepts are interrelated in that job satisfaction can contribute to morale and morale can contribute to job satisfaction.

The Satisfaction-Performance Controversy

For many years, managers have believed for the most part that a satisfied worker will automatically be a good worker. In other words, if management could keep all the workers "happy," then good performance would automatically follow. Charles Greene has suggested that many managers subscribe to this belief because it represents "the path of least resistance."[13] Greene's thesis is that increasing employees' happiness is far more pleasant than confronting employees with their performance if a performance problem exists.

Before exploring the satisfaction-performance controversy further, it might be wise to point out that there are subtle but real differences between being satisfied and being happy. Although happiness eventually results from satisfaction, satisfaction goes much deeper and is far less tenuous than happiness.

The incident below presents two propositions concerning the satisfaction-performance relationship.

> As Ben walked by smiling on the way to his office, Ben's boss remarked to a friend, "Ben really enjoys his job, and that's why he's the best damn worker I ever had. And that's reason enough for me to keep Ben happy." The friend replied, "No, you're wrong! Ben likes his job because he does it so well. If you want to make Ben happy, you ought to do whatever you can to help him further improve his performance."[14]

Job satisfaction—
individual's general attitude about his or her job.

Organizational morale—
individual's feelings of being accepted by, and belonging to, a group of employees through common goals, confidence in the desirability of these goals, and progress toward them.

The first is the traditional view that satisfaction causes performance. The second proposition is that satisfaction is the effect rather than the cause of performance. In this proposition, performance leads to rewards which result in a certain level of satisfaction. Thus, rewards constitute a necessary intervening variable in the relationship. Another position considers both satisfaction and performance to be functions of rewards. This position not only views satisfaction as being caused by rewards but also postulates that current performance affects subsequent performance if rewards are based on current performance.

Research evidence generally rejects the more popular view that satisfaction causes performance. The evidence does, however, provide moderate support for the view that performance causes satisfaction. The evidence also provides strong indications that: (1) rewards constitute a more direct cause of satisfaction than does performance; and (2) rewards based on current performance cause subsequent performance.[15]

Research has also investigated the relationship between intrinsic and extrinsic satisfaction and performance for jobs categorized as being either stimulating or nonstimulating.[16] The studies found that the relationship did vary, depending on whether the job was stimulating or nonstimulating. These and other studies further emphasize the complexity of the satisfaction-performance relationship. One relationship that has been clearly established is that job satisfaction does have a positive impact on turnover, absenteeism, tardiness, accidents, grievances, and strikes.[17]

In addition, recruitment efforts by employees are generally more successful if the employees are satisfied. Satisfied employees are preferred simply because they make the work situation a more pleasant environment. So, even though a satisfied employee is not necessarily a high performer, there are numerous reasons for cultivating satisfied employees.

As mentioned earlier, a wide range of both internal and external factors affect an individual's level of satisfaction. The top portion of Figure 13–7 summarizes the major factors which determine an individual's level of satisfaction (or dissatisfaction). The lower portion of the figure shows the organizational behaviors generally associated with satisfaction and dissatisfaction. Individual satisfaction leads to organizational commitment, while dissatisfaction results in behaviors detrimental to the organization (turnover, absenteeism, tardiness, accidents, etc.). For example, employees who like their jobs, supervisors, and other job-related factors will probably be very loyal and devoted employees. However, employees who strongly dislike their jobs or any of the job-related factors will probably be disgruntled and will often exhibit these feelings by being late, absent, or by taking more covert actions to disrupt the organization.

Satisfaction and motivation are not synonymous. Motivation is a drive to perform, while satisfaction reflects the individual's attitude or happiness with the situation. The factors that determine whether an individual is satisfied with the job differ from those that determine whether the individual is motivated. Satisfaction is largely determined by the comfort offered by

FIGURE 13–7
Determinants of Satisfaction and Dissatisfaction

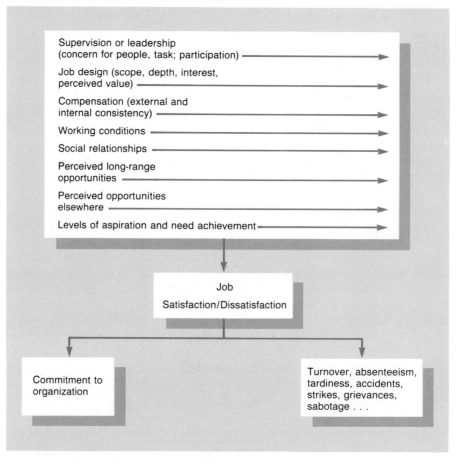

the environment and the situation. Motivation, on the other hand, is largely determined by the value of rewards and their contingency on performance. The result of motivation is increased effort, which in turn increases performance if the individual has the ability and if the effort is properly directed. The result of satisfaction is increased commitment to the organization, which may or may not result in increased performance. This increased commitment will normally result in a decrease in problems such as absenteeism, tardiness, turnover, and strikes.

SUMMARY

Motivation begins with needs which cause motives which lead to the accomplishment of goals. Needs are caused by deficiencies. Motives are stimuli that cause an action to be taken to satisfy the need. Achievement of the goal satisfies the need and reduces the motive. When the goal is reached, balance is restored, and of course, other needs arise. These new needs must also be satisfied by the motivation process.

Six basic theories of motivation are the traditional theory, need hierarchy theory, achievement-power-affiliation theory, motivation-maintenance theory, preference-expectancy theory, and reinforcement theory. Traditional ① theory is based on the assumption that money is a primary motivator. Employees will produce more to get a greater financial gain.

The need hierarchy theory is based on the assumption that workers are ② motivated to satisfy a variety of needs only some of which can be satisfied by money. The needs of an individual exist in a hierachy and range from low to high as follows: physiological, safety, social, esteem, and self-actualization. Once a need has been sufficiently satisfied, it can no longer be used to motivate an individual.

The achievement-power-affiliation theory holds that all people have three ③ needs—a need to achieve, a need for power, and a need for affiliation. Furthermore, the level of intensity of these needs varies among individuals. People are motivated in situations that allow them to satisfy their most intense needs.

The motivation-maintenance model states that there are two categories ④ of factors which relate to motivation. The first category is called hygiene, or maintenance, factors. They relate to the work environment and include status, interpersonal relations, supervision, company policy and administration, job security, working conditions, salary, and personal life. The hygiene factors are important and must be present in the job, or motivation cannot occur. However, providing the hygiene factors does not motivate employees. Rather, it keeps them from being dissatisfied. The second category of factors, called motivators, relates to the work itself. These factors include such things as recognition, advancement, achievement, growth potential, and responsibility. Only if both the hygiene and motivator factors are properly provided will motivation occur.

The preference-expectancy theory of motivation implies that moti- ⑤ vation depends on the preferences and expectations of an individual. The preference-expectancy theory emphasizes the need for organizations to relate rewards directly to performance and to ensure that the rewards provided are desired by the recipients.

The reinforcement theory of motivation is based on the idea that behavior ⑥ which appears to lead to a positive consequence tends to be repeated, while behavior which appears to lead to a negative consequence tends not to be repeated. Both positive and negative reinforcement can be used.

Although each of the basic motivation theories may appear to be quite different, most of them are not in conflict with one another. They rather look at different segments of the overall motivational process or look at the same segment from a different perspective.

Job satisfaction is an individual's general attitude about the job and is influenced by many factors. The relationship between job satisfaction and job performance is complex and has been debated for years. Current theory holds that performance should determine rewards. Rewards in turn affect an individual's level of satisfaction through their impact on current needs and desires. Research has shown that job satisfaction can have a direct impact on managerial concerns such as absenteeism, turnover, tardiness, grievances, and sabotage.

References and Additional Readings

[1] Cited in Paul Hersey and Kenneth H. Blanchard, *Management of Organizational Behavior: Utilizing Human Resources,* 4th ed. (Englewood Cliffs, N.J.: Prentice-Hall, 1982), p. 4.

[2] Richard M. Steers and Lyman W. Porter, *Motivation and Human Behavior* (New York: McGraw-Hill, 1983), pp. 3–4.

[3] Abraham H. Maslow, *Motivation and Personality,* 2d ed. (New York: Harper & Row, 1970).

[4] Edwin A. Locke, "The Nature and Causes of Job Satisfaction," in *Handbook of Industrial and Organizational Psychology,* ed. Marvin D. Dunnette (New York: John Wiley & Sons, 1983).

[5] David C. McClelland, *The Achievement Motive* (New York: Halsted Press, 1976).

[6] Frederick Herzberg, Bernard Mausner, and Barbara Synderman, *The Motivation to Work* (New York: John Wiley & Sons, 1959), p. ix.

[7] Victor H. Vroom, *Work and Motivation* (New York: John Wiley & Sons, 1967).

[8] McGregor's Theory X and Theory Y, which some authors consider to be basic theories of motivation, are discussed in Chapter 14, "Leading: Influencing Human Behavior." The authors of this text feel that the theories more logically fit into a discussion of leadership than of basic motivation theories.

[9] Steers and Porter, *Motivation,* chap. 4.

[10] Ibid., pp. 123–24.

[11] Ibid., pp. 162–63.

[12] P. M. Podsakoff, William D. Tudor, and Richard Skov, "Effects of Leader Contingent and Noncontingent Reward and Punishment Behaviors on Subordinate Performance and Satisfaction," *Academy of Management Journal,* December 1982, pp. 810–21.

[13] Charles N. Greene, "The Satisfaction-Performance Controversy," *Business Horizons,* October 1972, p. 31.

[14] Ibid., p. 32.

[15] Ibid., p. 40.

[16] John M. Ivancevich, "The Performance to Satisfaction Relationship: A Causal Analysis of Stimulating and Nonstimulating Jobs," *Organizational Behavior and Human Performance* 22 (1978), pp. 350–64.

[17] Donald P. Schwab and Larry L. Cummings, "Theories of Performance and Satisfactions: A Review," *Industrial Relations,* October 1970, pp. 408–29. Also see Locke, "Job Satisfaction," p. 1343, for a complete summary of the related research.

Review Questions

1. Explain the motivation sequence.
2. Describe the following theories of motivation:

   a. Traditional theory.
   b. Need hierarchy theory.
   c. Achievement-power-affiliation theory.

    d. Motivation-maintenance theory.
    e. Preference-expectancy theory.
    f. Reinforcement theory.
3. What is job satisfaction? What are the major components of job satisfaction?

4. What is organizational morale?
5. Discuss the satisfaction-performance controversy.
6. From a managerial standpoint, what are the real benefits of having satisfied employees?

Discussion Questions

1. Discuss your views on this statement: "Most people can be motivated with money."
2. Do you think that a very loyal employee is necessarily a good employee?
3. As a manager, would you prefer a motivated or a satisfied group of employees? Why?
4. The XYZ Company has just decided to take all of its employees (200 in number) to Las Vegas for a three-day expense-paid weekend to show its appreciation for their high level of performance this past year. What is your reaction to this idea?
5. Discuss the following statement: "A satisfied employee is one that is not being pushed hard enough."

Incident 13–1
Our Engineers Are Just Not Motivated

Situation: You are a consultant to the manager of mechanical engineering for a large company (8,000 employees, $200 million annual sales) that manufactures industrial equipment. The manager has been in this position for six months, having moved from a similar position in a much smaller company.

Manager: I just can't seem to get these people to perform. They are all extremely competent, but they just don't seem to be willing to put forth the kind of effort that we expect and need if this company is going to remain successful.

Consultant: What type of work do they do?

Manager: Primarily designing minor modifications to existing equipment lines to keep up with our competition and to satisfy special customer requirements.

Consultant: How do you evaluate their performance?

Manager: Mainly on whether they meet project deadlines. It's hard to evaluate the quality of their work, since most of it is fairly routine and the designs are frequently altered later by the production engineers to facilitate production processes.

Consultant: Are they meeting their deadlines reasonably well?

Manager: No, that's the problem. What's worse is that they don't really seem too concerned about it.

Consultant: What financial rewards do you offer them?

Manager: They are all well-paid—some of the best salaries for mechanical engineers that I know of anywhere. Base pay is determined mainly on the basis of seniority, but there is also a companywide profit-sharing plan. At the end of each year, the company distributes 10 percent of its profits after taxes to the employees. The piece of the pie that you get is in proportion to your basic salary. This kind of plan was used in the company I used to work for, and it seemed to have a highly motivating effect for them. They also get good vacations, insurance plans, and all the other usual goodies. I know of no complaints about compensation.

Consultant: How about promotion possibilities?

Manager: Well, all I know is that I was brought in from the outside.

Consultant: If they are so lackadaisical, have you considered firing any of them?

Manager: Are you kidding? We need them too much, and it would be difficult and expensive to replace them. If I even threatened to fire any of them for anything short of blowing up the building, my boss would come down on me like a ton of bricks. We are so far behind on our work as it is. Besides, I'm not sure that it's really their fault entirely.

Questions

1. Why are the engineers not motivated?
2. What should management do to correct the situation?

Incident 13–2
The Long-Term Employee

Bill Harrison is 57 years old and has been with Ross Products for 37 years. He is on a top-paying machine-operator job and has been for the last 20 years. Bill is quite active in community affairs and takes a genuine interest in most employee activities. He is very friendly and well liked by all employees, especially the younger ones, who often come to him for advice. He is extremely helpful to these younger employees and never hesitates to help when called on. When talking with the younger employees, Bill never talks negatively about the company.

Bill's one shortcoming, as his supervisor Alice Jeffries sees it, is his tendency to spend too much time talking with other employees. This not only causes Bill's work to suffer but perhaps more important, it hinders the output of others. Whenever Alice confronts Bill with the problem, Bill's performance improves for a day or two. It never takes long, however, for Bill to slip back into his old habit of storytelling and interrupting others.

Alice considered trying to have Bill transferred to another area where he would have less opportunity to interrupt others. However, Alice concluded that she needs Bill's experience, especially since she has no available replacement for Bill's job.

Bill is secure in his personal life. He owns a nice house and lives well. His wife works as a librarian, and their two children are grown and married. Alice has sensed that Bill feels he is as high as he'll ever go in the company. This doesn't seem to bother him since he feels comfortable and likes his present job.

Questions

1. What would you do to try and motivate Bill if you were Alice Jeffries?
2. Suppose Alice could transfer Bill. Would you recommend that she do it?

Exercise
Motivation-Maintenance

This exercise is designed to illustrate Herzberg's motivation-maintenance theory in terms of your personal experiences.

A. Think of a time when you were extremely motivated or "turned on" by a job (the instance could have taken place yesterday or several years ago and it could have been on a full or part-time job) and write a brief two- or three-sentence description of the situation. After you have completed the description, list the reasons that this situation had a motivational effect on you. Don't sign your name, but do pass your paper forward.

B. After completing the above, repeat the same procedure, for a situation which was highly demotivating. After all the papers have been passed forward your instructor will help you analyze them.

14

Leading:
Influencing
Human Behavior

Chapter Outline

Leadership is many things. It is patient. It is altering agendas so that new priorities get enough attention. It is being visible when things are going awry, and invisible when things are going well. It's listening carefully much of the time, frequently speaking with encouragement, and reinforcing words with believable action. It's being tough when necessary, and it's the occasional naked use of power. *

As we saw in Chapter 13, motivation comes from inside a person. Leadership—what one person can do to influence the behavior of others—and motivation are closely related. The leadership abilities of one person can certainly affect the motivation of other people.

Each year, new information is published about leadership. Checklists have been devised to find what style of leadership is used by people. Questionnaires try to determine the style of leadership used within an organization. New teaching aids and devices are designed to improve one's leadership abilities.

All of this activity would seem to show that managers today know a great deal about the leadership process. But this is not true. Many of them appear to have a hard time performing well in leadership roles. This chapter reviews and offers a perspective on leadership styles and processes.

LEADERSHIP: WHAT IS IT?

Leadership–process of influencing the behavior of members of a group.

Leader–occupies the central role in a leadership situation; has the ability to influence the behavior of others in a given situation.

Leadership is a process of influencing the activities of members of a group in their tasks of goal setting and goal achievement. The ability to obtain followers and influence them makes a leader. Generally, influence is the result when one person presents information in such a way as to convince the other members of the group that their situation will be improved if they behave in a certain way. A **leader** is the person who takes the central role in this interaction by influencing the behavior of other members of the group.

Managers are in a leadership role because they can influence the behavior of members of the formal work group. However, that does not mean the manager is effective in the role. A manager's leadership can be measured by the contribution of the group toward the organization's objectives (such as increased profit or service to customers).

Generally, there are two types of leaders in organizations: One is the

* Adapted from Thomas J. Peters and Robert H. Waterman, Jr., "How the Best-Run Companies Turn So-So Performers into Big Winners," *Management Review,* November–December 1982, p. 15.

formal or appointed leader (manager) who is assigned to the position by the organization; the other, informal leader is chosen by the group itself. Each type of leader relies on different sources of authority in performing the role. Note, however, that appointed leaders (managers) may or may not be informal leaders.

SOURCES OF AUTHORITY

The informal leader of a group is the one seen by the group as most capable of satisfying its needs. The authority of the leader can be removed, reduced, or increased, depending on the group's perceived progress toward its goals. The leader's authority may also be threatened by the emergence of different or additional goals.

A simple example of this point follows. Suppose a group of people were shipwrecked on a desolate island. The group's first goal would probably be to ensure their survival by finding food, water, and shelter. The person selected by the group as the leader would be the person seen by the group as the one who could best help the group survive. However, after this need is met, other needs will emerge. The need to escape from the island would probably emerge rather quickly. The person first selected as leader may not be perceived as the most capable to direct the attainment of these new needs. In this case, the group might select a new leader. This process of changing leaders might continue, depending on the group's view of its needs.

The role of manager and the role of the previous example's leader are different. The example shows an elective, or emergent, style of leadership. Under this system, the leader must know the needs of the group and must be seen by the group as being most capable in meeting those needs. In other words, the source of authority for the leader is the group being led. In most organizations, however, a manager's source of authority does not come from the group being managed but rather from higher management. Thus, the source of authority for a manager comes from above rather than below. Management in Action 14–1 describes a leader who emerged at a critical time in the Civil Rights movement.

POWER, AUTHORITY, AND LEADERSHIP

Power is the ability to command or apply force. It is not necessarily accompanied by authority. Through **power**, people can be influenced by someone to do something that they would not otherwise do. The use of or desire for power is often viewed negatively in our society because power

Power–ability or capacity to influence others to do something that they would not otherwise do.

MANAGEMENT IN ACTION 14–1

Martin Luther King, Jr., and the Southern Christian Leadership Conference

Martin Luther King, Jr., came to national attention in 1955 when the 26-year-old clergyman emerged as leader of the Montgomery bus boycott, the first massive and sustained black protest in the South following the Supreme Court's decision of May 1954. King and his associates went on to form the Southern Christian Leadership Conference in 1957 and lead the Birmingham protests of 1963, which contributed to the passage of the major civil rights legislation of 1964 and 1965. King's nonviolent philosophy won him the Nobel Peace Prize in 1965. He was recognized as one of the most important leaders of the civil rights movement.

Martin Luther King's leadership skills seemed to center around his faith in God, his vision of the future of the civil rights movement, and his ability to communicate. His "I have a dream" speech is well remembered for its eloquence in stating a vision for the future. On April 3, 1968, King stated:

"We've got some difficult days ahead. But, it really doesn't matter with me now. Because I've been to the mountain top. I won't mind. Like anybody, I would like to live a long life. Longevity has its place. But I'm not concerned about that now. I just want to do God's will.

And he's allowed me to go up to the mountain. And I've looked over, and I've seen the Promised Land. I may not get there with you, but I want you to know tonight that we as a people will get to the Promised Land."

On April 4, 1968, Martin Luther King, Jr., was assassinated.

Adapted from Martin Luther King, Jr., *The Measure of a Man* (Philadelphia: Pilgrim Press, 1968), p. 63; Melvin Drimmer, *Black History: A Reappraisal* (Garden City, N.Y.: Doubleday Publishing, 1968), pp. 440–54.

Authority–right to issue directives and expend resources.

Coercive power–based on fear.

Reward power–based on one's ability to provide rewards for compliance with one's wishes.

Legitimate power–based on one's position in an organization.

is often linked with the capacity to punish. There are, however, other forms of power, as shown in Figure 14–1.

Authority, which exists in the formal organization, is the right to issue directives and expend resources. Authority has been viewed in the past as a function of position in the organizational hierarchy, flowing from the top to the bottom of the organization. Basically, the amount of authority that a manager has depends on the amount of **coercive, reward** and **legitimate power** that the manager can exert in a certain position. Chester Bernard's acceptance theory of authority, discussed in Chapter 8, suggests that the source of a manager's authority lies with the subordinate: The subordinate has the power either to accept or to reject a superior's command; if the subordinate rejects the authority of a superior, it does not exist. Barnard viewed disobeying or ignoring a superior as a denial of the latter's authority. Basically, he was referring to the degree of legitimate power that a manager commands. The coercive and reward power a manager can exert affect how much legitimate power the manager holds. Power can also be exerted up from the bottom of an organization as well as from the top down. Employees can have some power over management. For instance, they can strike or threaten a strike.

Leadership has been described in this chapter as a process of influencing the behavior of other members of the group. Leaders may use one or several

FIGURE 14–1
Types of Power

Coercive power	Based on fear, the subordinate does what is required to avoid punishment or some other negative outcome. The disciplinary policies of organizations generally are based on this type of power.
Reward power	Based on the ability of one individual to provide rewards, either intrinsic or extrinsic, for compliance with this individual's wishes.
Legitimate power	Based on an individual's position in the organization; thus, when joining an organization, a person accepts the fact that the boss's orders are to be carried out.
Expert power	Based on the special skill, expertise, or knowledge that a particular individual possesses.
Referent power	Exemplified by the charismatic individual who has unusual traits that allow that person to control situations.

types of power to influence group behavior. For instance, some political leaders use **referent power;** others use a combination of coercive, reward, and referent power—Adolph Hitler is an example. Informal leaders generally combine referent power and **expert power.** Some managers rely only on their authority—which is the combination of coercive, reward, and referent power—while others use different combinations. In fact, David C. McClelland and David H. Burnham have extensively explored the relationship between power and effective management. They report as follows:

> Good managers are not motivated by a need for personal aggrandizement or by a need to get along with subordinates, but rather by a need to influence others' behavior for the good of the whole organization. In other words, good managers want power.[1]

However, these same authors also suggest that power can lead to authoritarianism; thus, it must be tempered by maturity and a high degree of self-control.

Referent power–based on the charismatic traits or characteristics of an individual.

Expert power–based on the special skill, expertise, or knowledge of an individual.

LEADER ATTITUDES

In the late 1950s, Douglas McGregor developed two attitude profiles, or assumptions, about the basic nature of people. These attitudes were termed **Theory X and Theory Y;** they are summarized in Figure 14–2. McGregor maintained that many leaders in essence subscribe to either Theory X or Theory Y and behave accordingly. A Theory X leader would likely use a much more authoritarian style of leadership than a leader who believes in Theory Y assumptions. The real value of McGregor's work was the idea that a leader's attitude toward human nature has a large influence on how that person behaves as a leader.[2]

Theory X and Theory Y–terms coined by Douglas McGregor to describe assumptions made by managers about basic human nature.

FIGURE 14–2
Assumptions about People

Theory X

1. The average human being has an inherent dislike of work and will avoid it if possible.
2. Because of their dislike of work, most people must be coerced, controlled, directed, or threatened with punishment to get them to put forth adequate effort toward the achievement of organizational objectives.
3. The average human being prefers to be directed, wishes to avoid responsibility, has relatively little ambition, and wants security above all.

Theory Y

1. The expenditure of physical and mental effort in work is as natural as play or rest.
2. External control and the threat of punishment are not the only means for bringing about effort toward organizational objectives. Workers will exercise self-direction and self-control in the service of objectives to which they are committed.
3. Commitment to objectives is a function of the rewards associated with their achievement.
4. The average human being learns, under proper conditions, not only to accept but to seek responsibility.
5. The capacity to exercise a relatively high degree of imagination, ingenuity, and creativity in the solution of organizational problems is widely, not narrowly, distributed in the population.
6. Under the conditions of modern industrial life, the intellectual potentialities of the average human being are only partially utilized.

Source: Douglas McGregor, *The Human Side of Enterprise* (New York: McGraw-Hill, 1960), pp. 33–34 and 47–48. Copyright © 1960 by McGraw-Hill, Inc. Used with permission of McGraw-Hill Book Company.

Others have also studied the relationship between a leader's attitudes and how individuals within the group perform. The relationship between a leader's expectations and the resulting performance have received much attention.

J. Sterling Livingston has looked at the link between a manager's expectations and how subordinates perform. If the manager's expectations are high, productivity is likely to be high. On the other hand, if the manager's expectations are low, productivity is likely to be poor. McGregor had earlier called this idea the **self-fulfilling prophecy.** Livingston called it "Pygmalion in management." He found that:

Self-fulfilling prophecy (Pygmalion in management)—describes the influence of one person's expectations on another's behavior.

> What a manager expects of his subordinates and the way he treats them largely determine their performance and career progress. A unique characteristic of superior managers is their ability to create high performance expectations that subordinates fulfill. Less effective managers fail to develop similar expectations, and as a consequence, the productivity of their subordinates suffers. Subordinates, more often than not, appear to do what they believe they are expected to do.[13]

Both McGregor and Livingston believed that leaders' attitudes or assumptions about their subordinates can greatly influence the performance of the subordinates.

GENERAL APPROACHES TO LEADERSHIP

Many studies have been done on leadership. Some of the more important ones are discussed here.

Trait Theory

Early research efforts devoted to leadership stressed what the leader was *like* rather than what the leader *did*—a **trait theory** of leadership. Many personality traits (such as originality, initiative, persistence, knowledge, enthusiasm), social traits (tact, patience, sympathy, etc.), and physical characteristics (e.g., height, weight, attractiveness) have been examined to differentiate leaders.[4]

At first glance, a few traits do seem to distinguish leaders from followers. These include being slightly superior in such physical traits as weight and height and in a tendency to score higher on tests of dominance, intelligence, extroversion, and adjustment. But the differences seem to be small, with much overlap.

Thus, the research in this area has generally been fruitless—largely because the traits related to leadership in one case usually did not prove to be predictive in other cases. In fact, many studies have shown that leadership traits that are effective in one situation may not be effective in other situations.[5] One study even concluded that the chance of finding a set of universally effective leadership traits is essentially nil.[6]

In general, it can be said that traits may to some extent influence the capacity to lead. But these traits must be analyzed in terms of the leadership situation (described in detail later in this chapter).

Trait theory–holds that certain physical and psychological characteristics, or traits, differentiate leaders from their groups.

Basic Leadership Styles

Other studies dealt with the style of the leader. They found three basic leadership styles: autocratic, laissez-faire, and democratic. The main difference among these styles is where the decision-making function rests. Generally, the **autocratic leader** makes most decisions for the group; the **laissez-faire leader** allows people within the group to make all decisions; and the **democratic leader** guides and encourages the group to make decisions. More detail about each of the leadership styles is given in Figure 14–3. (Figure 14–3 implies that the democratic style is the most desirable and productive. However, current research on leadership, discussed later in this chapter, does not necessarily support this conclusion.) The primary contribution of this research was identifying the three basic styles of leadership. Management in Action 14–2 describes the leadership style of Lucille Ball.

Autocratic leader–makes most decisions for the group.

Laissez-faire leader– allows individuals in the group to make the decisions.

Democratic leader– guides and encourages the group to make decisions.

FIGURE 14–3
Relationship between Styles of Leadership and Group Members

Autocratic Style

Leader
1. The individual is very conscious of his or her position.
2. He or she has little trust and faith in members of the group.
3. This leader believes that pay is a just reward for work and the only reward that will motivate employees.
4. Orders are issued to be carried out, with no questions allowed and no explanations given.

Group Members
1. No responsibility is assumed for performance, with people merely doing what they are told.
2. Production is good when the leader is present, but poor in the leader's absence.

Laissez-Faire Style

Leader
1. He or she has no confidence in his or her leadership ability.
2. This leader does not set goals for the group.

Group members
1. Decisions are made by whomever in the group is willing to do it.
2. Productivity generally is low, and work is sloppy.
3. Individuals have little interest in their work.
4. Morale and teamwork generally are low.

Democratic Style

Leader
1. Decision making is shared between the leader and the group.
2. When the leader is required or forced to make a decision, his or her reasoning is explained to the group.
3. Criticism and praise are given objectively.

Group members
1. New ideas and change are welcomed.
2. A feeling of responsibility is developed within the group.
3. Quality of work and productivity generally are high.
4. The group generally feels successful.

Source: Adapted from Leland B. Bradford and Ronald Lippitt, "Building a Democratic Work Group," *Personnel 22*, no. 3 (November 1945). Copyright © 1945 by American Management Association, inc. Reprinted by permission of the publisher.

Dimensions of the Leadership Process

A series of studies on leadership was conducted at Ohio State University to find out the most important activities of successful leaders. The researchers wanted to find out what a successful leader does, regardless of the type of group being led: a mob, a religious group, a university, or a business organization. To do this, they developed a questionnaire called the **Leader Behavior Description Questionnaire (LBDQ).** Both the original form or variations are still used today.

In using the questionnaire, two leader activities emerged consistently as

Leader Behavior Description Questionnaire (LBDQ)—developed at Ohio State University and designed to determine how successful leaders carry out their activities.

Lucille Ball and Desilu Productions

The television program "I Love Lucy" was the forerunner of modern-day situation comedies and was one of the most successful series ever produced for television. It gave its leading woman Lucille Ball her introduction to the business side of television and motion pictures. Lucy—no one calls her Ms. Ball—went on to become the first woman to head a major Hollywood film company, Desilu Productions, Inc.

During her early years as an actress, she studied how directors worked with cast and crew, how they motivated people, why some succeeded and others failed. "I never regretted all the B films because I was getting paid for learning. What more can one want?" Lucy's philosophy about employees is: "Anytime one of my people is unhappy, he or she is free to go; if that person is unhappy, you have nothing." In fact, however, Lucy treats her staff almost like family.

Her philosophy of work is: "Set high standards for yourself, be true to them, and give it your best shot, because you'll never be able to please everybody."

Source: Adapted from Tony Velvui, "The Real Lucille Ball, "Nation's Business, October 1981, pp. 75–78.

being the most important. These were "consideration" and "initiating structure." The term *consideration* refers to the leader activity of showing concern for individual group members and satisfying their needs. The term *initiating structure* refers to the leader activity of structuring the work of group members and directing the group toward the attainment of the group's goals.

Since the Ohio State research, many other studies have been done on the relationship between the leader activities of consideration and initiating structure and their resulting effect on leader effectiveness. The major conclusions that can be drawn from these studies are:[7]

1. Leaders scoring high on consideration tend to have more satisfied subordinates than do leaders scoring low on consideration.
2. The relationship between the score on consideration and leader effectiveness depends on the group that is being led. In other words, a high score on consideration was positively correlated with leader effectiveness for managers and office staff in a large industrial firm, whereas a high score on consideration was negatively correlated with leader effectiveness for production foremen.
3. There is also no consistent relationship between initiating structure and leader effectiveness; rather, the relationship varies depending on the group that is being lead.

Likert's Work

The Institute for Social Research of the University of Michigan conducted studies to discover principles contributing both to the productivity of a group and to the satisfaction derived by group members. The study was conducted at the home office of the Prudential Insurance Company in Newark, New Jersey.

Interviews were conducted with 24 section heads or supervisors and 419 nonsupervisory personnel. Results of the interviews showed that supervisors of high-producing work groups were more likely:

1.   To receive general rather than close supervision from their superiors.
2.   To like the amount of authority and responsibility they have in their job.
3.   To spend more time in supervision.
4.   To give general rather than close supervision to their employees.
5.   To be employee oriented rather than production oriented.

Supervisors of low-producing work groups had basically opposite characteristics and techniques. They were production oriented and gave close supervision.

Rensis Likert, then director of the institute, published the results of his years of research in the book *New Patterns of Management,* which is a classic in its field.[8] Likert feels that there are four patterns or styles of leadership or management employed by organizations. He has identified and labeled these styles as follows:

System 1: Exploitative authoritative. Authoritarian form of management that attempts to exploit subordinates.

System 2: Benevolent authoritative. Authoritarian form of management, but paternalistic in nature.

System 3: Consultative. Manager requests and receives inputs from subordinates but maintains the right to make the final decision.

System 4: Participative. Manager gives some direction, but decisions are made by consensus and majority, based on total participation.

Likert used a questionnaire to determine the style of leadership and the management pattern employed in the organization as a whole. The results of his studies indicated that System 4 was the most effective style of management and that organizations should strive to develop a management pattern analogous to this system.[9]

The Managerial Grid

Managerial Grid®–two-dimensional framework characterizing a leader according to concern for people and concern for production.

Robert Blake and Jane Mouton have also developed a method of classifying the leadership style of an individual.[10] The **Managerial Grid**®, depicted in Figure 14–4, is a two-dimensional framework rating a leader on the basis of concern for people and concern for production. (Notice that these activities closely relate to the leader activities from the Ohio State studies—consider-

FIGURE 14–4
The Managerial Grid®

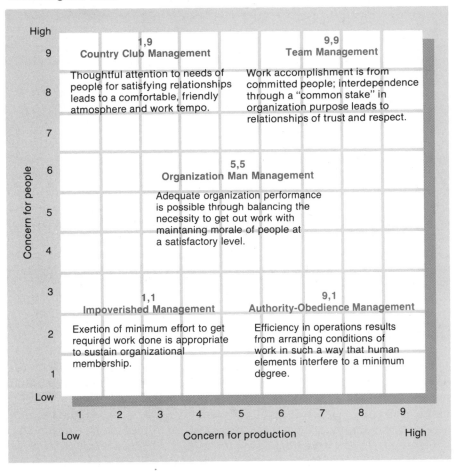

ation and initiating structure.) A questionnaire is used to locate a particular style of leadership or management on the grid.

Blake and Mouton identified five basic styles of management, using the Managerial Grid. Authority-obedience—located in the lower right-hand corner (9,1 position)—assumes that efficiency in operations results from properly arranging the conditions at work with minimum interference from other people. The opposite view; country club management—located in the upper left-hand corner (1,9 position)—assumes that proper attention to human needs leads to a comfortable organizational atmosphere and workplace. Team management—in the upper right-hand corner (9,9)—combines a high degree of concern for people with a high degree of concern for production. The other two styles on the grid are impoverished management (1,1) and organization man management (5,5). The Managerial Grid is intended to serve as a framework for managers to learn what their leadership style is and to develop a plan to move toward a 9,9 team management style of leadership.

SITUATIONAL (CONTINGENCY) APPROACHES TO LEADERSHIP

The leadership studies discussed so far are similar in that they do not specifically address the complex differences between groups (such as production workers versus accountants) and their influences on leader behavior. To imply that a manager should be employee oriented rather than production oriented (Michigan studies) or that the leader should exhibit concern for both production and people (Blake and Mouton) does not say much about what the leader should do in particular situations. Nor does it offer much guidance for daily leadership situations. Current research is largely concerned with the style of leadership that is most effective in a particular situation.[11] This is called the **contingency approach to leadership.**

Contingency approach to leadership–holds that the most effective style of leadership depends on the particular situation.

Continuum of Leadership Behaviors

Robert Tannenbaum and Warren Schmidt contend that different combinations of situational elements require different styles of leadership. They suggest that there are three important factors, or forces, involved in finding the most effective leadership style: forces involving the manager, the subordinate, and the situation.[12] Furthermore, all of the forces are interdependent.

Figure 14–5 describes in detail the forces that affect leadership situations. Since these forces differ in strength and interaction in differing situations, one style of leadership is not effective in all situations.

In fact, Tannenbaum and Schmidt argued that there is a continuum of behaviors that the manager may employ, depending on the particular situations (see Figure 14–6). Those authors further concluded that successful leaders are keenly aware of the forces that are most relevant to their behavior at a given time. Successful leaders accurately understand not only themselves but also the other persons in the organizational and social environment, and they are able to behave correctly in light of these insights.[13]

Fiedler's Contingency Approach to Leadership

Fred Fiedler further refined the idea of a situational approach to leadership. He tried to define the particular style of leadership needed for a given situation.[14] Fiedler defined two basic styles of leadership—task motivated

FIGURE 14-5
Forces in the Leadership Situation

Forces in the Manager	Forces in the Subordinates	Forces in the Situation
Value system: How the manager personally feels about delegating, degree of confidence in subordinates.	Need for independence: Some people need and want direction, while others do not.	Type of organization: Centralized versus decentralized.
Personal leadership inclinations: Authoritarian versus participative.	Readiness to assume responsibility: Different people need different degrees of responsibility.	Work group effectiveness: How effectively the group works together.
Feelings of security in uncertain situations.	Tolerance for ambiguity: Specific versus general directions.	The problem itself: The work group's knowledge and experience relevant to the problem.
	Interest and perceived importance of the problem: People generally have more interest in, and work harder on, important problems.	Time pressure: It is difficult to delegate to subordinates in crisis situations.
	Degree of understanding and identification with organizational goals: A manager is more likely to delegate authority to an individual who seems to have a positive attitude about the organization.	Demands from upper levels of management.
	Degree of expectation in sharing in decision making: People who have worked under subordinate-centered leadership tend to resent boss-centered leadership.	Demands from government, unions, and society in general.

and relationship motivated. The task-motivated style (similar to earlier discussed ideas of concern for production and initiating structure) fulfills the leader's need for satisfaction from the performance of a task. The relationship-motivated style of leadership (similar to concern for people and consideration) fulfills the leader's need to gain satisfaction from interpersonal relationships.

Fiedler used a questionnaire to find the leadership style of an individual. Respondents were asked to describe the person with whom they could work least effectively and the person with whom they could work most effectively. A person who described a least preferred co-worker in fairly favorable terms was presumed to be motivated to have close interpersonal relations with others; Fiedler classified these people as relationship-motivated leaders. On the other hand, people who rejected co-workers with whom they had difficulties were presumed to be motivated to accomplish or achieve the task: They were classified as task-oriented leaders.

Fiedler next turned to the situation in which the leader was operating. He placed leadership situations along a favorable-unfavorable continuum based on three major dimensions: leader-member relations, task structure, and position power. *Leader-member relations* refer to the degree that others trust and respect the leader, and to the leader's friendliness. This compares somewhat to referent power. *Task structure* is the degree to which job tasks

FIGURE 14–6
Continuum of Leadership Behavior

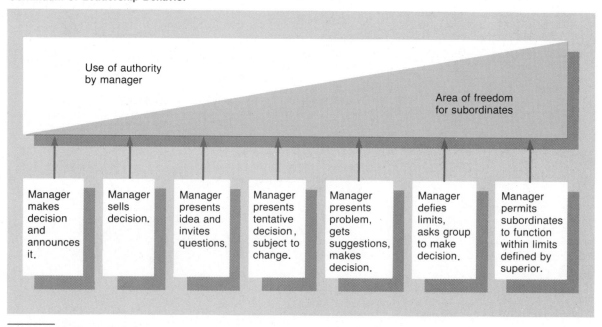

Use of authority
by manager

Area of freedom
for subordinates

| Manager makes decision and announces it. | Manager sells decision. | Manager presents idea and invites questions. | Manager presents tentative decision, subject to change. | Manager presents problem, gets suggestions, makes decision. | Manager defies limits, asks group to make decision. | Manager permits subordinates to function within limits defined by superior. |

Source: Robert Tannenbaum and Warren H. Schmidt, "How to Choose a Leadership Pattern," *Harvard Business Review*, May–June 1973. Copyright © 1973 by the President and Fellows of Harvard College; all rights reserved.

are structured. For example, assembly-line jobs are more structured than managerial jobs. *Position power* refers to the power and influence that go with a job. A manager has more position power who is able to hire, fire, and discipline. Position power compares to coercive, reward, and legitimate power. Using these three dimensions, an eight-celled classification scheme was developed. Figure 14–7 shows this scheme along the continuum.

Figure 14–8 shows the most productive style of leadership for each situation. In both highly favorable and highly unfavorable situations, a task-motivated leader was found to be more effective. In highly favorable situations, the group is ready to be directed and is willing to be told what to

FIGURE 14–7
Fiedler's Classification of Situations

Situation	1	2	3	4	5	6	7	8
Leader-member relations	Good	Good	Good	Good	Poor	Poor	Poor	Poor
Task structure	Structured	Structured	Unstructured	Unstructured	Structured	Structured	Unstructured	Unstructured
Position power	Strong	Weak	Strong	Weak	Strong	Weak	Strong	Weak

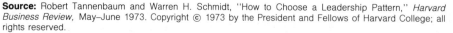

Favorable for leader   Unfavorable for leader

FIGURE 14–8
Relationship of Leadership Style to Situation

Situation	1	2	3	4	5	6	7	8
Leader-member relations	Good	Good	Good	Good	Poor	Poor	Poor	Poor
Task structure	Structured	Structured	Unstructured	Unstructured	Structured	Structured	Unstructured	Unstructured
Leader position power	Strong	Weak	Strong	Weak	Strong	Weak	Strong	Weak
	Favorable for leader						Unfavorable for leader	
Most productive leadership style	Task	Task	Task	Relation	Relation	No data	Task or relation	Task

do. In highly favorable situations, the group welcomes having the leader make decisions and direct the group. In moderately favorable situations, a relationship-motivated leader was found to be more effective. In Situation 7 (moderately poor leader-member relations, unstructured task, and strong position power), the task and relationship styles of leadership were equally productive. Thus, Fiedler has gone one step beyond Tannenbaum and Schmidt. He has shown which style of leadership is most effective in a given situation. Management in Action 14–3 describes Lee Iacocca's style of leadership during difficult times at Chrysler Corporation.

Path–Goal Theory of Leadership

The **path-goal theory of leadership** attempts to define the relationships between a leader's behavior and the subordinates' performance and work activities.[15] Leader behavior is acceptable to subordinates to the degree that they see it as a source of satisfaction now or as a step toward future satisfaction. Leader behavior influences the motivation of subordinates when it makes the satisfaction of their needs contingent on successful performance; and it provides the guidance, support, and rewards needed for effective performance (but which are not already present in the environment).

In path-goal theory, leader behavior falls into one of four basic types—role classification, supportive, participative, and autocratic. *Role classification leadership* lets subordinates know what is expected of them, gives guidance as to what should be done and how, schedules and coordinates work among the subordinates, and maintains definite standards of performance. *Supportive leadership* has a friendly, approachable leader who attempts to make the work environment more pleasant for subordinates. *Participative leadership* involves consulting with subordinates and asking for their suggestions in the decision-making process. *Autocratic leadership* comes from a leader who gives orders which are not to be questioned by subordinates.

Under the theory, each of these leadership behaviors results in different

Path-goal theory of leadership–holds that the leader's role is to increase personal payoffs to subordinates for work-goal attainment, make the path to payoffs easier, increase the opportunities for satisfaction enroute, and that the effectiveness of such efforts depends on the situation.

Lido "Lee" Anthony Iacocca and The Chrysler Corporation

Lee Iacocca joined Ford Motor Co. right out of school in 1946. After a series of marketing jobs, he was appointed as vice president and general manager of the Ford Division in 1960. By 1967, he was running all of Ford's North American car and truck operations as executive vice president and general manager. In December 1970, he was named company president and second in command to Henry Ford II. However, in 1978, he was fired by Henry Ford, after years of disputes over who should be on the management team and what the future direction of Ford's product line should be.

Later in 1978, Iacocca accepted the job as CEO of Chrysler Corporation, which was on its way to reporting a loss of $205 million on $13.6 billion in sales. Iacocca's description of what he found was as follows: "I found a mess. It was an absolute mess.

. . . At that point, you don't have time for strategies or philosophies. We had time to make a payroll every Friday."

Iacocca's charismatic leadership style was described as follows: "There were lots of times he had to rally the marketing troops. His speciality was speaking at company rallies. His own strength of character would mesmerize them. He's the only guy I know who can talk about the same thing four times in the same presentation and still not lose the audience's interest. People were fascinated by him."

In telling the management of Chrysler what it had to do, Iacocca says it was simple. "Our whole team had to learn one thing quickly—you're playing with live ammunition. If we have one failure, we're done. We're bankrupt."

Source: Adapted from Larry Marion, "CEO of the Year: Lee Iacocca of Chrysler," *Financial World*, March 31, 1983, pp. 22–26.

levels of performance and subordinate satisfaction, depending on the structure of the work tasks. Role clarification leads to high satisfaction and performance for subordinates engaged in unstructured tasks. Supportive leadership brings the most satisfaction to those who work on highly structured tasks. Participative leader behavior enhances performance and satisfaction for subordinates engaged in ambiguous tasks. Autocratic leadership behavior has a negative effect on both satisfaction and performance in both structured and unstructured task situations.

Life-Cycle Theory of Leadership

Life-cycle theory of leadership–holds that the maturity level of the followers determines the most appropriate leadership style for a situation.

Paul Hersey and Kenneth Blanchard include maturity of the followers as an important factor in style of leadership.[16] According to the **life-cycle theory of leadership,** as the level of maturity of followers increases, not only less and less structure (task) but also less and less socioemotional support (relationship) is needed in leader behavior. The maturity level of the followers is determined by their relative independence, their ability to take responsibility, and their achievement-motivation level.

FIGURE 14–9
Life-Cycle Theory of Leadership

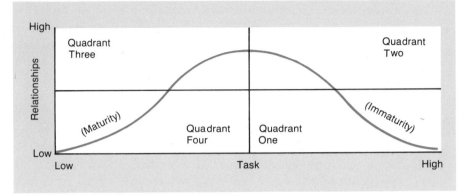

Figure 14–9 shows the cycle of the basic leadership styles that should be used by the leader, depending on the maturity of the followers. The life-cycle theory proposes that as the followers progress from immaturity to maturity, the leader's behavior should move from (1) high task–low relationships to (2) high task–high relationships to (3) low task–high relationships to (4) low task–low relationships.

IMPLICATIONS OF LEADERSHIP THEORIES FOR ORGANIZATIONS AND MANAGERS

How can all of these leadership theories be made relevant to the organization's need for effective managers? First, given the situational factors discussed in this chapter, it appears unlikely that a selection process will be developed to accurately predict successful leaders. The dynamic, changing nature of managerial roles further complicates the situation. Even if the initial process could select effective leaders, the dynamics of the managerial situation might make the selection invalid. Further, contrary to the conclusions of many studies, most leadership training today seems to assume that there is one best way to lead.

However, leadership training designed to help leaders or potential leaders identify the nature of the leadership situation appears to have potential in developing more effective leaders. Such training is not so much a process of changing individual traits as it is one of ensuring that the person is operating in an appropriate situation or of teaching the individual how to act in a given situation. The following points on effective leadership can tentatively be made:

1. High consideration and initiating structure often provide a successful leadership style.

2. Under emergency or high-pressure situations, emphasis on initiating structure is desirable and often preferred by subordinates.

3. When the manager is the only information source for subordinates regarding their tasks, they often expect the manager to structure their behavior.

4. Subordinates have differing preferences regarding the degree of consideration and initiating structure exhibited by their managers.

5. Higher management often has set preferences regarding the leadership styles employed by lower-level managers.

6. Some managers can adjust their behavior to fit the situation; while others, in attempting to make this adjustment, appear to be fake and manipulative.[17]

SUMMARY

Leadership is a process of influencing the activities of either formal or informal work groups in their tasks of goal setting and goal achievement. Generally, there are two types of leaders in organizations—the appointed leader (manager) and the informal leader. Power is defined as a relationship between people in which individuals can be influenced by another to do something that they would not do otherwise. Various types of power are: coercive, reward, legitimate, expert, and referent. Leaders may use one or several power types to influence group behavior.

Several important research studies on leadership were also reviewed. Trait theory focuses on the characteristics or traits of the leader. It was concluded, however, that traits must be analyzed in light of the leadership situation. Early studies also identified three basic styles of leadership—autocratic, laissez-faire, and democratic. The Ohio State studies attempted to describe what successful leaders do. They identified consideration for people and initiating structure as key dimensions of leadership behavior. Using leadership dimensions similar to the Ohio State studies, Blake and Mouton developed the Managerial Grid, which uses a two-dimensional grid for classifying leadership styles. The University of Michigan studies on leadership were designed to study the relationship between leadership style and productivity. Basically, these studies concluded that the employee-oriented manager had more-productive workers.

Most current leadership research has been concerned largely with the leadership situation. Tannenbaum and Schmidt contend that different combinations of situational elements require different styles of leadership. Fiedler further refined the idea of a situational approach to leadership by attempting to define the particular style of leadership that is appropriate for a given situation. The path-goal theory of leader effectiveness was discussed. This theory attempts to define the relationships between a leader's behavior and the subordinate's performance and work activities. The life-cycle theory of leadership considers the level of maturity of the followers in determining the appropriate leadership style for a particular situation.

The final section of the chapter dealt with the previously discussed leadership theories' relevance to the organization's need for effective managers. Several points were summarized concerning effective leadership.

References and Additional Readings

[1] David C. McClelland and David H. Burnham, "Power Is the Great Motivator," *Harvard Business Review,* March–April 1976, p. 100.

[2] For another view on Theory X and Theory Y, see T. C. Carbone, "Theory X and Theory Y Revisited," *Managerial Planning,* May–June 1981, pp. 24–27.

[3] J. Sterling Livingston, "Pygmalion in Management," *Harvard Business Review,* July–August 1969, p. 82.

[4] J. D. Barrow, "The Variables of Leadership: A Review and Conceptual Framework," *Academy of Management Review,* April 1977, p. 232.

[5] R. M. Stogdill, "Historical Trends in Leadership Theory and Research," *Journal of Contemporary Business,* Autumn 1974, p. 5.

[6] C. A. Schriesheim, J. M. Tolliver, and O. C. Behling, "Leadership Theory: Some Implications for Managers," *Business Topics,* Summer 1978, p. 35.

[7] Victor H. Vroom, "Leadership," in *Handbook of Industrial & Organizational Psychology,* ed. Marvin D. Dunnette (Skokie, Ill.: Rand McNally, 1976), p. 1531.

[8] Rensis Likert, *New Patterns of Management* (New York: McGraw-Hill, 1961).

[9] Rensis Likert, *The Human Organization* (New York: McGraw-Hill, 1967), p. 46.

[10] Robert R. Blake and Jane Srygley Mouton, *The New Managerial Grid* (Houston: Gulf Publishing, 1978); Robert R. Blake and Jane S. Mouton, "How to Choose a Leadership Style," *Training and Development Journal,* February 1982, pp. 38–45.

[11] C. L. Graeff, "The Situational Leadership Theory: A Critical Review," *Academy of Management Review,* April 1983, pp. 285–91.

[12] Robert Tannenbaum and Warren Schmidt, "How to Choose a Leadership Pattern," *Harvard Business Review,* May–June 1973, pp. 162–80.

[13] Ibid.

[14] Fred E. Fiedler, *A Theory of Leadership Effectiveness* (New York: McGraw-Hill, 1967).

[15] For an in-depth analysis of the path-goal theory, see J. F. Schriesheim and C. A. Schriesheim, "Test of the Path-goal Theory of Leadership and Some Suggested Directions for Future Research," *Personnel Psychology,* Summer 1980, pp. 349–71; Janet Falk and Eric R. Wendler, "Dimensionality of Leader-Subordinate Interactions: A Path-Goal Investigation, "*Organizational Behavior and Human Performance,* October 1982, pp. 241–64.

[16] Paul Hersey and Kenneth Blanchard, "Life-Cycle Theory of Leadership," *Training and Development Journal,* June 1979, pp. 94–100.

[17] Schriesheim et al., "Leadership Theory," pp. 34–40.

Review Questions

1. Define leadership. What is the source of a leader's authority?
2. Describe in detail the following three leadership styles:
   a. Autocratic.
   b. Laissez-faire.
   c. Democratic.
3. What was the purpose of the Ohio State leadership studies? What were the results of the Ohio State studies?
4. What was the purpose of the University of Michigan leadership studies? Explain the results of the Michigan studies.
5. Describe the Managerial Grid.
6. Describe three important forces, or factors, that Tannenbaum and Schmidt think should be considered in determining what leadership style is most effective.
7. What is Fiedler's contingency approach to leadership?
8. What is the path-goal theory of leader effectiveness?
9. Describe some of the implications of the studies on leadership for organizations and managers.

Discussion Questions

1. Discuss the following statement: "Leaders are born and cannot be developed."
2. "Leaders must have courage." Do you agree or disagree? Why?
3. Do you think the variance in leadership styles of such people as Adolph Hitler, Franklin D. Roosevelt, and Martin Luther King, Jr., can be explained by any of the theories discussed in this chapter? Elaborate on your answer.
4. "Leaders lead by example." Explain what people mean when they use this statement. Do you believe it? Explain your answer.

Incident 14–1

Does the Congregation Care?

Situation: You are talking with a young pastor of an independent church with 300 adult members. The pastor came directly to the church after graduating from a nondenominational theological school and has been in the job for eight months.

Pastor: I don't know what to do. I feel as if I've been treading water ever since the day I got here; and frankly, I'm not sure that I will be here much longer. If they don't fire me, I may leave on my own. Maybe I'm just not cut out for the ministry.

You: What has happened since you came to this church?

Pastor: When I arrived, I was really full of energy and wanted to see how much this church could accomplish. The very first thing I did was to conduct a questionnaire survey of the entire adult membership to see what types of goals they wanted to pursue. Unfortunately, I found that the members had such mixed (and perhaps apathetic) feelings about the goals that it was hard to draw any conclusions. There were also a few who strongly favored more emphasis on internal things, such as remodeling the sanctuary, developing our music program, and setting up a day-care center for the use of the members. Most of the members, however, didn't voice any strong preferences. A lot of people didn't return the questionnaire, and a few even seemed to resent my conducting the survey.

You: What have you done since you took the survey?

Pastor: To be honest about it, I've kept a pretty low profile, concentrating mainly on routine duties. I haven't tried to implement or even push any major new programs. One problem is that I've gotten the impression, through various insinuations, that my being hired was by no means an overwhelmingly popular decision. Evidently, a fairly substantial segment of the congregation was skeptical of my lack of experience and felt that the decision to hire me was railroaded through by a few members of the Pastoral Search Committee. I guess I am just reluctant to assume a strong leadership role until some consensus has developed concerning the goals of the church and I've had more time to gain the confidence of the congregation. I don't know how long that will take, though; and I'm not sure I can tolerate the situation much longer.

Questions

1. Analyze and explain the situation using any of the theories of leadership discussed in this chapter?

2. What would you recommend that the young pastor do?

Incident 14–2
Changes in the Plastics Division

Ed Sullivan was general manager of the Plastics Division of Warner Manufacturing Company. Eleven years ago, Ed hired Russell (Rusty) Means as general manager of the Plastics Division's two factories. Ed trained Rusty as a manager and feels that Rusty is a good manager, an opinion based largely on the fact that products are produced on schedule and are of such quality that few customers complain. In fact, for the past eight years, Ed has pretty much let Rusty run the factories independently.

Rusty believes strongly that his job is to see that production runs smoothly. He feels that work is work. Sometimes it is agreeable, sometimes disagreeable. If an employee doesn't like the work, he or she can either adjust or quit. Rusty, say the factory personnel, "runs things. He's firm and doesn't stand for any nonsense. Things are done by the book, or they are not done at all." The turnover in the factories is low; nearly every employee likes Rusty and feels that he knows his trade and that he stands up for them.

Two months ago, Ed Sullivan retired and his replacement Wallace Thomas took over as general manager of the Plastics Division. One of the first things Thomas did was call his key management people together and announce some major changes that he wanted to implement. These included: (1) bring the operative employees into the decision-making process; (2) establish a planning committee made up of three management members and three operative employees; (3) start a suggestion system; and (4) as quickly as possible, install a performance appraisal program agreeable to both management and the operative employees. Wallace also stated that he would be active in seeing that these projects would be implemented without delay.

After the meeting, Rusty was upset and decided to talk to Robert Mitchell, general manager of sales for the Plastics Division.

> **Rusty:** Wallace is really going to change things, isn't he?
>
> **Robert:** Yeah, maybe it's for the best. Things were a little lax under Ed.
>
> **Rusty:** I liked them that way. Ed let you run your own shop. I'm afraid Wallace is going to be looking over my shoulder every minute.
>
> **Robert:** Well, let's give him a chance. After all, some of the changes he's proposing sound good.
>
> **Rusty:** Well, I can tell you our employees won't like them. Having them participate in making decisions and those other things are just fancy management stuff that won't work with our employees.

Questions

1. What different styles of leadership are shown in this case?
2. What style of leadership do you feel that Wallace will have to use with Rusty?
3. Do you agree with Rusty? Discuss.

Exercise

Insubordination?

The company installed a new performance management system this year. You distributed the information and forms several weeks ago, and they were due to be completed two weeks ago. One manager reporting to you has not yet returned his. This morning, you ran into him in the parking lot and asked him about it. He reacted angrily with: "I haven't had time to do it—I don't have enough time to get my job done as it is, much less to take the time necessary to have my people write a bunch of meaningless information."

You ask him to stop by your office later to discuss it. As you think about how to handle this situation in the meeting, you consider several alternatives.

1. In view of his attitude and behavior, it clearly is appropriate to exercise your authority. Tell him, in no uncertain terms, that this must be done if he expects to continue as a supervisor.

2. Tell him why this program is important and use your best persuasion technique to sell him on doing it willingly.

3. Remind him that no salary increases, including his own, will be processed until the forms are completed. Establish another deadline and let him know you expect it to be done then.

4. Explain to him that appraising employee performance is a part of every supervisor's job and that he himself is being evaluated on his performance in implementing this program.

5. Tell him you understand the difficulties of his job and the shortage of time available to do it, but remind him that this is a mandatory program that has top management's backing.

Other alternatives may be open to you, but assume that these are the only ones you have considered. WITHOUT DISCUSSION with anyone, choose one of them and be prepared to defend your choice.

Objectives

1. To explore why informal work groups form in organizations.
2. To discuss some factors common to all informal work groups.
3. To describe the impact that informal work groups can have on individuals.
4. To examine the need for creativity and innovation in organizations.

15

Understanding Work Groups and Encouraging Creativity

Chapter Outline

Joe Marm was a young second lieutenant serving in South Vietnam. In the fall of 1965, he grabbed up two side arms and a pile of grenades and ran up a hill alone. He attacked and destroyed a machine gun nest killing eight Viet Cong. Afterwards, Lieutenant Marm was recommended for the Congressional Medal of Honor for his heroic actions. When asked why he had made the attack on his own, Marm replied, "What would the fellows have thought of me if I had been afraid to do it?"

New York Times*

The above quote describes the effect of a group on one individual. The importance of belonging to a group and its effect on human behavior in organizations was emphasized early by Elton Mayo in the famous Hawthorne Studies. He concluded that much of human behavior and attitudes can be explained by looking at the informal work group rather than at individuals themselves.[1] The major conclusion reached by the Hawthorne researchers was that workers react to the psychological and social conditions at work as well as to the physical conditions and that group pressures directly affect an individual's actions. A significant contribution of these studies was the recognition that an organization consists of individuals, groups, and inter-group relationships and that these components greatly influence the productivity and stability of the organization.

WORK GROUPS DEFINED

Group–number of persons who interact with one another on a face-to-face basis over a span of time and perceive themselves to be a group.

A **group** is a small number of people who communicate with one another often on a face-to-face basis over a span of time and who perceive themselves to be a group. Thus, small size, face-to-face communication, and awareness that a group exists are all characteristics of a group.

Primary Group–has all the characteristics of a group but also has feelings of loyalty, comradeship, and a common sense of values among its members.

Sociologists have further refined the definition of groups by distinguishing between a small group and a primary group. A small group must merely have all of the traits outlined in the previous paragraph. A **primary group,** in addition to the above traits, must have feelings of loyalty, comradeship, and a common sense of values among its members. Therefore, all primary groups are small groups, but all small groups are not necessarily primary groups. Both types of groups exist within organizations.[2]

Work groups–describes groups in organizations.

In this chapter, the term **work groups** will be used to describe groups in organizations. A further distinction will be made between formal and informal work groups. Formal work groups result primarily from the organiz-

* Source: *New York Times,* November 17, 1966.

ing function of management. Generally, **formal work groups** are defined by officially prescribed relationships between employees and a prescribed plan of effort directed toward the attainment of specific objectives.

Two popular forms of formal work groups are command and task groups. These groups can be either small or primary. Command groups are almost always shown on an organization chart. The vice presidents reporting to the president comprise a command group. The department heads reporting to a vice president comprise another command group. A task group is formed by employees that collaborate in order to accomplish a work task assigned by the organization. Engineers working on a particular project and committees are both examples of task groups.

Overlapping the formal work groups in organizations are **informal work groups.** These groups are not defined by the organizing function of management. Yet, all organizations have them. Groups of employees that regularly lunch together and office "cliques" are examples of informal work groups.

Formal work groups– have a defined structure and are formally recognized by the organization.

Informal work groups– result from personal contacts and interactions of people; usually not formally recognized by the organization.

THE LINKING–PIN CONCEPT

Rensis Likert has proposed the linking-pin concept to describe management's role in work groups. Likert suggests that an individual's interactions with the organization should contribute to maintaining a sense of personal worth and importance. Both formal and informal work groups are important sources of satisfaction in maintaining an employee's sense of personal worth and importance. Likert concludes:

> Management will make full use of the potential capacities of its human resources only when each person in an organization is a member of one or more effectively functioning work groups that have a high degree of group loyalty, effective skills of interaction, and high performance goals.[3]

Likert further contends that management should consciously attempt to build these groups. Managers have overlapping group memberships and link these groups to the total organization. Thus, the manager is viewed as a linking pin in the organization. The linking-pin concept is depicted in Figure 15–1.

TEAM BUILDING

Building the kind of work groups that Rensis Likert described is often called team building. **Team building** is a process that involves the work group developing an awareness of those conditions that keep it from functioning effectively and then requires the work group to take action to eliminate those conditions.

Team building–work group develops awareness of conditions that keep it from functioning effectively and takes action to eliminate these conditions.

FIGURE 15–1
Linking-pin Concept

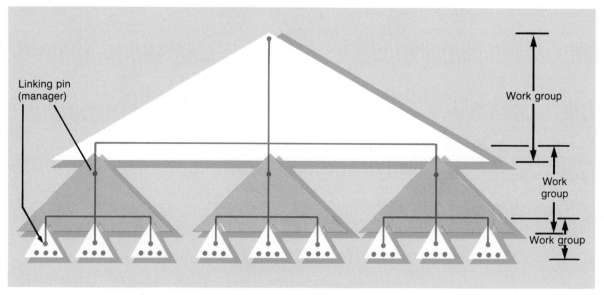

Source: Rensis Likert, *New Patterns of Management* (New York: McGraw-Hill, 1961), p. 104.

To build an effective team, the manager must first establish a working environment that is seen as fair and equitable. This cannot be done by one manager alone. All levels of management must contribute. However, if a manager does not establish this environment in the work unit, the efforts of higher levels of management will usually be wasted. Second, employee participation in working out changes, and keeping them informed about what is taking place, also helps build an effective team.

An effective manager also attempts to see and understand issues from the employees' point of view. However, the manager needs to be careful here. One who is always siding with the employees and taking an attitude of "it's us against them" can create a negative environment. The point is not to side with employees against management but to attempt to understand the issues from the employees' point of view.

FIGURE 15–2
Suggestions for Effective Team Building

---

1. Establish a working environment that is considered to be fair and equitable by employees.
2. Practice participation—listen to employees' ideas and get them involved in planning.
3. Show the employees that you, the manager who represents higher levels of management, also see issues from the employees' side.
4. Attempt to gain acceptance as the group's leader.

MANAGEMENT IN ACTION 15–1

Work Groups at Saab

Transformation of the workplace in Sweden is continuing. Saab, a manufacturer of automobiles, has replaced the traditional assembly line with semiautonomous groups in its body-welding area. Each group is composed of seven workers. Six work in pairs while the seventh is a coordinator, seeing that materials arrive and stepping in when someone is temporarily absent. The coordinator position is rotated among the members of the group on a weekly basis.

Each pair of workers has a buffer stock of work-in-process material, equal to an hour's work, on each side of them. They can set their own work tempo without affecting the workers feeding them or receiving their work. They can work more to fill the buffer and take an extra hour off to read, play cards, sleep, or satisfy the curiosity of visitors to the plant.

The team not only builds auto bodies but also performs many functions previously reserved for skilled craft workers and white-collar employees. It does most of the maintenance of its machinery, controls quality, and (in consultation with management) hires new members and controls a $100,000 to $150,000 budget for new equipment. It can also, within limits, hire temporary replacements for members who are ill. The team is also paid extra for taking on these additional duties.

Reduction in labor turnover and labor costs have been significant as a result of the changes. Quality has improved, and labor turnover is down. Annual savings are estimated at nine times annual costs.

Source: Adapted from John Logue "Semiautonomous Groups at Saab: More Freedom, High Output," *Management Review*, September 1982, pp. 32–33.

Finally, the manager should strive to gain acceptance as the group's leader. Certainly, a manager has formal authority that is delegated from higher levels of management. However, formal authority does not guarantee effective team building. Figure 15–2 summarizes these suggestions for effective team building. Management in Action 15–1 illustrates how teams operate at Saab.

WHY INFORMAL WORK GROUPS EXIST

Work is a social experience and provides an opportunity for employees to fulfill many needs. When people are brought together in an office or plant, they interact and work together in their formal job duties. Friendships naturally emerge out of these continuous contacts and from areas of common interest. Mutual interests, friendships, and the need to fulfill social needs are three reasons that help to explain both the formation of informal work groups and the desire of employees to become members of such groups.

Informal work groups provide a sense of security to the individual members, because group members usually exhibit a strong sense of loyalty and share common values. Further, membership in informal work groups facilitates social interaction and affiliation and fosters a feeling of pride or esteem by enabling an individual to be part of the in-group. One of the reasons why informal work groups evolve is to satisfy many of the needs that were described in the need hierarchy in Chapter 13.

Physical work conditions can also encourage the formation of informal work groups. People in close proximity to each other are almost forced to interact. The arrangement of furniture, desks, and offices can either encourage or discourage the formation of informal work groups. Generally, a physical work setting which facilitates social interaction increases the likelihood not only that an informal work group will exist but also that new employees will join.

Technology, which is closely aligned with physical work conditions, also heavily influences informal work group formation. Technology, in this broad sense, refers to how the overall work flows through the organization. The technology of an organization positions people in the work system, prescribes their activities, determines their interactions, and thus influences work group formation.

Like technology, management can influence the formation of informal work groups. For instance, suppose mangement decides to organize on a functional basis—accounting department, marketing department, and so forth. This facilitates the formation of informal work groups comprised of people performing similar functions. If, on the other hand, management organizes by product, customer, or geographical area, then people performing different functions are likely to form into groups.

In addition, the style of leadership employed by a manager can influence the formation of informal work groups. For instance, an autocratic manager and a participative manager can cause entirely different informal work group behavior.

In summary, there are many reasons for the formation of informal work groups within organizations. The reasons discussed here are by no means mutually exclusive or all-inclusive. The important point to remember is that overlapping the formal work groups in an organization are informal work groups which can have a significant impact on both individual and organizational performance.

FACTORS COMMON TO ALL INFORMAL WORK GROUPS

Once informal groups are formed, they evolve in such a manner that they take on a life of their own, separate and distinct from the work processes in which they originated. Informal group development is viewed as a self-generating process: Individuals who are formally required to interact with each other soon build favorable sentiments toward certain people. These sentiments serve to facilitate interactions and activities—eating lunch together, discussing problems, etc.—above and beyond those required by the job description. Simultaneously, these individuals become closer, and the group becomes an identifiable entity rather than just a collection of people. Over time, the informal group develops a set way of doing things and possesses several factors which seem to be common to all informal work groups. The implications of these factors for effective management can be better understood by examining them in more detail.

Group Norms

Group norms are the informal rules that a group adopts to regulate and regularize group members' behavior.[4] The various forms of informal group norms are limitless. One example of informal group norms that relates to the workplace is setting certain performance levels that may be either above, below, or the same as those set by management. Playing a joke or trick on all new employees is another example. Unfortunately, little is known about what factors determine whether an informal group will establish pro- or antiorganization norms.[5] However, a significant factor that determines whether group norms are closely adhered to by group members is the group's cohesiveness.[6]

Group norms–informal rules that a group adopts to regulate members' behavior.

Group Cohesiveness

Group cohesiveness basically refers to the degree of attraction that each member has for the group, or the "stick-togetherness' of the group. Cohesiveness is important for the group, because the greater the cohesiveness of the group, the more likely are members to pursue group norms and not individual norms. That is, the greater the cohesiveness, the greater the individual members' conformity to group norms.

Group cohesiveness–degree of attraction each member has for the group.

One variable affecting the cohesiveness of the group is its size. As discussed earlier, individuals in the group must interact in order for the group to exist; this interaction requirement limits the size of the group. Group cohesiveness decreases as the size of the group increases. It is impossible to specify an upper limit on the size of informal work groups. However, the interaction requirement generally limits the size of the group to a maximum of 15 to 20 members. If the informal work group becomes larger than 20, subgroups begin to form.

The success and status of the informal group also play an important part in group cohesiveness. The more successful a group is in achieving its goals, the more cohesive the group becomes. The relationship is circular in that success breeds cohesiveness and cohesiveness, in turn, breeds more success. Numerous factors contribute to the status of work groups. Some of these include: the skill required in performing the job (skilled versus semiskilled jobs); opportunities for promotion out of the group (some groups develop reputations such as "the way to the top is through marketing"); the degree of supervision required (groups requiring less supervision have a higher status); and the type of work that is performed by the group (the more dangerous or more financially rewarding the work, the greater the status). Several other factors can also contribute to the status of the group. However, the important point is that groups that are successful in achieving their goals and that have higher status generally exhibit more cohesiveness.

Outside pressures, stability of membership, ability to communicate, and degree of physical isolation also influence group cohesiveness. For instance, if management's demands or requests are perceived by informal work groups as threats, group cohesiveness increases to offset the perceived threat. Higher cohesion results from stable membership in the group, because the group members have a longer time to know each other, to learn the norms of the group, and to learn how to behave according to group norms. Production lines and office layouts designed to inhibit conversation can reduce group cohesiveness. And coal miners, in their geographical isolation from the rest of the country, have demonstrated in numerous strikes the cohesiveness that can result from physical isolation from other groups.

Group cohesiveness has significance to managers. If the goals of a highly cohesive group are compatible with the organization's productivity goals, then the group's output will be above average. However, if the group's goals are incompatible with the organization's performance goals, the group's output will be below average.

Other variables can also influence the degree of group cohesiveness.[7] Figure 15–3 summarizes many of the conditions that can either increase or decrease group cohesiveness.

Group Leadership

Informal group leadership has been the subject of numerous research studies. Two of the general conclusions reached regarding informal group leadership are:

1. The group selects as its leader the individual it perceives to have the most competence in helping the group achieve its objectives.
2. The group selects as its leader the individual with strong communication skills, especially in the areas of setting objectives for the group, giving direction, and summarizing information for the group.[8]

It may also be that many informal work groups require two leaders—a task and a social leader. The task leader pushes the group toward the accomplishment of its objectives; the social leader is primarily concerned with maintaining harmony within the group.

FIGURE 15–3
Conditions for Increasing or Decreasing Group Cohesiveness

Increasing Cohesiveness	Decreasing Cohesiveness
1. Smaller groups tend to have more cohesiveness. When the group becomes too large (generally larger than 20), subgroups begin to form.	1. When interpersonal conflict results from members' disagreements over ways to achieve group goals or solve group problems, the attractiveness of the group decreases. Members of highly cohesive groups may often have disagreements, but they try to eliminate the disagreements quickly.
2. The success and prestige of the group increases cohesiveness. Groups that are successful in achieving their goals are more cohesive. Higher-status groups are also more cohesive.	2. If participation in the group results in unpleasant experiences for an individual, the attractiveness of the group decreases. When group activities result in embarrassment for an individual, the individual's attraction is usually reduced.
3. Physical isolation from other groups increases group cohesiveness.	3. If membership in the group places limits on the individuals' participation in other activities or groups, cohesiveness may be lowered. In other words, if the group restricts the freedom of its members' activities outside the group, the attraction of the group may decrease.
4. The group becomes more attractive for individuals who gain prestige or status within the group.	4. If conditions exist in the group which prevent or restrict effective communication, cohesiveness decreases. Reduced communication may result if some members are too dominating or if some members are unpleasant or obnoxious in their communication behavior.
5. Cohesiveness is higher under conditions where group members are in cooperative relationships than under conditions where there is internal competition.	5. The cohesiveness may be reduced if group members feel the activities involve too great a personal risk. The risks could be physical danger or psychological threats. Risk could involve the group's engaging in activities which individuals feel may be illegal or immoral. Risk could involve group actions in an organization that the individual feels might result in getting disciplined or fired.
6. When group members can fulfill more needs through participating in the group, the attraction of the group increases.	6. If the evaluation of the group by outsiders who are respected becomes negative, this can result in the group becoming unattractive to its members.
7. When the group is attacked from the outside, the cohesiveness usually increases as the members deal with the external threat. When the group shares a common fate as a result of external attack, the reaction is usually to focus the group's resources on protecting the group. The response to an outside threat is reflected in the statement, "United we stand, divided we fall."	

Source: Adapted from Dan L. Costley and Ralph Todd, *Human Relations in Organizations*, 2d ed. (St. Paul, Minn.: West Publishing, 1983. Copyright © 1983 by West Publishing Company. Reprinted by permission. All rights reserved.

CONFORMITY AND INFORMAL WORK GROUPS

The earlier sections of this chapter were designed to give an understanding of the nature of informal work groups in organizations. The purpose of this section is to examine the role of informal work groups in obtaining conformity of individuals to group norms.

Conformity is the degree to which the members of a group accept and abide by the norms of the group. It is situationally determined: Conformity in one situation might be viewed as deviant behavior in another. Probably the most important variable in the situation is the individual's relationships with other people and their relationships with each other. Thus, the group defines conformity for any given situation.

Knowing that the group defines conformity does not offer much help to practicing managers. Managers need to know how the group maintains conformity and the effect it has on the individual in the group.

Conformity–the degree to which group members accept and abide by the norms of the group.

Group Pressures on the Individual

Informal work groups seek to control the behavior of their members for many reasons. One reason the group desires uniform, consistent behavior from each member is so that other members can predict with reasonable certainty how the individual member will behave. This certainty is necessary in order to achieve some degree of coordination in working toward the group's goals. On the other hand, groups are organizations in and of themselves; as a result, conformity is often required in order to maintain the group. Individualistic behavior among group members can threaten the survival of the group by causing internal dissention. Individual members tend to conform to group norms under the following conditions:

1. When the norm is congruent with the personal attitudes, beliefs, and behavioral predispositions of the members.
2. When the norm is inconsistent with the personal attitudes, beliefs, or behavioral predispositions, but strong pressures to comply are exerted by the group, and the rewards of complying are valued or the sanctions imposed for noncompliance are devalued.[9]

One study on the influence of group pressures on individuals placed college students in groups of seven to nine people.[10] Group members were told that they would be comparing lengths of lines on white cards. Figure 15–4 shows the cards and lines. The subjects in the study were then asked to pick the line on the second card that was identical in length to the line on the first card.

In the experiment, all but one member of each group were told to pick one of the two wrong lines on Card 2. In addition, the uninformed member of the group was positioned to always be one of the last individuals to

FIGURE 15–4
Cards in Asch Experiment

respond. Under ordinary circumstances, mistakes on the line selection occur less than 1 percent of the time. However, in this experiment, the uninformed member made the wrong selection in 36.8 percent of the trials.

An uninformed member confronted with only a single individual who contradicted the choice continued to answer correctly in almost all trials. When the opposition was increased by two, incorrect responses increased to 31.8 percent.

The experiment demonstrated that the group's behavior affected the behavior of the individual members; although some individuals remained independent in their judgments, other acquiesced on almost every judgment. Over all, group pressure caused individuals to make incorrect judgments in over one third of the cases. The experiment also showed that the more members that disagreed with the individual, the more likely the individual was to succumb to the judgment of the group.

Lester Coch and John R. P. French conducted a classic study on the influence of groups at Harwood Manufacturing Company, a textile firm in Marion, Virginia. Figure 15–5 illustrates a major finding of their study. In this case, a woman textile worker started to exceed the group norm of 50 units per day. On the 13th day, the group began to exert pressure on the woman and her output was quickly reduced to conform with the group norm. On the 20th day, the group was disbanded by moving all group members except the woman to other jobs. Once again, her production quickly climbed to almost double the group norm.

Individuals that Deviate from Group Norms

While evidence of conformity abounds in all group situations, there are also those members who deviate from group norms and are allowed to do so by group members. Certain members who have made or are making significant contributions to the group's goals are allowed to take some liber-

FIGURE 15–5
Effect of Group Norms on Member Productivity

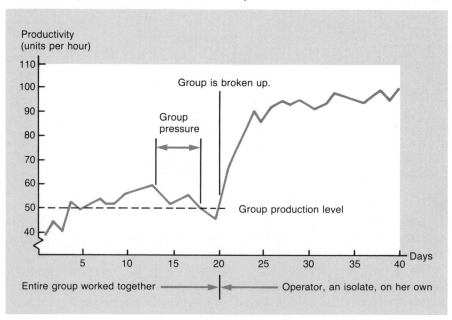

Source: Lester Coch and J. R. P. French, Jr., "Overcoming Resistance to Change," *Human Relations,* 1948, pp. 519–20.

Idiosyncrasy credit–form of credit or liberties a group gives to certain members who make a significant contribution to the group's goals.

ties within the group. This phenomenon has been called **idiosyncrasy credit.**[11]

People who contribute a great deal to the group also play a major role in developing group norms. Consequently, the group's norms largely reflect the attitudes of the major givers. This means that those who accumulate the most idiosyncrasy credit do not have to use it; the group norms largely reflect their own attitudes. People who make large contributions to the group are allowed to deviate from the group norms, but they are not likely to do so because of the similarity between their norms and group norms.

FIGURE 15–6
Potential Benefits from Informal Work Groups

---

1. Informal work groups blend with the formal organization to make a workable system for getting work done.
2. Informal work groups lighten the workload for the formal manager and fill in some of the gaps in the manager's abilities.
3. Informal work groups provide satisfaction and stability to the employees.
4. Informal work groups provide a useful channel of communication in the organization.
5. The presence of informal work groups encourages managers to plan and act more carefully than they would otherwise.

Source: Keith Davis, *Human Behavior at Work,* 6th ed. (New York: McGraw-Hill, 1981), pp. 275–76.

Conversely, those members who make little or no contribution to the group must learn to conform to norms which they had little or no part in establishing. Conformity, therefore, may be more difficult and more rigorously demanded from these members.

MANAGEMENT AND INFORMAL WORK GROUPS

As this chapter has discussed, much individual behavior is influenced by the informal work groups to which individuals belong. Unfortunately, many managers view informal work groups as being only negative toward organizational objectives. As summarized in Figure 15–6, however, informal work groups can be beneficial to management. In order to realize the potential benefits outlined there, the manager must be aware of the impact of informal work groups on individuals. Figure 15–7 indicates several key factors the manager should keep in mind in dealing with informal work groups.

CREATIVITY AND INNOVATION

Conformity is necessary if an organization is to function efficiently. However, too much conformity can result in little or no creativity and innovation. Providing an environment that fosters a healthy mix of conformity, creativ-

---

FIGURE 15–7
Key Factors in Dealing with Informal Work Groups

1. Participation in groups is a basic source of social need satisfaction for employees.
2. Informal groups try to protect their members and provide security. They will try to protect members from perceived threats from management.
3. Groups develop communication systems to provide information that members want. If management does not provide the information employees want, the informal group will try to obtain it.
4. Both informal and informal groups obtain status and prestige within an organization. Groups may use their status and prestige as a power base to influence others in the organization.
5. Groups develop and enforce norms for the behavior of members. The group norms may be supportive of management or may work against management objectives.
6. The more cohesive a group, the more control it has over the behavior of its members. The highly cohesive group can produce high achievement of organizational goals. But it can work just as effectively against organizational objectives when the group opposes management.
7. Both formal and informal groups within an organization establish roles that affect the activities and responsibilities of members. Accepting role responsibilities in an informal group may require that an individual violate the role expectations of management.

Source: Reproduced by permission from *Human Relations in Organizations* by Dan L. Costley and Ralph Todd. Copyright © 1978, West Publishing Company. All rights reserved.

MANAGEMENT IN ACTION 15–2

Creativity and Innovation at 3M

3M is 47th on the *Fortune 500* list with sales of $7.0 billion in 1983. Its businesses include graphic systems, abrasives, adhesives, building materials, chemicals, protective products, printing products, static control, recording materials, electrical products, and health care products. The largest segment of its business is tape and allied products, amounting to about 17 percent of sales.

The following story describes how the tape business started. The salesmen who visited the auto plants noticed that workers painting new two-toned cars were having trouble keeping the colors from running together. Richard G. Drew, a young 3M lab technician, came up with the answer: masking tape, the company's first tape. In 1930, six years after Du Pont introduced cellophane, Drew figured out how to put adhesive on it, and Scotch tape was born, initially for industrial packaging. It didn't really begin to roll until another imaginative 3M hero, John Borden, a sales manager, created a dispenser with a built-in blade.

Source: Adapted from Thomas J. Peters and Robert H. Waterman, Jr., *In Search of Excellence* (New York: Harper & Row, 1982), p. 228.

ity, and innovation is difficult at best. But the manager who understands each of these factors is better able to recognize the trade-offs involved and better prepared to manage these trade-offs.

It should also be reorganized that creativity and innovation, while similar, are not exactly the same. **Creativity** is the thinking process involved in producing an idea or concept that is new, original, useful, or satisfying to its creator or someone else. **Innovation** is doing new things.[12] Creativity involves coming up with a new idea, while innovation involves implementing the new idea. Thus, both creativity and innovation are crucial to the success of any company. Management in Action 15–2 illustrates creativity and innovation at 3M.

Creativity–thinking process that produces an idea or concept that is new, original, useful, or satisfying to its creator or someone else.

Innovation–doing new things.

The Creative Process

The creative process generally has four basic stages: (1) preparation, (2) incubation, (3) illumination, and (4) verification.[13] Preparation involves the hard, conscious, systematic, and often fruitless examination of a problem or area of study. The preparation stage involves getting ready to solve a particular problem. Preparation not only requires being aware of a problem area but also requires study of the problem area. The stage during which the individual or group is not consciously thinking about the problem forms the incubation stage. Unconscious mental exploration of the problem occurs during incubation. The illumination stage occurs with the appearance of the solution and is generally a very sudden occurrence. Finally, the verification stage of creativity involves testing and refining the solution.

For most people, the above four stages overlap each other as different problems are explored. A manager reading the morning mail may be accumulating knowledge in preparation for solving one problem, may be at the incubation stage on another problem, and also may be verifying another problem.

Aids in Creativity

Several techniques serve as aids for creative problem solving in organizations The following sections of this chapter describe some of those techniques.

Brainstorming

Alex F. Osborn developed brainstorming as an aid to producing creative ideas for an advertising agency. Basically, **brainstorming** involves presenting a problem to a group of people and allowing them to present ideas for solution to the problem. Brainstorming is intended to produce a large quantity of ideas or alternatives and generally follows a definite procedure.

In the first phase, members of the group are asked to present ideas off the top of their heads. The group is told that quantity is desired and that they should not be concerned about the quality of their ideas. Four basic rules for the first phase are:

1. No criticism of ideas is allowed.
2. No praise of ideas is allowed.
3. No questions or discussion of ideas is allowed.
4. Combinations and improvements on ideas that have been previously presented are encouraged.

During the second phase, the merits of each idea are reviewed. This review often leads to additional alternatives. Furthermore, alternatives with little merit are eliminated in this phase. In the third phase, one of the alternatives is selected. Frequently, the alternative is selected through group consensus.

Brainstorming—presenting a problem to a group and allowing them to produce a large quantity of ideas for its solution; no criticisms are allowed initially.

Gordon Technique

William J. J. Gordon developed a technique for the consulting firm of Arthur D. Little, Inc. to spur creative problem solving. The technique was initially devised to get creative ideas on technical problems. The **Gordon technique** differs from brainstorming in that no one but the group leader knows the exact nature of the real problem under consideration. A key word is used to describe a problem area; the group then explores that area, using the key word as a starting point. For instance, the word *conservation* might be used to start a discussion on energy conservation. The key word would direct discussion and suggestions on conservation to other areas in

Gordon technique—aid to producing creative ideas in which only the group leader knows the exact nature of the real problem; a key word is used to describe the problem area as a starting point for exploring solutions.

addition to the one under question. Proponents of the Gordon technique argue that it gives better-quality ideas because the discussion is not limited to one particular area as with the brainstorming technique.

Nominal Grouping Technique (NGT)

Nominal grouping technique (NGT)–highly structured technique for solving group tasks; minimizes personal interactions to encourage creativity and reduce pressures toward conformity.

The **nominal grouping technique** is a highly structured technique designed to keep personal interactions at a minimum. It involves the following steps:

1. Listing: Each group member, working alone, develops a list of possible solutions to a group task.
2. Recording: Each member offers an item from his or her listing in a round-robin manner to the group leader who records the ideas on a master list in full view of the group. The round-robin process continues until all items on each person's list have been recorded by the leader.
3. Voting: Each member records on an individual ballot his or her preference with respect to the priority or importance of the items appearing on the master list.

No verbal interaction is allowed during the first three steps. The results of the voting are tabulated, and scores are posted on the master list.

4. Discussion: Each item is then discussed for clarification as well as evaluation.
5. Final voting: Each member votes a second time with respect to the priority of the ideas generated.[14]

The NGT has been found to generate more unique ideas than brainstorming. However, both the NGT and brainstorming suffer from the problem that occurs when the participants are so close to the problem that they are blind to what appear to be obvious solutions.[15]

Brainwriting

Under this approach, group members are presented with a problem situation and then asked to jot their ideas down on paper without any discussion. The papers are not signed. The papers are then exchanged with others, who build upon the ideas and pass the papers on again until all have had an opportunity to participate.

Input-Output Scheme

This technique was developed by General Electric for use in solving energy-related problems. The first step under this method is to list the desired output. Once the desired output has been agreed upon, the next step is to list all possible combinations of inputs which could lead to the desired output. After the list of possible inputs has been exhausted, the group then discusses and prioritizes the desirability of the different possibilities. This process continues until one input eventually emerges as the preferred approach.

Synetics

Synetics is a relatively new technique used in creative problem solving. One method used in synetics is called "good wishes" and requires the participants to fantasize about how a particular problem could be solved if there weren't any fiscal or technical constraints. After developing a list of wishful solutions, the participants are encouraged to come up with the most absurd solutions they can imagine. Often, at least one or two of these absurd solutions can be refined into quite practical solutions.

A word of caution must be offered in the use of any of the previously described techniques. Much controversy exists regarding the effectiveness of all of the techniques as aids to creativity. Two researchers addressed this issue: "The evidence on balance does not seem encouraging enough to propose that managers who are seeking an extremely creative idea to help them on a problem situation should resort to a brainstorming session."[16] On the other hand, these same researchers concluded that brainstorming may be effective at generating a wider variety of solutions to a problem.

In conclusion, none of the techniques is a complete answer for improving creativity within organizations. Each should be viewed merely as a tool to serve a limited purpose in specific situations. Management in Action 15–3 tells of one company's approach to generating new ideas.

Encouraging Creativity and Innovation

A key challenge for any management team is to develop a corporate environment which encourages creativity and innovation. One inhibiting factor is fear of the consequences of failure. Failures are to be expected. If someone is fired every time an innovative effort fails, word quickly gets around and innovation is discouraged. Thus, it has been suggested that in areas of a business where risk is a factor in growth, special ground rules be established that permit innovative managers and employees to function without fear of being fired if they fail. The 3M Company, in its new-business activities, does this by setting up ventures in the same way that Junior Achievement businesses are formulated.[17]

Another factor that fosters creativity and innovation is the development of effective communication systems throughout the organization.[18] Rigid adherence to the formal channels of communication jeopardizes innovation. Upward and lateral communication must be fostered and encouraged.

Finally, the management of an organization must realize that highly cre-

MANAGEMENT IN ACTION 15-3

Annual Personnel Roundup at Texas Tool and Fastener

Bob Harding, who launched his Austin, Texas–based company seven years ago, is projecting fiscal year sales of close to $10 million—up from $7.2 million the previous year. He credits much of the success to the idea-sharing sessions he has conducted annually during the past four years.

The idea-sharing sessions are conducted with all employees present and amount to a four-day working vacation. Half of each working day is spent in formal meetings of the group as a whole; the other half consists of informal meetings in small groups where information is shared and ideas generated.

Source: Adapted from "Annual Personnel Roundup Spurs Texas Distributor's Flow of Ideas," *Industrial Distribution*, June 1982, p. 67.

ative and innovative people often do not fit the typical organizational mold. They generally shun highly regulated situations. They are often egoistic and can frequently be obnoxious. Thomas J. Watson, founder of IBM, stated his opinion on this issue: "We are convinced that any business needs its wild ducks. And in IBM, we try not to tame them."[19] Creativity and innovation must not only be encouraged but also be rewarded if an organization is to be successful in today's constantly changing environment.

SUMMARY

Small size, physical and psychological awareness, and interaction are all characteristics of groups. Sociologists have further refined the definition of groups by distinguishing between a small group and a primary group. A small group meets all of the requirements given above. A primary group, in addition to meeting the above requirements, must also have feelings of loyalty, comradeship, and a common sense of values among its members. Both types of groups exist within organizations.

The term *work groups* is used to describe groups in organizations. Both formal and informal work groups exist in organizations. Formal work groups result primarily from the organizing function of management. Team building is a process that involves developing an awareness on the part of the work group of those conditions that keep the group from functioning effectively and then requires the work group to take those actions that will eliminate those conditions.

Overlapping the formal work groups in organizations are informal work groups. Informal groups form for many reasons. Some of these reasons include mutual interests, friendships, the need to fulfill social needs, physical work conditions, technology, and management practices.

Once informal work groups are formed, they possess several factors in common. This chapter analyzed some of these factors: group norms, group cohesiveness, and group leadership. A group norm is an agreement among the members of the group concerning how the members should behave. Group cohesiveness refers to the degree of attraction that each member has for the group. Variables that affect group cohesiveness are size, success and status of the group, outside pressures, stable membership, ability to communicate, and degree of physical isolation from other groups.

Conformity is the degree to which the members of a group accept and abide by the norms of the group. Individual members tend to conform to group norms when the norm is congruent with their personal attitudes, beliefs, and behavioral predispositions. Even if the group norm is inconsistent with their personal attitudes, beliefs, and behavioral tendencies, individual members tend to conform when strong pressures to comply are applied by the group and the sanctions imposed for noncompliance are devalued.

While conformity is necessary to some degree in all organizations, it must not be at the expense of eliminating creativity. A balance of conformity and creativity is required in organizations, and management must provide an environment that fosters a healthy mix.

Creativity is the thinking process involved in producing an idea or concept that is new, original, useful, or satisfying to its creator or someone else. Innovation is doing new things. The creative process generally takes place in four stages: (1) preparation, (2) incubation, (3) illumination, and (4) verification. Brainstorming, the Gordon technique, the nominal grouping technique, brainwriting, the input-output scheme, and synetics were described as aids for fostering creativity in organizations. Finally, suggestions were offered for encouraging creativity and innovation in organizations.

References and Additional Readings

[1] Elton Mayo, *The Human Problems of an Industrial Civilization* (Cambridge, Mass.: Harvard University Graduate School of Business Administration, 1946).

[2] For an analysis on the impact of group size and absenteeism, see "Group Size and Absenteeism Rates: A Longitudinal Analysis," *Academy of Management Journal,* December 1982, pp. 921–27.

[3] Rensis Likert, *New Patterns of Management* (New York: McGraw-Hill, 1961), p. 104.

[4] Daniel C. Feldman, "The Development and Enforcement of Group Norms," *Academy of Management Review* 9 (January 1984), p. 47.

[5] J. Richard Hackman, "Group Influences on Individuals," in *Handbook of Industrial and Organizational Psychology,* ed. Marvin D. Dunnette (New York: John Wiley & Sons, 1983), p. 1517.

[6] Ibid.

[7] For a further discussion of components of group cohesion, see Joseph P. Stokes, "Components of Group Cohesion: Intermember Attraction, Instrumental Value, and Risk Taking," *Small Group Behavior,* May 1983, pp. 163–73.

[8] Beatrice Schultz, "Predicting Emergent Leaders: An Exploratory Study of the Salience of Communicative Functions," *Small Group Behavior,* February 1978, pp. 109–14.

[9] Hackman, "Group Influences," p. 1503.

[10] Solomon Asch, "Opinions and Social Pressure," *Scientific American,* November 1955, pp. 31–34.

[11] E. P. Hollander, "Conformity , Status, and Idiosyncrasy Credit," *Psychological Review* 65 (January 1958), pp. 117–27.

[12] Theodore Levitt, "Ideas are Useless unless Used," *Inc.,* February 1981, p. 96.

[13] Graham Walles, *The Art of Thought* (New York: Harcourt Brace Jovanovich, 1976), p. 80.

[14] Gene E. Burton, Dev S. Pathak, and David B. Burton, "The Gordon Effect in Nominal Grouping," *University of Michigan Business Review,* July 1978, p. 8.

[15] Ibid., p. 7.

[16] T. Richards and B. L. Freedman, "Procedures for Managers in Idea-Deficient Situations: An Examination of Brainstorming Approaches," *Journal of Management Studies,* February 1978, pp. 43–55.

[17] Maurice I. Zeldman, "How Management Can Develop and Sustain a Creative Environment," *Advanced Management Journal,* Winter 1980, p. 25.

[18] Thomas J. Peters and Robert H. Waterman, Jr., *In Search of Excellence* (New York: Harper & Row, 1982), pp. 223.

[19] Thomas J. Watson, *A Business and Its Beliefs* (New York: McGraw-Hill, 1963), p. 28.

Review Questions

1. Define the following terms:
   a. Group.
   b. Small group.
   c. Primary group.
   d. Work group.
2. What is team building?
3. Outline some of the reasons why informal work groups exist in organizations.
4. What is a group norm?
5. What is group cohesiveness?
6. Describe some of the variables that affect the cohesiveness of a group.
7. What is conformity?
8. Describe the results of two studies dealing with the influence of groups on individual behavior.
9. What is idiosyncrasy credit?
10. What is creativity? Describe the creative process.
11. Describe the following aids to creativity:
    a. Brainstorming.
    b. Gordon technique.
    c. Nominal grouping technique.
    d. Brainwriting.
    e. Input-output scheme.
    f. Synetics.
12. What are some suggestions for encouraging creativity and innovation in organizations?

Discussion Questions

1. Do you think it is possible to eliminate entirely the need for informal work groups?
2. Discuss the following statement: "Goals of informal work groups are never congruent with the goals of the formal organizations."
3. Some employees are described as "marching to the beat of a different drummer." In light of the discussion in this chapter, what does this statement mean to you?
4. "Creativity is born in an individual and cannot be developed." Do you agree?

Incident 15–1

One of the Gang?

Recently, Gary Brown was appointed as the supervisor of a group of machine operators in which he was formerly one of the rank and file employees. When he was selected for the job, the department head told him the former supervisor was being transferred because he could not get sufficient work out of the group. He said also that the reason Gary was selected was because he appeared to be a natural leader, that he was close to the group, and that he knew the tricks they were practicing in order to restrict production. He told Gary that he believed he could lick the problem and that he would stand behind him.

He was right about Gary knowing the tricks. When he was one of the gang, not only did he try to hamper the supervisor, but he was the ringleader in trying to make life miserable for him. None of them had anything personally against the supervisor; all of them considered it a game to pit their wits against his. There was a set of signals to inform the boys that the supervisor was coming so that everyone would appear to be working hard. As soon as he left the immediate vicinity, everyone would take it easy. Also, the operators would act dumb to get the supervisor to go into lengthy explanations and demonstrations while they stood around. They complained constantly and without justification about the materials and the equipment.

At lunchtime, the boys would ridicule the company, tell the latest fast one they had pulled on the supervisor, and plan new ways to harass him. All this seemed to be a great joke. Gary and the rest of the boys had a lot of fun at the expense of the supervisor and the company.

Now that Gary has joined the ranks of management, it is not so funny. He is determined to use his managerial position and his knowledge to win the group over to working for the company instead of against it. Gary knows that, if this can be done, he will have a top-notch group. The operators know their stuff, have a very good team spirit, and if they would use their brains and efforts constructively, they could turn out above-average production.

Gary's former buddies are rather cool to him now; but this seems to be natural, and he believes he can overcome it in a short time. What has him concerned is that Joe James is taking over his old post as ringleader of the group, and the group is trying to play the same tricks on him as they did on the former supervisor.

Questions

1. Did the company make a good selection in Gary?
2. What suggestions would you make to Gary?
3. Are work groups necessarily opposed to working toward organizational goals? Explain.

Incident 15–2
Talkative Mike

Mike was an exceptionally friendly and talkative man—to the extent that he bothered his supervisor by frequently stopping the whole work crew to tell them a joke or a story. It didn't seem to bother Mike that it was during working hours or that somebody other than his crew might be watching. He just enjoyed telling stories and being the center of attention. The trouble was that the rest of the crew enjoyed him, too.

The supervisor had just recently taken over the department, and he was determined to straighten the crew out. He felt that he would have no problem motivating such a friendly person as Mike. Because the crew was on a group incentive, the supervisor felt he could get them to see how much they were losing by standing around and talking. But there was no question about it: Mike was the informal leader of the crew, and they followed him just as surely as if he were the plant manger.

Mike's crew produced extremely well. When they worked—and that was most of the time—their output could not be equaled. But the frequent non-scheduled storytelling breaks did bother the supervisor. Not only could that nonproductive time be converted to badly needed production but they also were setting a poor example for the other crews and the rest of the department.

The supervisor called Mike in to discuss the situation. His primary emphasis was on the fact that Mike's crew could make more money by better using their idle time. Mike's contention was, "What good is money if you can't enjoy it? You sweat your whole life away to rake in money, and then all you've got to show for it is a lot of miserable years and no way of knowing how to enjoy what's left. Life's too short to spend every minute trying to make more money." The discussion ended with Mike promising that the group would quiet down; if their production didn't keep up the supervisor would let him know.

Things did improve for a while; but within a week or so, the old pattern was right back where it had been. The supervisor then arranged to talk with the other members of the crew individually. Their reactions were the same as Mike's. As before, some improvements were noted at first; then the crew gradually reverted to their old habits.

Questions

1. Do you agree with Mike and his group?
2. Does the supervisor really have a complaint in light of the fact that Mike's group produces well above average?
3. If you were the supervisor, what would you do next?

Exercise

Crash Project

You are told that you and your work group have two weeks to implement a new program. You feel two weeks are insufficient and that you and your employees would virtually have to work around the clock to complete it in that time. Morale has always been high in your group; yet you know that some people just don't like overtime. As you think about how best to handle the situation, you consider these alternatives:

1. Tell your group that the company is being pretty unreasonable about this. "I don't see what the big rush is. But it's got to be done, so let's all pitch in and help, shall we?"

2. Tell your group that you have told Bob Smith (your boss) that you have a superb group of people and that "if anyone in the company could get the job done, we could."

3. Tell the group that your job is on the line and that if they want you around for awhile, they will have to make a heroic effort.

4. Tell your group that you don't want to hear any griping. This is the nature of the job, and anyone who feels that he or she can't devote the extra time had better start looking for another job.

5. Tell the group that the job must be done and ask them to make suggestions on how it can be completed within the deadline.

Other alternatives may be open to you, but assume that these are the only ones you have considered.

WITHOUT DISCUSSION with anyone, decide which of these approaches you would take and be prepared to defend your choice.

16

Managing Conflict and Stress

Chapter Outline

As conflict—difference—is here in the world, as we cannot avoid it, we should, I think, use it. Instead of condemning it, we should set it to work for us. Why not? What does the mechanical engineer do with friction? Of course, his chief job is to eliminate friction, but it is true that he also capitalizes friction. The transmission of power by belts depends on friction between the belt and the pulley. The friction between the driving wheel of the locomotive and the track is necessary to haul the train. All polishing is done by friction. The music of the violin we get by friction. We left the savage state when we discovered fire by friction. We talk of the friction of mind on mind as a good thing. So in business, too, we have to know when to try to eliminate friction and when to try to capitalize it, when to see what work we can make it do.

Mary Parker Follet*

Conflict in organizations is often assumed to be unnatural and undesirable—to be avoided at all costs. Conflict can lead to rigidity in the system in which it operates, distort reality, and debilitate the participants in the conflict situation. Therefore, many organizations approach the management of conflict with the following assumptions:

1. Conflict is avoidable.
2. Conflict is the result of personality problems within the organization.
3. Conflict produces inappropriate reactions by the persons involved.
4. Conflict creates a polarization within the organization.

Recent studies in the behavioral sciences have reexamined these assumptions about organizational conflict. These studies suggest that conflict is perfectly natural and should be expected to occur. The key point in the study of conflict, however, is not that it is natural or unavoidable. As Mary Parker Follet states in the above quote, management must know when to eliminate conflict and when to build on it.

WHAT IS CONFLICT?

Conflict—overt behavior in which one party seeks to advance its own interests in its relationship with others.

Conflict is overt behavior in which one party seeks to advance its own interests in its relationship with others. Conflict begins when one party perceives that a second party has frustrated or is about to frustrate some

---

* Mary Parker Follet, "Constructive Conflict," in *Dynamic Administration*, ed. Henry C. Metcalf and L. Urwick (New York: Harper & Row, 1940), pp. 30–31.

concern of the first party.[1] The parties involved denote social units in a conflict situation. They can be individuals, groups, organizations, or nations.

Today's managers must accept the existence of conflict and realize that to attempt to stop all conflict is a mistake. In one survey, managers reported that they spend 20 percent of their time dealing with conflict and that their ability to manage conflict has become increasingly more important.[2] The general consensus today is that conflict itself is not undesirable, rather, it is a phenomenon that can have constructive or destructive effects. How positive the effect of the conflict is often depends on the participant's own point of view. However, the results of a conflict should also be evaluated from the organization's point of view.

For example, in a struggle between two people for a promotion, the winner will probably feel that the conflict was most worthwhile, while the loser will probably reach the opposite conclusion. However, the impact of the conflict on the organization must also be considered. If the conflict ends in the selection and promotion of the better person, then the effect is good from the organization's viewpoint. If, by competing, the parties have produced more or made improvements within their areas of responsibility, then the effect is also positive. At the same time, there may be destructive effects. The overall work of the organization may have suffered during the conflict. The loser may resign or withdraw as a result of the failure. The conflict may become chronic and inhibit the work of the organization. In extreme cases, the health of one or both of the participants may be adversely affected.

The destructive effects of conflict are often obvious. The constructive effects may be more subtle. The manager must be able to see these constructive effects and to weigh them against the costs. Some potentially useful effects of conflict are:

1. Conflict energizes people. Even if not all of the resulting activity is constructive, it at least wakes people up and gets them moving.

2. Conflict is a form of communication; the resolution of conflict may open up new and lasting channels.

3. Conflict often provides an outlet for pent-up tensions, resulting in catharsis. With the air cleansed, the participants can again concentrate on their primary responsibilities.

4. Conflict may actually be an educational experience: The participants may become more aware and more understanding of their opponents' functions and the problems with which they must cope.

The potential for conflict depends on how incompatible the goals of the parties are, the extent to which the required resources to achieve the objectives are scarce and shared, and how interdependent the task activities are. The potential for conflict is great at all levels of the organization. Management in Action 16–1 recounts a conflict at the top level of Ford Motor Company.

MANAGEMENT IN ACTION 16–1

Firing of Lee Iacocca

At about 3 P.M., Henry Ford summoned Lee Iacocca to his office for a meeting with him and Ford's brother William Ford. Henry Ford informed Iacocca that he was being fired and offered little explanation.

Since its earliest days, Ford Motor Co. has been known as a place of relatively short tenure for top nonfamily managers. However, Lee Iacocca had seemed to be more resilient and entrenched than his predecessors. But, one source commented on the firing as follows: "There's a saying at Ford: 'Nobody flies too close to Air Force One.' Maybe Lee just got too close."

Some attribute the friction to the differing styles of the two men. While Iacocca's automotive brilliance and ambition helped him climb to the top, some of these same attributes may have kept Henry Ford from ever being completely comfortable with him. "Henry Ford and Lee Iacocca were dissimilar styles, and it doesn't work well over a period of time," says Mr. Gadsden, a Ford Motor director. "The glue that held them together got dry and cracked."

Some sources believe Henry Ford may have feared that the ambitious Iacocca, if he achieved the top job in the company, might have interfered with Henry Ford's desire to eventually have his son Edsel B. Ford II run the company. The younger Ford, 29, is being groomed in the management ranks, and Henry Ford has publicly expressed the hope that someday he will take over.

In an interview with *Automotive News*, Iacocca is quoted as asserting that Ford "wants to diffuse and bureaucratize the company as he gets to be 61. He just doesn't want strong guys around."

Source: Adapted from "Henry Ford Threatened to Quit if Board Failed to Back Him on Iacocca," *The Wall Street Journal*, July 17, 1978, pp. 1, 23.

PROGRESSIVE STAGES OF CONFLICT

A manager must be aware of conflict's dynamic nature. Conflict does not usually appear suddenly. It passes through a series of progressive stages as tensions build. These stages of development are:[3]

1. Latent conflict: At this stage, the basic conditions for conflict exist but have not yet been recognized.
2. Perceived conflict: The cause of the conflict is recognized by one or both of the participants.
3. Felt conflict: Tension is beginning to build between the participants, although no real struggle has yet begun.
4. Manifest conflict: The struggle is under way, and the behavior of the participants makes the existence of the conflict apparent to others who are not directly involved.
5. Conflict aftermath: The conflict has been ended by resolution or suppression. This establishes new conditions that will lead either to more effective cooperation or to a new conflict that may be more severe than the first.

Conflict does not always pass through all of these stages. And those in conflict may not be at the same stage simultaneously. For example, one participant could be at the manifest state of conflict while the other is at the perceived stage.

ANALYZING CONFLICT

Conflict can be analyzed from two basic perspectives. One approach sees conflict as a process internal to the individual (intrapersonal conflict). The other views it as external to the individual—individual versus individual, individual versus group, group versus group, organization versus organization, or any combination of these. External conflict is of three general types: structural, interpersonal, and strategic. The following sections examine intrapersonal, structural, interpersonal, and strategic conflict in more detail.

Intrapersonal Conflict

Intrapersonal conflict is internal to the individual. It is probably the most difficult form of conflict to analyze. Basically, it relates to the need-drive-goal motivational sequence (see Figure 16–1) discussed in Chapter 13.

Intrapersonal conflict can result when barriers exist between the drive and the goal. This often leads to frustration for the person involved. Such conflict may also result when goals have both positive and negative aspects and when competing and conflicting goals exist. Figure 16–2 illustrates how it can occur in the motivational sequence.

Intrapersonal conflict–
internal to the individual;
relates to the need-drive-
goal motivational
sequence.

Frustration

Frustration results when a drive or motive is blocked before the goal is reached. Barriers can be either overt (rules and procedures) or covert (mental hang-ups). When a drive is blocked, people tend to react with defense mechanisms, which are behaviors used to cope with frustration. Figure 16–3 lists some typical defense mechanisms.

Frustration– results when
a drive or motive is blocked
before the goal is reached.

FIGURE 16–1
The Motivation Sequence

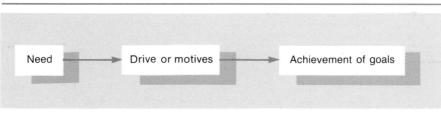

Need → Drive or motives → Achievement of goals

FIGURE 16–2
Sources of Intrapersonal Conflict

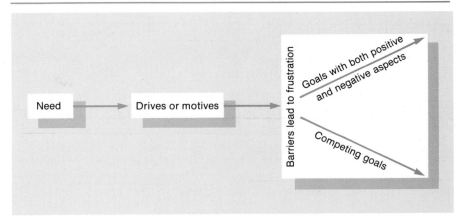

Responses to frustration vary and can be expressed through withdrawal behavior (higher absenteeism and turnover rates), aggression (sabotage and other destructive work acts), excessive drinking, drug abuse, and more subtle responses such as ulcers or heart trouble.

Goal Conflict

Goal conflict - results when a goal has both positive and negative features or when two or more competing goals exist.

Goal conflict occurs when a goal has both positive and negative features or when two or more competing goals exist. Basically, three forms of conflicting goals exist:

1. **Mutually exclusive positive goals.** Goal conflict results when a person is motivated toward two or more positive, mutually exclusive goals at the same time. Selecting an academic major is an example of this type of conflict. Economics, law, and medicine may all have positive aspects, but all cannot be pursued at once. Often, this form of conflict can be resolved by making a decision rather quickly, thereby ending the conflict.

2. **Positive-negative goals.** Conflict that exists when a person tries to achieve a goal that has both positive and negative effects. To pursue a top management position, people must often sacrifice their own time and time with their family. Thus, the goal of being a successful business leader can have both positive and negative aspects.

3. **Negative-negative goals.** Here the person tries to avoid two or more negative, mutually exclusive goals. Someone may dislike his or her job but finds quitting and looking for another job even less attractive. The likely outcome of this conflict is frustration.

Dissonance - feeling of disharmony within an individual.

Goal conflict forces the person to make a decision. Decision making often creates a feeling of conflict within the individual. A person feeling such disharmony, called **dissonance,** will always attempt to reduce it.

FIGURE 16–3
Reactions to Frustration

Adjustive Reactions	Psychological Process	Illustration
Compensation	Individual devotes himself to a pursuit with increased vigor to make up for some feeling of real or imagined inadequacy.	Zealous, hardworking president of the Twenty-Five Year Club who has never advanced very far in the company hierarchy.
Conversion	Emotional conflicts are expressed in muscular, sensory, or bodily symptoms of disability, malfunctioning, or pain.	A disabling headache keeping a staff member off the job the day after a cherished project has been rejected.
Displacement	Redirects pent-up emotions toward persons, ideas, or objects other than the primary source of the emotion.	Roughly rejecting a simple request from a subordinate after receiving a rebuff from the boss.
Fantasy	Daydreaming or other forms of imaginative activity provide an escape from reality and imagined satisfactions.	An employee's daydream of the day in the staff meeting when he corrects the boss' mistakes and is publicly acknowledged as the real leader of the group.
Negativism	Active or passive resistance, operating unconsciously.	The manager who, having been unsuccessful in getting out of a committee assignment, picks apart every suggestion that anyone makes in the meetings.
Rationalization	Justifies inconsistent or undesirable behavior, beliefs, statements, and motivations by providing acceptable explanations for them.	Padding the expense account because "everybody does it."
Regression	Individual returns to an earlier and less mature level of adjustment in the face of frustration.	A manager, having been blocked in some administrative pursuit, busies himself with clerical duties or technical details more appropriate for his subordinates.
Repression	Completely excludes from consciousness impulses, experiences, and feelings which are psychologically disturbing because they arouse a sense of guilt or anxiety.	A subordinate "forgetting" to tell his boss the circumstances of an embarrassing situation.
Resignation, apathy, and boredom	Breaks psychological contact with the environment, withholding any sense of emotional or personal involvement.	Employee who, receiving no reward, praise, or encouragement, no longer cares whether or not he does a good job.
Flight or withdrawal	Leaves the field in which frustration, anxiety, or conflict is experienced, either physically or psychologically.	The salesman's big order falls through, and he takes the rest of the day off; constant rebuff or rejection by superiors and colleagues pushes an older worker toward being a loner and ignoring whatever friendly gestures are made.

Source: Timothy W. Costello and Sheldon S. Zalkind, *Psychology in Administration: A Research Orientation* (Englewood Cliffs, N.J.: Prentice-Hall, 1963), pp. 148–49. Copyright © 1963 by Prentice-Hall, Inc. Reprinted by permission of the publisher.

Structural (Functional) Conflict

Structural (functional) conflict—results from the organizational structure; relatively independent of the individuals occupying the roles within the structure.

Structural (functional) conflict results from the organizational structure and is relatively independent of the individuals occupying the roles within the structure. The marketing department and the production department in Figure 16–4, for example, may have structural conflict. The marketing department, being customer-oriented, may believe that some exceptions can and should be made in production for the sake of current and future sales. The production department may view such exceptions as unreasonable and not in the best interests of the organization. Hence, a structural conflict occurs. Various types of structural conflict are discussed in the following sections.

Goal segmentation and rewards. Each functional unit of an organization has different functional goals. These can cause conflict which, when it emerges, may seem to be personality clashes. The classical problem of inventory levels shows this dilemma. The marketing department would like to keep finished-goods inventories high to supply all of the customers' needs on short notice. The finance department would like to keep inventories low because of the cost of maintaining these inventories. Another illustration of this dilemma concerns the product line. Marketing would like to carry a product line composed of all shapes, sizes, and colors. Because of the problems involved in producing multiple shapes, sizes, and colors, the production department would prefer one basic product. The end result in either case is often a conflict between departments.

Richard Walton and John Dutton suggest that the reward system is the key to reducing this type of conflict.[4] They believe that a reward system that stresses the separate performance of the departments feeds the conflict. However, rewarding the combined efforts of the conflicting departments reduces the conflicts.

Mutual departmental dependence. Sometimes, two departments or units of an organization are dependent on one another for the accomplish-

FIGURE 16–4
Functional Organization Structure

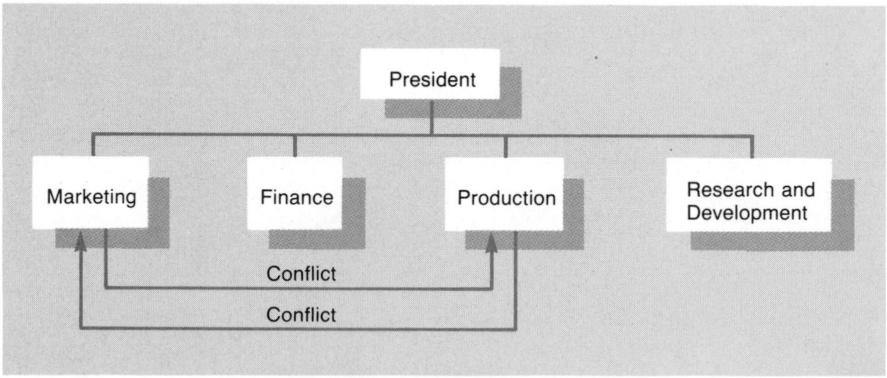

ment of their respective goals; a potential for structural conflict is then present. For instance, the marketing department's sales depend on the volume of production from the production department; at the same time, the production department's quotas are based on the sales of the marketing department. This type of mutual dependence exists in many organizations.

Unequal departmental dependence.   Often, departmental dependence is unequal and fosters conflict. In most organizations, for instance, staff groups are more dependent on line groups. The staff generally must understand the problems of the line, cooperate with the line, and sell their ideas to the line. However, the line does not have to reciprocate. One tactic in this form of conflict is an attempt by the more dependent unit to interfere with the work performance of the independent group. The more dependent group hopes that the other group will cooperate once they realize how the dependent group can hinder their progress.

Functional unit and the environment.   Functional units obviously perform different tasks and cope with different parts of the environment. Research has shown that the more the environments served by functional units differ, the greater the potential for conflict. Paul Lawrence and Jay Lorsch have developed four basic dimensions to describe these differences: (1) structure—this refers to the basic type of supervisory style employed; (2) environment orientation—this refers to the orientation of the unit to the outside world; (3) time-span orientation—this refers to the unit's planning-time perspectives; (4) interpersonal orientation—this refers to the openness and permissiveness of interpersonal relationships.[5]

Lawrence and Lorsch applied their scheme to six organizations in the plastics industry. The results are shown in Table 16–1: The environmental differences are a primary cause of structural conflict. Coordinating the activities of departments such as applied research, sales, and production is harder due to these differences.

Role dissatisfaction.   Role dissatisfaction may also produce structural conflict. Professionals in an organizational unit who receive little recognition

---

TABLE 16–1
Differences Related to Environment of Departments

Departments	Degree of Structural Formality	Orientation toward Environment	Orientation toward Time	Interpersonal Orientation*
Fundamental research	Medium (4)†	Technoeconomic and scientific	Long	Task (2)
Applied research	Medium (3)	Technoeconomic	Long	Relationship (3)
Sales	High (2)	Market	Short	Relationship (4)
Production	Highest (1)	Technoeconomic	Short	Task (1)

* Fiedler's questionnaire discussed in Chapter 14 was used in this analysis.
† Numbers refer to the relative ranking of the departments in that dimension.
Source: P. R. Lawrence and J. W. Lorsch, "Differentiation and Integration in Complex Organizations," *Administrative Science Quarterly* 12 (1967), pp. 16–22.

and have limited opportunities for advancement may initiate conflict with other units. Purchasing agents often demonstrate this form of conflict.

Role dissatisfaction and conflict often result when a group that has low perceived status sets standards for another group. For example, within academic institutions, administrators—who may be viewed by the faculty as having less status—often set standards of performance and make administrative decisions that affect the faculty.

Role ambiguity.   Ambiguities in the description of a particular job can lead to structural conflict. When the credit or blame for the success or failure of a particular assignment cannot be determined between two departments, conflict is likely to result. For instance, improvements in production techniques require the efforts of the engineering and production departments. After the improvements are made, credit is difficult to assign; thus, conflict often results between these two departments.

Common resource dependence.   When two organizational units are dependent on common but scarce resources, potential for conflict exists. This often occurs when two departments are competing for computer time. Each obviously feels that its projects are more important.

Communication barriers.   Semantic differences can cause conflict. For instance, purchasing agents and engineers generally use different language to describe similar materials, which can lead to conflict.

FIGURE 16–5
Summary of Types of Structural Conflict

Type	Example
Mutual departmental dependence	Marketing department's sales are dependent on the volume of production from the production department.
Unequal departmental dependence	Staff departments are generally more dependent on line departments.
Goal segmentation and rewards	Different inventory levels are desired by different functional departments.
Functional unit and environment	The environment faced by an applied research department and a sales department are different and can lead to conflict between these departments.
Role dissatisfaction	Professionals in an organizational unit who receive little attention.
Ambiguities	When the credit or blame for the success or failure of a particular assignment cannot be determined between two departments.
Common resource dependence	Two departments competing for computer time.
Communication barriers	Semantic differences. Purchasing agents and engineers may use different language to describe similar materials, and conflict can result from those semantic differences.

Communication-related conflict also occurs when a physical or organizational barrier to effective communication exists. Company headquarters and branch offices frequently suffer from this problem. Figure 16–5 summarizes types of structural conflict.

Interpersonal Conflict

Interpersonal conflict may result from personality conflicts as well as from structural conflict and many other factors. Interpersonal conflicts occur when barriers to communication exist between the involved parties. These barriers are often harder to overcome than the communication barriers discussed earlier as structural conflict. Communication barriers often create what is called *pseudoconflict.* This results when participants in a group fail to reach a group decision because of their failure to exchange information, opinions, or ideas. Although the group may really be in complete agreement, the situation has all the symptoms of a conflict caused by differences of opinion.

> **Interpersonal conflict** – between two or more individuals; can be caused by many factors.

A second major cause of interpersonal conflict occurs when individuals are dissatisfied with their roles as compared to the roles of others. An employee may be compatible with both his or her manager and fellow employees. However, when a peer is promoted to a management job, the employee may no longer accept his or her role in relation to the former peer.

Opposing personalities often cause conflict situations. Some people simply rub each other the wrong way. The extrovert and the introvert, the boisterous and the reserved, the optimist and the pessimist, the impulsive and the deliberate—these are but a few possible combinations that might bother each other.

Finally, there are special prejudices based on personal background or ethnic origin that cause conflict. This, of course, includes racial and religious conflicts; but there are also other, more subtle, prejudices. Examples include the college graduate versus the person with less education, the married versus the divorced person, or the longtime employee versus the new hiree.

Unlike structural conflicts, where both parties are actively involved, interpersonal conflicts may be one-sided. One of the parties may be totally unaware of the existing conflict.

Strategic Conflict

Intrapersonal, structural, and interpersonal conflicts are usually not planned. They simply develop as a result of existing circumstances. **Strategic conflicts** are often started purposely; they are sometimes fought with an elaborate battle plan. Such conflicts usually result from the promotion of self-interests on the part of an individual or group. There is a clear goal and those who stand in the way are the adversary. In organizations, the goal is usually to gain an advantage over the opponent within the reward

> **Strategic conflict** –results from promotion of self-interests by an individual or group; often deliberately planned.

system. The potential reward may be a bonus or commission, a choice assignment, a promotion, or an expansion of power. Whatever it is, usually only one of the participants will receive it (or the greatest portion of it).

The vice presidents of an organization may find themselves in a strategic conflict situation as the retirement of the president nears. An overly ambitious vice president, in an attempt to better his or her personal chances for the presidency, may create a strategic conflict with one or more of the other vice presidents. Strategic conflict can also occur between departments within a university when a new course is offered and two or more departments feel that they should be teaching a particular course.

Strategic conflict does not always imply that the participants are dishonest or unethical. Indeed, rewards are there to be pursued with vigor. But such conflicts can degenerate into unfair play because the participants cannot resist temptation.

Because it is usually impossible to isolate a single cause, few conflicts fit neatly into one of the above categories. Nevertheless, they do provide a useful framework for analyzing conflict.

MANAGING CONFLICT

There are five general methods of solving interpersonal conflict situations: (1) withdraw one or more of the participants; (2) smooth over the conflict and pretend it does not exist; (3) compromise for the sake of ending the conflict; (4) force the conflict to a conclusion by third-party intervention; and (5) have a confrontation between the participants in an effort to solve the underlying source of conflict. Confrontation, or problem solving, is generally considered to be the most effective method of resolving conflict, while forcing the conflict to a conclusion has been found to be the least effective method.

Much structural conflict results from interdependencies inherent in the organizational structure. Some of this conflict potential may be removed by decoupling the conflicting parties: reduce their common resource dependencies; give each control over their own resources; introduce large buffer inventories; or invoke impersonal, straightforward rules for resource allocation. Decoupling may also occur by duplicating facilities for dependent departments. However, this approach may be too expensive for the organization. Lawrence and Lorsch suggest the use of a "linking" position between dependent departments. The purpose is to ease communication and coordination between interdependent and potentially conflicting departments.[6] Another way is to design the work flow so that the system reflects more logical and complete work units where responsibility and authority are more consistent. Lastly, the matrix organization can offer a means for constructive confrontation, which (as stated earlier) is the most effective method of conflict resolution.

A Model for Conflict Management

Walton and Dutton have developed a general model (shown in Figure 16–6) for managing conflict in organizations. This model views the conflict situation from two perspectives. The first views the manager as an intervening force in the conflict cycle. The second involves the response patterns of higher-level managers.

FIGURE 16–6
Model for Conflict Management

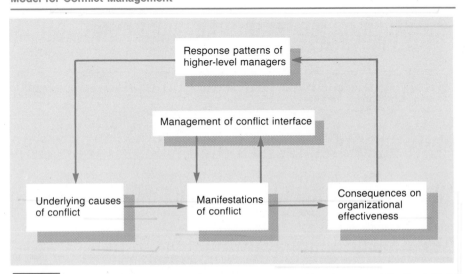

Source: Richard F. Walton and John M. Dutton, "The Management of Interdepartmental Conflict: A Model and Review," *Administrative Science Quarterly,* March 1969, p. 74.

The Conflict Interface

Management of the conflict interface is based on monitoring the behavior of the participant(s) as the conflict develops. The objective of the manager is not to resolve the conflict but to act as a referee and counselor in helping the participant(s) reach an acceptable solution. Understanding the type of conflict—intrapersonal, structural, interpersonal, strategic—and the stage of the conflict cycle will aid the manager. Figure 16–7 lists key questions that a manager should address to apply the concepts presented in this chapter to the resolution of a conflict situation.

To maximize the constructive aspects of the conflict and to speed its resolution while minimizing the destructive consequences, the manager should also know the following ground rules for verbal confrontations:

1. Review past actions and clarify the issues before the confrontation begins.

FIGURE 16–7
Key Questions to Be Answered in Conflict Resolution

1. What perceived loss or threat of loss has led each party to perceive a conflict?
2. How does each party define the conflict issue?
    - Does each party have an accurate perception of the other's concerns? Is the issue posed superficially rather than in terms of underlying concerns?
    - Would alternative definitions of the issue be more helpful in suggesting integrative solutions to the conflict?
3. How does each party pursue his or her objectives in dealing with the other party?
    - What is his or her underlying orientation in approaching the conflict issue—competive, collaborative, sharing, avoidance, accommodative?
    - What assumptions underlie the individual's choice of strategies and tactics?
4. How is each party's behavior influenced by the behavior of the other?
    - What ongoing dynamics seem to be producing the escalation or deescalation?
    - Is each party aware that the other's behavior is partly a response to his or her own?
    - What efforts are the parties making to manage their own conflict?
5. If things proceed as they are, what are likely to be the short-term and long-term results—both substantive and emotional?
    - What foreseeable effects will this episode have upon subsequent episodes?
6. Does the general makeup of either party predispose him or her toward the use of specific conflict-handling modes?
    - Are those predispositions compatible with the requirements of his or her position?
    - To what extent could a person's behavior be changed through training experiences?
7a. Is either party acting as representative for a larger set of individuals?
    - What expectations do they have of the representative's behavior?
    - How much power do they have over this person?
    - To what extent can they monitor his or her negotiation behavior?
7b. Who are the other, relatively neutral, onlookers?
    - What sort of behavior will they encourage or discourage?
    - How much power do they have over the parties?
8. What is the relative importance and frequency of competitive issues versus common problems in the relationship as a whole?
    - To what extent have resource scarcities created conflict of interest between the parties?
    - In what ways have differentiated responsibilities created conflict of interest?
9a. Are there many rules which dictate or constrain settlements on specific issues?
    - To what extent are the parties free to problem-solve on important issues?
9b. How are the behaviors of the parties shaped by the format of their negotiations?
    - How frequently do the parties interact?
    - When and where are meetings held?
    - What are the number and composition of people present?
    - How formally are the negotiations conducted?
9c. What provisions are there for involving third parties?
    - Are skilled third parties available to help the parties resolve their own disputes?
    - Does the larger system have provisions for terminating conflict episodes by imposing settlements when the parties deadlock?

Source: Kenneth Thomas, "Conflict and Conflict Management," in *Handbook of Industrial and Organizational Psychology,* ed. Marvin D. Dunnette (New York: John Wiley & Sons, 1983).

2. Communicate freely; do not hold back grievances.

3. Do not surprise the opponent with a confrontation for which the individual is not prepared.

4. Do not attack the opponent's sensitive spots that have nothing to do with the issues of the conflict.

5. Keep to specific issues; do not argue aimlessly.

6. Maintain the intensity of the confrontation and ensure that all participants say all that they want to say. If the basic issues have been resolved at this point, agree on what steps are to be taken toward resolving the conflict.

Besides acting as referees in enforcing these rules, managers can give valuable assistance to the participant(s) without interfering with their responsibility to resolve the conflict. Managers can help the participants understand why the conflict exists and what underlying issues must be resolved.[7] They can also help obtain information that may be needed to reach a solution. In interpersonal conflict, managers can regulate somewhat the frequency of contacts between the participants and perhaps establish a problem-solving climate when they meet. A manager's most important contribution, however, is to keep the individuals working toward a true resolution of the conflict. Confrontation of the conflict situation within the guidelines developed above should encourage constructive conflict within the organization.[8]

Responses of Higher-Level Managers

The second level of conflict management concerns the responses of higher-level managers to the conflict's consequences for the ongoing work of the organization. If the conflict itself or the nature of its aftermath has made conditions intolerable, management must step in and make whatever decisions and changes needed to restore order. The resulting actions either force a resolution to the conflict or change the solution that has been reached.

Such intervention is often regarded as arbitrary by the participant(s), especially by those who do not receive a favorable decision. In such cases, the intervening authority must not give the impression that the action has been taken because either or both of the participants have failed; rather, an immediate or different solution is in the best interest of the organization. There should be no doubt that the solution is final and that the conflict has been concluded.[9]

MANAGING STRESS

Just as conflict is an integral part of organizational life, so is stress. Stress is part of living and can contribute to personal growth, development, and mental health. However, excessive and prolonged stress generally becomes quite negative. Stress of this type can be related to health problems such as insomnia, asthma, ulcers, and heart disease.[10]

Stress involves an interaction between a person and an environment. The potential for **stress** exists when an environmental situation presents a demand threatening to exceed a person's capabilities and resources for meeting it, under conditions where the person expects a substantial difference in the rewards and costs resulting from meeting the demand versus not meeting it.[11]

Stress–results when an environment presents a demand threatening to exceed the person's capabilities and resources for meeting it.

Sources of Stress

Stress can result from many factors. Some of the more common sources of employee stress are a job mismatch, conflicting expectations, role ambiguity, role overload, fear/responsibility, working conditions, working relationships, and alienation. Each of these is described more fully in Figure 16–8.

Burnout

One reaction to stress is a phenomenon that has been described as burnout. Many writers view burnout and stress as being synonymous. However, for the purposes of this book, **burnout** is viewed as being a person's adaptation not only to stress but also to a variety of work-related and personal factors. In burnout, work is no longer a meaningful experience to the burned-out person. Burned-out people often show a combination of the following behavioral tendencies: to blame others in the organization for their burnout, to complain bitterly about aspects of work which in the past were not areas of concern, to miss work because of nonspecific and increasingly prevalent illness, to daydream or sleep on the job, to be the last to come to work and the first to leave, to bicker with coworkers or seem incooperative, and to become increasingly isolated from others. Figure 16–9 (p. 444) charts the path to professional burnout.

Burnout–adaptation an individual makes not only to stress but also to a variety of work-related and personal factors; work is no longer a meaningful experience.

Strategies for Reducing Stress and Burnout

Several strategies are used to reduce stress and burnout. The first involves self-help approaches; one of the most frequently mentioned is proper exercise and diet. Activities include exercising, paying attention to diet and nutrition, getting the proper amounts of sleep, and engaging in leisure activities.

Other self-help approaches to stress reduction include relaxation response, biofeedback, autogenic training, and meditation. **Relaxation response is trained control of major muscle groups.** A person learns to tense and relax each set of muscles for a short period while breathing deeply and regularly.

Relaxation response–trains a person to control major muscle groups.

FIGURE 16–8
Common Sources and Suggested Causes of Organizational Stress

Common Sources	Suggested Causes
Job mismatch	Job demands skills or abilities that the employee does not possess (job incompetence). Job does not provide opportunity for the employee to fully utilize skills or abilities (underutilization).
Conflicting expectations	The formal organization's concept of expected behavior contradicts the employee's concept of expected behavior. The informal group's concept of expected behavior contradicts the employee's concept. The individual employee is affected by two (or more) strong influences.
Role ambiguity	Employee is uncertain or unclear about how to perform on the job. Employee is uncertain or unclear about what is expected in the job. Employee is unclear or uncertain about the relationship between job performance and expected consequences (rewards, penalities, and so forth).
Role overload	Employee is incompetent at job. Employee is asked to do more than time permits (time pressure).
Fear/responsibility	Employee is afraid of performing poorly or failing. Employee feels pressure for high achievement. Employee has responsibility for other people.
Working conditions	The job environment is unpleasant; there is inadequate lighting or improper regulation of temperature and noise, for example. The requirements of the job may unnecessarily produce pacing problems, social isolation, and so forth. The machine design and maintenance procedures create pressure. The job involves long or erratic work hours.
Working relationships	Individual employees have problems relating to, and/or working with, superiors, peers, and/or subordinates. Employees have problems working in groups.
Alienation	There is limited social interaction. Employees do not participate in decision making.

Source: Adapted from Charles R. Stoner and Fred L. Fry, "Developing a Corporate Policy for Managing Stress, *Personnel,* May–June 1983, p. 70.

444   Human Relations Skills

FIGURE 16–9
The Path to Professional Burnout

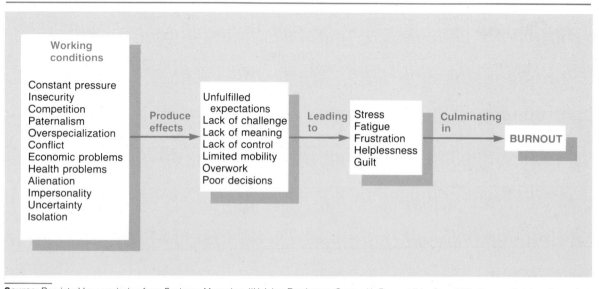

Source: Reprinted by permission from *Business* Magazine. "Helping Employees Cope with Burnout," by Donald P. Rogers, October–December 1984. Copyright © 1984 by the College of Business Administration, Georgia State University, Atlanta.

Biofeedback–monitoring devices give an individual feedback on the degree of relaxation or tension of various muscle groups.

Autogenic training–much like self-hypnosis; helps individuals gain control over their physiology through passive concentration.

Meditation techniques–focus attention on a constant object such as one's breath or a repetitive syllable.

In **biofeedback,** monitoring devices give feedback on the degree of relaxation of various muscle groups. The device is used first to learn to recognize the degrees of relaxation or tension in various muscle groups. Subsequently, the person learns to relax muscles without the aid of the monitoring devices. **Autogenic training** is closely related to self-hypnosis; it helps individuals gain control over their physiology through passive concentration. Finally, **meditation techniques** are relaxing methods that focus attention on a constant object such as one's breath or a repetitive syllable.[14]

Although useful, self-help stress reduction programs may not deal with the root of the problem causing the stress. For example, stress caused by a job mismatch may be reduced by some of the self-help approaches. However, organizationally supported training and education may be necessary to minimize or fully overcome this type of stress. Figure 16–10 lists specific actions to help overcome organizationally induced stress for individuals.

Finally, if the undesirable effects of stress are widespread in an organization or work group, organizationwide corrective actions are needed. Figure 16–11 (p. 446) outlines specific action programs to reduce stress at the organizational level. Management in Action 16–2 (p. 447) shows one organization's approach for reducing stress.

Stress can never be entirely eliminated. As was mentioned previously, some stress actually produces positive results. Effectively using the techniques described in this chapter should help to reduce the negative aspects of stress.

FIGURE 16–10
Actions for Reducing Stress at the Individual Level

Stress Dimension	Corrective Method	Possible Action Programs
Job mismatch	Placement	Relocate, transfer.
	Training	Set up programs to build and develop particular skills.
	Education	Set up formal program to enhance overall aptitude and ability.
Conflicting expectations	Communication	Establish clear picture of the organization's role and help employee realize how to fulfill this role.
	Training	Set up programs to build and develop skills that will enable the employee to fulfill role.
Role ambiguity	Communication	Clearly explain the nature of job dimensions and expectations.
Role overload	Training and education	Develop skills to weaken cause of job incompetence. Set up time management programs to deal more effectively with time pressures.
Fear/responsibility	Training	Develop skills to address problem areas more confidently.
	Counseling	Help the employee understand and deal constructively with underlying fears and apprehension.
Working conditions	Counseling	Help employee deal with behavioral difficulties (isolation feelings, for example).
	Communications	Help employee understand justification for work process and how employee fits into overall process.
Working relationships	Training	Set up encounter and team-building sessions.
	Counseling	Deal with personality conflicts, social isolates, and so forth.
	Communication	Develop better communication practices within groups. Help supervisors and subordinates learn to relate more effectively to each other.
Alienation	Counseling	Help employees deal constructively with their feelings.
	Communication	Provide avenues for upward communication, participation, and involvement.

Source: Adapted from Charles R. Stoner and Fred L. Fry, "Developing a Corporate Policy for Managing Stress," *Personnel*, May–June 1983, p. 72.

FIGURE 16–11
Actions for Reducing Stress at the Organizational Level

Stress Source	Corrective Method	Possible Action Programs
Job mismatch	Job redesign Personnel evaluation Training Communication	Set up job enrichment programs. Improve selection and placement procedures. Institute job-related skills training. Provide counseling to explore causes of conflict.
Conflicting expectations	Communication Job redesign Personnel evaluation	Examine and reduce misunderstandings that may cause conflict. Schedule, for example, flexitime, 4-day weeks, job sharing, and so forth to deal with particular conflict areas (that is, working woman versus family, work versus leisure). Improve selection and placement (transfer, for example).
Role ambiguity	Communication Structure	Provide more accurate job descriptions. Define responsibilities and authority structure more precisely.
Role overload	Job redesign Structure	Change work floor, layout, or process. Rewrite job description.
Fear/responsibility	Training Communication	Train in decision-making skills. Provide counseling programs for dealing with underlying problems.
Working conditions	Job redesign	Change physical conditions and work routine (rotate jobs, change hours of work, give relaxation breaks and "stress days" off, for example.)
Work relationships	Training Communication	Develop human relations skills; provide training to build more cohesive, team-oriented work groups. Set up various counseling programs.
Alienation	Training Job redesign Structure Rewards Communication	Help with career planning. Provide job enrichment programs. Utilize formal structural design that is most conducive to situation and individual needs (for example, use project or matrix format). Alter methods and timing of payment; aim incentives more directly at employees' needs and expectations. Provide for participation by employees.

Source: Adapted from Charles R. Stoner and Fred L. Fry, "Developing a Corporate Policy for Managing Stress," *Personnel*, May–June 1983, p. 73.

MANAGEMENT IN ACTION 16–2

Stanford University Hospital

The pressure-filled and emotional atmosphere in an acute-care hospital like Stanford University Hospital makes its staff members, especially its nurses, good candidates for burnout. The Stanford approach is an example of what managers and their organizations can do to identify and deal with stress.

First, a questionnaire was administered to 129 intensive care unit (ICU) nurses to determine the nature of their stress. An analysis of the questionnaires revealed the following ranking for the primary stressors:

1. Conflicts with staff, physicians, administrators, and residents.
2. Dealing with the deaths of patients and the unnecessary prolongation of life.
3. Problems with the management of the unit.
4. Physical work environment.

Some of the actions taken to deal with these stressors included:

1. Developing and conducting workshops dealing with conflict resolution.
2. Developing and conducting workshops on death and bioethics.
3. Intensified recruitment and retention efforts to improve inadequate-staffing problems, and options in work secheduling offered to nurses.
4. Remodeling of physical plant.

Finally, a full-time nurse consultant was hired to help the nurses deal with their stress when it happened. One result of this program has been that the attrition rate among Stanford ICU nurses has declined by 18 percent.

Source: Adapted from June T. Biley and Duane D. Walker "Rx for Stress: One Hospital's Approach," *Supervisory Management*, August 1982, pp. 32–37.

SUMMARY

Conflict in organizations is often assumed to be an unnatural and undesirable situation to be avoided at all costs. Management must realize that conflict exists in all organizations and is not necessarily negative. The goal of management should be to understand and manage conflict in order to obtain positive benefits.

Conflict is overt behavior arising out of a process in which one party seeks the advancement of its own interests in its relationship with others. Conflict begins when one party perceives that a second party has frustrated or is about to frustrate some concern of the first party. In this definition, the parties involved denote social units in conflict. They can therefore be individuals, groups, organizations, or nations. The potential for conflict depends on how incompatible the goals of the parties are, the availability of the resources required to achieve the goals, and the degree of interdependence of task activities.

Conflict does not usually appear suddenly. The stages of conflict development are: latent conflict, perceived conflict, felt conflict, manifest conflict, and the conflict aftermath.

Conflict was analyzed from two basic perspectives—internal (or intrapersonal) conflict and external conflict. External conflict can be divided into three types: structural, interpersonal, and strategic.

A model was presented in which conflict management is viewed from two perspectives. In the first perspective, the manager is an intervening force in the conflict cycle. The second perspective concerns the responses of higher-level managers to the consequences of the conflict as it affects the ongoing work of the organization. Questions were presented which need to be answered in order to resolve a conflict situation.

Stress involves an interaction between a person and an environment. The potential for stress exists when an environmental situation presents a demand which threatens to exceed a person's capabilities and resources for meeting it, under conditions where the person expects a substantial difference in the rewards and costs resulting from meeting the demand versus not meeting it. Common sources of stress include a job mismatch, conflicting expectations, role ambiguity, role overload, fear/responsibility, working conditions, working relationships, and alienation.

Burnout is the adaptation that an individual makes not only to stress but also to a variety of work-related and personal factors. Several strategies were described for reducing stress and burnout.

References and Additional Readings

[1] See Kenneth Thomas, "Conflict and Conflict Management," in *Handbook of Industrial and Organizational Psychology,* ed. Marvin D. Dunnette (New York: John Wiley & Sons, 1983).

[2] K. W. Thomas and W. H. Schmidt, "A Survey of Managerial Interests with Respect to Conflict," *Academy of Managment Journal* June 1976, pp. 315–18.

[3] Louis Pondy, "Organizational Conflict: Concepts and Models," *Administrative Science Quarterly,* September 1967, pp. 296–320.

[4] Richard F. Walton and John M. Dutton, "The Management of Interdepartmental Conflict: A Model and Review," *Administrative Science Quarterly,* March 1969, p. 75.

[5] P. R. Lawrence and J. W. Lorsch, *Organization and Environment* (Boston: Harvard Business School Division of Research, 1967).

[6] P. R. Lawrence and J. W. Lorsch, "New Management Job: The Integrator," *Harvard Business Review,* November–December 1967, pp. 142–51.

[7] C. G. Weiman, "A Study of Occupational Stressors and the Incident of Disease Risk," *Journal of Occupational Medicine,* February 1977, pp. 119–22; M. T. Matteson and J. M. Ivancevich, "Organizational Stressors and Heart Disease: A Research Model," *Academy of Management Review,* July 1979, pp. 347–58.

[8] See Joseph E. McGarth, "Stress and Behavior in Organizations," in *Handbook of Industrial and Organizational Psychology,* ed. Marvin D. Dunnette (New York: John Wiley & Sons, 1983).

[9] See John M. Ivancevich, Michael T. Matteson, and Cynthia Preston, "Occupational Stress, Type A Behavior, and Physical Well-Being," *Academy of Management Journal,* June 1982, pp. 373–91.

[10] Morley D. Glicken and Katherine Jantia, "Executives under Fire: The Burnout Syndrome," *California Management Review,* Spring 1982, p. 67. See also Donald P. Rogers, "Helping Employees Cope with Burnout," *Business,* October–December 1984, pp. 3–7.

[11] Much of the material in this paragraph was drawn from Heather R. Sailer, John Schlacter, and Mark R. Edwards, "Stress: Causes, Consequences, and Coping Strategies," *Personnel,* July–August 1982, pp. 39–40.

Review Questions

1. What two basic viewpoints can be used to analyze conflict? *Internal /external*

2. What causes intrapersonal conflict? *barries between goal + drive.*

3. What are some typical defense mechanisms used when an individual is frustrated? *drugs, leave abuse, apathy, withdrawal*

4. Describe three forms of goal conflict. *pos /neg, pos/pos, neg/neg*

5. Name at least four types of structural conflict. *Ambiguities, role dissatisfaction, Commun. common resource shares, barrier*

6. What are some of the causes of interpersonal conflict? *Personalities, struct. conflict etc.*

7. What is strategic conflict? *VP going for pres job.*

8. Describe some of the useful effects of conflict. *Energizes people, outlet, comm., educational*

9. Identify the five stages of conflict. *Latent, perceived, felt, manifest, aftermath*

10. What are some methods that can be used to resolve conflict? *Compromise, Confront. withdrawal, force, smooth*

11. Describe in detail a model for managing over conflict in organizations.

12. Outline some key questions that need to be answered in conflict resolution.

13. Outline several common sources of stress. *job*

14. What is burnout?

15. What is relaxation response? Biofeedback? Autogenic training? Meditation? *spasms of muscle. monitor, self-hypnosis, breathing*

Discussion Questions

1. Discuss the following statement: "Every manager should attempt to avoid conflict at all times."

2. "Conflict is inevitable." Do you agree or disagree? Discuss.

3. How can managers reduce destructive stress in organizations?

4. Describe how you would handle the situation in which you have two people working for you who "just rub each other the wrong way."

Incident 16–1
Problems at the Hospital

Smith County is a suburban area near a major midwestern city. The county has experienced such a tremendous rate of growth during the past decade that local governments have had difficulty providing adequate service to the citizens.

Smith County Hospital has a reputation of being a first-class facility, but it is inadequate to meet local needs. During certain periods of the year, the occupancy rates exceed the licensed capacity. There is no doubt in anyone's mind that the hospital must be expanded immediately.

At a recent meeting of the Hospital Authority the hospital administrator Kaye Austin presented the group with a proposal to accept the architectural plans of the firm of Watkins and Gibson. This plan calls for a 100-bed addition adjacent to the existing structure. Kaye announced that after reviewing several alternative plans, she believed the Watkins and Gibson plan would provide the most benefit for the expenditure.

At this point, Randolph (Randy) Lewis, the board chairman, began questioning the plan. Randy made it clear that he would not go along with the Watkins and Gibson plan. He stated that the board should look for other firms to serve as the architects for the project.

The ensuing argument became somewhat heated, and a 10-minute recess was called to allow those attending to get coffee as well as to allow tempers to calm down. Kaye was talking to John Rhodes, another member of the Hospital Authority Board, in the hall and said, "Randy seems to fight me on every project.

Randy, who was talking to other members of the board, was saying, "I know that the Watkins and Gibson plan is good, but I just can't stand for that woman to act like it's her plan. I wish she would leave so we could get a good administrator from the community who we can identify with."

Questions

1. Is Randy's reaction uncommon?
2. What type of conflict exists between Kaye and Randy?
3. What methods would you use to reduce or resolve the conflict?
4. Could Kaye have done anything in advance of the meeting to maximize her chances of success?

Incident 16–2
The Young College Graduate and the Old Superintendent

Situation: You are a consultant to the manager of a garment manufacturing plant in a small southern town. The manager has been having trouble with two employees: Ralph, the plant superintendent, and Kevin, the production scheduler. Ralph is 53 years old and has been with the company since he was released from military duty after World War II. He started as a warehouseworker with a sixth-grade education and worked his way up through the ranks. Until recently, Ralph handled—along with his many other duties—the production scheduling function. He was proud of the fact that he could handle it all "in my head." As the volume of production and the number of different products grew, however, the plant manager felt that significant savings could be attained through a more sophisticated approach to scheduling. He believed that he could save on raw materials by purchasing in larger lots, and on production setup time by making longer runs. He also wanted to cut down on the frequency of finished-goods stock-outs; when backlogs did occur, he wanted to be able to give customers more definite information as to when goods would be available. He wanted to have a schedule documented for at least two months into the future, with daily updates.

Kevin is 24 years old and grew up in the Chicago area. This is his first full-time job. He earned a master of science degree in industrial engineering from an eastern engineering school. He jumped right into the job and set up a computer-assisted scheduling system, using a time-sharing service with a teletype terminal in his office. The system is based on the latest production scheduling and inventory control technology. It is very flexible and has proven to be quite effective in all the areas that were of interest to the plant manager.

Plant manager: Sometimes I just want to shoot both Ralph and Kevin. If those two could just get along with each other, this plant would run like a well-oiled machine.

Consultant: What do they fight about?

Manager: Anything and everything that has to do with the production schedule. Really trivial things in a lot of cases. It all seems so completely senseless!

Consultant: Have you tried to do anything about it?

Manager: At first, I tried to minimize the impact of their feuds on the rest of the plant by stepping in and making decisions that would eliminate the point of controversy. I also tried to smooth things over as if the arguments were just friendly disagreements. I thought that after they had a chance to get accustomed to each other, the problem would go away. But it didn't. It got to the point that I was spending a good 20 percent of my time stopping their fights. Furthermore, I began to notice that other employees were starting to take sides. The younger people seemed to support Kevin; everybody else sided with Ralph. It began to look as if we might have our own little war.

Consultant: What's the current situation?

Manager: I finally told them both that if I caught them fighting again, I would take very drastic action with both of them. I think that move was a mistake though, because now they won't even talk to each other. Kevin just drops the schedule printouts on Ralph's desk every afternoon and walks away. Ralph needs some help in working with those printouts, and Kevin needs some feedback on what's actually going on in the plant. Frankly, things aren't going as well production spacewise now as when they were at each other's throats. And the tension in the plant as a whole is even worse. They are both good people and outstanding in their respective jobs. I would really hate to lose either of them, but if they can't work together, I may have to let one or both of them go.

Questions

1. Why is this conflict occurring?

2. What method did the manager use in dealing with this conflict situation? Was it effective?

3. Recommend an approach for resolving the conflict.

Exercise
Conflict over Quality

This morning, your department completed a large order and turned it over to quality control. The quality control manager has just come to tell you that she must tighten up on inspection standards because a number of complaints have been received from the field. She feels the order must be reworked by your department to pass inspection. You try to convince her to impose the stricter standards only on future lots, but she refuses.

Reworking these units will set you back a couple of days in your production schedule. This you can explain to your superiors. But the costs, which will be charged to your budget, will be much more difficult to explain later on.

As you reflect on what has happened, you are clearly annoyed. You decide something must be done, and you see your alternatives as follows:

1. You can calm down, issue instructions to rework the units, and do the best you can with the budgeting and scheduling problems.

2. You can send the quality control manager a memo clearly outlining the cost considerations and ask her to help you find a solution.

3. You can call the quality control manager and ask for a meeting at her earliest convenience to discuss the situation further.

4. You can go to the plant manager to whom both of you report, point out the budgeting and scheduling difficulties, and request that old standards be applied this one last time.

5. You can tell the quality control manager that if she does not go along with your suggestion to impose the stricter standards only on future production, you will no longer be able to lend her one of your operators for inspection work when she needs one.

Other alternatives may be open to you, but assume that these are the only ones you have considered. WITHOUT DISCUSSION with anyone, choose one of them and be prepared to defend your choice.

Section 4 Case

Chick-fil-A*

Chick-fil-A is a breast of chicken sandwich—garnished with a pickle and served on a fresh, buttered bun—around which a whole enterprise has been built. The fast-food restaurant chain is also called Chick-fil-A. Founded by S. Truett Cathy in 1967, Chick-fil-A had 280 outlets from coast to coast by 1983. In 1984, nationwide sales reached $134 million, a 29 percent increase over the previous year. Average outlet sales of $510,640 were up 21 percent from 1982. Average operator income was more than $40,000 per year. All of this was accomplished within the fast-food industry, which is quickly maturing and marked with tremendous competition in all of its segments. Chick-fil-A's high-quality, tasty breast of chicken sandwich recipe and other homemade accompaniments like fresh lemonade and lemon pie have resulted in so much financial success that 90 percent of financing for each new unit is generated internally.

Chick-fil-A is a special business entity in many ways. Its consistent record of success in the highly competitive fast-food business stems from various factors which involve all of Chick-fil-A's people. Basic to this is Truett Cathy's personality, which has greatly contributed to the people orientation at Chick-fil-A. First, Cathy is a Christian businessman with a deep religious faith. The corporate purpose statement of the enterprise reads: "To glorify God by being faithful stewards of all that is entrusted to us. To have a positive influence on all who come into contact with Chick-fil-A." Cathy is quick to tell anyone who questions the Christian orientation of the firm that a "business run by Christian principles" does not require that you be a Christian. What it does mean is to believe in service and in helping others. His whole life is a demonstration of this orientation.

One example of Cathy's people orientation is the pleasant surroundings at Chick-fil-A corporate headquarters. The 110,000-square-foot building featuring an 80-foot atrium lobby and a five-story spiral staircase cost $7.5 million. Each floor opens into the lobby, which is topped by a clear, sky-lighted roof. Two glass elevators ride up the outside of the elevator shaft. Mr. Cathy wanted the building to blend into its peaceful surroundings, and it seems to almost be lost among the surrounding trees. It is hard to believe that a busy major highway is nearby. The setting, with its emphasis on nature and open space, makes both staff and visitors feel right at home at Chick-fil-A headquarters.

Truett Cathy is committed to the quality of his product and to the excellence of his company. At the same time, he has spent as much time as possible helping others to develop their potential. Most fast-food operations

---

* This case was prepared by Jean Marie Hanebury, Georgia State University. Used by permission.

have grown through the franchise system. For a hefty entry fee, franchisees buy into such successful chains as McDonald's, Burger King, and Mrs. Winner's Chicken. In contrast, Chick-fil-A has used the people orientation of the founder. Their unique system, called the owner-operator system, is structured in a rather unusual manner. Going back to his experience as a young family man trying to make a living and to have a happy family life, Mr. Cathy incorporated his own philosophy into the conception of how his restaurants would be organized and staffed. His son Dan puts it this way: "Dad's vision is all based on his prior restaurant experience. You can handle any other pressure if you don't have financial pressure. Consequently, the Chick-fil-A system is designed to relieve our owner-operators from financial burdens and requires the initial investment of just $5,000."

For the initial $5,000 investment, an operator is completely trained in the operations end of the business. New operators are guaranteed a minimum income of $20,000 for each of the first two years. After this initial period, they are guaranteed $12,000 plus 50 percent of the net profits. The parent company receives 15 percent of gross sales each year, and 3.25 percent of sales are used in the national advertising program. All of these monies are spent back in the local markets. There are also three or four national advertising campaigns per year.

Additionally, hundreds of thousands of pounds of chicken are given away in front of stores each year. A minimum of 100 pounds is distributed at *each* location each month. Owner-operators are free to decide how their share of the advertising budget should be spent—on newspaper ads, free coupons given out at the location, or other promotions. This allows the feeling of autonomy that is emphasized in the loose-tight approach that marks Chick-fil-A's people-oriented business plan.

Each owner-operator must be ready and willing to invest long hours to make the restaurant unit a success. The units operate six days' each week. It is a cardinal rule with Truett Cathy that no Chick-fil-A will be open on Sunday; the only operator to violate this dictum is no longer with the company. The average operator can reasonably expect to make $40,000 after five years with the enterprise. In 1983, 62 of the owner-operators, or about 26 percent, made more than $50,000.

One of Chick-fil-A's rules forbids multiple ownership. Cathy and his staff feel that each operator can manage just one Chick-fil-A. "Absentee ownership just doesn't work," he firmly asserts. "Each operator must run his own store. Taking on more than one would disturb [the manager's] effectiveness." President James Collins sees this philosophy as another key to success. At the same time, unit managers are encouraged to make as much money as possible from *their own unit* each year. In fact, owner-operators can and do make more money each year than most of the headquarters staff.

Part of the people philosophy at Chick-fil-A is attracting the right people to do the best job. Previous restaurant experience is not a governing criteria for selection. Truett Cathy often says, "You can train anyone to cook chicken and make cole slaw. But it is more important to carefully select the person you train, because everything else follows from that initial personnel decision." Basic work habits and work attitudes must be established and reinforced. "When you have high expectations people will do their best," is one way to sum up how things are done at Chick-fil-A. Another analogy often used by the founder and his corporate headquarters staff is that of the well-trained sports team. "It's like a football team; if you pick the right players and inspire them to hard work, they will be doing their very best for the team."

Such people epitomize both the corporate staff and the owner-operators at Chick-fil-A. Someone with entrepreneurial spirit, a successful track record, a stable family background, and a history of community service is a prime candidate. Huie Woods, senior director of human resources, reiterates the philosophy: "The boss insists that human resources are the most important asset that we have. If you are right at the people end of the business, you can't fail."

Most emphasized is the selection end of this human resource process. All selections are made at the Atlanta headquarters, where much time is spent reviewing applications for staff and owner-operator positions. People with goals and values akin to those of the founder and other key managerial personnel are sought, as they are thought to exemplify the corporate purpose of Chick-fil-A.

The initial investment to become an owner-operator is small; yet Cathy has often helped finance candidates if they show potential. It is not unusual for an employee who started out making coleslaw at a Chick-fil-A location after school to aspire to and become an owner-operator.

Chick-fil-A offers owner-operators a special benefit package. Ongoing management training is one facet of the package. As noted in the 1983 annual message: "Every February, Chick-fil-A invites operators and their spouses to an expense-paid, five-day seminar at a luxury resort. For 1984, we held the seminar at the Southampton Princess Hotel in Bermuda." These yearly retreats are not just state-of-the-business reports, operational workshops, and new marketing plans. A large part of each meeting is spent on awards ceremonies. Operators are encouraged to get to know one another and their spouses so that they might enjoy the camaraderie of sharing with old and new friends.

An incentive package includes the Symbol of Success program: Operators who increase their restaurant sales by 40 percent or more are awarded the use of a new Lincoln Continental Mark VII for one year. If the operators continue the 40 percent sales growth through another year, the car is theirs to keep. In 1983, 46 operators were presented the Symbol of Success.

Lines of communication are also kept open between the owner-operators and corporate headquarters. Two house organs, *Chick-fil-A Operator Newsletter* and *Chicken Chatter,* keep the Chick-fil-A "family" in touch with each other. Operators are encouraged to share promotional ideas and get reports on new corporate directions. Personal milestones such as new babies, marriages, and other personal or family triumphs are shared in this manner.

There are usually only one or two full-time employees other than the operator at each location. In many instances, the operator's spouse or another family member makes up the core of the crew; other employees are called "crew members." Eighty percent of the employees are students. They are part-time employees with an average work week of 20 hours. Again, a people orientation makes the crew another ingredient in Chick-fil-A's recipe for success.

Owner-operators make all hiring decisions when it comes to the crew. They staff their own location and decide how much to pay each worker. Using tested methods developed over the years by the headquarters staff, each location trains its own crew. Dan Cathy, director of operations, described the kind of young people that Chick-fil-A operators attract: "Lots of these youngsters are class leaders. They are the kind of young people who attract other prospective employees. It is also not unusual for brothers and sisters to follow one another into the Chick-fil-A ranks. We have had as many as three members of the same family as crew members at the same time." This is the kind of relationship corporate and local managers strive to develop. It exemplifies the team and family spirit that Chick-fil-A emphasizes.

A friendly atmosphere is important at Chick-fil-A restaurants, so new crew members are introduced to public contact gradually. Almost all Chick-fil-A restaurants are located in regional malls where there is a heavy traffic of customers who want friendly service and tasty food. Pleasing the customer is another key to success, and Chick-fil-A crew members must keep that in mind.

Each new employee participates in an individual "Crew Member Training Program." Dan Cathy sees the crew member training as a "fulfilling experience. For many, Chick-fil-A is their first business exposure. Having the privilege of taking an active involvement in crew members' development is a great responsibility." Goals are set for each new employee. One of the corporate goals mentioned again and again in training manuals is to "provide a system of recognition and incentives to motivate crew members to constantly strive for increased levels of performance and productivity."

Student workers are offered special incentives to stay and grow with Chick-fil-A. Students who work an average of 20 hours a week for a period of two years or more and maintain a C average or better, receive a $1,000 scholarship to the college of their choice. More than $2 million in scholarships have been awarded since 1973; in 1983 alone, the amount exceeded $500,000.

A milestone was set for Chick-fil-A crew members in 1984: Chick-fil-A and Berry College—a four-year liberal arts institution located in Rome, Georgia—entered into a scholarship grant program. The founder of Berry College, Martha Berry, and Truett Cathy espouse the same goals: "to excel in work and study and to take pride in a job well done." Approximately

1,500 students from all over the United States and several foreign countries make up the student body at Berry.

The new joint grant program allows about 75 young people from Chick-fil-A restaurants nationwide to be housed in the Berry Academy, a former secondary school located near the main campus. To be eligible for this new program, crew members must have worked for Chick-fil-A for at least six months. They must apply and be accepted for admission to Berry before receiving approval from corporate headquarters to enter the grant program. Plans are made for more opportunities for individual growth and leadership development through company-sponsored recreational, academic, and religious programs.

Truett Cathy's President's Message of 1984 closed with these words: "The time is coming when a large number of operators and staff will come from this pool of young people who work in Chick-fil-A restaurants. For instance, one new Chick-fil-A operator, age 22, has nine years of experience with the company already. He started out as a crew member at age 13, wiping tables after school." A tremendous responsibility comes with the more conventional rewards of being a successful business manager. At Chick-fil-A, top management feels a responsibility to operators, crew members, corporate personnel, and the public in general. They have a strong commitment to people. In fact, it is said that they don't bring in an operator or a member of the staff unless it is a person they want to be with until "one of us retires or dies!"

5

Improving Organizational Performance

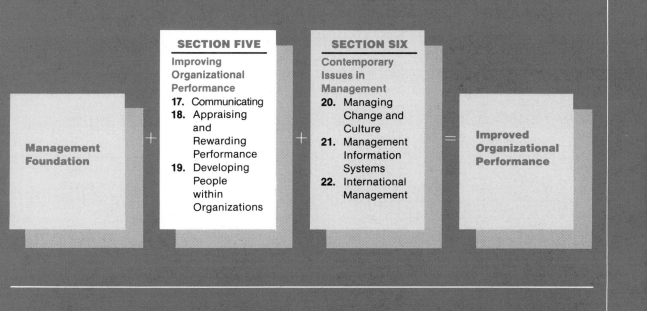

Management
Foundation

+

SECTION FIVE

Improving
Organizational
Performance

17. Communicating
18. Appraising
    and
    Rewarding
    Performance
19. Developing
    People
    within
    Organizations

+

SECTION SIX

Contemporary
Issues in
Management

20. Managing
    Change and
    Culture
21. Management
    Information
    Systems
22. International
    Management

=

Improved
Organizational
Performance

The first four sections of this text are designed to provide a sound management foundation. They outline what managers do and discuss the skills required to perform the job of management. Building on this management foundation, Section 5 is based on the realization that the ultimate goal of management is to improve organizational performance and that improved organizational performance is accomplished through people. A manager must apply the skills of management to elicit high levels of performance from individuals. Three of the primary methods of increasing performance in organizations are: having effective communication systems, appraising and rewarding performance, and developing the skills of employees.

Chapter 17 deals with the topic of communication, which is essential to improving performance. Both the formal and informal communication systems in organizations are analyzed.

The first part of Chapter 18 is devoted to a discussion of what determines performance. Next, several different methods for appraising performance are presented. Finally, the relationship between organizational rewards and employee performance is described.

Chapter 19 emphasizes the importance of developing people. The role of the manager in orienting new employees is described. In addition, the role of the manager in training new and longer-term employees is discussed. Finally, methods used by organizations to develop the skills of managers are presented.

Objectives

1. To analyze the interpersonal communication process.
2. To describe downward, upward, and horizontal communication systems in organizations.
3. To discuss the nature of the grapevine in organizations.
4. To present several suggestions for improving communication in organizations.

17

Communicating: Transmitting Understanding

Chapter Outline

A naturalist discovered that baboons have a language consisting of shrill alarm cries, contented chucklings and grunts, dissatisfied barks, silly happy chatterings, mourning wails for their dead, cries denoting pain, groans of dread, and calls for assembly and for action. He observed that at night there was a continuous soft mumbling among them which sounded so much like human talk that he was almost convinced that they were capable of articulated speech. A native confirmed this for him: "Baboons can talk," he said. "But they won't do it in front of men for fear they will put them to work."

*John Denton Scott**

Breakdowns in the communication process are said to cause divorces, wars, racial problems, business failures, and other problems too numerous to mention. Within organizations, there are endless places where poor communication can be costly if not disastrous. Therefore, poor communication is often named the culprit when any organizational problem arises. It may very well be the cause of the problem; but it is sometimes only a symptom of a more complex problem. Poor communication can be used as a scapegoat for other problems.

Good communication is not a cure-all for all organizational problems. It will not, for instance, make up for poor planning. However, even good plans must be communicated. Thus good communication is an essential element in achieving excellent performance. Management in Action 17–1 tells of the intensity of the communication process at Exxon and Citibank.

Communication has been estimated to occupy between 50 and 90 percent of the manager's time.[1] Unfortunately, however, research has revealed that as much as 70 percent of all business communications fail to achieve their intended purpose.[2]

WHAT IS COMMUNICATION?

Communication–transfer of information that is meaningful to those involved; the transmittal of understanding.

The problem in defining communication is best shown by the fact that one study found over 95 definitions of the term.[3] Many were supposed to be "the one true" definition. In this book, **communication** is defined as the transfer of information that is meaningful to those involved—in general, the transmittal of understanding. Communication can occur in many forms ranging from face-to-face contact involving facial expressions and body movements to written messages. One author states that communication occurs when a person takes something into account, whether it was something

* Adapted from John Denton Scott, "Speaking Wildly," *Reader's Digest,* May 1977, p. 144.

Communication Intensity at Exxon and Citibank

Two companies known for their no-holds-barred communications in characteristically uncommunicative industries are Exxon and Citibank. We've had the opportunity to observe senior managers in action at both companies. The difference between their behavior and that of their competitors is nothing short of astonishing. They make a presentation, and then the screaming and shouting begin. The questions are unabashed; the flow is free; everyone is involved. Nobody hesitates to cut off the chairman, the president, a board member.

And how that contrasts with the behavior of most companies we encounter! Senior people, who have sometimes worked together for 20 years or more, won't attend meeting unless there are formal agendas. At the extreme, people whose offices are on the same floor communicate only in writing.

Source: Adapted from Thomas J. Peters and Robert H. Waterman, Jr., *In Search of Excellence* (New York: Harper & Row, 1982), p. 219.

someone did or said or did not do or say, whether it was some observable event, some internal condition, the meaning of something being read or looked at, some feeling mixed with some past memory—literally anything that can be taken into account by human beings in general and that person in particular.

Communication in organizations can be viewed in one of two perspectives: between individuals (interpersonal communication) and within the formal organizational structure (organizational communication). These two basic forms are interdependent: interpersonal communication is almost always a part of organizational communication.

INTERPERSONAL COMMUNICATION

Effective communication between individuals, especially between a manager and subordinates, is critical to achieving organizational goals and, as a result, to effectively managing people. **Interpersonal communication occurs between individuals**. It is an interactive process that involves a person's effort to attain meaning and to respond to it. It involves sending and receiving verbal and nonverbal messages. These come not only from other people but also from the physical and cultural settings of both the sender and the receiver.[4]

Interpersonal communication– communication between individuals.

The basic purpose of interpersonal communication is to transmit ideas, thoughts, or information so that the sender of the message both is understood and understands the receiver. Figure 17–1 diagrams this dynamic and interactive process. An event or condition generates an idea, thought, or information. The desire to share the information or to inform another person about

FIGURE 17–1
Interpersonal Communication Process

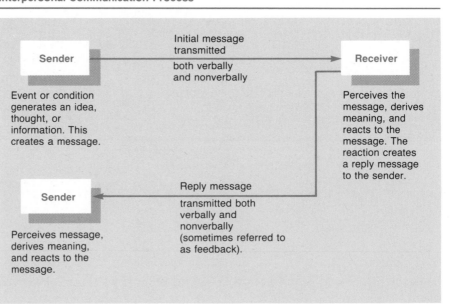

it provides the need to communicate. The sender then creates a message and transmits it both verbally and nonverbally. It is perceived and interpreted by the receiver. Hopefully, the receiver creates a reply message with a response or reaction to the initial message. This reply message may cause the sender to have responses which lead to a repeat of the process.

Often, many factors interfere and cause this process to fail. Some of the causes of communication failure are: different interpretations of the meaning of words (semantics), differences in perception, poor listening habits, inadequate feedback, and differences in the interpretation of nonverbal communications.

Semantics

Semantics—science or
study of the meaning of
words and symbols.

Semantics is the science or study of the meaning of words and symbols. Words themselves have no real meaning. They have meaning only in terms of peoples' reactions to them. A word may mean very different things to different people, depending on how it is used. In addition, a word may be interpreted differently, depending on the facial expressions, hand gestures, and voice inflection used.

The problems involved in semantics are of two general types. Some words and phrases invite multiple interpretations. For example, Figure 17–2 shows different interpretations of the word *fix*. Another problem is that groups

---

FIGURE 17–2
Interpretations of the Word *Fix*

An Englishman visits America and is completely awed by the many ways we use the word *fix*. For example:

1. His host asks him how he'd like his drink fixed. He meant *mixed*.
2. As he prepares to leave, he discovers that he has a flat tire and calls a repairman who says he'll fix it immediately. He means *repair*.
3. On the way home, he is given a ticker for speeding. He calls his host, who says, "Don't worry, I'll fix it." He means *nullify*.
4. At the office the next day, he comments on the cost of living in America, and one of his cohorts says, "It's hard to make ends meet on a fixed income." He means *steady* or *unchanging*.
5. He has an argument with a co-worker. The latter says, "I'll fix you." He means *seek revenge*.
6. A cohort remarks that he is in a fix. He means *condition* or *situation*.
7. He meets a friend at his apartment who offers to "fix him up" with a girl. You know what that means.

---

of people in specific situations often develop their own technical language, which may or may not be understood by outsiders. For example, physicians, government, and military employees are often guilty of using acronyms and abbreviations that only they understand.

Words are the most common form of interpersonal communication. Because of the real possibility of misinterpretation, words must be carefully chosen and clearly defined for effective communication.

Perception

Perception also plays an important role in interpersonal communication. **Perception** basically refers to how a message is processed by a person. Each individual's perception is unique; so people often perceive the same situation in entirely different ways.

Perception in communication depends primarily on three factors: personality, previous experience, and a stimulus (see Figure 17–3). The mix of these factors creates a unique perception for each person. The stimulus is the information received, whether it is conveyed in writing, verbally, or another way. Perception of the received information is modified by the individual's personality, previous experience, and other factors. Therefore, different people react differently to the same message, because no two have the same personal experiences, memories, likes, and dislikes. One study at Texas Instruments found that messages from management reach less than 15 percent of the intended audience because of the false assumption that all employees think alike and that the same message or methods of communication work equally well for everyone. This same study found seven different value systems that caused variations in how employees reacted to situations,

Perception—refers to how a person processes a message; influenced by the person's personality and previous experience and unique for each individual.

FIGURE 17–3
Perception Development in Communication

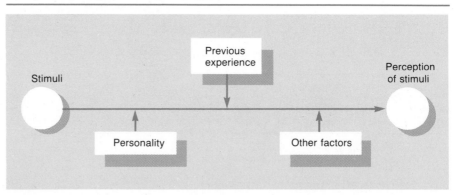

including messages from their supervisors.[5] In addition, the phenomenon of selective perception often distorts the intended message: People tend to listen to only part of the message, blocking out the rest for a number of reasons.

Two illustrations found in many introductory psychology texts show the influence of perception. Please answer the following questions before proceeding.

    1.   What characteristics do you perceive of the woman in Figure 17–4?

FIGURE 17–4
Picture of a Woman

Source: Edwin G. Boring, "A New Ambiguous Figure," *American Journal of Psychology,* July 1930, p. 444. Also see Robert Leeper. "A Study of a Neglected Portion of the Field of Learning—The Development of Sensory Organization," *Journal of Genetic Psychology,* March 1935, p. 62. Originally drawn by cartoonist W. E. Hill and published in *Puck,* November 8, 1915.

FIGURE 17–5
Shapes for Perception

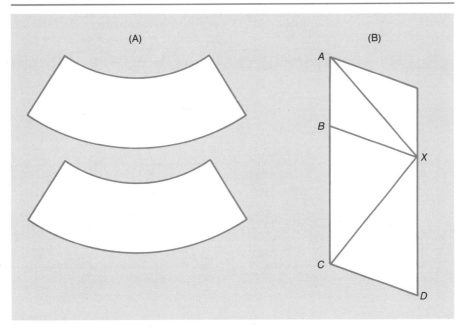

Source: Gregory A. Kimble and Normal Garmezy, *General Psychology* (New York: Ronald Press, 1963), pp. 324–25.

2. In Figure 17–5(A), what shape is the largest?
3. In Figure 17–5(B), which line—AX, CX, CB, or XD—is the longest?

About 60 percent of the people who see Figure 17–4 for the first time see an attractive, apparently wealthy young woman. About 40 percent see an ugly, poor old woman. (Figure 17–6 shows both figures clearly.) In Figure 17–5, both shapes in A are the same size; in B, the lines AX, CX, CB, and XD are of equal length. Obviously, if differences in perception exist in viewing physical objects, more subtle forms of communication such as facial expressions and hand gestures leave much room for differences in perception. Management in Action 17–2 gives a humorous example of differences in perception.

Listening—An Important Factor

Communication depends on the ability not only to send but also to receive messages. So the ability to listen effectively greatly enhances the communication process. Studies have concluded that 45 percent of the total time spent in verbal communication is devoted to listening.[6] Unfortunately, studies

FIGURE 17–6
Clear Picture of the Young and the Old Woman

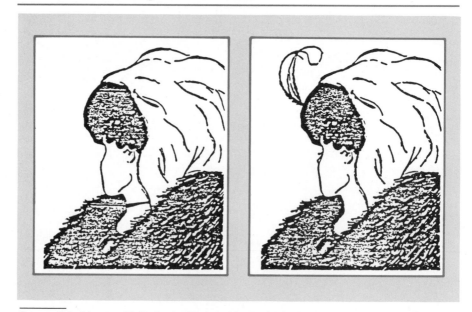

Source: Robert Leeper, "A Study of a Neglected Portion of the Field of Learning—The Development of Sensory Organization," *Journal of Genetic Psychology,* March 1935, p. 62.

have also revealed that most people are not very good listeners; they only retain about 25 percent of all the information they hear.[7]

Effective listening is not natural to most people. How well a person listens very much depends on the listener's attitude toward the speaker. The listener who respects the intelligence of the speaker and expects to profit from the communication will be more likely to listen effectively.

Daydreaming and concern with other matters also often keep individuals from listening to what a speaker is saying. It has been suggested that at any given point in a college lecture, 20 percent of both men and women are thinking about sex, 60 percent are off on some mental trip of their own, and only the remaining 20 percent are concentrating on the professor.[8]

Other barriers to effective listening include: mentally arguing with points being made by the speaker before the talk is finished; getting impatient with listening, and preferring active involvement by talking; lack of interest in the message; and other negative reactions toward the speaker.

Effective listening habits can be developed. Ralph Nichols has proposed a pattern of thought to follow in improving listening habits.[9]

1. Anticipate what a person is going to talk about. On the basis of what has already been said, ask yourself: What point is the person trying to make?

MANAGEMENT IN ACTION 17–2

Perception in the Examination Room

A woman of 35 came in one day to tell me that she wanted a baby but that she had been told that she had a certain type of heart disease which might not interfere with a normal life but would be dangerous if she ever had a baby. From her description, I thought at once of mitral stenosis. This condition is characterized by a rather distinctive rumbling murmur near the apex of the heart and especially by a peculiar vibration felt by the examining finger on the patient's chest. The vibration is known as the "thrill" of mitral stenosis.

When this woman had been undressed and was lying on my table in her white kimono, my stethoscope quickly found the heart sounds I had expected. Dictating to my nurse, I described them carefully. I put my stethoscope aside and felt intently for the typical vibration which may be found in a small but variable area of the left chest.

I closed my eyes for better concentration and felt long and carefully for the tremor. I did not find it, and with my hand still on the woman's bare breast, lifting it upward and out of the way, I finally turned to the nurse and said: "No thrill."

The patient's eyes snapped open, and with venom in her voice she said: "Well, isn't that just too bad? Perhaps it's just as well you don't get one. That isn't what I came for."

My nurse almost choked, and my explanation still seems a nightmare of futile words.

Source: Frederic Loomis, *Consultation Room* (New York: Alfred A. Knopf, 1939), p. 47.

---

2. Summarize what the person has been saying. What point(s), if any, have been made?
3. Mentally question the person's evidence. Ask yourself: Am I getting the full picture or only what will prove the person's point?
4. Listen between the lines. Voice tone and volume, facial expressions, hand gestures, and body movements also have meaning.

The 10 guides for effective listening shown in Figure 17–7 give some additional tips for improving listening habits. Management in Action 17–3 tells how Sperry Univac sponsored seminars in good listening habits.

Feedback

Effective communication is a two-way process. Information must flow back and forth between sender and receiver. The flow from the receiver to the sender is called **feedback.** It allows the sender to know if the receiver has received the correct message; it also lets the receiver know if he or she has the correct message. For example, asking a person if he or she understands a message often puts that person on the defensive and can result in little feedback. Instead of asking if a person understands a message, it

Feedback –flow of information from receiver to sender that indicates if the message was received as intended by sender.

FIGURE 17–7
Effective Listening Guides

1. *Stop talking.* Unfortunately, most of us prefer talking to listening. Even when we are not talking, we are inclined to concentrate on what to say next rather than on listening to others. So you must stop talking before you can listen.
2. *Put the talker at ease.* If you make the talker feel at ease, he or she will do a better job of talking. Then you will have a better input to work with.
3. *Show the talker you want to listen.* If you can convince the talker that you are listening to understand rather than oppose, you will help to create a climate for information exchange. Specifically, you should look and act interested. Doing things like reading, looking at your watch, and looking away distracts the talker.
4. *Remove distractions.* Things you do can also distract the talker. So don't doodle, tap with your pencil, shuffle papers, or the like.
5. *Empathize with the talker.* If you will place yourself in the talker's position and look at things from his or her point of view, you will help to create a climate of understanding. With such a climate established, a true exchange of information can result.
6. *Be patient.* You will need to allow the talker plenty of time. Remember that not everyone can get to the point as quickly and clearly as you. And do not interrupt. Interruptions merely serve as barriers to information exchange.
7. *Hold your temper.* From our review of the workings of our mental filters, we know that angry minds do not contribute to communication. Angry people build walls between themselves and others. They harden their positions and block their minds to the words of others.
8. *Go easy on argument and criticism.* Argument and criticism tend to put the talker on the defensive. Thus, he or she tends to "clam up" or get angry. Even if you win the argument, you lose. Rarely does either party benefit from such controversy.
9. *Ask questions.* By frequently asking questions, you display an open mind. You show that you are listening. And you assist in developing the message and in improving correctness of meaning.
10. *Stop talking!* The last guideline is to stop talking. It was also the first. All other guidelines depend on it.

Source: Raymond V. Lesikar, *Communication Theory and Application* (Homewood, Ill.: Richard D. Irwin, 1976), p. 480.

is much better to request that the receiver explain what he or she has heard.

In an experiment designed to show the importance of feedback, a person was asked to describe a series of rectangles (see Figure 17–8) to a group of people.[10] The experiment was conducted two different ways. First, the sender described the rectangles. The listeners could not ask questions or see the sender; thus, there was no feedback. In the second trial, the sender could see the listeners, and the listeners could ask questions. Thus, feedback was present.

The results showed that lack of feedback increased the speed of transmission. However, feedback caused the accuracy and the listeners' degree of confidence in the accuracy to improve greatly. In summary, feedback in the communication process takes more time but improves the quality of the communication.

MANAGEMENT IN ACTION 17–3

Sperry Univac: "The Computer People Who Listen"

It all started as an advertising slogan, "We understand how important it is to listen." Before undertaking the advertising campaign, however, Sperry management decided that the campaign should not be hollow. Management decided that efforts had to be made to ensure that people in the company really did listen to customers. Senior managers throughout Sperry were given seminars in good listening habits. Once the advertisements stressing Sperry's commitment to good listening and to training good listeners appeared on television, employees from throughout the company requested the training. Since then, over 10,000 employees have taken the training.

The 10 bad listening habits that the Sperry training program attempts to eliminate are:

1. Calling the subject uninteresting.
2. Criticizing the speaker's delivery or mannerisms.
3. Getting stimulated by something the speaker says.
4. Listening primarily for facts.
5. Trying to outline everything.
6. Faking attention.
7. Allowing interfering reactions.
8. Avoiding difficult material.
9. Letting emotion-laden words arouse personal antagonism.
10. Daydreaming.

One of the clear lessons learned from Sperry's experience is that people are much less efficient listeners than they imagine.

Source: Adapted from *International Management*, February 1981, pp. 201–21. Permission of McGraw-Hill International Publications Company Limited. All rights reserved.

Nonverbal Communication

Humans have a unique capacity for conveying meaning through silence and other nonverbal means of expression as well as through speech. Gestures, vocal intonations, facial expressions, and body posture are all used to communicate at the **nonverbal** level.

Estimates are that no more than 35 percent of the meaning of a message is conveyed by words in face-to-face communication.[11] This suggests that people are not good "nonverbal liars." In other words, people communicate nonverbally that part of the message which they wish least to communicate. Further, visual clues often lead to more accurate judgments about the meaning of a message than do vocal cues.

Nonverbal communication—conscious or unconscious behavior of the individual sending a message that is perceived consciously or subconsciously by the receiver.

ORGANIZATIONAL COMMUNICATION SYSTEMS

Organizational communication occurs within the formal organizational structure. In general, organizational communication systems are downward, upward, or lateral (horizontal). Overlapping these three formal systems is the informal communication system called the grapevine.

Organizational communication—communication occurring within the formal organizational structure.

FIGURE 17–8
Rectangles in Communication Experiment

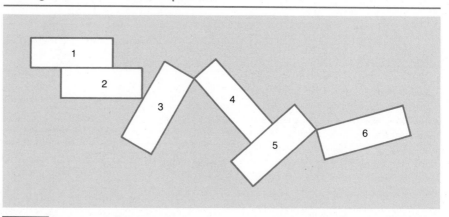

Source: Reprinted from *Managerial Psychology* by Harold J. Leavitt by permission of The University of Chicago Press. © 1972 by *(copyright holder).*

Two Early Approaches

Management pioneer Henry Fayol (see Chapter 2) was one of the first writers to analyze the communication process. He recognized that communication via the formal chain of command could produce unnecessary distortion. In Figure 17–9, suppose that F would like to transmit a message to G. Following the formal chain of command, the message would go from F to B to C to G. It is easy to see the potential for distortion. Fayol proposed

FIGURE 17–9
Fayol's Gangplank Concept

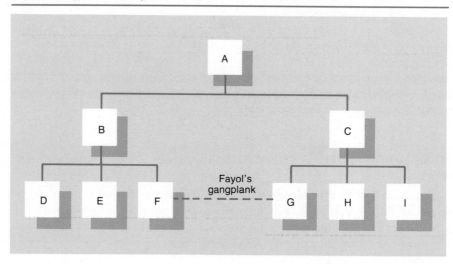

a shortcut between F and G. He stated the need for the shortcut (called Fayol's gangplank, or bridge) as follows:

> Allow the two employees . . . to deal, at one sitting and in a few hours, with some question or other which via the scalar chain would . . . inconvenience many people, involve masses of paper, lose weeks or months to get to a conclusion less satisfactory generally than the one which could have been obtained via direct contact.[12]

Chester Barnard also stressed the importance of communication in organizations.[13] In fact, he felt that it was basic to the existence of an organization—essential for establishing its authority structure. He contended that an employee can and will accept a communication as authoritative only if four conditions are met: the employee (1) understands the communication, (2) believes it to be consistent with the purpose of the organization, (3) believes it to be compatible with his or her personal interest as a whole, and (4) is physically and mentally able to comply with the communication. Barnard's coupling of authority with the communication process led to his development of the acceptance theory of authority, discussed in Chapter 8.[14]

Communication Patterns

Figure 17–10 shows six communication patterns which can exist in an organization.[15] Each falls into one of two classes, depending on the presence or lack of feedback. No pair of individuals can exchange messages in patterns A, B, and C; in other words, no feedback can occur. They do not encourage good coordination or the exchange of ideas.

Any pair of individuals in patterns D, E, and F can exchange messages either directly or indirectly. Thus, feedback can occur. Such patterns have advantages and disadvantages as outlined in Figure 17–11. The following conclusions about patterns of communication networks can be drawn from the figure.

1. They affect the accuracy and speed of messages.
2. They affect the task performance of the group.
3. They affect the satisfaction of group members.

Thus, no one communication pattern is best for all situations. The most effective one for a given situation depends on the required speed, accuracy, morale, and organization structure. For instance, the wheel pattern is most desirable in situations requiring a clear-cut leader and rapid decisions.

Numerous studies have researched the relationships between the pattern of the network and the communication process. Primarily, these studies have indicated that the network pattern is important in determining the effectiveness of the communication process.

FIGURE 17–10
Communication Patterns

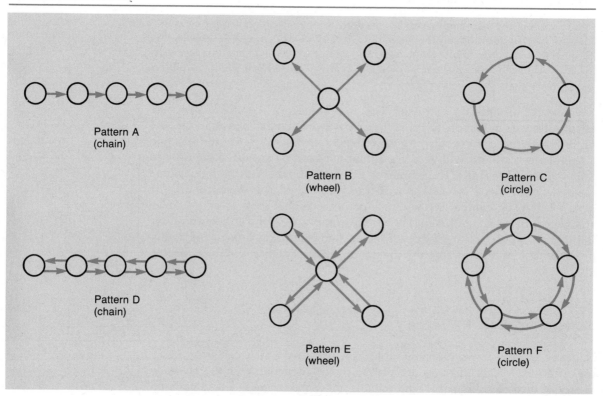

Downward Communication Systems

Downward communication—transmitting information from higher to lower levels of the organization through the chain of command.

Traditional views of the communication processes in organizations have been dominated by **downward communication** systems. Such systems transmit information from higher to lower levels of the organization. The chain of command determines the flow of downward information. Policy manuals, bulletins, organizational magazines, job descriptions, orders, and directives are all examples of downward communication.

Often, downward communication systems are assumed to be better than studies indicate that they actually are. For example, it has been reported that much of the material in employee handbooks and manuals is not understandable to the average employee.[16]

One important choice that must be made in such systems is the medium to use. Written communication is less likely to be filtered and provides an official record; but it does not enable immediate feedback. Oral communication provides no record and is subject to filtering; but it does facilitate immediate feedback. Figure 17–12 offers some guidelines for when to use oral and written communications.

FIGURE 17–11
Advantages and Disadvantages of Communication Patterns

Characteristics	Chain	Wheel	Circle
		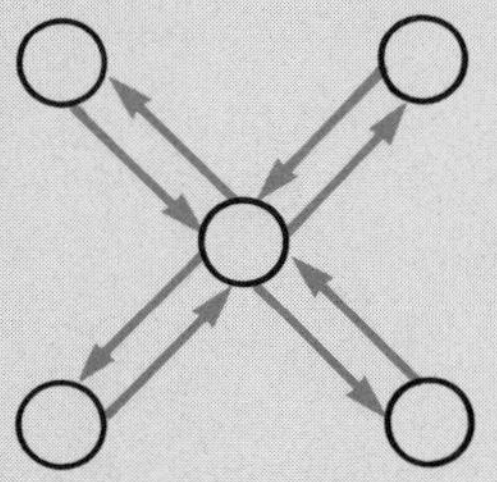	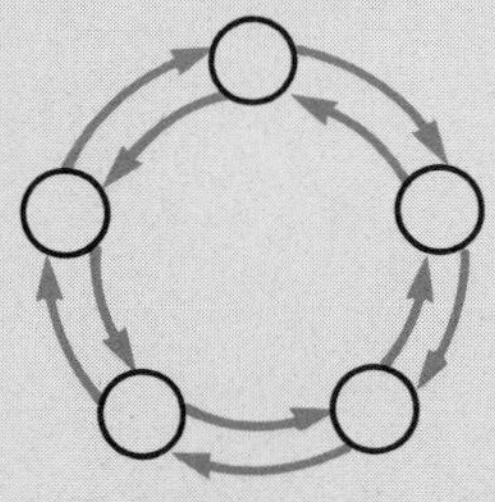
Speed	Fast	Fast	Slow
Accuracy	Good	Good	Poor
Organization	Slowly emerging but stable organization	Almost immediate and stable organization	No stable form of organization
Emergency of leader	Marked	Very pronounced	None
Morale	Poor	Very poor	Very good

Upward Communication Systems

Upward communication starts at the lower levels of the organization and flows toward the top. An upward communication system should help management judge the effectiveness of their downward communications and enable them to learn about organizational problems. Four major areas of information should be communicated from below: (1) the activities of subordinates in terms of their achievements, progress, and future plans; (2) unresolved work problems in which subordinates may need help currently or in the future; (3) suggestions or ideas for improvements within work groups or the organization as a whole; and (4) the feelings of subordinates about their jobs, associates, and the organization. Figure 17–13 lists several forms of upward communication.

The key to effective upward communication systems appears to be a superior-subordinate relationship in which subordinates do not feel that they will be penalized for candor. Subordinates often conceal and distort their real feelings, problems, opinions, and beliefs because they fear disclosure may cause the superior to punish them in some way. In fact, trust in one's superior appears to be a key variable in effective upward communica-

Upward communication—originates at the lower levels of the organization and flows toward the top.

FIGURE 17–12
Effective Communication Methods

Method of Communiction	Situations	
	Most Effective	Least Effective
Oral communication by itself.	Reprimanding employees. Resolving work-centered disputes.	Communicating information requiring future action. Communicating information of a general nature. Communicating directives or orders. Communicating information about an important policy change. Communicating with your immediate superior about work problems. Promoting a safety campaign.
Written communication by itself.	Communicating information requiring future action. Communicating information of a general nature.	Communicating information requiring immediate action. Commending an employee for noteworthy work performance. Reprimanding an employee for poor performance. Resolving work-related disputes.
Oral, then written communication.	Communicating information requiring immediate action. Communicating directives or orders. Communicating information about an important policy change. Communicating with your immediate superior about work-related problems. Promoting a safety campaign. Commending an employee for noteworthy work performance.	

Source: Dale Level, Jr., "Communication Effectiveness: Method and Situation," *Journal of Business Communication,* Fall 1972, pp. 19–25.

FIGURE 17–13
Techniques Used in Upward Communication

Informal inquiries or discussion with employees.
Exit interviews.
Discussion with first-line supervisors.
Grievance or complaint procedures.
Grapevine.
Union representatives.
Counseling.
Formal meeting with employees.
Suggestion system.
Formal attitude surveys.
Question and answer column in employee publication.
Gripe boxes.
Hot line system.

MANAGEMENT IN ACTION 17–4

Peugeot's Suggestion System

Peugeot's suggestion system was initiated in 1951 and encourages all employees to submit their ideas to the suggestion boxes found at central locations throughout the Peugeot plants.

An evaluation committee initially screens all the suggestions. The ideas accepted by this committee are then considered by all the departments affected by the idea. Accepted ideas are then rewarded on the basis of cost savings.

The person making the suggestion is paid 30 percent of the calculated savings over a three-month period. The other 70 percent is placed in a fund held by the plant where the idea is put into use. Twice a year, the fund pays out a generous bonus to workers and staff in that particular plant.

During 1981, Peugeot's suggestion system generated over 550,000 ideas and paid awards totaling $33 million for those ideas.

Source: Adapted from "Peugeot Pays $33 Million for Ideas," *Automotive News*, February 22, 1982, p. 82.

tion systems.[17] Management in Action 17–4 describes Peugeot's suggestion system.

Ideally, the organizational structure should provide for both upward and downward communication systems. Communication should flow in both directions through the formal organizational structure. Unfortunately, communication from the bottom does not flow as freely as communication from the top. Some deterrents to effective upward communication are:

1. Management fails to respond when subordinates bring up information or problems. Failure to respond will ultimately result in no communication.

2. Managers tend to be defensive about less-than-perfect actions. When subordinates see this defensiveness, information will be withheld.

3. The manager's attitude plays a critical role in the upward communication process. If the manager is really concerned and really listens, then upward communication improves.

4. Physical barriers can also inhibit the upward communication process. Separating a manager from subordinates creates communication problems.

5. Time lags between the communication and action can inhibit upward communication. If it takes months for the various levels of management to approve an employee's suggestion, upward communication is hindered.

Horizontal, or Lateral, Communication

The upward and downward communication systems generally follow the formal chain of command within the organization. However, greater size

**Horizontal (lateral)
communication**–
transmitting information
across the lines of the
formal organization's chain
of command.

and complexity increase the need for communication across the lines of
the formal chain of command. This is referred to as **horizontal or lateral
communication.**

Specialized departments (such as engineering, marketing research, and
quality control) perform functions such as gathering data, issuing reports,
preparing directives, coordinating activities, and advising higher levels of
management. Such specialized departments are generally quite active in horizontal communication because their activities influence several chains of
command rather than one. Departments that depend on one another for
achieving their respective goals also need horizontal communication. Finally,
matrix structures require much horizontal communication.

Interdepartmental committee meetings and distribution of written reports
are two of the more commonly used methods of horizontal communication.
A word of caution about memoranda that cross departmental lines: Too
many memos and reports—an excess of paperwork—lead to new communication problems. The recipient of too many memoranda may end up not
reading even the important ones.

Research on the influence of horizontal communication in organizations
has been limited.[18] One study did indicate that specialization of functions
in large organizations impairs communication between departments.[19] Another study concluded that employees generally are not rewarded or encouraged to communicate laterally within the organization.[20] Even so, horizontal
communication is essential to coordination among departments and to the
proper functioning of the upward and downward communication systems.

Grapevines

Grapevines–informal
channels of communication
resulting from casual
contacts in various
organizational units.

Many informal paths of communication also exist in organizations. These
informal channels are generally referred to as **grapevines.** During the Civil
War, intelligence telegraph lines hung loosely from tree to tree looked similar
to a grapevine. Messages sent over these lines were often garbled; thus,
any rumor was said to be "from the grapevine."[21] The organization grapevine
often results from the organization's informal work groups.

Although generally not sanctioned formally, the grapevine always exists.
As the name suggests, it does not follow the organizational hierarchy. It
may go from secretary to vice president or from engineer to clerk. Not
limited to nonmanagement personnel, the grapevine also operates among
managers and professional personnel.

One study of the grapevine in an organization reached the following
conclusions:

1. Males and females were equally involved in the activities of the
    grapevine.
2. Full-time employees were more active in the grapevine than part-
    time employees.

3. Managers were more knowledgeable about information on the grapevine than were nonmanagers.

4. Although managers accounted for only a small percentage of the employees studied, they initiated nearly 50 percent of the grapevine information and, on the average, told about eight other people. The average employee told only four other people.[22]

The grapevine generally has a poor reputation because it is regarded as a rumor factory. However, rumors and the grapevine are not identical. Rumors are only part of the grapevine—the part not based on fact or authority. Managers should correct all rumors as quickly as possible.

An estimated 75 to 95 percent of grapevine information is correct, though most of it is incomplete in detail.[23] This 5 to 25 percent error can, of course, completely change the information; so the grapevine probably produces more misunderstanding than its small percentage of wrong information indicates.

Some suggestions to aid management in effectively using the grapevine follow.[24]

1. The grapevine is a permanent part of the formal organizational structure. It should be used to facilitate effective communication.

2. Managers should have a knowledge of what the grapevine is communicating and why.

3. Managers' inputs into the grapevine are spread to a greater number of employees—most employees hear grapevine information for the first time from management. Therefore, all levels of management should be provided with total and accurate information so that the messages they communicate through the grapevine are accurate.

SUMMARY

Communication is defined as the transfer of information that is meaningful to those involved—the transmittal of understanding. Two forms of communication were discussed: interpersonal and organizational.

Interpersonal communication involves communication between individuals. It is an interactive process involving the transmission and reception of verbal and nonverbal signs and symbols which come from other people as well as from the physical and cultural settings of both the sender and the receiver. Obstacles to effective interpersonal communication can result from semantics, perception, poor listening, inadequate feedback, and nonverbal communication.

Analyzing the communication process from the organizational perspective involves viewing the organizational structure as the primary network through which the communication process flows. Several different communication patterns that occur in organizations were presented and evaluated. Downward communication, upward communication, horizontal or lateral communication, and grapevines were discussed as forms of organizational communication. Suggestions were given for making each of these forms of communication more effective.

References and Additional Readings

[1] Henry Mintzberg, *The Nature of Managerial Work* (New York: Harper & Row, 1973), p. 38.

[2] Ralph W. Weber and Gloria E. Terry, *Behavioral Insights for Supervisors* (Englewood Cliffs, N.J.: Prentice-Hall, 1975), p. 138.

[3] F. E. X. Dance, "The Concept of Communication," *Journal of Communication* 20 (1970), pp. 201–10.

[4] See Lyman W. Porter and Karlene H. Roberts, "Communication," in *Handbook of Industrial and Organizational Psychology,* ed. Marvin D. Dunnette (Skokie, Ill.: Rand McNally, 1976), p. 1558.

[5] "Hitting the Communication Bull's Eye," *Personnel Administrator,* June 1974, p. 16.

[6] Ralph G. Nichols, "Do We Know How to Listen? Practical Helps in a Modern Age," in *Communication Concepts and Processes,* ed. Joseph De Vito (Englewood Cliffs, N.J.: Prentice-Hall, 1971), p. 206.

[7] Phillip V. Lewis, *Organizational Communication: The Essence of Effective Management,* 2d ed. (Columbus, Ohio: Grid, 1975), p. 9.

[8] David R. Hampton, Charles E. Sumner, and Ross A. Webber, *Organizational Behavior and the Practice of Management,* 4th ed. (Glenview, Ill.: Scott, Foresman, 1978), p. 117.

[9] See Ralph G. Nichols, "Listening Is a 10-Part Skill," in *Readings in Interpersonal and Organizational Communication,* 3d ed., ed. Richard C. Huseman, Cal M. Logue, and Dwight L. Freshley (Boston: Holbrook Press, 1977), p. 560.

[10] Harold J. Leavitt, *Managerial Psychology,* 4th ed. (Chicago: University of Chicago Press, 1972), p. 116.

[11] Randall Harrison, "Non-Verbal Communication," in *Dimensions in Communication,* ed. J. H. Campbell and P. W. Harper (Belmont, Calif.: Wadsworth, 1970).

[12] Henri Fayol, *General and Industrial Management,* trans. Constance Storrs (London: Sir Isaac Pitman & Sons, 1949), p. 35.

[13] Chester I. Barnard, *The Functions of the Executive* (Cambridge, Mass.: Harvard University Press, 1938).

[14] For additional discussion on organizational communication, see J. S. Leipzig and E. More, "Organizational Communication: A Review and Analysis of Three Current Approaches to Field," *Journal of Business Communication,* Fall 1982, pp. 77–92.

[15] Alex Bavelas and Dermot Barrett, "An Experimental Approach to Organizational Communication," *Personnel,* March 1951, pp. 366–71.

[16] Earl Planty and William Machaner, "Upward Communication: A Project in Executive Method," in *Readings in Interpersonal and Organizational Communication,* eds. Huseman, et al., pp. 102–3. See also L. McCallister, "Predicted Employee Compliance to Downward Communication," *Journal of Business Communication,* Winter 1983, pp. 67–79.

[17] Karlene H. Roberts and Charles A. O'Reilly III, "Failures in Upward Communication in Organizations: Three Possible Culprits," *Academy of Management Journal,* June 1974, pp. 205–15.

[18] Ronald L. Smith, Gary M. Richetto, and Joseph P. Zima, "Organizational Behavior: An Approach to Human Communication," in *Read-*

ings in Interpersonal and Organization Communication, eds. Huseman et al., p. 14.

[19] Ibid., p. 13.

[20] Ibid.

[21] Keith Davis, *Human Relations at Work,* 6th ed. (New York: McGraw-Hill, 1981), p. 222.

[22] Jay Knippen, "Grapevine Communication: Management Employees," *Journal of Business Research,* January 1974, pp. 47–58.

[23] Keith Davis, "The Care and Cultivation of the Corporate Grapevine," in *Readings in Interpersonal and Organizational Communication,* eds. Huseman et al., p. 136.

[24] For additional information on the grapevine, see J. L. Esposito and R. L. Rosnow, "Corporate Rumors: How They Start and How to Stop Them," *Management Review,* April 1983, pp. 44–49.

Review Questions

1. What is communication?
2. Define interpersonal communication.
3. What is semantics?
4. What is perception, and what role does it play in communication?
5. What is feedback, and how does it affect the communication process?
6. Give some suggestions for improving listening habits.
7. What is the importance of nonverbal communication in interpersonal communication?
8. Identify the contributions of Henri Fayol and Chester Barnard to the understanding of the communication process.
9. Describe three conclusions which can be drawn concerning communication patterns in organizations.
10. Describe the following organizational communication systems:
    a. Downward communication systems.
    b. Upward communication systems.
    c. Horizontal, or lateral, communication systems.
    d. Grapevines.

Discussion Questions

1. Describe some ways in which the grapevine can be used effectively in organizations.
2. Explain why the following question is raised frequently by many managers: "Why didn't you do what I told you to do?"
3. Discuss the following statement: "Meanings are in people, not words."
4. "Watch what we do, not what we say." Is this good practice? Explain.
5. Poor communication of the organization's goals is often given as the reason for low performance of the organization. Do you think that this is usually a valid explanation?

Incident 17-1
Who Calls the Shots?

The financial reports for the last quarter of operations for the Brighton Cabinet Company were just received by the company's president John Branner. After looking over the reports, John decided that the purchasing department is paying too much for the company's raw materials, which include plywood, paneling, and flakeboard. He immediately called Joe Scott, vice president of manufacturing, and informed him of the decision. Exhibit 1 gives a partial organizational chart for Brighton Cabinet Company.

Joe called Bill Sloane, the supervisor of purchasing, and said, "Mr. Branner is upset over the cost figures for raw materials last quarter. You were well above budget. He wants them brought down, this quarter!"

As Bill hung up the phone, he asked himself who figured out the budget for his department and if they realized that plywood had gone up from $6.05 to $6.75 a sheet.

Instructed to cut costs, Bill was determined to do so. Two days later, Bill found a supplier who would sell Brighton Cabinet plywood for $5.95 a sheet. He ordered a two-week supply. Upon delivery, Bill's suspicions were confirmed. The plywood was a poorer quality, but it would work. Bill decided to continue to buy the less expensive plywood.

A month later, Bill was approached by Ted Brown, supervisor of the Assembly Department, who asked, "Bill, what's with this plywood? All

EXHIBIT 1
Partial Organization Chart for Brighton Cabinet Company

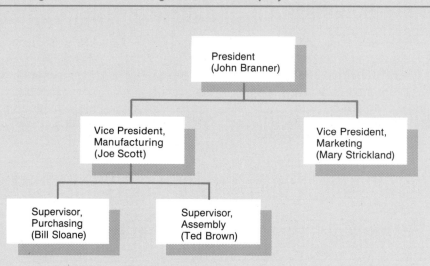

of a sudden, we've been having a lot of it split on us while trying to nail and staple the pieces together."

Bill replied, "Well, Ted, Mr. Branner sent orders down for me to cut costs. I don't know how else to do it other than purchasing the lower-grade plywood. It was the only way out."

Things were left as they were, and the quarter ended. The financial reports for the quarter showed a drop in sales and profits. According to forecasts and trends of previous years, the profits and sales should have been higher. John Branner immediately called Mary Strickland, vice president of marketing, to his office and demanded an explanation. Mary explained, "It seems that we have lost a couple of major builders as customers. They seem to think that our competitors have something better to offer. I have investigated the situation and have found that our cabinets are splitting more on installation due to the fact that we are using a lower-grade plywood now. I talked to Joe Scott: he told me you had ordered him to cut costs. And the purchase of the lower-grade plywood was one of the few ways that costs could be reduced."

Branner immediately ordered Scott to begin purchasing plywood of the necessary quality. Scott then informed Sloane. Later that day, Bill asked Joe Scott what should be done with the three-week supply of the lower-grade plywood. "That's your problem," Joe snapped. Apparently, he had gotten a good chewing out from Branner.

After making several calls, Bill decided that the only good offer for the plywood was made by the company who sold it to Brighton. But they would only pay 60 percent of what it cost Brighton. Bill agreed to the price, wanting to get rid of it to make room for the new supplies that would be coming in.

Three days later, Bill was called into Joe's office. Joe asked, "Bill, who gave you permission to sell that plywood at that price?"

"No one. It was my decision. It was the best deal that I could find, and I needed to get it out to make room for the new supplies coming in," Bill replied.

"Well Bill, with decisions like that, this company won't last very long," Scott commented. "You should have used up the other plywood a little at a time by mixing it in with the higher grade plywood. Don't let this happen again!"

Questions

1. How did this problem actually begin, and how could it have been avoided?
2. Describe the communications failures that occurred in this case.
3. Is Bill really responsible? Who else, if anyone, is responsible?
4. Comment on Joe Scott's talk with Bill at the end of the case.

Incident 17–2
Unions—Why?

George Abbott, 53 years old, sat back in his chair, totally bewildered. He had just been told by his first-shift supervisor Alice Moore that the paperworkers union was rapidly gaining support in the mill that he had managed for over 20 years. The way things were going, it looked like they would have enough supporters to demand an election within the next week. He couldn't believe it. The Marlan Textile Mill was a small mill, employing about 50 relatively unskilled employees. The work force was predominantly comprised of middle-aged females living in the small, rural, southern town of Tyson, where the mill was located.

Abbott could not understand why they would do this to him. He had always thought his employees were happy with the conditions at the mill. It was a small operation and was more like a large family than a place of employment. Surely, if there was something causing them to be so dissatisfied that they felt they had to turn to a union, he would have been aware of it. It made no sense whatsoever to him.

George: Alice, I just can't understand it. I can't help but take it personally. Why, I've done everything I could to see that they would get a fair deal. What could it be?

Alice: Well, George, I don't really know for sure, but rumor has it that it's not more money that they're after. Half of them couldn't earn near what you pay them anywhere else, and they know it. And I can tell you, they do appreciate it. I can't figure it out either. Everyone that's talked to me about the whole situation has agreed that you've been real fair with them.

George: Then why the union? I mean, they just didn't wake up one morning and say "Hey, let's unionize!" Something must be wrong—it just doesn't make sense.

Alice: You know, George, I've only been at the mill two months now. But I've heard that they've been asking for years for more washroom facilities. This may sound crazy, but I wonder what that might have had to do with it. I've heard a lot of talk about that lately.

George: No, we're in compliance with OSHA standards. Sure, at least once a month, someone suggests that additional washroom facilities be made available and the existing ones be made "prettier." But I don't take those suggestions seriously. You know, when I implemented the suggestion box, I knew people would feel like they had to participate. Asking for more washrooms is just one of the first things that would come into a woman's mind. You know how those ladies are. They want to be sure that I know they're interested in the company; so they feel like they have to make their share of suggestions. They don't really need another washroom.

Questions

1. What communication system has failed?

2. What do you think of George's perception of the situation? Is his perception typical of some managers?

Exercise

Meanings Are in People

1. Write down the maximum number of people you feel could live in a town and have the town be described as being small.

2. Write down the minimum number of people that you feel could live in a town and have the town be described as being large.

3. The instructor will collect this data and help you draw some conclusions.

Appraising and Rewarding Performance

Chapter Outline

It meant also informing the men each day just what they had done the day before and just what they were to do that day. In order to do that, as each man came in the morning he had to reach his hand up to a pigeonhole (most of them could not read or write, but they could all find their pigeonholes) and take out two slips of paper. One was a yellow slip and one was a white slip. If they found the yellow slip, those men who could not read and write knew perfectly well what it meant; it was just the general information: "Yesterday you did not earn the money that a first-class man ought to earn. We want you to earn at least 60 percent beyond what other laborers are paid around Bethlehem. You failed to earn that much yesterday; there is something wrong."

Frederick W. Taylor*

One of management's most effective motivation tools is the organizational reward system. It's design and use are often interpreted by employees as a reflection of management attitudes and intentions. Before performance can be rewarded, however, it must be measured. The purpose of this chapter is to explore methods of appraising and rewarding performance.

UNDERSTANDING PERFORMANCE

Performance–degree of accomplishment of the tasks that make up an individual's job.

Performance is the degree of accomplishment of the tasks that make up an individual's job. It reflects how well a person is fulfilling the requirements of a job. Often confused with effort, which refers to energy expended, performance is measured in terms of results. For example, a student may exert a great deal of effort in preparing for an exam and still make a poor grade. Thus, the effort expended is high, yet the performance is low.

Determinants of Performance

Job performance has been described as being "the net effect of a person's effort as modified by his abilities and traits and by his role perceptions."[1] This definition implies that performance in a given situation results from the interrelationships of effort, abilities, and role (or task) perceptions.

Effort, which results from being motivated, is the amount of energy (physical and/or mental) used by a person in performing a task. Abilities are personal characteristics used in performing a job. They usually do not change

* F. W. Taylor, *Addresses and Discussions at the Conference on Scientific Management* (Hanover, N. H.: Dartmouth College, 1911), pp. 39–40.

much over short periods of time. Role or task perceptions refer to the direction(s) in which employees believe they should channel their efforts on their jobs. The activities and behavior that people believe are necessary in the performance of their jobs define their role perceptions.

For acceptable performance, a minimum level of skill is needed in each of the performance components. Similarly, the level of skill in any one of the performance components can place an upper limit on performance. If employees put forth tremendous effort and have excellent abilities but lack a good understanding of their roles, performance will probably not be good in the eyes of their managers. A lot of work will be produced, but it will be misdirected. Likewise, a person probably will rate low on performance who puts forth a high degree of effort and understands the job but lacks ability. A final possibility is the person who has good ability and understanding of the role but is lazy and expends little effort. This person's performance will also probably be low. Of course, an individual can compensate, up to a point, for a weakness in one area by being above average in one or both of the other areas.

Environmental Factors as Performance Obstacles

Other factors beyond the control of an individual can also stifle performance. Although sometimes used merely as excuses, they are often very real and should be recognized. Common performance obstacles include lack of time or conflicting demands on the subordinate's time, inadequate work facilities and equipment, restrictive policies that affect the job, lack of cooperation from others, type of supervision, timing, and even luck.[2]

Environmental factors are not direct determinants of individual performance; but they modify the effects of effort, ability, and direction (see Figure 18–1). For example, poor ventilation or worn-out equipment might very easily affect the efforts of an employee. Unclear policies or poor management can also misdirect effort. Similarly, a lack of training could result in underuti-

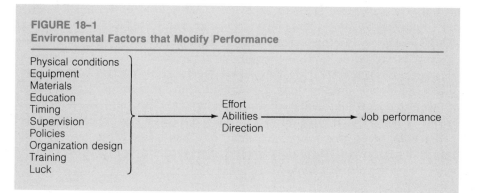

FIGURE 18–1
Environmental Factors that Modify Performance

Physical conditions
Equipment
Materials
Education
Timing
Supervision
Policies
Organization design
Training
Luck

Effort
Abilities —————→ Job performance
Direction

lized abilities. One of management's greatest responsibilities is to provide employees with adequate working conditions and a supportive environment to eliminate or minimize performance obstacles.

PERFORMANCE APPRAISAL: DEFINITION AND USES

Performance appraisal— process of determining and communicating to employees how they are performing the job, and establishing a plan for improvement.

Performance appraisal is a process that involves determining and communicating to employees how they are performing the job and, ideally, establishing a plan for improvement. When properly conducted, performance appraisals not only let employees know how well they are performing but should also influence their future level of effort and task direction. Effort should be enhanced if the employee is properly reinforced. The task perception of the employee should be clarified through the establishment of a plan for improvement.

One of the most common uses of performance appraisals is for making administrative decisions about employees' salary increases, promotions, transfers, and sometimes demotions or terminations.[3] For example, the job performance of an employee is often the primary consideration in deciding whether to promote the person. Successful performance does not necessarily mean that an employee will be effective in a higher-level job; but performance appraisals do provide some predictive information.[4]

Performance appraisals can also provide needed input for determining both individual and organizational training and development needs. For example, they can be used to identify individual strengths and weaknesses. These data can then be used to help pinpoint the organization's overall training and development needs. A completed appraisal should include a plan outlining the employee's specific training and development needs.

A final and important use of performance appraisals is to encourage performance improvement. In this regard, performance appraisals are used to communicate to employees how they are doing and to suggest needed changes in behavior, attitude, skill, or knowledge. This type of feedback clarifies for employees the job expectations of the manager. Often it must be followed by coaching and training by the manager to guide an employee's work efforts.

How often should performance appraisals be conducted? Annual appraisals are most common.[5] However, there seems to be no real consensus on how often they should be done. The answer seems to be as often as necessary to let employees know what kind of job they are doing and, if performance is not satisfactory, the measures that must be taken for improvement. For many employees, this takes more than one annual performance appraisal. Informal performance appraisals should also be conducted for most employees two or three times a year.

PERFORMANCE APPRAISAL: METHODS

The most common performance appraisal methods include:

1. Essay appraisal.
2. Graphic rating scale.
3. Behaviorally anchored rating scale (BARS).
4. Checklist.
5. Forced-choice rating.
6. Critical-incident appraisal.
7. Work standards.
8. Ranking methods.
9. Management by objectives.

Each of these methods is discussed in the following sections.

Essay Appraisal

The **essay appraisal** requires that the rater describe an individual's performance in written narrative form. Instructions are often provided as to the topics that should be covered. A typical essay appraisal question might be: "Describe in your own words this employee's performance, including quantity and quality of work, job knowledge, and ability to get along with other employees. What are his or her strengths and weaknesses?"[6] The primary problem with essay appraisals is that their length and content can vary considerably, depending on the rater. For instance, one rater may write a long statement about an employee's potential and little about past performance. Another rater might focus on the individual's past performance. Thus, essay appraisals are difficult to compare. The writing skill of the appraiser can also affect the appraisal. An effective writer can make an average employee look better than actual performance warrants.

Essay appraisal–requires the rater to prepare a written statement describing an individual's strengths, weaknesses, and past performances.

Graphic Rating Scale

One of the most popular methods used in performance appraisals is the **graphic rating scale.** With this method, the rater assesses an individual on factors such as quantity of work, dependability, job knowledge, attendance, accuracy of work, and cooperativeness. Graphic rating scales include both numerical ranges and written descriptions. Figure 18–2 gives an example of some of the items that might be included on a graphic rating scale using written descriptions.

Graphic rating scale–requires the rater to indicate on a scale where the employee rates on work-related factors.

FIGURE 18–2
Sample Items that Might Be Included on a Graphic Rating Scale Evaluation Form

Quantity of work—the amount of work an individual does in a workday.

( )	( )	( )	( )	( )
Does not meet mini-mum requirements.	Does just enough to get by.	Volume of work is satisfactory.	Very industrious, does more than is required.	Superior work pro-duction record.

Dependability—the ability to do required jobs well with a minimum of supervision.

( )	( )	( )	( )	( )
Requires close supervision; is un-reliable.	Sometimes requires prompting.	Usually completes necessary tasks with reasonable prompt-ness.	Requires little supervision, is reliable.	Requires absolute minimum of supervi-sion.

Job knowledge—information on work duties that an individual should have for satisfactory job performance.

( )	( )	( )	( )	( )
Poorly informed about work duties.	Lacks knowledge of some phases of job.	Moderately in-formed, can answer most questions about the job.	Understands all phases of job.	Has complete mas-tery of all phases of job.

Attendance—faithfulness in coming to work daily and conforming to work hours.

( )	( )	( )	( )	( )
Often absent without good excuse or fre-quently reports for work late, or both.	Lax in attendance or reporting for work on time, or both.	Usually present and on time.	Very prompt, regular in attendance.	Always regular and prompt, volunteers for overtime when needed.

Accuracy—the correctness of work duties performed.

( )	( )	( )	( )	( )
Makes frequent errors.	Careless, often makes errors.	Usually accurate, makes only average number of mistakes.	Requiries little supervision, is exact and precise most of the time.	Requires absolute minimum of supervi-sion, is almost al-ways accurate.

This method is subject to some serious weaknesses. Potentially, all raters are unlikely to interpret written descriptions in the same manner, due to differences in background, experience, and personality. Another problem can be the choice of rating categories. It is possible to choose categories with little relationship to job performance or to omit categories which greatly influence job performance. Regardless, a study of major national and interna-tional companies found that graphic rating scales were the primary appraisal technique used by these organizations.[7]

Behaviorally Anchored Rating Scale (BARS)

Behaviorally anchored rating scale (BARS)—determines employee's level of performance based on presence of specific job behaviors.

The **behaviorally anchored rating scale (BARS)** method of performance appraisal is designed to assess behaviors that are required for a job's success. To understand BARS, several key terms must be defined. First, most BARS use the term *job dimension* to mean those broad categories of duties and responsibilities that make up a job. Each job is likely to have several job dimensions and separate scales must be developed for each. Figure 18–3 is an example of a BARS written for the job dimensions found in many managerial jobs: planning, organizing, and scheduling project assignments and due dates. The scale values on the left side of Figure 18–3 define specific categories of performance. Anchors on the right side are specific written statements of actual behaviors that, when exhibited on the job, put the level of performance on the scale opposite that particular anchor.[8] As the anchor statements appear beside each of the scale values, they are said to "anchor" each of the scale values along the scale.

BARS require the rater to read the list of anchors on each scale to find the group of anchors that best describes the employee's job behavior during

FIGURE 18–3
Example of Behaviorally Anchored Rating Scale

Scale Values	Anchors
7 [ ] Excellent	Develops a comprehensive project plan, documents it well, obtains required approval, and distributes the plan to all concerned.
6 [ ] Very good	Plans, communicates, and observes milestones; states week by week where the project stands relative to plans. Maintains up-to-date charts of project accomplishments and backlogs and uses these to optimize any schedule modifications required. Experiences occasional minor operational problems but communicates effectively.
5 [ ] Good	Lays out all the parts of a job and schedules each part; seeks to beat schedule and will allow for slack. Satisfies customers' time constraints; time and cost overruns occur infrequently.
4 [ ] Average	Makes a list of due dates and revises them as the project progresses, usually adding unforeseen events; instigates frequent customer complaints. May have a sound plan, but does not keep track of milestones; does not report slippages in schedule or other problems as they occur.
3 [ ] Below average	Plans are poorly defined; unrealistic time schedules are common. Cannot plan more than a day or two ahead, has no concept of a realistic project due date.
2 [ ] Very poor	Has no plan or schedule of work segments to be performed. Does little or no planning for project assignments.
1 [ ] Unacceptable	Seldom, if ever, completes project, because of lack of planning; does not seem to care. Fails consistently due to lack of planning; does not inquire about how to improve.

Source: C. E. Schneier and R. W. Beatty, "Developing Behaviorally Anchored Rating Scales (BARS)." Reprinted from the August 1979 issue of *Personnel Administrator,* copyright 1979, The American Society for Personnel Administration, 606 North Washington Street, Alexandria, VA 22314, $30 per year.

MANAGEMENT IN ACTION 18–1

Reporter Evaluation at Gannett Company—America's Largest Communications Chain

In an attempt to develop a system for evaluating its reporters, the Gannett Company has developed a behaviorally anchored rating scale. It defined its standard of meeting deadlines as follows:

Meets daily deadlines with complete, accurate, well-written stories requiring minimal editing. Unnecessary for editors to supervise efforts to meet deadlines.

The behaviorally anchored scale developed and used by Gannett is shown below:

Outstanding — Meets the standard with rare exceptions.

Commendable — Usually meets the standard. Requires occasional help from editors in handling complicated stories on deadline.

Acceptable — Meets the standard more often than not. Deadlines are met, but stories sometimes are not complete, well organized, or tightly written.

Marginal — Frequently fails to meet the standard. Often misses deadlines with stories that are not complete, well organized, or tightly written. Copy usually requires reworking. Often requires supervision to meet deadlines.

Unacceptable — Rarely meets the standard. Seldom meets deadlines. Stories submitted on deadline are usually not complete, well organized, or tightly written. Copy requires substantial reworking. Even with close supervision, has difficulty meeting deadlines.

Source: Adapted from Robert Giles and Christine Landauer, "Setting Specific Standards for Appraising Creative Staffs," *Personnel Administrator,* March 1984, p. 38.

the review period. The scale value opposite that group is then checked. This process is used for all the known dimensions of the job. A total evaluation is obtained by combining the scale values checked for all the different job dimensions.

BARS are normally developed through a series of meetings attended by both managers and job incumbents. The usual steps are:

1. Managers and job incumbents identify the relevant job dimensions for the job.
2. Managers and job incumbents write behavioral anchors for each of the job dimensions. As many anchors as possible should be written for each dimension.
3. Managers and job incumbents reach a consensus concerning the scale values that are to be used and the grouping of anchor statements for each scale value.

The use of BARS has several advantages. First, BARS are developed through the active participation of managers and job incumbents. This increases the chances that the method will be accepted. A second advantage is that the anchors are developed from the observations and experiences of employees who actually perform the job. Finally, BARS can be used for specific feedback on an employee's job performance.

One of the major drawbacks to the use of BARS is that they take considerable time and commitment to develop. Also, separate forms must be developed for different jobs.[9] Management in Action 18–1 shows a behaviorally anchored rating scale on the activity of meeting deadlines for reporters at the Gannett Company.

Checklist

In the **checklist** method, the rater makes yes-or-no responses to a series of questions concerning the employee's behavior. Figure 18–4 lists some typical questions. The checklist can also have varying weights assigned to each question.

Checklist–requires the rater to answer yes or no to a series of questions about the behavior of the individual being rated.

FIGURE 18–4
Sample Checklist Questions

	Yes	No
1. Does the individual lose his or her temper in public?		
2. Does the individual play favorites?		
3. Does the individual praise employees in public when they have done a good job?		
4. Does the employee volunteer to do special jobs?		

Normally, the rater is not aware of weights for each question; but because the positive or negative thrust of each question can be seen, bias can be introduced. Also, it is time consuming to assemble the questions for each job category; a separate listing of questions must be developed for each job category; and the checklist questions can have different meanings to different raters.

Forced-Choice Rating

Many variations of the **forced-choice rating** method exist. The most common practice requires the rater to rank a set of statements describing an individual's strengths, weaknesses, and past performances. Figure 18–5 illustrates a group of forced-choice statements.

Normally, the statements are weighted, and the weights are not generally known to the rater. After the rater ranks all of the forced-choice statements, the human resource/personnel department applies the weights and computes a score.

Forced-choice rating–requires rater to rank a set of statements describing an individual's strengths, weaknesses, and past performances.

FIGURE 18–5
Sample Forced-Choice Item

Instructions: Rank the following statements according to how they describe the manner in which this employee carries out his/her duties and responsibilities. Rank 1 should be given to the most descriptive and Rank 4 to the least descriptive. No ties are allowed.

Rank

_____ Has complete mastery of all phases of job.

_____ Shows superior ability to express self.

_____ Requires close supervision.

_____ Careless and makes recurrent errors.

This method attempts to prevent rater bias by forcing the rater to rank statements that may seem either the same or unrelated. However, the forced-choice method tends to irritate some raters, who feel they are not being trusted. Furthermore, the results of the appraisal can be hard to communicate to employees.

Critical-Incident Appraisal

Critical-incident appraisal–rater records incidents of both positive and negative employee behavior and uses them to evaluate performance.

The **critical-incident** requires the rater to keep a written record of incidents (as they occur) involving job behaviors that illustrate both satisfactory and unsatisfactory performance of the person being rated. The recorded incidents provide a basis for performance evaluation and feedback to the employee.

The main drawback to this approach is that the rater must jot down incidents regularly; this can be burdensome and time consuming. Also, the definition of a critical incident is unclear—it may be interpreted differently by different people. This method can lead to friction between the manager and employees who feel that the manager is keeping a "book" on them.

Work Standards

Work standards approach–involves setting a standard or expected level of output and then comparing each employee's performance to the standard.

This method involves setting a standard or expected level of output and then comparing each employee's performance to the standard. Generally speaking, **work standards** should reflect the output of a normal person. Work standards attempt to answer the question: What is a fair day's output? The work standards approach is most often used for production employees.

Several methods can be used for setting work standards. Some of the more common methods are summarized in Figure 18–6.

An advantage of the work standards method is that the performance review is based on factors that are highly objective. Of course, to be effective,

FIGURE 18-6
Frequently Used Methods for Setting Work Standards

Methods	Areas of Applicability
Average production of work groups	When tasks performed by all employees are the same or approximately the same.
Standards based on the performance of specially selected employees	When tasks performed by all employees are basically the same and it would be cumbersome and time consuming to use the group average.
Time study	Jobs involving repetitive tasks.
Work sampling	For noncyclical types of work where many different tasks are performed, there is no set pattern or cycle.
Use of expert opinion	When none of the more direct methods (described above) applies.

the standards must be viewed as fair by the affected employees. The most serious criticism of work standards is a lack of comparability of standards for different job categories.

Ranking Methods

To compare the performance of two or more individuals, **ranking methods** can be used. Three common ranking methods are alternation, paired comparison, and forced distribution.

Ranking methods–the performance of an individual is ranked relative to the performance of others.

Alternation ranking.   The names of persons to be rated are listed down the left side of a sheet of paper. The rater is then asked to choose the "most valuable" employee on the list, cross that name off the left-hand list, and put it at the top of the right side of the paper. The rater is then asked to select and cross off the name of the "least valuable" employee and move it to the bottom of the right-hand column. The rater then repeats this process for all of the names on the list. The resulting right-hand column of names ranks the employees from most to least valuable.

Paired comparison ranking.   This method is best explained with an example. Suppose a rater is to evaluate six employees. Their names are listed on the left side of a sheet of paper. The rater then compares the first employee with the second employee on a chosen performance criterion, such as quantity of work. If the rater feels that the first employee has produced more work than the second employee, a check mark would be placed by the first employee's name. The first employee would then be compared to the third, fourth, fifth, and sixth employee on the same performance criterion. A check mark would be placed by the name of the employee who had produced the most work in each of these paired comparisons.

The process is repeated until each worker is compared to every other worker on all of the chosen performance criteria. The employee with the most check marks is considered to be the best performer. Likewise, the employee with the fewest check marks is the lowest performer. One major problem is that this method becomes unwieldly when comparing large numbers of employees.

Forced distribution. This method assumes that the performance level in a group of employees will be distributed according to a bell-shaped, or "normal," curve. The rater compares the performance of employees and places a certain percentage of employees at various performance levels.

Figure 18–7 illustrates how the forced distribution method works. The rater is required to rate 60 percent of the employees as meeting expectations, 20 percent as exceeding expectations, and 20 percent as not meeting expectations. One problem is that in small groups of employees, a bell-shaped distribution of performance may not apply. Also, though the distribution may approximate a normal curve, it is probably not a perfect curve. This means that some employees will probably not be rated accurately.

Management by Objectives

Management by objectives (MBO) was described in detail in Chapter 5 as it relates to the planning process. After objectives have been set using the guidelines described in that chapter, the objectives can then be used to evaluate an employee's performance, based on the achievement of the objectives. Normally, MBO is used in appraising the performance of professional and managerial employees.

FIGURE 18–7
Forced Distribution Curve

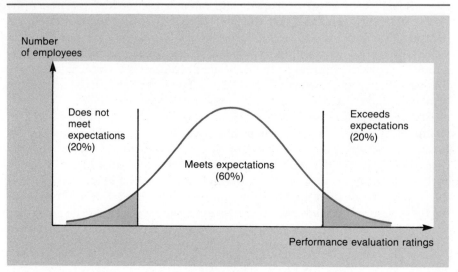

MANAGEMENT IN ACTION 18–2

New Appraisal System at General Electric

GE recently funded a major study on the practices used by its various divisions for measuring and appraising the performance of exempt employees. The findings suggested a wide diversity in performance appraisal systems and some level of frustration with most of them.

While this corporate study was being completed, one of GE's divisions, presently called the Contractor Equipment Business Operations, was discarding its appraisal system. The system was plagued with a number of problems and was failing. Managers had low confidence in it (only 50 percent used it), and employees denounced the entire program as unreliable, inaccurate, and a waste of everyone's time. Division management decided to design a new appraisal system.

The new system consisted of the following steps:

1. Work planned mutually by employee and manager—including setting specific objectives and identifying ways of obtaining them. This joint employee-manager process would occur at the start of the appraisal period.
2. Interim appraisals and coaching focused on monitoring progress toward objectives and coaching the employee accordingly when a behavior change is necessary.
3. A final appraisal, based on the work the employee actually accomplished, including planned and unplanned work.
4. The performance appraisal system linked to the compensation system by requiring a current appraisal for a salary action to be processed.

A recent survey found that 86 percent of the managers rated this system as an improvement over other performance appraisal systems. The survey also found that 85 percent of 100 randomly selected employees whose performance had been appraised under the system felt that the appraisal process was a helpful management tool.

Source: Adapted from Robert J. Butler and Lyle Yorks, "A New Appraisal System as Organizational Change: GE's Task Force Approach," *Personnel,* January–February 1984, pp. 31–42.

Essential to the successful use of MBO in performance appraisals is that the objectives and action plan must serve as a basis for regular discussions between the manager and employee concerning the employee's performance. These regular talks give the manager and employee a chance to modify objectives when necessary and discuss progress. Management in Action 18–2 describes how GE uses an MBO type of system for performance appraisals.

POTENTIAL ERRORS IN PERFORMANCE APPRAISALS

Several common errors have been identified in performance appraisals. **Leniency** is grouping ratings at the positive end instead of spreading them throughout the performance scale. **Central tendency** is rating all or most employees in the middle of the scale. Leniency and central tendency errors

Leniency–tendency to group performance ratings at the positive end instead of spreading them throughout the performance scale.

Central tendency—tendency to rate all or most employees in the middle of the performance rating scale.

Halo effect—raters allow their general impressions of an employee to influence judgment on separate items of the performance appraisal.

make it difficult, if not impossible, to separate the good performers from the poor performers. Also, these errors make it difficult to compare ratings from different raters. For example, it is possible for a good performer rated by a manager committing central tendency errors to receive a lower rating than a poor performer rated by a manager committing leniency errors.

Another common error in performance appraisals is the **halo effect.** This occurs when a rater allows general impressions of an employee to influence his or her judgment on each separate item in the performance appraisal. This often results in the employee receiving approximately the same rating on every item. An employee should not necessarily be evaluated at the same level on all items in the performance appraisal.

Personal preferences, prejudices, and biases can also cause errors in performance appraisals. Managers with biases or prejudices tend to look for employee behaviors that will confirm those biases. Appearance, social status, dress, race, and sex have influenced many performance appraisals. Managers have also allowed first impressions to influence later judgments of an employee. First impressions are only a sample of behavior; however, people tend to retain them, even when faced with opposite evidence.[10]

OVERCOMING ERRORS IN PERFORMANCE APPRAISALS

As can be seen, the potential for errors in performance appraisals is great. One approach to overcoming these errors is to refine the design of appraisal methods. It could be argued that the forced distribution method attempts to overcome the errors of leniency and central tendency. Also, BARS are designed to reduce halo, leniency, and central tendency errors. Unfortunately, even refined instruments often do not overcome all the obstacles.[11] Thus, it does not appear likely that refining appraisal instruments will totally overcome errors in performance appraisals.

A more promising approach is to improve the skills of raters. Several studies have shown that certain appraisal errors can be reduced through rater-training programs.[12] Suggestions on specific training is often vague but normally emphasizes that raters should be trained to observe behavior more accurately and judge it fairly. One study found that training raters in how to keep a diary of critical incidents significantly reduced leniency and halo errors.[13]

At this point, more research is needed before a definitive set of topics for rater training can be established. However, at a minimum, raters should be trained in the performance appraisal method(s) used by the company, the importance of the rater's role in the total process, and the communication skills necessary to provide feedback to the employee.

PROVIDING FEEDBACK THROUGH THE APPRAISAL INTERVIEW

After one of the performance appraisal methods has been used, the results must be communicated to the employee. Unless properly conducted, this interview can be and often is an unpleasant experience for the manager and the employee.

Many studies have researched the conditions associated with the success or failure of appraisal interviews. Some of the conclusions are:

1. The more the employee participates in the appraisal process, the more satisfied he or she is with the appraisal interview and with the manager and the more likely are performance improvement objectives to be accepted and met.

2. The more a manager uses positive motivational techniques (e.g., recognizing and praising good performance), the more satisfied the employee is likely to be with the appraisal interview and with the manager.

3. The mutual setting by the manager and the employee of specific performance improvement objectives results in more improvement in performance than does a general discussion or criticism.

4. Discussing and solving problems that may be hampering the employee's current job performance improve the employee's performance.

5. Areas of job performance needing improvement that are most heavily criticized are less likely to be improved than similar areas of job performance that are less heavily criticized.

6. The more employees are allowed to voice their opinions during the interview, the more satisfied they feel with the interview.

7. The interview benefits from how much thought and preparation employees independently devote to it beforehand.

8. The more employees perceive that performance appraisal results are tied to organizational rewards, the more beneficial is the interview.[14]

COMPENSATING EMPLOYEES

Compensation refers to the extrinsic rewards that employees receive in exchange for their work. Usually, it is composed of the base wage or salary, any incentives or bonuses, and any benefits. The base wage or salary is the hourly, weekly, or monthly pay that employees receive for their work.

Incentives are rewards offered in addition to the base wage or salary and are usually directly related to performance. Benefits are rewards which employees receive due to their employment and position with an organization. Paid vacations, health insurance, and retirement plans are examples of benefits. Figure 18–8 presents some examples of the different types of compensation. An organization's **compensation system** consists of the policies, procedures, and rules that it follows in determining employee compensation.

Compensation system—policies, procedures, and rules the organization uses to determine employee compensation.

FIGURE 18–8
Components of Employee Compensation

Base Wage or Salary	Incentives	Benefits
Hourly wage	Bonuses	Paid vacation
Weekly, monthly, or annual salary	Commissions	Health insurance
	Profit sharing	Life insurance
Overtime pay	Piece rate plans	Retirement pension

The Importance of Fair Pay

Employee motivation is closely related to the types of rewards offered and their method of disbursement. There is much debate over the motivational aspect of pay. But there is little doubt that inadequate pay can have a very negative impact on an organization. Figure 18–9 presents a simple model of the reactions of employees dissatisfied with their pay. According to this model, pay dissatisfaction can influence people's feelings about their jobs in two ways: (1) it can increase the desire for more money; (2) it can lower the attractiveness of the job. An individual with an increased desire for more money is likely to engage in actions that can increase pay. These actions might include joining a union, looking for another job, performing better, or going on strike. Except for performing better, all of the actions are generally classified by management as being undesirable. Better performance happens only in those cases where pay is perceived as being directly related to performance.

On the other hand, when the job becomes less attractive, the employee is more likely to be absent or tardy and become dissatisfied with the job itself. After studying compensation systems in Great Britain for more than 10 years, Elliot Jacques reported that "underpayment by more than 10 percent brings about enough dissatisfaction to make employees want to act to get their compensation boosted, and that underpayment by roughly 20 percent produces an explosive situation."[15] Thus, while its importance may vary somewhat from situation to situation, pay satisfaction can and usually does have a strong impact on both individual and organizational performance.

FIGURE 18–9
Model of the Consequences of Pay Dissatisfaction

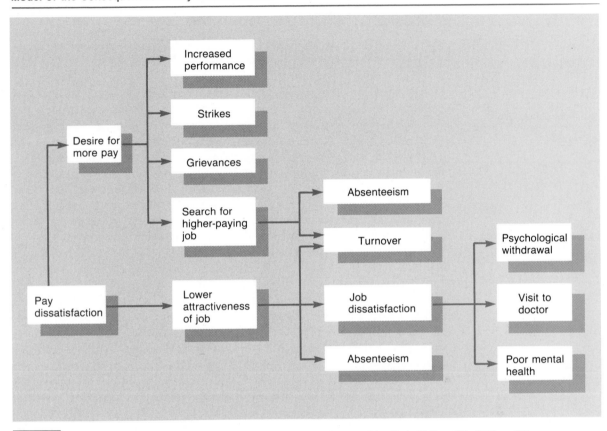

Source: E. E. Lawler III, *Pay and Organizational Effectiveness: A Psychological View* (New York: McGraw-Hill, 1971), p. 233.

Pay Equity

The question of fair pay involves two general factors: (1) what the employee is being paid for doing his or her job compared to what other employees in the same organization are being paid to do their jobs **(internal equity);** and (2) what employees in other organizations are being paid for performing similar jobs **(external equity).** It is not at all unusual for an individual to feel good about internal equity and bad about external equity, or vice versa. For example, employees may feel very good about their pay compared to what their friends working in other organizations are making. However, a person may be very unhappy about his or her pay relative to several other people in the same organization.

If organizations are to avoid discontent with pay, employees must be

Internal equity what an employee is paid compared to what other employees in the organization are paid to do their jobs.

External equity what employees are paid compared to employees performing similar jobs in other organizations.

convinced that both internal and external equity exist. A sound job evaluation system is usually the best method for ensuring internal equity. External equity is usually established through wage surveys.

JOB EVALUATION

Job evaluation–
systematic determination of the value of each job in relation to other jobs in the organization.

Job evaluation is a systematic determination of the value of each job in relation to other jobs in the organization. It is used for designing a pay structure, not for appraising the performance of employees. The general idea is to list a job's requirements and contribution to the organization and then to classify it according to its importance. For instance, a design engineer's job would be more complex and potentially contribute more than that of an assembler of the designed product. Although both jobs are important, the relative worth of each must be established. The main purpose of job evaluation is to establish the relative worth of jobs; however, it can serve several other purposes. Figure 18–10 presents a list of potential uses.

The first step in a job evaluation program is to gather information on the jobs in question. Normally, information comes from current job descriptions. If they do not exist, then it is usually necessary to analyze the jobs and create up-to-date descriptions. Then, the factor or factors are identified that will be used in determining the worth of different jobs to the organization. Factors often used are skill, responsibility, and working conditions.

The job evaluation process also involves developing and implementing a plan for using the chosen factors to evaluate the relative worth of the different jobs. Such a plan should always place jobs requiring more of the factors at a higher level in the job hierarchy than jobs requiring fewer of the factors.

It is expensive and difficult to keep job evaluations up to date. For example,

FIGURE 18–10
Potential Uses of Job Evaluations

- To provide a more workable internal wage structure to simplify and make rational the relatively chaotic wage structure resulting from chance, custom, and such individual factors as favoritism.
- To provide an agreed-upon device for setting rates for new or changed jobs.
- To provide a means whereby realistic comparisons may be made of the wage and salary rates of different organizations.
- To provide a base for measuring individual performance.
- To reduce grievances over wage and salary rates and provide an agreed-upon means for solving those disputes.
- To provide incentives for employees to strive for higher-level jobs.
- To provide facts for wage negotiations.
- To provide facts on job relationships for use in selection, training, transfers, and promotions.

Source: Adapted from David W. Belcher, *Compensation Administration*, © 1974, pp. 91–92. Reprinted by permission of Prentice-Hall, Inc., Englewood Cliffs, N.J.

the content of management and professional jobs can change significantly as incumbents change. Also, job evaluation and performance appraisal should not be confused. Job evaluation enables management to establish salary ranges for different jobs within an organization. Where an employee falls within a salary range should be determined by performance as rated by the performance appraisal process.

WAGE SURVEYS

Wage surveys are performed to collect reliable information on the policies, practices, and methods of wage payment from selected organizations in a given geographic location or particular type of industry so that comparisons can be made. Wage surveys are the primary method used to ensure external equity in an organization's wage and salary system. Data may be gathered from a variety of sources. The Bureau of Labor Statistics of the U.S. Department of Labor regularly publishes wage data broken down by geographic area, industry, and occupation. Industry and employee associations sometimes conduct surveys and publish their results. Trade magazines also may contain wage survey information. Beside using these sources, many organizations design and conduct their own surveys. To design a wage survey, the jobs, area, and organizations to be studied must be determined, as must the method for gathering data.

A geographic area, an industry type, or a combination of the two may be surveyed. The size of the geographic area, the cost-of-living index for the area, and similar factors define the scope of the survey. The organizations to be surveyed are often competitors or others who employ similar types of workers. The most important and most respected organizations in the area should be chosen from among those willing to cooperate.

The three basic methods of collecting wage data are personal interviews, telephone interviews, and mailed questionnaires. The most reliable and most costly method is the personal interview. Mailed questionnaires are probably used most often. However, they should only be used to survey jobs that have a uniform meaning throughout the industry. If there is any doubt concerning the definition of a job, the responses may be unreliable. Another potential problem with mailed questionnaires is that they can be answered by someone who is not thoroughly familiar with the wage structure. The telephone method, which yields quick but often incomplete information, may be used to clarify responses to mailed questionnaires.

Wage survey–survey of selected organizations to provide a comparison of reliable information on the policies, practices, and methods of payment.

PAY SECRECY

Some organizations have a policy of keeping pay-related information secret. Pay secrecy is usually to avoid any discontent that might result from employees knowing what others are being paid. Further, many employees (especially high achievers) feel strongly that their pay is nobody else's business.[16]

Pay secrecy makes it difficult for employees to determine whether pay is related to performance. Also, it does not eliminate pay comparisons, but it may (1) cause employees to overestimate the pay of their peers and (2) cause employees to underestimate the pay of supervisors.[17] Both situations can cause unnecessary feelings of discontent.

A good compromise on the issue of pay secrecy is to disclose the pay ranges for various job levels within the organization. This approach clearly gives the general ranges of pay for different jobs without telling just what any specific employee makes.

INCENTIVE PAY PLANS

Incentive pay plans relate pay to performance in order to reward above-average performance rapidly and directly. Good performance can be rewarded through the base wage or salary structure. But these rewards are often subject to delays and other restrictions. Therefore, they often are not viewed by the recipients as being directly related to performance. Incentive pay plans attempt to strengthen the performance-reward relationship and thus motivate the affected employees.

There are two basic requirements for an effective incentive plan.[18] First, if incentives are to be based on performance, then employees must feel that performance is accurately and fairly evaluated. Naturally, this is easier in some situations than in others. For example, the performance of a commissioned salesperson is usually easy to measure. On the other hand, the performance of a middle manager is often difficult to measure. A key issue in performance measurement is the degree of trust in management. If the employees distrust management, then it is almost impossible to establish a sound performance appraisal system.

The second requirement is that incentives (rewards) must be based on performance. This may seem obvious, yet it is often violated. Employees must see a relationship between what they do and what they get. Individual-based incentive plans require that employees perceive a direct relationship between their own performance and the rewards that follow. Group-based plans require employees to perceive a relationship between the group's performance and the subsequent rewards of the group's members. Furthermore, the group members must believe that their individual performances have an impact on the group's overall performance. Organization-based plans have the same basic requirements as group plans. Employees must see a relationship between the organization's performance and their individual rewards. Also, employees must believe that their individual performances affect the performance of the organization. Management in Action 18–3 shows how incentives have worked in China.

MANAGEMENT IN ACTION 18-3

Cotton Mills and Incentives in the People's Republic of China

Cotton Textile Mill No. 4 of Northwest China sits in the middle of Xian, a city of 2.5 million, some 550 miles southwest of Peking. Xian enjoys a measure of fame as the site of a fascinating archaeological find—thousands of life-sized terra cotta warriors and horses guarding the tomb of Qin Shi Huangdi, an emperor who ruled in the third century B.C. and is credited with unifying China.

Cotton Textile Mill No. 4 has more than a touch of an American company town of yesteryear about it. Besides several manufacturing buildings, the compound boasts company-operated stores, apartment buildings, schools, and a medical clinic.

Other paternalistic "fringes" abound. Company-sponsored recreational activities for workers range from a variety of athletic events, through amateur singing, dancing and opera performances, to a library. If a worker wants a big-ticket item but lacks the cash to buy, the company store will work out an installment plan.

The company also has an incentive pay plan. The average bonus comes to 20 yuan a month. This sum may seem low, but it takes on considerable luster when one learns that the average monthly wage at Mill No. 4 runs to only 60 yuan. For outstanding work, an employee may get a bonus as high as 30 to 40 yuan.

Source: Adapted from Edward R. Cony, "Beansprout Capitalism," *Barron's,* June 14, 1982, pp. 20, 32.

SUMMARY

Performance refers to the degree of accomplishment of the tasks that make up an individual's job. Performance in a given situation results from the interrelationship between effort, ability, and role perceptions, as modified by environmental forces.

Performance appraisal is a process that involves determining and communicating to an employee how he or she is performing the job and ideally involves establishing a plan for improvement. Methods of performance appraisal include: essay appraisal, graphic rating scale, behaviorally anchored rating scale, checklist, forced-choice rating, critical-incident appraisal, work standards, ranking methods, and management by objectives. Each of these methods was discussed in this chapter.

Several common errors have been identified in performance appraisals. Leniency occurs when ratings are grouped at the positive end instead of being spread throughout the performance scale. Central tendency occurs when all or most employees are ranked in the middle of the rating scale. The halo effect occurs when a manager allows a general impression of an employee to influence judgment of each separate item in the performance appraisal. Two approaches to overcoming these errors are refining performance appraisal instruments and improving the skills of raters.

Compensation is normally composed of the base wage or salary, incentives or bonuses, and any benefits. An organization's compensation system consists of the policies, procedures, and rules that it follows in determining employee compensation.

511

Pay dissatisfaction can influence a person's feelings about his or her job in two ways: (1) it can increase the desire for more money; (2) it can lower the attractiveness of the job. The question of fair pay involves both internal and external equity. Internal equity refers to what an employee is being paid for doing a job compared to what other employees in the same organization are being paid to do their jobs. External equity refers to what employees in other organizations are being paid for performing similar jobs.

Job evaluation is a systematic determination of the value of each job in relation to other jobs in the organization. In wage surveys, information is collected on the compensation policies, practices, and methods of wage payments of other organizations in the same or a related industry or in a given geographic area. Incentive pay plans attempt to relate pay to performance in an endeavor to reward above-average performance rapidly and directly.

References and Additional Readings

[1] L. W. Porter and E. E. Lawler III. *Managerial Attitudes and Performance* (Homewood, Ill.: Dorsey Press, 1968), p. 28.

[2] C. N. Greene, "The Satisfaction-Performance Controversy," *Business Horizons,* October 1972, p. 36.

[3] D. McGregor, "An Uneasy Look at Performance Appraisal," *Harvard Business Review,* May–June 1975, pp. 89–94.

[4] D. Yoder and H. Heneman, *Handbook of Personnel and Industrial Relations* (Washington, D.C.: Bureau of National Affairs, 1979), p. 4–168.

[5] *Management Performance Appraisal Programs,* Bureau of National Affairs PPF Survey No. 104 (Washington, D.C.: 1974), p. 13.

[6] Ibid., p. 4–168.

[7] K. S. Teel, "Performance Appraisal: Current Trends, Persistent Progress," *Personnel Journal,* April 1980, pp. 296–301.

[8] C. E. Schneier and R. W. Beatty, "Developing Behaviorally Anchored Rating Scales (BARS)," *Personnel Administrator,* August 1979, p. 63.

[9] For a further discussion of BARS, see P. O. Kingstrom and A. R. Bass, "A Critical Analysis of Studies Comparing Behaviorally Anchored Rating Scales (BARS) and Other Rating Formats," *Personnel Psychology* 34 (1981), pp. 263–89.

[10] For additional discussion of appraisal errors, see W. F. Cascio, *Applied Psychology in Personnel Management* (Reston, Va.: Reston Publishing, 1978), pp. 320–22.

[11] See, for instance, D. P. Schwab, H. G. Heneman, and T. A. DeCatiris, "Behaviorally Anchored Rating Scales: A Review of the Literature," *Personnel Psychology* 28 (1975), pp. 549–62.

[12] See J. M. Ivancevich, "A Longitudinal Study of the Effects of Rater Training on Psychometric Errors in Ratings," *Journal of Applied Psychology* 64 (1979), pp. 502–8; H. J. Bernardin and D. S. Walter, "Effects of Rater Training and Diary Keeping on Psychometric Error in Ratings," *Journal of Applied Psychology* 62 (1977), pp. 64–69.

[13] H. J. Bernadin and M. R. Buckley, "Strategies in Rater Training," *Academy of Management Review* 6 (1981), pp. 205–12.

[14] R. J. Burke, W. Weitzel, and T. Weir, "Characteristics of Effective Employee Performance Review and Development Interviews:

Replication and Extension," *Personnel Psychology* 31 (1978), pp. 903–19.

[15] E. Jacques, *Equitable Payments* (New York: John Wiley & Sons, 1961), p. 142.

[16] P. Thompson and J. Pronsky, "Secrecy or Disclosure in Management Compensation," *Business Horizons,* June 1975, pp. 67–74.

[17] E. E. Lawler III, "Should Managers' Compensation Be Kept under Wraps?" *Personnel,* January–February 1965, p. 17.

[18] J. G. Goodale and M. W. Mouser, "Developing and Auditing a Merit Pay System," *Personnel Journal,* May 1981, p. 391.

Review Questions

1. What is performance? What factors influence an employee's level of performance?
2. Define performance appraisal.
3. Give at least three uses of performance appraisal information.
4. Describe the following methods used in performance appraisal:

    a. Essay appraisal.
    b. Graphic rating scale.
    c. Behaviorally anchored rating scale.
    d. Checklist.
    e. Forced-choice rating.
    f. Critical-incident appraisal.
    g. Work standards.
    h. Ranking methods.
    i. Management by objectives.

5. Define the following types of performance appraisal errors:

    a. Leniency.
    b. Central tendency.
    c. Halo effect.

6. Outline some of the conditions associated with the success or failure of appraisal interviews.
7. Define the three basic components of compensation and give examples of each.
8. What is job evaluation?
9. What are wage surveys and how might they be conducted?
10. What are two basic requirements for an incentive plan to be effective?

Discussion Questions

1. Describe your thoughts on discussing salary raises and promotions during the performance appraisal interview.
2. Was your last exam a performance appraisal? Use your last exam to discuss both the reasons for using performance appraisals and their limitations.
3. It has been said that "incentive plans only work for a relatively short time." Do you agree or disagree? Why?
4. Suppose your organization's recently completed wage survey showed that pay rates of several jobs were either less than or more than they should be. How might you bring these jobs into line?

Incident 18–1
Does Money Motivate?

About four months ago, Judy Holcomb was promoted to supervisor of the Claims Department for a large, Eastern insurance company. It is now time for all supervisors to make their annual salary increase recommendations. Judy doesn't feel comfortable in making these recommendations since she has only been in her job for a short time. To further complicate the situation, the former supervisor has left the company and is unavailable for consultation.

There are no formal company restrictions on the kind of raises that can be given, but Judy's boss has said that the total amount of money available to Judy for raises would be 8 percent of Judy's payroll for the past year. In other words, if the sum total of the salaries for all of Judy's employees was $100,000, then Judy would have $8,000 to allocate for raises. Judy is free to distribute the raises just about any way she wants, within reason.

Summarized below is the best information on her employees that Judy can find from the files of the former supervisor of the Claims Department. This information is supplemented by feelings Judy has developed during her short time as supervisor.

John Thompson.   John has been with Judy's department for only five months. In fact, he was hired just before Judy was promoted into the supervisor's job. John is single and seems to be a carefree bachelor. His job performance, so far, has been above average, but Judy has received some negative comments about John from his co-workers. Present salary, $18,000.

Carole Wilson.   Carole has been on the job for three years. Her previous performance appraisals have indicated superior performance. However, Judy does not feel that the previous evaluations are accurate. She feels that Carole's performance is, at best, average. Carole appears to be well liked by all of her co-workers. Just last year, she became widowed and is presently the sole support for her five-year-old child. Present salary: $19,000.

Evelyn Roth.   Evelyn has been on the job for four years. Her previous performance appraisals were all average. In addition, she had received below-average increases for the past two years. However, Evelyn recently approached Judy and told her that she feels she was discriminated against in the past due to both her age and sex. Judy feels that Evelyn's work so far has been satisfactory but not superior. Most employees don't seem to sympathize with Evelyn's accusations of sex and age discrimination. Present salary: $17,000.

Jane Simmons.   As far as Judy can tell, Jane is one of her best employees. Her previous performance appraisals also indicate that she is a superior performer. Judy knows that Jane badly needs a substantial salary increase due to some personal problems. In addition, all of Judy's employees are aware of Jane's problems. She appears to be well respected by her co-workers. Present salary: $18,500.

Bob Tyson. Bob has been performing his present job for eight years. The job is very technical, and he would be difficult to replace. However, as far as Judy can discern, Bob is not a good worker. He is irritable and hard to work with. In spite of this, Bob has received above-average pay increases for the past two years. Present salary: $20,000.

Questions

1. Indicate the size of the raise that you would give each of these employees.
2. What criteria did you use in determining the size of the raise?
3. What do you think would be the feelings of the other people in the group if they should find out what raises you recommend?
4. Do you feel that the employees would eventually find out what raises others received? Would it matter?

Incident 18–2
The Lackadaisical Plant Manager

Plant manager Paul Dorn wondered why his boss Leonard Hech had sent for him. Paul thought that Leonard had been tough on him lately; he was slightly uneasy at being asked to come to Leonard's office at a time when such meetings were unusual. "Close the door and sit down, Paul," invited Leonard. "I've been wanting to talk to you." After preliminary conversation, Leonard said that because Paul's latest project had been finished, he would receive the raise that he had been promised on its completion.

Leonard went on to say that since it was time for Paul's performance appraisal, they might as well do that now. Leonard explained that the performance appraisal was based on four criteria: (1) the amount of high-quality merchandise manufactured and shipped on time, (2) the quality of relationships with plant employees and peers, (3) progress in maintaining employee safety and health, and (4) reaction to demands of top management. The first criterion had a relative importance of 40 percent; the rest had a weight of 20 percent each.

On the first item, Paul received an excellent rating. Shipments were at an all-time high, quality was good, and few shipments had arrived late. On the second item, Paul also was rated excellent. Leonard said that plant employees and peers related well to Paul, that labor relations were excellent, and that there had been no major grievances since Paul had become plant manager.

However, on attention to matters of employee safety and health, the evaluation was below average. His boss stated that no matter how much he bugged Paul about improving housekeeping in the plant, he never seemed to produce results. Leonard also rated Paul below average on meeting demands from top management. He explained that Paul always answered yes to any request and then disregarded it, going about his business as if nothing had happened.

Seemingly surprised at the comments, Paul agreed that perhaps Leonard was right and that he should do a better job on these matters. Smiling as he left, he thanked Leonard for the raise and the frank appraisal.

As weeks went by, Leonard noticed little change in Paul. He reviewed the situation with an associate. "It's frustrating. In this time of rapid growth, we must make constant changes in work methods. Paul agrees but can't seem to make people break their habits and adopt more efficient ones. I find myself riding him very hard these days, but he just calmly takes it. He's well liked by everyone. But somehow, he's got to care about safety and housekeeping in the plant. And when higher management makes demands he can't meet, he's got to say, 'I can't do that and do all the other things you want, too.' Now he has dozens of unfinished jobs because he refuses to say no."

As he talked, Leonard remembered something Paul had told him in confidence once. "I take Valium for a physical condition I have. When I don't take it, I get symptoms similar to a heart attack. But I only take half as much as the doctor prescribed." Now, Leonard thought, I'm really in a spot. If the Valium is what is making him so lackadaisical, I can't endanger his health by asking him to quit taking it. And I certainly can't fire him. Yet, as things stand, he really can't implement all the changes we need to fulfill our goals for the next two years.

Questions

1. Do you feel a raise was justified in Paul's situation?
2. What could have been done differently in the performance appraisal session?
3. What can be done now to change the situation?

Exercise
Compensation Factors

Outlined below is a list of items that might be considered in determining an employee's compensation. Rank the items (one being most important, and eleven being least important) according to what you feel should be considered for an executive secretary's job.

Education.

Quantity of work.

Quality of work.

Knowledge of job.

Experience.

Seniority.

Cooperation with others.

Working conditions.

Dependability.

Initiative.

Personal qualities such as personality, appearance, and integrity.

What implications does your ranking have for rewarding employees?

Objectives

1. To explore organizational activities and managerial responsibilities for developing people.
2. To describe the process of orienting new employees.
3. To discuss the process and methods used in training managers and employees in the acquisition of skills, concepts, or rules.
4. To describe methods for evaluating training and management development activities.

Developing People within Organizations

Chapter Outline

Few organizations would admit that they can survive without it—yet some act as though they could.

Everyone knows what it is—yet management, unions, and workers often interpret it in light of their own job conditions.

It is going on all the time—yet much of it is done haphazardly.

It is futile to attempt it without the needed time and facilities—yet often those responsible for it lack either or both.

It costs money—yet at times there is not adequate budgetary appropriation for it.

It should take place at all levels—yet sometimes it is limited to the lowest operating levels.

It can help everyone do a better job—yet those selected for it often fear it.

It is foolish to start it without clearly defined objectives—yet this is occasionally done.

It cannot be ignored without costing the company money—yet some managers seem blind to this reality.

It should permeate the entire organization and be derived from the firm's theory and practice of management—yet sometimes it is shunted off to one department that operates more or less in isolation from the rest of the business.

*F. A. Phillips, W. M. Berliner, and J. J. Cribbin** [*]

Newly hired employees must be introduced to the organization and to their jobs. They must be trained to perform their jobs. Furthermore, current employees must regularly have their skills updated and must learn new skills. An organization should also be very concerned about developing the skills of its management team. This chapter will explore organizational activities and managerial responsibilities for developing its human resources.

HUMAN ASSET ACCOUNTING

Human asset accounting–attempt to place a value on an organization's human assets by measuring the costs incurred by organizations in recruiting, hiring, training, and developing their human assets.

Human asset, or human resource, accounting attempts to place a value on an organization's human assets. It measures the costs incurred by organizations in recruiting, hiring, training, and developing their human assets.[1] Basically, the proponents of human asset accounting feel that the quality of the human resources in an organization should be reflected on its balance sheet.

_____

* F. A. Phillips, W. M. Berliner, and J. J. Cribbin, *Management of Training Programs* (Homewood, Ill.: Richard D. Irwin, 1960), pp. 5–6.

Several methods have been suggested for finding the financial value of an organization's human resources:

1. *Start-up costs:* Derive the original costs of hiring and training personnel as well as the costs of developing working relationships.
2. *Replacement costs:* Estimate the cost of replacing current employees with others of equivalent talents and experiences.
3. *Present-value method:* Multiply the present value of wage payments for the future five years times the firm's efficiency ratio (which is a measure of the firm's rate of return in relation to the average rate of return for the industry).
4. *Goodwill method:* Allocate a portion of the company's earnings in excess of the industry average (goodwill) to human resources.[2]

Human asset accounting is not presently an acceptable accounting practice for financial reporting purposes.[3] However, direct costing, introduced as a management technique in 1939, has become accepted managerial accounting for internal purposes, although it has never been an accepted practice for either tax or financial reporting.[4] Thus, in order for the use of human asset accounting to become widespread, it must first be proven to be useful in practice.

ORIENTATION

Orientation is the introduction of new employees to the organization, their work unit, and their job. It comes from co-workers and the organization. The orientation from co-workers is usually unplanned and unofficial and it can provide the new employee with misleading and inaccurate information.[5] This is one of the reasons that it is important to have an orientation provided by the organization. An effective orientation program has an immediate and lasting impact on the new employee and can make the difference between a new employee's success or failure.

Orientation—introduction of new employees to the organization, their work unit, and their job.

Job applicants get some orientation to the organization even before they are hired, sometimes through the organization's reputation—how it treats employees and the types of products or services it provides. Also, during the selection process, applicants often see other general aspects of an organization and what their duties, working conditions, and pay will be.

After the employee is hired, the organization's formal orientation program begins. For all types of organizations, orientation should usually be conducted at two distinct levels:

1. General organizational orientation—presents topics of relevance and interest to all employees.

2. Departmental and job orientation—covers topics unique to the new employee's specific department and job.

Normally, the general orientation is given by the human resources/personnel department. Departmental and job orientation is generally handled by the new employee's manager.

Organizational Orientation

Organizational orientation should cover the needs of both the organization and the employee. A good balance is essential if the orientation program is to have positive results. The organization is interested in making a profit, providing good service to customers and clients, satisfying employee needs and well-being, and being socially responsible. New employees, on the other hand, generally are more interested in pay, benefits, and specific terms and conditions of employment.

Figure 19–1 provides a listing of suggested topics for an organization's orientation program.

Departmental and Job Orientation

The content of departmental and job orientation depends on the needs of the department and the skills and past experience of the new employee. Figure 19–2 provides a checklist for departmental and job orientation programs.

Orientation Kit

Orientation kit–packet of written information given to a new employee to supplement the verbal orientation program.

Each new employee should receive a kit or packet of information to supplement the verbal orientation program. This **orientation kit** is normally prepared by the human resource department and can provide a wide variety of materials. Care should be taken in its design. Essential information should be provided, but not too much information given. Materials that might be included in an orientation kit include:[6]

Organizational chart.

Map of the organization's facilities.

Copy of policy and procedures handbook.

List of holidays and fringe benefits.

Copies of performance appraisal forms and procedures.

Copies of other required forms (e.g., expense reimbursement form).

Emergency and accident prevention procedures.

Sample copy of company newsletter or magazine.

Telephone numbers and locations of key company personnel (e.g., security).

Copies of insurance plans.

FIGURE 19–1
Possible Topics for an Organizational Orientation Program

1. Overview of the company:
   □ Welcoming speech.
   □ Founding, growth, trends, goals, priorities, and problems.
   □ Traditions, customs, norms, and standards.
   □ Current specific functions of the organization.
   □ Products/services and customers served.
   □ Steps in getting product/service to customers.
   □ Scope of activities.
   □ Organization, structure, and relationship of company and its branches.
   □ Facts on key managerial staff.
   □ Community relations, expectations, and activities.

2. Key policies and procedures review.

3. Compensation:
   □ Pay rates and ranges.
   □ Overtime.
   □ Holiday pay.
   □ Shift differential.
   □ How pay is received.
   □ Deductions: required and optional, with specific amounts.
   □ Option to buy damaged products, and costs thereof.
   □ Discounts.
   □ Advances on pay.
   □ Loans from credit union.
   □ Reimbursement for job expenses.
   □ Tax shelter options.

4. Fringe benefits:
   □ Insurance:
     □ Medical-dental.
     □ Life.
     □ Disability.
     □ Workers' compensation.
   □ Holidays and vacations (e.g., patriotic, religious, birthday).
   □ Leave: personal illness, family illness, bereavement, maternity, military, jury duty, emergency, extended absence.
   □ Retirement plans and options.
   □ On-the-job training opportunities.
   □ Counseling services.
   □ Cafeteria.
   □ Recreation and social activities.
   □ Other company services to employees.

5. Safety and accident prevention:
   □ Completion of emergency data card (if not done as part of employment process).
   □ Health and first-aid clinics.
   □ Exercise and recreation centers.
   □ Safety precautions.

□ Reporting of hazards.
□ Fire prevention and control.
□ Accident procedures and reporting.
□ OSHA requirements (review of key sections).
□ Physical exam requirements.
□ Use of alcohol and drugs on the job.

6. Employee and union relations:
   □ Terms and conditions of employement review.
   □ Assignment, reassignment, and promotion.
   □ Probationary period and expected on-the-job conduct.
   □ Reporting of sickness and lateness to work.
   □ Employee rights and responsibilities.
   □ Manager and supervisor rights.
   □ Relations with supervisors and shop stewards.
   □ Employee organizations and options.
   □ Union contract provisions and/or company policy.
   □ Supervision and evaluation of performance.
   □ Discipline and reprimands.
   □ Grievance procedures.
   □ Termination of employment (resignation, layoff, discharge, retirement).
   □ Content and examination of personnel record.
   □ Communications: channels of communication—upward and downward—suggestion system, posting materials on bulletin board, sharing new ideas.
   □ Sanitation and cleanliness.
   □ Wearing of safety equipment, badges, and uniforms.
   □ Bringing things onto, and removing things from, company grounds.
   □ On-site political activity.
   □ Gambling.
   □ Handling of rumors.

7. Physical facilities:
   □ Tour of facilities.
   □ Food services and cafeteria.
   □ Restricted areas for eating.
   □ Employee entrances.
   □ Restricted areas (e.g., from cars).
   □ Parking.
   □ First aid.
   □ Rest rooms.
   □ Supplies and equipment.

8. Economic factors:
   □ Costs of damage, by select items, with required sales to balance.
   □ Costs of theft with required sales to compensate.
   □ Profit margins.
   □ Labor costs.
   □ Cost of equipment.
   □ Costs of absenteeism, lateness, and accidents.

Source: "The Complete Employee Orientation Program," by Walter D. St. John, Copyright May 1980, pp. 376–77. Reprinted with the permission of *Personnel Journal,* Costa Mesa, California; all rights reserved.

FIGURE 19–2
Possible Topics for Departmental and Job Orientation Programs

1. Department functions:
   - Goals and current priorities.
   - Organization and structure.
   - Operational activities.
   - Relationship of functions to other departments.
   - Relationships of jobs within the department.

2. Job duties and responsibilities:
   - Detailed explanation of job, based on current job description and expected results.
   - Explanation of why the job is important, how the specific job relates to others in the department and company.
   - Discussion of common problems and how to avoid and overcome them.
   - Performance standards and basis of performance evaluation.
   - Number of daily work hours and times.
   - Overtime needs and requirements.
   - Extra-duty assignments (e.g., changing duties to cover for an absent worker).
   - Required records and reports.
   - Checkout on equipment to be used.
   - Explanation of where and how to get tools, have equipment maintained and repaired.
   - Types of assistance available; when and how to ask for help.
   - Relations with state and federal inspectors.

3. Policies, procedures, rules, and regulations:
   - Rules unique to the job and/or department.
   - Handling emergencies.
   - Safety precautions and accident prevention.
   - Reporting of hazards and accidents.
   - Cleanliness standards and sanitation (e.g., cleanup).
   - Security, theft problems and costs.
   - Relations with outside people (e.g., drivers).
   - Eating, smoking, chewing gum, etc., in department area.
   - Removal of things from department.
   - Damage control (e.g., smoking restrictions).
   - Time clock and time sheets.
   - Breaks/rest periods.
   - Lunch duration and time.
   - Making and receiving personal telephone calls.
   - Requisitioning supplies and equipment.
   - Monitoring and evaluating employee performance.
   - Job bidding and requesting reassignment.
   - Going to cars during work hours.

4. Tour of department:
   - Rest rooms and showers.
   - Fire-alarm box and fire extinguisher stations.
   - Time clocks.
   - Lockers.
   - Approved entrances and exists.
   - Water fountains and eye-wash systems.
   - Supervisors' quarters.
   - Supply room and maintenance department.
   - Sanitation and security offices.
   - Smoking areas.
   - Locations of services to employees related to department.
   - First-aid kit.

5. Introduction to department employees

Source: "The Complete Employee Orientation Program," by Walter D. St. John, Copyright May 1980, p. 377. Reprinted with permission of *Personnel Journal*, Costa Mesa, California; all rights reserved.

Many organizations require employees to sign a form stating that they have received and read the orientation kit. In unionized organizations, this protects the company if a grievance arises and the employee claims not to be aware of certain company policies and procedures. However, whether signing a document really encourages new employees to read the kit is questionable.

TRAINING EMPLOYEES

Training–process that involves acquiring skills or learning concepts to increase employee performance.

Training is a process that involves acquiring skills or learning concepts to increase the performance of employees. Generally, the new employee's manager has primary responsibility for training in how to perform the job.

Sometimes this is delegated to a senior employee in the department. Regardless, the quality of this initial training can greatly influence the employee's job attitude and productivity.

Economic, social, technological, and governmental changes also influence the skills needed in an organization. Changes in these areas can make current skills obsolete in a short time. Also, planned organizational changes and expansions can make it necessary for employees to update their skills or acquire new ones.

Determining Training Needs

Training must be aimed at the achievement of some organizational objective, such as more efficient production methods, improved quality of products/services, or reduced operating costs. An organization should only commit its resources to training that can help in achieving its objectives. Deciding specific training activities in an organization requires a systematic and accurate analysis of training needs.

A variety of methods can be used to determine an organization's training needs.[7] Company reports and records provide clues to internal trouble spots. Records on absenteeism, turnover, tardiness, and accident rates provide objective evidence of problems. Because this type of information already exists, it can be collected and examined with minimal effort and interruption of the work flow. Interviews with employees, questionnaires, and group discussions can also be used to locate training needs. Personal observations of work being performed can also give insight into performance problems that may be corrected through training.

Establishing Training Objectives

After training needs have been determined, objectives must be set for meeting these needs. Unfortunately, many training programs have no goals. "Training for training's sake" appears to be the maxim. With this philosophy, it is almost impossible to evaluate the strengths and weaknesses of a training program.

In general, objectives should define the skills to be acquired or concepts to be learned from the training. They should be in writing and be measurable. Until an organization decides what results it expects from training, it cannot determine the content or method of instruction.[8]

METHODS OF TRAINING

Several methods can be used to satisfy an organization's training needs and accomplish its objectives. Some of the more commonly used methods include on-the-job training, job rotation, vestibule training, apprenticeship training, classroom training, and programmed instruction.

On-the-Job Training and Job Rotation

On-the-job training (OJT)–normally given by a senior employee or supervisor; trainee is shown how to perform the job and allowed to do it under the trainer's supervision.

On-the-job training (OJT) is normally given by a senior employee or supervisor. The trainee is shown how to perform the job and allowed to do it under the trainer's supervision.

One form of on-the-job training is job rotation, sometimes called cross-training. Under OJT, an employee learns several different jobs within a work unit or department and performs each for a specified time period. One main advantage of job rotation is that it allows flexibility in the department. For example, when one member of a work unit is absent, another can perform that job.

One advantage of OJT is that no special facilities are required; also, the new employee does productive work during the learning process. Its major disadvantage is that the pressures of the workplace can cause training to be haphazard or neglected.

Several steps can be taken to ensure that job training is effective. The following five steps should be followed in any type of on-the-job training:

Prepare the employee for learning the job. The desire to learn a new job is almost always present in an employee. Showing an interest in the person, explaining the job's importance, and explaining why it must be done right enhance the employee's desire to learn. Knowing the employee's previous work experience in similar jobs enables the trainer to use that experience in explaining the present job or to eliminate explanations that are unnecessary.

Break down the work into components and identify the key points. This breakdown consists of defining the segments which make up the total job. In each segment, something is done to advance the work toward completion. The breakdown can be seen as a detailed road map which helps guide the employee through the entire work cycle in a rational, easy-to-understand manner, without injury to the person or damage to the equipment.

Any directive or information that helps the employee perform a work component correctly, easily, and safely is a key point. Key points are the "tricks of the trade" and are given to the employee to help reduce learning time. Observing and mastering the key points help the employee to acquire needed skills and perform the work more effectively.

Demonstrate the proper way to perform the job. Simply telling an employee how to perform a job is usually not enough. An employee must not only be told but also must be shown how to do the job. Each component of the job must be demonstrated. While each is being shown, the key points for that component should be explained. Employees should be encouraged to ask questions about each component.

<u>Allow the employee to perform the job.</u>   An employee should perform the job under the guidance of the trainer. Generally, an employee should be required to explain what to do at each phase of the job. If the explanation is correct, the employee is then allowed to perform the phase. If it is incorrect, the mistake should be corrected before the employee is allowed to actually perform the phase. Praise and encouragement are essential.

<u>Gradually put the employee on his or her own.</u>   When the trainer is reasonably sure that an employee can do the job alone, the employee should be allowed to work at his or her own pace and should be left alone while developing skills in performing the job. An employee should not be turned loose and forgotten. The trainer should return periodically to answer any questions and see that all is going well. An employee will have questions and will make better progress if the trainer is available to answer them and help with problems.

Figure 19–3 outlines the job instruction training (JIT) system, which is an old, yet still effective method for ensuring that on-the-job training is properly conducted.

FIGURE 19–3
Steps in the JIT System

Determining the training objectives and preparing the training area.
1. Decide what the trainee must be taught: so he or she can do the job efficiently, safely, economically, and intelligently.
2. Provide the right tools, equipment, supplies, and material.
3. Have the workplace properly arranged, just as the employee will be expected to keep it.

Presenting the instruction.
Step 1:   Preparation of the trainee.
   1. Put the trainee at ease.
   2. Find out what the trainee already knows about the job.
   3. Get the trainee interested in, and desirous of, learning the job.

Step 2:   Presentation of the operations and knowledge.
   1. Tell, show, illustrate, and question to put over the new knowledge and operations.
   2. Instruct slowly, clearly, completely, and patiently, one point at a time.
   3. Check, question, and repeat.
   4. Make sure the trainee understands.

Step 3:   Performance tryout.
   1. Test the trainee by having him or her perform the job.
   2. Ask questions beginning with why, how, when, or where.
   3. Observe performance, correct errors, and repeat instructions, if necessary.
   4. Continue until the trainee is competent in the job.

Step 4:   Follow-up.
   1. Put the trainee on his or her own.
   2. Check frequently to be sure the trainee follows instructions.
   3. Taper off extra supervision and close follow-up until the trainee is qualified to work with normal supervision.

Source: Adapted from *The Training within Industry Report* (War Manpower Commission: Bureau of Training, 1945), p. 195.

Vestibule Training

In **vestibule training,** procedures and equipment similar to those used in the actual job are set up in a special working area called a vestibule. The trainee is then taught how to perform the job by a skilled person and is able to learn the job at a comfortable pace without the pressures of production schedules.

The primary advantage of this method is that the trainer can stress theory and use of proper techniques rather than output, and the student can learn by actually doing the job. However, this method is expensive, and the employee still must adjust to the actual production environment. Vestibule training has been used for training typists, word processor operators, bank tellers, clerks, and others in similar jobs.

Apprenticeship Training

Apprenticeship training dates back to biblical times. It is frequently used to train personnel in skilled trades, such as carpenters, bricklayers, electricians, mechanics, and tailors. The apprenticeship period generally lasts from two to five years. During this time, the trainee works under the guidance of a skilled worker but receives lower wages than the skilled worker.

Classroom Training

Classroom training is conducted off the job and is probably the most familiar method of training. Classroom training is an effective means of getting information quickly to large groups with limited or no knowledge of the subject being presented. It is useful for teaching factual material, concepts, principles, and theories. Portions of orientation programs, some aspects of apprenticeship training, and safety programs are usually presented with some form of classroom instruction. However, classroom training is used more frequently for technical, professional, and managerial employees.

Programmed Instruction

The increased availability and lower cost of computers have made the use of programmed instruction more attractive. **Programmed instruction** requires the trainee to read material on a particular subject and then to answer questions about the subject. If the answers are correct, the trainee moves on to more advanced or new material. If the answers are incorrect, the trainee is required to reread the material and answer additional questions. The material in programmed instruction is presented either in text form

MANAGEMENT IN ACTION 19-1

SAFECO Offers Training by Computer

SAFECO, which operates computers in various aspects of the insurance business, is offering its 6,500 insurance agents the opportunity to take training courses in the comfort of their own offices. The courses are designed so agents can take them at their convenience and work at their own speed. The most important benefit is that agents can learn in their offices while still being able to service their clients.

The first course, which teaches the use of computer terminals, was introduced in 1980. A course on private passenger auto rating has also been added since then. It can be completed in four to six hours.

Two agents who recently discovered the convenience of the computer-taught courses are Cynthia Caldwell of the Frank B. Hall Agency in Seattle and Ruth McCoy of the Torrence Insurance Agency in Longview, Washington.

Caldwell was the first agent to complete the new auto rating course; McCoy was the first to complete the course for continuing-education credits. They not only received the training in their offices; they were able to take the examinations at their terminals. When they finished, the scores flashed on the screens immediately so they didn't have to wait to find out if they had passed.

Source: Adapted from Alfred G. Haggerty, "SAFECO Offers Training by Computer," *National Underwriter (Property and Casualty Insurance Edition)*, July 1, 1983, pp. 2, 14.

or on computer video displays. Regardless of the type of presentation, programmed instruction provides active practice, a gradual increase in difficulty over a series of steps, immediate feedback, and an individualized rate of learning. It normally is used to teach factual information. Management in Action 19-1 illustrates one form of computerized programmed instruction.

MAKING TRAINING MEANINGFUL

To make all types of training more meaningful, there are several common pitfalls that a manager should avoid. Lack of reinforcement is one. An employee who is praised for doing a job well is likely to be motivated to do it well again. Praise and recognition can very effectively reinforce an employee's learning. Too many managers only point out mistakes. And they often tell people, "I'll let you know if you do the job wrong." However, people also want to know when they do the job right. Feedback regarding progress is critical to effective learning. Setting standards for trainees and measuring performance against them encourage learning.

"Practice makes perfect" definitely applies to the learning process. Too many managers try to explain the job quickly—then they expect the person to do it perfectly the first time. Having trainees perform a job or explain how to perform it focuses their concentration and helps learning. Repeating a job or task several times also helps. Learning is always aided by practice and repetition.

Managers sometimes also have preconceived and inaccurate ideas about what certain people or groups of people can or can't do (the Pygmalion effect). A manager should realize that different people learn at different rates. Some learn rapidly; some learn more slowly. A manager shouldn't expect everyone to pick the job up right away. The pace of the training should be adjusted to the trainee. Also, if a person is not a fast learner, this does not mean that the person will always be a poor performer. The manager should take the attitude that all people can and want to learn.

MANAGEMENT DEVELOPMENT

Management development–developing the attitudes and skills necessary to become or remain an effective manager.

Management development is concerned with developing the attitudes and skills necessary to become or remain an effective manager. To be successful, it must have the full support of the organization's top executives. Management development should be designed, conducted, and evaluated on the basis of the goals of the organization, the needs of the managers involved, and probable changes in the organization's management team.

Needs Assessment

Numerous methods have been proposed for use in assessing management development needs. The management development needs of any organization are composed of the aggregate, or overall, needs of the organization and the development needs of each manager within the organization.

Organizational needs.   The most common method for determining organizational management development needs is an analysis of problem areas within the organization.[9] For example, increases in the number of grievances or accidents within an area of the organization often signal the need for management development. High turnover rates, absenteeism, or tardiness might also indicate management development needs. Projections based on the organization's objectives and on changes in its management team are also used to determine overall management development needs.

Needs of individual managers.   The performance of the person is the primary indicator of individual development needs. Performance evaluations of each manager can be examined to determine areas that need strengthening. The existence of problem situations within a manager's work unit can also signal needs. Planned promotions or reassignments also often indicate the need for development.

Establishing Management Development Objectives

After the management development needs of an organization have been determined, objectives for the overall management development program and for individual programs must be established to meet these needs. Both types of objectives should be written and measurable.

One classification system for overall management development objectives involves routine, problem-solving, and innovative objectives.[10] Routine, or regularly occurring, objectives might include supervisory training for new managers. Specifically, these might include targets for the number of trainees, hours of training, cost per trainee, and time required for trainees to reach a standard level of knowledge.

The second category of objectives is concerned with problem areas within the organization that are to be addressed through management development. They would result from a needs assessment of management reports on such factors as absenteeism, turnover, safety, and number of grievances. Also, managers could be interviewed or polled through questionnaires.

Innovative objectives are aimed at achieving higher levels of performance with new techniques to improve the quality of management, reduce the cost of management development, or ensure more effective development activities.

The difference between problem-solving and innovative objectives is shown by the following example:

An organization notices a sudden increase in employee grievances. To correct this, a new development program is designed to improve the human relations skills of supervisors. If the number of grievances then returns to normal or is reduced even further, the situation has been remedied. The problem-solving objective has been met. In another company, new supervisors have received most of their training in the form of classroom lectures; this method appears to be meeting the organization's needs. However, the human resource department, seeing room for improvement, starts a program of combined home study and programmed learning. If the new supervisors can now build their skills faster or at a lower cost, an innovative objective has been achieved.

After these overall management development objectives have been set, individual program goals must be identified. They should specify the skills or attitudes expected from the program. After these objectives have been developed, course content and method of instruction can be specified.

Methods Used in Management Development

Some of the most popular methods of management development, listed in Figure 19–4, are discussed below.

Understudy Assignments

Understudy assignments generally are used to develop an employee to fill a specific job. The person who will someday have a specific job works for the incumbent to learn the job. The title of the heir apparent is usually

Understudy assignments—OJT where an individual, designated as heir to a job, learns the job from the present jobholder.

FIGURE 19–4
Selected Methods Used in Management Development

On the Job	Off the Job
Understudy assignments	Classroom training
Coaching	Lectures
Experience	Case studies
Job rotation	Role playing
Special projects and committee	In-basket techniques
assignments	Business games
	University and professional association
	seminars

assistant manager, administrative assistant, or assistant to a particular manager.

There is one main advantage of understudy assignments. The heir realizes the purpose of the training and can learn in a practical and realistic situation without being directly responsible for operating results. On the negative side, however, the understudy learns the bad as well as the good practices of the incumbent. In addition, understudy assignments that last a long time can become expensive. If an understudy assignment system is used, one or more of the other management development methods should also be used.

Coaching

Coaching–management development conducted on the job, where experienced managers advise and guide trainees in solving managerial problems.

Coaching by experienced managers stresses the responsiblity of all managers for developing subordinates. Experienced managers advise and guide trainees in solving management problems. Coaching should allow the trainee to develop individual approaches to management with the counsel of a more experienced person.

One advantage to coaching is that the trainee gets practical experience and sees the results of decisions. The danger is that the coach may neglect the training or pass on incorrect management practices. The coach's expertise and experience are critical to this method.

Experience

Development through experience is used in many organizations. Employees are promoted into management jobs and allowed to learn on their own, from their daily experiences. The primary advantage is that the manager, trying to perform a certain job, may see the need for development and look for a way to get it. However, employees who have to learn on their own can create serious problems by making mistakes. Also, it is frustrating to try to manage without the needed background and knowledge. Serious problems can be avoided if experience is combined with other management development methods.

Job Rotation

Job rotation is designed to give an employee broad experience in many different areas of the organization. In understudy assignments, coaching, and experience, the trainee generally receives training and development for one particular job. In job rotation, the trainee goes from job to job within the organization, generally remaining in each from six months to a year. This technique is used often by large organizations for training recent college graduates.

Job rotation–employee learns several different jobs in a work unit or department and performs each for a specified time period.

Job rotation shows trainees how management principles can be applied in a cross section of environments. The training is practical; it also allows the trainee to become familiar with the company's entire operations. One disadvantage is that the trainee is often given menial work in each job. There is also a tendency to leave the trainee in each job too long.

Special Projects and Committee Assignments

Special projects require the employee to learn about a specific subject. For example, a trainee may be told to develop a training program on safety. This would require learning about the present internal safety policies and problems and about the safety training done by other companies. The person must also learn to work and relate to other employees. However—and this is critical—the special assignments must provide a developing and learning experience for the trainee and not just busywork.

Committee assignments, similar to special projects, can be used if the organization has standing or ad hoc committees. An employee works with the committee on its regular duties; thus, the person develops skills in working with others and learns through the activities of the committee.

Classroom Training

Classroom training is not only used in management development programs; it is also widely used in the orientation and training activities discussed earlier in this chapter. Therefore, some of the material in this section also applies to those activities. In addition, several of the approaches used in organization development (discussed later in this chapter) involve classroom training.

Lectures. With lecturing, the trainer has control and can present the material just as desired. The lecture is useful for presenting facts; however, its value in changing attitudes and in teaching skills is somewhat limited.

Case studies. This technique was popularized by the Harvard Business School. With this method, sample situations are presented for the trainee

Case study—classroom training where students analyze real or hypothetical situations and suggest what to do and how to do it.

to analyze. Ideally, the **case study** should force the trainee to think through problems, propose solutions, choose among them, and analyze the consequences of the decision. One primary advantage of the case study method is that it brings a note of realism to the instruction. However, case studies often are simpler than the real situations faced by managers. Also, when cases are discussed, there is often a lack of emotional involvement on the part of the participants; thus, attitude and behavioral changes are less likely to occur. Finally, the success of the case study method depends greatly on the skills of the instructor.[11]

Incident method—form of case study; students are given the general outline of a situation and are given additional information only as they request it.

One type of case study is the **incident method.** The trainee receives only the general outline of a situation. The trainer then provides more information as the trainee requests it. In theory, this method makes the trainee probe the situation and seek information, much as would be required in real life.

Role playing—trainees learn by acting out assigned roles in a realistic situation.

Role playing. In this method, trainees are required to act out assigned roles in a realistic situation. They learn from playing the roles. The success of this method depends on the ability of trainees to act realistically. Videotaping allows for review and evaluation of the exercise to improve its effectiveness.

In-basket technique—classroom training where trainee is required to handle a manager's mail and phone calls and react accordingly.

In-basket techniques. This technique simulates a realistic situation. It requires the trainee to answer one manager's mail and telephone calls. Important duties are interspersed with routine matters. One call may come from an important customer who is angry; another from a local civic club requesting a donation. The trainee analyzes the situation and suggests possible actions. Evaluation is based on the number and quality of decisions and on the priorities assigned to each situation. The **in-basket technique** has been used not only for management development but also in assessment centers. (They are discussed later in this chapter.)

Business game—classroom training that provides the setting of a company and its environment and requires team players to make operating decisions.

Business games. **Business games** generally provide a setting of a company and its environment and require a team of players to make operating decisions. Business games also normally require the use of computer facilities. Often, several different teams in a business game act as companies within an industry. This method forces trainees to work not only with other group members; they also must deal with competition within the industry. Advantages of business games are: they simulate reality; decisions are made in a competitive environment; feedback is provided about decisions; and decisions are made with less-than-complete data. The main problem is that many trainees simply attempt to determine the key to winning. When this occurs, the game is not used to its fullest potential as a learning device.[12]

University and Professional Association Seminars

Many colleges and universities offer both credit and noncredit courses to help meet the management development needs of various organizations. These courses range from principles of supervision to advanced executive management programs. Professional associations—such as the American

MANAGEMENT IN ACTION 19–2

Management Development at Young & Rubicam (Y&R) Advertising Agency

To keep on top of its growth, continue to turn out its own management talent pool, and ensure that all employees at Y&R's various new and old offices remain faithful to the Y&R modus operandi, this advertising agency has found it necessary to create what would be called its own in-house college.

There are 18 separate management development programs at Y&R, covering strategy, creative print, broadcast, direct marketing, selling, lawful interviewing, performance appraisal, time management, writing, and presentation skills. One of

the most grueling of the 18 courses is the Advertising Skills Workshop. Held twice a year, this course requires the Y&R managers to spend five and one-half weeks in a classroom, from 8:30 A.M. to 5:30 P.M. daily. Participants are taught the Y&R way of doing things, as well as key points in handling clients.

Throughout the course, the participants apply what they have learned to a case study which is either real or is based on a real-life situation. In a recent course, the test case was a hypothetical Better for You food line from General Foods. Ultimately, students make presentations based on what they've learned.

Source: Adapted from Christy Marshall, "Y&R a Heavy Investor in Executive Training," *Advertising Age*, March 14, 1983, p. 72.

Management Association—also offer a wide variety of management development programs. Many of the classroom techniques discussed in this chapter are used in these programs.

The Appendix at the end of this chapter provides, in summary form, a comparison of the strengths and weaknesses of several methods of employee development. Management in Action 19–2 demonstates one company's approach to employee development.

ASSESSMENT CENTERS

An **assessment center** utilizes a formal procedure to evaluate a person's potential as a manager and determine that person's development needs. Assessment centers are used in both the selection and development of managers. Basically, these centers simulate the problems that a person might face in a real managerial situation. Presently, more than 2,000 companies use assessment centers. Because of its validity, assessment center use has continued to grow.[13] AT&T was one of the earliest and best-known users of assessment centers.

In the typical center, 10 to 15 employees of about equal rank are brought together for three to five days to work on individual and group exercises typical of a managerial job. Business games, situational problems, interviews, and cases are normally used. These exercises involve the employees in decision making, leadership, written and oral communication, planning, organiz-

Assessment center– evaluates an individual's potential as a manager and determines the person's development needs based on his or her reactions in a simulated, "real world" environment.

ing, and motivation. Assessors observe the participants, rate their performance, and provide feedback to them about their performance and developmental needs.

Assessors are often selected from management ranks several levels above those of the participants. Also, psychologists from outside the organization often serve as assessors. For a program to be successful, the assessors must be thoroughly trained in the assessment process, the mechanics of the exercises to be observed, and the techniques of observing and providing feedback.

One attractive feature of assessment centers is extensive research showing the technique is valid in predicting managerial success.[14] Furthermore, participants learn from the feedback what their strong and weak points are and they are often advised how to improve their skills in a particular area.

However, some operational problems can arise in using assessment centers. First, the organization must recognize that they are often more costly than other methods of management assessment and development.[15] Problems can occur when employees come from different levels in the organization. When their differences become apparent, lower level participants often defer in the group exercises to those at higher levels; thus, the assessment results are biased. Finally, certain "canned" exercises may only be remotely related to the on-the-job activity at the organization in question. Care must be taken to ensure that exercises used in the assessment center bring out the specific skills and aptitudes needed in the position for which participants are being assessed. Management in Action 19–3 describes an assessment center at Burlington Northern Railway.

EVALUATING EMPLOYEE TRAINING AND MANAGEMENT DEVELOPMENT ACTIVITIES

When the results of employee training and management development are evaluated, certain benefits accrue. Less effective programs can be withdrawn to save time and effort. Weaknesses within programs can be identified and remedied.[16]

Evaluation of training and management development can be broken down into four logical steps:

Step 1: Reaction. How well did the trainees like the program?

Step 2: Learning. What principles, facts, and concepts were learned in the program?

Step 3: Behavior. Did the job behavior of the trainees change because of the program?

Step 4: Results. What were the results of the program in terms of factors such as reduced costs or reduction in turnover?

Reaction evaluation generally uses questionnaires administered at the end of the training program. Trainee reactions can be checked just after the

MANAGEMENT IN ACTION 19–3

Assessment Centers at Burlington Northern Railroad (BN)

BN wanted to create a reservoir of people to compete for higher-level jobs, make sure its managers had the skills that would make them promotable, and make sure its sales representatives could gain some experience in what the management environment is all about so that they could decide whether they're cut out to compete for managerial-level positions.

It used assessment centers to meet its needs. In 1982, it conducted 10 assessment centers of 10 persons each. It ensured assessments would be fair by qualifying 30 people as assessors and by having each participant assessed by four assessors.

Two weeks after each session, results were sent to the participants, showing what their pattern of performance had been, where they were strong and where they were weak, and indicating their needs for skill development.

Source: Adapted from "Sharpening Sales Skills," *Railway Age*, August 1983, pp. 56–57.

training and again several weeks later. The major flaw in using only reaction evaluation is that the enthusiasm of trainees is not necessarily evidence of improved ability and future performance.

Learning evaluation measures how well the trainee has learned the principles, facts, and concepts presented in the program. Behavior evaluation measures how the training has influenced the employees' behavior on the job. Each requires testing of the trainee's knowledge and behavior both before and after training. Also, control groups—which do not receive the training but match the training group as closely as possible in all other respects—are required for learning and behavior evaluations. Comparison of pretest and posttest data on trainees identifies the changes in knowledge and behavior. Comparison of data from the control group and the trainee group helps to identify factors other than training that may have produced the change.

Results evaluation attempts to measure changes in variables such as turnover, absenteeism, accident rates, tardiness, and productivity. As with learning and behavior evaluation, pretests, posttests, and control groups are required in performing an accurate results evaluation.

Even when great care is taken in designing evaluation procedures, it is hard to determine the exact effect of training and management development activities on learning, behavior, and results. Because of this, the evaluation of training and management development is still limited and often superficial.

SUMMARY

Human asset accounting attempts to place a value on an organization's human assets by measuring the costs incurred by organizations in recruiting, hiring, training, and developing their human assets. Orientation is the introduction of new employees to the organization, their work unit, and their job. Orientation is conducted at two distinct levels—general organizational and departmental and job orientation.

Training is a process that involves acquiring skills or learning concepts to increase one's performance. Training must be objective oriented. Some of the methods for achieving training objectives are on-the-job training, job rotation, vestibule training, apprenticeship training, and classroom training.

Management development is concerned with developing the attitudes and skills needed to become or remain an effective manager. If it is to be effective, a needs assessment must be made, and objectives must be set. Some of the more popular methods used in management development include understudy assignments, coaching, experience, job rotation, special projects and committee assignments, and classroom training.

Assessment centers utilize a formal procedure aimed at evaluating a person's potential as a manager and determining his or her development needs. Presently, more than 2,000 companies use assessment centers.

Evaluation of training and management development can be broken down into four logical steps: reaction evaluation, learning evaluation, behavior evaluation, and results evaluation.

References and Additional Readings

[1] Bruce E. Meyers and Hugh H. Shane, "Human Resource Accounting for Managerial Decisions; Capital Budgeting Approach," *Personnel Administrator,* January 1984, p. 29.

[2] Michael H. Gilbert, "The Asset Value of the Human Organization," *Management Accounting,* July 1970, pp. 26–27.

[3] Jacob B. Paperman and Desmond D. Martin, "Human Resource Accounting: A Managerial Tool?" *Personnel,* March–April 1977, p. 45.

[4] Ibid.

[5] See, for instance, M. R. Louis, "Surprise and Sense Making: What Newcomers Experience in Entering Unfamiliar Organizational Settings," *Administrative Science Quarterly,* June 1980, pp. 226–51.

[6] Walter D. St. John, "The Complete Employee Orientation Program," *Personnel Journal,* May 1980, p. 375.

[7] S. V. Steadman, "Learning to Select a Needs Assessment Strategy," *Training and Development Journal,* January 1980, pp. 56–61.

[8] For more information, see R. F. Mager, *Preparing Instructional Objectives* (Belmont, Calif.: Fearon Publishers, 1972).

[9] L. A. Digman, "Determining Management Development Needs," *Human Resource Management,* Winter 1980, p. 13.

[10] George Odiorne, *Personnel Administration by Objectives* (Homewood, Ill.: Richard D. Irwin, 1971), pp. 338–51.

[11] For an in-depth discussion on the case method, see C. Argyris, "Some Limitations of the Case Method: Experiences in a Management Development Program," *Academy of Management Review,* April 1980, pp. 291–98.

[12] For a further discussion of business games, see B. Hunter and M. Price, "Business Games: Underused Learning Tools?" *Industry Week,* August 18, 1980, pp. 52–56.

[13] L. A. Digman, "How Well-Managed Organizations Develop Their Executives," *Organizational Dynamics,* Autumn 1978, pp. 65–66. See also the entire February 1980 issue of *Personnel*

Administrator, which is devoted to an analysis of assessment centers.

[14] Louis Olivas, "Using Assessment Centers for Individual and Organizational Development," *Personnel,* May–June 1980, p. 63.

[15] Donald H. Brush and Lyle F. Schoenfeldt, "Identifying Managerial Potential: An Alterna-

tive to Assessment Centers," *Personnel,* May–June 1980, p. 71.

[16] For a discussion of evaluation procedures for management development activities, see L. A. Digman, "How Companies Evaluate Management Development Programs," *Human Resource Management,* Summer 1980, pp. 9–13.

Review Questions

1. What is human asset accounting?
2. What is orientation?
3. Describe the two distinct levels at which orientation is normally conducted within organizations.
4. What is training?
5. Describe the following methods of training.
   a. On-the-job.
   b. Job rotation.
   c. Vestibule.
   d. Apprenticeship.
   e. Programmed instruction.
6. What is management development?
7. Describe the following methods used in management development:
   a. Understudy assignments.
   b. Coaching.
   c. Experience.
   d. Job rotation.
   e. Special projects and committee assignments.
   f. Classroom training.
8. What is an assessment center?
9. Describe four logical steps in the evaluation of training and management development.

Discussion Questions

1. "Why should we train our employees? It is a waste of money because they soon leave and another organization gets the benefits." Discuss.
2. Outline a system for evaluating a development program for supervisors.
3. "Management games are fun, but you don't really learn anything from them." Discuss.
4. Why are training programs generally one of the first areas to be eliminated when an organization must cut its budget?

Incident 19–1
Starting a New Job

Jack Smythe, branch manager for a large computer manufacturer, has just been told by his marketing manager Bob Sprague, that Otis Brown has given two weeks' notice. When Jack had interviewed Otis, he had been convinced of the applicant's tremendous potential in sales. Otis was bright and personable, an honor graduate in electrical engineering from Massachusetts Institute of Technology who had the qualifications that the company looked for in computer sales. Now he was leaving after only two months with the company. Jack called Otis into his office for an exit interview.

Jack: Come in, Otis, I really want to talk to you. I hope I can change your mind about leaving.

Otis: I don't think so.

Jack: Well, tell me why you want to go. Has some other company offered you more money?

Otis: No. In fact, I don't have another job. I'm just starting to look.

Jack: You've given us notice without having another job?

Otis: Well, I just don't think this is the place for me!

Jack: What do you mean?

Otis: Let me see if I can explain. On my first day at work, I was told that my formal classroom training in computers would not begin for a month. I was given a sales manual and told to read and study it for the rest of the day.

   The next day I was told that the technical library, where all the manuals on computers are kept, was in a mess and needed to be organized. That was to be my responsibility for the next three weeks.

   The day before I was to begin computer school, my boss told me that the course had been delayed for another month. He said not to worry, however, because he was going to have James Chess, the branch's leading salesperson, give me some on-the-job training. I was told to accompany James on his calls. I'm supposed to start the school in two weeks, but I've just made up my mind that this place is not for me.

Jack: Hold on a minute, Otis. That's the way it is for everyone in the first couple months of employment in our industry. Any place you go will be the same. In fact, you had it better than I did. You should have seen what I did in my first couple of months.

Questions

1. What do you think about the philosophy of this company pertaining to a new employee's first few months on the job?

2. What suggestions do you have for Jack to help his company avoid similar problems of employee turnover in the future?

Incident 19-2
Development—For What?

The Matlock Corporation began an extensive management development program several years ago. The company's personnel director felt that this program would benefit the company by providing a ready source of promotable people for filling vacancies as they occurred in the company. Up to this point, promotions had often been filled by personnel from outside the company.

Managers at all levels of the organization became involved in the management development program. They took in-company classes on subjects such as general management and time management. Also, they were encouraged to improve other skills by taking night courses at the local college at company expense. Many of the managers did in fact enroll in several of the courses.

At the time the program was initiated and at subsequent management development meetings, the participants were advised by top management that the program was designed to improve their management skills and to qualify them for future promotions within the company.

Jane Martin, a section supervisor, has been with the company for over 10 years. She has diligently participated in the management development program and has completed several night courses at the local college. Jane originally felt that this diligence on her part would be rewarded by a promotion when an opening developed. However, twice during the last year, outsiders have been hired to fill managerial positions within the company. In each case, Jane and other supervisors had applied for the vacancy; they felt that their experience plus the additional knowledge gained through the management development program made them better qualified than the outsider who was hired.

At a recent appraisal interview, Jane brought up this problem for discussion with her department manager. She was told that in each case, no supervisor within the company was thought to be qualified for the managerial opening. Jane expressed the opinion that the company management development program was a waste of time for the supervisors if the knowledge and experience gained were not recognized by higher levels of management. Jane's department manager explained that it takes time to develop a supervisor for higher-level responsibility. He also reminded Jane that employees are rewarded for their self-improvement by extra merit salary increases during their annual performance appraisals.

Questions

1. Do you think that Jane has a legitimate complaint?
2. Do you think the organization is "training for training's sake"?
3. How do you think that Jane's manager should have handled the problem?

Exercise
OJT

Assume you are training director for a large, local retail company. The company has seven department stores in your city. One of your biggest problems is adequately training new salesclerks. Because salesclerks represent your company to the public, the manner in which they conduct themselves is highly important. Especially critical aspects of their job include knowledge of the computerized cash register system, interaction with the customers, and knowledge of the particular products being sold.

A. Design a three-day orientation/training program for these salesclerks. Be sure to outline the specific topics (subjects) to be covered and the techniques to be used.
B. Specify what methods could be used to evaluate the success of the program.

Chapter 19 Appendix
Comparison of Training Methods

Method	Definition	Strengths	Weaknesses
1. Lecture	Speech by the instructor with very limited discussions.	Clear and direct methods of presentation. Good if there are more than 20 trainees. Materials can be provided to trainees in advance to help in their preparation. Trainer has control over time. Cost effective (cheap).	Since there is no discussion, it is easy to forget. Sometimes it is not effective. Requires high level of speaking ability. Requires high level of quick understanding by trainees.
2. Group discussion (conference)	Speech by the instructor with a lot of participation (questions and comments) from the listeners. Sometimes instructor not necessary; however, a leader is needed.	Good if the participants are small groups. Each participant has opportunity to present own ideas. More ideas can be generated.	Sometimes they get away from the subjects. Some group leaders or instructors do not know how to guide discussions. Sometimes one strong individual can dominate others.
3. Role playing	Create a realistic situation and have trainees assume parts of specific personalities in the situation. Their actions are based on the roles assigned to them. Emphasis is not on problem solving but rather on skill development.	Good if the situation is similar to the actual work situation. Trainees receive feedback which gives them confidence. Good for interpersonal skills. Teaches individuals how to act in real situations.	Trainees are not actors. Trainees sometimes are not serious. Some situations cannot be implemented in role playing. Uncontrolled role playing may not lead to any sufficient results. If it is very similar to actual life, it may produce adverse reactions.
4. Sensitivity training (laboratory training)	It is used for organizational development. Create situations and examine the participants' reaction and behavior, then having feedback about behavior. Group members exchange thoughts and feelings in unstructured ways.	Helps individuals to find the reasons for their behavior (self-insight). Helps individuals to know the effects of their behavior on others. Creates more group interactions.	People may not like information about their behavior, especially if it is negative. May lead to conflict and anger among the group. May not be related or transferrable to jobs.
5. Case study	A written narrative description of a real situation, issue, or incident which a manager faced in a particular organization. Trainees are required to propose suitable solution or make appropriate decision.	Cases are usually very interesting. High group discussion and interaction about many solutions, since there is no absolute solution. Develops trainees' abilities in effective communication and active participation.	Slow method of training. Often difficult to select the appropriate case study for specific training situation. Requires high level of skills by both trainees and trainer, as the discussion can become boring. Can create frustration on

Method	Definition	Strengths	Weaknesses
		Develops' trainees' ability to figure various factors that influence their decision building. Develops trainees' ability to make proper decisions in real-life situations (transfer of learning).	part of trainees, especially if they fail to arrive at specific solution.
6. Management games	Giving the trainees information about the organization and its environment, then dividing into teams. Each team is required to make operational decision and then evaluate its decision.	Develops practical experience for the trainees. Helps in transferring knowledge and in applying administrative thoughts. Helps to evaluate and correct the trainees' behavior.	Often, it is difficult to study the results of each team's decision. Some teams may not take it seriously. May be a slow process.
7. Simulation exercises	Same as management games, except a digital computer is used to input information and analyze the team decisions. Then, results of trainees' actions are evaluated and discussed.	Same as management games.	Same as management games. Very costly. Difficult to simulate very complex system.
8. Wilderness training	Several managers meet out of the workplace and live in cabins or tents for up to seven days. They test their survival skills and learn about their own potentials—for creativity, cooperation, etc.	People learn limits and capabilities.	Very costly. May not be transferable.
9. In-basket training	Create the same type of situation trainees face in daily work. Then observe them, how they arrange the situations, and their actions regarding them. Then evaluate on the basis of the number and quality of decisions. Used for MD and assessment centers.	Effective for corrective action or reinforcement. Widely used in assessment centers for measuring supervisory potential.	Tendency to be or become overly simplistic.
10. Incident process (problem solving)	Simple variation of the case study method. The basic elements are given to the trainee, who then asks the instructor for the most sufficient information which will help him in making his decision.	Has an immediate feedback from the instructor. Develops supervisory skills in seeking facts and decision making.	Requires high degree of instructing skills in forming answers.

Method	Definition	Strengths	Weaknesses
	The instructor will only give the requested information.		
11. Vestibule training	Setting up training area very similar to the work area in equipment, procedures and environment, but separated from the actual one so trainees can learn without affecting the production schedule. Used for training typists, bank tellers, etc.	Fast way to train employees. Trainees can get the most from this method.	Very expensive.
12. Apprenticeship training	Trainee works under guidance of skilled, licensed instructor and receives lower pay than licensed workers.	Develops special skills like mechanical, electronic, tailoring, etc. Extensive training.	Takes a long time.
13. Internship training	According to agreement, individuals in these programs earn while they learn, but at a lower rate than if they worked full-time.	More chance for trainees to apply what they have learned. Trainee gets exposure to both organization and job.	Takes a long time.
14. Projects	Like group discussion method. Trainees together analyze data and reach conclusion.	Helps trainees to know more about the subject.	Requires instructor's time to ensure the group is going in the right direction.
15. Video tapes and movies	Recording and producing certain events or situations with clear descriptions in order to cover certain subjects. Can be shown many times, then reviewed and discussed to help trainees understand more fully.	Tapes can be played many times to ensure individual's understanding. Many events and discussions can be put on one tape. Because length time is known, presentation and follow-up can be scheduled.	Recording and producing has to be done by professionals to get good quality. Expensive (a typical 20- to 30-minute cassette costs $50, without projector or screen).
16. Multiple management	Lower- and middle-level managers participate formally with top management in planning and administration.	Helps top management to identify top management candidates. Enhances employees' participation in the organization.	

Source: Sulaiman M. Al-Malik, unpublished paper, Georgia State University, Winter 1985.

Section 5 Case
The Coca-Cola Company*

A three-legged brass pot stands in the middle of one of U.S. industry's most colorful corporate legends. From this pot, Dr. John Smyth Pemberton is said to have poured a syrup which he carried to Jacobs' Pharmacy in Atlanta, Georgia, on May 8, 1886. The product was mixed with soda water and served as a fountain beverage. Sold for 5 cents a glass, Coke sales averaged $.65 a day (13 drinks!) for the remainder of 1886. Since that time, Coca-Cola has become one of the world's most common trademarks; the brass pot has been replaced by an organization selling soft-drink, food, and entertainment products to people in more than 135 countries.

With 1984 revenues in excess of $7.3 billion, the company is easily the world's largest producer of soft-drink beverages, producing more than 35 percent of the soft drinks consumed worldwide. In addition to sheer size, several developments during the last decade have pointed to the increasing demands on personnel and the importance of human resource development.

With the beginning of Roberto C. Goizueta's chairmanship in 1981, Coca-Cola shed its conservative image in favor of an aggressive new strategy with growth in earnings as a primary objective. With 1982 earnings of $512 million, the management team set a goal for annual earnings of $1 billion by 1990. In developing a strategy for attaining this goal, the planning process identified seven areas of particular concern—finance, competition, bottling, consumer, energy, technical, and human. To acknowledge the importance of the human factor, Chairman Goizueta made the following statement in his "Strategy for the 1980s" statement published in the company's 1982 Annual Report:

> Finally, let me comment on this vision as it affects our "lifestyle"—or business behavior—as a viable international business entity. I have previously referred to the *courage* and *commitment* that will be indispensable as we move through the 1980s. To this I wish to add *integrity* and *fairness* and insist that the combination of these four ethics be permeated from top to bottom throughout our organization so that our behavior will produce leaders, good managers, and—most importantly—entrepreneurs. It is my desire that we take initiatives as opposed to being only reactive and that we *encourage intelligent individual risk taking.*
>
> As a true international company with a multicultural and multinational employee complement, we must foster the "international family" concept which has been a part of our tradition. All employees will have equal opportunities to grow, develop and advance within the company. Their progress will depend only on their abilities, ambition, and achievements.

To foster the growth and development of Coca-Cola personnel, the Human Resources Development (HRD) area has the objectives of "attracting,

---

* This case was prepared by Thomas K. Glenn II, Emory University. Used by permission.

evaluating, developing, and retaining outstanding employees." Comprised of approximately 40 individuals, the HRD area is organized into four groups—Employment, Employee Training, Bottler Training, and Employee Development. In addition to full-time HRD personnel, the company retains a "faculty" made up of professors and experts in various areas who teach courses and provide specialized consultation.

Though the company is obviously dedicated to enhancing the quality of existing personnel, considerable effort is focused on the screening process prior to hiring. The employment group administers a one-and-a-half-day assessment process in evaluating an applicant's potential. Usually perceived as a positive experience, the procedure is frequently praised by applicants—some of whom do not eventually become Coke employees—for its thoroughness and effectiveness in pointing to logical career directions. Having hired individuals who meet established criteria, the company looks to the other three HRD groups—employee development, employee training, and bottler training to provide counseling and educational assistance as necessary.

Employee Development

The Employee Development Group addresses three primary objectives: staffing, evaluation, and development. The group's role in accomplishing these objectives is viewed as an iterative process, as shown in Exhibit 1.

As suggested by Exhibit 1, the Employee Development Group develops procedures for evaluating individuals and matching them with appropriate jobs. Additionally, the group develops and conducts evaluations to assist in training, guidance, and promotions. Programs produced by Employee Development are used by the Employee and Bottler Training groups, as well as by the Employment Group in its initial screening process.

More specific objectives are itemized as follows:

1. To develop talent in depth and in advance of anticipated staffing needs, enabling the company to promote from within wherever possible.
2. To attract and retain the most qualified employees available.
3. To identify employees with demonstrated potential and see that they have the opportunity to test themselves in positions with expanded responsibilities.
4. To match job abilities to job requirements effectively.
5. To maintain integrity in the selection and promotion process.
6. To improve employee and department performance levels.

Several important principles undergird the employee development process, two of which are employee participation and employee initiative. Written policy emphasizes the necessity of employee participation at every stage of the career development process—from establishing objectives to discussing

EXHIBIT 1
Career Development System

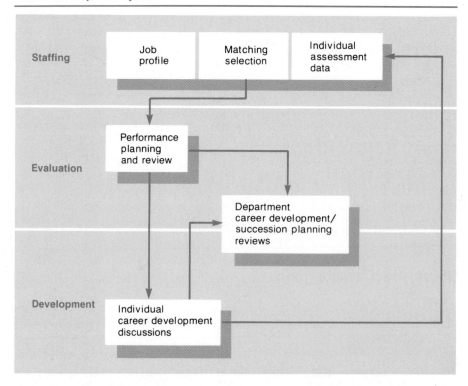

career interests and plans. Where employee initiative is concerned, it is felt that both the manager and the employee share responsibility for the employee's career. Despite the manager's role in this process, the employee must take the initiative in deciding personal goals and then making commitments to reach them.

Employee Training

Results from evaluation procedures developed by the Employee Development Group may lead a manager to conclude that certain employees need training to improve performance in their present jobs. Conversely, high-level achievers may show potential for assuming greater levels of responsibility or performing more-demanding tasks. In either case, the Employee Training Group provides a wide "curriculum" of in-house training and educational programs.

To communicate the group's activities to employees throughout the organization, a course catalog (similar in format to that used by many colleges) is made available to all employees and updated periodically through the

Employee Training Update. The catalog groups skills into various areas, such as effective business writing or project management, and lists courses which correspond to these areas. Exhibit 2 provides a partial list of courses adminis-tered by the Employee Training Group. As suggested by the course titles, programs are available for virtually all levels of employment.

EXHIBIT 2
Partial List of Course Offerings

Assertive Skills for On-the-Job Effectiveness
Leadership Workshop
The Changing Office Environment
Speed and Accuracy in Handling Numbers
Managing Programs and Projects
Basic Finance
Career Strategies for Managers and Professionals
The Computer: A Management Resource
The Personal Computer
Introduction to LOTUS 1–2–3™

In addition to performing a function that is purely educational in nature, the Employee Training Group plays a vital role in the area of communication. Three courses entitled "Orientation: The Coca-Cola Company," "Coca-Cola USA: In-Depth Orientation for Managers and Professionals," and "Employee Update" provide systematic briefings which address company history, values, policies, and recent changes.

If employees have educational needs that cannot be met by in-house programs, the Training Information Procedure (TIP) can help to find courses and seminars offered by outside sources. Such assistance ranges from provid-ing recommendations of programs to handling registration procedures for individuals enrolling in educational institutions.

Bottler Training

Though the Employee Training Group develops programs that are used in almost all areas of the company, a separate group within the HRD area is responsible for disseminating these and many other programs throughout the vast bottler network.

The Bottler Training Group provides an important service that is unique when compared to training facilities in many other large organizations. To better appreciate this, one must first understand some of the basic differences among types of franchise agreements.

A basic dimension of franchise agreements is their comprehensiveness. At one extreme lies the *product distribution* franchise in which franchisors provide the franchisees with goods in salable form. The franchisees operate under their own names, usually pay no franchise fee, and are frequently licensed to sell additional products offered by other franchisors. Compared with other types of franchises, product distribution agreements are not comprehensive. They seldom impose requirements on the franchisee's marketing or management activities. Such agreements simply provide a license to sell certain goods or services and are common in the marketing of furniture and home appliances.

At the other extreme lies the *pure,* or *comprehensive,* franchise. This type of arrangement provides the franchisee with a license to use a trade name, products or services to be sold, and a complete operating format. Procedures for production and quality control are usually specified, as well as design and appearance of the physical plant. Training of supervisors and employees is a frequent requirement. This type of agreement is common among fast-food franchises, of which McDonald's is a notable example.

Coca-Cola markets soft-drink products through more than 1,500 bottlers worldwide. Though some of these operations are company owned, the vast majority operate under franchise agreements. The comprehensiveness of these agreements falls somewhere between the two extremes described above. The franchised bottlers purchase Coca-Cola product ingredients, pay for the privilege of using the company trademark, and agree to adhere to various production and quality control standards. Beyond these requirements, bottlers operate in a decentralized structure that allows them considerable freedom in marketing, management, and personnel decisions. In stark contrast to the McDonald's franchisee, who must attend Hamburger University, or the Burger King operator, who must enroll in Whopper College, owners of Coca-Cola bottling franchises may obtain training for themselves and/or their employees from the Bottler Training Group, from some other sources, or may simply prefer to use their own approaches to train bottling plant employees internally.

A significant implication of this arrangement is that the Bottler Training Group does not have a "captive market" for its services. As a result, the group must "sell" its programs—a situation creating incentive to develop meaningful and productive training packages. Though evaluation techniques developed by the Employee Development Group and educational programs provided by the Employee Training Group are available to bottlers, Bottler Training offers additional training packages that are custom designed for bottling plant applications. Training systems are designed for seminar and in-plant video formats. Exhibit 3 provides a list of courses suggesting the industry-specific nature of the curriculum.

Basic Philosophies

Several characteristics appear as basic philosophies throughout the HRD area. First, there is a strong strategic planning orientation: Objectives and

> **EXHIBIT 3**
> **Examples of Bottler Training Courses**
>
> Line Supervisor's Training Seminar
> Empty Bottle Inspection
> Microbiological Testing
> Distribution Management Workshop
> In-Plant Safety
> Forklift and Materials Handling
> Product Handling on the Route
> Successful Selling in a Changing Market
> Managing Today's Fleet
> Train-the-Trainer Workshops

means of accomplishing them are carefully articulated and put in writing. Next, all HRD personnel are aware that they are performing roles which go beyond the functions of education and training. Communication and public/employee relations are of equal importance. "Selling the company" is a constant objective.

Reflecting Chairman Goizueta's statements about the importance of personal initiative, HRD's operating philosophy rests on the assumption that employees will take the initiative to utilize development and training opportunities. For the most part, access to programs is limited only by the employee's desire to participate. Programs are developed for capitalizing on initiative (as opposed to developing it). As a result, entry-level screening procedures attempt to identify individuals who possess initiative from the outset.

Finally, and in keeping with the strategic planning orientation, program implementation holds a level of importance equal to that of formulation. Once a training or evaluation technique is developed and validated, procedures for administration are systematized to assure proper usage.

6

Contemporary Issues in Management

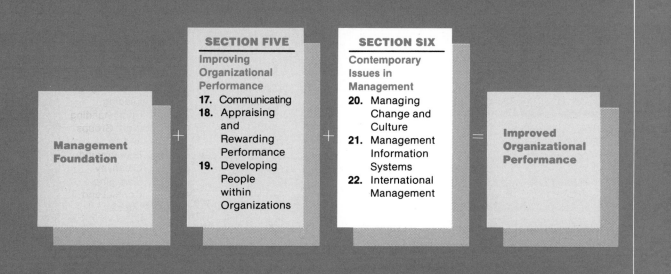

Management Foundation

+

SECTION FIVE

Improving Organizational Performance
17. Communicating
18. Appraising and Rewarding Performance
19. Developing People within Organizations

+

SECTION SIX

Contemporary Issues in Management
20. Managing Change and Culture
21. Management Information Systems
22. International Management

=

Improved Organizational Performance

The first five sections of this text concentrated on providing the foundation and ingredients necessary for developing a successful manager. All of the major segments of a manager's day-to-day job were covered. The purpose of this final section is to develop an appreciation for contemporary issues and possible future trends and thus develop not only successful managers but also responsible managers.

Chapter 20 is designed to develop an understanding for how today's pace of rapid change affects organizations. It also identifies and analyzes the role of corporate culture and its influence on corporate performance.

Management information systems are described in Chapter 21. This chapter is designed to develop an understanding of the role that computerized information systems play in modern organizations.

The final chapter in this text, Chapter 22 explores international management. The chapter emphasizes the growing necessity for managers to understand the nature of international management.

Objectives

1. To develop an understanding of how today's rapid rate of change affects organizations.
2. To present several methods for implementing change and reducing resistance to change.
3. To define the concept of corporate culture.
4. To identify and diagnose different types of corporate cultures.

20 Managing Change and Culture

Chapter Outline

MANAGING CHANGE
  Employee Reactions to Change
  Resistance to Change
  Reducing Resistance to Change
  Planned Change
  Organizational Development

MANAGING ORGANIZATIONAL
  CULTURE
  Cultural Forms of Expression
  How Does Culture Originate?
  Identifying Culture
  Changing Culture
SUMMARY

The serious business of modern American culture is that of taming, harnessing, subduing, tempering, rationalizing, and understanding the powerful and mystifying thing that we believe to be within us and around us, and to animate all things—which we call "nature." Our personal and collective values are all measured by this enterprise, whether we speak of health, sanity, performance, sportsmanship, morality, or progress. Our collective culture is a vast accumulation of material and spiritual achievements and resources stemming from the conquest of nature and necessary to the continuance of this effort. It includes the substantial foundations of our cities and economic life, the massive banks of "information" and "knowledge" that fill our libraries and computers, the triumphs of art and science, and the arcane and ubiquitous labryinths of technology. These are our heritage, our property, our life and our work, and our means of carrying forth our ideals and commitments.

Roy Wagner *

The two major topics of this chapter—<u>organizational change and organiza-tional culture—are inextricably related</u>. Both of these topics have recently been pushed to the forefront in management circles. The many reasons for heightened interest in these topics all relate to the increasing rate of change in today's world. The following analogy shows the rate of change in the modern world:

Suppose that we reduce to 12 months the total duration of the known period of history of man: some 30,000 years. In these 12 months which represent the life of all our ancestors from the Stone Age until the present, it is toward the 18th of October that the Iron Age begins. On the 8th of December, the Christian era begins.

On the 29th of December, Louis XVI ascends the throne of France. What mechanical power does mankind possess at that epoch? Exactly the same as that which the caveman had possessed plus whatever he was able to derive from draft animals after the invention of the yoke.

On the 30th of December, in the first 18 minutes of the morning, Watt invents the steam engine. Later that same day, at 4 P.M., the first railway begins to operate.

And thus we reach the last day of the year. The 31st of December. Before daybreak, Edison invents the first incandescent lamps. By early afternoon, Bleriot crosses the English Channel. And not until mid- to late afternoon does World War I begin. At this late hour, Western man disposes of $8/10$ of a horsepower. This is notable and brutal progress because:

During the whole year, he has lived with only $1/10$ of a horsepower. In one day, he has multiplied it by 8; but only five hours suffice to bring this figure to 80.

* Reprinted from *The Invention of Culture,* rev. ed. by Roy Wagner, p. 140, by permission of The University of Chicago Press. © 1981 by (The University of Chicago Press).

MANAGEMENT IN ACTION 20-1

A Changing Business Environment

In *Megatrends,* author John Naisbitt notes that one of the most significant changes of the 1970s was the move away from a focus on the national economy toward a focus on the world economy. During the 1950s and 60s, U.S. productivity growth increased more than 3 percent per year. In 1960, the United States had a 25 percent share of the world market in manufacturing, and American companies produced 95 percent of the automobiles, steel, and consumer electronic goods sold in the United States.

But the United States, the world, and the world economy have changed. During the 1970s, U.S. productivity growth fell to 1 percent per year and in some years actually declined. In 1979, the U.S. share of world manufacturing was 17 percent, and American companies produced 79 percent of the automobiles, 86 percent of the steel, and less than 50 percent of the consumer electronic goods sold in the United States.

Source: Adapted from John Naisbitt, *Megatrends* (New York: Warner Books, 1982), pp. 55–56.

The following events took place during the last few minutes of the day: The first atomic bomb exploded, Neil Armstrong walked on the moon, and 50 million computers were in use.[1]

The faster rate of change forced organizations to adapt at an equally increasing rate. Management in Action 20–1 describes several recent worldwide changes that have affected modern organizations. At this point, organizations first discovered that they could not always change their cultures as quickly as desired. Because of this problem, increasing attention has been focused on the study of organizational culture.

MANAGING CHANGE

Change as it applies to organizations can be classified into three major categories: (1) technological, (2) environmental, and (3) internal to the organization. **Technological changes** are such things as new equipment and new processes. The technological advances since World War II have been dramatic, with computers being the most notable. **Environmental changes** are all those nontechnological changes that occur outside the organization. New government regulations, new social trends, and economic changes are all examples of environmental change. **Changes internal** to the organization include such things as budget adjustments, policy changes, and personnel changes. Figure 20–1 illustrates the three major categories of change.

Any of the types of changes previously discussed can greatly impact on a manager's job. Different people react in different ways to changes, and this complicates the manager's job. The next section discusses possible employee reactions to change.

Technological changes—such things as new equipment and new processes.

Environmental changes—all nontechnological changes that occur outside the organization.

Internal changes—budget adjustments, policy changes, personnel changes, and the like.

FIGURE 20–1
Types of Changes Affecting Organizations

Technological	Environmental	Internal
Machines	Laws	Policies
Equipment	Taxes	Procedures
Processes	Social trends	Methods
Automation	Fashion trends	Rules
Computers	Political trends	Reorganization
	Economic trends	Budget adjustment
	Interest rates	Restructuring of jobs
	Consumer trends	Personnel

Employee Reactions to Change

How an employee perceives a change greatly affects how that person reacts to the change. While many variations are possible, there are four basic situations that can occur:

1. If employees cannot foresee how the change will affect them, they will resist the change or be neutral at best. Most people shy away from the unknown. The attitude often is that the change may make things worse.

2. If it is clearly seen that the change does not fit employees' needs and hopes, they will resist the change. In this instance, employees are confident that the change will make things worse.

3. If employees see that the change is going to take place regardless, they may first resist and then resign themselves to the change. The first reaction is to resist. Once the change appears inevitable, employees often see no other choice but to go along with the change.

4. If employees view the change as in their best interests, then they will be motivated to accept it. The key here is for the employees to feel sure that the change will make things better.

Note that three out of four of these situations result in some form of resistance to change. Also, the way in which employees resist change can vary greatly. For example, an employee may mildly resist by not acting interested in the change. At the other extreme, an employee may resist by trying to sabotage the change.

Resistance to Change

Most people profess to be modern and up-to-date. However, they still resist change. This is most true when the change affects their jobs. Resistance to change is a natural, normal reaction. It is not a reaction reserved only for troublemakers.

Resistance to change may be very open, or it may be very subtle. The employee who quits a job because of a change in company policy is showing resistance to change in a very open and explicit manner. Another employee who stays but becomes very sullen is resisting in a more passive manner.

Barriers to Change

There are many reasons why employees resist change. Some of the reasons found most often are discussed below.

1. Fear of the unknown. It is natural human behavior for people to fear the unknown. With many changes, the outcome is not foreseeable. When it is, the results are often not made known to all of the affected employees. For example, employees may worry about and resist a new computer if they are not sure what its impact will be on their jobs. Similarly, employees may resist a new manager simply because they don't know what to expect. A related fear is the uncertainty that employees may feel about working in a changed environment. They may fully understand a change, yet really doubt whether they will be able to handle the change. For example, an employee may resist a change in procedure because of a fear of not being able to master it.

2. Economics. Employees fear any change that they think threatens their job or income. The threat may be real or only imagined. In either case, the result is employee resistance. For example, a salesperson who believes that a territory change will result in less income will resist the change. Similarly, production workers will oppose new standards that they believe will be harder to achieve.

3. Inconvenience. Many changes result in personal inconveniences to the affected employees. If nothing else, they often have to learn new ways. This may mean more training, schooling, or practice. In either case, the employee will probably be inconvenienced. A common reaction by employees is, "it isn't worth the extra effort required."

4. Threats to interpersonal relations. The social and interpersonal relationships between employees can be quite strong. These relationships may appear unimportant to everyone but those involved. For example, eating lunch with a particular group may be very important to the involved employees. When a change, such as a transfer, threatens these relationships, the affected employees often resist. Employees naturally feel more at ease when working with people that they know well. Also, the group may have devised methods for doing their work based on the strengths and weaknesses of group members. Any changes in the group would naturally disrupt the routine.

Reducing Resistance to Change

Most changes come from management. The way in which management implements a change often has great impact on acceptance of the change.

Several suggestions for reducing resistance to change are prescribed in Figure 20–2 and discussed in the following paragraphs.

FIGURE 20–2
Suggestions for Reducing Resistance
to Change

Build trust.
Discuss upcoming changes.
Involve the employees in the changes.
Make sure the changes are reasonable.
Avoid threats.
Follow a sensible time schedule.
Implement in the most logical place.

Build trust. If employees trust and have confidence in management, they are much likely to accept change. If there is an air of distrust, change is likely to be strongly resisted. Trust does not come overnight; it is built over a period of time. Management's actions determine the degree of trust among employees. If employees see management as fair, honest, and forthright, trust develops. If they feel that management is always trying to put something over on them, they will not exhibit trust. Managers can go a long way toward building trust if they discuss upcoming changes with the employees and if they actively involve the employees in the change process.

Discuss upcoming changes. Fear of the unknown is one of the major barriers to change. This fear can be greatly reduced by discussing any upcoming changes with the affected employees. During this discussion, the manager should be as open and honest as possible. The manager should explain not only what the change will be but also why the change is being made. The more background and detail the manager gives, the more likely that the change will be accepted by the employees. The manager should also outline the impact of the change on each affected employee. (Everyone is mainly interested in how the change will affect them personally.) A critical requirement for success is that managers give employees a chance to ask questions. Regardless of how thorough the explanation might be, employees usually have questions. Managers should try to answer each question as fully as possible.

Involve the employees. Another way to reduce resistance to change and build trust is to involve employees in the change process. While not always possible, it can be very effective. It is only natural for employees to want to go along with a change they have helped implement. A good approach is to ask for employee ideas and input as early as possible in the change process. In other words, don't wait until the last minute to ask the employees what they think; ask them as soon as possible. When affected employees have been involved in a change from or near the beginning, they will most often actively support the change. The psychology involved here is simple: Few people oppose something they have helped develop.

Make sure the changes are reasonable.   The manager should always do everything possible to ensure that any proposed changes are reasonable. Often, proposals for changes come from other parts of the organization. These proposals are sometimes not reasonable, because the originator is unaware of all the pertinent circumstances. It then becomes the manager's job to do what can be done to straighten out such a situation.

Avoid threats.   The manager who attempts to force change through the use of threats is taking a negative approach. This is likely to decrease rather than increase employee trust. Most people resist threats or coercion. A natural reaction is, "this must be bad news if it requires a threat." Even though threats may get results in the short run, they are often damaging in the long run. Such tactics usually have a negative impact on employee morale.

Follow a sensible time schedule.   A manager can often influence the timing of changes. Some times are doubtless better than others for making certain changes. The week before Christmas, for instance, would usually not be a good time to make a major change. Similarly, a major change should normally not be attempted during the height of the vacation season. The manager can often provide valuable insight into the proper time for a change. If nothing else, the manager should always use common sense when proposing a time schedule for implementing a change.

Implement in the most logical place.   Managers often have some choice as to where a change takes place. For example, a manager usually decides who will get a new piece of equipment. Those who make it a point to know their employees usually have a pretty good idea as to who will most likely be adaptable to change and who will not. Changes should, where possible, be made in such a way so as to minimize their effect on interpersonal relationships. Attempts should be made not to disturb smooth-working groups. The effect of a change on social relationships should also be considered.

All of the above suggestions require planning for successful implementation. Unfortunately, many managers do not plan for change but rather merely react to it.

Planned Change

Many times the need for change can be foreseen and plans made. It is desirable then to develop a program of planned change. A **program of planned change** has been defined as "the deliberate design and implementation of a structural innovation, a new policy or goal, or a change in operating philosophy, climate, and style."[2] A program of planned change is most needed when the change will pervade most or all of the organization, as opposed to only a small segment of it.

Program of planned change–deliberate design and implementation of a structural innovation, a new policy or goal, or a change in operating philosophy, climate, and style.

A program of planned change usually involves a change agent—the person responsible for coordinating and overseeing the change process. A change agent can be an employee of the organization or an outside consultant.

Implementing a planned change. Basically, three elements of an organization can be altered to make a change: its organizational structure, its technology, and/or its human resources.[3] Usually, a change in one affects the others. For example, a structure change in the form of a reorganization would impact on the organization's human resources.

Structural and technological changes would be fairly simple to make except for their impact on the organization's human resources. One of the primary approaches used to change an organization's human resources is organizational development.

Organizational Development

Organizational development (OD)—organizationwide, planned effort managed from the top, to increase organizational performance through planned interventions.

Organizational development (OD) is an organizationwide, planned effort managed from the top, with a goal of increasing organizational performance through planned interventions in the organization. In particular, OD looks at the human side of organizations. It seeks to change attitudes, values, and management practices in an effort to improve organizational performance. The ultimate goal of OD is to structure the organizational environment so that managers and employees can use their skills and abilities to the fullest.

An OD effort starts with a recognition by management that organizational performance can and should be improved. Following this, most OD efforts include the following phases:

1. Diagnosis.
2. Strategy planning.
3. Education.
4. Evaluation.

Diagnosis involves gathering and analyzing information about the organization to determine the areas in need of improvement. Information is usually gathered from employees through the use of questionnaires or attitude surveys. Strategy planning involves developing a plan for organization improvement based on the obtained data. This planning identifies specific problem areas in the organization and outlines steps that are to be taken to resolve the problems. Education consists of sharing diagnostic information with people who are affected by it and helping them to realize the need for change. The education phase often involves the use of outside consultants working with individuals or employee groups. It can also involve the use of management development programs. The evaluation phase in effect repeats the diagnostic phase. In other words, after diagnosis, strategy planning, and education, data is gathered to determine the effects of the OD effort on the total organization. This information can then, of course, lead to more planning and education.

Sensitivity Training

Sensitivity training is often used in OD programs. It is designed to make one more aware of oneself and one's impact on others. Unfortunately, some people tend to equate sensitivity training and OD. Sensitivity training, however, is only one technique used in OD. It does not have to be used at all in organizational development.

Sensitivity training involves a group, normally called a training group or T-group, which meets and has no agenda or particular focus. Normally, the group has between 10 and 15 people who may or may not know each other. With no planned structure and/or no prior common experiences, the behavior of individuals in trying to deal with the lack of structure becomes the agenda. While engaging in group dialogue, members are encouraged to learn about themselves and others in the nonstructured environment.

Although sensitivity training sessions have no agenda, there is a desired pattern of events. The group meets with no directive leadership patterns, no authority positions, no formal agenda, and no power and status positions. Therefore, a vacuum exists. Nonevaluative feedback received by individuals on their behavior from other group members is the method of learning. From this feedback and from limited guidance by the trainer, a feeling of mutual trust follows. Openness and mutual trust emerge as the members of the group serve as resources to one another. Collaborative behavior develops. Finally, the group explores the relevance of the experience as it relates to the organization.

Sensitivity training has been both passionately criticized and defended as to its relative value for organizations. In general, the research shows that people with sensitivity training tend to show increased sensitivity, more open communication, and increased flexibility.[4] However, these same studies indicate that it is difficult to predict exactly the outcome of sensitivity training for any one person. The outcomes of sensitivity training are beneficial in general, but the impact of such training for any one person cannot be predicted.

Sensitivity training—method used in OD to make one more aware of oneself and one's impact on others.

Grid Training

Another approach used in OD is grid training. **Grid training** is an extension of the Managerial Grid, which was discussed in Chapter 14. The methods used in grid training can be divided into six phases:[5]

1. *Laboratory-seminar training:* Designed to introduce the participant to the Managerial Grid concepts and material. Each manager determines where he or she falls on the Managerial Grid.

Grid training—method used in OD to make managers and organizations more team oriented.

MANAGEMENT IN ACTION 20–2

OD at Sherwin-Williams

Sherwin-Williams, the paint and finishes company, has been involved in an organizational development effort for several years. This effort has had vigorous support from the start by the company's CEO and is guided by an outside consultant. Sherwin-Williams' OD program is based on the premise that for individuals and the organization to continue to grow and keep up with the rapid changes in the environment, change strategies must be continually explored and tried at all levels of the company. The primary mode used by Sherwin-Williams to facilitate organization and individual change is to consult with employees who are ready to initiate a change in themselves or in their organizational unit. The posture of consultation can vary from firm directives to supportive listening.

Source: Adapted from Ernest C. Miller, "Organization Development: A Dynamic New Force?" *Personnel,* November–December 1977, pp. 4–9.

2. *Team development:* Involves establishing the ground rules and relationships necessary for 9,9 management.

3. *Intergroup development:* Involves establishing the ground rules and relationships necessary for 9,9 management for group-to-group working relationships.

4. *Organizational goal setting:* Management by objectives is used to establish individual and organizational goals.

5. *Goal attainment:* Goals established in Phase 4 are pursued.

6. *Stabilization:* Changes brought about by the other phases are evaluated, and an overall evaluation of the program is made.

As with sensitivity training, grid training has met with mixed success in organizations. Little research has been conducted on grid training; more is needed before conclusions can be drawn regarding its effectiveness.[6]

Evaluations of OD

OD has been applied in many organizations during the past 25 years (see Management in Action 20–2 for one example). There have also been many attempts to evaluate the effectiveness of different OD programs. These studies have produced both positive and negative results; in fact, the studies themselves have been criticized.[7] At this time, a lot of the supposed value of OD has to be taken on faith.[8]

MANAGING ORGANIZATION CULTURE

The word *culture* is derived in a roundabout way from the Latin verb *colere,* which means "to cultivate."[9] In later times, the word *culture* came

MANAGEMENT IN ACTION 20–3

Potential Culture Clash

Electronic Data Systems (EDS) has a highly competitive atmosphere with low pay, strict discipline (including a dress code), and extremely loyal, hardworking employees. Excellent job performance is rewarded with large bonuses and merit raises. The key to success at EDS is "Work hard, keep your nose clean, and keep that nose to the grindstone."

When General Motors acquired EDS in 1984, many observers expected a clash of cultures and wondered whether GM would stifle Electronic Data Systems' innovative, energetic spirit. However, EDS seems to be changing GM. GM has recently announced plans to abolish cost-of-living raises, and GM chairman Roger Smith has indicated he likes the aggressive, innovative EDS style.

Source: Damon Darlin and Melinda Grenier Guiles, "Some GM People Feel Auto Firm, Not EDS, Was the One Acquired," *The Wall Street Journal*, December 19, 1984, p. 1.

to indicate a process of refinement and breeding in domesticating some particular crop. The modern-day meaning draws upon this agricultural derivation: It relates to society's control, refinement, and domestication of itself. A contemporary definition of **culture** is "the set of important understandings (often unstated) that members of a community share in common."[10]

Culture in an organization compares to personality in a person. Humans have fairly enduring and stable traits which help them protect their attitudes and behaviors. So do organizations. In addition, certain groups of traits or personality types are known to consist of common elements. Organizations can be described in similar terms. They can be warm, aggressive, friendly, open, innovative, conservative, and so forth. An organization's culture is transmitted in many ways, including long-standing and often unwritten rules, shared standards about what is important, prejudices, standards for social etiquette and demeanor, established customs for how to relate to peers, subordinates and superiors, and other traditions that clarify to employees what is and is not appropriate behavior. Thus, **corporate culture** communicates how people in the organization should behave, by establishing a value system conveyed through rites, rituals, myths, legends, and actions. Simply stated, corporate culture means "the way we do things around here."[11] Management in Action 20–3 describes the culture at Electronic Data Systems (EDS).

> **Culture**–set of important understandings (often unstated) that members of a community share in common.

> **Corporate culture**–communicates how people in an organization should behave, by establishing a value system conveyed through rites, rituals, myths, legends, and actions.

Cultural Forms of Expression

Culture has two basic components: (1) its substance, or the meanings contained in its ideologies, values, and norms; and (2) its forms, or the practices whereby these meanings are expressed, affirmed, and communicated to members.[12] Figure 20–3 defines many of the most often encountered forms of cultural expression.

FIGURE 20–3
Frequently Encountered Forms of Cultural Expression

Form	Definition
Rite	Relatively elaborate, dramatic, planned sets of activities that consolidate various forms of cultural expressions into one event, which is carried out through social interactions, usually for the benefit of an audience.
Ceremonial	System of several rites connected with a single occasion or event.
Ritual	Standardized, detail set of techniques and behaviors that manage anxieties but seldom produce intended, technical consequences of practical importance.
Myth	Dramatic narrative of imagined events, usually used to explain origins or transformations of something. Also, an unquestioned belief about the practical benefits of certain techniques and behaviors that is not supported by demonstrated facts.
Saga	Historical narrative describing the unique accomplishments of a group and its leaders—usually in heroic terms.
Legend	Handed-down narrative of some wonderful event that is based in history but has been embellished with fictional details.
Story	Narrative based on true events—often a combination of truth and fiction.
Folktale	Completely fictional narrative.
Symbol	Any object, act, event, quality, or relation that serves as a vehicle for conveying meaning, usually by representing another thing.
Language	A particular form or manner in which members of a group use vocal sounds and written signs to convey meanings to each other.
Gesture	Movements of parts of the body used to express meanings.
Physical setting	Those things that surround people physically and provide them with immediate sensory stimuli as they carry out culturally expressive activities.
Artifact	Material objects manufactured by people to facilitate culturally expressive activities.

Source: Harrison M. Trice and Janice M. Beyer, "Studying Organizational Cultures through Rites and Ceremonials," *Academy of Management Review* 9, no. 4 (1984), p. 655.

How Does Culture Originate?

There is no question that different organizations develop different cultures. Figure 20–4 summarizes certain cultural characteristics of some well-known companies. What causes an organization to develop a particular type of culture? Many trace their culture to one person who provided a living example of the major values of the organization. Robert Wood Johnson of Johnson & Johnson, Harley Procter of Procter & Gamble, Walt Disney of Walt Disney Productions, and Thomas J. Watson, Sr., of IBM all left their imprint on the organizations they headed. Research indicates, however, that fewer than

FIGURE 20–4
Culture Characteristics of Some Well-Known Companies

Company	Characteristics
IBM	Concern for marketing drives a service philosophy that is almost unparalleled. The company maintains a hot line around the clock, seven days a week, to service its products.
ITT	Financial discipline demands total dedication. Once, an executive phoned former chairman Harold Geneen at 3 A.M. to beat out the competition in a merger deal.
Digital Equipment Corporation	Emphasis on innovation creates freedom with responsibility. Employees are allowed to set their own hours and working styles, but they are expected to show evidence of progress.
Delta Air Lines	Focus on customer service produces a high degree of teamwork. Employees will gladly substitute in other jobs to keep planes flying and baggage moving.
Atlantic Richfield Company	Emphasis on entrepreneurship encourages individual action. Operating employees have the autonomy to bid on promising fields without getting approval from top management.

Source: Adapted from "Corporate Culture: The Hard-to-Change Values that Spell Success or Failure," *Business Week,* October 27, 1980, pp. 148.

half of a new company's values reflect the values of the founder or chief executive. The rest appear to develop in response both to the environment in which the business operates and to the needs of the employees.[13] Four separate factors contribute to an organization's culture: its history, its environment, its selection process, and its socialization processes.[14]

History.   Employees are aware of the organization's past, and this awareness builds culture. Much of the "way things are done" is a continuation of how things have always been done. The existing values which may have been established originally by a strong leader are constantly and subtly reinforced by experiences. The status quo is also protected by the human tendency to embrace beliefs and values fervently and to resist changes. Executives for Walt Disney Productions reportedly pick up litter on the grounds unconsciously, because of the Disney vision of an immaculate Disneyland.

Environment.   Because all organizations must interact with their environments, the environment has a role in shaping their cultures. In the case of AT&T (see Management in Action 20–4), the highly formalized and risk-adverse culture was in large part a product of the regulatory environment in which it operated for so long. No longer sheltered by its monopoly power, the culture must change. The question is whether the change can come fast enough to ensure success and survival.

Staffing.   Organizations tend to hire, retain, and promote persons who are similar to current employees in important ways. A person's ability to fit in can be important in these processes. This "fit" criterion ensures that current values are accepted and that potential challengers of "how we do things" are screened out. For example, organizations are often as interested in the way applicants dress and handle themselves as in their work experiences.

Entry socialization.   While an organization's values, norms, and beliefs may be widely and uniformly held, they are seldom written down. The new employee, least familiar with the culture, is most likely to challenge it. It is, therefore, important to help the newcomer adopt the organization's culture. Companies with strong cultures attach great importance to the process of introducing and indoctrinating new employees. This process is called the **entry socialization** process. Entry socialization not only reduces threats to the organization from newcomers; it also lets newly hired employees know what is expected of them. It may be handled in a formal or informal manner, as well as on an individual or group basis.

Entry socialization—adaption process by which new employees are introduced and indoctrinated into an organization.

Identifying Culture

Researchers have identified <u>seven characteristics</u> that taken together capture the <u>essence of an organization</u>'s culture:[15]

1. *Individual autonomy:* The degree of responsibility, independence, and opportunities for exercising initiative that individuals in the organization have.

2. *Structure:* The number of rules and regulations and the amount of direct supervision that is used to oversee and control employee behavior.

3. *Support:* The degree of assistance and warmth provided by managers to their subordinates.

4. *Identification:* The degree to which members identify with the organization as a whole rather than with their particular work group or field of professional expertise.

5. *Performance-reward:* The degree to which reward allocations (i.e., salary increases, promotions) in the organization are based on performance criteria.

6. *Conflict tolerance:* The degree of conflict present in relationships between peers and work groups, as well as the willingness to be honest and open about differences.

7. *Risk tolerance:* The degree to which employees are encouraged to be aggressive, innovative, and risk seeking.

Each of these traits should be viewed as existing on a continuum that ranges from low to high. A picture of the overall culture can be formed by appraising an organization on each of these.

MANAGEMENT IN ACTION 20–4

Culture Change—by Choice or by Force

A company may be forced to reevaluate its culture following an upheaval in its environment or may choose to alter its culture as part of a planned strategic change. Before their court-ordered breakup in January 1984, AT&T had a strong corporate culture that focused on delivering reliable, inexpensive phone service. Now AT&T is in the middle of what one insider termed "a cultural train wreck." The company culture that advocated consensus decision-making, lifetime employment, promotion from within, and pride in service—all within the regulated environment of guaranteed profits—is now suffering in the aftermath of the divestiture. The company is now having to come to terms with a highly competitive market, a declining reputation for quality service, poor employee morale, and a totally new organization structure.

In contrast, Johnson & Johnson, the maker of Band-Aids, baby shampoo and Tylenol, is undergoing a company-initiated culture change. For years, J&J has been a strong example of a market-driven, decentralized organization with 170 virtually autonomous "companies." As part of a diversification effort, J&J has acquired 25 companies in 5 years. Many of the companies are in high-technology health care markets such as surgical lasers and magnetic resonance scanners. However, changing the company's mix of businesses has been easier than changing management attitudes. Marketing and sales are unaccustomed to selling products that are used more than once, and management is unaccustomed to the cooperation among units that now seems to be necessary.

For AT&T and J&J, how well they adapt their cultures to their new environments will determine the ultimate success of the organizations.

Sources: Jeremy Main, "Waking UP AT&T: There's Life after Culture Shock," *Fortune*, December 24, 1984, pp. 66–74; "Changing a Corporate Culture," *Business Week*, May 14, 1984, pp. 130–38.

There are as many distinct cultures as there are organizations. Most can be grouped into one of four basic types, determined by two factors:[16] (1) the degree of risk associated with the organization's activities and (2) the speed with which organizations and their employees get feedback indicating the success of decisions. Figure 20–5 shows in matrix form the four generic types of cultures.

Tough-guy, macho culture. This type of culture is characterized by individualists who regularly take high risks and get quick feedback on whether their answers are right or wrong. Teamwork is not important, and every colleague is a potential rival. In this culture, the value of cooperation is ignored; there is no chance to learn from mistakes. It tends to reward employees who are temperamental and shortsighted. *Examples:* Big advertising campaigns, the fall television season, an expensive construction project, a high-budget film.

> **Tough-guy, macho culture**–characterized by individualists who take high risks and get quick feedback on whether their answers are right or wrong.

Work-hard/play-hard culture. The **work-hard/play hard culture** encourages employees to take few risks and to expect rapid feedback. In this culture, activity is the key to success. Rewards accrue to persistence and the ability to find a need and fill it. Because of the need for volume, team players who are friendly and outgoing thrive. *Examples:* Sales organizations

> **Work-hard/play-hard culture**–encourages employees to take few risks and to expect rapid feedback.

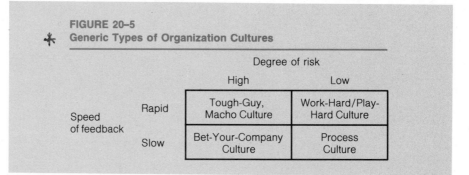

FIGURE 20–5
Generic Types of Organization Cultures

		Degree of risk	
		High	Low
Speed of feedback	Rapid	Tough-Guy, Macho Culture	Work-Hard/Play-Hard Culture
	Slow	Bet-Your-Company Culture	Process Culture

of all types, including retail stores, door-to-door sales, and mass-consumer sales.

Bet-your-company culture—requires big-stakes decisions; considerable time passes before the results are known.

The bet-your-company culture.   These cultures require big-stakes decisions, with considerable time passing before the results are known. Pressures to make the right decisions are always present in this environment. *Examples:* Capital goods companies, oil companies, investment banks, architectural firms.

Process culture—involves low risk with little feedback; employees focus on how things are done rather than on the outcomes.

Process culture.   This culture involves low risk coupled with little feedback; employees must focus on how things are done rather than the outcomes. Employees in this atmosphere become cautious and protective. Those who thrive are orderly, punctual, and detail oriented. *Examples:* Banks, insurance companies, government agencies, utilities.

These generic types are often not detailed enough to apply to an organization without some modifications. In fact, within an organization, there may be a mix of cultures. For example, sales may be closer to the work-hard/ play-hard designation; research and development may be closer to a bet-your-company situation. While these generic cultures help to identify major types of cultural orientation, they represent only a starting point.

Use of Consultants versus Inside Diagnosis

Examinations of culture by consultants run the risk of being superficial; but they can still be useful. Information can come from the physical setting, public statements of the organization, the way the organization greets outsiders, how people in the organization spend their time, and what employees say about the company. The major advantage of an outside diagnosis is the likelihood of objectivity.

Insiders have the chance to make a more detailed study of culture but may find it hard to be objective. They must be careful to observe rather than judge. The insider can examine career paths, tenure in jobs, specific issues which consume the time of employees, and the anecdotes and stories that are passed around.

Changing Culture

Implicit in this discussion has been the fact that strong cultures can contribute greatly to an organization's success. The opposite is also true: Weak cultures can inhibit success. Figure 20–6 summarizes some characteristics of a weak culture.

FIGURE 20–6
Characteristics of a Weak Culture

They have no clear values or beliefs about how to succeed in their business.

They have many beliefs as to how to succeed but cannot agree on which are most important.

Different parts of the organization have fundamentally different beliefs about how to succeed.

Those that personify the culture are destructive or disruptive and don't build upon any common understanding about what is important.

The rituals of day-to-day organizational life are disorganized and/or working at cross-purposes.

Source: Terrence E. Deal and Allan A. Kennedy, *Corporate Cultures: The Rites and Rituals of Corporate Life* (Reading, Mass.: Addison-Wesley Publishing, 1982), pp. 135–36.

Executives who have successfully changed organization cultures estimate that it usually takes from 6 to 15 years.[17] Because organization culture is difficult and time consuming to change, any attempts should be well thought out. Allen Kennedy, an expert on organization culture, believes that there are only five reasons to justify a large-scale cultural change.[18]

1. The organization has strong values that don't fit a changing environment.
2. The industry is very competitive and moves with lightning speed.
3. The organization is mediocre or worse.
4. The organization is about to join the ranks of the very large companies.
5. The organization is small but growing rapidly.

As we saw earlier, in Management in Action 20–4, some organizations attempt to change their culture only when they are forced to; others anticipate a necessary change. While massive cultural reorientation may be unreasonable in most situations, it is still possible to strengthen or "fine-tune" the current situation. A statement of corporate mission consistently reinforced by systems, structures, and policies is a useful tool for strengthening the culture.

Because of the cost, time, and difficulty involved in changing culture, many people believe it is easier to change (physically replace) the people. This view assumes that most organizations promote people who fit the prevailing norms of the organization. Therefore, the easiest if not the only way to change an organization's culture is to change its people.

Because the best time to make changes in people's values is when they are new to the organization, many companies attempt to shape the desired culture through the employee orientation process and indoctrination period.

SUMMARY

Organizational change and culture are inextricably related. Both topics have recently been pushed to the forefront in management circles. Change, as it applies to organizations, can be classified into three major categories: technological, environmental, and internal to the organization.

How an employee perceives a change greatly affects how that person will react to it. Most employees tend to resist change; there are several reasons why. These include fear of the unknown, economics, inconvenience, and threats to interpersonal relations. Resistance to change can be reduced by building trust, discussing upcoming changes with employees, involving the employees in the changes, making sure the changes are reasonable, avoiding threats, following a sensible time schedule, and implementing the change in the most logical place.

A program of planned change is the deliberate design and implementation of a structural innovation, a new policy or goal, or a change in operating philosophy, climate, and style. There are three elements of an organization that can be altered to accommodate a change: its structure, its technology, and/or its human resources.

Organizational development (OD) is one of the primary approaches used to alter an organization's human resources. OD is an organizationwide, planned effort managed from the top, with a goal of increasing organizational performance through planned interventions in the organization. Sensitivity training is frequently used in OD programs and is designed to make one more aware of oneself and one's impact on others. Grid training, an extension of the Managerial Grid, is another approach used in OD.

Corporate culture communicates how people in the organization should behave, by establishing a value system and conveying that value system through rites, rituals, myths, legends, and actions. An organization's culture originates with its history and environment and is reinforced by its staffing decisions and the socialization process.

While every organization has a unique culture, most cultures can be grouped into one of four generic types according to the risk of the organization's activities and the speed at which feedback about success is delivered. Outside consultants or inside resources can be used to diagnose an organization's culture.

Because changing culture is costly, time consuming, and very difficult, it should only be attempted under certain circumstances. Many believe that the easiest way to change an organization's culture is to change (replace) its people.

References and Additional Readings

[1] Adapted from R. Nordling, "Social Responsibilities of Today's Industrial Leader," quoting Jean Predseil, *S.A.M. Advanced Management Journal,* April 1957. © 1957 by Society for Advancement of Management, pp. 19–20.

[2] John M. Thomas and Warren G. Bennis, eds., *The Management of Change and Conflict* (New York: Penguin Books, 1972), p. 109.

[3] Harold J. Leavitt, "Applied Organization Change in Industry; Structural, Technical, and Human Approaches," in *New Perspectives in Organization Research,* eds. W. W., Cooper, H. J. Leavitt, and M. W. Shelly II (New York: John Wiley & Sons, 1964), pp. 55–71.

[4] Michael Beer, "The Technology of Organization Development," in *Handbook of Industrial and Organizational Psychology,* ed. Marvin D. Dunnette (New York: John Wiley & Sons, 1983), p. 941; Michael Beer, *Organization Change and Development: A System View* (Santa Monica, Calif.: Goodyear Publishing, 1980), pp. 194–95.

[5] Robert R. Blake, Jane S. Mouton, Louis B. Barnes, and Larry E. Greenes, "Breakthrough in Organization Development," *Harvard Business Review,* November–December 1964, pp. 137–38.

[6] Beer, "Organization Development," p. 943; John M. Nicholas, "Evaluation Research in Organizational Change Interventions: Considerations and Some Suggestions," *Journal of Applied Behavioral Science,* January–February–March 1979, pp. 23–40.

[7] For example, see Jerry I. Porras and Per Olaf Berg, "Evaluation Methodology in Organization Development: An Analysis and Critique," *Journal of Applied Behavioral Science,* April–May–June 1978, pp. 151–73.

[8] Stephen P. Robbins, *Organizational Behavior,* 2d ed. (Englewood Cliffs, N.J.: Prentice-Hall, 1983), p. 485; Peggy Morrison, "Evaluation in OD: A Review and Assessment," *Group and Organizational Studies,* March 1978, pp. 42–70.

[9] Roy Wagner, *The Invention of Culture,* rev. ed. (Chicago: University of Chicago Press, 1981), p. 21.

[10] Vijay Sathe, "Implications of Corporate Culture: A Manager's Guide to Action," *Organizational Dynamics,* Autumn 1983, p. 6.

[11] Terrence E. Deal and Allan A. Kennedy, *Corporate Cultures: The Rites and Rituals of Corporate Life* (Reading, Mass.: Addison-Wesley Publishing, 1982), p. 4.

[12] Harrison M. Trice and Janice M. Beyer, "Studying Organizational Cultures through Rites and Ceremonials," *Academy of Management Review* 9, no. 4 (1984), p. 645.

[13] "The Corporate Culture Vultures," *Fortune,* October 17, 1983, p. 72.

[14] Stephen P. Robbins, *Essentials of Organizational Behavior* (Englewood Cliffs, N.J.: Prentice-Hall, 1984), pp. 174–76.

[15] S. P. Robbins, *Essentials of Organizational Behavior,* © 1984, p. 171. Reprinted by permission of Prentice-Hall, Inc., Englewood Cliffs, N.J.

[16] Deal and Kennedy, *Corporate Cultures,* p. 107.

[17] This section is drawn from Deal and Kennedy, *Corporate Cultures,* pp. 129–35.

[18] "The Corporate Culture Vultures," p. 70.

Review Questions

1. Name the three major categories of change that apply to organizations.
2. Describe the four basic reactions of employees to change.
3. Name four common barriers (reasons for resistance) to change.
4. Discuss seven methods or approaches for reducing resistance to change.
5. What is a program of planned change?
6. What is organizational development (OD)? Describe the following techniques used in OD:

   a. Sensitivity training.
   b. Grid training.
7. What are the organizational characteristics which determine corporate culture?
8. How is corporate culture originated and maintained?
9. Name and briefly define the four generic types of corporate culture.
10. Under what circumstances might a change in corporate culture be attempted?

Discussion Questions

1. Take a position and be prepared to defend it with regard to the following statement: "Most people resist change, not because the change is harmful but because they are lazy."
2. "Everyone should be exposed to sensitivity training at some point in his or her career." Do you agree? Explain.
3. Choose a not-for-profit organization of which you are a member (church, sorority, campus club, professional group) and analyze its culture. How is your behavior as a member shaped by the culture? How are expectations transmitted to new members?
4. Pick an actual organization or industry that you think will need to change its culture if it is to thrive in the future (like AT&T in Management in Action 20–3). Be prepared to explain why you feel this change must occur.

Incident 20–1
Upgrading Quality

Bob Franklin, the plant manager of Smart Manufacturing Company, was reviewing the Quality Control Department figures with despair. Once again, the department's figures indicated that quality improvements were not being made. Bob was annoyed. "I don't understand it," he thought. "I've been stressing to my staff for over a year that I want to see some quality improvements, but it just doesn't seem to be happening. Quality may actually be worse now than it was a year ago!"

Bob called in David Berg, the quality control manager, and production manager Stuart Lewicki. "Look," Bob said, "I told both of you over a year ago I wanted to see some improvements in quality around here, and we've talked about it at every staff meeting since then. But nothing has happened. What's going on?"

David Berg spoke up. "My department just inspects the products. The quality problems occur in production. All I can do is what I've been doing all along—tell Stuart about the problems we are seeing. I've already told him that 50 percent of the quality problems are caused by worker carelessness."

"I know," said Stuart Lewicki. "I don't understand it. I've been stressing to my shift supervisors that we need to see quality improvements. They have all told me they are coming down really hard on quality problems and are telling their people they need to work harder on getting out a quality product. Just the other day, Francis Stanfield threatened to fire Joe Duncan if she got any more complaints from quality control about Joe's work."

Questions

1. Why have efforts to improve quality failed?
2. Describe a quality improvement program that would have a better chance of being successful.

Incident 20–2
The Way We Do Things

The Fitzgerald Company manufactures a variety of consumer products for sale through retail department stores. For over 30 years, the company has held a strong belief that customer relations and a strong selling orientation are the keys to business success. As a result, all top executives have sales backgrounds and spend much of their time outside the company with customers. Because of the strong focus on the customer, management at Fitzgerald emphasizes new-product development projects and growth in volume. The company rarely implements cost reduction or process improvement projects.

Between 1965 and 1975, Fitzgerald's 10 percent share of market was the largest in the industry. Profitability was consistently better than the industry group average. However, in the last 10 years, the markets for many of Fitzgerald's products have matured, and Fitzgerald has dropped from market share leader to the number three company in the industry. Profitability has steadily declined since 1980, although Fitzgerald offers a more extensive line of products than any of its competitors. Customers are complaining that Fitzgerald's prices are higher than those of other companies.

In June 1985, Jeff Steele, the president of Fitzgerald Company, hired Valerie Stevens of Management Consultants, Inc. to help him improve the company's financial performance. After an extensive study of Fitzgerald Company and its industry group, Valerie met with Jeff and said, "Jeff, I believe the Fitzgerald Company may have to substantially change the way it does business."

Questions

1. Describe the corporate culture at the Fitzgerald Company.
2. What does Valerie mean when she says the Fitzgerald Company may have to change the way it does business? What are the some of the necessary changes?
3. Discuss the problems the company may encounter in attempting to implement changes.

Exercise
Resisting Change

One of the problems you face involves mistakes being made by employees who perform a particular operation. The same mistakes seem to occur in more than one department. You feel that a training program for the people concerned will help reduce errors.

You are aware, however, that your supervisors may defend existing procedures simply because the introduction of training may imply criticism of the way they have been operating. You realize, too, that the supervisors may fear resistance by employees afraid of not doing well in the training program. All in all, you plan to approach the subject carefully.

You consider the following methods of approaching the matter:

1. Add to the agenda of your weekly staff meeting a recommendation that training be undertaken to help reduce errors.

2. Talk to all your supervisors individually and get their attitudes and ideas about what to do before bringing the subject up in the weekly staff meeting.

3. Ask the corporate training staff to come in, determine the training needs, and develop a program to meet those needs.

4. Since this training is in the best interests of the company, tell your supervisors that they will be expected to implement and support it.

5. Appoint a team to study the matter thoroughly, develop recommendations, then bring it before the full staff meeting.

Other alternatives may be open to you, but assume that these are the only ones you have considered. WITHOUT DISCUSSION with anyone, choose one of them and be prepared to defend your choice.

Objectives

1. To develop an understanding of the role that computerized information systems play in modern organizations.
2. To introduce management information systems (MIS) and to define the related terminology.
3. To present a series of steps for successfully implementing an MIS.
4. To discuss potential pitfalls and cautions relating to MIS.

21

Management Information Systems

Chapter Outline

If the aviation industry had developed at the same rate as electronic data processing, we would have landed people on the moon less than six months after the Wright brothers made their first flight at Kitty Hawk. If the cost of a 1955 Cadillac (introduced about the same time as computers were introduced in business) had been reduced as much as that of computer memories while efficiencies were raised to an equal degree, the Cadillac would now cost $5 and go 20,000 mph.

James A. Senn*

Successful implementation of the basic planning, organizing, and controlling functions of management requires that managers have adequate information: Managers must first identify and then acquire the necessary information. Identifying and acquiring adequate information have historically been two of the biggest challenges of managers.

The advent and maturing of electronic computers have greatly altered not only the availability of information but also the manner by which it is identified and acquired. The purpose of this chapter is to introduce and discuss information systems that can be especially useful to managers.

THE INFORMATION EXPLOSION

Until the past 20 or so years, managers almost never felt that they had enough information to make decisions. Of course, information has always been available, but it has not always been so easy to obtain, synthesize, and analyze. In the 1950s, a manager could always send a team of researchers to the local library; even then, much of the data would not be current. Other available information sources included the radio, newspapers, and professional meetings and publications. Contrast that scenario with one today! Today's managers are often burdened not with a lack of information but rather from information overload. **Information overload** occurs when managers have so much information that they have trouble distinguishing between the useful and the useless information. Management in Action 21–1 describes how the Securities and Exchange Commission is attempting to deal with the huge amounts of information that it receives.

Information overload— occurs when managers have so much information available that they have trouble distinguishing between the useful and the useless information.

The Computer Evolution

The first electronic computer, the ENIAC, was developed by the University of Pennsylvania in conjunction with the U.S. Army Ordnance Corps. The

---

* James A. Senn, *Information Systems in Management,* 2d ed. (Belmont, Calif.: Wadsworth, 1982), p. 83.

MANAGEMENT IN ACTION 21-1

SEC Moves to a Paperless System

The Securities and Exchange Commission (SEC) receives more than 6 million pages of financial reports from corporations each year. In order to streamline the process of reviewing and analyzing tons of paper copy, the SEC plans to install a computerized system. Instead of sending printed 10–Ks and other forms, companies will send data over telephone lines to the SEC from their own computers. The information will then be stored in a data base. SEC staff members will be able to use the computer system to cross-reference industry information, check arithmetic, perform calculations on reports, and compare current reports to those previously filed. The new system should be more efficient and more accurate than the existing manual system. According to Kenneth A. Fozash, SEC deputy executive director, "The current process is costly, untimely, and error prone."

Source: Adapted from "The SEC's Plan to Put a Mountain of Paper into a Computer," *Business Week*, April 2, 1984, pp. 72–74.

ENIAC was eight feet high, eight feet long, weighed 30 tons, and required about 174,000 watts of power to run.[1] On the average, it took about two days to set up ENIAC to carry out a program.

In the 1960s, large and very costly mainframe computers (such as the IBM 360 series) were in use by only the very largest companies and government organizations. Not only was the hardware for these systems expensive but they also required highly paid operators, service personnel, programmers, and systems specialists. Because of the physical size and costs of these systems, they were almost always highly centralized and, more often than not, considered an extension of the accounting function.

The large computers were followed by the minicomputers of the 1970s. The minicomputers were much smaller in size and cost and they were often programmed to do specific functions for a specific business activity. Minicomputers ushered in the concept of distributed data processing—each operational area of an organization has control of its own computer to better respond to the needs of the area.

The decentralization first made possible by minicomputers has been taken even farther by the personal computer. For just a few hundred dollars, a manager today can buy a personal computer capable of processing mammoth amounts of data—and it occupies no more space than a typewriter! Management in Action 21–2 highlights some of the advances made in computer technology.

The phenomenal improvements in computer hardware have been accompanied by improvements in software and user compatibility. Modern computers are much more **user-friendly** than those of the past. Managers today do not have to know sophisticated programming languages and computer jargon to use the computer.

User-friendly computer—requires very little technical knowledge to use.

Computer technology improvements have also created some new problems for managers. Diverse computers and communication technologies operate on a wide array of information at many different levels in the organization.

MANAGEMENT IN ACTION 21–2

The Growth of Computers

The electronic revolution that we are living through now is expected to affect society as dramatically as the Industrial Revolution. Just consider these facts about business computers:

- The first electronic business computer was delivered in 1955. Less than 30 years later, there are more than half a million computers in the United States, and available power is growing by 40 percent per year.
- Since the 1950s, prices for general-purpose computers have been dropping at an annual compound rate of about 20 percent per year.

- Circuits today are 10,000 times more reliable than 25 years ago.
- The number of circuits that can be placed on a silicon chip has been increasing exponentially for about 20 years.
- Sixty-five silicon chips with enough capacity to store 260 copies of the Declaration of Independence can now be fabricated simultaneously on a wafer 82 millimeters in diameter.

Source: John C. Papageorgiou, "Decision Making in the Year 2000," *Interfaces,* April 2, 1983, pp. 77–86.

Therefore, it is no longer possible to place the information function neatly on the organization chart.[2] The need to integrate and coordinate information in an organization has led to the development of systems for doing just that.

WHAT IS A MANAGEMENT INFORMATION SYSTEM?

Data–raw material from which information is developed; it is composed of facts that have not been interpreted.

Information–data that have been interpreted and that meet the need of one or more managers.

Management information system (MIS)–integrated approach for providing interpreted and relevant data that can help managers make decisions.

Before defining management information systems (MIS), it is necessary to define some other, more basic terms first. Many people make a clear distinction between the terms *data* and *information*. **Data** is the raw material from which information is developed; it is composed of facts that describe people, places, things, or events and that have not been interpreted.[3] Data that have been interpreted and that meet the need of one or more managers are **information**.[4]

In simple terms, an **MIS** is an integrated approach for providing interpreted and relevant data that can be used to help managers make decisions. An MIS should interpret, organize, and filter data so that it reaches managers in an efficient and timely manner.

MIS can be viewed as a computer-based system or, more broadly, as the total communication system—including oral, published, and data-based information storage and retrieval.[5] In the broader sense, management information systems have existed for many years. However, in most people's minds and in this chapter, the term *MIS* requires the use of computers to process data at some point in the system.

Knowing that most MIS involves the computer, it is important to note that MIS is not the same as data processing. **Data processing** is the capture, processing, and storage of data, whereas MIS uses that data to produce information for management.[6] In other words, data processing provides the data base of the MIS.

Transaction-processing systems substitute computer processing for manual record-keeping procedures. Examples include payroll, billing, and inventory record systems. By definition, transaction processing requires routine and highly structured decisions. It is actually a subset of data processing. Therefore, an organization can have a very effective transaction-processing system and not have a MIS. Figure 21–1 shows the relationships between MIS, data processing, and transaction processing. Management in Action 21–3 describes how some hospitals are using MIS to help control costs.

Data processing–capture, processing, and storage of data.

Transaction-processing systems–substitutes computer processing for manual record-keeping procedures.

FIGURE 21–1
Relationship between MIS, Data Processing, and Transaction Processing

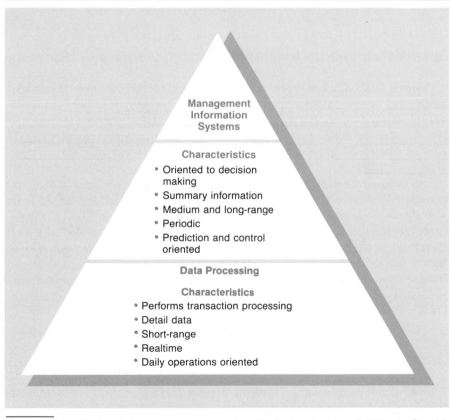

Management
Information
Systems

Characteristics
• Oriented to decision making
• Summary information
• Medium and long-range
• Periodic
• Prediction and control oriented

Data Processing

Characteristics
• Performs transaction processing
• Detail data
• Short-range
• Realtime
• Daily operations oriented

MANAGEMENT IN ACTION 21–3

Management Information System Helps Hospitals Control Costs

The federal government has created a new medicare fixed-fee system that is forcing hospitals to do a better job of keeping track of costs. If the cost of treating a patient exceeds the fixed fee for that particular disease, the hospital takes a loss. If the cost is less than the fixed fee, the hospital keeps the difference. As such, hospitals now have a real initative to keep costs down and to know exactly what goes into the cost of treating each patient. Hospital administrators are turning to computers to help them structure and maintain the extensive information files needed to better control costs.

At Arnot Ogden Memorial Hospital in Elmira, New York, treatment information, prescription records, supply charges, and room charges are all recorded by patient number in a computerized file. The hospital can then track costs by patient, by doctor, and by disease. The specific cost information can then be used to spotlight everything from doctors who order more tests than average to supplies that are too costly. According to Phillip D. Cusans, the president and CEO of Stamford Hospital in Connecticut, hospitals are "making an investment in information."

Source: Adapted from "The Medicare Squeeze Pushes Hospitals into the Information Age," *Business Week*, June 18, 1984, pp. 87, 90.

Operational versus Strategic MIS

Historically, MIS has been used mostly to assist managers in making operational decisions. Recently, however, MIS has begun to help managers with more-strategic decisions. **Operational MIS** basically provides information to assist in making decisions about current operations; **strategic MIS** is more concerned with decisions that affect the accomplishment of long-range objectives.

Operational MIS—basically provides information to assist in making decisions related to current operations.

Strategic MIS—concerned with decisions that affect the organization's long-range objectives.

The following example should help distinguish between operational and strategic MIS.[7] Several discount department store chains have changed from centralized to point-of-sale warehousing by using strategic MIS. They designed their MIS to focus on inventory management and make sure that all stores are well stocked at all times. This nearly eliminates the cost of central warehousing. On the other hand, an operational MIS plan would focus on reducing central-warehousing costs. Many people contend that MIS must move from mainly an operations orientation to a more strategic one if certain organizations are to remain competitive.

Decision Support Systems (DSS)

Decision support systems (DSS)—extension of an MIS; provides information for making decisions and becomes a part of the process.

Management information systems do not make decisions for managers. Rather, they provide information to assist managers in making decisions. **Decision support systems (DSS)** not only provide inputs to the decision process; they actually become a part of the process.[8] Thus, a DSS may be viewed as an extension of an MIS. Decision support systems allows a manager to use computers directly to retrieve information for decisions on semistructured problems. Such problems contain some elements that are well defined and can be quantified and some that are not. Examples of decisions that lend themselves to DSS include plant locations, acquisitions, and new products/services.

MIS Components

Certain basic components are needed for a successful MIS.[9] The actual computer, known as **hardware,** is one requirement. The selection is abundant and continues to expand.

All computers need instructions or programs to run them. These instructions and programs are referred to as **software.** Software can be purchased off the shelf for most applications. However, some organizations elect to write their own software. This can require anything from a single programmer to several programmers and systems analysts. **Programmers** are the people who write the instructional programs that tell the computer what to do. **Systems analysts** study a potential computer application and determine the type of programs needed. Systems analysts basically serve as intermediaries between the users and the programmers.

A third necessary component is the data base. **A data base** includes the data needed by the user. Usually a data base has information about the organization's operations. It is stored so as to be readily accessed. Information for a data base can be very expensive.

The final necessary component of the system is the management staff and executive leadership. Other components can produce information; but this information must be used by information-oriented managers. They must know what information they need and how to use it. And they must be

Hardware–actual computer and its peripheral equipment.

Software–instructions and programs used to run a computer.

Programmer–writes instructional programs that tell computers what to do.

Systems analyst–studies a potential computer application and determines the type of programs needed.

Data base–contains the data required to meet the user's need; usually, readily accessible information about the organization's operations.

FIGURE 21–2
Components of an MIS

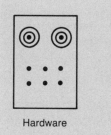

| Hardware | Software | Data base | Information-oriented managers and executives |

willing to make the effort needed to improve the information and the MIS itself. Top managers or executives must actively endorse and support the MIS. If the middle- and lower-level managers see that top management is really not committed to the MIS, the system will surely fail. Figure 21–2 on page 587 summarizes the necessary components of a successful MIS.

DEVELOPING AN MIS

The development of an MIS consists of the design phase and the implementation phase. Each is discussed in the following sections.[10]

The Design Phase

Designing an MIS includes everything that occurs prior to buying the equipment and putting the new MIS into operation. The design phase involves the following steps:

1. **Identify the needs of managers.**   What problems do managers encounter? What are their informational needs? The most common and possibly most effective method for determining such needs is to interview the different managers. Once this information has been collected, it should be classified as either (1) important enough or used often enough to be provided by the MIS or (2) used so rarely that it is cheaper to search for it when it is needed.

2. **Set objectives for the system.**   The objectives of the MIS should be expressed in writing. They should be based upon the managers' needs, the associated costs, and the expected benefits of the system. Remember that an MIS can not be all things to all people. The MIS objectives should, above all else, help the organization achieve its objectives and mission.

3. **Prepare a project proposal.**   The project proposal should contain both a general description of why the system is needed and an estimate of its cost and implementation schedule. The project proposal is used by top management to evaluate whether to pursue the project.

4. **Prepare a conceptual design of the MIS.**   The conceptual design specifies the main subsystems and components, the arrangement and relationships of these subsystems, the general nature of the inputs and outputs, and the anticipated performance of the MIS. The major purpose of the conceptual design is to consider and evaluate alternative concepts.

5. **Prepare a detailed design.**   The detailed design extends the conceptual design. It includes a detailed narrative, charts, tables, and diagrams for setting up the proposed MIS. The detailed design should provide all the technical information necessary to implement the system. Figure 21–3 gives the steps in the design phase and some examples of each step.

FIGURE 21–3
Steps in MIS Design

Step	Examples
1. Find out the *information needs* of all managers.	Study the position description for the marketing manager. This manager states a need for monthly information about sales by product and area for the company and for competitors.
2. Write down the *objectives* of the MIS, based upon the needs of all managers, the costs, and the anticipated benefits.	One objective will be to supply managers with productivity analyses at the end of each month. Another objective will be to make financial and cost reports available within three days after the end of each month.
3. Prepare a *plan* and *proposal* for the design of MIS, including schedule and estimated cost.	A revised financial and new marketing MIS will be completed in preliminary form by May 17, 1985. The estimated cost is $57,500.
4. Prepare a preliminary, *conceptual* design of the MIS.	A table listing each manager, their responsibilities, their information needs, and source of such information. An outline of files and records. General computer configuration.
5. Prepare the *detailed* design of all aspects of the MIS.	Specific report received by each manager. The customer-record file. A flowchart of the environmental scanning system. Computer programs. Hardware architecture. (Obviously, the detailed design of the MIS is a very lengthy document.)

Source: Robert G. Murdick, *MIS Concepts and Design*, © 1980, pp. 17–18. Reprinted by permission of Prentice-Hall, Inc., Englewood Cliffs, N.J.

The Implementation Phase

Designing an MIS can be an expensive and lengthy process. Turning the design into a working system can be even more difficult and expensive.[11] Implementation includes the purchase and integration of the resources necessary to form a working MIS, as well as testing and actually putting the system into operation. Specifically, implementation consists of the following steps:

1. Acquiring the necessary facilities, equipment, and personnel.
2. Training the personnel.
3. Conversion from the old to the new MIS (if an old one existed).
4. Testing the new MIS.
5. Operating the MIS.
6. Evaluating the MIS to see if it is doing what it was designed to do.

Once an MIS operates as designed, it must be maintained. Needed changes in procedures or the structure of the data files must be made to handle

MANAGEMENT IN ACTION 21-4

MIS at MTA

In 1982, New York's Metropolitan Transportation Authority (MTA) embarked on a $7.2 billion, five-year improvement plan. As part of the plan, MTA has installed a specifically developed online management information system that allows MTA to monitor the status and costs of the many projects that are part of the improvement plan. The system is designed to track the contracts, labor, and materials of the various capital, maintenance, and procurement programs.

The system, called central, has 10 subsystems: budgeting/funding, scheduling/resource allocation, task detailing, procurement, real estate, change order, contract payment, force account, system reporting,

and system maintenance. All of the subsystems share a common data base which means a change of one field updates information across the system. The continual updating of project completion status and costs allows MTA management to know immediately about problems that might lead to delays and cost overruns.

MTA is counting heavily on the central system. If the new information system allows MTA to complete the renovation on time and within budget, service will be better, and future renovation programs will have a greater chance of being approved.

Source: Peter Derrick, "Space-Age Computer to Keep MTA Project on Track," *Mass Transit,* November 1982, pp. 16–22.

changing inputs and management needs. Management in Action 21–4 describes how New York's Metropolitan Transportation Authority has implemented an MIS.

Organization/People Strategies

Discussion of both the design and implementation phases focused on the technical requirements of each phase. However, merely attending to these does not ensure that the MIS will work. In fact, a recent study reported that "for the MIS practitioner, the research results in this area carry a clear message—worry less about how up-to-date your hardware is and whether or not the latest data base system is in place, and worry more about how user interaction takes place, how employees are managed, and how computer resources are allocated within the organization."[12]

A successful MIS must have the cooperation of many groups of people. So certain organization and people–related factors must be considered. The following strategies have been suggested to overcome potential organization- and people-related problems.[13]

1. Get top management involved.   Top management must be committed to MIS if the system is to be successful. Not only must they approve the expenditures (which may be significant); they also must outwardly exhibit interest in the project. Subordinates sense when their superiors are genuinely interested in a project, and they act accordingly.

2. Determine if there is a felt need for the system.   Make sure that the ultimate users and those who must provide inputs to the MIS feel the need for it. One helpful approach is to make sure that the users understand how the system can help them.

3. Get the users involved.   As discussed in the previous chapter, most people resist change. One of the best ways to overcome this is to involve the users in the project as early as possible. Ask for their ideas and keep them fully informed as to what is going on. Involving users early in the design phase will also help ensure that the system will be compatible with the different users' needs and their organizational constraints.

4. Provide training and education.   Users must be taught how to input data and how to get answers from the system. In addition, training should include educating users in the overall purpose of the system, what it is supposed to do, how it does it, why it needs to be done, and who must do it.

5. Consider user attitudes.   Studies have shown that user attitudes have a great impact on system effectiveness, especially when use of the system is mandated.[14] It is helpful to establish rewards for successful implementation of the system. These rewards do not have to be monetary but can be some form of recognition or other type of extrinsic reward.

6. Keep the interface simple.   Even when the system is complex, the interface with users should be kept as simple as possible. Usually, users do not need to see the complex flow-diagrams and programming of the system design. Systems that appear very complicated to users often frighten them and make them leery of the entire system.

7. Let the ultimate users (managers) determine information usefulness.   MIS designers should remember that what counts is what the users think is important. If users feel the information is neither useful nor important for making decisions, the system implementation will likely fail.

All of the above strategies are closely related to each other. They are not necessarily sequential but rather may be used at the same time. Also, they not only apply to the initial implementation but should be regularly reviewed and used to improve the system after it is operational. Figure 21–4 summarizes the above strategies.

FIGURE 21–4
Organization/People Strategies for Implementing an MIS

1. Get top management involved.
2. Ascertain that there is a felt need for the system.
3. Get the users involved.
4. Provide training and education.
5. Consider user attitudes.
6. Keep the interface simple.
7. Let the ultimate users determine information usefulness.

INFORMATION CENTERS

Learning to interact with their companies' computer systems is a major problem for many of today's managers. Most managers do not have the time or interest to become experts in data processing. What managers want and need is to be able to gain direct access to data without becoming frustrated and confused.

Information centers— in-house centers that companies establish to teach their managers to use their information systems.

Many companies—such as Exxon, Standard Oil of California, Bank of America, and New York Telephone—have formed internal **information centers.** There managers can learn how to interact with their information systems from staff specialists whose job it is to train and support noncomputer people.[15] Typically, a manager contacts the center and describes the problems encountered and the type of information needed. A center consultant then works one-on-one with the manager, showing how to access needed data and use the software to get the desired information. The key to the information center concept is that managers use a hands-on approach and learn how to generate their own reports.

CRITICISMS OF MIS

There is little doubt that an MIS can have a very positive effect on organizational performance. Yet, it is still subject to frequent criticism. Much criticism relates to shortfalls in methods of implementation. Figure 21–5 mentions some of the most frequent criticisms of MIS.

FIGURE 21–5
Criticisms of MIS

Weakness	Criticism
Inadequate information	Managers often complain that they do not get the information they need but they do get much information that is irrelevant.
Ignorance about what managers actually do	Understanding a manager's job is a natural prerequisite to providing that manager with useful information.
Centralized control of MIS	There is a tendency to centralize the development of an MIS. However, because of the large number and variety of activities that go on in an organization, this frequently leads to problems.
Complex user procedures	The rule of thumb is to keep the system as simple and user-friendly as possible.
Poor communication	Any system is almost doomed to failure if there is not open communication between the users and those responsible for developing the MIS.

Source: David Lynch, "MIS: Conceptual Framework, Criticisms, and Major Requirements for Success," *Journal of Business Communication,* Winter 1984, pp. 23–25.

CAUTIONS CONCERNING MIS

Tremendous strides have been made regarding computers and management information systems. Still, managers must realize that technology will never replace certain aspects of a manager's job. Managers must surely become familiar with and be able to use computerized information systems. Yet, they must guard against being too dependent upon any computer system. In fact, it has been said that "too many cut-and-dried computer printouts have usurped the human aspect and put forth the fallacy that a corporation is equal to (and not more than) the sum of its parts."[16] Thomas Peters and Robert Waterman emphasize this same point in their book *In Search of Excellence* by attacking the tendency of many managers to become "overly rational."[17] Information systems can be of tremendous help in making managerial decisions. But the fact remains that successful management is still heavily dependent on human interaction.

SUMMARY

The advent and maturing of computers has greatly altered not only the availability of information but also the manner by which it is identified and acquired. Because of this, today's managers are often overloaded with information.

Computer technology has made huge leaps. It has moved from primarily large computers to distributed minicomputers to small personal computers. The vast improvements in hardware have been accompanied by improvements in software and user compatibility.

A management information system (MIS) is an integrated approach for providing interpreted and relevant data that can be used to help managers make decisions. For most situations, an MIS must include the use of computers to process data at some point in the system. Data processing is oriented toward the capture, processing, and storage of data, whereas MIS is oriented toward using that data to produce information for management.

Operations MIS basically provides information to assist in making decisions about current operations, while strategic MIS is more concerned with decisions that affect how the organization will compete. Decision support systems (DSS) not only provide inputs to the decision process; they actually become a part of the process. A DSS may be viewed as an extension of an MIS.

The following components are basic to any MIS: hardware, software, data base, and information-oriented managers and executives. Programmers and systems analysts may also be required.

Developing an MIS can be broken down into two phases: the design phase and the implementation phase. The design phase includes everything that occurs prior to buying the equipment and putting the MIS into operation.

Implementation includes the acquisition and integration of the resources to form a working MIS as well as testing and actually putting the system into operation. Several steps were suggested for designing and implementing an MIS.

Meeting the technical requirements of a MIS does not ensure that it will work. Because a successful MIS must involve the cooperation of many groups of people, certain organization and people–related factors must be considered. Several of these factors were discussed.

Many large companies have established information centers to assist managers in learning to use an MIS. Inadequate information, ignorance about what managers actually do, centralized control of MIS, complex user procedures, and poor comunication are criticisms that are frequently made about a MIS and those responsible for its development.

References and Additional Readings

[1] Stan Augarten, *Bit by Bit: An Illustrated History of Computers* (New York: Ticknor & Fields, 1984), pp. 124–25, 128.

[2] Herbert R. Brinberg, "Effective Management of Information: How to Meet the Need of All Users," *Management Review,* February 1984, p. 11.

[3] David Lynch, "MIS: Conceptual Framework, Criticisms, and Major Requirements for Success," *Journal of Business Communication,* Winter 1984, p. 20.

[4] Ibid.

[5] James O. Hicks, Jr., *Management Information Systems: A User Perspective* (St. Paul, Minn.: West Publishing, 1984), p. 21.

[6] "Using MIS Strategically," *Management Review,* April 1984, p. 5.

[7] For example, see F. Warren McFarlan, "Information Technology Changes the Way You Compete," *Harvard Business Review,* May–June 1984, pp. 98–103.

[8] James A. Senn, *Information Systems in Management,* 2d ed. (Belmont, Calif.: Wadsworth, 1982), p. 284.

[9] This section is adapted from Raymond McLeod, Jr., *Management Information System,* 2d ed. (Chicago: Science Research Associates 1983), pp. 16–17.

[10] Much of the material in the following two sections is drawn from Robert G. Murdick, *MIS Concepts and Design* (Englewood Cliffs, N.J.: Prentice-Hall, 1980), pp. 16–18, 210–11, 308–31.

[11] Ibid., p. 308.

[12] Paul H. Cheney and Gary W. Dickson, "Organizational Characteristics and Information Systems: An Exploratory Investigation," *Academy of Management Journal,* March 1982, pp. 181–82.

[13] Jugoslan S. Multinovich and Vladimir Vlahovich, "A Strategy for a Successful MIS/DSS Implementation," *Journal of Systems Management,* August 1984, pp. 8–16.

[14] For example, see D. Robey, "User Attitudes and Management Information System Use," *Academy of Management Journal* 22, no. 3 (1979), pp. 527–38.

[15] William Clarke, "How Managers with Little DP Know-How Learn to Go Online with the Company Data Base," *Management Review,* June 1983, pp. 9–11. Much of this section is based on this article.

[16] Robert E. McGarrah, "Ironies of Our Computer Age," *Business Horizons,* September–October 1984, p. 34.

[17] Thomas J. Peters and Robert Waterman, Jr., *In Search of Excellence* (New York: Harper & Row, 1982), pp. 29–54.

Review Questions

1. Define "information overload." *each area*
2. What is distributed data processing? *own computer*
3. Distinguish between data and information. *raw material / processed*
4. What is a management information system (MIS)?
5. How does a transaction-processing system differ from an MIS? *substitute computer processing for manual record-keeping*
6. Contrast operational MIS with strategic MIS. *current vs. long-term*
7. What is a decision support system (DSS)? *part of*
8. What are the four basic components of a *decision* MIS? *hardware, software, data base, managers* *process*

9. Name the five basic steps involved in designing an MIS?
   1. identify needs of mgr. 4.prepare conceptual design
   2. set obj. for system
   3. prepare project proposal 5.prepare detailed design
10. What steps are involved in implementing an MIS? *acq., integration, testing, on-line*
11. Briefly describe seven organization and people-related strategies that should be considered when developing an MIS. *p.591*
12. What is an information center? *in house center to teach mgrs to use MIS*
13. Summarize at least five criticisms that are frequently made about management information systems.
    1. inadequate info.
    2. Centralized control of MIS
    3. Poor comm.
    4. Complex user procedures
    5. Ignorance about what mgr does

Discussion Questions

1. How would you respond to the following statement: "Learning about management information systems should be reserved for computer specialists"?
2. When you go into a fast-food store and the salesperson keys your order into the cash register type of device, how might this information be used as part of a MIS?
3. Assume your boss has just assigned you a special project to introduce all middle and top managers (a total of 20 managers) to personal computers. Describe in outline form how you might go about this project. Assume that none of the managers has ever worked with a personal computer.
4. Why do you think that some people like to talk about computers and MIS as if you have to be a genius to work with them?

Incident 21–1
Overburdened with Paperwork

Frank Bierman is a pharmacist and owner of a small, suburban drugstore. In recent years, his business has grown to the point where he could live comfortably—if he could just relax! Every working hour of every day he works at a breakneck speed just to fill prescriptions and keep up with all of the drugstore records.

When a customer wants a prescription filled, Frank pulls the customer's chart from a file cabinet and scans it for any potential drug interactions. He then types a prescription label that lists the patient's name, prescription number, name of the medicine, dosage, quantity, and the name of the prescribing physician. Finally, he fills the prescription, prepares a sales slip, and accepts payment.

During his few slow periods, Frank updates the customers' charts by hand with the same information that is printed on the prescription label. He also has to prepare his third-party billing forms. "Third-party billing" involves billing insurance companies directly for those customers who are covered by medicare, medicaid, or special group insurance programs. If a customer has a charge account with the store, Frank "files" a copy of the sales slip in a shoe box. Once a month, he and his wife spend an entire weekend totaling accounts, writing out bills, and addressing envelopes in order to bill customers. Frank has two clerks working in the store. They make deliveries and wait on customers, but they do not help Frank with the paperwork.

With all of the paperwork, Frank never leaves the store at closing time and rarely has a work-free weekend. He has been reading in the trade journals about small computer systems for retail drugstores that can help the pharmacist manage all of the drug, patient, and billing information. Frank thinks maybe a computer system could help him get control of the paperwork in his store.

Questions

1. What are Frank's information needs?
2. Assume you are Frank Bierman and that you have decided to look into purchasing a small computer system. Write a list of objectives that you would like for this system to achieve. Make any assumption you feel are necessary, but note them in your answer.

Incident 21–2
The First Assignment

Julie Shorski has recently been hired as assistant manager for a small local restaurant chain that includes five stores. Julie was hired to take over many of the day-to-day administrative functions so that the owner, who is also the manager, would have more time to plan further expansions. One specific problem that Julie discovered right away is that the company has very little information about what their customers order, what their supply levels are, and when supplies should be ordered. Julie would like to have more control over what is going on and be able to predict roughly what items will be most in demand on particular days and at particular times of the day. The manager has encouraged Julie to make any recommendations that she thinks might better enable her to do her job.

Question

What recommendations do you think Julie should make? In formulating your response, consider the following:
a. The process Julie should use to determine information needs.
b. The objectives of the system.
c. Any problem that Julie might confront in implementing the system.

Exercise

Recall*

Your instructor will read several series of digits to you. Listen carefully to each number. *When told to do so,* recall the digits and record them on a sheet of paper in their proper order as shown by the spaces provided below. Remember, do not write down the numbers until your instructor tells you to.

		Did You Get It Correct?	
		Yes	*No*
String 1:	___ ___ ___ ___ ___ ___ ___ ___ ___ ___	___	___
String 2:	___ ___ ___ ___ ___ ___ ___ ___ ___ ___	___	___
String 3:	___ ___ ___ ___ ___ ___ ___ ___ ___ ___	___	___
String 4:	___ ___ ___ ___ ___ ___ ___ ___ ___ ___	___	___
String 5:	___ ___ ___ ___ ___ ___ ___ ___ ___ ___	___	___
String 6:	___ ___ ___ ___ ___ ___ ___ ___ ___ ___	___	___

Compare the following sets of outcomes by noting whether you got the string correct or not.

Comparison I

Did you get String 1 correct?   Yes   No
Did you get String 2 correct?   Yes   No
Did you get String 3 correct?   Yes   No
How are 1, 2, and 3 different? _____
What does this show? _____
_____

Comparison II

Did you get String 3 correct?   Yes   No
Did you get String 5 correct?   Yes   No
How are Strings 3 and 5 different? _____
What does this show? _____
_____

_____

* This exercise is adapted from Henry J. Tosi and Jerald W. Young, *Management Experiences and Demonstrations* (Homewood, Ill.: Richard D. Irwin, 1982), pp. 154–55.

Comparison III

Did you get String 4 correct?   Yes   No

Did you get String 6 correct?   Yes   No

How are Strings 4 and 6 different? _____

What does this show? _____
_____

Objectives

1. To emphasize the growing necessity for managers to understand the nature of international management.
2. To introduce the basic approaches to, and problems associated with, international management.
3. To discuss multinational corporations (MNCs).
4. To describe some lessons that can be learned from the management practices in other countries.

International Management

Chapter Outline

INTERNATIONAL BUSINESS
  INVOLVEMENT
EXPORTING AND IMPORTING
PROBLEMS IN INTERNATIONAL
  BUSINESS ACTIVITIES
  Tariffs
  Quotas
  Payment for International
    Transactions
  Government Control over Profits

Taxation
Cultural Differences
MULTINATIONAL
  CORPORATIONS (MNCs)
  Problems Facing MNCs
  Managers in MNCs
LEARNING FROM FOREIGN
  MANAGEMENT
SUMMARY

Of the 500 largest industrial corporations in the United States, at least 25 earn more than half of their profits overseas. Today, 68 of the 156 largest multinational organizations are U.S. firms.

David Ricks and Vijay Mahajan*

Throughout this text, management has been discussed in terms of American organizations operating in the United States. An important trend is the increasing internationalization of business activity. International business activities range from exporting goods to other nations to establishing manufacturing operations in other nations. These activities present new challenges to managers.

While not all organizations are directly involved in international business activities, events that impact on American organizations occur almost daily in other nations. Thus, it is increasingly important that all managers understand the nature of international business activity.

The trading of goods and services across national boundaries results from the principle of comparative advantage. A country has a **comparative advantage** when it can produce goods and services more efficiently or cheaply than other countries. Factors determining a country's comparative advantage include the presence of natural resources, adequate quality and quantity of labor and capital, available technology, and the costs of these resources.

Comparative advantage—
a country produces those goods and services it can produce more efficiently or cheaply than other countries.

INTERNATIONAL BUSINESS INVOLVEMENT

Generally, the decision to extend an organization's operations to other countries has two objectives: profit and stability. In terms of profit, international operations give organizations the chance to meet the increasing demand for goods and services in foreign countries. In addition, new sources of demand (in other countries) for an organization's output may have a stabilizing effect on the organization's production process.

Organizations deciding to move into international operations can usually be classified as following one of four basic strategies:[1]

1. Exploit a technological lead. When an organization creates a new product, it at first enjoys a distinct competitive advantage. As the product becomes less unique and this advantage erodes, the organization often attempts to build new markets elsewhere. In addition, as costs begin to play a more critical part in the production of the product, the organization often sets up production and/or marketing facilities nearer to the markets it is serving.

* David A. Ricks and Vijay Mahajan, "Blunders in International Marketing: Fact or Fiction," *Long-Range Planning,* February 1984, p. 78.

2. Exploit a strong trade name. A successful product often induces organizations to set up operations on an international basis. Foreign brands often are considered better—as a result of snob appeal or on the basis of superior quality. This is especially evident in the foreign car market.

3. Exploit advantages of scale. Larger organizations can more easily assemble the funds, physical assets, and human resources needed to produce and distribute goods on a larger scale than can smaller organizations.

4. Exploit a low-cost resource. When costs of production are a critical concern, an organization may set up international operations in areas where the resource and/or labor costs are relatively lower than they are domestically.

EXPORTING AND IMPORTING

An organization may become involved in international business activities by exporting, importing, or manufacturing in a foreign country.

Exporting refers to the selling of an organization's goods in another country; **importing** is the purchasing of goods or services from a foreign country. Some of the more common reasons for exporting and importing are listed in Figure 22–1.

Exporting–selling an organization's goods or services to another country.

Importing–purchasing goods or services from foreign countries.

FIGURE 22–1
Reasons for Exporting and Importing Goods

Why Export?

1. If the production process requires high volume to reduce cost per unit, the home market may be too small to absorb the output. Thus, the output may be sold overseas. Stoves, for example, are purchased by households only when needed to replace an old one or when a new home is built. To restrict selling stoves only to the U.S. market would limit the number of stoves demanded below that amount which is cost efficient to produce.
2. The demand for the firm's product may be seasonal and irregular. By expanding the firm's market to other countries, production costs may be lowered by more effective production scheduling.
3. All products undergo what is called the product life cycle: When the product is first introduced, there is usually a big demand and the introducing firm is the only supplier. As the product reaches maturity, this competitive edge is reduced and can be maintained only by creating new markets, where it reenters the growth stage.
4. In selling goods overseas, the organization may not face competition as stiff as it does in the United States; thus, its marketing costs may be reduced. By selling its established goods in new overseas markets, the organization is also able to increase its profits without risking new-product development.

Why Import?

1. The goods may be needed but not available in the importing country (e.g., crude oil).
2. Many foreign-made products have prestige value and are demanded by the home market (e.g., French perfumes, sports cars from Germany).
3. Some foreign goods are less expensive due to lower production costs.

MANAGEMENT IN ACTION 22–1

Bethlehem Steel Corporation

Agreements have been signed between Bethlehem Steel Corporation of the United States and two European steelmakers for licenses to manufacture Bethlehem's aluminum-zinc alloy coated sheet. Ensidesa (Empress Siderargica Nacional SA) of Madrid, Spain, and La Magona D'Italia of Florence, Italy, announced the agreement in April 1984. The coated sheet is used in the building and roofing industry, automotive and appliance markets, and for solar heating panels.

Both European companies are major producers of sheet steel, Ensidesa being the largest integrated steel company in Spain and La Magona being Italy's main precoated sheet steel producer. This agreement brings to 13 the number of licenses granted for this technology by Bethlehem Steel. Many of the world's largest steelmakers have signed agreements, including those in Japan, Australia, and Canada.

Source: Adapted from *Iron and Steel International*, June 1984, p. 74.

Organizations that make a commitment to selling their products overseas must decide how to organize their exporting/importing activities. The organizational structure that is used depends on how critical these activities are to the overall organization. The organization may establish its own internal structure. This requires special expertise in international accounting, finance, marketing, and law. As a result, many organizations either cannot or do not desire to establish such divisions. Some contract with an outside person who is sometimes called a combination export-import manager. An **export-import manager** serves a group of exporting/importing organizations and handles all activities involved in the exporting/importing of the organization's goods or services.

Export-import manager–serves a group of exporting/importing organizations and handles all activities involved in the exporting/importing of their goods or services.

Over time, many organizations find that it is economically better to expand their production operations overseas than to continue exporting goods to their markets abroad. Furthermore, in recent years, less-developed countries have sought local production of goods. As a result, American organizations are finding that they must produce in these countries in order to maintain their overseas markets.

Parent organization–organization that extends its operations beyond its nation's boundaries.

Host country–country in which a foreign organization does business.

The ways in which international organizations expand their production activities differ in the degree of control retained by the **parent organization** (the organization extending its operations beyond its nation's boundaries). The country which it is entering is referred to as the **host country.** The parent company may set up assembly operations in a foreign country: Parts are exported overseas, and the finished product is assembled there. Also, the parent organization may contract with a foreign organization to produce its product, but retain control over the marketing of the product in that country. Licensing arrangements are an extension of this latter type of expansion. The parent organization enters into an agreement with a foreign organization, licensing it to produce and market the parent organization's product in return for a set percentage of sales revenues. Often, the parent organization provides technical and/or managerial support to the foreign organization. Management in Action 22–1 describes a licensing agreement between Bethlehem Steel and two European Steelmakers.

PROBLEMS IN INTERNATIONAL BUSINESS ACTIVITIES

When an organization decides to extend its operations abroad, some new problems must be dealt with if the activities are to be managed effectively.

Tariffs

Tariffs are government-imposed taxes charged on goods imported into, or exported from, a country. They serve (1) to raise revenues for the country or (2) to protect the country's producers from the competition of imported goods. The tariffs charged on parts are often less than those charged on finished goods. Therefore, foreign assembly operations (discussed earlier) have become quite popular.

Tariffs–government-imposed taxes charged on goods imported into, or exported from a country.

Quotas

A **quota** establishes the maximum quantity of a good that can be imported (or exported) during a given time period. A quota can be set in physical or in value terms. Quotas can be imposed unilaterally, or they can be negotiated on a voluntary basis. Voluntary negotiation generally means that the quotas have been negotiated with threats of even worse restrictions if voluntary cooperation is not forthcoming.[2] Management in Actice 22–2 describes how import quotas have been set for Japanese cars sold in the United States.

Quotas–establish the maximum quantity of a good that might be imported (or exported) during a given time period.

Payment for International Transactions

International trade requires exchanging currency from one country into that of another. Foreign exchange rates (the rate of exchange for one currency to another currency, e.g., French francs to American dollars) present certain problems as the rates fluctuate in value. For example, in 1985, it was estimated that the overvalued American dollar had helped to cause exports to be 15 percent lower and imports to be 15 percent higher than would have been the case with a normal dollar value.

MANAGEMENT IN ACTION 22-2

Import Quotas on Japanese Cars

The U.S. and Japanese governments in 1981 entered into an arrangement which called for an annual ceiling of 1.68 million Japanese cars which could be imported into the United States. This agreement expired on March 31, 1984. However, the Japanese minister of international trade and industry and the U.S. trade representative reached agreement in late 1983 on new restraints, limiting the number of Japanese cars imported into the U.S. to 1.85 million cars. The new agreement was described as a transitional measure to ensure full recovery of the American auto industry.

Reactions to the agreement were negative in both the U.S. and Japan, but for different reasons. For example, Ford Motor Co. Chairman Philip Caldwell said his company ''is disappointed to see any increase in Japanese auto exports at a time of continuing high U.S. unemployment and record high U.S. trade deficits with Japan.'' On the other hand, Toshio Okamoto, president of Isuzu Motors, Ltd., expressed strong dissatisfaction with the new agreement, saying that it would adversely affect Isuzu's plans to supply 100,000 small cars annually to General Motors.

Source: Adapted from Geoff Lundstrom, ''1.85 Million Japan Cars Rapped by Both Sides,'' *Automotive News*, November 7, 1983, p. 2.

Government Control over Profits

A firm owning facilities in another country naturally expects to receive profits from its operations. The amount of profits the parent company receives is often controlled by the host country's government, which regulates the access foreigners have to its currency.

Taxation

Firms operating in another country are subject to that country's laws and regulations. As taxes are a primary source of government revenue, many countries tax foreign investments located within their boundaries. These taxes may be quite high, since some of these foreign countries have few other businesses to tax.

Cultural Differences

International business activities bring people of many different cultures together. This results in language problems. A more subtle but equally important problem is that of differences in cultural values, tastes, and attitudes. Countries differ socially, economically, technically, and politically. To be successful in the international business environment requires that these differences be recognized and considered in managing international activities.

MULTINATIONAL CORPORATIONS (MNCs)

The multinational corporation (MNC) has become a well-known entity in international business. Yet a common definition of that entity does not seem to exist. Measures used to determine if a business is multinational include percentage of total sales accounted for by majority-owned foreign affiliates, percentage of earnings due to foreign operations, and percentage of new capital investment destined for overseas facilities.[3] However, for the purposes of this book, an **MNC** is defined as any business that maintains a production, assembly, sales, or service presence in two or more countries.[4]

The internationalization of American companies has been dramatic, with companies such as IBM, Eastman Kodak, Exxon, Bank America, and American Express having large and growing international activities. The same kind of experience can be observed among non-American multinationals such as Volkswagen, Nestle, British Petroleum, Phillips, Toyota, Olivetta, and numerous others. In fact, Management in Action 22–3 shows that many of the world's largest companies are not American.

Multinational corporation (MNC)–any business organization that maintains a production, assembly, sales, or service presence in two or more countries.

Problems Facing MNCs

As would be expected, MNCs must deal with the normal problems in international business activities, such as tariffs, quotas, cultural differences, taxation, payment for international transactions, and government control over profits. Each of these problems was discussed earlier in this chapter. However, MNCs also face other difficult and challenging problems.

Human Rights

Should Ford Motor Co. and General Electric close their South African plants as long as apartheid exists in that country? Should Coca-Cola establish minimum labor standards for all of its bottlers around the world to prevent abuses of workers in certain countries? Such questions present dilemmas for managers of MNCs which are accompanied by ethical predicaments and hard choices. Most MNCs have yet to develop a coherent, effective response to the challenge of human rights.[5] In each specific situation, management of an MNC must strike a balance between the interests and ideals of all of its various publics. There are no clear and easy choices.

Terrorism

Over the past decade, MNCs have become a favorite target of numerous forms of terrorism. The U.S. Central Intelligence Agency (CIA) has concluded that "because of the tighter security measures that have been introduced

The Biggest Companies Aren't Always American Anymore

When U.S. securities dealers talk of investing in an industry, they don't consider that some of the biggest or most profitable companies in that industry today may be foreign. The figures below clearly illustrate foreign companies are significant in several industries.

Rank	Top 5 Companies in U.S. Company	Sales ($millions)	Top 5 Companies in the World Company	Sales ($millions)
	Automotive			
1	General Motors	$74,582	General Motors	$74,582
2	Ford Motor	44,455	Ford Motor	44,455
3	Chrysler	13,240	Toyota Motor	21,470
4	American Motors	3,272	Nissan Motor	16,309
5			Volkswagen Group	15,701
	Banking (by assets)			
1	Citicorp	$134,655	Citicorp	$134,655
2	Bank America	121,176	Bank America	121,176
3	Chase Manhattan	81,921	Dai-ichi Kangyo Bank	110,036
4	Manufacturers Hanover	64,332	Fuji Bank	102,979
5	J. P. Morgan	58,023	Banque Nationale de Paris	101,019
	Chemicals			
1	E. I. du Pont	$35,173	E. I. du Pont	$35,173
2	Dow Chemical	10,951	BASF Group	14,824
3	Union Carbide	9,001	Bayer Group	14,623
4	Monsanto	6,299	Hoechst Group	14,565
5	W. R. Grace	6,219	Imperial Chemical Inds	12,524
	Electrical Equipment			
1	General Electric	$26,797	General Electric	$26,797
2	Westinghouse Electric	9,533	Hitachi	18,479
3	Texas Instruments	4,580	Matsushita Electric	16,745
4	Motorola	4,328	NV Philips Lamp	16,181
5	North America Philips	3,800	Siemens Group	15,730
	Food Processing			
1	Consolidated Foods	$6,789	Nestlé	$13,312
2	H. J. Heinz	3,843	Consolidated Foods	6,789
3	Campbell Soup	3,483	Dalgety	4,592
4	United Brands	2,232	Taiyo Fisheries	4,295
5	Castle & Cooke	1,642	Associated British Foods	4,127
	Steel			
1	US Steel	$16,869	US Steel	$16,869
2	Bethlehem Steel	4,898	Nippon Steel	11,602
3	Armco	4,165	Thyssen Group	11,306
4	Inland Steel	3,046	Krupp Group	6,765
5	National Intergroup	2,993	Nippon Kokan KK	6,265

Source: *FORBES,* July 2, 1984, p. 105.

at U.S. military and diplomatic installations, the continuing lure of lucrative ransom and extortion payments, and the symbolic value of U.S. firms (e.g., as 'capitalistic foreign exploiters' of the local working class), there is a real danger that terrorist attacks on the U.S. business community abroad will become even more frequent in the future."[6] Forms of terrorism include but are not limited to kidnapping of executives of MNCs, bombings, assassinations, and hijackings.

One way MNCs defend against terrorism is to increase security. It is now fairly standard practice for executives of MNCs in such high-risk cities as Paris, Rome, New York, and Mexico City to be accompanied by at least one bodyguard. Measures have also been taken to ensure a high level of security for the MNCs plants and other productive assets. Finally, most MNCs now have substantial insurance coverage to protect themselves against financial losses as a result of terrorism.

Marketing Practices

The approach used by many MNCs has been to simply take products designed to meet consumer needs and desires at home and market them in foreign markets. The tendency has been to treat foreign countries as an extension of the U.S. marketplace, which creates very significant potential for conflict.[7] For example, should a drug banned in the United States be sold by an MNC in an underdeveloped country? Should infant formula—safe to use in developed countries—be advertised, promoted, and sold in underdeveloped countries, where poverty and illiteracy may make the product unsafe? Pricing, distribution, advertising and promotion, and product quality and safety often pose unique problems for managers in the international environment.

Some MNCs have attempted to better understand the unique nature of a country's market by extending the concept of consumer affairs departments to foreign markets. Consumerism and consumer affairs departments were discussed in detail in Chapter 3. For example, Coca-Cola decided to expand its consumer affairs departments to its foreign subsidiaries.[8] In order to consider the worldwide nature of its market, Gillette has a vice president of product integrity, who can veto product introductions, order packaging changes, and stop advertising claims for any Gillette division anywhere in the world.[9]

Managers in MNCs

Using local nationals in management positions in foreign operations seems preferable. Two reasons given for this are lower costs and more thorough knowledge of the culture and market. In some countries, the development of local management is legally required by the host government as a condition of entry.

One problem with the use of local nationals as managers is that many of them may not be transferable to other company operations, which may contribute to frustration and nationalistic feelings. Another problem is that poor communications can develop unless someone in the parent company knows the local environment well enough to be able to represent the local operation to the rest of management. For these reasons, many MNCs assign American managers to their international operations.

International managers must possess several traits to be successful. First and foremost, they must be able to do the job. As one study put it, "Resident nationals will overlook qualities in an American they believe are abrasive— if he is efficient and knowledgeable and can get results for them."[10] Other desirable traits include cultural empathy, language skills, personal adaptability, and adaptability of the candidate's family.

LEARNING FROM FOREIGN MANAGEMENT

Obviously, many lessons can be learned from the management practices in other countries. Peter Drucker has outlined six lessons which he feels can be learned from foreign management, especially Western European and Japanese. These lessons are:[11]

1. Foreign managements increasingly demand responsibility from their employees.

2. Foreign managements have thought through their benefits policies more carefully and, especially in Japan and Germany, structure benefits according to the needs of recipients.

3. Foreign managements take marketing more seriously in that they attempt to know what is value for the customer.

4. Foreign managements base their marketing and innovation strategies on the systematic and purposeful abandonment of the old, the outworn, and the obsolete.

5. Foreign managements keep separate and discrete those areas where short-term results are the proper measurement and those where results should be measured over longer time spans—innovation, product development, product introduction, manager development, etc.

6. Managers in large Japanese, German, and French companies see themselves as national assets and leaders responsible for the development of proper policies in the national interest.

Drucker readily admits that each of those lessons is American in origin. However, reexamining and possibly reinstituting practices developed earlier is never bad, especially when they have been emulated so successfully by foreign managements.

SUMMARY

The increasing internationalization of business activity is an important trend. International business activities range from the exporting of goods to other nations to the establishment of manufacturing operations in other nations.

Organizations deciding to move into international operations usually follow one of four basic strategies: exploiting a technological lead, exploiting a strong trade name, exploiting advantages of scale, and exploiting a low-cost resource. An organization may become involved in international business activities by exporting, importing, or manufacturing in a foreign country. Problems encountered in international business activities include tariffs, quotas, payment for international transactions, government control over profits, taxation, and cultural differences.

A multinational corporation (MNC) is defined as any business that maintains a production, assembly, sales, or service presence in two or more countries.

References and Additional Readings

[1] Raymond Vernon and Louis T. Wells, Jr., *Manager in the International Economy,* 3d ed. (Englewood Cliffs, N.J.: Prentice-Hall, 1976), p. 5.

[2] Stefan H. Robock, Kenneth Simmonds, and Jack Zwick, *International Business and Multinational Enterprises* (Homewood, Ill.: Richard D. Irwin, 1977), p. 123.

[3] Thomas N. Gladwin and Ingo Walter, *Multinationals under Fire* (New York: John Wiley & Sons, 1980), p. 2.

[4] Ibid., p. 2.

[5] Ibid., p. 131.

[6] Directorate of Intelligence, U.S. Central Intelligence Agency, "International Terrorism in 1976," RP77–10034U (Washington, D.C.: July 1977), p. 4.

[7] Gladwin and Walter, *Multinationals,* p. 334.

[8] "Corporate Clout for Consumers," *Business Week,* September 12, 1977, p. 148.

[9] Richard Martin, "Gillette's Giovacchini Rules on Quality Safety of 850 Products," *The Wall Street Journal,* December 12, 1975, p. 1.

[10] Jean E. Heller, "Criteria for Selecting an International Manager," *Personnel,* May–June 1980, p. 48.

[11] Peter F. Drucker, "Learning from Foreign Management," *The Wall Street Journal,* June 4, 1980, p. 1.

Review Questions

1. In what ways may an organization enter into international business activities?
2. What are four basic strategies used by organization that decide to move into international operations?
3. What is exporting? Importing?

4. What are tariffs? Quotas?
5. Describe some problems faced by organizations in international business activities.
6. What is a multinational corporation (MNC)?

7. Describe some unique problems faced by MNCs.
8. Outline six lessons that can be learned from foreign management.

Discussion Questions

1. Do you think that the old saying "When in Rome, do as the Romans do" applies to international business activities?
2. What problems would you face if you were asked to serve as manager in a foreign country?

3. What are some management practices that are typical in the U.S. that would be difficult to apply in foreign countries?

Incident 22-1
Staying at Home

With the increased interest in doing business overseas, many large organizations have found it necessary to assign Americans to managerial positions in other countries. The prospect of seeing the world at the company's expense has enticed many Americans to seek overseas assignments in the past. Furthermore, overseas assignment has been used by organizations as a mechanism by which managers are groomed for higher-level positions when they are returned to America. Equally appealing has been the "hardship pay" awarded to those relocated managers to help ease the transition into another society for them and their families. In the past, these managers and their families generally have been relocated in European countries such as England, France, and Belgium.

However, many organizations have found recently that they are having trouble recruiting managers for overseas assignments. The opportunities, while plentiful, are increasingly being turned down. While some organizations have attempted to solve this problem by filling managerial positions from within the country in which they are operating, many others are reluctant to do so. These organizations feel that it is necessary to have managers who understand the workings of the American parent company as well as the complexities of international business. While local people may serve well in lower-level managerial positions, organizations are hesitant to place them in higher positions of authority.

The problem for these organizations is a perplexing one. It is especially critical since most new foreign opportunities are in the middle East and the underdeveloped countries, where capable local human talent does not exist in great quantities. Even if organizations wanted to use local people in these managerial positions, it is unlikely that they would possess the abilities and experience to perform successfully in these positions.

Questions

1. Why are firms facing this problem? Why would individuals today be less likely to accept overseas assignments?
2. What would an individual consider in deciding whether or not to accept an overseas assignment?
3. Can organizations do anything about this problem? Can they make the opportunity of an overseas assignment any more attractive for American managers?

Incident 22–2

Impose Quotas?*

Suppose that a labor union official testified as follows in a recent hearing before a senate committee investigating the need for trade legislation:

> Free trade policies are based on traditional trade theory which is no longer valid in a world dominated by international investment and multinational companies. When the American business firm is faced with severe foreign competition, it can move abroad and meet this competition by producing in a foreign location for the U.S. market. Businesses can adjust. The American workers cannot.
>
> Furthermore, is it in the United States' interest for American companies to invest abroad as rapidly as they are doing? U.S. advances in technology, often financed by government tax dollars, are being shipped abroad. The production overseas for foreign markets substitutes for U.S. production. We lose the foreign exchange that might be earned by exports. We lose American jobs, tax revenues, and so forth. We want protection while the United States works out a program to control international business. In order to slow down the disruptive impacts on American society and help to provide an orderly expression of trade, quotas should be placed on imports into the United States for those goods and product lines that are displacing significant percentages of U.S. production and employment.

Questions

1. Do you agree or disagree with the union official?
2. Does the United States lose or benefit from multinational business?
3. Do you feel that import quotas should be established for certain industries? Which ones?

---

* Adapted from Stefan H. Robock, Kenneth Simmonds, and Jack Zwick, *International Business and Multinational Enterprises* (Homewood, Ill.: Richard D. Irwin, 1977), pp. 125–26.

Exercise

Blunders

Multinational corporations have on occasion experienced unexpected troubles due to culture, language, and custom differences. The following examples demonstrate problems encountered by some companies with regard to product and company names:*

A. When Chevrolet introduced its Nova in Puerto Rico, sales were less than brisk. When spoken, the word *Nova* sounded like "no va," which in Spanish means "it doesn't go."

B. Ford introduced a low-cost truck, the Fiera, into some less developed countries and also experienced slow sales. Unfortunately, Fiera meant "ugly old woman" in Spanish.

C. A private Egyptian airline, Misair, proved to be rather unpopular with Frenchmen. When pronounced in French, the name means "misery."

D. The phonetic pronunciation of Esso in Japanese means "stalled car." Obviously this name did not go over well in Japan.

Questions

1. Assume that you have been considering opening a McDonald's franchise in either Central America or Spain. Develop a list of internationally related factors that you would need to investigate in evaluating the feasibility of this idea.

2. Prioritize the list you developed in Part A.

---

* These examples are taken from David A. Ricks, *Big Business Blunders: Mistakes in Multinational Marketing* (Homewood, Ill.: Richard D. Irwin, 1983), pp. 37–47.

Section 6 Case
International Harvester*

A revolutionary idea in 1831—a horse-powered reaper built and operated by West Virginia farmer Cyrus McCormick—sparked the evolution of the company that was to become International Harvester,[1] a company that went from the production of 1,500 reapers for the 1849 harvest to recognized leadership in the agricultural equipment industry through the 1950s, only to find itself struggling for survival during the past 20 years.

Looking Back

The Company

The company's earliest products were agricultural implements, primarily for harvesting and a full line of equipment was featured by the turn of the century. In 1908, the first International Harvester tractor was manufactured; 14 years later, the first successful row-crop tractor was introduced by the company. It was complemented only two years later with cultivators, plows, and other implements to revolutionize the farm equipment industry and farming as well. In another 10 years, IH introduced the diesel engine for tractors, and the first successful cottonpickers were manufactured in 1941.

In 1907, International Harvester entered the truck business with the production of the autobuggy, a vehicle designed to carry produce from farm to marketplace. Within 20 years, the company was the leading producer of a complete line of trucks. In 1928, IH was the first company to build a truck with a three-speed transmission and a two-speed rear axle. Truck production expanded in the 1950s with several different models and changes. In 1957, the company build the first heavy-duty, cab-over-engine truck to allow for a longer trailer and thus increase capacity. Truck production greatly expanded in the 1960s with a wide range of IH models in all sizes. The 1980s line includes a vast array of models with hundreds of different trucks, each tailored to specific needs.

Another natural evolution—from farm equipment to construction equipment—occurred in 1924, when solid rubber tires were mounted on a 10–20 McCormick Deering tractor. This became Harvester's first industrial tractor. In 1928, the 10–20 tractor was modified with a tracklaying device, enabling the company to enter the crawler-tractor business. A Construction Equipment Division was created in 1944, with a full line of construction equipment developing in the early 1950s. In 1974, the Pay Line Division

---

* This case was prepared by Nita Satterfield, Georgia State University. Used by permission.

was formed, which covered all phases of the construction, mining, materials handling, and light-industry fields.

The Company Leaders

Cyrus Hall McCormick initially manufactured a small number of reapers in the family blacksmith shop with the help of his father and brothers. Upon establishing the McCormick, Ogden & Co. in 1847 in Chicago, he was joined within three years by both brothers. McCormick directed the business until his death in 1884 and was succeeded by his son C. H. McCormick, Jr., who was the first actual president of the International Harvester Company. He was, in turn, succeeded by his brother Harold McCormick, who was president from 1918 to 1922. A non-McCormick president, Alex Legge, served from 1922 to 1941, although during that period, both C. H. McCormick III and Fowler McCormick (son of Harold) held vice presidencies. Fowler McCormick succeeded Legge and directed the company until 1951. A second non-McCormick, John L. McCaffery, led IH from 1951 until Harry O. Bercher took over in 1962. In 1971, the great-grandnephew of its founder, Brooks McCormick took over, returning the company to family rule for six more years. Presently, D. D. Lennox, who is not a family member, serves as CEO of IH.

A Closer Look

The Company

Though characterized in its own recent literature as "a distinctly American enterprise [that] has grown with the nation and helped the nation grow," International Harvester has not remained solely in the American market. From the 1850s, the company had exported to Canada and Europe. The 1902 incorporation enabled further development of foreign trade, and by 1906, the company's trade with Russia equaled their entire international export trade prior to that time. With Europe, Russia, Great Britain, South America, and Africa all buying from International Harvester, it was indeed an international company.

With 90,000 employees in 1950, IH had a reputation for quality, service, and good employee relations. Company employees recognized that the company was "steeped in tradition." As one executive described the phenomenon,

> In 1950, people were still talking about the Depression, how everyone was so well treated. No one was ever fired. The company was as solid as the Rock of Gibralter. Indeed, when I first joined the company and was in a management training program, I was told by one of the group, a son of an executive, that I had already achieved the most important thing in my career and that was getting hired.[2]

It was not surprising, then, when International Harvester celebrated its 50th anniversary, that a dinner was given for 26 men who had stayed with the company for that entire period.

Immediately following World War II, International Harvester did indeed hold a "Rock of Gibralter" stance; but then began to deteriorate and lose its market leadership. Ending the war as still essentially a farm implement company, IH began a diversification strategy. Tapping into the postwar home appliance boom, IH made large capital investments in that industry. But this pursuit never resulted in more than 5 to 6 percent of total sales, and those assets were sold in 1956.

While Harvester had held its own with major competitor Caterpillar Tractor Company prior to the war, it found itself outranked in the postwar international arena. Having been favored for military use throughout the world, Caterpillar capitalized on that position for international distribution and developed a reliable product line that emphasized the larger construction equipment. Fighting for parity, IH again made large capital investments—unfortunately, without equal quality control—and fell further behind, dogged by questions of reliability.

Other investments—individually sound—diverted attention from research and development in the core agriculture business. Meanwhile, major competitors made large investments in product improvements in the agricultural equipment industry.

With problems obscured by continuing sales growth in the 1950s—growth attributed to the Korean War—domestic sales lagged. And when defense sales evaporated in the mid-50s, Harvester's catch-up position was clearly noticeable.

Leadership from the 1960s

The problems of the 1950s accelerated with the leadership in the following decade. Led by a president with strong orientation to the Wisconsin Steel Division, who became overly involved with minute day-to-day details of operations, International Harvester was in rapid decline by the end of 1970. In 1971, Brooks McCormick became president.

With a power base firmly established on the prevailing feeling of the legitimacy of a McCormick in the presidency, "Mr. Harvester"[3] (as McCormick was described by an older employee) set a course to "save the company and rejuvenate it."[4] Faced with a weak financial picture and with organization and management systems intact from the 1940s, McCormick started with curing the ailments centered in people and planning. With the help of consultants, a shakey but nonetheless visible strategic planning process was operational by 1975. Climate studies were conducted, and accountabilities were established with individual performance rewarded. Effort was made to transform the autocratic, paternalistic company into one of true decentralization that allowed autonomous operation.

In addition, McCormick began to investigate sources of excess labor costs—and a 1977 consultant's report indicated that some $300 million in excess costs did indeed plague the company. Capital and engineering investments were given high priority, with emphasis on end-product development. Finally, divestiture of unprofitable operations was pursued.

Under McCormick's leadership from 1971 to 1976, net income grew from $45.2 million to $174.1 million, return on sales from 1.5 percent to 3.2 percent, and return on equity from 3.9 percent to 12.1 percent. One executive commented, "Brooks saved this company. He did a tremendous job of initiating change and getting the new programs going. His actions showed a lot of fortitude."[5]

In 1976, the consulting group advised a complete company reorganization—including a new president, preferably from outside the company. Brooks McCormick announced the reorganization in December 1976 and followed the basic recommendations. In September 1977, Archie McCardell was brought in as the number two man; in January 1978, he was named chief executive officer. Also in 1978, International Harvester underwent a structural reorganization which resulted in four major business units (Agricultural Equipment; Trucks; Pay Line—construction and industrial equipment; and Solar Turbines International—turbo machinery and component parts manufacturer for the other groups). The reorganization was designed to reduce the span of expertise required in particular management areas, and so set the stage to improve profitability by improving operational efficiency.

Archie McCardell. Archie McCardell was recruited from Xerox Corporation, where he had a reputation as a cost cutter. His 1978 game plan to improve profit margins was a defensive strategy of turnaround underscored by business strategies that emphasized extensive cost reductions. A goal of reducing costs by as much as $500 million or 10 percent of operating expenses was set for the next five-year period. McCardell's strategic plan also included a five-year program to redirect capital expenditures by modernizing plant and equipment holdings and substantially boosting expenditures in R&D, both of which had suffered considerable neglect in the past.

By July 1978, McCardell had laid off 3,000 employees (3.2 percent of IH's total work force). Between 1978 and 1979, the work force expanded due to increased production, then was again reduced between 1979 and 1981.

When the fiscal year closed on October 31, 1979, International Harvester's contract with the United Auto Workers (UAW) expired. On November 1, UAW members (35.8 percent of Harvester's employees) went on strike. McCardell's cost-cutting strategies and attempts to remedy an ailing profit margin included issues related to the union's contract which—as seen by McCardell—were major contributors to plant operational inefficiencies.

Friction had developed between the UAW and McCardell long before the expiration of the employment contract. The UAW was incensed by the large bonuses being paid to the management group while UAW workers were being laid off to conserve costs. With an irritated UAW on the one hand and a determined—if not stubborn—Archie McCardell on the other, the strike wore on for six months. It was the longest strike ever recorded in the history of the UAW.

The outcome of the strike was negligible contract gains for International Harvester, losses totaling $479 million, a severe cash drain, exhausted levels of inventories, and an embittered work force. The strike also took its toll on the company's suppliers and distributors, many of which suffered financial hardship.

Borrowing increased; losses abounded. It became necessary to scrap much of McCardell's plans for revitalizing plant and equipment and increasing the R&D work force. From 1980 through 1983, a total of $848.1 million was spent, considerably less than the $2 billion planned for that period. Indeed, IH barely matched the amount invested during the previous four-year period. The focus of all energies became the necessity to reduce costs dramatically in order to improve cash flow. As the full effects of the strike were understood, so was the need to replace Archie McCardell.

Donald D. Lennox.   On May 2, 1982, Archie McCardell's resignation was accepted, and a new management team was brought in. To head the new team, Louis W. Menk was named chief executive officer and Donald D. Lennox was named president and chief operating officer. Lennox moved to the position of chief executive officer on December 1, 1982.

The new corporate strategy was that of retrenchment, with concentration on turnaround and liquidation of unprofitable segments. Businesses that were not liquidated were to focus their strategic efforts on overall cost reduction.

In 1981, under McCardell, IH's Solar Turbine International Division was sold, two unprofitable truck plants were closed, and inventories were reduced by $210 million. Costs were reduced by $430 million in 1981 by drastic reductions in inventory levels, numbers of suppliers used, the use of more economic order sizes, and worker layoffs. In contrast, 1982's strategic plan did not consist of scattered cost cutting. Instead, it boldly addressed Harvester's needs by requiring liquidation of all businesses not directly related to its core business. International Harvester was to return to concentrating on the production of heavy-duty trucks and farm equipment; all other lines were to be divested. Continued emphasis was placed on improving the efficiency of operation. Plant utilization was to be maximized (which would require the closing of underutilized plants).

In November 1984, International Harvester made the decision to break further with its past and get out of the farm-related industry by selling most of its farm equipment operations to Tenneco's J. I. Case farm tractor and construction business. According to the November 17, 1984, issue of *The Wall Street Journal,* "In selling off the farm equipment operations, Harvester is taking a gamble. It is selling off the potential of future profits when the farm equipment market finally turns around. Meanwhile, it is increasing its exposure to a downturn in the truck market, an eventual certainty in such a cyclical business."

Notes

[1] Cyrus McCormick moved to Chicago in 1847 and built his first factory; McCormick, Ogden & Co. was formed October 7, 1847. In 1849, Ogden and Jones sold out to McCormick and in 1873, the firm became C. H. and L. J. McCormick. In 1879, the partnership merged into the corporation McCormick Harvesting Machines Company. In 1902, the corporation merged with Deering Harvester Co., Plano Harvester Co., and Warder, Breshnel, Glassner Co. to form International Harvester Company.

[2] Quotations taken from "International Harvester (A)," case study from C. Roland Christensen, Kenneth R. Andrews, Joseph L. Bower, Richard G. Hamermesh, and Michael E. Porter, *Business Policy: Text and Cases* (Homewood, Ill.: Richard D. Irwin, 1982), p. 760.

[3] Ibid., p. 762.

[4] Ibid.

[5] Ibid., p. 767.

Glossary of Key Terms

ABC classification system—Method of managing inventories, based on their values.

Acceptance sampling—Statistical method predicting the quality of a batch or large group of products by inspecting a sample or group of samples.

Achievement-power-affiliation theory—Holds that people have three needs—achievement, power, and affiliation; the level of intensity varies among individuals; people are motivated in situations that allow them to satisfy their most intense need(s).

Activity scheduling—Develops the precise timetable to be followed in producing a product or service.

Affirmative action plan—Written document outlining specific goals and timetables for remedying past discriminatory actions.

Age Discrimination in Employment Act of 1968—Amended in 1978; protects individuals from 40 to 70 years of age from discrimination in hiring, retention, compensation, and other conditions of employment.

Aggregate production planning—Concerned with overall operations and balancing major sections of the operating system; matches resources with demands for goods and services.

Apprenticeship training—Used in skilled trades; trainee works under the guidance of a skilled worker.

Assembly chart—Depicts the sequence and manner in which components of a product or service are assembled.

Assessment center—Evaluates an individual's potential as a manager and determines the person's development needs based on his or her reactions in a simulated, "real world" environment.

Audit—Method of control normally involved with financial matters; also can include other areas of the organization.

Authority—Right to issue directives (command) and expend resources.

Autocratic leader—Makes most decisions for the group.

Autogenic training—Much like self-hypnosis; helps individuals gain control over their physiology through passive concentration.

Behavior (personal) control—Based on direct, personal surveillance.

Behaviorally anchored rating scale (BARS)—Determines employee's level of performance; based on whether specific job behaviors are present.

Bet-your-company culture—Requires big-stakes decisions; considerable time passes before the results are known.

Biofeedback—Monitoring devices give an individual feedback on the degree of relaxation or tension of various muscle groups.

Bottom-up management—Philosophy popularized by William B. Given that encouraged widespread delegation of authority to solicit the participation of all employees from the bottom to the top.

Brainstorming—Involves presenting a problem to a group and allowing them to produce a large quantity of ideas for its solution; no criticisms are allowed initially.

Break-even chart—Depicts graphically the relationship of volume of operations to profits.

Budget—Statement of expected results or requirements expressed in financial or numerical terms.

Burnout—Adaptation an individual makes to stress and work-related and personal factors; results in a situation where work is no longer meaningful.

Business game—Classroom training that provides the setting of a company and its environment and requires team players to make operating decisions.

Business strategies—Focus on how to compete in a given business.

Captains of industry—Dominated and built corporate giants during the last 25 years of the 19th century; included John D. Rockefeller, James B. Duke, Andrew Carnegie, Cornelius Vanderbilt, and others.

Case study—Classroom training where students analyze real or hypothetical situations and suggest what to do and how to do it.

Central tendency—Tendency to rate all or most employees in the middle of the performance rating scale.

Centralization—Little authority is delegated to lower levels of management.

Certainty situation—Decision situation in which the decision maker knows the state of nature and can calculate exactly what will happen.

Checklist—Performance appraisal in which the rater answers yes or no to questions about the behavior of the person being rated.

Civil Rights Act of 1964—Title VII of this act eliminates discrimination in employment based on race, color, religion, sex, or national origin in organizations that conduct interstate commerce.

Clifford Trust—Company turns over some of its assets for a set time period during which all of the income earned on the assets goes to charity.

Coaching—Management development conducted on the job, where experienced managers advise and guide trainees in solving managerial problems.

Coercive power—Based on fear.

Committee—Organization structure in which a group of people are formally appointed, organized, and superimposed on the line or line and staff structure to consider or decide certain matters.

Communication—Transfer of information that is meaningful to those involved; the transmittal of understanding.

Comparative advantage—A country produces those goods and services it can produce more efficiently or cheaply than other countries.

Compensation system—Policies, procedures, and rules the organization uses to determine employee compensation.

Conflict—Overt behavior in which one party seeks to advance its own interests in its relationship with others.

Conformity—Refers to the degree to which group members accept and abide by the norms of the group.

Consumer Product Safety Act of 1972—Protects consumers against unreasonable risks of injury associated with consumer products.

Consumerism—Social movement that seeks to redress the perceived imbalance between buyers and sellers.

Contingency approach to leadership—Holds that the most effective style of leadership depends on the particular situation.

Contingency approach to management—Theorizes that different situations and conditions require different management approaches.

Contingency approach to organization structure—States that the most appropriate structure depends on the technology used, the rate of environmental change and other dynamic forces.

Control (controlling)—Management function that measures performance against an organization's objectives, determines causes of deviations, and takes corrective action when necessary.

Corporate culture—Communicates how people in an organization should behave, by establishing a value system conveyed through rites, rituals, myths, legends, and actions.

Corporate philanthropy—Donations of money, property, or work by organizations to needy persons or for social purposes.

Corporate strategies—Address what businesses an organization will be in and how resources will be allocated among those businesses.

Council on Environmental Quality—Assists and advises the president on environmental issues.

Creativity—Thinking process that produces an idea or concept that is new, original, useful, or satisfying to its creator or someone else.

Criterion—Measure of job success or performance.

Critical-incident appraisal—Method in which the rater records incidents of both positive and negative employee behavior and uses them to evaluate performance.

Critical path method (CPM)—Planning and control technique that graphically depicts the relationships between the various activities of a project; used when time durations of project activities are accurately known and have little variance.

Culture—Set of important understandings (often unstated) that members of a community share in common.

Customer departmentation—Organization units based on division by customers served.

Data—Raw material from which information is developed; composed of facts that have not been interpreted.

Data base—Contains the data required to meet the user's need; usually, readily accessible information about the organization's operations.

Data processing—Capture, processing, and storage of data.

Decentralization—Great deal of authority is delegated to lower levels of management.

Decision-making process—Involves searching the environment for conditions requiring a decision, developing and analyzing possible alternatives, and selecting a particular alternative.

Decision support systems (DSS)—Extension of an MIS; provides information for making decisions and becomes a part of the process.

Democratic leader—Guides and encourages the group to make decisions.

Departmentation—Grouping activities into related work units.

Dissonance—Feeling of disharmony within an individual.

Downward communication—Transmitting information from higher to lower levels of the organization through the chain of command.

Economic order quantity (EOQ)—Optimum number of units to order at one time.

Employee development—Process concerned with improvement and growth of the capabilities of individuals and groups within the organization.

Entrepreneur—Person who conceives the product or service idea, starts the organization, and builds it to the point where additional people are needed.

Entry socialization—Adaptation process by which new employees are introduced and indoctrinated into an organization.

Environmental changes—All nontechnological changes that occur outside the organization.

Environmental impact statement (EIS)—Written report required of federal government agencies on proposed actions that affect the human environment.

Environmental Protection Agency (EPA)—Interprets and administers the environmental protection policies of the federal government.

Equal employment opportunity—Right of all people to work and advance on the basis of merit, ability, and potential.

Equal Pay Act of 1963—Became effective June 1964; prohibits wage discrimination on the basis of sex.

Essay potential—Requires the rater to prepare a written statement describing an individual's strengths, weaknesses, and past performance.

Ethics—Standards of principles of conduct that govern the behavior of an individual or a group of individuals.

Exception principle—States that managers should concentrate on matters that deviate significantly from normal and let subordinates handle routine matters.

Expert power—Based on the special skill, expertise, or knowledge of an individual.

Export-import manager—Serves a group of exporting/importing organizations and handles all activities involved in the exporting/importing of their goods or services.

Exporting—Selling an organization's goods or services to another country.

External equity—What employees are paid compared to employees performing similar jobs in other organizations.

Federal Fair Packaging and Labeling Act of 1967—Regulates labeling procedures for businesses.

Federal Rehabilitation Act of 1973—Prohibits discrimination in the hiring of the handicapped by federal agencies and contractors.

Feedback—Flow of information from receiver to sender that indicates if message was received as intended by the sender.

Flat structure—Organization with few levels and relatively large spans of management at each level.

Flexible budget—Allows certain expenses to vary with the level of sales or output.

Flow process chart—Outlines what happens to a product or service as it progresses through the facility.

Forced-choice rating—Requires rater to rank a set of statements describing how an employee carries out the duties and responsibilities of the job.

Forecasting—Fourth step in the planning process; involves making predictions about the future.

Foreign Corrupt Practices Act of 1977—Prohibits American companies operating abroad from bribing foreign officials, political candidates, and party leaders; requires company's books and records to accurately and fairly reflect transactions.

Formal plan—Written, documented plan developed through an identifiable process.

Formal work groups—Have a defined structure and are formally recognized by the organization.

Frustration—Intrapersonal conflict that results when a drive or motive is blocked before the goal is reached.

Functional departmentation—Organization units are defined by the nature of the work.

Functional plans—Originate from the functional areas of an organization like production, marketing, finance, and personnel.

Functional strategies—Concerned with the activities of the different functional areas of a business.

Gantt chart—Control device that graphically shows work planned and work accomplished in their relation to each other and to time.

Geographic departmentation—Organization units are defined by territories.

Goal (objectives)—Statement designed to give an organization and its members direction and purpose.

Goal conflict—Intrapersonal conflict that results when a goal has both positive and negative features or when two or more competing goals exist.

Gordon technique—Aid to producing creative ideas in which only the group leader knows the exact nature of the real problem and uses a key word to describe the problem area as a starting point for exploring solutions.

Grand strategy—Describes the way the organization will pursue its objectives, given the threats and opportunities in the environment and its own resources and capabilities.

Grapevines—Informal channels of communication resulting from casual contacts in various organizational units.

Graphic rating scale—Requires rater to indicate on a scale where the employee rates on work-related factors.

Grid training—Method used in organizational development to make managers and organizations more team oriented.

Group—Number of persons who interact with one another over a span of time on a face-to-face basis and perceive themselves to be a group.

Group cohesiveness—Degree of attraction each member has for the group.

Group norm—Informal rules that a group adopts to regulate members' behavior.

Halo effect—Occurs when raters allow a single prominent characteristic to dominate their judgment of all traits, or allow general impression of employee to influence judgment on separate items of a performance appraisal.

Hardware—Actual computer and its peripheral equipment.

Hierarchy of needs—Maslow's five levels of individual needs: physiological, safety, social, esteem or ego, and self-actualization.

Horizontal (lateral) communication—Transmitting information across the lines of the formal organization's chain of command.

Host country—Country in which a foreign organization does business.

Human asset accounting—Measuring the costs incurred by organizations in recruiting, hiring, training, and developing their human assets.

Human resource forecasting—Process that determines future human resource needs.

Human resource planning (HRP)—Process of getting the right number of qualified people into the right jobs at the right time.

Idiosyncrasy credit—Form of credit or liberties a group gives to certain members who make significant contributions to the group's goals.

Importing—Purchasing goods or services from foreign countries.

In-basket technique—Classroom training where trainee is required to handle a manager's mail and phone calls and react accordingly.

Incident method—Form of case study where students are given the general outline of a situation and are given additional information only as they request it.

Informal organization—Aggregate of the personal contacts and interactions and the associated groupings of people working within the formal organization.

Informal work groups—Result from personal contacts and interactions of people within formal work groups; usually not formally recognized by the organization.

Information—Data that have been interpreted and that meet the need of one or more managers.

Information centers—In-house centers that companies set up to teach their managers how to use their information systems.

Information overload—Occurs when managers have so much information available that they have trouble distinguishing between the useful and the useless information.

Innovation—Doing new things.

Internal changes—Budget adjustments, policy changes, personnel changes, and the like.

Internal equity—What an employee is paid compared to what other employees in the organization are paid to do their jobs.

Interpersonal communication—Communication between individuals.

Interpersonal conflict—Between two or more individuals, can be caused by many factors.

Intrapersonal conflict—Internal to the individual; relates to the need-drive-goal motivational sequence.

Intuitive approach to decision making—Making decisions based on hunches and intuition.

Inventory—Quantity of raw materials, in-process goods, or finished goods on hand; serves as a buffer between different rates of flow associated with the operating system.

Japanese management style—Information and initiative flow from the bottom up; top management facilitates decision making rather than issuing edicts; middle management shapes solutions to problems; consensus decision making; fosters personal well-being of employees.

Job analysis—Determining, through observation and study, information relating to the nature of a specific job.

Job content—Aggregate of all the work tasks the jobholder may be asked to perform.

Job depth—Freedom of employees to plan and organize their own work, to work at their own pace, and to move around and communicate as desired.

Job design—Designates specific work activities of an individual or group of individuals.

Job description—Written statement that identifies the tasks, duties, activities, and performance results required in a specific job.

Job enlargement—Making a job structurally larger by giving an employee more similar operations or tasks to perform.

Job enrichment—Upgrading a job with factors like more meaningful work, recognition, responsibility, and opportunities for advancement.

Job evaluation—Systematic determination of the value of each job in relation to other jobs in the organization.

Job method—Manner in which the human body is used, workplace arrangement, and design of the tools and equipment used.

Job rotation—Requires employee to learn several different jobs in a work unit or department and perform each for a specified time period.

Job satisfaction—An individual's general attitude about the job.

Job scope—Number of different types of operations performed on the job.

Job specification—Written statement that identifies the abilities, skills, traits, or attributes necessary for a particular job.

Judeo-Christian ethic—Generally, the basis of Western ethical codes; primary goal is love, including love of God and neighbor.

Laissez-faire leader—Allows individuals in the group to make the decisions.

Leader—Occupies the central role in a leadership situation and has the ability to influence the behavior of others in a given situation.

Leader Behavior Description Questionnaire (LBDQ)—Developed at Ohio State University and designed to determine how successful leaders carry out their activities.

Leadership—Process of influencing the behavior of other members of the group.

Leading—Management function that directs and channels human behavior toward the accomplishment of objectives.

Legitimate power—Based on one's position in an organization.

Leniency—Grouping performance ratings at the positive end instead of spreading them over the performance scale.

Level of aspiration—Level of performance a person expects or hopes to attain.

Life-cycle theory of leadership—Holds that the maturity level of the followers determines the most appropriate leadership style for a situation.

Line and staff structure—Organization structure that results when staff specialists are added to a line organization.

Line balancing—Process of determining the optimum number of work stations.

Line functions—Functions and activities directly involved in producing and marketing the organization's goods or services.

Line structure—Organization structure with direct vertical links between the different levels of the organization.

Long-range objectives—Objectives that extend beyond the current fiscal year of the organization.

Long-range plans—Generally start at the end of the current year and extend into the future.

Management—Process that involves guiding or directing a group of people toward organizational goals or objectives.

Management audit—Attempts to evaluate the overall management practices and policies of the organization.

Management by objectives (MBO)—Superior and subordinate jointly define the objectives and responsibilities of the subordinate's job; superior uses them to evaluate subordinate's performance; subordinate's rewards are directly related to performance.

Management development—Concerned with developing the experience, attitudes, and skills necessary to become or remain an effective manager.

Management functions—Activities a manager performs in doing the work of management: planning, controlling, organizing, staffing, and leading.

Management information system (MIS)—Integrated approach for providing interpreted and relevant data that can help managers make decisions.

Management theory jungle—Term developed by Harold Koontz; refers to the division of thought that resulted from the multiple approaches to studying the management process.

Managerial Grid®—Two-dimensional framework characterizing a leader according to concern for people and concern for production.

Matrix structure—Hybrid organization structure in which individuals from different functional areas are assigned to work on a specific project or task.

McCormick multiple-management plan—Developed by Charles McCormick; uses participation as a training and motivational tool by selecting promising young employees from various company departments to form a junior board of directors.

Meditation techniques—Focus attention on a constant object such as the breath or a repetitive syllable.

Motivation—Causative sequence concerned with what activates, directs, and sustains human behavior: needs → drives or motives → goal attainment.

Motivation-maintenance theory—States that all work-related factors can be grouped into one of two categories: *maintenance factors,* which will not produce motivation but can prevent it, and *motivators,* which can encourage motivation.

Multinational corporation (MNC)—Any business organization that maintains a production, assembly, sales, or service presence in two or more countries.

National Environmental Policy Act of 1969—Committed the federal government to preserving the country's ecology, established a White House Council on Environmental Quality, and required filings of environmental impact statements.

Need hierarchy theory—Based on the assumption that individuals are motivated to satisfy a number of needs and that money can satisfy only some of these needs.

Nominal grouping technique (NGT)—Highly structured technique for solving group tasks; minimizes personal interactions to encourage activity and reduce pressures toward conformity.

Nonverbal communication—Conscious or unconscious behavior of the individual sending a message that is perceived consciously or unconsciously by the receiver.

Objectives (goals)—Statements outlining what you are trying to achieve; they give an organization and its members direction.

On-the-job training (OJT)—Normally given by a senior employee or supervisor; trainee is shown how to perform the job and allowed to do it under the trainer's supervision.

Operating system—Consists of the processes and activities necessary to transform various inputs into goods and/or services.

Operational MIS—Basically provides information to assist in making decisions relating to current operations.

Operations management—Application of basic management concepts and principles to the segments of the organization that produce the goods or services.

Operations planning—Designing the systems of the organization that produce goods or services; planning the day-to-day operations within these systems.

Optimizing—Practice of selecting the best possible alternative.

Organization—Group of people working together in a concerted or coordinated effort to attain objectives.

Organization structure—Framework that defines the boundaries of the formal organization and within which the organization operates.

Organizational communication—Occurs within the formal organizational structure.

Organizational development (OD)—Organization-wide, planned effort managed from the top, to increase organizational performance through planned interventions.

Organizational morale—Individual's feeling of being accepted by, and belonging to, a group of employees through common goals, confidence in the desirability of these goals and progress toward them.

Organizational purpose—Identifies an organization's current and future business; the primary objective of the organization.

Organizing— Management function that groups and assigns activities and provides the authority necessary to carry out the activities.

Orientation—Introduction of new employees to the organization, their work unit, and their job.

Orientation kit—Packet of written information given to a new employee to supplement the verbal orientation program.

Output (impersonal) control—Based on the measurement of outputs.

Parent organization—Organization that extends its operations beyond its nation's boundaries.

Parity principle—States that authority and responsibility must coincide.

Path-goal theory of leadership—Holds that the leader's role is to increase personal payoffs to subordinates for work-goal attainment, make the path to payoffs easier, and increase the opportunities for satisfaction enroute; the effectiveness of such efforts depends on the situation.

Perception—Refers to how a person processes a message; is influenced by the person's personality and previous experience and is unique for each individual.

Performance—Degree of accomplishment of the tasks that make up an individual's job.

Performance appraisal—Process of determining and communicating to employees how they are performing on the job, and establishing a plan of improvement.

Performance evaluation and review technique (PERT)—Planning and control technique that graphically depicts the relationships between the various activities of a project; used when the durations of the project activities are not accurately known.

Peter principle—Idea, popularized by Lawrence Peter, that managers tend to be promoted to their level of incompetence.

Physical layout—Process of planning the optimum physical arrangement of facilities, including personnel, operating equipment, storage space, office space, materials-handling equipment, and room for customer or product movement.

Planning—Management function that decides what objectives to pursue during a future time period and what to do to achieve those objectives.

Policies—Broad, general guides to action which relate to objective attainment.

Policies by fiat—Those that are arbitrarily announced by an individual or a group; they may lack precedence or clear-cut rationale.

Power—Ability or capacity to influence another to do something that the person would not otherwise do; ability to command or apply force; not necessarily accompanied by authority.

Preference-expectancy theory—Holds that motivation is based on a combination of the individual's expectancy that increased effort will lead to increased performance, which will lead to rewards, and the individual's preference for those rewards.

Primary group—Meets all the characteristics of a group but also has feelings of loyalty, comradeship, and a common sense of values among its members.

Principle—Accepted rule of action.

Pro forma statements—Forecast the future financial impact of a particular course of action.

Procedures—Series of related steps or tasks expressed in chronological order to achieve a specific purpose.

Process approach to management—Focuses on the management functions of planning, controlling, organizing, staffing, and leading.

Process control chart—Time-based graphic display that shows if a machine or process is producing items that meet preestablished specifications.

Process culture—Involves low risk with little feedback; employees focus on how things are done rather than on the outcomes.

Process physical layout—Equipment or services of a similar functional type are arranged or grouped together.

Process selection—Specifies in detail the processes and sequences required to transform inputs into products or services.

Product departmentation—All activities necessary to produce and market a product or service are under one manager.

Product physical layout—Equipment or services are arranged according to the progressive steps by which the product is made or the customer is served.

Production planning—Concerned primarily with aggregate production planning, resource allocation, and activity scheduling.

Productivity—Output per person-hour of input.

Professional manager—Career manager who does not necessarily have an ownership interest in the organization and who realizes a responsibility to employees, stockholders, and the public.

Program of planned change—Deliberate design and implementation of a structural innovation, a new policy or goal, or a change in operating philosophy, climate, and style.

Programmed instruction—Classroom training in which material is presented in text form or on computers; students must answer questions correctly before advancing.

Programmer—Writes instructional programs that tell computers what to do.

Promotion—Moving an employee to a job with higher pay, status, and performance requirements.

Quality circle—Members of a work unit who meet on a regular basis to discuss quality problems and generate ideas for improving quality.

Quality control—Process of ensuring or maintaining a certain level of quality for materials, products, or services.

Quotas—Establish the maximum quantity of a good that might be imported (or exported) during a given time period.

Ranking methods—Performance appraisal in which the performance of an individual is ranked relative to the performance of others.

Rational approach to decision making—Involves these steps: recognize the need for a decision; establish, rank, and weight criteria; collect data; identify alternatives; evaluate alternatives; and make the final choice.

Rational policies—These include policies set by the board of directors or a policy committee and may be altered by conditions.

Recruitment—Process of seeking and attracting a supply of people from which qualified candidates for job vacancies can be selected.

Referent power—Based on the charismatic traits or characteristics of an individual.

Reinforcement theory—Motivation approach based on the idea that behavior that appears to lead to a positive consequence tends to be repeated, while behavior that appears to lead to a negative consequence tends not to be repeated.

Relaxation response—Trains a person to control major muscle groups.

Resource allocation—Efficient allocation of people, materials, and equipment in order to meet the demand requirements of the operating system.

Responsibility—Accountability for the attainment of objectives, the use of resources, and the adherence to organizational policy.

Reverse discrimination—Alleged preferential treatment of one group (minority or sex) over another rather than merely providing equal opportunity.

Reward power—Based on an individual's ability to provide rewards for compliance with his or her wishes.

Risk situation—Decision situation in which the decision maker has some information and can calculate probalistic estimates about the outcome of each alternative.

Role—Organized set of behaviors belonging to an identifiable job.

Routing—Finds the best sequence of operations for attaining a desired level of output with a given mix of equipment and personnel.

Rules—Guidelines that require specific and definite actions be taken or not taken in a given situation.

Safety stocks—Inventory maintained to accommodate unexpected changes in demand and supply and to allow for delivery time.

Satisficing—Selecting the first alternative that meets the decision maker's minimum standard of satisfaction.

Scalar principle—States that authority in the organization flows, one link at a time, through the chain of managers ranging from the highest to lowest ranks.

Scanlon plan—Incentive plan developed in 1938 by Joseph Scanlon to give workers a bonus for tangible savings in labor costs.

Scientific management—Philosophy of Frederick W. Taylor that sought to increase productivity and make the work easier by scientifically studying work methods and establishing standards.

Self-audit—First step in the planning process; it answers the question "Where are we now?" and is an evaluation of all relevant factors internal to the organization.

Self-fulfilling prophecy (Pygmalion in management)—Describes the influence of one person's expectations on another's behavior.

Semantics—Science or study of the meaning of words and symbols.

Sensitivity training—Method used in organizational development to make one more aware of oneself and one's impact on others.

Separation—Voluntary or involuntary termination of an employee.

Short-range objectives—Generally tied to a specific time period of a year or less and are derived from an in-depth evaluation of long-range objectives.

Skills inventory—Contains basic information on all employees of an organization.

Short-range plans—Generally cover up to one year.

Social audit—Attempt to report in financial terms the expenditures and investments made by an organization for social purposes.

Social responsibility—Moral and ethical content of managerial and corporate decisions over and above the pragmatic requirements imposed by legal principle and the market economy.

Sociotechnical approach—Approach to job design that considers both the technical system and the accompanying social system.

Software—Instructions and programs used to run a computer.

Soldiering—Describes the actions of employees who intentionally restrict output.

Span of management—Number of subordinates a manager can effectively manage.

Staff functions—Advisory and supportive in nature; designed to contribute to the efficiency and maintenance of the organization.

Staffing—Management function that determines human resource needs; recruits, selects, trains, and develops human resources for jobs created by an organization.

Standard—Value used as a point of reference for comparing other values.

Strategic conflict—Results from promotion of self-interests by an individual or group; often deliberately planned.

Strategic management—Process through which top management determines the long-run direction and performance of an organization by ensuring careful formulation, proper implementation, and continuous evaluation of plans and strategies.

Strategic MIS—Concerned with decisions that affect the organization's long-range objectives.

Strategic planning—Covers a relatively long period of time; affects many parts of the organization; includes the formulation of objectives and the selection of the means by which they are to be attained.

Strategy—Outlines the fundamental steps management plans to undertake in order to reach an objective or set of objectives.

Stress—Results when an environment presents a demand threatening to exceed the person's capabilities and resources for meeting it.

Structural conflict—Result of the organizational structure; relatively independent of the individuals occupying the roles within the structure.

Survey environment—Second step in the planning process; answers the question "Where are we now?" and involves surveying factors that may influence the operation and success of the organization but are not under its control.

Systems analyst—Studies a potential computer application and determines the type of programs needed.

Systems approach to management—Views the human, physical, and informational facets of the manager's job as linking together to form an integrated whole.

Tactical planning—Presupposes a set of objectives handed down by a higher level in the organization and determines ways to attain them.

Tall structure—Organization with many levels and relatively small spans of management.

Tariffs—Government-imposed taxes charged on goods imported into, or exported from, a country.

Team building—Work group develops awareness of conditions that keep them from functioning effectively and takes action to eliminate these conditions.

Technological changes—Such things as new equipment and new processes.

Test reliability—Consistency or reproducibility of the results of a test.

Test validity—Extent to which a test measures what it purports to measure (generally, how well it predicts future job success or performance).

Tests—Provide a sample of behavior that is used to draw inferences about the future behavior or performance of an individual.

Theory X and Theory Y—Terms coined by Douglas McGregor to describe assumptions made by managers about basic human nature.

Tough-guy, macho culture—Characterized by individualists who take high risks and get quick feedback on whether their answers are right or wrong.

Traditional policies—Those that emerge from history, tradition and earlier events. Some may be desirable; others may inhibit organizational performance.

Traditional theory of motivation—Based on the assumption that money is the primary motivator: if the reward is great enough, employees will produce more.

Training—Learning process that involves the acquisition of skills or concepts to increase employee performance.

Trait theory—Holds that certain physical and psychological characteristics, or traits, differentiate leaders from their groups.

Transaction-processing systems—Substitutes computer processing for manual record-keeping procedures.

Transfer—Moving an employee to another job at about the same level, with about the same pay, performance requirements, and status.

Uncertainty situation—Decision situation in which the decision maker has no knowledge about the relative probabilities associated with the possible outcomes.

Understudy assignments—On-the-job training where an individual, designated as the heir to a job, learns the job from the present jobholder.

Unity-of-command principle—States that an employee should have one and only one immediate manager.

Upward communication—Originates at the lower levels of the organization and flows toward the top.

User-friendly computer—Requires very little technical knowledge to use.

Value—Conception, explicit or implicit, defining what an individual or group sees as desirable.

Vestibule training—Procedures and equipment similar to those used in the actual job are set up in a special working area called a vestibule.

Wage survey—Survey of selected organizations to provide a comparison of reliable information on policies, practices, and methods of payment.

Work groups—Describes groups in organizations.

Work-hard/play-hard culture—Encourages employees to take few risks and to expect rapid feedback.

Work standards approach—Involves setting a standard or expected level of output and then comparing each employee's level to the standard.

Name Index

A

Abels, Jules, 35
Absell, Gernard, 20
Age Discrimination in Employment Act, 622
Ajemain, Robert, 103
Alexander, L. D., 75
Al-Malek, Sulaiman M., 545
Alutto, Joseph A., 252
American Management Association, 238
American Society of Mechanical Engineers, 40
Apple Computer, 243
Aquilano, N. J., 176, 320, 325
Argenti, John, 149, 161
Argyris, Chris, 538
Asch, Solomon, 422
Ashland Oil, 94
Atkins, Orrin E., 94
Augarten, Stan, 594
Avon, 159

B

Baker, Arthur D., 161
Bakke, Allen, 272
Ball, Lucille, 385, 387
Barnard, Chester, 42, 57, 96, 392, 477
Barnes, Louis, 575
Barnfather, Maurice, 94
Barrett, Dermot, 484
Barrett, M. E., 484
Barrow, J. D., 397
Barth, Carl, 37
Bartlett, C. J., 4
Bavelas, Alex, 484
Bedeian, Arthur G., 219
Beer, M., 575
Behling, Orlando, 397
Belasco, James A., 252
Belcher, David W., 508
Bem, D. J., 112
Benetar, Leo, 125
Bernis, Warren G., 575
Berg, Norman A., 575
Berliner, W. M., 520
Bethlehem Steel, 37
Black & Decker, 132
Blake, Robert, 388, 389, 575
Blanchard, Kenneth, 355, 372
Boring, Edwin G., 470
Bork, Robert H., 74
Boulton, William R., 161
Bradford, Leland B., 386
Brennan, Charles W., 51
Bristol Meyers, 18
Brown, Alvin, 210
Buffa, Elwood S., 194

Burnham, D. H., 383, 397
Burns, Tom, 246
Burton, David B., 422
Burton, Gene E., 422
Byars, Lloyd L., 161

C

Campbell, J. H., 484
Carbone, T. C., 397
Carey, Alex, 51
Carnegie, Andrew, 34
Carroll, Archie B., 71, 75
Carzo, Rocco, 242
Chandler, Alfred D., 51
Chase, Richard B., 179, 320, 325
Chick-fil-A, 454–58
Child, John, 252
Churchill, Neil C., 74
Civil Rights Act, 266
Clarke, Peter B., 312
Cleland, David, 240
Coca-Cola, 131–32, 546–51
Coch, Lester, 413
Comrey, A. L., 161
Cooke, Morris, 38
Cooper, C. L., 575
Copley, Frank B., 51
Costello, Timothy W., 433
Costley, Dan L., 411
Cribben, J. J., 520
Cross, Kevin, 182
Cummings, Larry L., 372
Cummings Engine, 72
Cyert, Richard M., 100

D

Dale, Ernest, 251
Dallas Cowboys, 8
Dalton, Dan, 251
Dalton, Gene, 296
Dalton, M., 251
Davis, Keith, 414, 485
Davis, Louis, 181, 186
Davis, Ralph C., 45, 52
Deal, Terrence E., 573
Delta, Airlines, 8
D'Lites, 196–202
Dennison, Henry S., 43
Digman, L. A., 538
Dilworth, James B., 185
Dow Corning, 241
Drucker, Peter, 24, 120–21
Duke, James B., 34
Duke Power Company, 275

Subject Index

Material requirements planning (MRP), 185–86
  definition, 185
Matrix structure, 239
  definition, 239
Mechanistic systems, 246
Meditation techniques, 444
Method, ranking, 501–02
  definition, 501
Methods, job, 180
  definition, 180
Moody, Albermarle Paper Company v., 275
Morale, 368
  definition, 368
  versus job satisfaction, 369
Motivation, chapter 13
  definition, 355
  maintenance theory, 361
    compared with need hierarchy theory, 363
    definition, 361
    versus satisfaction, 369–70
Motivator factors, 362
Motive, 355

N

National Air Quality Standards Act of 1970, 69
Need hierarchy theory, Maslow's, 357
  definition of, 358
Needs
  definition, 357
  esteem/ego, 358
  Maslow's hierarchy of, 357, 358
  physiological, 358
  safety, 358
  self-actualization, 358
  social, 358
Nominal grouping technique, 418
  definition, 418
  steps, 418
Nonverbal communication, 475
  definition, 627
Norm, group, 409
  definition, 409

O

OD; *see* Organization development
OSHA; *see* Occupational Safety and Health Act of 1970
Objectives, Chapter 5
  areas for setting, 124
  cascade approach to setting, 121–122
  categories of, 124
  definition, 120
  guidelines for setting individual, 127
  integrating with policies and personnel planning, 125
  integrating with strategies and policies, 125
  long-range, 123
    definition, 123

Objectives—*Cont.*
  management by (MBO), 124
    definition, 124
    process, 126
    requirements of, 125
    steps for achieving objectives, 125–26
  short-range, 123
    definition, 123
On-the-job training, 526
  definition, 627
Operating
  system, 171–73
    definition, 171
    designing, 174
    types of, 172
Operations management, 170
  definition, 170
  importance of, 170
  and other areas, 170
  planning, Chapter 7
Optimizing, 99
  definition, 99
Organic systems, 239
Organization
  centralized, 221
    versus decentralized, 220
    definition, 220
  committee, 242–45
    definition, 242
  decentralized, 221
    versus centralized, 220
    definition, 221
  definition, 210
  development (OD), 564
    definition, 564
  flat versus tall, 241
  informal, 210
    definition, 210
  line, 237
    definition, 238
  line and staff, 238
    conflict, 238
    definition, 238
  matrix, 239
    definition, 239
  parent, 604
    definition, 628
  project; *see* Matrix organization
  structure, Chapter 9
    contingency approach to, 232
    definition, 232
Organizational
  communication, 475
    definition, 475
    early approaches to, 475
  development, 564
    definition, 210
    reasons for, 210–211
Orientation, employee, 521
  definition, 521

This book has been set VideoComp, in 10 and 9 point Compano leaded 2 points. Section and chapter numbers and titles are 72 and 27 point Spectra Bold. The size of the type page is 37 by 49 picas.